Fromme

D1054926

Amalfi Coast
with Naples, Capri & Pompeii
1st Edition

by Bruce Murphy & Alessandra de Rosa

Here's what the critics say about Frommer's:

"Amazingly easy to use. Very portable, very complete."

—*Booklist*

"Detailed, accurate, and easy-to-read information for all price ranges."
—*Glamour Magazine*

"Hotel information is close to encyclopedic."

—*Des Moines Sunday Register*

"...a way of gi... ...ou a real feel for a place."

Published by:

Wiley Publishing, Inc.
111 River St.
Hoboken, NJ 07030-5774

Copyright © 2006 Wiley Publishing, Inc., Hoboken, New Jersey. All rights reserved. No part of this publication may be reproduced, stored in a retrieval system or transmitted in any form or by any means, electronic, mechanical, photocopying, recording, scanning or otherwise, except as permitted under Sections 107 or 108 of the 1976 United States Copyright Act, without either the prior written permission of the Publisher, or authorization through payment of the appropriate per-copy fee to the Copyright Clearance Center, 222 Rosewood Drive, Danvers, MA 01923, 978/750-8400, fax 978/646-8600. Requests to the Publisher for permission should be addressed to the Legal Department, Wiley Publishing, Inc., 10475 Crosspoint Blvd., Indianapolis, IN 46256, 317/572-3447, fax 317/572-4355, or online at http://www.wiley.com/go/permissions.

Wiley and the Wiley Publishing logo are trademarks or registered trademarks of John Wiley & Sons, Inc. and/or its affiliates. Frommer's is a trademark or registered trademark of Arthur Frommer. Used under license. All other trademarks are the property of their respective owners. Wiley Publishing, Inc. is not associated with any product or vendor mentioned in this book.

ISBN-13: 978-0-7645-9590-5
ISBN-10: 0-7645-9590-3

Editor: Jennifer Reilly
Production Editor: M. Faunette Johnston
Cartographer: Andrew Murphy
Photo Editor: Richard Fox
Production by Wiley Indianapolis Composition Services

Front cover photo: Positano: Cityscape amongst the cliffs, Bay of Naples behind
Back cover photo: Pompeii: House of the Vettii, Wall fresco

For information on our other products and services or to obtain technical support, please contact our Customer Care Department within the U.S. at 800/762-2974, outside the U.S. at 317/572-3993 or fax 317/572-4002.

Wiley also publishes its books in a variety of electronic formats. Some content that appears in print may not be available in electronic formats.

Manufactured in the United States of America

Contents

aviali' — Sta Agata dei Moti

Cancello

List of Maps

An Invitation to the Reader

In researching this book, we discovered many wonderful places—hotels, restaurants, shops, and more. We're sure you'll find others. Please tell us about them, so we can share the information with your fellow travelers in upcoming editions. If you were disappointed with a recommendation, we'd love to know that, too. Please write to:

Frommer's Amalfi Coast, 1st Edition
Wiley Publishing, Inc. • 111 River St. • Hoboken, NJ 07030-5774

An Additional Note

Please be advised that travel information is subject to change at any time—and this is especially true of prices. We therefore suggest that you write or call ahead for confirmation when making your travel plans. The authors, editors, and publisher cannot be held responsible for the experiences of readers while traveling. Your safety is important to us, however, so we encourage you to stay alert and be aware of your surroundings. Keep a close eye on cameras, purses, and wallets, all favorite targets of thieves and pickpockets.

About the Authors

Bruce Murphy has lived and worked in New York City, Boston, Chicago, Dublin, Rome, and Sicily. His work has appeared in magazines ranging from *Cruising World* to *Critical Inquiry*. In addition to guidebooks, he has published fiction, poetry, and criticism, most recently the *Encyclopedia of Murder and Mystery* (St. Martin's Press).

Alessandra de Rosa was born in Rome and has lived and worked in Rome, Paris, and New York City. She did her first cross-Europe trip at age 2, from Rome to London by car. She has continued in that line ever since, exploring three out of five continents so far. Her beloved Italy remains her preferred destination.

Other Great Guides for Your Trip:

Frommer's Italy
Frommer's Italy from $90 a Day
Frommer's Italy Best-Loved Driving Tours
Frommer's Northern Italy
Suzy Gershman's Born to Shop Italy

Frommer's Star Ratings, Icons & Abbreviations

Every hotel, restaurant, and attraction listing in this guide has been ranked for quality, value, service, amenities, and special features using a **star-rating system.** In country, state, and regional guides, we also rate towns and regions to help you narrow down your choices and budget your time accordingly. Hotels and restaurants are rated on a scale of zero (recommended) to three stars (exceptional). Attractions, shopping, nightlife, towns, and regions are rated according to the following scale: zero stars (recommended), one star (highly recommended), two stars (very highly recommended), and three stars (must-see).

In addition to the star-rating system, we also use **seven feature icons** that point you to the great deals, in-the-know advice, and unique experiences that separate travelers from tourists. Throughout the book, look for:

Finds	Special finds—those places only insiders know about
Fun Fact	Fun facts—details that make travelers more informed and their trips more fun
Kids	Best bets for kids and advice for the whole family
Moments	Special moments—those experiences that memories are made of
Overrated	Places or experiences not worth your time or money
Tips	Insider tips—great ways to save time and money
Value	Great values—where to get the best deals

The following **abbreviations** are used for credit cards:

AE	American Express	DISC	Discover	V	Visa
DC	Diners Club	MC	MasterCard		

Frommers.com

Now that you have the guidebook to a great trip, visit our website at **www.frommers.com** for travel information on more than 3,000 destinations. With features updated regularly, we give you instant access to the most current trip-planning information available. At Frommers.com, you'll also find the best prices on airfares, accommodations, and car rentals—and you can even book travel online through our travel booking partners. At Frommers.com, you'll also find the following:

- Online updates to our most popular guidebooks
- Vacation sweepstakes and contest giveaways
- Newsletter highlighting the hottest travel trends
- Online travel message boards with featured travel discussions

The Best of Campania & the Amalfi Coast

Campania—the region that encompasses Naples and the Amalfi Coast—is, for many tourists, *terra incognita*. But for Italians, it is a place of myth. In fact, centuries before the rise of Rome, it was coveted by Greek settlers and other immigrants, and the ancient Romans may have valued this region more than all their far-flung possessions. In this chapter, we'll help you discover the best of the region by pointing you toward its major treasures.

1 The Best Travel Experiences

- **Visiting Naples and its *Centro Antico:*** One of Italy's lesser-known art cities, Naples will surprise you with its stunning collection of exquisite frescoes, paintings, and sculptures, which cover its numerous monasteries, palaces, churches, and museums. From the early Greek settlers to modern times, Naples has been the most important harbor in the south of Italy. Kings and noble families have lavished art on the city as nowhere else in Italy except Rome, making Naples a competitor with Florence and Venice. A key stop for art lovers during the "Grand Tour," Naples was later forgotten due to the complete abandonment of its monuments. But thanks to sustained efforts over the past 10 to 15 years, Naples is again experiencing a tourism boom. See "Exploring Naples" in chapter 4.

- **Arriving in Naples by Boat:** You don't have to book a transatlantic cruise to have this marvelous experience. While arriving in Naples by car can be nerve-racking, confusing, and hot, with most landmarks annoyingly out of view, gliding into the bay with a sea breeze behind you and the city spread out ahead can be magnificent. The majestic and somewhat ominous presence of Vesuvius looming over the bay makes it that much more dramatic. You can arrive by regular ferry from one of the islands or even from one of the other harbors in Campania, such as Salerno or Sorrento. We recommend arriving during the very early morning or in the evening when the sun is sinking below the horizon, bathing the city in gold and orange; upon soaking in the sight, you'll instantly understand the motivation behind the old saying, "See Naples and die."

- **Hiking the Ancient Paths of the Amalfi Coast:** Even if you're not in great shape, taking a stroll on one of the Amalfi Coast's footpaths—once the only means of communication between the region's towns—ratchets up the intensity of this amazing seascape. The region's main road— the famed Amalfi Drive—was built in 1840 and made the area more accessible, perhaps too much so. The old trails, on the other hand, are unique, and lead you through the Amalfi Coast missed by so many tourists. Trails come in all levels of difficulty, from flat stretches (such as the footpath from Amalfi to Atrani) to downhill ones (such as the footpath from Ravello to Minori) to more demanding ones (including the Sentiero degli Dei and the Via degli Incanti from Positano). See chapter 7.

- **Exploring Greek Ruins:** The first colony the Greeks established in Italy was Cuma, near Pozzuoli. From there, they expanded south to the rest of the Campanian coast. The heritage they left in Campania is immense—rivaled in Italy only by Sicily—and in a state of conservation seen only in Greece itself. This is *Magna Grecia,* where ancient Greece first spread its influence into Italy, setting the stage for what we call Western culture. In these temples and towns, you literally get the chance to walk in the footsteps of Plato and Aristotle's contemporaries. See chapters 4 and 10.

- **Eating Pizza Neapolitan Style:** For Neapolitans, there is no other "style" of pizza, because they invented it. Whether you prefer a simple pizza joint or an elaborate restaurant, you'll share the pride Neapolitans feel for their invention, now taken over by the whole planet. The decor may be simple and traditional (sometimes nonexistent), and you'll usually have a modest choice of toppings—only two at Da Michele, reputed to make the best pizza in Naples. Yet at whichever place you choose, the outcome will be tasty, satisfying, and distinctive, because in Naples, no two pizzas are alike. See "Where to Dine" in chapter 4.

- **Shopping in Capri and Positano:** The best exclusive shopping in the region can be found at these two famous and trendy resorts, which stock treasure troves of unique, handmade clothes and shoes. You can still find tailors in Positano and cobblers in both towns who will make you sandals or garments on the spot, while you wait—or, even better, while you go for a swim. See chapter 7 for addresses in Positano and chapter 9 for Capri.

- **Wandering through Ancient Roman Lanes:** Walking the streets of Pompeii and Herculaneum gives you an eerie feeling; it's romantic and sad, and even a little scary. At the center of the lanes' mesmeric attraction is the knowledge that their violent destruction and miraculous preservation both happened on one terrible day, nearly two thousand years ago. And, with a little imagination, it can feel like it's *still* that day here. The Villa dei Papiri in Herculaneum and the Terme Suburbane in Pompeii have been opened to the public for the first time in 2004 and 2002, respectively—but the best sites here might be some of the lesser known, such as the magnificent Villa di Poppea in Oplontis with its wonderful frescoes, the Villa Arianna and the Villa di San Marco in Castellammare di Stabia, and the Villa Romana of Minori. See chapters 5, 7, and 10.

- **Listening to a Concert in a Typical Campanian Medieval Cloister:** The unique blend of cultures operating in Campania gave birth to some of the most splendid medieval cloisters ever built. Intertwined arches of Sicilian-Norman architecture are used here to support the loggias of delightful inner gardens where the sun, more often than not, is shining on fruit-laden citrus trees and ancient stone and tile work. During the summer, music festivals are held in most coastal towns to take advantage of these magical spaces. The best of the medieval marvels are the Chiostro del Paradiso in Amalfi, the Villa Rufolo in Ravello, and the cloister of San Francesco in Sorrento. See chapters 6 and 7.

2 The Best Ruins

- **The Temples of Paestum:** The three temples and the complete set of walls here are the best Greek ruins in existence outside Greece. One of the three temples—the grandiose **Temple of Neptune,** whose restoration was finished in 2004, is simply the best-preserved Greek temple in the world, along with the Theseion in Athens. Try to time your visit in spring or fall, when the roses are in bloom and the ruins are at their most romantic. The site is also stunning at dawn and sunset in any season, when the temples' travertine surfaces glow golden in the sun. See chapter 9.

- **The Acropolis of Cuma:** The first Greek colony in Italy and a beacon of Greek culture, Cuma was built on one of the most picturesque promontories in Campania. In the enchanting area of the Phlegrean Fields, where so many myths reside (the Cave of the Sybil, Lake Averno and the entrance to the underworld, and so on), Cuma offers a stunning panorama and atmospheric ruins. See "Phlegrean Fields" in chapter 4.

- **The Anfiteatro Campano:** The largest Roman amphitheater after the Colosseum, the Campano offers a glimpse at ancient artistry in spite of active pillage here from the 9th century onwards. On-site is the Museo dei Gladiatori, a permanent exhibit reconstructing the life of a gladiator; it is housed in a building located on the probable site of Capua's Gladiator School—whose most famous graduate was Spartacus, the slave made famous by the 1960 Stanley Kubrick film. Santa Maria Capua Vetere occupies the ground of Roman Capua, the city that Cicero considered second only to Rome. The area is rich in other noteworthy ruins, such as the splendid Mitreo (Temple to the Persian god Mithras), and museum collections. See chapter 10.

- **Pompeii and Herculaneum:** Will enough ever be said to describe these incredible sites? Even if you have already visited them in the past, new findings are reason enough for a return visit. The magnificent Villa dei Papiri in Herculaneum was opened to the public for the first time in 2004; the Terme Suburbane in Pompeii was opened in 2002. The riches of the archaeological area are best complemented by a visit to the Museo Archeologico Nazionale in Naples (see below), to view its massive array of frescoes and mosaics from earlier excavations at both sites. See chapter 5.

- **Oplontis:** Also called the Villa of Poppea, these are the ruins of a splendid Roman villa—believed to be that of Nero's wife—with magnificent frescoes and decorations. Less known than other sites and often passed by hurried tourists who stop only in Pompeii or Herculaneum, this villa is unique, not only for its state of conservation, but because modern archaeology requires materials to be left *in situ*. The frescoes and statuary grant you a fuller experience of the Romans' daily lives. See chapter 5.

- **Trajan's Arch in Benevento:** This is the world's best-preserved example of an ancient Roman triumphal arch. Recently restored—it took 14 years of work before the arch was opened again to the public in 2001—it is a masterpiece of carving that depicts the deeds of the admired (and fairly benevolent) Roman Emperor Trajan. Careful cleaning has eliminated darker areas in the marble, making the reliefs much easier to read. Inside a little Longobard church nearby is a permanent exhibit on the arch, its restoration, and Roman life under Trajan. See chapter 10.

- **Pozzuoli:** The ruins of the ancient Roman town of Puteoli have been difficult to excavate since the busy modern town occupies exactly the same area as the original (much as Rome does). In the splendid frame of Pozzuoli's bay, you'll find an underground Pompeii—buried not by a volcanic explosion, but by sinking under unstable volcanic ground. The main attractions are the Rione Terra, with Roman streets and shops; the 1st-century Greco-Roman market (Serapeo); and the Roman amphitheater (Anfiteatro Flavio), where musical performances are held during summer. See chapter 4.

- **The Underwater Archeological Park of Baia:** Due to subsiding ground, a large part of the ancient Roman town of Baia was submerged by the sea. Excavated and transformed into an archaeological park, it can now be visited with scuba equipment (if you dive, you can rent gear directly through the park when you sign in for a guided visit)—or if you don't like to get wet, you can tour the park in a glass-bottom boat. The itinerary leads you through the streets of the ancient town and inside its beautiful villas, now water-filled. This magical experience truly deserves the word *unique.* See "Phlegrean Fields" in chapter 4.

- **Velia:** Overshadowed by Paestum and just a bit too far from Naples for a day trip, Velia was the site of an important Greek settlement started around 540 B.C. It gave birth to one of the most important philosophical schools of antiquity—the Eleatic school of Parmenides and Zeno. Velia is one of the only Greek archaeological sites showing remains not only of an acropolis with its ruined temples, but also of a lower town with some houses. Portions of the walls here date from the 5th and 4th centuries B.C. A stretch of the original Greek pavement climbs towards the town gate, the famous Porta Rosa. A highlight of the Roman period is the thermal baths. See chapter 9.

3 The Best Churches & Cathedrals

- **Casertavecchia Cathedral:** This medieval church is one of the most beautiful extant examples of Norman-Arab architecture, built with two colors of tufa stone and white marble, and dotted with strange human and animal figures. See chapter 10.

- **Naples's Duomo:** The most splendid of Naples's churches, and home of superb artwork, you'll find that the Duomo is three churches in one. The Cappella di San Gennaro is really a church, with a fantastic treasure on display in the attached museum. Santa Restituta, the original 6th-century

church, contains a magnificent 4th-century baptistery. See chapter 4.

- **Complesso Monumentale di Santa Chiara:** Another star on the Neapolitan scene, this splendid church-cum-monastery holds splendid examples of 14th-century sculpture that escaped the tragic bombing of World War II. (Other parts of the massive structure were not so lucky but have been restored.) The spacious majolica cloister holds a plethora of mythological, pastoral, and whimsical scenes enchanting to behold in the open air. See chapter 4.

- **San Lorenzo Maggiore:** Originally built in the 6th century, this is a lesser-known church in Naples, but it's famous for its literary guests—Boccaccio (who met his darling Fiammetta here), Francesco Petrarca, and others. It holds splendid Renaissance masterpieces and a multilayered archaeological site, where you can descend like a time traveler through layers of buildings all the way down to a paleochristian basilica and the 1st-century Roman Macellum (Market). See chapter 4.

- **Chiesa della Santissima Annunziata:** This church is located in Minuto, one of the medieval hamlets of the township of Scala, which stretches along the cliffs of the Amalfi Coast. The church offers not only some of the region's best examples of Romanesque architecture and beautiful 12th-century frescoes, but also a superb panorama. See chapter 7.

- **Duomo di Santa Maria Capua Vetere:** Dating originally from the 5th century, this beautiful paleochristian church has been redecorated in later centuries, but it contains artworks reaching back to Roman times (its columns and capitals), as well as examples of Renaissance frescoes and carvings. See chapter 10.

- **Sant'Angelo in Formis:** This is one of the most important Romanesque churches in the whole country. Its entire interior is graced with beautiful frescoes. The church's lovely setting is Mount Tifata, near Capua. See chapter 10.

- **Santa Sofia:** Dating back to the early Longobard kingdom in Benevento, this small medieval church is famous for its unique star-shaped floor plan and the integration of Longobard and Catholic symbols. See chapter 10.

- **Certosa di Padula (Carthusian Monastery of San Lorenzo):** Begun in the 14th century, this magnificent monastery—one of the largest in the world—is a baroque masterpiece, chock-full of art and architectural details, and only a short distance from Salerno. See chapter 9.

- **San Guglielmo al Goleto:** Located in Sant'Angelo dei Lombardi—way off the beaten track in Irpinia—this magnificent 12th-century fortified monastery is one of the most scenic and picturesque sights in all Italy. See chapter 10.

4 The Best Castles & Palaces

- **Castel dell'Ovo:** The symbol of Naples and the most picturesque icon of the Naples waterfront, this castle is the city's oldest fortification—dating back to its origin in the 9th century B.C. Greek settlement. Its foundations are said to be built over a magic egg hidden by the poet-magician Virgil for the defense of the city (which will crumble into ruin if the egg is destroyed). See chapter 4.

- **Reggia di Caserta:** The Versailles of Italy, this splendid royal palace was built by the famous architect Vanvitelli for the Bourbon kings in the 18th century. It holds fantastic art pieces (it's completely covered with decorations) and is famed for one of the most beautiful Italian gardens in the world. The massive scale of the palace, and the quality of the artwork, have to be seen to be believed. See chapter 10.

- **Castel Nuovo (Maschio Angioino):** This 13th-century castle was the residence of Neapolitan kings until the 17th century. Although a fire in the 16th century destroyed its beautiful frescoes by Giotto, there is still enough in this majestic fortress to impress visitors. See chapter 4.

- **Palazzo Reale:** The beautiful Royal Palace of Naples dominates wide Piazza del Plebiscito with its neoclassical facade and statues of kings. Inside, you'll find a rich collection of art and decorations as well as a wonderful library. See chapter 4.

- **Castel Lauritano:** This ruined castle in Agerola, a town on the Amalfi Coast, is incredibly picturesque and offers extensive views over both the coast and the interior. See chapter 7.

- **Villa Rufolo:** This splendid villa in Ravello has been made famous by its terrace and gardens, which inspired Wagner to write some of his *Parsifal*, so moved was he by its vistas. Today, you can listen to concerts of Wagner's work in the same setting. See chapter 7.

- **Villa Cimbrone:** The second most famous villa in Ravello, also with a splendid panoramic terrace, the Villa Cimbrone has another attraction: It houses a small hotel and a restaurant, which was opened to the public in 2005. See chapter 7.

5 The Best Museums

- **Museo Nazionale di Capodimonte:** Created by the Bourbon kings, this picture gallery is one of the best in the world, holding paintings from the 13th century onwards. The catalogue looks like a book on art history, complete with all the famous names of Italian art and many members of the Flemish school. The regular special exhibits draw visitors from all over Italy, Europe, and the world. (The success of these special exhibits is such that you'll need advance reservations to get in, unless you don't mind standing in line for several hours.) See chapter 4.

- **Museo Archeologico Nazionale:** Even if you are only mildly interested in archaeology, you should not miss this wonderful museum, which holds the largest collection of ancient Roman artifacts in the world. Created in the 17th century—with original Roman mosaics re-used in the floors and statues incorporated in the facade decoration—this is where the best finds from Pompeii and other sites were placed on display. The huge quantity of frescoes, statuary, and precious objects has benefited from a

reorganization, which was finished in 2005. See chapter 4.

- **Museo Nazionale della Ceramica Duca di Martina:** Housed in the splendid Villa Floridiana up in Naples's Vomero neighborhood, this rich ceramic collection includes the most important assemblage of Capodimonte porcelain in the world. See chapter 4.

- **Museo Campano:** This museum in Capua has a tall order, as the repository of the history and culture of the whole Campania region. It does a great job, though, with its several collections, covering the whole ancient history of the area, from the Oscans (about 6th century B.C.) to the Renaissance. It has a magnificent collection of parchment and illuminated manuscripts. See chapter 10.

- **Museo del Duomo:** This museum in Salerno is not large, but it holds a number of invaluable masterpieces ranging from Roman times to the Renaissance and baroque periods. It includes a unique collection of ivory carvings, a great picture gallery, and a rich collection of illuminated manuscripts. See chapter 9.

- **Museo del Sannio:** Housed in the beautiful cloister of Santa Sofia in Benevento, this is a small but well-rounded collection of artifacts from a local temple. It includes the largest collection of Egyptian art found at any archaeological site in Italy. See chapter 10.

- **Museo Irpino:** This modern museum displays a collection of artifacts found in the rich archaeological sites in the outlying region of Avellino. The objects date back into the distant past long before the Romans (or even the Greeks) came to the region—as far back as 4000 B.C. See chapter 10.

- **Museo Archeologico dei Campi Flegrei:** Housed in the picturesque Aragonese Castle of Baia, this is another great treasure trove of Roman and Greek art in the vicinity of Naples. See chapter 4.

6 The Best Swimming & Sunbathing Spots

- **Vico Equense:** This lesser-known resort town on the Sorrentine peninsula is endowed with several beaches—most of them small and hidden away inside picturesque coves, including **Marina di Equa,** dominated by a powerful 17th-century tower. See chapter 6.

- **Punta del Capo:** This lovely beach near Sorrento under the cliffs has attracted visitors from time immemorial. Nearby, you'll find the ruins of a Roman villa and a small pool of water enclosed by rocks, known as the Bath of Queen Giovanna. See chapter 6.

- **Bay of Ieranto:** Part of the Marine Preserve of Punta Campanella, this unique fjord was almost lost to developers, who would have spoiled its beauty forever. When the light is just right at day's end, the clarity of the waters here creates the illusion of boats floating in mid-air. See chapter 6.

- **Grotta dello Smeraldo:** Although this grotto in the village of Conca dei Marini on the Amalfi Coast is usually visited by boat, it is also the destination of a scuba procession on Christmas night. The pretty beach can be visited anytime, however. See chapter 7.

- **Positano:** The most famous resort on the Amalfi Coast, Positano has several very nice beaches—although they're hardly deserted. Besides the central **Spiaggia Grande** by the Marina, you'll find **Fornillo** to the west of town, and **La Porta, Ciumicello, Arienzo,** and **Laurito** to the east. See chapter 7.

- **Spiaggia di Citara:** This is the most beautiful beach on the island of Ischia, near the little town of Forio. Besides the lovely scenery, there are several natural thermal springs. See chapter 8.

- **Lido dei Maronti:** Also on Ischia, this beach is a delightful 2km (1¼-mile) stretch of fine sand. See chapter 8.

- **Marina di Paestum:** Greek temples are not the only reason to come to Paestum. The sandy beach here is one of the best in Italy, extending for miles along the clear blue sea. See chapter 9.

- **Baia della Calanca:** In beautiful Marina di Camerota, this is one of the nicest beaches in the Cilento, and is famed for its clear waters. See chapter 9.

- **Bagni di Tiberio:** This is the best of the rare and tiny beaches of Capri. As the name suggests, it lies near the ruins of one of Emperor Tiberius's notorious pleasure palaces. It is accessible by a rocky steep path or by boat. See chapter 8.

7 The Best Spas

- **Parco Termale Giardini Poseidon:** This is our favorite thermal spa. Located on beautiful Ischia, the Poseidon boasts scenic outdoor thermal pools from which you can enjoy great views and a variety of aesthetic and health treatments. See chapter 8.
- **Ischia Thermal Center:** In the small town of Ischia, this is one of the most modern spas on the island, where you can enjoy a variety of state-of-the-art modern services. See chapter 8.
- **Terme della Regina Isabella:** Among the most famous and elegant spas on Ischia, this historical establishment in exclusive Lacco Ameno offers state-of-the-art facilities. See chapter 8.

- **Castellammare di Stabia:** This pleasant seaside resort is blessed with 28 natural thermal springs which you can enjoy at one of the two public spas: the historical one built by the Bourbon kings or the modern establishment on the slopes of Mount Faito. Both offer a wide range of services, from beauty and relaxation treatments to medical ones. See chapter 5.
- **Scrajo Terme:** At the beginning of the Sorrentine peninsula, just outside the pleasant resort town of In Vico Equense, you'll find this historic thermal establishment dating back to the 19th century. Stayovers are offered so that visitors can "take the waters" in style. See chapter 6.

8 The Best Vistas

- **Lungomare di Salerno:** Italy's best-kept secret may be the seaside promenade of laid-back Salerno. A splendid and completely pedestrian walkway lined with palm trees, it offers views encompassing the whole bay from Capri to Punta Licosa in the Cilento. See chapter 9.
- **Deserto:** From the terraces of this Carmelite hermitage near Sant'Agata dei Golfi, you can enjoy the famous, unique circular panorama encompassing both the Gulf of Naples with Sorrento and the islands, and the Gulf of Salerno with the Amalfi Coast. On a good day, you can see almost the whole region, from the Cilento—way off to the south of Paestum—to Capo Miseno, to the islands of Ischia and Procida, and to Capri. See chapter 6.
- **Belvedere dello Schiaccone:** This is the best lookout along the whole Amalfi Drive, located just west of Positano and accessible from the

road; the views are indeed superb. See chapter 7.
- **Lake Fusaro:** In the picturesque Phlegrean Fields, not far from Pozzuoli, this beautiful lake was chosen by the Bourbon kings as the site for the Casina Reale, a structural jewel designed by the architect Vanvitelli. Today, as back then, the Casina Reale commands royal views perfect for picture taking. See chapter 4.
- **Monte Cervati:** The highest peak of the Cilento massif, Cervati is famous for its beauty in summer—when it turns purple with lavender fields—and for the magnificent views from its top. See chapter 9.
- **Agropoli:** From the walls of the medieval citadel you can look down on vast stretches of coastline—a view that helped the Saracens hold onto Agropoli as the base for their incursions until they were finally dislodged in the 11th century. See chapter 9.

9 The Best Restaurants

- **Don Alfonso 1890:** This is one of the top Italian gourmet addresses and the best restaurant south of Naples, created and maintained by hosts Lidia and Alfonso Iaccarino. The restaurant, a member of the Relais & Châteaux association, has a luxurious decor and offers superb food made of ingredients mainly from the chefs' own organic farm. See chapter 6.

- **Taverna del Capitano:** Competing for the title of best restaurant on the Sorrento peninsula with Don Alfonso, this is our preferred spot to eat in the area. It might not have the elegance of Don Alfonso (though it's not a place to drop by in your bathing attire, either); it has a more down-to-earth atmosphere and an enthusiasm for homegrown food that we find irresistible. See chapter 6.

- **Faro di Capo d'Orso:** Owned by a young, emerging chef—Rocco Iannone—the Faro (Lighthouse) is one of the culinary highlights of the Amalfi Coast, supplemented by a unique location that offers stunning views of this stretch of coast. See chapter 7.

- **Ristorante Il San Pietro:** The restaurant of the famous hotel in Positano with the same name (see later in this chapter), Il San Pietro offers the fine cuisine of chef Alois Vanlangenacker—all based on ingredients from the hotel's own farm—and a delightfully romantic setting which is worth a visit all by itself. See chapter 7.

- **La Stanza del Gusto:** This small restaurant in Naples is the kingdom of Mario Avallone, chef and perfect host. The "Hall of Tastes," as it might be called in English, is a wonderful world where only the best ingredients and most pleasurable associations—some based on traditional Neapolitan cuisine—are to be found. The decor is intimate and vaguely bohemian, serving as the perfect background for the chef's inventive dishes. The prix-fixe menu is an adventure more than a sampler, and the wine list is a tome. See chapter 4.

- **George's:** Located on the roof terrace of the Grand Hotel Parker's (see below), this is a truly elegant restaurant happily devoid of stuffiness or ostentation. There's no snobbery here, only the best that money can buy. Chef Baciòt brings together the ingredients of tasty and healthy dishes which marry tradition with nutrition. The service and surroundings are impeccable, and the wine list is among the best in Italy. See chapter 4.

- **La Cantinella:** This well-known restaurant proudly serves a classic version of traditional Neapolitan cuisine, with a large share of the menu dedicated to seafood. You'll have to make your reservations early, because it is very popular with local crowds. See chapter 4.

10 The Best Luxury Stays

- **Grand Hotel Parker's** (© 081-7612474): This is Naples's most romantic luxury hotel, competing with the Vesuvio (see below) for the title of best hotel in town. Housed in a magnificent Liberty-style building, it offers superb service, classy accommodations, and one of the best restaurants in the country (see earlier). See chapter 4.

- **Grand Hotel Vesuvio** (© 081-7640044): This is generally considered the best hotel in Naples, offering palatial accommodations and exquisite service. You will be pampered the moment you step through the doors. A turndown service includes signature quality chocolates, not mere mints, on your pillow. You can have dinner in the gourmet roof-restaurant where you'll be fussed over by a professional maitre d'. Every detail here is truly first-class. See chapter 4.

- **Hotel San Pietro Positano** (© 800-7352478): A member of the Relais & Châteaux group, this elegant hotel is one of our preferred places to stay in the whole of Italy. You'll understand why as soon as you step inside. The romantic views from their terraces, the kind and attentive service, the colorful and cheerful—yet magnificently tasteful—furnishing details: We love everything about this place. See chapter 7.
- **Grand Hotel Excelsior Vittoria** (© 081-8071044): This gorgeous hotel is the best in Sorrento, housed in what once was a palatial residence overlooking the sea. The antiques in the guest rooms, the picturesque terraces, and the service make this an ideal hotel, right in the center of town (but with its own elevator down to a private beach). See chapter 6.

- **Hotel Santa Caterina** (© 089-871012): Amalfi's most luxurious hotel, on a cliff just out of town, this is where you'll want to come to be pampered away from the crowds—and to enjoy the hotel's beautiful private beach, swimming pool, and lush gardens. See chapter 7.
- **Hotel Le Sirenuse** (© 089-875066): Competing for the title of best hotel in Positano with the San Pietro above, this gorgeous hotel is housed in a beautiful 18th-century villa overlooking the sea. It offers palatial accommodations and fine service. See chapter 7.
- **Grand Hotel Quisisana Capri** (© 081-8370788): The glitziest resort on Capri, this luxury hotel provides its guests with splendid accommodations and exquisite service. The hotel's bar and restaurant are popular spots for visiting socialites, so it's worth stopping by just to enjoy the atmosphere. See chapter 8.
- **Capri Palace** (© 081-9780111): This is the best hotel on Capri, which naturally means elegance, breathtaking views, and deluxe furnishings in rooms decorated with artwork and antiques. The service is impeccable. See chapter 8.

2

Planning Your Trip to Campania & the Amalfi Coast

This chapter is devoted to the where, when, and how of your trip. Because you might not know exactly where in Campania you want to go, we'll start off with a quick rundown of the various regions that make up this larger region. To see Campania's highlights, plan on spending at least 5 to 7 days; 10 days will give you the leisure to enjoy things without feeling too pressed for time, and 14 days is about perfect.

1 The Regions in Brief

More than any other region, **Campania** reverberates with the memories of antiquity, from the Greeks, to the Etruscans, to the ancient Romans, who favored its strong sunlight, fertile soil, and bubbling sulfurous springs so much they made the region their preferred vacation destination.

Its marvelous spas, beaches, and islands still attract visitors from all around the world, but Campania also has a few surprises for those who take time to go off the beaten path. Norman and Longobard castles, delightful medieval bourgs, huge and rich monasteries, and high mountains and wonderful caves compose only part of what Campania has to offer. Campania has both one of the lowest population areas in Italy—in the mountain area of the Cilento—as well as the highest—in the urban area of Naples. The latter is what most tourists experience, which is good news—it means some of Campania's best attractions are still undiscovered.

THE AMALFI COAST

The most famous destination in the region, the Amalfi Coast will charm you with its dramatic coastline and beautiful cliff villages. Starting at **Vietri sul Mare,**

famous for its ceramics and majolica, Amalfi Drive is home to leading resorts (even though they're not exactly undiscovered) in **Ravello** (not on the sea) and **Positano** (on the sea). **Amalfi** is a harbor town rich in history and beauty, but its beaches tend to be crowded. It is the best starting point for walking tours along the coast and up the cliffs, and boasts a number of hotels cheaper than other towns on the coast. Amalfi is also an excellent base for exploring the area's lesser-known little towns. **Cetara, Atrani, Conca dei Marini, Praiano,** and **Vettica Maggiore** are all delightful towns right by the sea, while the interior—or, more appropriately, the cliff tops—hides such wonderful places as **Scala, Furore, Agerola,** and **Tramonti.**

NAPLES

Allow at least 2 days for Naples, which has amazing museums and incredible churches, to compensate for the world's worst traffic outside Cairo. The historic center of the city has changed so much since the renovations and reorganization of the 1990s that you will hardly recognize the city if you've visited earlier. Also, police work has been effective in reducing crime. Though the tourist areas are safer than ever, Naples *is* a big city, and you should still keep a careful eye on your belongings.

THE PHLEGREAN FIELDS

Campania contains many sites identified in ancient mythology, and most of them are in this region to the northwest of Naples, a volcanic area where bubbling springs and hot mud conjure up images of the underworld. (Lake Averno, the mythical entrance to the Kingdom of the Dead, can be found here.) This beautiful area is well worth a visit both for its rich archaeological remains and splendid natural attractions. The **Solfatara** volcano, the volcanic lakes, the beautiful promontory of **Capo Miseno,** and the delightful bay are enough reasons to come, but you should also visit the splendid ruins of **Cuma**—the first Greek colony in Italy, which includes the rich Roman archaeological sites of **Pozzuoli** and **Baia**—with its magical and unique underwater archeological park.

ISCHIA & PROCIDA

The natural continuation of the Phlaegrean fields, small and exclusive Procida, and peaceful Ischia, are volcanic islands of great beauty. Procida is where the most fortunate of VIPs have their hideaway villas overlooking one of the most beautiful bays in the world, while other mortals—us for instance—come to enjoy fantastic meals in remote, romantic restaurants. Ischia is where those in the know come for delicious spa vacations. The volcano of Ischia—Monte Epomeo—was still quite active when the Greeks tried to establish their first colony on this coast, but today, the inactive volcano serves only to feed the mineral hot springs and therapeutic muds which are used by the over 150 spas on the island.

CAPRI

The most famous of Campania's islands, Capri is the preferred destination for those seeking fun in the sun. The island is indeed spectacular, with postcard-worthy soaring cliffs, surrounded by a deep-blue sea. Besides being a choice destination for VIPs and wannabes, it has also traditionally been an important gay destination. Positively overcrowded during the summer with day visitors, Capri is at its best if you stay overnight.

THE VESUVIAN AREA

What would Naples's skyline be like without Mount Vesuvius? You'll discover the love-fear relationship that Neapolitans have with their volcano when you climb its slopes and when you taste its marvelous *Lacrima Christi* wine. Along the coast and its slopes are some of the world's most renowned ancient ruins: **Pompeii** and **Herculaneum,** and some worthwhile lesser-known ones, including the Roman Villa of **Oplonti** with its magnificent frescoes (a UNESCO World Heritage Site), the rural roman villas of **Boscoreale,** and the thermal resort of **Stabiae,** by the very active **Castellammare di Stabia.** These, together with the seaside town of **Torre del Greco**—modern in appearance but home to one of the oldest crafts on this coast, the carving of *cameos*—are great places to stay overnight if you'd like a more in-depth visit.

SORRENTO & ITS PENINSULA

The beautiful seaside setting of **Sorrento** has long been celebrated, and justly so. The Sorrento peninsula also has much to offer, including off-the-beaten-track splendid destinations to get away from the crowds, from elegant **Vico Equense** to out-of-the-way **Massa Lubrense** and **Sant'Agata sui due Golfi** with its incredible views.

Campania & the Amalfi Coast

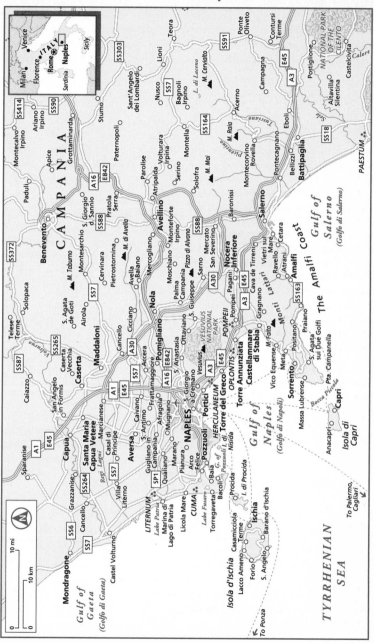

SALERNO

This lively town at the edge of the Amalfi Coast boasts Italy's most beautiful seafront promenade, but it's hardly visited by foreign tourists. It has a delightful medieval center—rich in small shops and restaurants—and a superb 11th- century Duomo, which, with its nearby museum, are enough to justify a visit to Campania. Salerno has the advantage, too, of being little crowded and having advantageously low hotel and restaurant rates.

THE CILENTO

Completely unknown to foreign tourists and very little known to Italians, the Cilento is Italy's second largest natural park, containing some of the most exciting natural attractions—including two huge caves, delightful fishing towns, and seaside resorts with fine sand beaches. The famous Greek ruins of **Paestum** have the best conserved Greek temple after the Theseion in Athens.

BENEVENTO

This is Campania's prettiest large town, situated up in the hilltops and well off-the-beaten-track. It hides some wonderful art treasures, including the best-preserved ancient Roman arch in existence and an intriguing Longobard star-shaped church.

Some of Italy's best D.O.C. wines, through the special label *Denominazione di Origine Controllata,* come from the hilly areas nearby.

AVELLINO

This small town, with its beautiful cathedral and wonderful archeological museum, is the capital of Irpinia, a region known for its food and wine. Also worth visiting in the area are the village of **Sant'Angelo dei Lombardi** and the nearby Convento di San Marco, one of the most romantic monasteries around (now being restored).

CASERTA

If the Caserta were to compete with the Versailles in France on matters of elegance and beauty, in our opinion the Reggia di Caserta would emerge the winner. Truly, the palace is reason enough for a visit to Campania. Nearby you'll find the medieval bourg of **Casertavecchia,** one of the best preserved in Italy. Also nearby is the very little-visited **Basilica of Sant'Angelo** in Fornmis, with its magnificent 11th-century frescoes, and the Old Roman Capua—**Santa Maria Capua Vetere.** During Roman times, this was the most prosperous city in the empire after Rome.

2 Visitor Information

For information before you go, contact the Italian National Tourist Board.

In the United States: 630 Fifth Ave., Suite 1565, New York, NY 10111 (© **212/245-4822;** fax 212/586-9249); 500 N. Michigan Ave., Suite 2240, Chicago, IL 60611 (© **312/644-0996;** fax 312/644-3019); and 12400 Wilshire Blvd., Suite 550, Los Angeles, CA 90025 (© **310/820-1898;** fax 310/820-6357).

In Canada: 175 Bloor St. E., South Tower, Suite 907, Toronto, ON, M4W 3R8 (© **416/925-4882;** fax 416/925-4799).

In the United Kingdom: 1 Princes St., London W1R 8AY (© **020/7408-1254;** fax 020/7399-3567).

You can also write directly (in English or Italian) to the provincial or local tourist boards of the areas you plan to visit.

There are five Provincial tourist boards (Ente Provinciale per il Turismo) in Campania:

EPT Napoli (also for Phlaegrean Fields, Pompeii and Herculaneum, and the Sorrento Peninsula): Piazza dei Martiri 58, 80121 Napoli (© **081-4107211;** www.ept.napoli.it).

EPT Salerno (also for the Amalfi Coast and the Cilento): Via Velia 15, Cap 84100 Salerno (© **089-230411;** www. crmpa.it/ept).

EPT Caserta (also for Capua): Palazzo Reale, 81100 Caserta (© **0823-322233;** www.casertaturismo.it).

EPT Avellino: Via Due Principati 5, 83100 Avellino (© **0825-74731** or 0825-74695; fax 0825-74757; www. provincia.avellino.it and www.e-irpinia.it).

EPT Benevento: Via Sala 31, 82100 Benevento (© **0824-319911;** www. eptbenevento.it).

Local tourist boards **(Azienda Autonoma di Cura, Soggiorno e Turismo)** operate in all places of tourist interest; we have listed their addresses in each chapter, but check with the Italian National Tourist Board for updated fax numbers, or on the Web at **www.enit.it** or **www.italiantourism.com**.

3 Entry Requirements & Customs

ENTRY REQUIREMENTS

U.S., Canadian, U.K., Irish, Australian, and New Zealand citizens with a **valid passport** don't need a visa to enter Italy or Campania if they don't expect to stay more than 90 days and don't expect to work there. If, after entering Italy, you want to stay more than 90 days, you can apply for a permit for an extra 90 days, which as a rule is granted immediately. Go to the nearest *questura* (police headquarters) or to your home country's consulate. If your passport is lost or stolen, head to your consulate as soon as possible for a replacement

For information on how to get a passport, go to "Passports" in the "Fast Facts" section of this chapter—the websites listed provide downloadable passport applications as well as the current fees for processing passport applications. For an up-to-date, country-by-country listing of passport requirements around the world, go to the "Foreign Entry Requirement" Web page of the U.S. State Department at **http://travel.state.gov**.

CUSTOMS

WHAT YOU CAN BRING INTO ITALY OR CAMPANIA   Foreign visitors can bring along most items for personal use duty-free, including fishing tackle, a pair of skis, two tennis rackets, a baby carriage, two hand cameras with 10 rolls of film, and 400 cigarettes or a quantity of cigars or pipe tobacco not exceeding 500 grams (1.1 lb.). There are strict limits on importing alcoholic beverages. However, for alcohol bought tax-paid, limits are much more liberal than in other countries of the European Union.

WHAT YOU CAN TAKE HOME Rules governing what you can bring back duty-free vary from country to country and are subject to change, but they're generally posted on the Internet.

Returning **U.S. citizens** who have been away for at least 48 hours are allowed to bring back, once every 30 days, $800 worth of merchandise duty-free. You'll pay a flat rate of duty on the next $1,000 worth of purchases. Any dollar amount beyond that is subject to duties at whatever rates apply. On mailed gifts, the duty-free limit is $200. Be sure to keep your receipts for purchases accessible to expedite the declaration process. *Note:* If you owe duty, you are required to pay on your arrival in the United States—either by cash, personal check, government or traveler's check, or money order (or, in some locations, a Visa or MasterCard).

To avoid paying duty on foreign-made personal items you owned before your trip, bring along a bill of sale, insurance policy, jeweler's appraisal, or receipts of purchase. Or you can register items that can be readily identified by a permanently affixed serial number or marking—think laptop computers, cameras, and CD players—with Customs before you leave. Take the items to the nearest Customs office or register them with Customs at the airport from which you're departing. You'll receive, at no cost, a Certificate of Registration, which allows duty-free entry for the life of the item.

With some exceptions, you cannot bring fresh fruits and vegetables into the United States. For specifics on what you can bring back, download the invaluable free pamphlet *Know Before You Go* online at **www.cbp.gov**. (Click on "Travel," and then click on "Know Before You Go! Online Brochure.") Or request the pamphlet from the **U.S. Customs & Border Protection (CBP)**, 1300 Pennsylvania Ave. NW, Washington, DC 20229 (© **877/287-8667**).

For a clear summary of **Canadian** rules, write for the booklet *I Declare,* issued by the **Canada Border Services Agency** (© **800/461-9999** in Canada, or 204/983-3500; www.cbsa-asfc.gc.ca). Canada allows its citizens a C$750 exemption, and you're allowed to bring back duty-free 1 carton of cigarettes, 1 can of tobacco, 40 imperial ounces of liquor, and 50 cigars. In addition, you're allowed to mail gifts to Canada valued at less than C$60 a day, provided they're unsolicited and don't contain alcohol or tobacco. (Write on the package: "Unsolicited gift, under $60 value.") All valuables should be declared on the Y-38 form before departure from Canada, including serial numbers of valuables you already own, such as expensive foreign cameras. *Note:* The $750 exemption can only be used once a year and only after an absence of 7 days.

Citizens of the U.K. who are **returning from a European Union (E.U.) country** will go through a separate Customs Exit (called the "Blue Exit") especially for E.U. travelers. In essence, there is no limit on what you can bring back from an E.U. country, provided the items are for personal use (this includes gifts), and you have already paid the necessary duty and tax. Customs law, however, sets out guidance levels. If you bring in more than these levels, you may be asked to prove that the goods are for your own use. Guidance levels on goods bought into the E.U. for personal use are 3,200 cigarettes, or 200 cigars, or 400 cigarillos, or 3 kilograms of smoking tobacco, 10 liters of spirits, 90 liters of wine, 20 liters of fortified wine (such as port or sherry), and 110 liters of beer.

The duty-free allowance in **Australia** is A$400 or, for those under 18, A$200. Citizens can bring in 250 cigarettes or 250 grams of loose tobacco, and 1.125 liters of alcohol. If you're returning with valuables you already own, such as foreign-made cameras, you should file form B263. A helpful brochure available from Australian consulates or Customs offices is *Know Before You Go*. For more information, call the **Australian Customs Service** at © **1300/363-263,** or log on to www.customs.gov.au.

The duty-free allowance for **New Zealand** is NZ$700. Citizens over 17 can bring in 200 cigarettes, 50 cigars, or 250 grams of tobacco (or a mixture of all three if their combined weight doesn't exceed 250g); plus 4.5 liters of wine and beer, or 1.125 liters of liquor. New Zealand currency does not carry import or export restrictions. Fill out a certificate of export, listing the valuables you are taking out of the country; that way, you can bring them back without paying duty. Most questions are answered in a free pamphlet available at New Zealand consulates and Customs offices: *New Zealand Customs Guide for Travellers, Notice no. 4.* For more information, contact **New Zealand Customs,** The Customhouse, 17–21 Whitmore St., Box 2218, Wellington (© **04/473-6099** or 0800/428-786; www.customs.govt.nz).

4 Money

CURRENCY

The **euro,** the single European currency, became the official currency of Italy and 11 other participating countries on January 1, 1999. You will still occasionally run into prices quoted in both euros and lire, but for all other purposes, the old currency, the Italian lira, was completely replaced by the euro on January 1, 2002. The euro's official abbreviation is "EUR." Exchange rates of participating countries are locked into a common currency that fluctuates against the dollar.

For more details on the euro, check out **www.europa.eu.int/euro**.

FOREIGN CURRENCIES VS. THE U.S. DOLLAR

Conversion ratios between the U.S. dollar and other currencies fluctuate, and their differences could affect the costs of your holiday. The figures reflected in the currency chart below were valid at the time of writing, but they might not be valid by the time of your departure. Check for more updated rates prior to making any serious commitments.

Exchange rates are more favorable at the point of arrival. Nevertheless, it's often helpful to exchange at least some money before going abroad. (Standing in line at the *cambio* [exchange bureau] in the Milan or Rome airport could make you miss the next bus leaving for downtown.) Check with any local American Express or Thomas Cook offices or major banks. Or order euros in advance from the following: **American Express** (© 800/ 221-7282;** www.americanexpress.com), **Thomas Cook** (© 800/223-7373;** www.thomascook.com). Note the rates and ask about commission fees; it can sometimes pay to shop around and ask the right questions.

ATMS

The easiest and best way to get cash away from home is from an ATM (automated teller machine). ATMs are prevalent in all Italian cities and even the smaller towns. ATMs are linked to a national network that most likely includes your bank at home. The **Cirrus** (© 800/424-7787; www.mastercard.com) network is much more common in Italy than **PLUS** (© 800/843-7587; www.visa.com), but both networks have automated ATM locators listing the banks in Italy that will accept your card. Or just search out any machine with your network's symbol emblazoned on it.

Make sure that the PINs on your bank cards and credit cards will work in Italy. You'll likely need a **four-digit code** (six digits may not work), so if you have a six-digit code you'll want to go into your bank and get a new PIN for your trip. If you're unsure about this, contact Cirrus or PLUS (see above). Be sure to check the daily withdrawal limit at the same time. *Note:* Remember that many banks impose a fee every time you use a card at another bank's ATM, and that fee can be higher for international transactions (up to $5 or more) than for domestic ones (where they're rarely more than $2). In addition, the bank from which you withdraw cash may charge its own fee. To compare banks' ATM fees within the U.S., use **www.bankrate.com**. For international withdrawal fees, ask your bank.

TRAVELER'S CHECKS

Traveler's checks are something of an anachronism from the days before the ATM made cash accessible at any time. Given the fees you'll pay for ATM use at banks other than your own, however, you might be better off with traveler's checks if you're going to withdraw money often.

The Euro, the U.S. Dollar & the British Pound

For American Readers Since the euro's inception, the U.S. dollar and the euro have traded on par (in other words, $1 approximately equals 1€). But as this book went to press, the euro continued to gain strength against the dollar. In converting prices to U.S. dollars, we used a conversion rate of 1€ = $1.25. For up-to-the-minute exchange rates between the euro and the dollar, check the currency converter website **www.xe.com/ucc**.

For British Readers At this writing, £1 = approximately $1.85, and approximately €1.48. These were the rates of exchange used to calculate the values in the table below.

Euro €	US$	UK£	Euro €	US$	UK£
1.00	1.25	.68	75.00	93.75	50.68
2.00	2.50	1.35	100.00	125.00	84.46
3.00	3.75	2.03	125.00	156.25	84.46
4.00	5.00	2.70	150.00	187.50	101.35
5.00	6.25	3.38	175.00	218.75	118.24
6.00	7.50	4.05	200.00	250.00	135.14
7.00	8.75	4.73	225.00	281.25	152.03
8.00	9.20	5.41	250.00	312.50	168.92
9.00	10.00	6.08	275.00	343.75	185.81
10.00	12.50	6.76	300.00	375.00	202.70
15.00	18.75	10.14	350.00	437.50	236.49
20.00	25.00	13.51	400.00	500.00	270.27
25.00	31.25	16.89	500.00	625.00	337.84
50.00	62.50	33.78	1000.00	1250.00	675.68

You can buy traveler's checks at most banks. **American Express** offers denominations of $20, $50, $100, $500, and (for cardholders only) $1,000. You'll pay a service charge ranging from 1% to 4%. By phone, you can buy traveler's checks by calling ⓒ **800/807-6233**. American Express cardholders should dial ⓒ **800/ 221-7282**; this number accepts collect calls, offers service in several foreign languages, and exempts Amex gold and platinum cardholders from the 1% fee.

Visa offers traveler's checks at Citibank locations nationwide, as well as at several other banks. The service charge ranges between 1.5% and 2%; checks come in denominations of $20, $50, $100, $500, and $1,000. Call ⓒ **800/732-1322** for information. AAA members can obtain Visa checks for a $9.95 fee (for checks up to $1,500) at most AAA offices or by calling ⓒ **866/339-3378**. **MasterCard** also offers traveler's checks; call ⓒ **800/223- 9920** for a location near you.

Foreign currency traveler's checks are useful if you're traveling to one country, or to the Euro zone; they're accepted at locations where dollar checks may not be, such as bed-and-breakfasts, and they minimize the currency conversions you'll have to perform while you're on the go. **American Express, Thomas Cook, Visa,** and **MasterCard** offer foreign currency traveler's checks. You'll pay the rate of exchange at the time of your purchase (so it's a good idea to monitor the rate before you buy), and most companies charge a transaction fee per order (and a shipping fee if you order online).

CREDIT CARDS

Credit cards are a safe way to carry money, they provide a convenient record of all your expenses, and they generally offer good exchange rates. You can also withdraw cash advances from your credit cards at banks or ATMs, provided you know your PIN. If you don't know yours, call the number on the back of the card and ask the bank to send it to you. It usually takes 5 to 7 business days, though some banks will provide the number over the phone if you tell them your mother's maiden name or some other personal information. Keep in mind that many banks now assess a 1% to 3% "transaction fee" on **all** charges you incur abroad (whether you're using the local currency or U.S. dollars). But credit cards still may be the smart way to go when you factor in things like exorbitant ATM fees and the higher exchange rates and service fees you'll pay with traveler's checks.

5 When to Go

From **April to June** and **September to October** are generally the best months for traveling to Campania—temperatures are usually mild and the crowds aren't quite so intense. Starting in mid-June, the summer rush really picks up, especially at the seaside resorts, and from **July to August** the coast teems with visitors. The interior never gets really crowded. **August** is the worst month on the coast: The entire country goes on vacation at least from August 15 to the end of the month—and many Italians take off the entire month to head for the beach. In the cities—Naples, but also Benevento, Avellino, Caserta, and Salerno, many hotels, restaurants, and shops are closed (except at the spas, beaches, and islands, where 70% of the Italians head). On the other hand, from **late October to Easter,** most attractions go on shorter winter hours or are closed for renovation. Many hotels and restaurants take a month or two off between **November and February,** spa and beach destinations become padlocked ghost towns, and it can get much colder than you'd expect (it might even snow).

High season on most airline routes to Naples usually stretches from June to the beginning of September. This is the most expensive and most crowded time to travel. **Shoulder season** is from April to May, early September to October, and December 15 to 24. **Low season** is from November 1 to December 14 and from December 25 to March 31.

WEATHER

In summer, it can be very hot in Campania, especially in the flat areas. The high temperatures (measured in Italy in degrees Celsius) begin in Naples in May, often lasting until sometime in October. Winters are mild by the sea, with temperatures averaging 50°F (10°C), but it gets much colder in the interior and on the mountains, with rain and snow.

For the most part, it's drier in Campania than in North America, so high temperatures don't seem as bad because the humidity is lower. In Naples, temperatures can stay in the 90°F (30°C) range for days, but nights are often comfortably cooler.

Campania's Average Daily Temperature & Monthly Rainfall

Naples	Jan	Feb	Mar	Apr	May	June	July	Aug	Sept	Oct	Nov	Dec
Temp. (°F)	50	54	58	63	70	78	83	85	75	66	60	52
Temp. (°C)	9	12	14	17	21	26	28	29	24	19	16	11
Rainfall (in.)	4.7	4	3	3.8	2.4	.8	.8	2.6	3.5	5.8	5.1	3.7
Salerno	Jan	Feb	Mar	Apr	May	June	July	Aug	Sept	Oct	Nov	Dec
Temp. (°F)	50	53	55	60	66	75	78	81	75	66	59	55
Temp. (°C)	10	11	13	16	19	24	26	27	24	19	15	13
Rainfall (in.)	6.2	5.4	4.5	3.7	2.9	1.5	.7	1.1	4.1	6.5	7.5	7.1
Benevento	Jan	Feb	Mar	Apr	May	June	July	Aug	Sept	Oct	Nov	Dec
Temp. (°F)	45	46	52	57	64	71	77	77	71	63	54	50
Temp. (°C)	7	8	11	14	18	22	25	25	22	17	12	10
Rainfall (in.)	2.8	2.8	2.1	2	2.1	1.4	.6	1.2	2.1	3	3.7	3.5

HOLIDAYS

Offices and shops in Campania are closed on the following **national holidays:** January 1 (New Year's Day), Easter Monday, April 25 (Liberation Day), May 1 (Labor Day), August 15 (Assumption of the Virgin), November 1 (All Saints' Day), December 8 (Feast of the Immaculate Conception), December 25 (Christmas Day), and December 26 (Santo Stefano).

Closings are also sometimes observed on **feast days** honoring the patron saint of each town and village. In Naples, September 19 is the Feast of St. Gennaro; in Avellino, February 14 is the Feast of St. Modestino.

CAMPANIA CALENDAR OF EVENTS

For major events in which tickets should be procured well before your arrival, check with **Global Edwards & Edwards** in the United States at *©* **800/223-6108.** An excellent Italy-based service is **TicketOne** (*©* **023-92261** for an English-speaking operator). You can also make all your reservations and purchase your tickets online (www.ticketone.it) if you can read a bit of Italian. Note that most of these performance events are in Italian.

January

Il Presepe nel Presepe (Manger in a Manger), Morcone. This suggestive little town near Benevento is a natural background for the reenactment of Jesus's birth. Each January, the villagers here transform their town into a version of Bethlehem, and open their homes to visitors. January 3.

Epiphany celebrations, regionwide. All Roman Catholic holidays are deeply felt in Campania, and festive celebrations for the Epiphany include numerous fairs and processions celebrating the arrival of the Three Kings at Christ's manger. January 6.

February

Carnival, regionwide. During the period before Lent, float parades and histrionic traditional shows take place in most towns, big and small, throughout the region. Some of the best are in **Capua,** which puts on a grand parade and cabaret and theater performances (call the tourist office at *©* **0823-321137**); and in **Montemarano,** where celebrations start on January 17 (call the tourist office at *©* **082-524013** for a schedule of events). **Paestum** schedules great parade and dance shows (call the tourist office at *©* **0828-811016**). Dates vary, but it's generally held the week before Ash Wednesday.

Carnevale Irpino, Avellino. This festival includes traditional representations such as the famous *Zeza*—a musical farce, parades, and the **Concorso della**

Zeza, a large competition for group mummers (masked performers). Contact the **EPT** (© **0825-74732** or 0825-74695) for a schedule of the events. The 2 weeks before Ash Wednesday.

March

Nauticsud, Mostra d'Oltremare, Napoli. Spanning both land and water, this boat show boasts displays of the latest motor and sailing boats and equipment. Check their website for information at www.nauticsud.info. Mid-March.

Comicon, Napoli. This international event at Castel Sant'Elmo, in its eighth year in 2006, is a must-see for fans of comic books and animation. Each year the fair picks a country as its main theme, but includes a large number of previews and presentations of new productions. Contact the organization for a schedule of events (© **081-4238127;** www.comicon.it). First weekend in March.

April

Easter (Pasqua), regionwide. Processions for the benediction of the symbolic palm—usually olive tree branches—take place on the Sunday before Easter Sunday. Stations of the Cross processions (reenacting Jesus' ascent to Golgotha) are staged in almost every church on Holy Friday. Easter Sunday is marked by special religious celebrations. Generally, at the end of March, but often in April.

Pasqua a Sorrento (Easter in Sorrento), Sorrento. These Easter celebrations last a whole week; religious processions and concerts are scheduled in the town's cathedral and in the delightful cloister of San Francesco. Other processions take place on the night of Holy Thursday through Holy Friday in the towns surrounding Sorrento: Meta, Piano di Sorrento, and Sant'Agnello. Week before Easter.

Processione dei Misteri (Procession of the Mysteries), Procida. This is one of the most famous traditional religious events in Campania, a procession of plastic scenes from the Passion of Christ sculpted by local craftspeople. Evolving from its original procession in 1627, it is now a glorious show of entire scenes depicting the betrayal of Judas, the Last Supper, and so on, as well as large statues of the Christ and the Madonna. Holy Thursday night into Holy Friday morning.

Salerno Film Festival (Linea d'ombra), Salerno. This major international event, in its 11th year in 2006, is dedicated to new talent in Europe and focuses on the passage from adolescence to adulthood—the "shadow line" written about by Joseph Conrad. Contact the festival office (© **089-2753673;** fax 089-2571125; www.shadowline.it). Varying weeks in April.

May

Feast of St. Costanzo, Marina Grande, Capri. Honors St. Constanzo, whose remains preserved in the local basilica protected the island from the Saracens' attacks during the Middle Ages. Bishop Costanzo died on the island during his apostolic mission in Capri on his way to Constantinople around A.D. 677. Call the local tourist office for a program at © **081-8370424.** Third week of May.

Maggio dei Monumenti (Monuments in May), Napoli. The *centro storico* (city center) of Naples comes alive with cultural events and extraordinary openings of private collections and monuments for a whole week. The year 2005 marked the 11th anniversary of this successful special event. Contact the tourist office for a schedule of events. Last week of May.

June

Music Festival, Sorrento. During this annual summer music festival, classical concerts and other musical events are organized throughout town, in churches and in gardens. Ask the tourist office (© **081-8074033**) for a schedule of events. June through September.

Concerti al Tramonto, Anacapri. Each summer, the Foundation Axel Munthe organizes a series of sunset classical concerts in the Villa San Michele, in a spectacular setting overlooking the island and the sea. Contact the tourist office for details (© **081-8371401;** www.sanmichele.org). June through August.

Summer Music Festival, Minori. Classical and jazz music concerts are scheduled throughout the summer along the Amalfi Coast, but the setting here in Minori is particularly pleasant. Contact the tourist office (© **089-877087** or 089-877607) for a program. June through September.

Historic Regatta of the Maritime Republics, Amalfi. Each of Italy's four historical towns—Genova, Pisa, Venice, and Amalfi—alternate turns hosting this annual regatta. Amalfi's turn was in 2005 and will occur again in 2009. Contact the tourist office (© **089-871107**). First Sunday in June.

July

Opera and Drama Season at the Roman Theater, Benevento. The ancient Roman theater of Benevento is the venue for a full-fledged summer season of opera and drama. Contact the tourist office (© **0824-319911**). July through August.

Sagra del Tonno (Tuna Festival), Cetara. At this traditional celebration of tuna fishing, the town's main activity, you can partake in tuna tastings and musical events. Contact the tourist

office (© **089-261474**) for more information. July.

Festival di Ravello, Ravello. This international music festival includes jazz, dance, and visual arts; you must make reservations well in advance for the most important performances. Contact the festival office (© **089-857096** or 199-109910; fax 089-858422; www.ravellofestival.com) for reservations. July through September.

Summer Program, Atrani. This rich program of music and art events is part of the Amalfi Coast Summer Festival. The events vary each summer but usually include classical music sunset concerts and exhibits by local and international artists. Contact the tourist office (© **089-871185**) for a schedule of events. July and August.

Summer Theater Festival, Scala. Each summer, Casa Romano becomes the setting of drama and concert performances. Contact the tourist office (© **089-858977** or 089-857325) for a schedule of events. July and August.

Summer Fest, Conca dei Marini. This little town's special take on the Amalfi Coast Summer Festival is the performing arts, including theater, ballet, and art shows. Contact the tourist office (© **089-831301**) for a program. June through September.

Jazz on the Coast, Minori. This international festival heralds jazz singers and musicians from around the world who come to perform with the Amalfi Coast as their backdrop. Concerts are usually scheduled over a period of 2 weeks starting at the end of July. Contact the local tourist office (©/fax **089-877087;** www.proloco.minori.sa.it). Last week in July and first week of August.

August

Estate Amalfitana, Amalfi. Starting in June, the town of Amalfi organizes this series of musical and artistic events. At the end of July and into August, the splendid Chiostro del Paradiso near Amalfi's cathedral becomes the setting for concerts, usually of classical music, including piano soloists and vocal performances. Contact the tourist office (© **089-871107**) for a program. Friday evenings, June through September.

Sagra della Sfogliatella di Santa Rosa, Conca dei Marini. This delicious event celebrates the local version of *sfogliatella,* the most famous of Neapolitan pastries, filled with pastry cream and a sour cherry confection. August.

Summer Festival, Furore Marina. Art and music events take place in the *monazzeri.* Call © **089-830525** for a schedule. July and August.

Festival of the Assunta, Positano. In the 9th and 10th centuries A.D., when the Saracens had established themselves in nearby Agropoli (see chapter 9), the whole coast was endangered by their repeated incursions and bloody robberies. This festival reenacts the Saracens' attack on Positano and the miraculous intervention of the Madonna who, legend has it, saved the town. August 14 and 15.

Festa del Mare, town of Ischia. These spectacular celebrations mark the occasion of the Festival of Sant'Anna. A procession of boats and floats crosses the harbor under the town's illuminated castle. July 26.

September

Festival Musica d'Estate (Summer Festival of Music), Positano. Celebrating its 39th year in 2006, this series of concerts focuses on chamber music. In addition to the concerts—which include everything from classical to jazz—you can sign up for classes taught by internationally renowned musicians. Call © **089-875067** for a

schedule of events. End of August to beginning of September.

Salerno Etnica, Salerno. This music festival is part of the celebrations for Salerno's patron saint, San Matteo. The focus is on music as an expression of culture and tradition. Contact the tourist office for a schedule of events (© **089-224744**). Week of September 21.

Santa Maria della Libera, Capri. Starting from the St. Costanzo in Marina Grande church and crossing the town of Capri, grand processions are staged at this festival, which includes music, fireworks, and market stalls. The Sunday closest to September 12.

Ischia Jazz Weekend, Ischia. This event is organized by the famous Umbria Jazz group, with important international performers. Call © **081-4972777** for information. Usually second weekend of September.

October

Annali delle Arti (Arts Yearbook), regionwide. At this annual event exploring contemporary art around the world, museums, historical palaces, and archaeological areas throughout Campania become the seat for exhibits by important artists from the international art scene. Contact the regional tourist office at © **081-6174239** for information. October through January.

November

Bread and Olive Oil, Vico Equense. At the heart of the production area of one of the best olive oils in Italy, this little town celebrates the pressing of the new olive harvest with extra-virgin olive-oil tastings, and an open house of one of the facilities. Contact the local tourist office for more information, at © **081-8015752.** Last Sunday of November.

Feast of St. Andrew, Amalfi. St. Andrew, the patron of Amalfi and the protector of fishermen, is honored

---

Tips Before You Leave Home: Tickets & Seats in Advance

You absolutely need advance reservations for the Capodimonte Museum in Naples (the one museum in Campania where lines are always several hours long in occasion of the many special exhibits) and for special guided tours of Pompeii, but you might want to make reservations for a number of other attractions and events as well. The best place to make reservations is **Pierreci** (© 063-9967050; www.pierreci.it), the official advance reservation service for a number of museums and events in Campania and in Italy. For all kinds of events, the best place to get tickets is **TicketOne** (© 023-92261 for an English-speaking operator). Or visit www.ticketone.it, though, so far, their website is in Italian only. U.S.-based companies offering advance tickets for a variety of museums and events in Italy are convenient, but they are usually more expensive and cover only a small selection of monuments and events. The best of these is **Culturalitaly.com** (© 800/380-0014; fax 928/639-0388; www.cultural italy.com), a Los Angeles–based company which offers seats and reservations for operatic performances in Naples, special guided tours in Pompeii, and even tickets to the famed Festival of Ravello. Most reservations carry a $10 fee, plus the cost of the event.

---

annually by local fishermen who run with his heavy statue on their shoulders from the beach up the hundreds of steps of the cathedral, and then present him with offerings of fish—both fresh and carved. The town also celebrates with games, folk shows, and magnificent fireworks. The feast is repeated in a mellower form on June 27, when the saint miraculously saved the town from an attack by the Saracens, 9th-century Muslim Turks who based themselves in nearby Agropili. November 30.

December

Sagra della Salsiccia e Ceppone, Sorrento. This is a great way to celebrate Saint Lucia, the shortest night of the year. Locals and visitors cook—and eat—about 200 pounds of delicious local sausages barbecued over a huge fire (prepared in the heart of the Santa Lucia neighborhood). The food is accompanied by bottles of the excellent local wine. December 13.

Avellino Christmas Concerts, Avellino. For 5 days, the town is alive with music as local choirs give concerts inside the town's beautiful cathedral. Contact the tourist office (© **0825-74695**) for a program. Usually December 13 through 18.

Feast of the *Torrone,* San Marco dei Cavoti. The typical Christmas candy, the torrone, becomes an occasion for celebrations in the little town that has been famous for making its special version—the *croccantino*—since the Middle Ages. You can taste all the variations of the treat along Via del Torrone (Via Roma), and then watch the building of a giant *croccantino* by local masters in the town's main square. Call the tourist office at © **0824-984009.** December 8 and the following weekends until Christmas.

Divers' Procession to Grotta dello Smeraldo, Conca dei Marini. Each December and January, a special pilgrimage embarks to this town's greatest attraction, Grotta dello Smeraldo. Local and guest scuba divers swim from the beach to an underwater manger inside the grotto (see chapter 7). Call the visitor center in Amalfi at ℭ **089-871107** for more information. December 24 and January 6.

Live Manger, Belvedere di San Leucio, Caserta. Come to see this hamlet turn the clock back to the 18th century with historical reenactments, music, and performances during the Christmas period. Contact ℭ **333-8283690** or e-mail info@presepevaccheria.it for information. December 25 to January 6.

Live Manger, Pietrelcina. This picturesque little town near Benevento hosts another reenactment of Christmas, involving the whole town, with events spread over several days. December 27 through 29.

Sagra della Zeppola (Feast of the Zeppola), Positano. Celebrants at this feast ring in the New Year by feasting on zeppolas, delicious fried sweet pastries, and by enjoying the Kermesse of dances, music, and fireworks on the beach of Marina Grande. December 31 through January 1.

6 Travel Insurance

Check your existing insurance policies and credit card coverage before you buy travel insurance. You may already be covered for lost luggage, canceled tickets, or medical expenses.

The cost of travel insurance varies widely, depending on the cost and length of your trip, your age and health, and the type of trip you're taking, but expect to pay between 5% and 8% of the vacation itself. You can get estimates from various providers through **InsureMyTrip.com**. Enter your trip cost and dates, your age, and other information, for prices from more than a dozen companies.

TRIP-CANCELLATION INSURANCE Trip-cancellation insurance will help you retrieve your money if you have to back out of a trip or depart early, or if your travel supplier goes bankrupt. Permissible reasons for trip cancellation can range from sickness to natural disasters to the State Department's declaration that a destination is unsafe for travel. (Insurers usually won't cover vague fears, though, as many travelers discovered when they tried to cancel their trips in Oct 2001.) In this unstable world, trip-cancellation insurance is a good buy if you purchase tickets well in advance—who knows what the

state of the world, or of your airline, will be in 9 months? Insurance policy details vary, so read the fine print—and make sure that your airline or cruise line is on the list of carriers covered in case of bankruptcy. A good resource is **"Travel Guard Alerts,"** a list of companies considered high-risk by Travel Guard International (see website below). Protect yourself further by paying for the insurance with a credit card—by law, consumers can get your money back on goods and services not received if you report the loss within 60 days after the charge is listed on your credit card statement.

Note: Many tour operators, particularly those offering trips to remote or high-risk areas, include insurance in the total trip cost or can arrange insurance policies through a partnering provider, which is a convenient and often cost-effective way for the traveler to obtain insurance. Make sure the tour company is a reputable one, however, and be aware that some experts suggest you avoid buying insurance from the tour or cruise company you're traveling with. They contend it's more secure to buy from a "third party" than to put all your money in one place.

For more information, contact one of the following recommended insurers: **Access America** (✆ 866/807-3982; www.accessamerica.com); **Travel Guard International** (✆ 800/826-4919; www.travelguard.com); **Travel Insured International** (✆ 800/243-3174; www.travelinsured.com); and **Travelex Insurance Services** (✆ 888/457-4602; www.travelex-insurance.com).

MEDICAL INSURANCE

For travel overseas, most health plans (including Medicare and Medicaid) do not provide coverage. The ones that do often require you to pay for services upfront and reimburse you only after you return home. Even if your plan does cover overseas treatment, most out-of-country hospitals make you pay your bills upfront, and send you a refund only after you've returned home and filed the necessary paperwork with your insurance company. As a safety net, you may want to buy travel medical insurance, particularly if you're traveling to a remote or high-risk area where emergency evacuation is a possible scenario. If you require additional medical insurance, try **MEDEX Assistance** (✆ 410/453-6300; www.medexassist.com). Or try **Travel Assistance International** (✆ 800/821-2828;

www.travelassistance.com); for general information on Travel Assistance's services, call the company's Worldwide Assistance Services, Inc. (✆ **800/777-8710**).

LOST-LUGGAGE INSURANCE

On international flights (including U.S. portions of international trips), baggage coverage is limited to approximately $9.07 per pound, up to approximately $635 per checked bag. If you plan to check items more valuable than what's covered by the standard liability, see if your homeowner's policy covers your valuables, get baggage insurance as part of your comprehensive travel-insurance package, or buy Travel Guard's "BagTrak" product. Don't buy insurance at the airport, where it's usually overpriced. Be sure to take any valuables or irreplaceable items with you in your carry-on luggage, because many valuables (including books, money, and electronics) aren't covered by airline policies.

If your luggage is lost, immediately file a lost-luggage claim at the airport, detailing the luggage contents. Most airlines require that you report delayed, damaged, or lost baggage within 4 hours of arrival. The airlines are required to deliver luggage, once found, directly to your house or destination free of charge.

7 Health & Safety

THE HEALTHY TRAVELER

In general, Campania and Italy are viewed as "safe" destinations, although problems, of course, can and do occur anywhere. You don't need to get shots; most food is safe, and the water in cities and towns is potable. Naples has a water problem, but hotels, restaurants, and bars have their own water-purification systems. If you're still concerned, order bottled water. Prescriptions are easily filled in towns and cities. You'll find English-speaking doctors at hospitals with well-trained medical staff nearly everywhere.

In other words, Campania is part of the civilized world.

Vegetarians can go into any restaurant in Campania, even those specializing in meat and fish, sure to find a variety of vegetarian dishes on the menu—from antipasti to pasta dishes—and most restaurants will try their best to accommodate your dietary restrictions.

WHAT TO DO IF YOU GET SICK AWAY FROM HOME

Any foreign consulate can provide a list of area doctors who speak English. If you get sick, consider asking your hotel concierge to recommend a local doctor—even his or her own. You can also try the emergency room at a local hospital. Many hospitals have walk-in clinics for emergency cases that are not life-threatening; you may not get immediate attention, but you won't pay the high price of an emergency-room visit. Hospitals and emergency phone numbers are listed under "Fast Facts."

If you suffer from a chronic illness, consult your doctor before your departure. For conditions like epilepsy, diabetes, or heart problems, wear a **MedicAlert identification tag** (© 888/ 633-4298; www.medicalert.org), which will immediately alert doctors to your condition and give them access to your records through MedicAlert's 24-hour hot line.

Pack **prescription medications** in your carry-on luggage, and carry them in their original containers, with pharmacy labels—otherwise they won't make it through airport security. Also carry copies of your prescriptions in case you lose your pills or run out. Carry the generic names of prescription medicines, in case a local pharmacist is unfamiliar with the brand name. Don't forget an extra pair of contact lenses or prescription glasses.

For travel abroad, you may have to pay all medical costs upfront and be reimbursed later. See "Medical Insurance" under "Travel Insurance," above.

STAYING SAFE

The most common menace, especially in Naples, is the plague of pickpockets. In spite of valiant police activity, the feared Camorra gang is still a problem in poor areas of distant Naples suburbs.

If you rent a car, never leave valuables in the car, and never travel with your car unlocked. Never, except in the most remote and quiet rural areas, leave your car unattended, unless you have a solid steering and pedal block. In Naples, park your car only inside private garages, where attendants will get it in and out for you. A U.S. State Department travel advisory warns that every car (whether parked, stopped at a traffic light, or moving) can be a potential target for robbery. In these uncertain times, it is always prudent to check the U.S. State Department's travel advisories at http://travel.state.gov.

8 Specialized Travel Resources

TRAVELERS WITH DISABILITIES

Laws in Campania and in Italy have compelled train stations, airports, hotels, and most restaurants to follow a stricter set of regulations for **wheelchair accessibility** to restrooms, ticket counters, and the like. Museums and other attractions have conformed to the regulations, which mimic many of those presently in effect in the United States. Always call ahead to check on the accessibility in hotels, restaurants, and sights you want to visit.

Many travel agencies offer customized tours and itineraries for travelers with disabilities. **Flying Wheels Travel** (© 507/451-5005; fax 507/451-1685; www.flyingwheelstravel.com) offers escorted tours and cruises that emphasize sports and private tours in minivans with lifts. **Accessible Journeys** (© 800/846-4537 or 610/521-0339; www.disability travel.com) caters specifically to slow walkers and wheelchair travelers as well as their families and friends.

Two organizations that offer assistance to travelers with disabilities are **MossRehab** (www.mossresourcenet.org), which provides a library of accessible-travel resources online, and **Society for Accessible Travel and Hospitality (SATH;** © 212/447-7284; www.sath.org). SATH offers a wealth of travel resources for all types of disabilities, as well as informed recommendations on destinations, access guides, travel agents, tour operators, vehicle rentals, and companion services.

For more information specifically targeted to travelers with disabilities, the community website **iCan** (www.ican online.net) has destination guides and several regular columns on accessible travel.

GAY & LESBIAN TRAVELERS

Since 1861, Campania and Italy have had liberal legislation regarding homosexuality, Ischia and Capri have long been gay meccas, and there is a somewhat active gay life in Naples. Still, open displays of same-sex affection are sometimes frowned upon in the Catholic country (despite the fact that people in Campania are very physical, and men and women alike embrace when saying hello and goodbye).

ARCI Gay (www.arcigay.it) is the country's leading gay organization, with branches throughout Campania and Italy.

The International Gay & Lesbian Travel Association (IGLTA; ⓒ 800/ 448-8550 or 954/776-2626; fax 954/ 776-3303; www.iglta.org) links travelers with gay-friendly hoteliers, tour operators, and airline and cruise-line representatives. It offers monthly newsletters, mailings, and a membership directory updated once a year. Membership is $200 yearly, plus a $100 administration fee for new members.

Many agencies offer tours and travel itineraries specifically designed for gay and lesbian travelers. **Above and Beyond Tours** (ⓒ **800/397-2681;** www.above beyondtours.com) is the exclusive gay and lesbian tour operator for United Airlines. **Now, Voyager** (ⓒ **800/255-6951;** www.nowvoyager.com) is a well-known San Francisco–based gay-owned and operated travel service. **Olivia Cruises & Resorts** (ⓒ **800/631-6277** or 510/655- 0364; www.olivia.com) charters entire

resorts and ships for exclusive lesbian vacations and offers smaller group experiences for both gay and lesbian travelers.

The following travel guides are available at most travel bookstores and at gay and lesbian bookstores; or you can order them from **Giovanni's Room** bookstore, 1145 Pine St., Philadelphia, PA 19107 (ⓒ **215/923-2960;** www.giovannisroom. com): *Frommer's Gay & Lesbian Europe* (Wiley Publishing, Inc.), an excellent travel resource; *Out and About* (ⓒ **800/929-2268** or 415/644-8044; www.outandabout.com), which offers guidebooks and a newsletter 10 times a year packed with solid information on the global gay and lesbian scene; and *Spartacus International Gay Guide* (Bruno Gmunder Verlag; www.spartacus world.com/gayguide).

SENIOR TRAVEL

Mention the fact that you're a senior when you first make your travel reservations. Most major airlines and many Italian hotels offer discounts for seniors.

Members of **AARP** (formerly known as the American Association of Retired Persons), 601 E St. NW, Washington, DC 20049 (ⓒ **800/424-3410** or 202/ 434-2277; www.aarp.org), might get discounts on hotels, airfares, and car rentals also abroad. AARP offers members a wide range of benefits, including *AARP: The Magazine* and a monthly newsletter. Anyone over 50 can join.

Many reliable agencies and organizations target the 50-plus market. **Grand Circle Travel** (ⓒ **800/221-2610** or 617/ 350-7500; www.gct.com) offers package deals for the 50-plus market, mostly of the tour-bus variety, with free trips thrown in for those who organize groups of 10 or more. **Elderhostel** (ⓒ **877/426- 8056;** www.elderhostel.org) arranges study programs for those aged 55 and over (and a spouse or companion of any age) in the U.S. and in more than 80 countries around the world, including Italy.

Recommended publications offering travel resources and discounts for seniors include: the quarterly magazine *Travel 50 & Beyond* (www.travel50andbeyond. com); *Travel Unlimited: Uncommon Adventures for the Mature Traveler* (Avalon); and *Unbelievably Good Deals and Great Adventures That You Absolutely Can't Get Unless You're Over 50* (McGraw-Hill), by Joann Rattner Heilman.

FAMILY TRAVEL

Most Italian hoteliers will let children 12 and younger stay in a room with their parents for free; others do not. Sometimes this requires a little negotiation at the reception desk. Italians love *bambini* but don't offer a lot of special amenities for them: Italians bring their kids everywhere, and even the largest hotels will offer babysitting only on request. Also, a kiddies' menu in a restaurant is a rarity. You can, however, order a half-portion *(mezza porzione),* and most waiters will oblige. At attractions, even if it isn't posted, inquire if a kid's discount is available. Italians call such deals *"sconto bambino."* E.U. members younger than age 18 are admitted free to all state-run museums.

To locate accommodations, restaurants, and attractions that are particularly kid-friendly, refer to the "Kids" icon throughout this guide.

Familyhostel (© **800/733-9753;** www.learn.unh.edu/familyhostel) takes the whole family, including kids ages 8 to 15, on moderately priced domestic and international learning vacations. Lectures, field trips, and sightseeing are guided by a team of academics.

How to Take Great Trips with Your Kids (The Harvard Common Press) is full of good general advice that can apply to travel anywhere, including Italy. **Family Travel Files** (www.thefamily travelfiles.com) offers an online magazine and a directory of off-the-beaten-path tours and tour operators for families.

9 Planning Your Trip Online

SURFING FOR AIRFARES

The "big three" online travel agencies, **Expedia.com, Travelocity.com,** and **Orbitz.com,** sell most of the air tickets bought on the Internet. (Canadian travelers should try Expedia.ca and Travelocity.ca; U.K. residents can go for Expedia. co.uk and Opodo.co.uk.) Each has different business deals with the airlines and may offer different fares on the same flights, so it's wise to shop around. Expedia and Travelocity will send you **e-mail notification** when a cheap fare to your favorite destination becomes available. Of the smaller travel agency websites, **SideStep** (www.sidestep.com) has gotten the best reviews from Frommer's authors. It's a browser add-on that purports to "search 140 sites at once," but, in reality, only beats competitors' fares as often as other sites do.

Remember to check **airline websites,** especially those for low-fare carriers such as Ryanair, whose fares are often misreported or simply missing from travel agency websites. Even with major airlines, you can often shave a few bucks from a fare by booking directly through the airline and avoiding a travel agency's transaction fee. But you'll get these discounts only by **booking online:** Most airlines now offer online-only fares that even their phone agents know nothing about. For the websites of airlines that fly to and from your destination, see "Getting There," below.

Great **last-minute deals** are available through free weekly e-mail services provided directly by the airlines. Most of these are announced on Tuesday or Wednesday and must be purchased online. Most are valid only for travel that weekend, but some can be booked weeks or months in advance. Sign up for weekly e-mail alerts at airline websites; or check mega-sites that compile comprehensive lists of last-minute specials, such as **Smarter Travel** (www.smartertravel. com). For last-minute trips, **Last-minute.com** in Europe often has better deals than the major sites.

If you're willing to give up some control over your flight details, use an **opaque fare service** like **Priceline** (www. priceline.com; www.priceline.co.uk for Europeans). It offers rock-bottom prices in exchange for travel on a "mystery airline" at a mysterious time of day, often with a mysterious change of planes en route. The mystery airlines are all major, well-known carriers and the airlines' routing computers have gotten a lot better than they used to be. But your chances of getting a 6am or 11pm flight are pretty high. Hotwire tells you flight prices before you buy. Priceline usually has better deals than Hotwire, and you no longer have to play their "name our price" game. You can now pick low-priced flights, times, and airlines from a list. If you're new at this, the helpful folks at **Bidding-ForTravel** (www.biddingfortravel.com) do a good job of demystifying Priceline.

SURFING FOR HOTELS

Shopping online for hotels is much easier in certain parts of Europe, including Italy and Campania, than it is in the rest of the world. Of the "big three" sites, **Expedia** may be the best choice, thanks to its long list of special deals. **Travelocity** runs a close second. Hotel specialist sites **hotels.com** and **hoteldiscounts.com** are also reliable. However, since most Italian hotels—including some of the most famous luxury hotels such as the San Pietro in Positano—are private, often family-run businesses, you'll do much better checking an Italy-based search engine such as **Venere Net** (www.venere.com). Always check the hotel's website directly, since these often list the same rates as some supposed discount agencies, without the extra fee. Other sites to check are **Italyhotels** (www.italyhotelink.com), **ITWG.com** (www.italyhotels.com), **Welcome to Italy** (www.wel.it), **Europa Hotels** (www.europa-hotels.com), and **Italy Hotels** (www.hotels-in-italy.com).

Priceline is even better for hotels than for airfares; you're allowed to pick the neighborhood and quality level of your hotel before offering up your money, but it's much better at getting five-star lodging for three-star prices than at finding anything at the bottom of the scale.

SURFING FOR RENTAL CARS

For booking rental cars online, the best deals are usually found at rental car company websites, although all the major online travel agencies offer rental car reservations services. Priceline and Hotwire work well for rental cars, too; the only "mystery" is which major rental company you get. For most travelers, the difference between Hertz, Avis, and Budget is negligible.

10 The 21st-Century Traveler

INTERNET ACCESS AWAY FROM HOME

Travelers have any number of ways to check e-mail and access the Internet on the road. Of course, using a laptop, PDA (personal digital assistant), or electronic organizer with modem gives you the most flexibility. If you don't have one of these, you can access your e-mail and office computer from hotels and cybercafes.

WITHOUT YOUR OWN COMPUTER

It's hard nowadays to find a city that *doesn't* have a few cybercafes. Although there's no definitive directory for cybercafes—these are independent businesses, after all—three places to start looking are at **www. cybercaptive.com**, **www.netcafeguide. com**, and **www.cybercafe.com**.

Most major airports now have **Internet kiosks** scattered throughout their gates. These kiosks, which you'll also see in shopping malls, hotel lobbies, and tourist information offices around the world, give you basic Web access for a per-minute fee that's usually higher than cybercafe prices. The kiosks' clunkiness and high prices mean they should be avoided whenever possible.

To retrieve your e-mail, ask your **Internet Service Provider (ISP)** if it has a Web-based interface tied to your existing e-mail account. If your ISP doesn't have such an interface, you can use the free **mail2web** service (www.mail2web.com) to view and reply to your home e-mail. For more flexibility, you may want to open a free, Web-based e-mail account with **Yahoo! Mail** (http://mail.yahoo. com). Microsoft's Hotmail, another popular option, has severe spam problems. Your home ISP may be able to automatically forward your e-mail to the Web-based account.

If you need access to files on your office computer, look into a service called **GoToMyPC** (www.gotomypc.com). The service provides a Web-based interface for you to access and manipulate a distant PC from anywhere—even a cybercafe—provided your "target" PC is on and has an always-on connection to the Internet (such as with Road Runner cable). The service offers top-quality security, but if you're worried about hackers, you can use your own laptop rather than a cybercafe to access the GoToMyPC system.

WITH YOUR OWN COMPUTER

More and more hotels, cafes, and retailers are signing on as Wi-Fi (wireless fidelity) "hotspots," from where you can get high-speed connection without cable wires, networking hardware, or a phone line (see below). You can get Wi-Fi connection one of several ways. Many laptops sold in the last year have built-in Wi-Fi capability (an 802.11b wireless Ethernet connection). Mac owners have their own networking technology, Apple AirPort. For those with older computers, you can plug in an 802.11b/**Wi-Fi card** (around $50). You sign up for wireless access service much as you do for cellphone service, through a plan offered by one of several commercial companies that have made wireless service available in airports, hotel lobbies, and coffee shops, primarily in the U.S. (followed by the U.K. and Japan). **T-Mobile Hotspot** (www.t-mobile.com/hotspot) serves up wireless connections at more than 1,000 Starbucks coffee shops nationwide. **Boingo** (www.boingo.com) and **Wayport** (www.wayport.com) have set up networks in airports and high-class hotel lobbies. IPass providers (see below) also give you access to a few hundred wireless hotel lobby setups. Best of all, you don't need to be staying at the Four Seasons to use the hotel's network; just set yourself up on a nice couch in the lobby. (Pricing policies can be Byzantine, but in general you pay around $30 per month for unlimited access, and prices are dropping as Wi-Fi access becomes more common.) To locate other hotspots that provide **free wireless networks** in cities around the world, go to **www.personaltelco.net/index.cgi/ WirelessCommunities**.

For dial-up access, most business-class hotels throughout the world offer dataports for laptop modems, and a few thousand hotels in Europe now offer free high-speed Internet access using an Ethernet network cable. You can bring your own cables, but most hotels rent them for around $10. **Call your hotel in advance** to see what your options are.

In addition, major Internet Service Providers (ISPs) have **local access numbers** around the world, allowing you to go online by placing a local call. Check your ISP's website or call its toll-free number and ask how you can use your current account away from home, and how much it will cost. See "Fast Facts" later in this chapter for more information.

The **iPass** network also has dial-up numbers around the world. You'll have to sign up with an iPass provider, who will then tell you how to set up your computer for your destination(s). For a list of iPass providers, go to www.ipass.com and click on "Individuals Buy Now." One solid provider is **i2roam** (www.i2roam.com; 𝄐 **866/811-6209** or 920/235-0475).

Wherever you go, bring a **connection kit** of the right power, phone adapters, a spare phone cord, and a spare Ethernet network cable—or find out whether your hotel supplies them to guests.

USING A CELLPHONE OUTSIDE THE U.S.

The three letters that define much of the world's **wireless capabilities** are GSM (Global System for Mobiles), a big, seamless network that makes for easy cross-border cellphone use throughout Europe and dozens of other countries worldwide. In the U.S., T-Mobile, AT&T Wireless, and Cingular use this quasi-universal system; in Canada, Microcell and some Rogers customers use GSM; and all Europeans and most Australians use GSM.

If your cellphone is on a GSM system, and you have a world-capable phone such as many (but not all) Sony Ericsson, Motorola, or Samsung models, you can make and receive calls across civilized areas on much of the globe, from Andorra to Uganda. Call your wireless operator and ask that "international roaming" be activated on your account. Unfortunately, per-minute charges can be high—usually $1 to $1.50 in Western Europe and up to $5 in places such as Russia and Indonesia.

World-phone owners can bring down your per-minute charges with a bit of trickery. Call your cellular operator and say you'll be going abroad for several months, so you want to "unlock" your phone to use it with a local provider. Usually, they'll oblige. Then, in your destination country, pick up a cheap, prepaid phone chip at a mobile phone store and slip it into your phone. (Show your phone to the salesperson, as not all phones work on all networks.) You'll get a local phone number in your destination country—and much, much lower calling rates.

Otherwise, **renting** a phone is a good idea. While you can rent a phone from any number of overseas sites, including kiosks at airports and at car-rental agencies, it might be smart to rent the phone before you leave home. That way you can give loved ones your new number, make sure the phone works, and take the phone wherever you go—especially helpful when you rent overseas, where phone-rental agencies bill in local currency and may not let you take the phone to another country.

Rentacell (𝄐 **877/736-8355** in the U.S.; 028-86337799 in Italy; www.rentacell.com) will deliver a phone to you anywhere for free. You can also pick it up in the U.S. before you leave. Incoming calls are free. **Easyline** (𝄐 **800-010600** toll-free within Italy) also delivers phones for free. Both will give you your number upon reservation, before you leave for your trip.

11 Getting There

BY PLANE

High season on most airlines' routes to Campania is usually from June to the beginning of September. This is the most expensive and most crowded time to travel. **Shoulder season** is from April to May, early September to October, and December 15 to December 24. **Low season** is from November 1 to December 14 and from December 25 to March 31.

Campania is served by Naples's **Capodichino airport** (℡ 081-7896259; www.gesac.it), only about 7km (4 miles) from the city center. Buses from the airport will transport you to Naples, as well as nearby towns such as Sorrento and Castellammare di Stabia.

Alitalia's vacation company **Eurofly** (℡ 091-5007704; www.eurofly.it) started offering a direct flight to Naples—the first of many, we hope, during summer 2005. They fly three times a week during summer only from New York's John F. Kennedy airport. From elsewhere in North America, you will have to fly first into Rome or Milan and take a connecting flight. Rome is only 50 minutes away, and the flight from Milan is about 90 minutes. You can fly into Naples from many other Italian and European cities as well.

FROM NORTH AMERICA   Fares to Italy are constantly changing, but you can expect to pay somewhere in the range of $460 to $1,460 for a direct round-trip ticket from New York to Rome in coach class.

Flying time to Rome from New York, Newark, and Boston is 8 hours; from Chicago, 10 hours; and from Los Angeles, 12½ hours. Flying time to Milan from New York, Newark, and Boston is 8 hours; from Chicago, 9¼ hours; and from Los Angeles, 11½ hours.

Alitalia (℡ 800/223-5730; www.alitalia.com), the Italian national airline, offers the most nonstop flights to Rome and Milan from different North American cities, including Atlanta, Boston, Chicago, Miami, New York (JFK), Newark, Toronto, and Washington. From Milan or Rome, Alitalia can easily book connecting domestic flights if your final destination is Naples. Alitalia participates in the frequent-flier programs of other airlines, including Continental and US Airways.

American Airlines (℡ 800/433-7300; www.aa.com) offers daily nonstop flights to Rome from Chicago's O'Hare airport, with flights from all parts of American's vast network making connections into Chicago. **Delta** (℡ 800/241-4141; www.delta.com) flies from New York's JFK airport to Milan, Venice, and Rome; separate flights depart every evening for both destinations. **US Airways** (℡ 800/428-4322; www.usairways.com) offers one flight daily to Rome out of Philadelphia (you can connect through Philly from most major U.S. cities). And **Continental** (℡ 800/525-0280; www.continental.com) flies five times a week to Rome and Milan from its hub in Newark.

Air Canada (℡ 888/247-2262; www.aircanada.ca) has flights daily from Toronto to Rome. Two of the flights are nonstop; the others touch down en route in Montreal, depending on the schedule.

British Airways (℡ 800/AIRWAYS; www.britishairways.com), **Virgin Atlantic Airways** (℡ 800/862-8621; www.virginatlantic.com), **Air France** (℡ 800/237-2747; www.airfrance.com), **Northwest/KLM** (℡ 800/374-7747; www.klm.com), and **Lufthansa** (℡ 800/399-LUFT; www.lufthansa-usa.com) offer attractive deals for anyone interested in

---

Tips Cutting Air Costs

Regardless of how you opt to fly, it's cheaper for transatlantic passengers book-ing a flight to Italy from North America to have your flight to Naples written into your overall ticket. If you book a flight to Naples once you have arrived in Italy, it will cost much more.

---

combining a trip to Campania with a stopover in, say, Britain, Paris, Amsterdam, or Germany.

FROM THE UNITED KINGDOM Operated by the European Travel Net-work, **www.discount-tickets.com** is a great online source for regular and dis-counted airfares to destinations around the world. You can also use this site to compare rates and book accommodations, car rentals, and tours. Click on "Special Offers" for the latest package deals.

British newspapers are always full of classified ads touting slashed fares to Italy. One good source is *Time Out.* London's *Evening Standard* has a daily travel sec-tion, and the Sunday editions of almost any newspaper will run many ads. Although competition is fierce, one well-recommended company that consolidates bulk ticket purchases and then passes the savings on to its consumers is **Trailfinders** (© 020/7937-5400; www.trailfinders. com). It offers access to tickets on such carriers as SAS, British Airways, and KLM.

Both **British Airways** (© 0870/850-9850 in the U.K.; www.britishairways. co.uk) and **Alitalia** (© 0870/544-8259; www.alitalia.it) offer frequent flights from London's Heathrow airport to Naples. Flying time from London to Naples is about 2 hours.

GETTING THROUGH THE AIRPORT
With the federalization of airport secu-rity, security procedures at U.S. airports are more stable and consistent than ever. Generally, you'll be fine if you arrive at the airport **1 hour** before a domestic flight and **2 hours** before an international flight; if you show up late, tell an airline employee that you've done so, and she'll probably whisk you to the front of the line.

Bring a **current, government-issued photo ID** such as a driver's license or passport, and if you've got an e-ticket, print out the **official confirmation page;** you'll need to show your confirmation at the security checkpoint, and your ID at the ticket counter or the gate. (Children younger than age 18 do not need photo IDs for domestic flights, but the adults checking in with them need them.)

Security lines are getting shorter, but some doozies remain. If you have trouble standing for long periods of time, tell an airline employee; the airline will provide a wheelchair. Speed up security by **not wearing metal objects** such as big belt buckles or clunky earrings. If you've got metallic body parts, a note from your doctor can prevent a long chat with the security screeners. Keep in mind that only **ticketed passengers** are allowed past security, except for folks escorting dis-abled passengers or children.

Federalization has standardized **what you can carry on and what you can't.** The general rule is that sharp things are out, nail clippers are okay, and food and beverages must be passed through the X-ray machine—but that security screen-ers can't make you drink from your coffee cup. Bring food in your carry-on rather than checking it, as explosive-detection machines used on checked luggage have been known to mistake food (especially chocolate, for some reason) for bombs. Travelers in the U.S. are allowed one carry-on bag, plus a "personal item" such as a purse, briefcase, or laptop bag. Carry-on hoarders can stuff all sorts of things into a laptop bag; as long as it has a laptop in it, it's considered a personal item. The Transportation Security Administration (TSA) has issued a list of restricted items; check its website (www.tsa.gov/public/index.jsp) for details.

At presstime, the TSA recommends that you **not lock your checked luggage,** so screeners can search it by hand if necessary. The agency says to use plastic "zip ties" instead, which can be bought at hardware stores and can be easily cut off.

BY BOAT & FERRY

Naples, a major Mediterranean port and the major port of central Italy, receives daily ships and ferries from international destinations.

A number of cruise-ship companies sail to Naples, especially in the good season, from spring well into fall. Arriving in the Naples by ship is a magnificent experience and the best approach to Campania. You'll land at **Stazione Marittima,** only steps from the Maschio Angioino in the heart of the historical district, the *città antica.*

Most hydrofoil regular service operates from nearby **Mergellina's Terminal Aliscafi.** The major companies offering regular service are **Tirrenia** (© 199-123199 or 081-2514711; www.tirrenia.it), with boats to Cagliari and Palermo; **Siremar** (© 081-5800340; www.siremar.it), with ships to the Aeolian Islands and Milazzo; **TTTLines** (© 800-915365), with ships to Catania and Palermo; **Medmar** (© 081-5513352), with boats to Tunis and (©081-3334411); **SNAV** (© 081-4285555 or 081-4285111; www.snav.it), with boats to Palermo, Sardinia, and the Aeolian and Pontine islands.

Salerno is a major harbor, with regular international service from Valencia in Spain, Malta (La Valletta), and Tunis via **Grimaldi Ferries** (© 081-496444; www.grimaldi-ferries.com), which also offers regular service to Palermo. **Caronte & Tourist** (© 800-627414 toll-free within Italy, or 089-2582528; www.carontetourist.it) travels from Salerno to Catania and Messina.

BY CAR

If you're already on the continent, particularly in a neighboring country such as Austria, you may want to drive to Naples. It's possible to drive from London to Naples, a distance of 1,951km (1,210 miles), via Calais/Boulogne/Dunkirk, or 1,888km (1,170 miles) via Oostende/Zeebrugge, not counting channel crossings by hovercraft, ferry, or the Chunnel. If you cross over from England and arrive at one of the continental ports, you still face a 24-hour drive. Most drivers play it safe and budget 3 days for the journey.

Most of the roads from Western Europe leading into Italy are toll-free, with some notable exceptions. If you use the Swiss superhighway network, you'll have to buy a special tax sticker at the frontier. You'll also pay to go through the St. Gotthard Tunnel into Italy. Crossings from France can be through the Mont Blanc Tunnel, for which you'll pay; or you can leave the French Riviera at Menton and drive directly into Italy along the Italian Riviera toward San Remo.

If you don't want to drive such distances, ask a travel agent to book you on a Motorail arrangement whereby the train carries your car. This service, however, is good only to Milan, as there are no car-and-sleeper expresses running the 785km (487 miles) south to Naples.

If you are driving to save money, think again. All highways in Italy are toll roads, and fuel prices are quite high, with gasoline in Europe rating among the highest prices around. Also, we don't recommend using a car to explore the most remote areas of Campania; if these areas are on your travel itinerary, you'll be much happier—and safer—using public transportation.

BY TRAIN

The train is the most convenient way to reach Naples and Salerno, which lie on the main line from Rome to Reggio Calabria. Other main cities in Campania are also easily reached by train from Naples and Salerno. The train ride from Rome to Naples is less than 2 hours; from Firenze about 4 hours; and from Venice less than 7. For fares and information, contact **Trenitalia** (℃ **892021** from anywhere in Italy; www.trenitalia.it), the Italian railroad company.

If you plan to travel heavily on the European rails, you'll do well to secure the latest copy of the *Thomas Cook European Timetable of Railroads.* This 500-plus-page timetable accurately documents all of Europe's mainline passenger rail services. It's available from **Forsyth Travel Library,** 44 S. Broadway, White Plains, NY 10604 (℃ **800/FORSYTH;** www.forsyth.com), for $29 (plus $4.95 shipping in the U.S. and $6.95 in Canada); or you can find it at online travel specialty stores such as **Rand McNally** (www.randmcnally.com).

Electric high-velocity trains have made travel within Europe and Italy faster and more comfortable than ever. Italy's **ETRs** travel at speeds of up to 233kmph (145 mph). A new **TAV** (high-velocity train) line recently added to Naples is being extended south.

If you plan to travel extensively in Europe by train, you might want to take advantage of one of the greatest travel bargains, the **Eurailpass,** which permits unlimited first-class rail travel in any country in western Europe (except the British Isles), and in Hungary in eastern Europe. Oddly, it doesn't include travel on the rail lines of Sardinia, which are organized independently of the rail lines of the rest of Italy.

The advantages are tempting: There are no tickets; simply show the pass to the ticket collector and then settle back to enjoy the scenery. Seat reservations are required on some trains. Many of the trains have couchettes (sleeping cars), for which an extra fee is charged. Obviously, the 2- or 3-month traveler gets the greatest economic advantages. To obtain full advantage of a 15-day or 1-month pass, you'd have to spend a great deal of time on the train.

Eurailpass holders are entitled to considerable reductions on certain buses and ferries as well. You'll get a 20% reduction on second-class accommodations from certain companies operating ferries between Naples and Palermo or for crossings to Sardinia and Malta.

A **Eurailpass** is $588 for 15 days, $762 for 21 days, $946 for 1 month, $1,338 for 2 months, and $1,654 for 3 months. Children age 3 and younger travel free, provided that they don't occupy a seat; children age 4 to 11 are charged half-fare. If you're younger than age 26, you can buy a **Eurail Youthpass,** entitling you to unlimited second-class travel for $414 for 15 days, $534 for 21 days, $664 for 1 month, $938 for 2 months, and $1,160 for 3 months. Other options exist; discuss them with the travel or rail agent where you'll buy the pass.

In **North America,** you can buy these passes from travel agents or rail agents in major cities such as New York, Montreal, and Los Angeles. Eurailpasses are also available through **Rail Europe** (℃ **877/ 272-RAIL;** www.raileurope.com). No matter what everyone tells you, you can buy Eurailpasses in Europe as well as in America (at the major train stations), but they're more expensive. Rail Europe can give you information on the rail or drive versions of the passes.

For details on the rail passes available in the **United Kingdom,** stop at or contact the **International Rail Centre,**

Victoria Station, London SW1V 1JZ (© 087-05848848). The staff can help you find the best option for the trip you're planning. Some of the most popular are the **Inter-Rail** and **Under 26** passes, entitling you to unlimited second-class travel in 26 European countries.

12 Package Deals, Escorted Tours & Special-Interest Tours

Before you start your search for the lowest airfare, you may want to consider booking your flight as part of an escorted or package tour. What you lose in adventure, you gain in time and money when you book accommodations, and maybe even food and entertainment, along with your flight.

PACKAGE TOURS

Package tours are not the same as escorted tours. With a package tour, you travel independently but pay a group rate. Packages usually include airfare, a choice of hotels, and car rentals, and packagers often offer several options at different prices. In many cases, a package that includes airfare, hotel, and transportation to and from the airport will cost you less than the hotel alone would have if you had booked it yourself. That's because packages are sold in bulk to tour operators—who resell them to the public at a cost that drastically undercuts standard rates.

One good source of package deals is the airlines themselves. Most major airlines offer air/land packages: **Italiatour**, a company of the Alitalia Group (© 800/845-3365; fax 212/765-2183; www.italiatour.com), specializes in packages for independent travelers who ride from one destination to another by train or rental car. In most cases, the company sells pre-reserved accommodations, which are usually less expensive than if you had reserved them yourself. Because of the company's close link with Alitalia, the prices quoted for air transport are sometimes among the most reasonable on the retail market.

Other good sources of package deals are **American Airlines Vacations** (© 800/321-2121; www.aavacations.com), **Delta Vacations** (© 800/221-6666; www.deltavacations.com), **US Airways Vacations** (© 800/455-0123 or 800/422-3861; www.usairwaysvacations.com), **Continental Airlines Vacations** (© 800/301-3800; www.coolvacations.com), and **United Vacations** (© 888/854-3899; www.unitedvacations.com).

Vacation Together (© 800/839-9851; www.vacationtogether.com) allows you to search for and book packages offered by a number of tour operators and airlines. The **United States Tour Operators Association** (© 212/599-6599; www.ustoa.com) has a search engine that allows you to look for operators offering packages to specific destinations. Travel packages are also listed in the travel section of your local Sunday newspaper. **Liberty Travel** (© 888/271-1584; www.libertytravel.com), one of the biggest packagers in the Northeast, often runs full-page ads in Sunday papers. Or check ads in the national travel magazines such as *Arthur Frommer's Budget Travel Magazine*, *Travel & Leisure*, *National Geographic Traveler*, and *Condé Nast Traveler*.

ESCORTED GENERAL-INTEREST TOURS

Escorted tours are structured group tours with a group leader. The price usually includes everything from airfare to hotels, meals, tours, admission costs, and local transportation.

Most escorted tours include Campania as part of a larger tour covering other destinations in Italy, at least Rome or Sicily.

Italiatour, part of the Alitalia Group (✆ 800/845-3365; fax 212/765-2183; www.italiatour.com), is the only company that offers tours with Campania as its main focus; it's no wonder its tours are the best as well. The best deal is a 7-day, 5-night package starting from $1,299 round-trip and taking in Rome, Pompeii, Sorrento, the Amalfi Coast, and Capri.

You can cover some of Campania with **Perillo Tours** (✆ 800/431-1515; www.perillotours.com), family operated for three generations—perhaps you've seen the TV commercials featuring the "King of Italy," Mario Perillo, and his son, Steve. Since it was founded in 1945, it has sent more than a million travelers to Italy on guided tours. Perillo's tours cost much less than you'd spend if you arranged a comparable trip yourself. Accommodations are in first-class hotels, and guides tend to be well qualified and well informed. They offer a "Vesuvius Tour" taking in Naples, Sorrento, and Pompeii; and a "South and Sicily Tour" stopping in Sorrento, Capri, the Amalfi Coast, and Naples.

Trafalgar Tours (✆ 800/854-0103; www.trafalgartours.com) is one of Europe's largest tour operators, offering affordable guided tours with lodgings in unpretentious hotels. Its "Italian Concerto" tour takes in the Amalfi Coast, Capri, and Pompeii and lasts 12 days. Check with your travel agent for more information on these tours (Trafalgar takes calls only from agents).

One of Trafalgar's leading competitors is **Globus+Cosmos Tours** (✆ 800/338-7092; www.globusandcosmos.com). Globus has first-class escorted coach tours of various regions lasting from 8 to 16 days (for a more in-depth review of an Italian Globus tour, check our website, www.Frommers.com); several of these include important destinations in Campania. Cosmos, a budget branch of Globus, has a 15-day "Southern Italy and Sicily" tour with in-depth visits of Capri, Mount Vesuvius, Pompeii, Sorrento, and the Amalfi Coast. Tours must be booked through a travel agent, but you can call the 800 number for brochures. Another competitor is **Insight Vacations** (✆ 800/582-8380; www.insightvacations.com), which books superior, first-class, fully escorted motorcoach tours, and offers a 14-day "Country Roads of Southern Italy and Sicily" stopping in Naples and Capri.

Tour Italy Now (✆ 800/955 4418; www.touritalynow.com), a Connecticut-based company, offers a variety of tours to the Amalfi Coast, which take in other destinations in Campania as well.

Abercrombie & Kent (✆ 800/323-7308 in the U.S. or 020/7730-9600 in the U.K.) offers luxurious premium packages. Your overnight stays will be in meticulously restored castles and exquisite villas, most of which are government-rated four- and five-star accommodations. Among the trips offered are "Classical Treasures of Southern Italy" and "Italy: A Family Adventure," taking in Naples, Capri, and the Amalfi Coast. The company's website is **www.abercrombiekent.com**.

The oldest travel agency in Britain, **Cox & Kings** (✆ 020/7873-5000; www.coxandkings.co.uk), specializes in unusual, if pricey, holidays. Their Italy offerings include organized tours through the country's gardens and sites of historic or aesthetic interest, opera tours, pilgrimage-style visits to sites of religious interest, and food- and wine-tasting tours. They never fail to offer their "Pompeii and Herculaneum" tour, taking in Sorrento, Paestum, Naples, the Phlegrean Fields, Amalfi, Ravello and, of course, Herculaneum and Pompeii. The company is noted for its focus on tours of ecological and environmental interest.

SPECIAL-INTEREST TRIPS

If you're interested in a wide range of special tours, chances are you'll find it in Campania.

For a truly special vacation, check out the "Cilento Sea Kayak" tour offered by **Vacations in Italy** (www.vacationsin italy.com). They've offered this tour for 2 years in a row and we certainly hope they'll keep it. They have the right attitude: Beginners are welcome, and the focus is on fun, comfort, and good food.

The best company for a variety of special-interest tours is the lively Napoli-based **Rising Incoming Organizer** (R.I.O., Via Monte di Dio 9, 80132 Napoli; ✆ 081-7644934; www.riorimontitours.com), a family business now in its third generation. They offer unique and off-the-beaten-path tours, covering all kinds of special interests, from ceramics—a 12-day course and tour in Naples, Vietri, the Amalfi Coast, and Cerreto Sannita (near Benevento)—to golf, sailing, and culinary adventures, including one on Neapolitan pastries.

Tour Italy Now (✆ 800/955 4418; www.touritalynow.com), a Connecticut-based company, offers two Amalfi Coast hiking tours which take in some of the Cilento, and a bicycle tour of southern Italy that goes through Campania.

La Dolce Vita Wine Tours (✆ 888/746-0022; www.dolcetours.com) organizes a great walking tour of the Amalfi Coast, taking in Capri, Mount Vesuvius, and Pompeii, as well as some of the best vineyards in the region.

For both art-and-architecture and food-and-wine tours, **Amelia Tours International,** 176 Woodbury Rd., Hicksville, NY 11801 (✆ 800/742-4591 or 516/433-0696; fax 516/822-6220; www.ameliainternational.com), is the leader of the pack, offering a standard tour of the Amalfi Coast as well as a culinary trip of the region.

As home to some of the best culinary traditions in Italy, Campania offers a number of other food-oriented tours. From her home in Ravello, Mamma Agata—who in her past life was the cook for such Hollywood stars as Humphrey Bogart and Liz Taylor—conducts small classes with great warmth and skill. This is only one of the many tour-courses offered by **Epiculinary** (✆ 888/380-9010 toll-free in the U.S.; www.epiculinary.com).

Romantica Tours (✆ 888/666 3158 in the U.S. and ✆ 06-7142017 in Italy; www.romanticatours.com) bases its Amalfi Coast tour in Minori and alternates cooking lessons with visits to the best destinations in the area, including Pompeii, Ravello, and Amalfi, as well as tours of limoncello- and mozzarella-producing establishments.

Located in Sorrento, **Sorrento Cooking School** (✆ 081-8783255; www. sorrentocookingschool.com) offers tour-package courses from a half-day to 8 days in length, as well as a variety of wine tours. You can work a number of their daily excursions into your own itinerary.

13 Getting Around Campania

BY TRAIN

Trains provide a great medium-priced means of transport around Campania. In addition to the national railway system **FFSS** (✆ 892021 from anywhere in Italy; www.trenitalia.it), Campania is served by three other local companies: **Alifana** (✆ 800-127157 toll-free within Italy, or 081-5993254; www.alifana.it), from Benevento to Napoli and serving the region of Benevento; **Circumvesuviana** (✆ 800-053939 toll-free within Italy; www.vesuviana.it), connecting Naples with the Vesuvian area and Sorrento; and **Metronapoli** (✆ 800-568866 toll-free within Italy; www.metro.na.it), connecting Naples with Pozzuoli and the Phlegrean Fields.

The national service offers fast EuroStar and InterCity trains (designated

ES and IC on train schedules, respectively): modern, air-conditioned trains that make limited stops and are ideal for longer trips. The supplement can be steep, but a second-class ES or IC ticket will provide a first-class experience. Children age 4 to 11 receive a discount of 50% off the adult fare, and children age 3 and younger travel free with their parents. Seniors and travelers younger than age 26 can purchase discount cards. Seat reservations are highly recommended during peak season and on weekends or holidays, and are obligatory on ES trains; they must be booked in advance.

If you intend to travel a lot by train, one of the best Italian railway ticket deals for Campania is the **Italy Rail 'n Drive Pass,** which combines rail and car travel, allowing you 4 days of unlimited train travel in Italy and 2 days of car rental with unlimited mileage. You have 2 months to complete your trip and are given a choice of three categories. Under this pass, two adults, for example, can travel first class for $249 per person, or second class for $209 per person.

The **Italian Flexi Rail Card** entitles you to a predetermined number of days of travel on any rail line in a certain time period. It's ideal for passengers who plan in advance to spend several days sightseeing before boarding a train for another city. A pass giving 4 possible travel days out of a block of 2 months is $239 first class and $191 second class; a pass for 8 travel days stretched over a 2-month period costs $335 first class and $267 second class; and a pass for 10 travel days within 2 months costs $383 first class and $305 second class. The **Italy Flexi Rail Card Youth** grants 4 days in 2 months for $160 second class only.

You can buy these passes from any travel agent or by calling © **800/848-7245.** You can also call © **800/4EURAIL** or **800/EUROSTAR.**

BY BUS

Local bus companies operate in all areas of the region, particularly in the hill sections and mountain areas where rail travel isn't possible or available. One of the leading bus operators is **SITA** (© **081-5522176;** www.sita-on-line.it), serving the Sorrento Peninsula and the Amalfi Coast; another is **SEPSA** (© **800-001616** toll-free within Italy; www.sepsa. it), serving the area of Pozzuoli, Baia, Cuma, and Miseno, as well as Procida and Ischia; **CTP** (© **800-482644** toll-free within Italy; www.ctpn.it), serving Naples and connecting the city with neighboring small towns; **AIR** (© **0825-204250;** www.air-spa.it), performing the same service for the Avellino area; and **CSTP** (© **800-016659** toll-free within Italy or 089-487001; www.cstp.it), servicing Salerno, with Paestum and the Cilento.

For more information, see "Getting There" in the individual city, town, and village sections throughout this book.

BY FERRY

Some of the most charming destinations in Campania are right on the water, making the sea a very important means of transportation in the region, and one of the most satisfying because of its unique views.

Naples is the region's major harbor. Other important hubs are Salerno, Amalfi, and Sorrento, plus a number of minor harbors.

Hydrofoil service (suspended in winter) operates mostly from Naples, at the **Terminal Aliscafi** of **Mergellina,** with frequent and fast runs to Capri, Ischia, Procida, Sorrento, Positano, Amalfi, Salerno, and Sicily (Milazzo and the Aeolian Islands). The major operators are **Tirrenia** (© 199-123199 or 081-2514711; www.tirrenia.it), with ships to Cagliari and Palermo; **Siremar** (© 081-5800340;

www.siremar.it), with ships to the Aeolian Islands and Milazzo; **TTTLines** (© 800-915365), with ships to Catania and Palermo; **Medmar,** with ships (© 081-5513352) to Tunis and with ferries (© 081-3334411) to Ischia; **Caremar** (© 081-5513882; www.caremar.it), with ferries and hydrofoils to Ischia, Capri, and Procida; **Alilauro** (© 081-7611004; www.alilauro.it), with hydrofoils to Ischia and Positano; **SNAV** (© 081-4285555 or 081-4285111; www.snav.it), with hydrofoil service to Ischia, Capri, and Procida, and with ships to Palermo, Sardinia, and the Aeolian and Pontine islands; **LMP** (© 081-5513236), with hydrofoils to Sorrento; and **NLG** (© 081-5527209), with hydrofoils to Capri.

BY CAR

U.S. and Canadian drivers don't need an **International Driver's License** to drive a rented car in Italy. However, if you will drive a private car, you do need the international license.

You can apply for an International Driver's License at any **American Automobile Association (AAA)** branch. You must be at least 18 and have two 2×2-inch photos and a photocopy of your U.S. driver's license with your AAA application form. The actual fee for the license can vary, depending on where it's issued. To find the AAA office nearest you, check the local phone directory, or contact **AAA's national headquarters** (© 800/222-4357 or 407/444-4300; www.aaa. com). Remember that an International Driver's License is valid only if physically accompanied by your original driver's license and only if signed on the back. In Canada, you can get the address of the **Canadian Automobile Association** closest to you by calling © 613/247-0117; or go to www.caa.ca.

The **Automobile Club d'Italia (ACI),** Via Marsala 8, 00185 Roma (© 06-49981), is open Monday through Friday from 8am to 2pm. The ACI's 24-hour **Information and Assistance Center (CAT)** is at Via Magenta 5, 00185 Roma (© 06-491716). Both offices are near the main rail station (Stazione Termini).

RENTALS   Many of the loveliest parts of Campania are situated away from the main cities, far away from the train stations. For that, and for sheer convenience and freedom, renting a car is usually the best way to explore out-of-the-way areas, especially if time is a concern. But you have to be a pretty aggressive and alert driver who won't be fazed by super-high speeds on the *autostrade* (national express highways) or by narrow streets in the cities and towns.

Neapolitans have truly earned their reputation as bad but daring drivers. To rent a car here, a driver must have nerves of steel, a sense of humor, a valid driver's license, and a valid passport; and you must (in most cases) be over 25. Insurance on all vehicles is compulsory, though any reputable rental firm will arrange this in advance before you're even given the keys.

Besides the international major rental companies **Avis** (© 800/331-1212; www.avis.com), **Budget** (© 800/472-3325; www.budget.com), and **Hertz** (© 800/654-3131; www.hertz.com), the primary rental company in Campania and Italy is **Maggiore** (© 1478-67067 toll-free in Italy; www.maggiore.it), associated with **National** in the U.S. (© 800/CAR-RENT; www.nationalcar.com), through which you can book your rental. Other U.S.-based companies specializing in European car rentals are **Auto Europe** (© 800/223-5555; www.autoeurope. com), **Europe by Car** (© 800/223-1516 or 212/581-3040 in New York; www. europebycar.com), and **Kemwel Holiday Auto** (© 800/678-0678; www.kemwel. com).

In some cases, slight discounts are offered to members of the American

Automobile Association (AAA) or the AARP (formerly called American Association of Retired Persons). Be sure to ask when you book.

GASOLINE   Gasoline (known as *benzina*) is expensive in Italy. Be prepared for sticker shock every time you fill up even a medium-size car with super, which has the octane rating appropriate for most of the cars you'll be able to rent. It's priced throughout the country at around 1.20€ ($1.50) per liter (about 4.50€/$5.63 per gal.). Gas stations on the autostrade are open 24 hours, but on regular roads only a few gas stations have self-service areas accessible during the lunch recess, on Sunday, and after 7pm. Do make sure the pump registers zero before an attendant starts refilling your tank. A popular scam is to fill your tank before resetting the meter, so you pay not only your bill but also the charges run up by the previous motorist.

DRIVING RULES   The Italian Highway Code follows the Geneva Convention, and Campania and Italy use international road signs. Driving is on the right; passing is on the left. Violators of the highway code are fined; serious violations might also be punished by imprisonment. In cities and towns, the speed limit is 50kmph (31 mph). For all cars and motor vehicles on main roads and local roads, the limit is 90kmph (56 mph). For the autostrade, the limit is 130kmph (81 mph). Use the left lane only for passing. If a driver zooms up behind you on the autostrade with his or her car lights on, that's your signal to get out of the way! Use of seat belts is compulsory.

BREAKDOWNS & ASSISTANCE   In case of car breakdown or for any tourist information, foreign motorists can call ⓒ **800-116800** (24-hr. nationwide telephone service). For road information, itineraries, and all sorts of travel assistance, call ⓒ **064-91716.** For emergency assistance, dial ⓒ **116.**

14 Tips on Accommodations

Hotels along the Amalfi Coast and in the interior of Campania tend to be different from those you might be used to in the U.S. or U.K. While the differences are only a question of character in the most expensive luxury hotels, cultural idiosyncrasies become more and more apparent as you go down in the level of accommodations. Buildings are old—sometimes centuries old—and there is only so much you can do to update a medieval tower without spoiling its character. The biggest difference can be found in the bathrooms, which tend to be small, with fixtures that sometimes look old-fashioned even if they are in perfect working order. Rooms also tend to be smaller than you might expect. On these southern shores, carpeting is the exception, while tiles—often hand-decorated ones from the local industry—are the rule. The climate is mild, so hotels are structured to maximize outdoor enjoyment. This is why most hotels have balconies and terraces, and why many guest rooms open onto a patio or terrace/garden.

Amenities tend to be different, too—or rather, you might have a different picture in your mind based on your past experience. Air-conditioning, for example, is far from standard. Yet the climate is so nearly perfect—warm and breezy—that you will rarely need it, provided you don't mind sleeping with your window open. Although TVs are almost everywhere, make sure they offer satellite service for access to English-speaking programs; satellite TVs are not standard. Internet access (a terminal, usually in the lobby) is becoming standard, but Wi-Fi has not taken off in southern Italy the way it has in the U.S. or U.K.

A Home Away from Home: Renting Your Own Apartment or Villa

If you're looking to rent a villa or an apartment, one of the best agencies to call is **Rent Villas** (ⓒ **800/726-6702** or 805/641-1650; fax 805/641-1630; www.rentvillas.com). It represents the Cuendet properties, some of the best in Campania and in Italy, and its agents are very helpful in tracking down the perfect place to suit your needs. Cuendet's representative in the United Kingdom, and one of the best all-around agents in London, is **International Chapters** (ⓒ **08450/700-618**; www.villa-rentals.com). Also in the U.K., contact **Cottages to Castles** (ⓒ **1622/775-217**; www.cottagestocastles.com). For some of the top properties, call **The Parker Company, Ltd.** in the U.S. (ⓒ **800/280-2811** or 781/596-8282; fax 781/596-3125; www.theparker company.com). This agency rents apartments, villas, restored farmhouses, and even castles throughout Campania. One of the most reasonably priced agencies is **Villas and Apartments Abroad, Ltd.** (ⓒ **800/433-3020** or 212/213-6435; fax 212/213-8252; www.ideal-villas.com). A popular but very pricey agency is **Villas International** (ⓒ **800/221-2260** or 415/499-9490; www.villasintl.com).

Again, because of the climate—and also because of the southerners' love for the sun—swimming pools are almost always outdoors. You will find indoor pools in spas, but they are rarely big enough for actual swimming. Tennis courts are almost always outdoors, too.

Most hotels have a restaurant and, in summer, the smaller operations like to offer a meal plan to go with the room. You can usually choose among B&B service (breakfast only), half-board (breakfast and either lunch or dinner), and full board (breakfast, lunch, and dinner). Sometimes, however, you are bound to half- or even full-board service. This is often the case during August, the busiest month. Although many hotels cater to families, they rarely offer more than quads or connected rooms in terms of special amenities for children. In rare cases you'll find a playground or a special swimming pool. Babysitting is usually available upon request.

You'll also find that few hotels have their own private garage, especially in Naples. Some hotels in smaller towns and in the country have their own parking lot, but sometimes you might have to just park in the street nearby. Daily parking rates are specified whenever they're available under each hotel listing.

One last local peculiarity: Since many moderate and inexpensive hotels along the coast cater to families who come for their summer vacations, summer rates are based on longer stays—often they'll have a minimum of 3 days or even a week.

AGRITURISMO (STAYING ON A FARM)

Campania is certainly part of the *agriturismo* movement in Italy, whereby a working farm or agricultural estate makes accommodations available for visitors who want to stay in the countryside. The rural atmosphere is ensured by the fact that an operation can call itself "agriturismo" only if: (a) It offers fewer than 30 beds total; and (b) the agricultural component of the property brings in a larger economic share of profits than the hospitality part—in other words, the property has to remain a farm and not become a glorified hotel.

Agriturismi are generally a crapshoot. They're loosely regulated, and the price, quality, and types of accommodations can vary dramatically. Some are sumptuous apartments or suites with hotel-like amenities; others are a straw's width away from sleeping in the barn on a haystack. Most, though, are miniapartments, often furnished from secondhand dealers and usually rented out with a minimum stay of 3 days or a week. Sometimes you're invited to eat big country dinners at the table with the family; other times you cook for yourself. Rates can vary from 15€ ($17) for two people per day all the way up to 250€ ($288)—as much as a board-rated four-star hotel in town. I've reviewed a few choice ones throughout this book, but there are hundreds more.

Probably the best, most fantastic resource—because it is both user-friendly and has an English version—is **www. agriturismo.regione.toscana.it**, with databases of hundreds of farm stays searchable by text or by clickable map down to the locality, with info about each property, a photo or two, and a direct link to the property's website.

15 Tips on Dining

Meals are structured differently here than in the U.S. or elsewhere in the world. Here you will usually start with a first course of pasta or rice *(il primo)*—the appetizer *(antipasto)* before that is optional and locals often skip it—followed by a second course *(il secondo)* of meat or fish accompanied by a vegetable side dish or a salad *(il contorno)*. You can follow all that with cheese *(formaggio),* a piece of fruit *(frutta),* or dessert *(dolce)* and, of course, a *caffè* (coffee). Ordering a *cappuccino,* though, is a social blunder, because *cappuccino* is reserved for the morning. Don't ask for a *latte,* either, if you are used to the American version; what you'll get in Italy is a glass of milk, which is what *latte* means in Italian.

Ordering pasta as the main course *(il secondo)* is still looked upon with puzzlement. The practice is accepted at lunch, when an increasing number of working people will have a pasta dish as their midday snack, but it remains completely unheard-of at dinner.

If pasta is all you want, some restaurants that specialize in first courses—called *spaghetterie*—serve a large variety of pasta dishes; they are usually youth-oriented hangouts. *Pizzerie* will also serve pasta dishes, and a meal there is less strictly structured. Typically, you will get an array of appetizers, followed by a pizza or a pasta dish. Dessert is optional, and locals will often opt for a gelato at a nearby ice-cream parlor, unless a good home-made cake or pastry is on the menu.

Pizza a taglio indicates a place where you can order pizza by the slice, but *pizza a metro* and *pizzeria* are both casual sit-down restaurants, the first a place where long pizzas are sold by weight, and the second a spot that sells individual, round pizzas made in wood-burning ovens. A *tavola calda* (literally "hot table") serves ready-made hot foods you can take away or eat at one of the few small tables. The food is usually very good. A *rosticceria* is the same type of place; you'll see chickens roasting on a spit in the window. *Friggitoria* usually sell pizza and deep-fried *calzone.*

For a quick bite, go to a **bar.** Although bars in Campania do serve alcohol, they function mainly as cafes. Prices have a split personality: *Al banco* is the price you pay standing at the bar, while *à tavola* means you are charged two to four times as much for sitting at a table where you'll be waited on. In bars, you can find local pastries, panino sandwiches on various kinds of rolls, and *tramezzini* (white-bread sandwich triangles with the crusts cut off). The sandwiches run 1€ to 3€ ($1.25–$3.75) and are traditionally put in a kind of tiny press to flatten and toast them so the crust is crispy and the filling is hot and gooey. (Unfortunately, microwaves have invaded the region recently, turning panini into something resembling a soggy hot tissue.)

A full-fledged restaurant will go by the name **osteria, trattoria,** or **ristorante.** Once upon a time, these terms meant something—*osterie* were basic places where you could get a plate of spaghetti and a glass of wine; *trattorie* were casual places serving full meals of filling peasant fare; and *ristoranti* were fancier places, with waiters in bow ties, printed menus, wine lists, and hefty prices. Nowadays, fancy restaurants often go by the name of *trattoria* to cash in on the associated charm factor; trendy spots use *osteria* to show they're hip; and simple, inexpensive places sometimes tack on *ristorante* to ennoble themselves. Many restaurants double as *pizzerias,* with a regular menu and a separate selection for pizza, sometimes offering a separate casual dining area as well.

The **pane e coperto (bread and cover)** is a 1€ to 3€ ($1.25–$3.75) cover charge that you must pay at most restaurants for the mere privilege of sitting at a table. Most Italians eat a leisurely full meal—appetizer and first and second courses—at lunch and dinner and will expect you to do the same, or at least eat a first and second course. To request the bill, say, *"Il conto, per favore"* (eel *con*-toh, pore fah-*vohr*-ay). A tip of 15% is usually included in the bill these days but, if you're unsure, ask, *"È incluso il servizio?"* (ay een-*cloo*-soh eel sair-*vee*-tsoh?).

At many restaurants, especially larger ones and in cities, you'll find a **menu turistico (tourist's menu),** sometimes called **menu del giorno (menu of the day).** This set-price menu usually covers all meal incidentals—including table wine, cover charge, and 15% service charge—along with a first course *(primo)* and second course *(secondo),* but it almost always

Campanian Nightlife

By American and British standards, nightlife in Campania's provincial towns tends to be lame. There isn't a bar culture in southern Italy, and often what's called a pub here is a rather pale imitation. Cultural and social life, though, are always lively, from strolling to and fro along the main street, to going out for dinner, to having an aperitivo, to eating handmade gelato ice cream, to going to the theater or to a movie.

Clubs can be found, but you may not want to go out of your way to be seen there. While there are some great clubs in Naples, the situation is quite different in the rest of the region. You'll find some good ones along the Amalfi Coast in summer, but in the interior you are in a very different atmosphere—it isn't at all unusual for young people to drive all the way to Naples for a good evening out. Your best option will often be a concert. Musical events (both classical and pop, though the pop is in Italian) are sometimes staged in even the most remote little towns and villages.

offers an abbreviated selection of pretty bland dishes: spaghetti in tomato sauce and slices of pork. Sometimes a better choice is a *menu à prezzo fisso* (**fixed-price menu**). It usually doesn't include wine but sometimes covers the service and often offers a wider selection of better dishes, occasionally house specialties and local foods. More elegant restaurants offer a *menu degustazione* (**tasting menu**), and that is usually the way to go for the best selection of food at the best price. Except in those special restaurants, ordering a la carte will offer you the best chance of a memorable meal. Even better,

forego the menu entirely and put yourself in the capable hands of your waiter.

The *enoteca* wine bar is a growing, popular marriage of a wine bar and an *osteria,* where you can sit and order from a host of local and regional wines by the glass while snacking on finger foods (and usually a number of simple first-course possibilities) that reflect the area's fare. Relaxed and filled with ambience and good wine, these are great spots for light and inexpensive lunches—perfect for educating your palate and recharging your batteries.

16 Recommended Books & Films

BOOKS
GENERAL
Besides his more famous *Italian Neighbors* (Grove Press, 2003), Tim Parks wrote a delightful account of his encounters with Italian culture (his wife is Italian) full of humor and insight, in *Italian Education* (Harper Perennials, 1996).

TRUE STORIES
If you want to bone up on the ancient Romans, Edward Gibbon's *History of the Decline and Fall of the Roman Empire* (begun in 1776) is still unrivaled today, but it will take you a minimum of 3 months to get through the several volumes (Penguin classics, 1983).

Among the many travel writers who wrote on this region, one of the first is also one of the best and most charming: Johann Wolfgang von Goethe's *Italian Journey* (1816; reprinted by Penguin Books, 1992). Goethe much preferred Naples to Rome and writes vividly about a wide range of social and natural phenomena, from his mingling with the aristocracy to a trip up Mount Vesuvius during an eruption. The 19th century saw an explosion of travel writing by eminent authors on the "Grand Tour"; William Dean Howells recorded his

impressions in *Roman Holidays and Others* (Kessinger Publishing, 2004). The impoverished English "slum novelist" George Gissing was finally able to travel to Italy toward the end of his life and wrote with great enthusiasm about his experiences in *By the Ionian Sea* (Marlboro Press, 1996). Henry James's *Italian Hours* (Penguin Classics, 1995) is a collection of essays, one of which describes the novelist's visit to the bay of Naples and its islands. Barbara Grizzuti Harrison describes her time in Italy, including a stay Naples, in *Italian Days* (Atlantic Monthly Press, 1998).

ART HISTORY
For a modern history of art, the touchstone is the massive *History of Italian Renaissance Art* (H. N. Abrams, 1994) by Frederick Hartt. Naples was not central to the art of that great period—Rome, Florence and Venice were the major focal points—but you will find an interesting treatment of Naples's renaissance legacy in Laurie Scheider Adams's *Italian Renaissance Art* (Westview Press, 2001). To hone in on Naples's baroque heritage, try John Varriano's *Italian Baroque and Rococo Architecture* (Oxford, 1986). Giorgio Vasari's *Lives of the Artists Vols.*

I and II (Penguin Classics, 1987) is a collection of biographies of the great artists from Cimabue up to Vasari's own 16th-century contemporaries.

FICTION

The English writer Norman Douglas came to the bay of Naples early in the 20th century and began a lifelong fascination with the region. His most famous novel, *South Wind* (IndyPublishing, 2002), is set on a fictional version of Capri, and reproduces the glamorous and eccentric expatriate community. Susan Sontag's historical novel, *The Volcano Lover* (Anchor, 1997), is set in the Napoleonic era, and is based on the true story of the love triangle between Sir William Hamilton (British ambassador to the Kingdom of the Two Sicilies), his wife, and her lover, Lord Horatio Nelson.

The Uncle from Rome (Viking, 1992), by American author Joseph Caldwell, is the story of an opera singer from Indiana who comes to Naples to play a role. He befriends a family of Neapolitans, and becomes involved in family dynamics at least as theatrical as his stage performance. For a look at Naples's dark side, there is the tragicomic *Così fan Tutti* (Vintage/Black Lizard, 1998) a mystery by English novelist Michael Dibdin in his detective Aurelio Zen series.

Several Italian authors have written movingly of the harsh and beautiful rural life of southern Italy. Most famous perhaps is Carlo Levi's *Christ Stopped at Eboli* (English translation Farrar, Straus & Giroux, 2000), about the author's sojourn in a small village where he was exiled during the Fascist period.

FAST FACTS: Campania & the Amalfi Coast

American Express Travel agencies representing American Express are found in major cities. In Naples, check out **Dusila Travel,** also at Capodichino airport (Viale Fulco Ruffo di Calabria; ✆ 081-2311281).

Area Codes See the "Telephone Tips" in the inside front cover of this book.

ATMs See "Money," earlier in this chapter.

Business Hours Regular business hours are generally Monday through Friday from 9am (sometimes 9:30am) to 1pm, and 3:30pm (sometimes 4pm) to 7 or 7:30pm. In July and August, **offices** might not open in the afternoon until 4:30 or 5pm. **Banks** are open Monday through Friday from 8:30am to 1 or 1:30pm, and from 2 or 2:30pm to 4pm. They are closed Saturday, Sunday, and national holidays. The *riposo* (mid-afternoon closing) and Sunday closing are most commonly observed, except for certain tourist-oriented stores that are now permitted to remain open on Sunday during the high season. If you're in Campania during the summer and the heat is intense, we suggest that you, too, learn the custom of the *riposo.*

Car Rentals See "Getting Around Campania," earlier in this chapter.

Currency See "Money," earlier in this chapter.

Driving Rules See "Getting Around Campania," earlier in this chapter.

Drugstores At every drugstore *(farmacia)* there's a list of those that are open at night and on Sunday.

Electricity The electricity in Campania varies considerably. It's usually alternating current (AC), varying from 42 to 50 cycles. The voltage can be anywhere

from 115 to 220. It's recommended that any visitor carrying electrical appli-
ances obtain a transformer. Plugs have prongs that are round, not flat; therefore, an adapter plug is also needed.

Embassies & Consulates All consulates are in Naples. The **U.S. Consulate** is at
Piazza della Repubblica 2 (© **081-5838111;** fax 081-7611869; www.usis.it); the
Canadian Consulate is at Via Carducci 29 (© **081-401338;** fax 081-406161; www.
canada.it); the **U.K. Consulate** is at Via Crispi 122 (© **081-663511** or 081-663589;
fax 081-7613720; www.britain.it).

Emergencies Dial © **113** for ambulance, police, or fire. In case of a breakdown
on an Italian road, dial © **116** at the closest telephone box; the nearest Automobile Club of Italy (ACI) will be notified to come to your aid.

Etiquette & Customs Volumes have been written on Italian etiquette, and it
would be too much to summarize here. One hint: Look around, see what locals
do, how they dress, and how they behave, and mold your behavior to theirs.
You can't go wrong.

   Among the things that would bother a local: Don't cut in line. Italians might
not queue in an orderly manner like the English, but they respect the order of
arrival at the ice-cream counter, as at the post office. If you ask someone a
question and discover that he or she doesn't speak English, don't loudly repeat
the question—try gesturing, or ask for help instead. Don't assume everyone is
a crook trying to get you into a tourist trap. Crooks exist here as everywhere,
but most people are honest; use your judgment and you'll be fine. Also, get up
for the elderly and for women—especially on public transportation. Hold doors
open for people—particularly those hampered by packages and small children.
Say "Hello" when entering a shop, and "Thank you" when exiting (or *"Buon-
giorno"* and *"Grazie"*), even if you didn't buy anything.

Holidays See "Campania Calendar of Events," earlier in this chapter.

Information See "Visitor Information," earlier in this chapter.

Internet Access See "Fast Facts" in the destination chapters throughout the
book.

Language Italian is the language spoken in Campania, together with the local
dialect, but English is generally understood at most attractions such as museums, and at most hotels and restaurants that cater to visitors. Even if not all the
staff at a restaurant or other business speaks English, almost always one person
does and can be summoned. As you travel in remote towns and villages, a
Berlitz Italian phrase book is a handy accompaniment.

Laundromats Public laundromats are extremely rare (they are called *lavanderia a gettoni*), but you can leave your laundry with most *tintoria (dry cleaners)*
and come back to pick it up folded and clean.

Legal Aid The consulate of your country is the place to turn for legal aid,
although offices can't interfere in the Italian legal process. They can, however,
inform you of your rights and provide a list of attorneys. You'll have to pay for
the attorney out of your pocket—there's no free legal assistance. If you're
arrested for a drug offense, about all the consulate will do is notify a lawyer
about your case and perhaps inform your family.

Liquor Laws Wine with meals has been a normal part of family life for hundreds of years in Campania and in Italy. Children are exposed to wine at an early age, and consumption of alcohol isn't out of the ordinary. There's no legal drinking age for buying or ordering alcohol. Alcohol is sold day and night throughout the year because there are almost no restrictions in Italy. If you are curious about the results of such a policy, alcoholism is almost unknown in Italy, and drinking-related accidents on the road are extremely rare. There are, though, serious problems with young tourists, and the U.S. government has issued a travel advisory about young Americans who regularly get in trouble faced with so much freedom.

Mail Mail delivery in Italy had a remarkably bad record, but things have improved enormously in recent years. Postcards (not in regular letter envelopes) pay a reduced rate, but are also the slowest. Your family and friends back home might receive your postcards in 1 week, or it might take 2 weeks (sometimes longer). Letters mailed to locations outside Europe with *Posta Prioritaria* take 4 to 8 days depending on the destinations; letters to Europe and Mediterranean countries take 3 days. Postcards and letters weighing up to 20 grams sent to the United States, Canada, Australia, and New Zealand cost .80€ ($1); to the United Kingdom and Ireland, .62€ (78¢). You can buy stamps at all post offices and at *tabacchi* (tobacco) stores.

Maps D'Agostini as well as the Touring Club d'Italia (TCI) publish excellent maps of Campania, which are available for sale at most newsstands and some bookstores in every town, as well as from rest stops on the highway. You might want to check out the **Touring Club d'Italia** store in Naples (© 008-56710157).

Newspapers & Magazines In major cities, it's possible to find the *International Herald Tribune* or *USA Today,* as well as other English-language newspapers and magazines, including *Time* and *Newsweek,* at hotels and news kiosks.

Passports **For Residents of the United States:** Whether you're applying in person or by mail, you can download passport applications from the U.S. State Department website at **http://travel.state.gov**. For general information, call the **National Passport Agency** (© 202/647-0518). To find your regional passport office, either check the U.S. State Department website or call the **National Passport Information Center** (© 900/225-5674); the fee is 55¢ per minute for automated information and $1.50 per minute for operator-assisted calls.

   For Residents of Canada: Passport applications are available at travel agencies throughout Canada or from the central **Passport Office,** Department of Foreign Affairs and International Trade, Ottawa, ON K1A 0G3 (© 800/567-6868; www.ppt.gc.ca).

   For Residents of the United Kingdom: To pick up an application for a standard 10-year passport (5-year passport for children younger than age 16), visit your nearest passport office, major post office, or travel agency. You can also contact the **United Kingdom Passport Service** at © 0870/521-0410, or search its website at www.ukpa.gov.uk.

   For Residents of Ireland: You can apply for a 10-year passport at the **Passport Office,** Setanta Centre, Molesworth Street, Dublin 2 (© 01/671-1633; www.irlgov.ie/iveagh). Those younger than age 18 and older than 65 must apply for a 12€, 3-year passport. You can also apply at 1A South Mall, Cork (© 021/ 272-525) or at most main post offices.

For Residents of Australia: You can pick up an application from your local post office or any branch of Passports Australia, but you must schedule an interview at the passport office to present your application materials. Call the Australian Passport Information Service at © 131-232, or visit the government website at www.passports.gov.au.

For Residents of New Zealand: You can pick up a passport application at any New Zealand Passports Office or download it from their website. Contact the Passports Office at © 0800/225-050 in New Zealand or 04/474-8100, or log on to www.passports.govt.nz.

Police Dial © 113, the all-purpose number for police emergency assistance in Italy.

Restrooms All airport and train stations have restrooms, often with attendants who expect to be tipped. Bars, nightclubs, restaurants, cafes, gas stations, and hotels should have facilities as well. Public toilets are found near many of the major sights. Usually they're designated WC (water closet) and bear international symbols or the signs DONNE (women) and UOMINI (men). The most confusing designation is SIGNORI (gentlemen) and SIGNORE (ladies), so watch that final i and e! Many public toilets charge a small fee or employ an attendant who expects a tip. It's a good idea to carry some tissues in your pocket or purse—they often come in handy.

Safety Refer to "Health & Safety," earlier in this chapter.

Smoking Smoking is very common but is forbidden in enclosed public spaces, except those with separate ventilated smoking areas. If smoking is important to you, call the restaurant or club of your choice to find out if it's allowed.

Taxes As a member of the European Union, Italy imposes a value-added tax (called IVA in Italy) on most goods and services. The tax that most affects visitors is the one imposed on hotel rates, which ranges from 9% in first- and second-class hotels to 19% in deluxe hotels.

Non-E.U. (European Union) citizens are entitled to a refund of the IVA if you spend more than 155€ ($194) at any one store, before tax. To claim your refund, request an invoice from the cashier at the store and take it to the Customs office *(dogana)* at the airport to have it stamped before you leave. *Note:* If you're going to another E.U. country before flying home, have it stamped at the airport Customs office of the last E.U. country you'll be in (for example, if you're flying home via Britain, have your Italian invoices stamped in London). Once you're back home, mail the stamped invoice (keep a photocopy for your records) back to the original vendor within 90 days of the purchase. The vendor will, sooner or later, send you a refund of the tax that you paid at the time of your original purchase. Reputable stores view this as a matter of ordinary paperwork and are businesslike about it. Less-honorable stores might lose your dossier. It pays to deal with established vendors on large purchases. You can also request that the refund be credited to the card with which you made the purchase; this is usually a faster procedure.

Many shops are now part of the "Tax Free for Tourists" network (look for the sticker in the window). Stores participating in this network issue a check along with your invoice at the time of purchase. After you have the invoice stamped at Customs, you can redeem the check for cash directly at the Tax Free booth in the airport (in Rome, it's past Customs; in Milan's airports, the booth is inside the duty-free shop) or mail it back in the envelope provided within 60 days.

Telephone Check the inside front cover of this book for international and domestic telephone codes.

A **local phone call** in Italy costs around .10€ (13¢). **Public phones** accept coins, precharged phone cards (*scheda* or *carta telefonica*), or both. You can buy a *carta telefonica* at any *tabacchi* (tobacconists; most display a sign with a white "T" on a black/brown background) in increments of 5€ ($6.25), 10€ ($12.50), and 20€ ($25). To make a call, pick up the receiver and insert .10€ (13¢) or your card (break off the corner first). Most phones have a digital display that'll tell you how much money you've inserted (or how much is left on the card). Dial the number, and don't forget to take the card with you after you hang up.

Italy has recently introduced a series of **international phone cards** *(scheda telefonica internazionale)* for calling overseas, which are by far the most economical way to call abroad. They come in increments of 50, 100, 200, and 400 *unità* (units), and they're usually available at *tabacchi* and bars. Each *unità* is worth .15€ (19¢) of phone time; it costs 5 *unità* (.65€/81¢) per minute to call within Europe or to the United States or Canada and 12 *unità* (1.55€/$2) per minute to call Australia or New Zealand. You don't insert this card into the phone; instead, dial ℂ **1740** and then *2 (star, 2) for instructions in English, when prompted.

To make **collect or calling card calls,** drop in .10€ (13¢) or insert your card and dial one of the numbers here; an American operator will shortly come on the line to assist you. (Because Italy has yet to discover the joys of the touch-tone phone, you'll have to wait for the operator.) The following calling-card numbers work all over Italy: **AT&T** ℂ 172-1011, **MCI** ℂ 172-1022, and **Sprint** ℂ 172-1877. To make collect calls to a country besides the United States, dial ℂ **170** (free), and practice your Italian counting in order to relay the number to the Italian operator. Tell him or her that you want it *a carico del destinatario* (charged to the destination, or collect).

Don't count on all Italian phones having touch-tone service! You might not be able to access your voice mail or answering machine if you call home from Italy.

Time Zone In terms of standard time zones, Campania is 6 hours ahead of Eastern Standard Time in the United States. Daylight saving time goes into effect in Italy each year from the end of March to the end of September.

Tipping In **hotels,** the service charge of 15% to 19% is already added to a bill. In addition, it's customary to tip the maid .50€ (65¢) per day, the doorman (for calling a cab) .50€ (65¢), and the bellhop or porter 1.50€ to 2.50€ ($1.90–$3.15) for carrying your bags to your room. A concierge expects about 15% of his or her bill, as well as tips for extra services performed, which could include help with long-distance calls. In expensive hotels, these euro amounts are often doubled.

In **restaurants and cafes,** 15% is usually added to your bill to cover most charges. If you're not sure whether this has been done, ask, *"È incluso il servizio?"* (ay een-*cloo*-soh eel sair-*vee*-tsoh). An additional tip isn't expected, but it's nice to leave the equivalent of an extra couple of dollars if you've been pleased with the service. Checkroom attendants expect .75€ (95¢), and washroom attendants should get .50€ (65¢). Restaurants are required by law to give customers official receipts.

Taxi drivers expect at least 15% of the fare.

Water In restaurants, most Campanians drink mineral water with their meals; however, tap water is safe everywhere, as are public drinking fountains. Some areas of Naples have had long-term problems with the water supply, and this is why all public establishments in the city—hotels, bars, cafes, restaurants, and so on—have their own filtering devices. If you are staying in a private home, though, make sure you ask about the water supply. Elsewhere, if tap water comes out cloudy, it's because of the calcium or other minerals inherent in a water supply that often comes untreated from fresh springs. Unsafe sources and fountains will be marked ACQUA NON POTABILE.

3

Suggested Campania & the Amalfi Coast Itineraries

Campania is a moderately sized region, but there is so much to see that you can split it up in any number of ways. Public transportation in Campania is good, so you can easily move about from one destination to the other by train or bus. Exploring the countryside, though, will require a car, which you can rent in any large town for just the time you need it—with the rocketing car theft rates in Campania, having a car is more a liability than a commodity. Another possibility is renting a car with a driver, an increasingly popular option for the famous Amalfi Drive.

While Naples is usually thought of as the place to start your visit in Campania—it is the largest city, and has an airport and all—we recommend that you don't. Naples can be overwhelming, literally bursting with life and noise, and you'll appreciate it a lot more if you ease yourself slowly into this special cultural universe by starting your visit in smaller towns. The itineraries below take in all our preferred destinations; you can vary them depending on the amount of time you have, and on your particular interests.

1 Campania & the Amalfi Coast in 1 Week

One week is not long to visit the whole Amalfi Coast region, but you'll certainly be able to get a good idea of its key attractions. Since your time is short, you'll have to pare your exploration to the essentials. You'll miss a lot of the pleasurable lingering, which is so suitable to this region, but you'll have enough time to plunge right into the most phenomenal sights.

You can do a lot of this itinerary by public transportation (including ferries), but you might want to have a car for days 2 and 3, while exploring the region's southern area.

Days ❶ to ❷: Sorrento & the Amalfi Coast

Fly into Naples's Capodichino Airport and get yourself directly to **Sorrento** (there's bus and limo service from the airport, or you can rent a car if you feel more daring). Once there, allow yourself a day of relaxation to recover from jet lag. Stroll the **Lungomare,** do some swimming and, if you are more ambitious, catch a concert in the evening. The best, if you are lucky enough to get tickets, are

those offered in the cloister of San Francesco. On day 2, get an early start and explore the **Sorrento peninsula** and **Amalfi Coast.** (Hire a limo, use the public bus system, or drive a rental car.) Hike, swim, visit the splendid **Amalfi cathedral** (don't miss the interior). and some of the smaller towns off the beaten track. Have dinner at the **San Pietro, Faro di Capo d'Orso, Taverna del Capitano,** or even **Don Alfonso 1890**—on this stretch of coast you'll find the region's best gourmet haunts, as well as those with the best views. See chapters 6 and 7.

Day ❸: Padula, Paestum & Salerno

In the morning, go to **Certosa di Padula** (you can use public transportation, but you'll have to keep a strict timetable) and devote a few hours to this architectural marvel. In the afternoon, drive or take a bus to **Paestum** to visit the stunning temples at sunset—on the way, you'll cross through wild Cilento Park. Spend the night in **Salerno** (where you can relinquish your car if you rented one), and have dinner in the **medieval town.** See chapter 9.

Day ❹: Salerno & Capri

After an early stroll through **Salerno,** enjoying its splendid **Lungomare,** take a ferry to **Capri,** where you can shop and see the sights. Stay overnight to get the flavor of this mythical island, when the crowds—some of them—have gone back to the mainland. From Capri you can easily make it to **Naples** in the morning via the very frequent ferry and hydrofoil services. See chapter 8.

Days ❺ to ❻: Naples

At this point you'll be ready for the big city and its enormous amount of artistic riches. Start your visit with the **Maschio Angioino, Palazzo Reale,** and **Museo Nazionale di Capodimonte** before you proceed to the **Lungomare** to enjoy the panoramic views from picturesque **Borgo Marinari** (and have a nice dinner, too).

On day 6, take the **walking tour of SpaccaNapoli.** Have a pizza lunch in one of the historical *pizzeria.* We recommend completing your experience in Old Naples. Spend the afternoon at the **Museo Archeologico Nazionale** in preparation for your last day. See chapter 4.

Day ❼: Herculaneum, Pompeii & Mount Vesuvius

Catch a train on the Circumvesuviana railroad to **Herculaneum** if you want a relaxing, quiet excursion; or go to **Pompeii** if you like grandiose stretches of excavations. Both sites offer enormous amounts to see, but covering both in 1 day is impossible. Use the other half of your day to climb **Mount Vesuvius,** the burning heart of Campania. Alternatively, linger a few hours longer in Naples in the morning to visit more attractions there before heading for the excavation sites. See chapter 5.

2 Campania & the Amalfi Coast in 2 Weeks

Two weeks is an ideal amount of time to explore this culturally and naturally rich region. You'll be able to see some of the best art treasures in Italy, but you can also relax and enjoy the sea, coastline, and mountains. Again, there is much that you can do by public transportation, so it will generally be easiest not to bother with car rentals. You'll want to rent one, though, to explore the countryside at your own pace. The itinerary below has been organized so that you can follow it straight through, or follow it from day 3 through day 9, or from days 6, 7, and 8 on, depending on if you rent a car or not.

Day ❶: Sorrento

Recover from jet lag by relaxing in **Sorrento** (see chapter 6) on your first day. If you decide to rent a car, do not rent one at the airport unless you don't mind leaving it behind on day 2. (You can pick one up in Sorrento on day 3.)

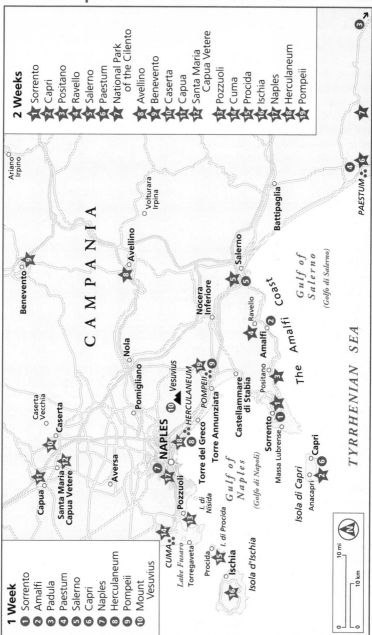

Campania & the Amalfi Coast in 1 Week & 2 Weeks

1 Week
1 Sorrento
2 Amalfi
3 Padula
4 Paestum
5 Salerno
6 Capri
7 Naples
8 Herculaneum
9 Pompeii
10 Mount Vesuvius

2 Weeks
1 Sorrento
2 Capri
3 Positano
4 Ravello
5 Salerno
6 Paestum
7 National Park of the Cilento
8 Avellino
9 Benevento
10 Caserta
11 Capua
12 Santa Maria Capua Vetere
13 Pozzuoli
14 Cuma
15 Procida
16 Ischia
17 Naples
18 Herculaneum
19 Pompeii

Day ❷: Capri

Take a ferry to **Capri,** where you can spend your day hiking, bathing, sunbathing, and shopping. See chapter 8.

Days ❸ to ❹: The Sorrento Peninsula & the Amalfi Coast

Stretch out day 2 in "The Amalfi Coast in 1 Week" itinerary and spend an extra day exploring the Amalfi Coast. Take in **Positano, Ravello,** and some of the interior's more remote towns. You can do this by bus and ferry, car service, or car rental. See chapters 6 and 7.

Day ❺: Salerno & Paestum

After a stroll along the **Lungomare** of **Salerno,** have lunch in the **medieval town** and visit the splendid **Cathedral.** In the afternoon, head for **Paestum** and its unique temples, and be sure to stay until sunset to enjoy the views. Both Salerno and Paestum are well connected by bus service if you don't care to rent a car. See chapter 9.

Day ❻: Padula & the Cilento

Take time to explore the **Park of the Cilento** and its memorable coast in the morning. Then make your way to the Certosa di Padula for an afternoon visit, crossing through the imposing Cilento Massif, with its eerie caves and soaring peaks. You can rely solely on public transportation here, but you'll have to keep to a strict timetable. See chapter 9.

Day ❼: Avellino & Benevento

These two towns are each the capital of a sub-region rich in cultural, natural, and artistic heritage. You'll have to satisfy yourself with the highlights; having a car will allow you to enjoy it most. We recommend that you start early in the morning with Sant'Angelo dei Lombardi and stop in **Avellino** for its **museum,** on your way to **Benevento.** There you'll want to

spend the night in order to take in all of the town's attractions. See chapter 10.

Day ❽: Caserta & Surroundings

Leave early in the morning for **Caserta** and start with a visit to the awesome **Reggia.** You'll also be able to visit the **Cathedral of Casertavecchia** or, alternatively, the **Belvedere di San Leucio,** before it is time to break for lunch. Spend the afternoon in **Capua** and nearby **Santa Maria Capua Vetere,** where you can stay overnight. See chapter 10.

Day ❾: Pozzuoli, Cuma & the Phlegrean Fields

Arrive in the morning in the splendid Bay of **Pozzuoli,** home to treasures from antiquity and views beloved by Neapolitans. Spend the day visiting the **Parco Archeologico Subacqueo di Baia** and the **Acropolis of Cuma.** (See chapter 4.) In the evening, catch a ferry from Pozzuoli to have dinner on the island of **Procida,** where you can spend the night. See chapter 8.

Day ❿: Ischia

From Pozzuoli (or Procida), catch a ferry to **Ischia.** On the island, hire a local taxi to take you on a tour, or use the excellent public bus system. Then spend a few hours in **Giardini Poseidon**—our favorite spa on the island—or pick one of the others we recommend. For another kind of relaxation, you can head for the beach; **Spiaggia di Citara** and **Lido dei Maronti** are the best on the island. See chapter 8. In the evening, catch a ferry for Naples, in order to arrive in its famous harbor—under the towering shadow of Vesuvius—at sunset. See chapter 4.

Days ⓫ to ⓬: Naples

Follow days 5 and 6 of the **Naples** itinerary for "Campania & the Amalfi Coast in 1 Week," but save some attractions of the

SpaccaNapoli walking tour for your last day. See chapter 4.

Day ⓭: Pompeii or Herculaneum
Follow day 7 of the itinerary for "Campania & the Amalfi Coast in 1 Week." See chapter 5.

Day ⓮: More Naples
Spend your last day exploring more of this magical city's many attractions: **Chiesa di Monteoliveto** obviously tops the list, but you'll also want to visit attractions along the SpaccaNapoli walking tour. See chapter 4.

3 Campania & the Amalfi Coast for Families

If you had any concerns before starting on this vacation with your kids, they'll melt away as soon as you travel through this warm and welcoming region. Depending on the attention span and specific interests of your family members, you might have to cut short some artistic attractions, but you'll be more than rewarded with outdoor activities.

Day ❶: Massa Lubrense & the Amalfi Coast
Fly into Naples's Capodichino Airport and get directly to **Massa Lubrense.** This lesser-known town is more geared to families than its neighbor Sorrento is, with lots of water activities and a choice of hotels that are beautiful but less expensive and stuffy than the ones in Sorrento. Enjoy the view from the Cathedral, then pack a picnic with goodies from **Antico Panificio Gargiulo** and descend to the Marina della Lobra's sandy beach. See chapter 6.

Day ❷: The Amalfi Coast
Make an early start and explore the **Amalfi Coast** (hire a limo service, use the good public bus system, or drive a rental car). You'll want to allot more time to swimming and hiking than to visiting churches and driving; still, do not miss the splendid **Amalfi cathedral** in Amalfi. See chapter 7.

Day ❸: Paestum & National Park of the Cilento
Head to the **Paestum** area and spend the better part of your day in the **National Park of the Cilento** (in the mountains or on the coast, according to your family's preferences). Whatever you choose, make sure to arrive in Paestum in time for a visit to the temples at sunset; it's an evocative sight for all ages. Spend the night by the beach, where you can go swimming if the weather's nice. See chapter 9.

Day ❹: Salerno & Capri
Get to **Salerno** early enough for a stroll along its splendid **Lungomare** and its **medieval** area—there is another noteworthy cathedral here if your kids can bear it—before your ferry to **Capri** is due. Spend the rest of the day and night on this mythical island, enjoying its beaches and hiking trails. Climb the **Fenician Staircase** and take a boat tour of the island (much better than waiting in line for the Blue Grotto if you're there in high season). See chapters 8 and 9.

Days ❺ to ❻: Naples
Leave Capri in the morning via one of the many ferries or hydrofoils for **Naples;** your whole family will delight in the glorious views of this city from the water. Visit the **Maschio Angioino,** a mighty castle that will interest any kid, and continue on to the **Museo Nazionale di**

Campania & the Amalfi Coast for Families

1. Masa Lubrense
2. Amalfi
3. Paestum
4. National Park of the Cilento
5. Salerno
6. Capri
7. Naples
8. Herculaneum
9. Pompeii
10. Mount Vesuvius

Capodimonte. On day 6, take our **walking tour of SpaccaNapoli.** Among all the churches we indicate, a great pick is the church of **San Lorenzo Maggiore,** where you can explore several layers of excavations—most kids should find this exciting. Also, do not miss a pizza lunch at the historical **Pizzeria Di Matteo.** (These are individual pizzas; order one each plus a deep-fried one for the table, to share as appetizer.) Spend the afternoon at the **Museo Archeologico Nazionale;** if you have little ones along, this has a nice playground where they are sure to make a friend or two. (This was greatly appreciated by our own little guy—so much so that we now have to squeeze in an hour there every day we are in Naples.) See chapter 4.

Day 7: Herculaneum, Pompeii & Mount Vesuvius

Catch a train via the Circumvesuviana railroad to **Herculaneum.** This site is smaller than Pompeii and your family is less likely to be overwhelmed or to overtire; besides, the casts of dead bodies in the museum here might be just the thing if your teenagers and pre-teens are like someone we know. Use the other half of your day to visit **Pompeii** or to climb **Mount Vesuvius.** Definitely hire a guide to descend into the crater—your kids will be thrilled at the sight—and hike the nature trail on the north slope of the volcano. See chapter 5.

4 The Natural Wonders of Campania & the Amalfi Coast

If you think Campania is museums, churches, and archaeological areas, you'll miss out on its great masterpieces not made by human hands. This region offers manifold opportunities to combine culture with outdoor activities and superb natural attractions. The itinerary below is designed for a week, but you can shorten or lengthen it at your leisure to accommodate your other plans. Having a car will allow for the greatest freedom, but it is not necessary.

Days ❶ to ❷: Vico Equense & the Sorrento Peninsula

Start with one of the lesser-known resorts on the Sorrento peninsula, **Vico Equense.** (A bus service for Sorrento directly from the airport stops at Vico, if you are interested), where you can have your first encounter with the sea at **Marina di Equa,** the best beach in town, dominated by a powerful 17th-century tower.

Reserve the afternoon for a beautiful hike through the peninsula (difficulty: moderate) and take the footpath from Sorrento towards **Punta Sant'Elia;** this scenic point overlooks the islets of Li Galli in the Bay of Salerno, which have made Positano famous. See chapter 6.

On day 2, continue on to the tip of the peninsula and the beach of **Punta del Capo.** Beloved by the locals, it is located near the ruins of a Roman villa. Nearby, a small pool of water enclosed by rocks is known as the Bath of Queen Giovanna.

In the afternoon, hire a boat from Marina del Cantone to reach the Bay of Ieranto and its marine preserve. You will be rewarded with magical surroundings—when the light is just right towards the end of the day, the boats appear to float in mid-air. See chapter 6.

Day ❸: The Amalfi Coast

Start the day with a swim (or have a rowboat take you) into the Grotta dello Smeraldo in the village of **Conca dei Marini.** Continue with a great hike from **Furore** down to **Furore Marina,** the deep fjord

graced by a small beach, over the ancient footpath. You can then hike the Sentiero degli Dei or the Via degli Incanti, and finish your day visiting the natural preserve of Capo d'Orso. From here, walk to the 11th-century monastery and have dinner at the lighthouse. See chapter 7.

Day ❹: Capri

Hop on a ferry or hydrofoil to **Capri** (from Positano or Salerno) and explore the island, taking the chairlift to **Monte Solaro** and descending the famous **Scala Fenicia.** End your day with a swim at the **Bagni di Tiberio,** near the ruins of one of Emperor Tiberius's notorious pleasure palaces. See chapter 8.

Days ❺ to ❻: Paestum & the Cilento

Head for the **National Park of the Cilento,** starting with the beautiful coast where you can enjoy a variety of watersports, including diving and water-skiing. The best beach is **Baia della Calanca,** in Marina di Camerota. Don't forget the interior, though. Schedule a visit to the **Grottoes of Castelcivita** or **Grottoes of Pertosa** for fantastic spelunking (nothing demanding athleticism or ropes), as well as a hike on **Monte Cervati,** the highest peak of the Cilento massif; or hike nearby **Monte Alburno.**

In the afternoon of day 6, head back towards **Paestum** to visit its temples, walk its walls, and swim from one of the best beaches in Italy. See chapter 9.

The Natural Wonders of Campania & the Amalfi Coast

① Vico Equense
② Punta del Capo
③ Conca dei Marini
④ Furore
⑤ Capri
⑥ National Park of the Cilento
⑦ Paestum
⑧ Baia
⑨ Mount Vesuvius

Benevento

Mondragone   Capua   Caserta Vecchia   Caserta

Santa Maria Capua Vetere

CAMPANIA

Aversa

Lake Patria   LITERNUM   Nola   Avellino

Pomigliano   Volturara Irpina

Licola Mare   NAPLES   Vesuvius ⑨

CUMA   Pozzuoli

Lake Fusaro   Baia ⑧   HERCULANEUM

Torregaveta   I. di Nisida   Torre del Greco   OPLONTIS   POMPEII   Nocera Inferiore

Procida   I. di Procida   Torre Annunziata   Castellammare di Stabia

Ischia   Gulf of Naples   Vico Equense ①   Salerno

Isola d'Ischia   (Golfo di Napoli)   Sorrento   Positano   Conca dei Marina ④③   Ravello   Amalfi

Massa Lubrense   Furore   The Amalfi Coast   Battipaglia

Isola di Capri   Gulf of Salerno   (Golfo di Salerno)

Anacapri ⑤ Capri   Punta del Capo ②

0   10 mi
0   10 km   N   TYRRHENIAN SEA   PAESTUM ⑦   ⑥

Day ⑦: Baia and Bay of Pozzuoli

For your last day, get yourself back to the Naples area and head for the **Bay of Pozzuoli.** Start your visit with some of the best scuba diving you'll ever do, visiting the **Underwater Archeological Park of Baia.** (If you don't scuba-dive, take a tour in one of the glass-bottom boats.) You can then take the archaeological hike from the **Monumental Park** to the **Parco Archeologico Terme di Baia.**

Alternatively—or if you have some time left—take your leave of the region with a hike to the crater of **Mount Vesuvius.** What could be more appropriate than ending your trip with a blast? See chapters 4 and 5.

4

Naples

This famous—and at times infamous—city keeps surprising us, no matter how many times we visit. Napoli ("Napule," in local parlance) is a city of many faces, a village and a metropolis at the same time. The first adjective that comes to mind to define it is "ebullient." You'll feel this energy in the traffic, the noise, but also in the cultural life—in the people's deep love and pride in their city and in their fervent religiosity. Above all, you'll pick up on a sense of enthusiasm for what the city has to offer, from romantic evening walks along the shore; to magnificent views over the bay with Mount Vesuvius in the background; to the beauty of Piazza del Plebiscito, Maschio Angioino, and Castel dell'Ovo. And, of course, this being Italy, Neapolitans are proud of all the good things to eat here, especially the fresh seafood; local tomatoes, which make the best fresh sauces; and the pizza they invented.

The second adjective that describes Naples is "welcoming." If you take the time to notice, you will see that Neapolitans really reach out to visitors and relish in others' enjoyment of their beloved city. Maybe that is the most truly fascinating thing about Naples: It has incredible architectural and artistic attractions, natural beauty, and fantastic food and wines, but ultimately, when you fall in love with the city—as you will if you let it get to you—you'll do so because of its humanity. When you walk the streets of Naples, you'll understand that its underlying character hasn't changed much in 2 millennia. It takes a certain kind of people, surely, to live in the shadow of a very dangerous volcano, century after century, and to find it beautiful.

This appreciation should not make you less careful: Naples is legendary for its pickpockets and other petty criminals. Also, a large part of Naples is unbelievably poor, and it's as plagued as anywhere in the modern world by drugs and thievery. Though depressed areas of Naples are well in the outskirts, pickpockets and thieves from those areas come regularly into the city to conduct their "business." This sort of thing gave Naples a bad name for many years, but police have recently been doing an excellent job at curbing crime.

The other unsavory thing about Naples is the traffic; the resulting confusion and dirt have put off many visitors. If you get past—or literally, away from—the noise, you can relax and discover a city that many visitors over the centuries have described in justly heavenly terms.

1 Essentials

GETTING THERE

BY PLANE   Naples's airport, **Aeroporto Capodichino** (© **081-7896259;** www.gesac. it), is only about 7km (4 miles) from the city center. It is a small but practical airport, receiving flights from many Italian and European cities. Alitalia offers daily flights from New York and Boston to Naples with one stop in Milan or Rome. From the airport you can take a taxi; the flat rate for the 15-minute trip is 19.50€ ($24) including all extras such as luggage and evening and Sunday supplements (but not gratuities). Many hotels offer a limousine service, but you have to spend a minimum of 35€ ($44). For 3€ ($3.75) one-way, a convenient ANM bus (© **800-639525;** www.anm.it) runs to Piazza Municipio in the town center (it stops across from the Teatro Mercadante), with an intermediary stop in Piazza Garibaldi (by the post office at Corso Novara). Buses run every 30 minutes from the airport (Mon–Fri 6:30am–11:39pm; Sat–Sun 6:30am–11:50pm) and from Piazza Municipio (Mon–Fri 6am–12:12am; Sat–Sun 6am–midnight).

BY TRAIN *Eurostar* (marked ES) or *intercity* (IC) trains run frequent and fast service from most Italian towns into Naples. It now takes less than 2 hours to reach Naples from Rome for a fare of about 23€ ($29). Trains arrive at the **Stazione Centrale** (© **081-5543188**) on Piazza Garibaldi. You will find taxis just outside the station. *Note:* You will be approached by "taxi" drivers—actually Gypsy taxis—inside the station. Turn them down firmly; they ask for outrageous rates and are one of the sources for Naples's bad rap on dishonesty. Official taxis are painted white, sometimes with a *Comune di Napoli* (Naples municipality) mark; written on the back of the seat inside are flat rates to central hotels and major attractions in town.

Under the station is the subway *(Metropolitana)* as well as the urban rail *(Cumana)*. Across from the station on Piazza Garibaldi, you can also catch the city bus no. R2 or tram no. 1 to the city center, and all kinds of buses and trams to other destinations. Slower trains also stop at the **Stazione Mergellina** (© **081-7612102**), on Piazza Piedigrotta, to the northwest of Naples's center. Taxis, subways, and buses connect this station with the town center and other destinations nearby.

BY BOAT Arriving into the bay of Naples by boat is the best introduction to the city. The major port of central Italy, **Stazione Marittima** (just off Via Cristoforo Colombo, steps from the Maschio Angioino, in the *città antica*) receives both cruise ships and regular ferry service from many destinations in Italy, including Ischia, Capri, Sicily (Messina, Siracusa Catania, Palermo, and the Aeolian Islands), and Sardinia (Cagliari). Hydrofoil service (suspended in winter) operates mostly from Mergellina's nearby **Terminal Aliscafi,** with frequent and fast runs to Capri, Ischia, Procida, Sorrento, Positano, Amalfi, Salerno, and Sicily (Milazzo and the Aeolian Islands). The major operating companies—all offering similar levels of service and fares but varying hours of operation—are **Tirrenia** (© **199-123199** or 081-2514711; www.tirrenia.it) ships to Cagliari and Palermo; **Siremar** (© **081-5800340;** www.siremar.it) ships to the Aeolian Islands and Milazzo; **TTTLines** (© **800-915365**) ships to Catania and Palermo; **Medmar** ships (© **081-5513352**) to Tunis as well as ferries (© **081-3334411**) to Ischia; **Caremar** (© **081-5513882;** www.caremar.it) ferries and hydrofoils to Ischia, Capri, and Procida; **Alilauro** (© **081-7611004;** www.alilauro.it) hydrofoils to Ischia and Positano; **SNAV** (© **081-4285555** or 081-4285111; www.snav.it) hydrofoil service to Ischia, Capri, and Procida, as well as ships to Palermo, Sardinia, and the Aeolian and Pontine islands; **LMP** (© **081-5513236**) hydrofoils to Sorrento; and **NLG** (© **081-5527209**) hydrofoils to Capri.

BY CAR Car theft—even from guarded parking lots—fierce traffic, and the local passion for speed make driving in Naples a real hassle. Still, arriving or leaving the city by car is not horribly difficult: major highways connect the city to most other destinations in Italy. From the north, take the *autostrada* A1 MILANO ROMA NAPOLI, whereas from the south take the *autostrada* A3 REGGIO CALABRIA SALERNO NAPOLI. If you are not return-ing your rental car, you can leave it at one of the large and well-posted public parking lots at the city's entrance. The most convenient is the **Parcheggio Brin** at the Via Brin corner of Via Volta (𝄐 **081-7632855;** .30€/40¢ per hour). Although most hotels offer (expensive) parking, arriving at your hotel is a challenge best left to those who know the city, with its narrow and labyrinthine streets, pedestrian areas, and one-way streets (which sometimes suddenly turn into one-way streets going *against* your direction of travel). Unless you have very precise and up-to-date driving directions or an excellent and recent driving map of Naples (one that marks every street and its driving direction), do not attempt it.

VISITOR INFORMATION

Naples's Provincial Tourist Office, **APT** (Piazza dei Martiri 58, by the Riviera di Chi-aia; 𝄐 **081-4107211;** bus no. 152; Mon–Fri 9am–2pm) maintains tourist booths in the Stazione Centrale (𝄐 **081-268799;** Metro: Piazza Garibaldi; Mon–Sat 9am–7pm) and at the Stazione Mergellina (Piazza Piedigrotta 1; 𝄐 **081-761-2102;** Metro: Mergellina; Mon–Sat 9am–7pm). The city's office, **AASCT** (𝄐 **081-2525711;** www.inaples.it), has two excellent tourist information points, one in Via San Carlo 9, off Piazza del Plebiscito (𝄐 **081-402394;** Mon–Sat 9am–1:30pm and 2:30–7pm); and one in Piazza del Gesù (𝄐 **081-5512701;** Mon–Sat 9am–1:30pm and 2:30–7pm). **Museo Aperto Napoli** (𝄐 081-5636062; www.museoapertonapoli.com) maintains a cultural center offering free information and guided tours (with a guide or audioguide) in six languages for the *città antica*. It's at Via Pietro Colletta 85 and is open daily 10am to 6pm; the center also houses a cafe, bookshop, and small exhibit space selling crafts.

CITY LAYOUT

A crescent-shaped city resting along the shores of a bay, Naples extends vertically up the steep hills that surround it. Proceeding from west to east, you will find **Posillipo,** then **Mergellina, Chiaia, Santa Lucia,** the *città antica* (old city and center of town) with the **Quartieri Spagnoli** along its western side, **Piazza Garibaldi** with the **Stazione Centrale** and **Stazione Circumvesuviana,** and finally the more industrial neighborhoods of Naples.

Above Chiaia and the *città antica* lies the **Vomero;** farther north and east is **Capodi-monte.** The *città antica* is the fat part of the crescent, crossed north-south by three major avenues: **Via Toledo, Via Medina,** and **Via Agostino Depretis.** These are crossed west-east by the continuous **Via Armando Diaz–Via G.Sanfelice–Corso Umberto I** and by the continuous Via Benedetto Croce–Via San Biagio dei Librai, also known as **Spaccanapoli,** both leading to **Piazza Garibaldi** and the **Stazione Centrale.**

THE NEIGHBORHOODS IN BRIEF

In this section, we give you a short description of each of Naples's central neighborhoods—including its major monuments—to give you some idea of what each is like and where you might want to stay.

Posillipo This residential neighbor-hood is graced by a number of dra-matic villas perched on rocky cliffs over the sea, as well as a few restaurants offering great food and fantastic views.

Mergellina Situated far from the center, this residential neighborhood lies near Naples's pleasant marina. The small harbor is lined with restaurants and cafes, where Neapolitans come for dinner by the sea and a romantic promenade.

Chiaia Charming and elegant, this neighborhood is graced by the public park. **Villa Comunale.** The hillside area has elegant villas but only a couple of hotels and restaurants, which enjoy quiet and fantastic views over the bay. The shore area around Riviera di Chiaia is famous for its upscale shopping and clubs, where Neapolitan nightlife congregates. The monuments of the *città antica* (old city) are a short public transportation ride away, but it is possible to walk.

Santa Lucia Once a village by the sea and retaining some of that character, Santa Lucia is separated from the *città antica* by steep Monte Echia. This is probably Naples's most famous neighborhood, lined with the elegant hotels of **Via Partenope**—the promenade created in the 19th century by filling in part of the harbor—which overlooks the bay and **Castel dell'Ovo.** This is another popular nightlife spot, boasting many restaurants along the shore and in the **Borgo Marinari** by Castel dell'Ovo. Behind the major hotels, you'll find a less-explored neighborhood filled with grocery shops and small cafes.

Quartieri Spagnoli Just north of **Piazza del Plebiscito**—the monumental heart of the city—this neighborhood of closely knit narrow streets on the western side of **Via Toledo** (called "Via Roma" by Neapolitans) lies only steps from most of Naples's major attractions. While the streets farther in from Via Toledo are still very authentic—to the point of being grungy—the blocks closer to that busy and famous street are experiencing genuine urban renewal, and old buildings have been transformed into charming small and moderately priced

hotels. A few nice restaurants have also appeared, making this a perfect base for visitors.

Città Antica This is Naples's heart, extending from the **Maschio Angioino** by the sea to the **Museo Archeologico Nazionale** to the north and **Castel Capuano** to the east. Not only are most of Naples's major historical and religious monuments here, but a number of political and administrative offices and the University of Naples reside in the area—along with the cascade of small restaurants, bars, and clubs such institutions create. This area is a perfect base because you'll be close to major attractions. While most of the hotels here are small, and housed in historical buildings, larger and more modern hotels line Via Medina and parallel Via Agostino Depretis, at the southern edge of the *città antica.*

Piazza Garibaldi Just across from the train station, this area is within walking distance of the *città antica's* eastern edge; **Castel Capuano** is only steps away. Not as glamorous as other areas of the city center, hotels here are moderately priced and have the advantage of being very well connected through public transportation to all destinations. You'll also be near a full range of shopping—from grocery to clothing stores—if you stay here.

Vomero This is the dwelling place of the *Napoli bene* (the city's middle and upper classes), where residents enjoy fresher air and spectacular views. A quiet and residential neighborhood, Vomero is mostly composed of elegant 19th- and early-20th-century buildings, with basically no hotels and only a few choice restaurants, but good shopping. Three famous attractions are located up here: the **Castel Sant'Elmo, Certosa SanMartino,** and **Villa Floridiana.**

Capodimonte A middle-class and blue-collar residential neighborhood, this is a good choice in summer, when the air is cooler up in the hills. This is also a good base if you plan to spend a lot of your time in the giant **Museo di**

Capodimonte and the wonderful public park that surrounds it. There are plenty of local grocery shops and bars to be had, but only a couple of hotels and restaurants.

GETTING AROUND

Walking is the best way to explore the historical heart of Naples. Public transportation is a better choice when you're traveling farther distances and if you want to take in some local color, although at rush hours there might be too much of the latter on the major subway and bus lines. Time your movements so that you can avoid rush hours. If you have to travel during those hours, take the diminutive electric buses which service the city center and are rarely crowded, or take a taxi.

On Foot Naples is a beautiful city to discover on foot; its attractions are close together and the sea is always present in the background. Walking is also an excellent way to notice the thousands of details that make this city so special, including small shops and craft "laboratories" (think workshops, not test tubes).

While the free city map given by the tourist office is perfectly sufficient for your general orientation, you might want to purchase a more detailed map with a *stradario,* or an alphabetical list of streets (see "Fast Facts," below).

By Public Transportation When you're tired of walking, the best ways to get around Naples are bus or subway. The small electric buses serving the city center are particularly good for reaching points of interest to tourists, while regular buses, trams, the Metro, and funiculars provide transporation farther out. Naples's **Transportation Authority** (© 800-482644 toll-free in Italy; www.ctpn.it) provides information on all the above and keeps an information booth on Piazza Garibaldi where, if you are in luck, you can get an excellent public transportation map. Public transportation tickets are sold at tobacconists' and at some bars and newsstands. You can get a regular *biglietto* (ticket) valid 90 minutes for 1€ ($1.25); or a *giornaliero* (day pass) valid until midnight for 3€ ($3.75). Both cover the whole metropolitan area of Naples, including funicular, tram, bus, Metro, and urban railway service.

The **Metropolitana** has two lines, line 1 from Piazza Dante to the Vomero and beyond (daily 6am–11pm); and line 2 from beyond Piazza Garibaldi to Pozzuoli (daily 5:30am–11pm). The **Cumana** (urban railroad) runs from Montesanto to Pozzuoli and beyond (daily 5am–11pm). Among the **buses,** the *linee rosse* (red lines marked by the letter **R**) are special fast lines serving tourist destinations with frequent service; they run daily from 5:30am to midnight. Regular buses tend to be slower; most stop as early as 8:30pm. A few lines are actually **tramways** with dedicated tracks, but because of traffic invading their lines, these can be as slow as the regular buses. At nightime, the few *linee notturne* (night lines) start around midnight and run every hour.

Heads Up

Always beware of pickpockets and purse grabbers in Naples; they favor crowded places such as public transportation and busy streets like Via Toledo. At night, avoid badly lit and solitary places because mugging is not completely unknown in these parts.

Dear to the hearts of Neapolitans is the **Funicolare,** a cable railway tunneled through rock to reach the cliffs surrounding the bay. Three funiculars reach the Vomero: **Montesanto** (at Metro station Montesanto; daily 7am–10pm), **Chiaia** (from Piazza Amedeo; daily 7am–10pm), and **Centrale** (from Via Toledo, off Piazza Trieste e Trento; Mon–Tues 6:30am–10pm and Wed–Sun 6:30am–12:30am). **Mergellina** also has a funicular, from Via Mergellina by the harbor up to Via Manzoni (daily 7am–10pm). (A public *ascensore* or elevator is located in Via Acton at the corner of Palazzo Reale, to climb Piazza Plebiscito. On the Vomero, there are escalators.)

Recently established, the **Metrò del Mare** (✆ 199-446644; www.metrodelmare. com) offers launch service between Naples and most destinations all the way down to Capri and Salerno. It doesn't operate in winter.

By Taxi Taxis are an excellent, relatively inexpensive way to get around the city. If you've heard that they're dishonest, these stories originate with people who have not visited Naples in the past decade or two. Today, taxis are very reliable and strictly regulated (as long as they are official city taxis, not Gypsy taxis). *Note:* Don't fret if your driver doesn't use the meter—*not* using the meter is legal for all rides that have established flat rates (for example from Piazza Municipio to the Museo Capodimonte, the rate is 9.50€/$12). As elsewhere in Italy, taxis do not cruise but can be found waiting at the many taxi stands around town, or can be called by phone (restaurants and hotels will do this for you): **Consortaxi** (✆ 081-5525252); **Radio Taxi Napoli** (✆ 081-5564444); **RadioTaxi Free** (✆ 081-5515151); **Radio Taxi Co.Ta.Na** (✆ 081-5707070); and **Radio Taxi Partenope** (✆ 081-5560202; www.taxivagando.it).

Naples also has a water taxi that offers private and public service, **Taxi del Mare** (✆ **081-8773600;** www.taxidelmare.it).

FAST FACTS: Naples

American Express **Every Tours** travel agency on Piazza del Municipio 5 (✆ **081-5518564;** bus: no. R2 or R3 to Piazza del Municipio) handles American Express business. It is open Monday through Friday from 9:30am to 1pm and 3:30 to 7pm, Saturday 9:30am to 1pm.

Banks Most banks are located in the city center and near the major hotels, and have **ATMs** outside their doors. **BNL (Banca Nazionale del Lavoro;** ✆ **081-7991111)** offers the PLUS network you'll likely need for your ATM card. Its several locations in Naples include Via Toledo 126 and Piazza dei Martiri 23.

Currency Exchange Among the numerous choices in town, the most convenient exchange places are the ones at the airport and around the Stazione Centrale on Piazza Garibaldi (Metro: Piazza Garibaldi). There are four *cambios* on Corso Umberto at nos. 44, 92, 212, and 292 (bus: no. R2 to Corso Umberto). Thomas Cook is on Piazza del Municipio (bus: no. R2 or R3 to Piazza del Municipio).

Doctors **Guardia Medica Specialistica** (✆ **081-431111)** is on call 24 hours a day. Consulates maintain a list of English-speaking doctors.

Embassies & Consulates See "Fast Facts: Campania & the Amalfi Coast," in chapter 2.

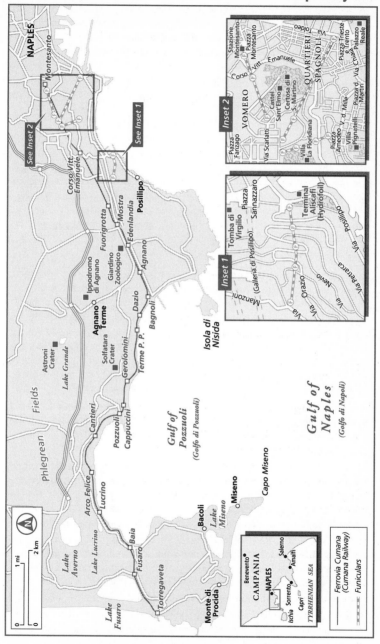

Emergencies For an **ambulance,** call ✆ **118;** for the **fire department** call ✆ **115;** for **first aid** *(pronto soccorso),* call ✆ **081-7520696.**

Hospital **Ospedale Fatebenefratelli,** the central hospital, is at Via Manzoni 220 (✆ **081-7697220).**

Internet Access The three locations of **Internet Point** (✆ **081-4976090** or 081-19568227) are conveniently located and offer ADSL connection at 1€ ($1.25) for 30 minutes: They are Vico Tre Re a Toledo 59/a (off Via Toledo to the left coming from Piazza Trieste e Trento, across from the Banco di Napoli); Via Montecalvario 9 (also off Via Toledo to the left, a few streets farther up); and Via Francesco Sav Correra 245 (3 blocks north and then left from Piazza Dante).

Laundry/Dry Cleaning Self-service laundromats are rare in Naples; your best bet is a *tintoria* (dry cleaner's) or a *lavanderia* (dry cleaner's and laundry service). A couple of good and central addresses are **Lavanderia Tintoria** at Via San Tommaso d'Aquino 43 (✆ **081-5511895**), **Lavanderia Helvetia** (Via San Mattia 1; ✆ **081-415635**), and the *lavanderia* at Salita Sant'Anna di Palazzo 4 (✆ **081-407222**).

Mail The **Central Post Office (Ufficio Postale)** is at Piazza Matteotti (✆ **081-5511456;** bus: no. R3 to Piazza Matteotti).

Maps You can buy a good map with a *stradario* (street directory) of Naples at any newspaper stand in town (usually the very good **Pianta Generale** by N. Vincitorio); if you prefer something smaller, buy the excellent, foldable, credit card–size **Mini-City** sold at museum shops in town (try the shop at Palazzo Reale).

Newspapers & Magazines Foreign newspapers and magazines are sold at train station kiosks and near the American Consulate. Do not miss *QuiNapoli,* the dashing free monthly (bilingual Italian/English) prepared by the city tourist office, which lists all the latest events as well as opening hours of monuments and museums. (It's also online at www.inaples.it/quinapoli.htm.)

Pharmacies There are several pharmacies open weekday nights and taking turns on weekend nights. A good one is located in the Stazione Centrale (Piazza Garibaldi 11; ✆ **081-5548894;** Metro: Piazza Garibaldi).

Police Call ✆ **113** for emergencies or ✆ **112.**

Safety Pickpocketing and car thefts are fairly common throughout Naples. In dark alleys and outside the city center, getting mugged is possible, particularly at night. Steer clear of the area behind the Stazione Centrale at dark, when it gets particularly seedy. The poorest suburbs in the outskirts of Naples to the east and southeast are where crime rates tend to be highest, but these are removed from the major tourist areas.

Smoking Thanks to a 2005 law, smoking is not allowed in public areas, including cafes and restaurants. It remains very common, however, and you will find that separate smoking areas are often available.

Taxis See "Getting Around," earlier in this chapter.

Toilets Public bathrooms are basically nonexistent. Your best bet is to use those in bars and cafes. Note, though, that they are reserved for clients, so to use them, you'll have to buy at least a coffee or a glass of mineral water.

Weather For forecasts, your best bet is the TV news (there's no "weather number" by telephone as there is in the U.S.). On the Internet, you can check out www.meteo.tiscalinet.it.

2 Where to Stay

POSILLIPO   *1-15*   *90€*   *80€*
MODERATE

Hotel Paradiso   Magnificent views over the bay and Vesuvius compensate for this hotel's distance from the center of town, away from traffic and noise. The Paradiso is located in the residential area of Posillipo, where lucky Neapolitans get to live. Although part of a chain—it was bought by Best Western—it maintains its personality, with a pleasant garden terrace and restaurant. Comfortable, tastefully appointed rooms (some of them quite large) all enjoy views; most of them have small sun terraces. Bathrooms are good sized.

Via Catullo 11, 80122 Napoli. © **800/528-1234** in the U.S., or 081-2475111. Fax 081-7613449. www.hotelparadiso napoli.it. 74 units. 160€–199€ ($200–$249) double; low season 140€–170€ ($175–$213) double. Rates include buffet breakfast. Extra bed 25€ ($31). Internet and other specials available. Children under 12 stay free in parent's room. AE, DC, MC, V. Parking: 15€ ($19) nearby. Metro: Mergellina. **Amenities:** Restaurant; bar; tennis court; concierge; room service; babysitting; laundry service; nonsmoking rooms. *In room:* A/C, satellite TV, dataport, minibar, hair dryer, safe.

SANTA LUCIA
VERY EXPENSIVE

Grand Hotel Santa Lucia 🏵🏵   At this historic hotel, you'll find old-fashioned atmosphere mixed with elegant decor. The professional service is impeccable, and the public spaces are grand—if a bit dusty and worn in places—graced by curving staircases, marble floors, and Murano chandeliers. Guest rooms are good-sized but not enormous, with wood or carpet floors, period or reproduction furniture, marble bathrooms, and great views over the Castel dell'Ovo and the bay. Most rooms have balconies to take in the view—they're too small for a table and chairs, though. The buffet breakfast is excellent and the hotel's restaurant elegant. One drawback is the lack of a fitness center if you are keen on exercising.

Via Partenope 46, 80121 Napoli. © 081-7640666. Fax 081-7648580. www.santalucia.it. 96 units. 280€–330€ ($350–$413) double, from 400€ ($500) suite; low season 215€–265€ ($269–$331) double, from 310€ ($388) suite. Extra bed 60€ ($75). Children under 3 stay free in parent's room. Rates include buffet breakfast. AE, DC, MC, V. Parking: 23€ ($29). Bus: 152, 140, or C25. **Amenities:** Restaurant; bar; business center; room service; same-day laundry service. *In room:* A/C, TV/VCR/DVD, dataport, minibar.

Grand Hotel Vesuvio 🏵🏵🏵   This elegant hotel claims to be the best in Naples, and indeed, it is up there with Parker's (see later in this section) when it comes to exquisite service. It compensates for a less romantic atmosphere with the most comfortable accommodations in town. Even the standard doubles are very roomy (with large marble bathrooms and Jacuzzi tubs), and come furnished with special details such as linen sheets and extra-firm mattresses. Superior rooms and suites have large balconies from which you can enjoy views over Borgo Marinari or Mount Vesuvius. The breakfast buffet—served in a delightful bright room with a view—is superb, including several kinds of juice, fresh fruit, bacon, and eggs, along with Neapolitan

Where to Stay in Naples

Grand Hotel Oriente **6**
Grand Hotel
   Parker's **18**
Grand Hotel
   Santa Lucia **12**
Grand Hotel Vesuvio **11**
Hotel Britannique **19**
Hotel Excelsior **13**
Hotel Executive **5**
Hotel Il Convento **9**
Hotel Majestic **17**
Hotel Miramare **14**

Hotel Palazzo
   Alabardieri **16**
Hotel Palazzo Turchini **7**
Hotel Paradiso **20**
Hotel Rex **15**
Hotel Toledo **8**
Mercure Angioino
   Napoli Centro **10**
Nuovo Rebecchino **2**
Starhotel Terminus **3**
Suite Esedra **4**
Villa Capodimonte **1**

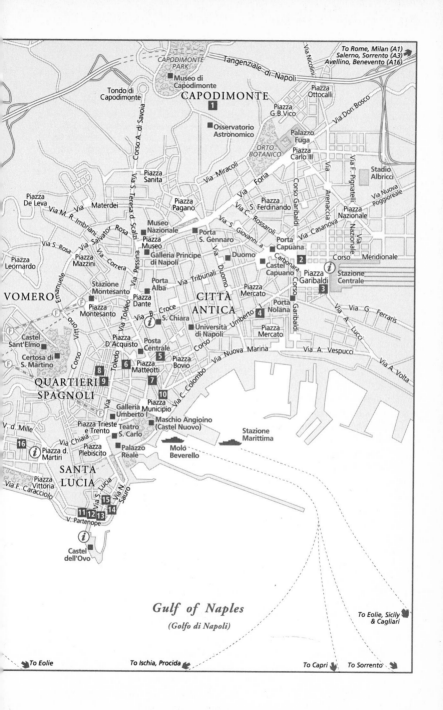

To Rome, Milan (A1)
Salerno, Sorrento (A3)
Avellino, Benevento (A16)

CAPODIMONTE
PARK

Via Nicolini

Tangenziale di Napoli

Museo di
Capodimonte

Via Don Bosco

CAPODIMONTE

1

Piazza
Ottocalli

Piazza
G.B. Vico

Tondo di
Capodimonte

Corso A. di Savoia

Osservatorio
Astronomico

Palazzo
Fuga

Piazza
Carlo III

ORTO
BOTANICO

Piazza
Sanita

Via Miracoli

Via Foria

Stadio
Albricci

Piazza
De Leva

Via M.R. Imbriani

Via

Materdei

Piazza
Pagano

Via C. Rossaroli

Piazza
S. Ferdinando

Corso Garibaldi

Piazza
Nazionale

Via F. Pignatelli

Via Nuova
Poggioreale

Via S. Teresa d. Scalzi

Via S. Rosa

Via Salvator Rosa

Museo
Nazionale

Via S. Giovanni a

Porta
S. Gennaro

Porta
Capuana

Via Atenacia

Via Casanova

Via Nazionale

Piazza
Leonardo

Piazza
Mazzini

Via Correra

Via Pessina

Piazza
Museo

Galleria Principe
di Napoli

Via Duomo

Duomo

Carbonara

Castel
Capuano

Corso   Meridionale

Stazione
Centrale

2

Porta
Alba

Via Tribunali

(i)

Stazione
Montesanto

Piazza
Dante

CITTÀ
ANTICA

Piazza
Mercato

Piazza
Garibaldi

3

VOMERO

Emanuele

Piazza
Montesanto

Via B. Croce

S. Chiara

Porta
Nolana

Via G. Ferraris

Via Toledo

(i)

Università
di Napoli

Corso Garibaldi

Via A. Lucci

Castel
Sant'Elmo

Vito

Piazza
D'Acquisto

Posta
Centrale

5

Corso

Piazza
Mercato

Via A. Volta

Certosa di
S. Martino

Piazza
Bovio

Corso   Umberto

Via Nuova Marina

Via A. Vespucci

8

Piazza
Matteotti

6

9

7

QUARTIERI
SPAGNOLI

Via C. Colombo

Via A. Vespucci

10

Piazza
Municipio

Via   Toledo

Galleria
Umberto

Maschio Angioino
(Castel Nuovo)

Stazione
Marittima

V. d. Mille

Via Chiaia

Piazza Trieste
e Trento

Teatro
S. Carlo

16

(i)

Piazza d.
Martiri

Piazza
Plebiscito

Palazzo
Reale

Molò
Beverello

SANTA
LUCIA

Via F. Caracciolo

Piazza
Vittoria

Via S. Lucia

Via N. Sauro

11 **12** **13** **14**

15

V. Partenope

(i)

Castel
dell'Ovo

Gulf of Naples
(Golfo di Napoli)

To Eolie, Sicily
& Cagliari

To Eolie

To Ischia, Procida

To Capri

To Sorrento

71

pastries, local cheeses and cold cuts, and several breads. The **Caruso Roof Garden** restaurant is very good and affords splendid views. A couple of caveats: At these prices, they should provide guests with free Internet access and free use of the fitness room (part of the beautiful spa, which charges an entrance fee of 32€/$40).

Via Partenope 45, 80121 Napoli. ℂ 081-7640044. Fax 081-7644483. www.vesuvio.it. 161 units. 410€ ($513) double; from 600€ ($750) suite. Low season 270€ ($338) double; 400€ ($500) suite. Extra bed 60€ ($75). Children under 6 stay free in parent's room. Internet and other specials available. Rates include buffet breakfast. AE, DC, MC, V. Parking: 22€ ($28). Bus: 152, 140, or C25. **Amenities:** Roof garden restaurant; bar; fitness center and spa; business center; room service; same-day laundry service. *In room:* A/C, TV/VCR/DVD, dataport, minibar, hair dryer, safe.

Hotel Excelsior ⭐ *Kids*   The third of three biggie hotels fronting the bay on Via Partenope, this one has more moderate prices than the Hotel Santa Lucia and the Vesuvio. It has the same gorgeous views, of course, and five-star service, plus a splendid roof garden-terrace. The rooms are good-sized and tastefully decorated, with marble bathrooms and linen sheets, as well as all the amenities you expect at this level (and price). However, everything comes at a slightly smaller scale than the Grand Hotel Vesuvio's (see above).

Via Partenope 48, 80121 Napoli. ℂ 081-7640111. Fax 081-7649743. www.excelsior.it. 121 units. 340€ ($425) double, from 550€ ($688) suite; low season 330€ ($413) double, from 460€ ($575) suite. Rates include buffet breakfast. Extra bed 55€ ($69). Children under 3 stay free in parent's room. AE, DC, MC, V. Parking: 21€ ($26). Bus: 152, 140, or C25. **Amenities:** Restaurant; bar; health club; concierge; business center; room service; babysitting; same-day laundry service; roof garden. *In room:* A/C, TV/VCR/DVD, dataport, minibar, hair dryer, safe.

MODERATE

Hotel Miramare *Value*   On the waterfront overlooking Castel dell'Ovo, this famous hotel offers excellent value. Family-run, it affords kind and warm service tailored to individual needs. Originally a private villa built in 1914, it briefly housed the American Consulate before opening as a hotel in 1944. For decades it was known for its Shaker Club—a restaurant and piano bar hot spot of Neapolitan elegant nightlife—until it closed in the mid-1980s. The public areas are still decorated in Liberty style, but the guest rooms have been renovated using colorful Venetian fabrics, large mirrors, and a whimsical assortment of furniture. The homey atmosphere is reflected in little touches like free Internet access and linen sheets in the summer (they make a big difference when it's hot). The rooms overlooking the sea have splendid views; rooms above the mezzanine level have balconies; and deluxe rooms are very large, with balconies at double the size. In clement weather, breakfast is served on the roof terrace overlooking the bay. You'll get discounts and special treatment at the nearby affiliated restaurants **La Cantinella** (see later in this chapter) and **Il Posto Accanto** (Neapolitan cuisine and pizza); and at the nightclub restaurants **Rosolino** and **Cantinella Privé.**

Via Nazario Sauro 24, 80132 Napoli. ℂ 081-7647589. Fax 081-7640775. www.hotelmiramare.com. 18 units. 262€–329€ ($328–$411) double; low season 212€–305€ ($265–$381) double. Extra bed 55€ ($69). Children under 6 stay free in parent's room. Weekend and Internet rates available. Rates include buffet breakfast. AE, DC, MC, V. Bus: 152, C25, or 140. Parking: 21€ ($26) in nearby garage. **Amenities:** Bar; lounge; concierge; room service; babysitting; laundry service. *In room:* A/C, satellite TV/VCR (free videos), minibar, hot-water pot w/tea, hair dryer, safe, radio.

INEXPENSIVE

Hotel Rex ⭐⭐ *Value*   This hotel is a steal: Housed in a 19th-century palace, only steps from the most famous harborside areas of Naples in the pleasant neighborhood of Santa Lucia, it offers spacious accommodations at moderate prices. Word is out that this family-run spot is ever-solicitous; it's very popular, especially with groups, so you must reserve well in advance. Guest rooms are simply but carefully decorated; some come with views over the harbor or Vesuvio, and some come with private balconies. Bathrooms are modern and roomy. A simple continental breakfast, served in your room, is included in the rates.

Via Palepoli 12, 80132 Napoli. ② 081-7649389. Fax 081-7649227. www.hotel-rex.it. 34 units. 135€ ($169); low season 100€ ($125). Rates include continental breakfast. Extra bed 25€ ($31). Children under 4 stay free in parent's room. AE, DC, MC, V. Parking: 21€ ($26) in nearby garage. Bus: 152, C25, or 140. **Amenities:** Lounge; concierge; babysitting. *In room:* A/C, TV, dataport.

CHIAIA

EXPENSIVE

Grand Hotel Parker's 𝓚𝓚𝓚   A landmark building of the Liberty (Italian Art Nouveau) style, Parker's served as Allied headquarters in World War II and still boasts most of its original architectural details and statuary. The hotel has seen good times as well as bad; now is definitely one of the good times: It looks absolutely splendid after renovations that took a whole decade (1980–1990), during which the hotel was completely closed. The commodious guest rooms are decorated with elegant period furniture (different floors are decorated in various styles—Louis XIV, Empire, and so on). Some suites—truly elegant duplex apartments on two levels—seem like places where you could happily live. The views from the rooms fronting the bay are particularly spectacular. The spa (a separate fee is charged depending on the treatment) is world class, with hydrotherapy, inhalation therapy, Turkish bath, and other treatments for whatever ails you. **George's,** on the roof garden, is one of the best restaurants in Naples (see later in this chapter).

Corso Vittorio Emanuele 135, 80121 Napoli. ② 081-7612474. Fax 081-663527. www.grandhotelparkers.com. 83 units. 325€–360€ ($406–$450) double; from 570€ ($713) suite. Extra bed 60€ ($75). Children under 6 stay free in parent's room. Internet and other specials available. Rates include buffet breakfast. AE, DC, MC, V. Parking: 18€–21€ ($23–$26). Bus: C24 or C27 to Via Tasso-Corso Vittorio Emanuele II. Metro: Piazza Amedeo. **Amenities:** Restaurant; bar; health club; spa; concierge; business center; room service; babysitting; same-day laundry service; nonsmoking floor. *In room:* A/C, TV/VCR/DVD, fax, dataport, minibar, hair dryer, safe.

MODERATE

Hotel Majestic 𝓚   Popular with Italian businesspeople and well-to-do travelers, this hotel is located at the end of the elegant shopping strip in Chiaia and offers upscale accommodations. Guest rooms are large, with marble bathrooms and hardwood floors. Decorated with sober elegance, they sport low-key colors in black, tan, and beige; streamlined modern high-quality furniture; and so on. Many of the rooms afford great views over the bay. **La Giara,** the hotel's restaurant, is quite good.

Largo Vasto a Chiaia 68. ② 081-416500. Fax 081-410145. www.majestic.it. 210€ ($263) double; 370€ ($463) suite. Rates include buffet breakfast. Extra bed 35€ ($44). Children under 6 free in parent's room. Internet and other specials available. AE, DC, MC, V. Parking: 20€ ($25). Metro: Piazza Amedeo. **Amenities:** Restaurant; piano bar; lounge; concierge; room service; babysitting; laundry service. *In room:* A/C, satellite TV/VCR, minibar, tea kettle and tea, hair dryer, safe.

Hotel Palazzo Alabardieri 𝓚𝓚   Opened in September 2004, this hotel is a great addition to Naples's accommodations scene. Housed in an elegant palace built in 1870 over the ancient cloister of the convent of Santa Caterina a Chiaia, it has been redone in a modern style that respects its history. Sleek marble floors in the public areas complement the warm hardwood floors in the guest rooms, which are furnished with period furniture and all the comforts you'd expect. The junior suites are extremely nice, with stylish furnishings and designer accents. All units come with good-sized marble bathrooms. Some rooms are wheel-chair accessible.

Via Alabardieri 38, 80121 Napoli. ℃ 081-415278. Fax 081-19722010. www.palazzoalabardieri.it. 33 units. 195€–220€ ($244–$275) double; 310€ ($388) junior suite. Rates include buffet breakfast. Internet and other specials available. Extra bed 40€ ($50). Children 3–12 20€ ($25) in parent's room; younger than 3 stay free in parent's room. AE, DC, MC, V. Parking: 20€ ($25). Metro: Piazza Amedeo. **Amenities:** Bar; health club; business center; concierge; room service; babysitting; same-day laundry service. *In room:* A/C, satellite TV w/pay movies, Internet, minibar, hair dryer, safe.

INEXPENSIVE

Hotel Britannique *Kids* Next door to Grand Hotel Parker's, the Britannnique is a good solution for those who don't want to shell out money for the luxury of staying at that landmark hotel, but who would like to enjoy its perfect location. Housed in a less grand building than its neighbor, it offers a beautiful garden and the same spectacular views. The rest of the hotel, though, is a bit dusty and in need of a face-lift, which justifies the lower prices. Guest rooms are large and decorated in Louis XVI or Empire style; most of them offer beautiful views over the Gulf. Bathrooms are old-fashioned but functional. Some rooms have cooking facilities, an added value for families with young children.

Corso Vittorio Emanuele 133, 80121 Napoli. ℃ 081-7614145. Fax 081-660457. www.hotelbritannique.it. 86 units. 170€–190€ ($213–$238) double; 220€ ($275) junior suite. Internet specials available. Rates include buffet breakfast. Extra bed 28€ ($35). Children under 6 stay free in parent's room. AE, DC, MC, V. Free parking. Bus: C24 or C27 to Via Tasso-Corso Vittorio Emanuele II.Metro: Piazza Amedeo. **Amenities:** Restaurant; bar; concierge; room service; babysitting; laundry service. *In room:* A/C, TV, radio, dataport, minibar, hair dryer.

QUARTIERI SPAGNOLI
MODERATE

Hotel Il Convento *⚡* Family-run, this hotel offers very pleasant accommodations at moderate prices in the heart of Napoli. Housed in a 17th-century palace, guest rooms have been carefully restored and are decorated with pastel-colored plaster walls that highlight varying architectural details, such as wooden beams in some rooms and arches in others; the two junior suites on the top floor enjoy delightful private roof gardens, while each of the two very nicely appointed family rooms has a loft bedroom. All have modern bathrooms and are furnished with quality modern furniture in dark wood. Breakfast is served in two small breakfast rooms; the buffet includes breads and jams, fruit, cold cuts, and cheese. Guests have access to sauna facilities at the Executive Hotel (see later in this chapter) and can check their e-mail in the reception area.

Via Speranzella 137/a, 80134 Napoli. ℃ 081-403977. Fax 081-400332. www.hotelilconvento.com. 14 units. 180€ ($225) double; 230€ ($288) junior suite; 280€ ($350) 4-person family room. Rates include buffet breakfast. Extra bed 60€ ($75). Children under 3 stay free in parent's room. Internet and other specials available. AE, DC, MC, V. Parking: 18€ ($23) in garage nearby. Bus: R2 to Piazza Municipio. **Amenities:** Bar; concierge; room service; babysitting; laundry service. *In room:* A/C, TV/VCR, dataport, minibar, hair dryer, safe.

Hotel Toledo *⚡* Renovated in 2004, this picturesque small hotel is on a narrow side street off Via Toledo. Less charming than the Convento above, but equally convenient, it offers good-sized guest rooms with modern bathrooms. The hotel also offers Internet access free for guests and a fitness room, as well as a bar and a restaurant on the roof garden, where the buffet breakfast included in the hotel rate is served.

Via Montecalvario 15, 80134 Napoli. ℃ 081-406800. Fax 081-406871. www.hoteltoledo.net. 35 units. 150€ ($188) double. Rates include buffet breakfast. Extra bed 25€ ($31). Children under 3 free in parent's room. AE, MC, V. Parking: 18€ ($23) in nearby garage. Bus: R2 to Piazza Municipio. **Amenities:** Bar; babysitting. *In room:* A/C, satellite TV, minibar, hair dryer, safe.

CITTA ANTICA
EXPENSIVE

Grand Hotel Oriente   This modern hotel belongs to the same group as the Grand Hotel Santa Lucia (p. 69), and offers a less pricey but convenient location in the heart of Naples. Guest rooms are spacious and pleasantly furnished, with good-sized, modern bathrooms. The rooms on the higher floors have balconies opening onto Vesuvio and the Gulf. The excellent restaurant is popular for its Neapolitan cuisine.

Via Armando Diaz 44, 80134 Napoli. ✆ 081-5512133. Fax 081-5514915. www.oriente.it. 131 units. 280€–310€ ($350–$388). Rates include buffet breakfast. Extra bed 55€ ($69). Internet and other specials available. Children under 3 stay free in parent's room. AE, DC, MC, V. Parking: 21€ ($26). Bus: C25, E2, or R2 to Via Toledo; C57, E3, or R3 to Via Medina. **Amenities:** Restaurant; bar, business center; concierge; room service; same-day laundry service. *In room:* A/C, satellite TV/VCR, dataport, minibar.

Hotel Palazzo Turchini   Recently opened in 2004, this centrally located hotel offers modern accommodations that become quite affordable during their great specials (sometimes you'll find discounts of over 50% off rack rates). Inside the shell of a 17th-century palace—once part of an orphanage specializing in musical studies—the guest rooms have been redone using state-of-the-art technology to completely soundproof every room. All guest rooms have hardwood floors and are furnished with a stylish mix of modern and period furniture; the marble bathrooms are good sized. Their "executive" doubles are larger and brighter than the "classics." Some executive doubles come with small private terraces, and others come with lounge areas. All rooms come with an Internet terminal attached to the TV (at an extra charge of 15€/$19 per day). Some units are accessible for travelers with disabilities. Breakfast is served on the roof terrace in clement weather.

Via Medina 21, 80132 Napoli. ✆ 081-5510606. Fax 081-5521473. www.palazzoturchini.it. 27 units. 300€–420€ ($375–$525) double, 650€ ($813) suite; low season 160€–220€ ($200–$275) double, 380€ ($475) suite. Rates include buffet breakfast. Extra bed 50€ ($63). Internet and other specials available. Children under 6 stay free in parent's room. AE, DC, MC, V. Parking: 18€ ($23) in nearby garage. Bus: C57, E3, or R3 to Via Medina. **Amenities:** Bar; concierge; babysitting; laundry service. *In room:* A/C, satellite TV, radio, dataport, minibar, hair dryer, safe.

MODERATE

Mercure Angioino Napoli Centro   Located within sight of the Angioino castle, this modern hotel offers comfortable, no-frills accommodations at a moderate price. Catering to the business crowd and the modern traveler, it is housed in a substantial 19th-century building. Guest rooms are good-sized and furnished in contemporary style, with large beds, modern furniture, and wall-to-wall carpeting. One whole floor is nonsmoking.

Via Depretis 123, 80133 Napoli. ✆ 081-4910111 or 081-5529500. Fax 081-5529509. mercure.napoliangioino@accorhotels.it. 85 units. 180€ ($225) double. Rates include buffet breakfast. Extra bed 30€ ($38). Internet and other specials available. Children under 3 stay free in parent's room. AE, DC, MC, V. Parking: 20€ ($25) in nearby garage. Bus: C25, C57, R2, or R3. Tram: 1 or 2 to Piazza Municipio. **Amenities:** Snack bar; business center; concierge; room service; babysitting; laundry service. *In room:* A/C, satellite TV w/pay movies, dataport, minibar, hair dryer, safe.

INEXPENSIVE

Hotel Executive *Value*   This comfortable hotel enjoys an excellent location in central Naples and offers a lot for its price, making it a good address for both moderately oriented business travelers and tourists. Guest rooms are nicely appointed, with tiled floors and tasteful modern furniture. Bathrooms are good-sized and modern. The one available suite is definitely "executive" level, with two balconies and a Jacuzzi in the bathroom. The hotel also offers a sizeable sauna and a delightful roof garden, where in good weather breakfast is served buffet-style: a variety of juices, cereals, breads, and platters of fresh fruit, cheese, and cold cuts.

Via del Cerriglio 10, 80134 Napoli. ⓒ 081-5520611. Fax 081-5520611. info@sea-hotels.com. 19 units. 165€–180€ ($206–$225) double; 238€ ($298) suite. Rates include buffet breakfast. Extra bed 30€ ($38). Internet and other specials available. Children under 3 stay free in parent's room. AE, DC, MC, V. Parking: 15€ ($19). Bus: CS, CD, or C25 to Via San Felice. Pets accepted. **Amenities:** Bar; health club; sauna; concierge; room service; babysitting; laundry service; roof garden. *In room:* A/C, satellite TV, dataport, minibar, hair dryer, safe.

Suite Esedra *Value* This pleasant small hotel offers moderately priced rooms in the heart of Naples. Housed in an aristocratic palace which has been completely restored, the guest rooms are tastefully furnished with excellent care to details; many have sweet little balconies. Of the two suites, one of them offers a fantastic private terrace equipped with a small pool. A buffet breakfast, served in a pleasant room, includes a variety of beverages, cold cuts, cheeses, fresh fruits, breads, jams, and homemade cakes.

Via Arnaldo Cantani 12, 80134 Napoli. ⓒ 081-5537087. Fax 081-5537087. info@sea-hotels.com. 17 units. 165€– 180€ ($206–$225) double; 310€ ($388) suite. Rates include buffet breakfast. Extra bed 40€ ($50). Internet and other specials available. Children under 6 free in parent's room. AE, DC, MC, V. Parking: 18€ ($23) in nearby garage. Metro: Piazza Garibaldi. **Amenities:** Bar; health club; outdoor pool; concierge; room service; babysitting; laundry service. *In room:* A/C, satellite TV, minibar, hair dryer, safe.

PIAZZA GARIBALDI
MODERATE
Starhotel Terminus 👄👄 This hotel, reopened at the end of 2004, offers elegant accommodations with full amenities and excellent service. Its less-than-glamorous location near the train station is more than compensated for by its moderate price convenience—it's within walking distance of the *città antica* and very well connected to the city's other major attractions. The commodious guest rooms are stylishly furnished, with warm wood, modern furniture, tasteful carpeting and fabrics, and elegant bathrooms. The "executive" doubles have extras such as trouser presses, a second TV in the bathroom, a cutting-edge CD/cassette system, and a complimentary tea/coffee/hot chocolate tray. The panoramic restaurant and bar on the roof garden have become quite a hit with Neapolitan socialites (see "Naples After Dark," later in this chapter).

Piazza Garibaldi 91, 80142 Napoli. ⓒ 081-7793111. Fax 081-206689. terminus.na@starhotels.it. 170 units. 175€– 225€ ($219–$281) double; 355€ ($444) suite. Rates include buffet breakfast. Extra bed 20€ ($25). Internet and other specials available. Children under 12 stay free in parent's room. AE, DC, MC, V. Free parking in garage. Metro: Piazza Garibaldi. Pets accepted. **Amenities:** Restaurant; bar; roof garden; gym; concierge; business center; room service; babysitting; same-day laundry service. *In room:* A/C, satellite TV w/pay movies and Internet, dataport, Wi-Fi, minibar, hair dryer, safe, radio.

INEXPENSIVE
Nuovo Rebecchino *Value* Not far from the Stazione Centrale and within walking distance of the ancient city, this hotel offers pleasant accommodations at reasonable rates. One of the oldest hotels in Naples, it was redone in 2004, and its pleasant public spaces have been completely restored. Guest rooms are ample and elegantly furnished in classic style, with carpeting. Bathrooms are good sized.

Corso Garibaldi 356, 80142 Napoli. ⓒ 081-5535327. Fax 081-268026. www.nuovorebecchino.it. 58 units. 160€ ($200) double; low season 110€ ($138) double. Rates include buffet breakfast. Extra bed 35€ ($44). Specials available. Children under 3 stay free in parent's room. AE, DC, MC, V. Parking: 16€ ($20) in nearby garage. Metro: Piazza Garibaldi. **Amenities:** Restaurant; bar; concierge; business center; limited room service; babysitting; laundry service. *In room:* A/C, TV, minibar, hair dryer.

CAPODIMONTE
MODERATE
Villa Capodimonte ✪ This 1995 hotel is just steps from the Royal Park of Capodi-monte and is surrounded by its own park with splendid views. Family-run, it offers a variety of public rooms, including several terraces, a solarium, a pleasant garden, and even a chapel and an auditorium. Guest rooms are large and nicely appointed, with classic furniture and wooden floors; each is basically a junior suite opening onto either the garden or a terrace. Many enjoy vistas of Mount Vesuvius and the Gulf.

Via Moiariello 66, 80131 Napoli. ✆ 081-459000. Fax 081-299344. www.villacapodimonte.it. 57 units. 220€ ($275). Rates include buffet breakfast. Extra bed 40€ ($50). Internet and other specials available. Children under 3 stay free in parent's room. AE, DC, MC, V. Free parking. Bus: C66 or 24 to Via Ponti Rossi. Pets accepted. **Amenities:** Restaurant; bar; garden; concierge; room service; babysitting; laundry service. *In room:* A/C, satellite TV w/pay movies, dataport, minibar, hair dryer, safe.

3 Where to Dine

Although Naples has not yet been hit by the trendy-restaurant syndrome—and prob-ably never will—new, fashionable restaurants are opening and old ones are getting face-lifts. You will find a number of good restaurants respectful of the local culinary traditions as well as many innovative ones. Seafood and **pizza** dominate the scene (see appendix A for an introduction to local cuisine and wines, and see appendix B for a glossary), but it is possible to enjoy a good meat dinner here and there.

POSILLIPO
EXPENSIVE
Giuseppone a Mare ✪✪ NEAPOLITAN/SEAFOOD This restaurant has been in Naples going on 200 years, and it rightfully commands a beautiful view of the bay looking back toward Napoli. The menu is large—two pages are devoted to pastas—but the specialty here is seafood. You can have *gamberoni* (king-size shrimp), *mazzan-colle* (prawns), *astice* (highly prized local lobster), you name it. Seafood cooked to order is priced by the kilo, or you can have one of the set dishes such as delicious *polpi Giuseppone* (squid in a tomato and black olive sauce). Pasta often comes with fish sauces like the excellent *fusilli della Baia* (pasta with swordfish and pumpkin served in a crunchy cheese crust), but vegetarian options are available. The space is bright and airy, with an antique majolica floor in lemon hues. Towards the back wall, you can see how the building was literally hewn out of the looming cliff above it. During warm months, you can dine on the terrace outside.

Via Ferdinando Russo 13. ✆ 081-5756002 or 081-7691384. Reservations recommended. Secondi 8€–15€ ($10–$19). AE, DC, MC, V. Tues–Sat 10:30am–3:30pm and 8–11:30pm; Sun 10:30am–5:30pm. Closed 2 weeks in Aug. Bus: C3 to Mergellina (end of line); switch to 140.

MODERATE
Ristorante La Fazenda ✪ NEAPOLITAN/SEAFOOD With a beautiful view over the bay and an informal atmosphere, La Fazenda pleases both locals and visitors. La Fazenda is famous for its fish specialties, and we loved their *pasta alle vongole* (pasta with clams) and fresh grilled seafood. The terrace here is popular in summer (don't try to go then without a reservation).

Via Mare Chiaro 58/a. ✆ 081-5757420. Reservations required. Secondi 12€–20€ ($15–$25). AE, MC, V. Tues–Sun noon–3pm; Mon–Sat 8–11:30pm; closed 1 week in Aug. Bus: C3 to Mergellina (end of line); switch to 140.

Where to Dine in Naples

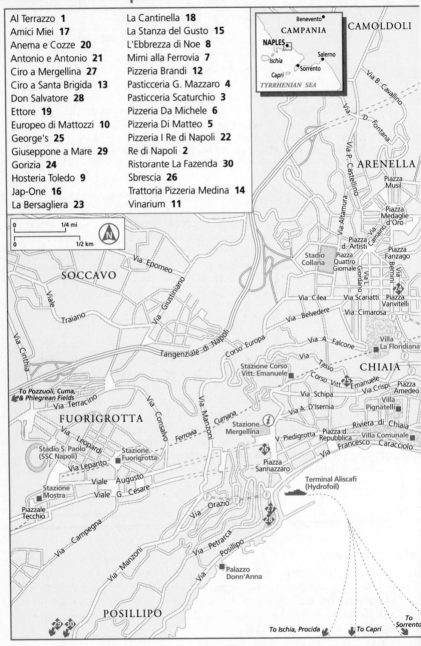

Al Terrazzo **1**
Amici Miei **17**
Anema e Cozze **20**
Antonio e Antonio **21**
Ciro a Mergellina **27**
Ciro a Santa Brigida **13**
Don Salvatore **28**
Ettore **19**
Europeo di Mattozzi **10**
George's **25**
Giuseppone a Mare **29**
Gorizia **24**
Hosteria Toledo **9**
Jap-One **16**
La Bersagliera **23**

La Cantinella **18**
La Stanza del Gusto **15**
L'Ebbrezza di Noe **8**
Mimi alla Ferrovia **7**
Pizzeria Brandi **12**
Pasticceria G. Mazzaro **4**
Pasticceria Scaturchio **3**
Pizzeria Da Michele **6**
Pizzeria Di Matteo **5**
Pizzeria I Re di Napoli **22**
Re di Napoli **2**
Ristorante La Fazenda **30**
Sbrescia **26**
Trattoria Pizzeria Medina **14**
Vinarium **11**

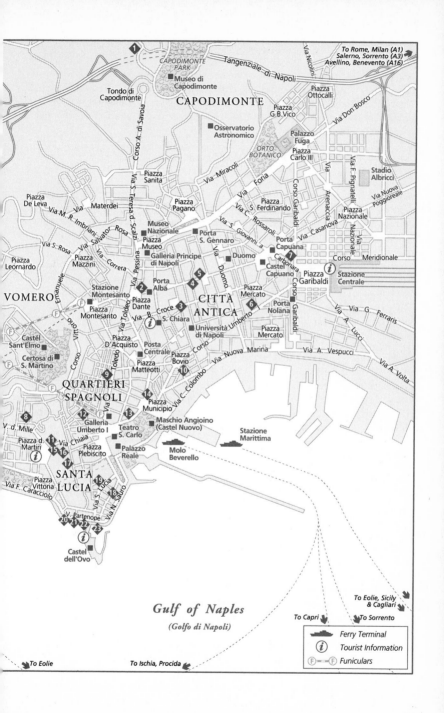

To Rome, Milan (A1)
Salerno, Sorrento (A3)
Avellino, Benevento (A16)

CAPODIMONTE PARK

Museo di Capodimonte

Via Nicolini

Tangenziale di Napoli

Piazza Ottocalli

Tondo di Capodimonte

CAPODIMONTE

Piazza G.B.Vico

Via Don Bosco

Osservatorio Astronomico

ORTO BOTANICO

Palazzo Fuga

Piazza Carlo III

Stadio Albricci

Corso A. di Savola

Via Miracoli

Via Foria

Corso Garibaldi

Via F. Pignatelli

Via Nuova Poggioreale

Piazza Sanita

Piazza Pagano

Via S. Teresa d. Scalzi

Via S.C. Rossaroli

Piazza Ferdinando

Arenaccia

Piazza Nazionale

Via Nazionale

Piazza De Leva

Via Materdei

Via M. R. Imbriani

Porta S. Gennaro

Porta Capuana

Via Casanova

Corso Meridionale

Museo Nazionale

Via S. Giovanni, a

Via Pessina

Piazza Museo

Galleria Principe di Napoli

Duomo

Castel Capuano

Stazione Centrale

Piazza Garibaldi

Via S. Rosa

Via Salvator Rosa

Via S. Correra

Piazza Mazzini

Porta Alba'

Via Duomo

Piazza Leonardo

Stazione Montesanto

Piazza Dante

B. Croce

S. Chiara

CITTÀ ANTICA

Piazza Mercato

Porta Nolana

Via A. Lucci

Via G. Ferraris

VOMERO

Via Toledo

Università di Napoli

Piazza Mercato

Piazza Montesanto

Piazza D'Acquisto

Posta Centrale

Piazza Bovio

Corso Umberto

Via Nuova Marina

Via A. Vespucci

Via A. Volta

Castel Sant'Elmo

Certosa di S. Martino

Corso V. Emanuele

Corso Vittorio

Piazza Matteotti

Via C. Colombo

QUARTIERI SPAGNOLI

Piazza Municipio

Galleria Umberto I

Teatro S. Carlo

Maschio Angioino (Castel Nuovo)

Stazione Marittima

V. d. Mille

Via Chiaia

Piazza d. Martiri

Piazza Plebiscito

Palázzo Reale

Molo Beverello

Piazza Vittoria

SANTA LUCIA

Via S. Lucia

Via N. Sauro

Via F. Caracciolo

V. Partenope

Castel dell'Ovo

Gulf of Naples

(Golfo di Napoli)

To Eolie, Sicily & Cagliari

To Capri

To Sorrento

To Eolie

To Ischia, Procida

Ferry Terminal

Tourist Information

Funiculars

79

Sbrescia *(Finds)* NEAPOLITAN/PIZZA   This is a real local hangout where Neapolitans of all ages come to enjoy the view of the nearby bay and the classic cuisine. The menu varies, but when you're in luck, this is a great place to taste Naples's traditional specialty, *sartù* (a baked rice dish filled with baby meatballs, cheese, and other ingredients). You'll find many other classics of Neapolitan cuisine, among them the well-prepared *fritto misto* (deep-fried seafood). They also have a wood-fired oven and prepare excellent pizza here.

Rampe Sant'Antonio 109. © **081-669140**. Reservations recommended. Secondi 6€–14€ ($7.50–$18). AE, MC, V. Tues–Sun noon–3:30pm and 7:30–11pm. Bus: C3 to Mergellina (end of line); switch to 140.

MERGELLINA
MODERATE
Ciro a Mergellina *(★★)* NEAPOLITAN/PIZZA/SEAFOOD   This historic restaurant is among Naples's preferred destinations for tourists and locals alike, who come for the fish prepared many ways, from sautés of mussels and small clams to pasta dishes and entrees, but also for the excellent pizza, still made with *mozzarella di bufala* (buffalo mozzerela), and for the excellent service. Try the *spaghetti alle vongole* (spaghetti with baby clams), *pasta all'aragosta* (pasta with local lobster), or *spigola fritta* (deep-fried sea bass). Among the appetizers, the seafood salad is a particular favorite. Their wonderful, homemade ice cream comes in a variety of flavors.

Via Mergellina 18. © **081-681780**. Reservations recommended. Secondi 6€–18€ ($7.50–$23). Tues–Sun 11:30am–11:30pm. AE, DC, MC, V. Bus: 140. Metro: Mergellina. Tram: 1.

Don Salvatore NEAPOLITAN/SEAFOOD   On the Mergellina waterfront, near the dock where the ferries leave for Capri, Don Salvatore is a perfect example of a Neapolitan seaside trattoria. In this atmospheric restaurant, housed in what was once a boat shed, you can enjoy nicely grilled fresh fish, accompanied by local vegetables, or opt for a risotto or seafood pasta, like the winning *linguine incaciate* (linguine with cheese). The restaurant features an excellent wine list.

Strada Mergellina 4/a. © **081-681817**. Reservations recommended. Secondi 10€–21€ ($13–$26). AE, DC, MC, V. Thurs–Tues 11:30am–3:30pm and 8–11:30pm (daily in summer). Bus: 140. Metro: Mergellina. Tram: 1.

CHIAIA
EXPENSIVE
George's *(★★★)* NEAPOLITAN   A temple of good taste, located on the top floor of Grand Hotel Parker's, this place has a view second to none. You can watch the sun on the Gulf as your taste buds are pampered by chef Baciòt's preparations; he likes to revisit the ancient dishes of Neapolitan tradition, removing a bit of fat and adding a bit of imagination. The menu is seasonal and might include *pizzelle foglia* (eggless homemade leaves of pasta with sauteed garden vegetables) or *pezzogna arrosto in guazzetto di tartufi* (local fish in a light sauce with truffles). For dessert we recommend the *gelato di fiordilatte con confettura di pomodori acerbi* (made with *bufala* milk and served with green tomato jam). In addition to its regular menu, George's serves a "de light" menu, in line with the therapies proposed in the hotel's spa and based on the principles of Marc Messegué, the herbal specialist; it's detoxifying yet extremely satisfying. The wine list is extensive, including a large variety of Campanian and Italian wines (no foreign wines, not even French, which apparently is why this restaurant has no Michelin rating). You can actually sign up for a Cordon Bleu class with the chef (call the hotel for a class schedule; you have to join well in advance if you're interested).

Corso Vittorio Emanuele 135. ☎ 081-7612474. www.grandhotelparkers.com. Reservations required. Secondi 22€–25€ ($28–$31). AE, DC, MC, V. Daily 12:30–2:30pm and 8–10:30pm. Bus: C24 or C27 to Via Tasso-Corso Vittorio Emanuele II. Metro: Piazza Amedeo.

MODERATE

Amici Miei ☆ *Finds* NEAPOLITAN/ITALIAN   If you are tired of seafood, this restaurant located on the hill between Chiaia and the Quartieri Spagnoli is for you. The menu focuses on meat—including a number of unusual choices such as ostrich and goose—as well as pasta dishes with vegetables and meat sauces. Try *pappardelle al sugo di agnello* (fresh large noodles with a lamb sauce) or *risotto ai fiori di zucchine* (risotto with zucchini flowers); or go for the daily choice of grilled meat. Just try not to fill up on the tasty homemade bread before your meal.

Via Monte di Dio 77. ☎ 081-7646063. Reservations required. Secondi 11€–13€ ($14–$16). AE, DC, MC, V. Tues–Sun 12:30–3:30pm; Tues–Sat 7:30–11:30pm; closed 2 weeks in July and Sept. Tram: 1 to Piazza dei Martiri.

Jap-One *Finds* SUSHI   This trendy sushi bar, hidden away at the end of a winding narrow alley under the cliff of Monte di Dio (taking a cab is the best way to find it), opened in March 2002. Since then, it has become popular with young and not-so-young Neapolitans, thanks to the care and friendliness of owner Roberto Goretti. The dining room is stylishly decorated with modern furniture, and looks more New York than Napoli. The atmosphere is relaxed, however, with cool jazz in the background and chefs preparing food at the sushi bar in view of the diners. Although the restaurant is Japanese, it has that irrepressible Neapolitan flair, seen in the use of local fish—for example the *maki di astice* (local lobster maki), or the coccio sashimi (sashimi of coccio, a local fish), depending on the day's catch.

Via Santa Maria Cappella Vecchia 30/i, off Piazza dei Martiri. ☎ 081-7646667. Reservations required. Secondi 14€–36€ ($18–$45). AE, DC, MC, V. Tues–Sat 8:30–11pm. Tram: 1 to Piazza dei Martiri.

L'Ebrezza di Noè ☆☆ *Finds* WINE/NEAPOLITAN   Beloved by locals, this elegant and trendy winery serves a simple menu of cured meats, cheeses, and appetizers to accompany the wide selection of wines from its excellent cellar. Their specialty is the discovery of unusual and lesser-known wines and vintages of great quality. Don't be afraid to ask for guidance from the experienced staff.

Vico Vetriera 9. ☎ 081-400104. Reservations recommended. Secondi 8€–15€ ($10–$19). AE, DC, MC, V. Daily 7:30pm–12:30am. Tram: 1 to Piazza dei Martiri.

La Stanza del Gusto ☆☆☆ CREATIVE NEAPOLITAN   Self-taught chef Mario Avallone has attracted a loyal following to this one-of-a-kind restaurant, which caters to gourmet tastes and wine aficionados. With its dark paneling, lemon-yellow walls, coffered ceiling, and array of curios, it can be best described as old-world funky. The extensive wine list has lots of local vintages that you would be hard-pressed to find elsewhere in Italy, let alone abroad, and offers a "wine of the week." (Prices for a bottle of wine start around 12€ ($15), and from there on, the sky's the limit.) The meal is built around a series of *assaggi*—small portions of skillfully prepared, beautifully presented dishes, some of them the chef's creations. (His delicious *Timballetto di palamiti e scarole* is fish wrapped in escarole, forming a sort of cake with pinoli nuts, tomatoes, olives, and pickles.) Other dishes are his reinterpretation of Neapolitan classics *(sartù di riso)*. These are presented as a prix-fixe menu (definitely the way to go), but you can order a la carte; just remember that portions are not exactly hearty, so this isn't a great place for young children or the famished.

Vicoletto Sant'Arpino 21, a ramp of steps off Via di Chiaia to the right, coming from Piazza dei Martiri. ⓒ 081-401578. Reservations required Vegetarian menu 45€ ($56); tasting menu 60€ ($75); secondi 8€–22€ ($10–$28). MC, V. Mon–Sat 7:30–10:30pm. Tram: 1 to Piazza dei Martiri.

Vinarium ✿ WINE/NEAPOLITAN   This popular winery is a bit less upscale than L'Ebrezza (see above), but just as welcoming. Boasting a simple, somewhat rustic decor, Vinarium serves a more rounded menu, with entrees in addition to appetizers, although here, too, the emphasis is on the wine. You can taste all of Campania's best D.O.C.s (see appendix A) as well as others from farther afield. A specially priced selection of wines is introduced each day.

Vico Cappella Vecchia 7. ⓒ 081-7644114. Reservations recommended. Secondi 6€–12€ ($7.50–$15). AE, DC, MC, V. Mon–Fri 10:30am–4:30pm; Mon–Sat 7pm–2:30am. Tram: 1 to Piazza dei Martiri.

SANTA LUCIA
EXPENSIVE
La Cantinella ✿✿✿ CREATIVE NEAPOLITAN/SEAFOOD   Bound to become one of the centuries-old, historic restaurants of Naples, this local favorite is always bursting with chic clientele. The stylish old-fashioned nightclub atmosphere doubles with excellent—and mostly strictly traditional—Neapolitan food. The choice of *antipasti* is good and savory. You can follow it with *pappardelle "sotto il cielo di Napoli"* (homemade pasta with zucchini, prawns, and green tomatoes) or *tubetti con le cozze* (short pasta with mussels). For your *secondo,* the *frittura* (deep-fried seafood) is a winner. Do not skip dessert—all are deliciously homemade (such as the superb soufflé, if you have the patience to wait). The attached club, **Privé,** features live music and a similar menu. The wine list is huge at both spots.

Via Cuma 42. ⓒ 081-7648684. Reservations required. Secondi 19€–30€ ($24–$38). AE, DC, MC, V. Mon–Sat 12:30–3:30pm and 7:30pm–midnight. Closed 1 week in Jan and 3 weeks in Aug. Bus: 152, C25, or 140.

MODERATE
Antonio e Antonio ✿✿ PIZZA/NEAPOLITAN   Located on the beautiful *lungomare* (oceanfront), this restaurant is popular with locals, many of whom come for its youthful atmosphere. The two Antonios who created this restaurant grew up and were trained in two of Naples's most famous, historic restaurants, Zi Teresa and Giuseppone a Mare. The open kitchen zips out 40 types of pizza and all the great Neapolitan classics, including *fusilli di pasta fresca ai pomodorini del Vesuvio* (fresh pasta with cherry tomatoes from Mt. Vesuvius, an especially tasty variety) and *polipetti affogati in cassuola* (squid cooked in an earthware pot with tomatoes and herbs). Appetizers and side dishes are served buffet style. A second location in Chiaia is located on the slopes of the Vomero, at Via Francesca Crispi 89 (ⓒ **081-682528** or 081-682438).

Via Partenope 24. ⓒ 081-2451987. Reservations recommended. Secondi 6€–17eu ($7.50–$21). AE, DC, MC, V. Daily 12:30–3:30pm and 7:30–11:30pm. Bus: 152, C25, or 140.

La Bersagliera ✿✿ *Kids* NEAPOLITAN/SEAFOOD   One of Naples's most historic restaurants, La Bersagliera has been managed by the same family for generations. Signora Elvira Chiosi, the current owner/manager, is the granddaughter of the original, 19th-century founder. Overlooking the yachts and fishing boats of the harbor at the Castel del' Ovo, the restaurant has kept much of its original decor and offers terrace dining in the summer. On the walls you'll see signed pictures of famous guests—Sophia Loren, Tyrone Power, Omar Sharif, and Pavarotti (who even indulged in a little *bel canto*). The food is still excellent, with seafood, not surprisingly, the centerpiece:

Try *tagliatelle Santa Lucia* (homemade pasta with swordfish and artichokes) or excellent *grigliata mista* (which includes prawns, shrimp, red mullet, and calamari). The highly professional, courteous staff is very kind to children, who can get highchairs and half-portions. There's a good selection of local wines, and a more extensive and expensive list of offerings from farther afield.

Borgo Marinari 10, Santa Lucia. ℂ 081-7646016. www.labersagliera.it. Secondi 8€–15€ ($10–$19). AE, MC, V. Wed–Mon 11:30am–3:30pm and 7:30–11pm. Closed 1 week after Epiphany (Jan 6). Bus: 152, C25, or 140.

INEXPENSIVE

Anema e Cozze ☞ PIZZA/SEAFOOD   A busy restaurant with a youthful, casual atmosphere, this is mostly a pizza place—but as the name suggests (it translates as "Soul and Mussels"), it focuses on mussels and seafood. Popular with locals who come here to enjoy the *lungomare*, it is a good place to eat typical Neapolitan *impepata di cozze* (steamed mussels with white pepper) and *cozze in padella* (sauté of mussels and tomatoes), and of course to enjoy great pizza. You can take the Garibaldi Metro to the second location at Via Caracciolo 13 (ℂ **081-2482158**).

Via Partenope 15. ℂ 081-2400001. Reservations not necessary. Secondi 6€–12€ ($7.50–$15). AE, MC, V. Daily noon–3:30pm and 7:30–11:30pm. Bus: 152, C25, or 140.

Ettore *Finds* NEAPOLITAN/PIZZA   This unpretentious and untrendy restaurant is a real neighborhood place. It's so popular with locals, in fact, that you might want to come early to get a seat. The menu is simple but varies often according to the season. They make excellent pizza, and their specialty is *pagnottiello*—calzone filled with mozzarella, ricotta, and prosciutto.

Via Santa Lucia 56. ℂ 081-7640498. Reservations recommended. Secondi 6€–15 € ($7.50–$19). AE, DC, MC, V. Tues–Sun 12:30–3:30pm and 7:30–11:30pm. Bus: 152, C25, or 140.

Pizzeria I Re di Napoli PIZZA/NEAPOLITAN   Not to be confused with the restaurant I Re di Napoli (p. 84), this is run by the same folks as nearby Anima e Cozze but is a bit more upscale. The dining rooms—a second one is up a spiral staircase—are warm and welcoming, and there are tables outside under umbrellas. The menu focuses not only on pizza and a nice choice of appetizers and side dishes, but also on pasta and secondi (mostly meat, depending on the market offerings).

Via Partenope 29. ℂ 081-7647775. Secondi 8€–15€ ($10–$19). AE, MC, V. Daily noon–1am. Closed Dec 25. Bus: 152, C25, or 140.

QUARTIERI SPAGNOLI
INEXPENSIVE
Hosteria Toledo NEAPOLITAN   A picturesque restaurant, Hosteria Toledo serves up tasty but not too expensive meals in a lively atmosphere. It's been serving traditional Neapolitan food to locals and visitors since 1951, and people keep coming, for the great pasta—*alle cozze e vongole* (mussels and clams)—and main courses—*polipo in guazzetto* (squid in a tomato sauce), *arrosto di maiale* (pork roast), and *salsicce* (sausages). If you have room left after those entrees, try one of the luscious desserts, which often include such great classics as *babà* (a sort of brioche with rum) and *pastiera* (a creamy sort of thick pie).

Vico Giardinetto 78/a. ℂ 081-421257. Secondi 6.50€–14€ ($8.15–$18). AE, DC, MC, V. Mon–Sat 12:30–3pm and 7:30–11pm. Bus: R2 or R3 to Piazza Trieste e Trento. Coming from Piazza Trieste e Trento, it's off Via Toledo to the left, across from the Banco di Napoli.

Pizzeria Brandi ☆ *(Kids)* PIZZA   Opened in 1780, Brandi was so renowned for the quality of its pizza that in 1889, the "pizzaiolo" (maker of pizzas) was invited to prepare pizza for the royal family. He created a special one for the first queen of Italy, Margherita di Savoia, which he named *pizza alla margherita* (pizza with mozzarella, basil, and tomatoes), whose colors were those of the newly unified country's flag. This pizzeria maintains the tradition of Neapolitan pizza, and the restaurant succeeds in being good but touristy at the same time. Among the many pizzas on the menu, try the *alla Totò*, a deep-fried pizza somewhat like a calzone. Children are welcomed with highchairs, child-size pizzas, and infinite patience from the staff.

Salita Sant'Anna di Palazzo 1, at the corner with Via Chiaja. © 081-416928. Reservations recommended. Secondi 7€–18€ ($8.75–$23). No credit cards accepted. Tues–Sun 12:30–3:30pm and 7:30pm–midnight. Bus: R2 or R3 to Piazza Trieste e Trento.

CITTA ANTICA
EXPENSIVE
Europeo di Mattozzi ☆ NEAPOLITAN/PIZZA/SEAFOOD   This landmark of Neapolitan dining is a bit on the expensive side but is consistently very rewarding. The chef/owner has created a welcoming atmosphere and offers a winning interpretation of traditional dishes. Among the *primi* you can have a very tasty *zuppa di cannellini e cozze* (bean and mussel soup) or *pasta e patate con provola* (pasta and potatoes with melted local cheese); for a *secondo* you could try *scorfano all' acquapazza* (a local fish in a light tomato and herb broth) or *stoccafisso alla pizzaiola* (dried codfish in a tomato, garlic, and oregano sauce). Pizza is also on the menu and is very well prepared, as are the desserts, including hometown favorites such as *babà* and *pastiera*.

Via Marchese Campodisola 4. © 081-5521323. Reservations required. Secondi 11€–16€ ($14–$20). AE, DC, MC, V. Mon–Sat noon–3:30pm and Thurs–Sat 7:30–11pm; in summer, dinner Thurs–Fri only. Closed 2 weeks in Aug. Bus: R2 or R3 to Piazza Trieste e Trento.

MODERATE
Ciro a Santa Brigida ☆ NEAPOLITAN   A traditional restaurant with a formal—but absolutely not stuffy—atmosphere and very professional service, Ciro a Santa Brigida is one of the most famous, and most typical, Neapolitan restaurants around. The restaurant was opened in 1932 by the father of the current owner/managers at Via Foria, and transferred here by his children. Since then, Santa Brigida has become a gastronomical institution, serving cuisine in a warm atmosphere laden with traditional decor. Popular with locals for its *fritto* (deep-fried seafood or cutlet), and for side dishes like hard-to-find traditional vegetables, it also serves good pizza and excellent desserts. Of the traditional Neapolitan specialties on hand, try *rigatoni ricotta e polpettine* (pasta with ricotta and baby meatballs) and *polpi alla Luciana* (squid cooked in a pocket with tomato and herbs). Counted among the restaurant's famous and faithful customers were the writers Pirandello, the artist De Filippo, and the actors Gassman and Totò.

Via Santa Brigida 71, off Via Toledo. © 081-5524072. Reservations required. Secondi 7.50€–15€ ($9.40–$18). AE, DC, MC, V. Mon–Sat noon–3:30pm and 7–11:30pm. Bus: R2 or R3 to Piazza Trieste e Trento.

INEXPENSIVE
I Re di Napoli NEAPOLITAN/PIZZA   This is a simple restaurant offering good food at inexpensive prices in two convenient locations. Their specialty is pizza—which they prepare in their brick oven. All of the many pizza options here are tasty, but if you decide you don't want pizza, they have a small menu of other dishes and a substantial buffet of appetizers/side dishes, including wonderful *involtini di melanzane*

(rolled-up fried eggplant filled with mozzarella and basil in a tomato sauce) and *peperonata* (sauté of sweet peppers). You can take bus R2 or R3 to their second location at Piazza Trieste e Trento 7

Piazza Dante 16. © 081-423013. Reservations recommended on weekends. Pizza: 5€–9€ ($6.25–$11). AE, DC, MC, V. Daily 11:30am–1am. Bus: R4, 24, CS, or 201. Metro: Piazza Dante.

Pizzeria Da Michele *Finds* PIZZA   Many say that this place serves the best pizza in Naples, period. The restaurant, small and authentic, has been in business since 1888, and for Naples that means it's had a chance to prove itself. It is usually quite crowded, so you'll have to come early or wait in line. Wonderful pizza (prepared with their secret dough recipe) will be your reward. It really is very good—but do brace yourself for the lack of frills: The pizza comes in only two varieties, *margherita* or *marinara,* basically with or without cheese. (You wanted traditional, right?) You are allowed to choose the size: small, medium, or maxi.

Via Sersale 1, off Via Forcella. © 081-5539204. Reservations not accepted. Pizza 5€–10€ ($6.25–$13). No credit cards. Mon–Sat 10am–10pm. Bus: R2 to Duomo.

Pizzeria Di Matteo *Value* PIZZA   The decor may be minimal, not to say nonexistent, but the pizza is succulent and incredibly cheap here. An old-fashioned Neapolitan pizzeria, Di Mateo opened in 1936, with a wood-burning oven, a counter, a couple of tables downstairs, and a set of small dining rooms upstairs crammed with plain Formica tables—it still looks the same. Locals come for a quick bite—fast food Neapolitan style—squeezing themselves at a table and choosing one of the individual pizzas and a drink (water, beer, and Coke are served). Service is efficient and curt; we wouldn't be surprised if they were brusque with President Clinton, when he came here during his stay in Naples for the G7 summit in 1994. Make up your mind fast and do not miss the *pizza fritta,* a delicacy of fluffy thin dough filled with a mix of ham, tomatoes, and local cheese—provola, ricotta, and mozzarella—that you can split as an appetizer or have on your own.

Via dei Tribunali 94, at Vico Giganti. © 081-455262. Pizza 3€–8€ ($3.75–$10). No credit cards. Mon–Sat 9am–3pm. Bus: R2 to Duomo.

Trattoria Pizzeria Medina NEAPOLITAN/PIZZA   This is the kind of place that is so large and glitzy from the outside, and so centrally located, that it has to be a tourist trap. In fact, it has a simple and very good pizzeria downstairs, and upstairs a full restaurant (you can eat pizza upstairs, too) set amid a series of huge rooms with 6m (20-ft.) beamed ceilings and painted scenes of Napoli. The pizza is excellent and comes in many varieties, but the regular dishes are very good, too. Try, for example, *tortelli al sugo* (filled homemade pasta in a tomato sauce), *trancio di cefalo in guazzetto* (steak of gray mullet in a light tomato sauce), or *costolette in padella* (sautéed cutlets). The *secondi* come—unusual in Italy—garnished with vegetables. The self-serve buffet of side dishes is ample, with a large choice of vegetable dishes.

Via Medina 32. © 081-5515233. Reservations recommended on weekends. Secondi 6.50€–13€ ($8.15–$17). AE, DC, MC, V. Daily noon–3pm and 7pm–midnight. Bus: R2.

PIAZZA GARIBALDI
MODERATE
Mimì alla Ferrovia *Finds* NEAPOLITAN   This is another of Naples's long-running restaurants that recently got a face-lift but has stayed popular with locals and true

For Those with Sweet Tooths

Naples is famous for its desserts, which include such world-famous specialties as *babà*, *sfogliatelle*, and *pastiera* (see appendix B, "Molto Italiano"). To taste those and many others, head to the **Pasticceria Scaturchio** ✿✿ (Piazza San Domenico Maggiore 19; ✆ 081-5516944). This historical pastry and coffee shop opened in 1903 and has been a favorite with locals ever since. Locals come here for a pick-me-up (there's nothing better than a *sfogliatella* as a mid-morning or mid-afternoon snack), or to buy dessert to bring to their hosts and family for dinner. Beside the excellent typical pastries, a chocolate candy developed here made them famous: the *Ministeriale*, a medallion of dark chocolate with a special liqueur cream filling.

Another excellent dessert stop is **Caffetteria Pasticceria Gelateria G. Mazzaro** ✿ (Palazzo Spinelli, Via Tribunali 359; ✆ 081-459248; www.pasticceriamazzaro.it; Wed–Tues 7am–midnight), which makes scrumptious pastries and excellent gelato in many flavors.

to Neapolitan tradition. The chef prepares excellent renditions of local favorites, varying according to the season. Depending on the time of year, you'll probably find *scialatielli ai frutti di mare* (eggless homemade pasta with seafood), *polipo alla Luciana* (squid cooked in a pocket with tomato and herbs), *in guazzetto* (squid in a light tomato sauce), and sometimes *sartù* (rice with baby meatballs and cheese). Not surprisingly, the desserts are those of the Neapolitan tradition—*babà* and *pastiera*.

Via Alfonso d'Aragona 21. ✆ 081-5538525. Reservations recommended on weekends. Secondi 8€–15€ ($10–$19). AE, DC, MC, V. Mon–Sat noon–3pm and 7:30–10:30pm. Metro: Piazza Garibaldi.

VOMERO
INEXPENSIVE

Gorizia ✿ *Finds* NEAPOLITAN/PIZZA   This excellent pizzeria was started in 1916 by the grandfather of the current owners (brothers Salvatore and Antonio), who are real traditionalists and don't believe pizza needs to be dressed up with fancy toppings. According to them, the crust is important above all: puffy but not gummy, with a slightly crunchy edge. Once you taste the result, you can only agree. Pizza's not the only thing here, however; they have a small yet varied menu which changes daily and always includes soup and a nice selection of appetizers/side dishes. If they have it, try the pasta with artichokes, olives, and tomatoes; or *pasta e ceci* (a thick soup made of garbanzo beans). The delicious escarole is stuffed with bread crumbs, olives, pinoli nuts, and raisins. This is a popular place for business lunches, and it helps to have a reservation in the evening.

Via Bernini 31, off Piazza Vanvitelli. ✆ 081-5782248. Reservations recommended for dinner. 5€–18€ ($6.25–$23). AE, DC, MC, V. Tues–Sun 12:30–4pm and 6pm–1am. Bus: V1. Funicolare to Vomero .

CAPODIMONTE
INEXPENSIVE

Al Terrazzo NEAPOLITAN/PIZZA   This large, simple neighborhood restaurant has been around since 1945 and is a convenient stop before or after visiting the Museo Capodimonte. It makes excellent pizza—try the *Antica Capri* (with smoked provola and fresh tomatoes)—and has a large menu including specialties such as *scialatielli ai* *frutti di mare* (eggless fresh pasta with seafood). The restaurant prides itself on its large buffet of antipasti and side dishes, offering 50 choices daily. During clement weather, you can dine on the terrace, which is on the second floor and above the traffic and street noise.

Viale Colli Aminei 99, off Via Capodimonte. (© **081-7414400** or 081-7414680. Secondi 4€–10€ ($5–$13). AE, DC, MC, V. Daily 11am–3:30pm and 6:30–11pm, later on Fri and Sat. Bus: R4.

4 Exploring Naples

Full of fun, surprise, and often wonder, Naples is particularly loved by art lovers and history buffs. To brush up on local history and art, see appendix A for help understanding this complex and multilayered city.

If you intend to visit at least three major attractions during your stay, the *Artecard* is a great deal (see box below). The **City Sightseeing** hop-on-and-off tour is another good idea; it will give you a great introduction to the city and provide convenient

---

Value   **Campania Artecard**

This recently introduced "region-" or "city-pass" gives you discounted admission to certain attractions, access to public transportation, and discounts to a number of participating businesses. The **Artecard** ((© 800-600601 or 063-9967650; www.campaniartecard.it) comes in several versions:

- The **"3 days all sites"** for 25€ ($31) grants free admission to the first two attractions you visit in Campania (plan the most expensive ones first) and a 50% discount on all the others, plus access to all public transportation—including regional trains and special buses—for 3 days.
- The **"3 days Naples and Campi Flegrei"** for 13€ ($16) also grants free admission to the first two attractions you visit (again, plan the most expensive ones first) and a 50% discount on all the others, plus access to all public transportation for 3 days, but only within Naples and the Campi Flegrei. (Even if you are not going to the Campi Flegrei, this is a great deal for Naples alone.)
- Each of the cards above also comes in a "youth" version for young people between 18 and 25; for 18€ ($23) and 8€ ($10) respectively, you get free admission to all sites plus public transportation.

  The sites that qualify for free or 50% admission are Museo Archeologico, Museo di Capodimonte, Certosa and Museo Di San Martino, Castel Sant'Elmo, Museo Civico di Castelnuovo, Palazzo Reale, and Città Della Scienza, within Naples. Also qualifying are the Campi Flegrei's five sites (counted as one admission), Pompeii, Herculaneum, Caserta, Capua, Paestum, Velia, and Padula, outside Naples. A 10% or 20% discount is offered at a number of participating attractions (see listings throughout the book). The card is for sale at all participating sites as well as at Capodichino airport; the Molo Beverello (harbor); the train stations of Napoli Cantrale and Mergellina; major hotels; and news kiosks.

What to See & Do in Naples

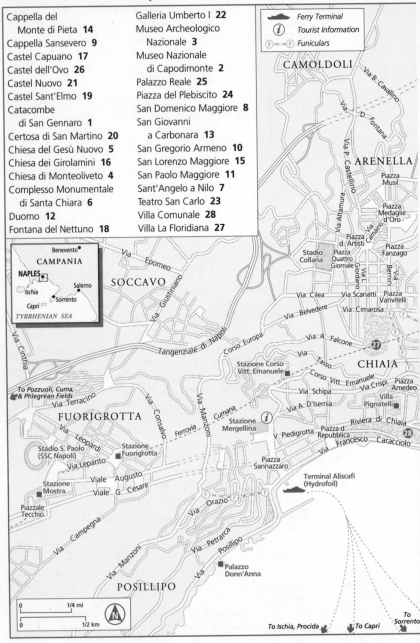

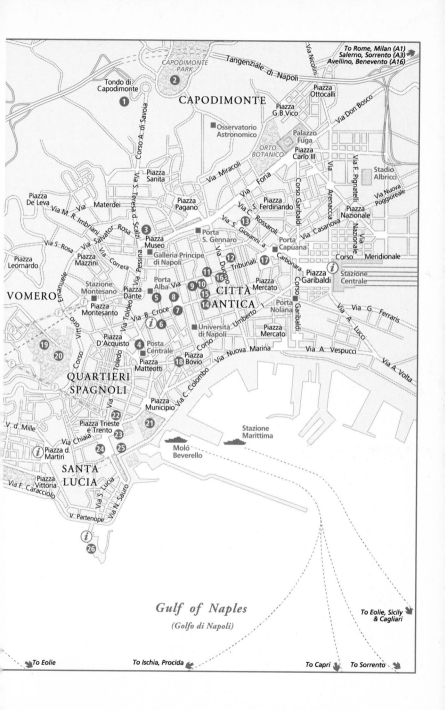

To Rome, Milan (A1)
Salerno, Sorrento (A3)
Avellino, Benevento (A16)

CAPODIMONTE PARK

Tondo di
Capodimonte

CAPODIMONTE

Tangenziale di Napoli

Via Nicolini

Piazza
Ottocalli

Piazza
G.B.Vico

Via Don Bosco

Corso A. di Savoia

Osservatorio
Astronomico

Palazzo
Fuga

ORTO
BOTANICO

Piazza
Carlo III

Via F. Pignatelli

Stadio
Albricci

Via S. Teresa d. Scalzi

Piazza
Sanita

Via Miracoli

Via Foria

Arenaccia

Via Nuova
Poggioreale

Piazza
De Leva

Via M. R. Imbriani

Materdei

Via

Piazza
Pagano

Via Fonia

Piazza
S. Ferdinando

Corso Garibaldi

Piazza
Nazionale

Piazza
Leonardo

Via S. Rosa

Via Salvator Rosa

Piazza
Mazzini

Via Correra

Piazza
Museo

Porta
S. Gennaro

Via C. Rossaroli

Via S. Giovanni a.

Porta
Capuana

Via Casanova

Via Nazionale

Corso Meridionale

VOMERO

Via C. Pessina

Galleria Principe
di Napoli

Via S. Giovanni a.

Via Duomo

Tribunali

Porta
Carbonara

Stazione
Centrale

Emanuele

Stazione
Montesano

Piazza
Dante

Porta
Alba

Via

CITTÀ

Piazza
Mercato

Corso Garibaldi

Piazza
Garibaldi

Piazza
Montesanto

ANTICA

Porta
Nolana

Corso Vittorio

Via B. Croce

Piazza
D'Acquisto

Università
di Napoli

Corso Umberto

Piazza
Mercato

Via G. Ferraris

QUARTIERI
SPAGNOLI

Posta
Centrale

Piazza
Bovio

Via Nuova Marina

Via A. Lucci

Piazza
Matteotti

Corso C. Colombo

Via A. Vespucci

Via A. Volta

Via Toledo

Piazza
Municipio

V. d. Mille

Piazza Trieste
e Trento

Stazione
Marittima

Via Chiaia

Molo
Beverello

Piazza d.
Martiri

SANTA
LUCIA

Via S. Lucia

Via N. Sauro

Piazza
Vittoria

Via F. Caracciolo

V. Partenope

Gulf of Naples

(Golfo di Napoli)

To Eolie, Sicily
& Cagliari

To Eolie

To Ischia, Procida

To Capri

To Sorrento

transportation between major attractions without forcing you to worry about bus numbers and tickets (see the "Guided Tours" section later in this chapter).

ROYAL NAPLES: PALACES & CASTLES

Castel Capuano   A fortress built by Guglielmo I d'Altavilla in the 12th century and restored in the 13th century by Carlo d'Angió, the Castel Capuano was transformed into a royal residence by the Aragona dynasty in 1484. In 1540, Don Pedro di Toledo, the viceroy of Naples, decided to change the residence to the seat of tribunals, a function it has to this day. The castle takes its name from the nearby gate, Porta Capuana, once at the head of the road for the city of Capua. Inside the courtyard, the medieval structure is visible. You can visit some of the decorated halls and the Cappella (Chapel) Sommaria, with its 16th-century frescoes.

Via Concezio Muzy, off Via dei Tribunali. Free admission. Daily 9am–6pm. Metro: Piazza Garibaldi.

Castel dell'Ovo 𝄞   Built over the small island where the first Greek colony was created in the 9th century B.C., this castle is one of Naples's most famous sites; its profile graces most pictures of the bay. According to legend, its name, "Castle of the Egg," refers to the magic egg that Virgil—the author of the *Aeneid* and a reputed magician—placed under the castle's foundations to protect it. The fortress evolved from the villa of the Roman Lucullus (a celebrated gourmand), which was fortified in the Middle Ages and transformed into a castle by Frederick II. Enlarged and strengthened between the 16th and the 18th centuries, it remained a royal residence until the 20th century. The castle now houses the Museum of Ethno-Prehistory, but it is open only for special exhibits. The rest of the castle can be visited: You will be able to admire the **Sala delle Colonne (Hall of the Columns)** 𝄞, and the **Loggiato** 𝄞—both architectural masterpieces, and great views from **Torre Maestra** and **Torre Normanna.** The castle occupies only part of the island, which is connected to the shore in front of the Santa Lucia neighborhood; around it are the picturesque alleys and fishermen's houses of the **Borgo dei Marinari** 𝄞—many of which have been transformed into restaurants.

Borgo Marinari. 📞 081-2400055. Admission depends on exhibit; 10% discount with Artecard. Mon–Sat 8:30am–5pm; Sun 8:30am–2pm. Bus: 152, C25, or 140.

Castel Sant'Elmo   Up on the Vomero near the Certosa di San Martino (see later in this chapter), this majestic star-shaped construction, with its six points and several moats, is visible from everywhere in the city. It was originally built by the Angevins in 1329 and called Belforte, then was remade into the present fortress by Viceroy Pedro Toledo in the 16th century. Used as a prison during the Masaniello revolution in 1799, it has been recently restored. You can visit the prisons and the terraces, which offer great views over Naples and the bay.

Via Tito Angelini 20. 📞 081-5784030. Admission 3€ ($3.75); included in admission to the Certosa di San Martino. Tues–Sun 8:30am–7:30pm. Ticket booth closes 1 hr. before. Closed Jan 1 and Dec 25. Metro: Vanvitelli. Bus: V1 from Piazza Vanvitelli. Funicolare to Vomare.

Castel Nuovo, aka Maschio Angioino & Museo Civico 𝄞   An imposing fortress dominating the bay and only steps from the shore, this castle was created by the French architect Pierre d'Angicourt for the new king, Carlo I d'Angió of the Angevin dynasty, who wanted a more suitable residence than the existing castles—Castel dell'Ovo and Castel Capuano. Started in 1279 and finished in 1282, it was enlarged in the 15th century by Alfonso I d'Aragona, first king of the Aragonese dynasty. The castle has five towers—del Beverello (overlooking the harbor), di San Giorgio, di Mezzo, di

Guardia, and dell'Oro (showing its tufa stone structure)—and a facade (facing inland) graced by the grandiose **Triumphal Arch of Alfonso I of Aragona** ✿. This is a splendid example of early Renaissance architecture by Francesco Laurana and Pietro de Martino, commemorating Alfonso I's ascent to power after his victory over the Angevins in 1443.

Across from the entrance in the courtyard and up a 15th-century staircase, you can access the magnificent **Sala dei Baroni** ✿✿, an architectural masterpiece. The monumental room is shaped like a cube, 27m (89 ft.) wide and 28m (92 ft.) high, with a star-shaped vaulted ceiling originally decorated by Giotto in the 14th century. (His frescoes, together with most of the sculptures that decorated the room, were unfortunately lost in a fire in 1919.)

Today, the castle houses the **Museo Civico (Civic Museum)** ✿, holding a rich collection of artworks from the castle itself and other important monuments in Naples. Part of the exhibit is inside the **Cappella Palatina** ✿, the only surviving part of the Angevin castle, opening onto the courtyard. The facade is decorated with a beautiful carved **portal** and **rose window** ✿ from the 15th century, added after the original ones were destroyed by an earthquake (the theme of destruction-and-renewal is a common one in Naples). Built in 1307, the chapel was completely decorated by Giotto, but only a few fragments remain. Inside you'll see a fine selection of 14th- and 15th-century sculptures, including a **Tabernacle** ✿✿ by Domenico Gagini (a pupil of Donatello and Brunelleschi) depicting a Madonna with Child, and two **Madonnas with Child** ✿ by Francesco Laurana—one from the portal of this chapel and the second from a nearby church. On the second floor, in the vestibule, is the beautiful **bronze door** ✿ of the castle, a 15th-century work by Guglielmo Monaco and Pietro de Martino. The broken hole in the door is from a cannon ball of uncertain origin, but probably dates to when the door was taken as war booty by the French in 1496. In the other rooms, you'll find a collection of 16th- and 17th-century paintings, including works by Luca Giordano and Francesco Solimena. On the third floor is an interesting collection of paintings dating from the 18th to the 20th centuries.

Piazza Municipio. ✆ 081-7955877. Admission 5€ ($6.25). Mon–Sat 9am–7pm; Sun 9am–2pm. Ticket booth closes 1 hr. before closing. Bus: R1 or R4.

Palazzo Reale ✿   This imposing palace was designed by Domenico Fontana and built from 1600 to 1602 for the Spanish king Filippo III—who never made it to Naples; it was then enlarged in the 18th century. Luigi Vanvitelli worked on the **facade** ✿✿, closing some of the arches to strengthen the walls and creating niches that were filled in 1888 by Umberto I, king of Italy, with eight statues of Neapolitan kings. Badly damaged during World War II, the building has been completely restored. Today, you can admire much of the interior, and we recommend doing so by guided tour to get a full appreciation of the sprawling place. Key stops start with the **Royal Apartment** ✿, which is furnished with original furniture but includes some important paintings from Neapolitan churches that have closed. From the elegant **Cortile d'Onore (Court of Honor)**, the double ramp of the main staircase leads to the first floor and the **Teatrino di Corte,** the private "home theater" of the royal family. Continuing throughout the palace, you enter the *appartmento* proper with its semi-public rooms, including the **Throne Room.** Beyond the corner begins the **Private Appartmento** (where the kings lived until the fire of 1837 obliged them to move upstairs), opening onto the beautiful elevated gardens and its views over the Gulf. Decorated with colored marble, tapestries, frescoes, and 19th-century furniture, the rooms are quite splendid, especially the beautifully furnished **Studio del Re (King's Study),** where you can admire a **desk** and two *secretaires* ✹ made for Napoleon Bonaparte by Adam Weisweiler. The following room contains the paintings *San Gennaro* and a *Crucifixion* by Luca Giordano, and two paintings by Andrea Vaccaro.

There's a seemingly endless array of other rooms here, most with 18th-century white and gilt original ceilings, marble floors, and dozens of paintings. The magnificent **Hall of Hercules** ✹, the ballroom, is hung with tapestries and boasts some beautiful Sèvres vases. The chapel, **Cappella Palatina,** is worth a visit for its carved wooden **doors** ✹ dating from the 16th century and its beautiful baroque **marble altar** ✹✹ by Dionisio Lazzari, with inlays of lapis lazuli, agate, amethyst, and gilt. The ceiling painting here, of the *Assunta* by Domenico Morelli, was being restored at presstime (no date is set for the end of the work). The most noteworthy aspect of the chapel, however, is the splendid 18th-century **Presepio del Banco di Napoli (Manger Scene)** ✹✹, which is one of the best examples of this art, and includes many figures carved by great Neapolitan sculptors of the time.

On the other half of the first floor is the **Appartamento delle Feste** ✹, with elegant rooms dedicated to public celebrations and festivities. It is now, together with the second floor, occupied by the **Biblioteca Nazionale di Vittorio Emanuele III,** the library which was originally established by Charles de Bourbon. Accessible from a separate entrance on the ground floor, the library is one of the greatest in the south, with about two million volumes (including 32,950 manuscripts, 4,563 incunabula, and 1,752 papyrus manuscripts from Herculaneum).

Piazza del Plebiscito 1. ☎ 081-5808111. Admission 4€ ($5); courtyard and gardens free. Guided tour by reservation 3€ ($3.75). Thurs–Tues 9:30am–8pm. Ticket booth closes 1 hr. before closing. Bus: R2 or R3 to Piazza Trieste e Trento.

Villa La Floridiana & Museo Nazionale della Ceramica Duca di Martina ✹✹

Surrounded by a magnificent park, this museum was once the 18th-century *casale* (country house) of Lucia Migliaccio, duchess of Floridia and second wife of Ferdinand II di Borbone. It now houses the **Museo Nazionale della Ceramica Duca di Martina** ✹, a rich collection of ceramics. The core of the museum is the private collection of Duc Placido De Sangro di Martina who, through his travels in Europe, collected precious objects not only in majolica and porcelain, but also glass, ivory, and coral. The collection was then expanded with objects from other museums in Naples. The stars of the show are the collection of **porcellane di Capodimonte (Capodimonte porcelain)** ✹, the most important collection in the world of this kind, with works from 1743 to 1759 by important artists such as Giuseppe Gricci; and the collection of **Japanese and Chinese porcelain** ✹, including precious Ming and Edo dynasty pieces. Decorating the walls are **sketches** by great Neapolitan artists of the 18th century, including Francesco Solimena, Domenico Antonio Vaccaro, and Corrado Giaquinto.

Note: Visits to the museum are only possible during fixed hours with an official guide. Even if you are not interested in ceramics, the villa is well worth a stop both for its architecture and for the splendid views over the whole bay.

Via Domenico Cimarosa 77. ☎ 081-407881 or 081-5788418. Admission 2.50€ ($3.15); 10% discount with Artecard. Wed–Mon 8:30am–2pm; ticket booth closes 1 hr. before closing. Closed Jan 1, May 1, and Dec 25. Museum visit only by guided tour starting at 9:30am, 11am, and 12:30pm. Funicolare to Piazza Fuga.

GREAT MUSEUMS

Museo Archeologico Nazionale ✹✹✹ *Kids*   This 16th-century palace was redone in the 17th century with the specific purpose of housing the National Archaeological

Museum; according to the fashion of the time, precious antiquities were embedded in the building as decoration. Notice the Roman marble statues on the facade—they come from the excavations of Pompeii. Inside, the mosaics on many of the floors don't just look Roman, but are original mosaics from the ancient Roman villas excavated in the 17th century. The whole collection is jaw-dropping and very extensive; no matter who you are, you'll find something to interest you. Children, for example, will love the Egyptian section, as well as the mosaics and the precious object collection.

The original core of the collection, the Farnese Collection, was moved here in 1777 and was enriched with treasures found during the archaeological excavations of Pompeii, Herculaneum, Stabia, and the rest of the region. The first-floor galleries here hold a superb collection of Roman sculptures, illustrating the integration of Hellenic principles into Roman art, and including such masterpieces as the **Doriforo (Spear Bearer)** ✯✯ from Pompeii, a unique, complete copy of the famous 5th-century-B.C. bronze statue by the Greek sculptor Policleto (in the Galleria dei Grandi Maestri, section 2). You'll also want to take note of the Roman marble statues that decorate the facade and the Roman mosaics on some of the floors. Other great masterpieces on display in the Farnese Collection include the famous *Ercole Farnese* ✯✯, a Hercules copied from a 4th-century-B.C. bronze by Greek sculptor Lisippo (found in the Terme di Caracalla in Rome, this sculpture had enormous influence on Renaissance artists); and the famous *Toro Romano* or *Toro Farnese* ✯✯, one of the largest existing sculpture groups from antiquity. Standing over 4m (13 ft.) high, the Toro Farnese is a copy of a Greek original from the 2nd century B.C., representing the torment of the queen of Beotia as she is tied to a bull. Also part of the Farnese Collection are the three rooms of the **Gemme della Collezione Farnese** ✯✯, a unique collection of precious objects (over 2,000 pieces), including the famous *tazza farnese* ✯✯, one of the largest cameos ever created. It was carved from a single piece of agate into the shape of a drinking cup in Alexandia in the 2nd century B.C.

From the first floor, you can also access the **Epigraphic Collection** (inscriptions) ✯✯— the most important epigraphic collection in the world that pertains to ancient Roman and Greek civilizations—and the **Egyptian Collection** ✯, holding artifacts from 2,700 B.C. up to the Ptolemaic-Roman period of the 2nd and 1st centuries B.C.

On the mezzanine level, you'll find a reorganized **Numismatic Collection** ✯, with over 200,000 coins and medals from antiquity, and a unique collection of **mosaics** ✯✯✯. This is the richest such mosaic collection in the world, boasting pieces from the 2nd century B.C. to the 1st century A.D. Among the many works of art here is the celebrated mosaic of **Alexander the Great defeating Darius of Persia** ✯✯✯, found in the Casa del Fauno in Pompei—it's a huge piece covering 201 sq. cm (216 sq. ft.). At your discretion, you can make a reservation for a guided tour to the collection of Roman erotica (famous already in Goethe's day) in the **Gabinetto Segreto (Secret Room)** ✯✯. These objects document how much sexuality was acknowledged in everyday Roman life—later Christian ages found this sort of art positively indecent.

On the second floor are the beautiful **Salone della Meridiana** ✯ and the **Prehistoric and Protohistoric Collection,** holding important findings from Naples and its surroundings and with Roman mosaics on many of the floors. (Note that at presstime, this area was being reorganized.) Also on this floor is the **Sala della Villa dei Papiri** ✯✯, a room holding the complete findings of a villa in Herculaneum. Still on the second floor, you'll find a superb collection (extending over several rooms and starting from room 66) of **paintings** ✯✯✯ from the 1st century B.C. to the 1st century A.D., all from Roman cities destroyed by the eruption of Mount Vesuvius in A.D. 79. *Note:* If you have time for only one section of the museum, make it this one: Entire rooms have been reconstructed from villas in Pompeii, Herculaneum, Boscoreale, Boscotrecase, and other locations. Head for room 77; it has beautiful **landscapes** and a portrait of the girl **Saffo.** (At presstime, the frescoes of this room were under restoration and only visible on selected days, so call before your visit.)

Further collections here include precious objects—silver, ivory, pottery, and glass, as well as marble and bronze objects, mostly from Herculaneum and Pompeii. Audioguides are available and well done; we definitely recommend them.

Piazza Museo 19. (✆) 081-440166. Admission 6.50€ ($8.15). Audioguide 4€ ($5) in Italian or English. Guided tours (90 min.) 4€ ($5). Wed–Mon 9am–8pm. Ticket booth closes 1 hr. earlier than general closing. Closed Jan 1 and Dec 25. Metro: Museo or Piazza Cavour.

Museo Nazionale di Capodimonte 🐿🐿🐿   Much more than a museum, the complex of Capodimonte was built by Carlo III di Borbone in 1743 to house his mother's (Elisabetta Farnese) art collection and to serve as a hunting preserve; the magnificent park is referred to as the *bosco reale* (royal wood) by locals, who love to come for a stroll, especially on weekends. In 1739, the king also founded the Capodimonte workshops for the production of artistic ceramics here, which went on to introduce a unique ceramic technique and style, made famous around the world. The laboratories slowed down considerably in 1759, when the king left Naples to become king of Spain, but his son Ferdinando kept it going until 1805. The museum is housed in the palace and includes several collections.

The **19th-century Gallery** on the mezzanine level includes a number of interesting paintings, but the star of the show is the **Farnese Gallery** 🐿🐿 on the second floor. This holds the richest members of the collection, with several paintings by the Italian artist elite—**Tiziano, Raffaello, Masaccio, Botticelli, Perugino, Luca Signorelli, Sandro Botticelli, Correggio, Giovanni Bellini, Mantegna, Parmigianino, Guido Reni, Caravaggio**—the list is almost endless. It also boasts paintings by artists from the Flemish school, such as **Pieter Bruegel the Elder** and **Van Dyck.** Besides paintings, the collection holds sculptures and precious tapistries. Also on this level, the small **Borgia Collection** 🐿 has paintings by **Mantegna** and other Spanish artists, as well as precious Renaissance **ivory** and **enamel** pieces.

The **Royal Apartment** 🐿 takes up much of the second floor. In the small **Porcelain Gallery** 🐿, you'll find a number of unique pieces, with objects and dinner plates from all the royal palaces of Naples, including *bisquits* (a firing process) of **Sèvres** and **Vienna,** and porcelains of **Meissen** and, of course, **Capodimonte.** Nearby is the **De Ciccio Collection** with more porcelain, but also paintings and precious objects. **The Armory** has interesting pieces, but is overshadowed by the famous **Salottino di Porcellana** 🐿🐿, a small room completely inlaid with porcelain, made for Maria Amalia in the 18th century for the royal palace of Portici.

A **gallery** 🐿🐿 dedicated to "Painting in Naples from the 13th to the 19th Centuries" occupies the third floor, and provides a unique overview of artists who worked in Naples. It includes works by **Sodoma, Vasari, Tiziano, Caravaggio,** and **Luca Giordano;** here you can also admire the seven beautiful 16th-century **tapestries** 🐿🐿 from the **d'Avalos Collection,** and also their picture collection including work by **Ribera** and **Luca Giordano.** The contemporary art collection extends from the third to the fourth floor, with works by Alberto Burri, Jannis Kounellis, Andy Warhol, and Enzo Cucchi, among others. On the fourth floor you can also find a **Photography**

Collection and the **Galleria dell'Ottocento** focusing on painters of the 19th century (Neapolitans, but also other Italians and foreigners).

Palazzo Capodimonte, Via Miano 1; also through the park from Via Capodimonte. ℭ 081-7499111. Admission 8€ ($10); 6.50€ ($8.15) after 2pm. Audioguide 4€ ($5). Tues–Sun 8:30am–7:30pm. Ticket booth closes 1 hr. before closing. Closed Jan 1 and Dec 25. Bus: R4 or 24.

RELIGIOUS NAPLES: CHURCHES & MONASTERIES

Perhaps the most religious city in Italy, Naples rivals Rome when it comes to the number and beauty of its churches. It is impossible to list them all; although we wanted to, we could cover only the best.

Cappella del Monte di Pietà *Finds*   This sober 16th-century palace of the Monte di Pietà hides one of Naples's real treasures: a perfectly preserved and richly decorated 16th-century chapel. Opening onto the palace's courtyard, the chapel is decorated by important artists of the 16th and 17th century, including the two **sculptures** on each side of the entrance by Pietro Bernini, father of the famous Lorenzo. Inside the church, the **ceiling** bears a beautiful **fresco** depicting scenes from the life of Jesus by Belisario Corenzio. Farther on, you can visit the adjoining rooms, in particular the **Sacristy** 𝄞 at the beginning and the **Sala delle Cantoniere** 𝄞 at the end, perfectly preserved in 17th-century style, down to the furnishings and floors.

Via Biagio dei Librai 114. ℭ 081-5807111. Free admission. Sat 9am–7pm; Sun 9am–2pm. Bus: R1, R2, or R3. Metro: Dante.

Cappella di Sansevero 𝄞   In the 18th century, Prince Raimondo de Sangro of Sansevero remodeled this funerary chapel—built in the 16th century for his family—and lavishly decorated it with sculptures. Among those are some particularly renowned works, starting with Giuseppe Sanmartino's *Cristo Velato* **(Veiled Christ)** 𝄞, created by the Neapolitan sculptor in 1753, and still with the original patina. Depicting veiled figures in stone seems to have obsessed the prince: Other sculptures here are the *Disinganno,* a technical virtuoso by Queirolo showing a standing figure of a man disentangling himself from a net; and *Pudicizia,* a masterpiece by Corradini showing a veiled naked woman. The prince—a student of science, an inventor, and an alchemist—achieved fame as a master of the occult, and the decoration of the chapel has contributed to this reputation. The most striking (and weird) objects here are two actual human bodies conserved in the crypt, whose circulatory systems are perfectly preserved after 2 centuries. The chapel is also used for art exhibits and concerts—call for schedules.

Via Francesco De Sanctis 19. ℭ 081-5518470. www.museosansevero.it. Admission 6€ ($7.50); 20% discount with Artecard. Mon and Wed–Sat 10am–6pm; Sun 10am–1:30pm. Bus: R1, R2, or R3. Metro: Dante.

Catacombe di San Gennaro (Catacombs of St. Gennaro) 𝄞   Attached to the church of San Gennaro extra Moenia (where the natural entrance to the catacombs used to be), these are the most important catacombs of southern Italy, famous both for their length of use—until the 10th century—and the well-preserved **fresco cycles** 𝄞 from the 2nd to the 10th centuries that decorate the large corridors and chapels. Organized on two levels, they have broad corridors and halls, differing in that respect from Roman catacombs. On the upper level, you'll also find the **Cripta dei Vescovi** 𝄞, decorated with magnificent mosaics from the 5th century. The lower level holds the **Basilica di Sant'Agrippino** *ipogea* ("pogean," or terranean) where St. Agrippino, the 3rd-century bishop of Naples, is buried. Also nearby is the **Cubicolo di San Gennaro,**

with the tomb of the patron saint of Naples, whose remains were moved here in the 5th century.

Via Capodimonte 13. ⓒ 081-7411071. Admission 3€ ($3.75). By guided tour only: Tues–Sun 9am, 10am, 11am, and noon. Bus: 24 or R4 to Via Capodimonte, and then down an alley alongside the church Madre del Buon Consiglio.

Certosa e Museo Nazionale di San Martino (Carthusian Monastery and National Museum of St. Martin) 🦋   Originally built in 1325 and redone in the 17th century, this great monastery has been restored to all its original beauty. Entering from the courtyard, you first come to the **church** 🦋, a masterpiece of baroque decoration, from the marble **floor** to the various works of art by artists such as Jusepe de Ribera (various paintings), Giuseppe Sanmartino (sculptures), and Battistello Caracciolo (frescoes). Do not overlook the marble **transenna** of the presbytery, decorated with precious stones (lapis lazuli and agate), and the **Cappella del Tesoro** 🦋, with a rich altar made of the same materials; beautiful **frescoes** by Luca Giordano—including the *Trionfo di Giuditta*—decorate the ceiling. You can also view the *Deposizione* by Jusepe de Ribera. You can then continue to the **Chiostro Grande** 🦋🦋. The **Quarto del Priore** 🦋🦋—the elegant apartment used for the reception of important personalities—contains a number of masterpieces, including a *Madonna col Bambino e San Giovannino* by Pietro Bernini. The monastery also houses the **Museo Nazionale di San Martino,** which has several sections. The recently restored collection of *presepi* 🦋 (or **manger scenes,** with unbelievable variation) is off the Chiostro dei Procuratori, among which the star is the *presepio* **Cuciniello,** created in 1879 with a collection of 18th-century figures and accessories. The **Images and Memories of Naples exhibit** 🦋🦋 on the first and second floors includes paintings, sculpture, porcelain, and precious objects. The **Collezione Rotondo** 🦋 has paintings and bronze sculpures by Neapolitan artists of the 19th century. In the Gothic **cellars** of the monastery you will find sections dedicated to sculpture and epigraphy. On the second floor is the library that houses the **Prints and Drawings Collection,** with over 8,000 pieces.

Largo San Martino 8. ⓒ 081-5781769. Admission 6€ ($7.50) includes Castel Sant'Elmo. Tues–Sun 8:30am–7:30pm; ticket booth til 1 hr. before closing. Closed Jan 1 and Dec 25. Bus: V1 from Piazza Vanvitelli. Any one of the Funicolare to Vomero. Metro: Vanvitelli. .

Chiesa del Gesù Nuovo 🦋   Built by Jesuits in 1470, this church has a striking facade in *bugnato a punta di diamante* (ashlar work), a rare technique which was preserved from the original facade of the great Sanseverino Palace, from which the church was transformed. A baroque portal englobes the original Renaissance portal and gives access to the majestic interior, featuring stucco, frescoes, and marble decorations by some of Naples's best artists from the 16th century to the beginning of the 19th. Among the masterpieces are the impressive **fresco** 🦋 by Francesco Solimena depicting the *Expulsion of Eliodorus from the Temple,* and the rich decorations in the left transept, including a beautiful **altar** 🦋 and Franzago's **statues** 🦋 of Jeremiah and David.

On the piazza outside the church, you'll find one of Naples's several baroque spires, the **Guglia dell'Immacolata,** a tall pile of statues and reliefs from 1750. Typically Neapolitan, this religious monument is modeled after processional objects—part float, part conglomeration of statues and figures—built for religious celebrations from baroque times until the 1950s. This particular spire was built to celebrate one of the major points of the Jesuits' teachings, and boasts sculptures of Jesuit saints and the story of Mary by Matteo Bottighero and Francesco Pagano.

Piazza del Gesù. ℭ 081-5518613. Free admission. Mon–Sat 9am–1pm and 4–7pm; Sun 9am–1pm. Bus R1, R2, R3, or R4. Metro: Dante.

Chiesa di Monteoliveto (aka Sant'Anna dei Lombardi, aka Santa Maria di Monteoliveto) ✵✵ Built in 1411, the Chiesa di Monteoliveto was one of the most acclaimed churches of the Aragonese dynasty. It opens onto a pretty square graced by the **Fontana di Monteoliveto,** considered to be the most beautiful baroque fountain in Naples. This fountain was built for Don Pedro de Aragona in 1699, based on a design by Cosimo Fanzago, and the bronze statue topping it is of King Carlo II d'Asburgo.

Behind the church's facade is the atrium, housing the tomb of the architect Domenico Fontana. Inside the church are three superb Renaissance chapels: **Cappella Correale** ✵ to the right of the entrance, with an altar by Benedetto da Maiano and the *San Cristoforo* over the altar by Francesco Solimena; **Cappella Piccolomini** ✵ to the left of the entrance—an almost perfect replica of the Chapel of the Cardinal of Portugal in the Florentine San Miniato al Monte church, graced by the tomb of Maria d'Aragona by Antonio Rossellino and Benedetto da Maiano; and **Cappella Tolosa** ✵, also to the left, attributed to Giuliano da Maiano and decorated in the styles of Brunelleschi and della Robbia. This last chapel is a triumph of sculpture, and gives a good overview of 15th- and 16th-century Neapolitan sculpture. From the right of the presbytery you can access the old **sacristy** ✵ with its vaulted ceilings frescoed by Giorgio Vasari. Its walls, decorated with wood inlays depicting classical panoramas, musical instruments, and other scenes, were created by Giovanni da Verona between 1506 and 1510.

Piazza Monteoliveto 44. ℭ 081-5513333. Free admission. Mon–Fri 9am–noon; Sat 9am–noon and 5:30–6:30pm. Bus R1, R2, R3, or R4. Metro: Dante.

Chiesa dei Girolamini ✵ *Finds* Rarely visited, this church and its attached convent hide a great collection of artwork by some prominent Italian Renaissance artists. The church was built between the end of the 16th century and the beginning of the 17th. Among the masterpieces you'll find inside are: in the counter-facade, a **fresco** by Luca Giordano; in the first chapel to the right, *Sant'Alessandro Moribondo* by Pietro da Cortona; in the transept, **frescoes** by Francesco Solimena and **statues** by Pietro Bernini; and over the altar in the sacristy, the painting *San Giovanni Battista* by Guido Reni.

In the annexed **Casa dei Padri dell'Oratorio** (entrance on Via Duomo 142), you can visit the beautiful **Chiostro Maggiore** ✵ and the **Quadreria dei Girolamini** ✵✵, a rich collection of paintings donated to the convent and including notable artists such as Cavalier d'Arpino, Sermoneta, Guido Reni, and Jusepe de Ribera. You can also visit the splendid **library** ✵, with its beautiful halls, especially the **Sala Grande.**

Chiesa: Via dei Tribunali. ℭ 081-292316. Free admission. Mon–Sat 9am–1pm and 4–7pm; Sun 9am–1pm. Quadreria: Via Duomo 142. ℭ 081-449139. www.girolamini.it. Admission 3€ ($3.75). Tues–Sun 9am–3pm. Bus R1, R2, R3, or R4. Metro: Dante.

Complesso Monumentale di Santa chiara (Monumental Complex of St. Clare) ✵✵ The most famous basilica in Naples, the Santa Chiara was built in 1310 by Roberto I d'Angió as the burial church for the d'Angió dynasty. In the 18th century, it was lavishly decorated by the best artists of the time, but bombings in 1943 destroyed much of the art. A subsequent restoration in 1953 reintroduced the original Gothic structure. Today, the facade is decorated with a large rose window and flanked by a majestic bell tower (the lower part is 14th century) which dominates the neighborhood.

Inside, 10 chapels open onto the central nave and royal tombs, including the monumental **tomb of Roberto d'Angió** ❀, a magnificent example of Tuscan-style Renaissance sculpture. From the sacristy you can access the **Coro delle Clarisse (Choir of the Clarisses)** ❀, where the basilica's nuns sit protected from the public during Mass, and its beautiful 14th-century marble portal; only fragments remain, sadly, of Giotto's frescoes. The **Chiostro delle Clarisse** ❀❀, the cloister behind the church (to the right), is strikingly decorated with bright majolica tiles.

The museum here, **Museo dell'Opera di Santa Chiara,** is dedicated to the history of the religious complex and includes the remains of thermal baths from the 1st or 2nd century A.D., as well as important local artists' sculptures and reliefs such as *Crocefissione* and *Visitazione* by Tino di Camaino.

Church: Via Santa Chiara 49. Ⓒ 081-5526280. Free admission. Thurs–Tues 9:30am–1pm and 4–6pm; Sun 9am–1pm. **Cloister & Museum:** Via Benedetto Croce 16. Ⓒ 081-7971256. www.santachiara.info. Admission 3€ ($3.75); 10% discount with Artecard. Mon–Sat 9:30am–1pm and 2:30–5:30pm; Sun 9:30am–1pm. Bus R1, R2, R3, or R4. Metro: Dante.

Duomo (aka Cattedrale di Santa Maria Assunta) ❀❀❀   A monumental construction, graced inside by 110 ancient granite columns which support its Latin Cross structure, the Duomo was begun by King Carlo II d'Angió sometime in the 13th century and finished by his successor Roberto d'Angió in 1313. When it was built, the cathedral incorporated two Paleochristian churches, Santa Stefania—of which there is no more trace—and **Santa Restituta** ❀, which you can still access from the Duomo's atrium to the left, and which is today the oldest basilica in Naples. Built in the 6th century by the Emperor Constantine, it was redone in Gothic style when it was annexed to the Duomo and lost its facade, its atrium, and two of the original five naves.

The interior of Santa Restitutea was redecorated in the 17th century but still features a luminous 14th-century **mosaic** by Lello da Orvieto and two beautiful 13th-century reliefs, all in the sixth chapel on the left. On the right, at the end of the nave, is the entrance to the **Baptistery of San Giovanni in Fonte** ❀❀. Founded in the 4th century, it is the world's oldest Western baptistery; its cupola is decorated with beautiful **mosaics** from the 5th century (unfortunately, some of them are damaged).

The Duomo itself is decorated with precious artwork. The painting of the *Assunta* on the right side of the transept is by **Perugino;** farther to the right is the entrance to the Gothic **Cappella Minutolo** ❀❀❀, with its beautiful 13th-century frescoes and mosaic floor. You'll also want to descend downstairs to access the **Succorpo** or **Cappella Carafa** ❀, one of the most elegant Renaissance architectural structures, attributed to **Bramante.**

To the right of the Duomo's atrium is the monumental **Cappella di San Gennaro** ❀❀, dedicated to the patron saint of Naples. Richly decorated with precious marbles, gold leaf, frescoes, and artwork, this is the highest achievement of Neapolitan baroque. The fresco cycle around the dome, illustrating the life of San Gennaro, is by Domenichino, while the oil painting over copper, depicting San Genarro, is by Jusepe de Ribera—the rich frame of gilded bronze and lapis lazuli is by Onofrio D'Alessio. The famous reliquaries containing the skull and the blood of San Gennaro—which is said to miraculously liquefy each September 19 (Feast Day of San Gennaro) as well as the first Sunday in May and December 16—are over the main altar and inside a safe.

If you like precious religious artwork, you should not miss the **Museum of the Treasure of San Gennaro** (entrance adjacent to the Duomo); the amount of the treasure is so great that the museum has to rotate its holdings over several years. From the museum you can also visit the **Sacristy** ✶✶, beautifully decorated with **frescoes** by Luca Giordano and paintings by **Domenichino.** In the sacristy, you can arrange an appointment to visit Santa Restituta and the Cappella Minutolo if you find them closed.

Cathedral: Via Duomo 147. ✆ 081-449097. Free admission. Mon–Sat 8am–12:30pm and 4:30–7pm; Sun and holidays 8am–1:30pm and 5–7:30pm. **Museum:** Via Duomo 149. ✆ 081-421609. www.museodeltesorodisan gennaro.info. Admission 2.60€ ($3.25); 25% discount with Artecard. Tues–Sat 9am–6:30pm; Sun and holidays 9am–7pm. Metro: Piazza Cavour.

San Domenico Maggiore ✶✶

You'll have to enter this church from the back because its facade faces an inner courtyard, according to Angevin tradition. Built by Carlo II d'Angiò between 1283 and 1324, San Domenico Maggiore encloses the older church of **San Michele Arcangelo a Morfisa,** which is still accessible from the transept. Inside both are innumerable works of art, including many **Renaissance monumental tombs** graced by sculptures and carvings, as well as 14th-century **frescoes** and 15th- and 16th-century **paintings.** The main **altar** is a beautiful work of marble inlay from the 16th century. On the square—one of Naples's most beautiful squares—is the **Guglia San Domenico,** a marble spire erected between 1658 and 1737 in gratitude for the end of that century's plague.

Piazza San Domenico Maggiore. ✆ 081-449097 or 081-459298. Free admission. Daily 9am–noon and 5–7pm. Metro: Piazza Cavour.

San Giovanni a Carbonara ✶ *Finds*

Built in 1343 with the annex convent, this church was used to bury the last members of the Angevin dynasty and remains one of Naples's undiscovered jewels, which is not surprising, considering that it's rather difficult to find. First, you'll need to climb a staircase leading to the baroque Consolazione a Carbonara church, and continue farther up until you reach three portals. You should ignore the central one—the Gothic entrance to the Cappella Santa Monica—and take the portal to the left. This will lead you into a terraced courtyard, and there you will finally find the entrance to San Giovanni, which you can access from its 15th-century lateral portal. Inside the church are several important works of art, including, in the apse—flat, not rounded as is usual—the **Monumental Tomb of King Ladislao,** a 15th-century masterpiece by several Tuscan artists. Behind the monument is the circular **Cappella Caracciolo del Sole,** with a majolica floor and beautiful **frescoes** from the 15th century, very handsome but less harmonious than the other circular chapel in this church—**Cappella Caracciolo di Vico.** This chapel, located to the left of the presbytery, is an architectural tour-de-force from the beginning of the 16th century, graced by a beautifully carved 16th-century altar.

Impressions

It would be rash to say that the whole population of Naples is always in the street, for if you look into the shops or cafes, or, I dare say, the houses, you will find them quite full . . . . Then there is the expansive temperament, which if it were shut up would probably be much more explosive than it is now. As it is, it vents itself in volleyed detonations and scattered shots which language can give no sense of. For the true sense of it you must go to Naples, and then you will never lose the sense of it.

—William Dean Howells, *Naples and her Joyful Noise,* 1908

Via San Giovanni a Carbonara 5. ✆ 081-295873. Free admission. Mon–Sat 8am–noon and 4:30–8:30pm; Sun 8am–2pm. Metro: Piazza Cavour.

San Gregorio Armeno   This church is little known and little visited—even if its name is famous worldwide for the manger artists and vendors lining the street that bears its name (see "Shopping" later in this chapter). Yet this church and its adjoining monastery—dating from the 8th century but redone in 1580—are well worth a visit to admire the bell tower and the richly decorated interior (all in gold leaf and with a beautifully carved **wooden ceiling** ✿), as well as the **frescoes** ✿ in the counter-facade by Luca Giordano. You should also visit the pretty **cloister** ✿ of the attached monastery (through the entrance outside the church, beyond the bell tower), beautifully preserved and graced by a marble **fountain** depicting Jesus meeting the Good Samaritan.

Via San Gregorio Armeno 44. Free admission. Daily 9:30am–noon. Metro: Piazza Cavour.

San Lorenzo Maggiore ✿✿   The most beautiful of Naples's medieval churches, San Lorenzo is famous for its literary past—here Giovanni Boccaccio met his Fiammetta in 1334, and the attached convent hosted Francesco Petrarca for a period. Built in the 6th century A.D., the church was redone in 1270 by Carlo I d'Angiò and his successor, and was reworked again in baroque style. Not surprisingly, the airy interior holds innumerable works of art, including 13th- and 14th- century **frescoes,** as well as beautiful **altars** and monumental tombs spanning the centuries. If you're interested in antiquity, the **Greek and Roman excavations** in the cloister will prove particularly appealing. There you'll see the building's layers of construction, from the Forum complete with merchant stalls, to the Roman Macellum, to the city market dating from the 1st century A.D., to a paleochristian basilica, to a medieval building to, finally, the existing buildings. The best pieces from the excavations are displayed in the **museum,** which also features a collection of historical ceremonial religious attire and a collection of 18th-century *presepio* figures.

Church: Piazza San Gaetano. ✆ 081-290580. Free admission. Mon–Sat 8am–noon and 5–7pm. Museum: ✆ 081-454948. www.sanlorenzomaggiorenapoli.it. Admission 2€ ($2.50). Tues–Sun 9am–6pm. Metro: Piazza Cavour.

San Paolo Maggiore ✿   Founded between the 8th and 9th centuries A.D. over a pre-existing Roman Temple of the Dioscuri—two of its columns remain on the facade—San Paolo Maggiore was completely redone in the 16th century. The interior was decorated by many important artists of the 17th and 18th century, but the standouts here are the statue of *Angelo Custode* by Domenico Antonio Vaccaro to the left of the central nave; the **frescoes** in the sacristy—considered the best work of Francesco Solimena; and the **Cappella Firrao** to the left of the presbytery, one of the most beautiful baroque chapels in Naples.

Piazza San Gaetano. ✆ 081-454048. Free admission. Daily 8am–noon and 5–7pm. Metro: Piazza Cavour.

Sant'Angelo a Nilo   Built in 1385 for the Brancaccio family and redone in the 18th century, this church merits a visit for its **Funerary Monument of Cardinal Rinaldo Brancaccio** ✿✿. This monument to the church's founder was created in Pisa by **Donatello** and **Michelozzo** between 1426 and 1427, and shipped by sea to Naples. Very modern for its time, the work merges Gothic and Renaissance movements in a noteworthy manner. The two portals to the right of the presbytery, one from the 14th and the other from the 16th century, are also noteworthy.

The Church of Sant'Angelo a Nilo gets its name from the Greek-Roman **Statue of the Egyptian God Nile,** in the small square near the church. Originally carved for merchants from Alexandria who worked in the area, the statue was lost for centuries and was found again in the 15th century. In typical Neapolitan spirit, the statue of the river god, with his babies representing the river tributaries, was interpreted as a representation of motherly Naples, nourishing its children; hence the nickname still in use today among the locals—*cuorp'e Napule* or "body of Naples."

Piazzetta Nilo, off Via Benedetto Croce. Free admission. Mon–Sat 8:30am–1pm and 4:45–7pm; Sun 8:30am–1pm. Bus: E1 or R2. Metro: Piazza Cavour.

PUBLIC NAPLES

Fontana del Nettuno   Naples's most beautiful fountain is famous for its mobility. Originally built for Viceroy Enrico Guzman, Count of Olivares, it was located in front of the Arsenal for 30 years. In 1622, the Duca d'Alba had it moved to the Piazza del Palazzo Reale. In 1637, it was moved again in front of the Castel dell'Ovo. A few years later, worried that it was dangerously positioned (open to attacks from the sea), the city authorities moved it "temporarily" to Piazza delle Corregge. It stayed there until the beginning of the 20th century, when it was moved again to its present—and maybe permanent—position.

Piazza G.Bovio off Via Medina. Bus: C57, E3, or R3.

Galleria Umberto I   Built at the end of the 19th century—20 years after its larger Milanese counterpart—this is an exemplary Italian Liberty-style building built with obvious Parisian inspiration. The gallery is an elegant glass-and-iron covered passage following a Greek cross shape, with each of its four arms opening onto a street on one end and meeting at a rotunda, covered with a cupola, on the other. Inside, the galleria is lined with elegant shops and cafes.

You'll find a second Liberty-era gallery in town, **Galleria del Principe di Napoli** (off Piazza Cavour to the right; Metro Piazza Cavour), which is virtually unknown, probably because of its location outside the most touristy area of Via Toledo.

4 entrances: To the right off Via Toledo as you come from Piazza del Plebiscito, Via Giuseppe Verdi, Via Santa Brigida, and Via San Carlo. Bus: R2 or R3 to Piazza Trieste e Trento.

Piazza del Plebiscito 🐨🐨   This is the most beautiful piazza in Naples, defined by the majestic colonnade of **San Francesco di Paola**—an 1817 church built in full neoclassical style and inspired by the Roman Pantheon—and the elegant neoclassical facade of the Royal Palace. In the square are two equestrian statues, one of **Carlo III** by Antonio Canova and one of **Ferdinando I** (only the horse is by Canova). The square is fittingly called the "salotto" (living room) by Neapolitans, since it has been completely closed to traffic. Nearby is Piazza Trieste e Trento, with the Fontana del Carciofo, and the start of Via Toledo (Neapolitans call this Via Roma), an extremely popular promenade and shopping street.

Off Piazza Trieste e Trento, between Via Chiaia and Via C. Console. Bus: R2 or R3 to Piazza Trieste e Trento.

Teatro San Carlo 🐨   Built for Carlo Borbone by Antonio Medrano, the Teatro San Carlo is among Europe's most beautiful opera houses and one of the most famous. A neoclassical jewel with an ornate gilded interior, the San Carlo was the first opera theater in the world; it was inaugurated on November 4, 1737. The facade was added in 1812 by Antonio Piccolini, who rebuilt the interior after a fire destroyed it in 1816. The theater hall, which holds 1,470 seats, is said to have even better acoustics than

Milan's famous La Scala, and such artists as Donizetti, Rossin, and Verdi produced and directed masterpieces here. You can appreciate its architecture and decoration by taking the free guided tour (by reservation), or come for a performance (see "Naples After Dark," later in this chapter) and see the building in its full glory.

Via San Carlo 93. (€ 081-400300 or 081-7972111 for reservations. Bus: R2 or R3 to Via San Carlo.

Villa Comunale ☝ Created in 1780 according to a design by Luigi Vanvitelli, as the private Royal Promenade for King Ferdinando IV Bourbon, this park was later transformed by the king into a public garden. The park is a baroque creation graced by statues, fountains—including the famous **Fontana delle Paperelle** ("fountain of the ducks")—and several elegant buildings such as **Casina Pompeiana, Chiosco della Musica,** and **Stazione Zoologica** with Europe's oldest **Aquarium,** specializing in the study of local marine life. On the first Saturday of each month, the Villa Comunale hosts an antiques market, which is open 8:30am to 1pm.

Park: Piazza Vittoria. (€ 081-7611131. Daily 7am–midnight. Aquarium: (€ 081-5833111 or 081-2452099. Tues–Sun 9am–5pm. Bus: C82 or R2.

GUIDED TOURS

If you only have a short time in the city, the best way to familiarize yourself with Naples is the **CitySightseeing** hop-on-and-off double-decker bus tour (€ **081-5517279;** www.napoli.city-sightseeing.it). Three buses start from Piazza Municipio/Parco Castello: Line A travels up to the Museo di Capodimonte from 9:45am to 6:45pm every 45 minutes; line B winds along the seashore to Posillipo Monday to Wednesday and Friday from 9:30am to 7:15pm every 45 minutes, and Thursday, Saturday, and Sunday from 9:30am to 7:30pm every 30 minutes; line C journeys to the Certosa di San Martino on Saturday, Sunday, and holidays with departures at 10am, noon, 2pm, 4pm, and 6pm from Piazza Municipio, and at 11am, 1pm, 3pm, and 7pm from the San Martino. Tickets are valid for 24 hours on all buses and can be purchased on board for 16€ ($20) adults and 8€ ($10) for children ages 5 to 15. There's a special 3€ ($3.75) ticket for the Museo Archeologico–Museo di Capodimonte, but only if you ride on the lower deck. Artecard (p. 87) offers a 10% discount.

Museo Aperto Napoli (€ **081-5636062;** www.museoapertonapoli.com) maintains a cultural center offering free information and guided tours (with a guide or audioguide) in six languages for the *città antica.* It's at Via Pietro Colletta 85 and is open daily 10am to 6pm; the center also houses a cafe, a bookshop, and a small exhibit space with crafts for sale.

Napoli Extra Moenia (€ **081-7769086;** www.viviquartiere.it) offers special art-history guided tours in Italian or English, with the option of adding on a show for 5€ to 10€ ($6.25–$13), depending on the program. For an art history tour more tailored to your personal must-see list in Naples and Campania, contact **Napolidentro** (€ **081-5789512** or 335-7773808; www.antonellanapoliguida.it); prices vary depending on the number of people and itinerary.

For more classic city tours, contact the agency **Every Tours** (Piazza del Municipio 5; € **081-5518564**) through the American Express outlet in Naples, which organizes tours of the city as well as day excursions to Vesuvio and other sights. It's open Monday through Friday from 9am to 1:30pm and 3:30 to 7pm and Saturday from 9am to 1pm. Another good agency is **NapoliVision** (€ **081-5595130;** www.napolivision.it), offering guided tours of Naples, Pompei, and Capri.

5 Spaccanapoli: A Walking Tour along the Very Heart of Naples

Spaccanapoli refers to the street that divides the *città antica* into two equal halves (*spacca* means "cracks in half"), at the heart of Naples. As its name indicates, this is the oldest part of town, dating back to Greek and Roman origins. If you have only one afternoon in Naples, you should definitely dedicate it to this street, which functions as a mini-itinerary through Naples's artistic and cultural highlights. Along Spaccanapoli and its cross streets, you will find Naples's most interesting churches, as well as notable small shops and traditional craftmakers.

Start:	Piazza del Gesù.
Finish:	Duomo.
Time:	2 hours plus interior visits.
Best Times:	Tuesday to Saturday 9am to 1pm and 5 to 7pm, when most of the churches and museums are open.
Worst Times:	Evening, when everything is closed. Sunday morning, because many churches cannot be visited during Mass. Monday, when some of the museums are closed. Lunchtime is also tricky, because only some of the attractions are open then.

❶ Piazza del Gesù

This pretty square houses the **Guglia dell'Addolorata,** one of Naples's famous baroque spires. (This particular spire commemorates Jesuit principles.) Across from it is the **Chiesa del Gesù,** the facade of which was once that of the Palazzo Sanseverino, sold to the Jesuits in the 15th century and preserved when the church was built. Inside, you'll find several noteworthy works of art, including a **fresco** by Solimena.

Follow the square a bit farther up until you get to the start of the Via Benedetto Croce. Immediately to the right is the:

❷ Complesso Monumentale di Santa Chiara

This huge complex includes a church, a monastery, a cloister, and a museum. The church itself contains some beautiful **monumental tombs** and the **Choir of the Clares,** but if you have little time, walk along the church's outer wall and take the little door to the right. This is the entrance to **The Clares' Cloister,** a majolica masterpiece that shouldn't be missed.

Emerge from the complex, and continue on Via Benedetto Croce to:

❸ Palazzo Filomarino

Located to your left at no. 12, this palace was built in the 14th century and redone in the 16th; go through its portal and peek at its **Monumental Internal Court** from the 16th century. Here lived and died the Italian 20th-century historian and philosopher Benedetto Croce.

Continue on Via Benedetto Croce, taking note of the palaces that line it until you reach:

❹ Piazza San Domenico Maggiore

This is one of the most beautiful squares in Naples, graced in the center by the **Guglia di San Domenico,** another of Naples's spires. This one was built between 1658 and 1737, in thanks for the end of a plague that struck in 1656. It is lined by beautiful *palazzi,* among them no. 17, the 18th-century **Palazzo di Sangro di Casacalenda,** finished by Vanvitelli and with a beautiful inner court; and no. 3, the 15th-century **Palazzo Petrucci,** with its striking original portal and loggias. Also in the square is the **San Domenico Maggiore** church, whose artwork spans everything from 14th-century **frescoes** to spectacular 16th-century **sculptures.**

PASTICCERIA SCATURCHIO
If you need a break, stop at Pasticceria Scaturchio (Piazza San Domenico Maggiore 19; ⓒ 081-5516944), a historical pastry and coffee shop right on the square across from the church, where you can sample wonderful pastry or try their *Ministeriale,* a medallion of dark chocolate with a liqueur cream filling.

Go back to the church and walk along its side on Vicolo San Domenico. Take the first right, to Via Francesco de Sanctis. At no. 19 you will find the:

❺ Cappella di Sansevero

This private chapel is decorated with some of the best Neapolitan sculptures from the 17th and 18th centuries. It is imbued with the spirit of its decorator, the mysterious alchemist and scientist Prince Raimondo de Sangro (see earlier in this chapter).

Going back to Piazza San Domenico Maggiore and continuing east, you'll find yourself in the:

❻ Piazzetta Nilo

This piazza was named after the Hellenistic Egyptian statue of the Nile that graces one of its corners. Believed in medieval times to depict a mother with her children, the statue was adopted as an image of the city of Naples, hence its name in local parlance—*cuorp'e Napule,* or body of Naples. You'll also find the **Sant'Angelo a Nilo** church here, with its monumental tomb of Cardinal Brancaccio, designed and partly sculpted by **Donatello.**

Continue east to the beginning of Via Biagio dei Librai, named after the bookstores which traditionally have lined this street (and still do). At no. 114 is the:

❼ Cappella del Monte di Pietà

This small chapel is a beautiful example of 16th-century art, while its sacristy and adjoining rooms are in perfectly preserved 18th-century style, down to the very floors and furnishings.

Facing the Cappella, cross to the right onto Vicolo San Severino e San Sossio. On that street is the:

❽ Chiesa di San Severino e San Sossio with Adjoining Monastery and State Archives

San Severnino church—beautifully decorated with 16th-, 17th-, and 18th-century art, is annexed to one of the oldest and richest monasteries of Naples. This is now the seat of the State Archives (access from Piazzetta Grande Archivio; ⓒ **081-563811**), as well as site of some 16th-century cloisters and beautifully frescoed rooms.

Going back to Via San Biagio dei Librai and continuing east, you will see, opening on your left:

❾ Via San Gregorio Armeno

This is one of Naples's most famous streets because of the many craft merchants that line it, specializing in the art of the *presepio* (see "Shopping," below). On this lively street (hide your jewelery and other precious belongings), you'll find the **Church and Convent of San Gregorio Armeno** to your left, with its stunningly preserved cloister and artwork.

At the end of Via San Gregorio Armeno, turn right onto:

❿ Piazza San Gaetano

This piazza is home to two of Naples's major churches, **San Lorenzo Maggiore** and **San Paolo Maggiore,** both rich in art and history. In San Lorenzo Maggiore, you can descend into an archaeological excavation going back to the Greek layer of town, ancient Neapolis.

CAFFETTERIA PASTICCERIA GELATERIA G. MAZZARO
For a snack or a great gelato, head to the **Caffetteria Pasticceria Gelateria G. Mazzaro** (Palazzo Spinelli, Via Tribunali 359; ⓒ 081-459248; www.pasticceriamazzaro.it).

If you're hankering for something more substantial, head to **Pizzeria Di Matteo** (Via dei Tribunali 94; ⓒ 081-455262) for its excellent pizza.

① Piazza del Gesù
② Complesso Monumentale
   di Santa Chiara
③ Palazzo Filomarino
④ Piazza San Domenico
   Maggiore
🍴 Pasticceria Scaturchio
⑤ Cappella Sansevero
⑥ Piazzetta Nilo
⑦ Cappella del
   Monte di Pietà
⑧ Chiesa di San Severino
   e San Sossio
⑨ Via San Gregorio Armeno
⑩ Piazza San Gaetano
☕ Pasticceria G. Mazzaro &
   Pizzeria Di Matteo
⑪ Chiesa and Quadreria
   dei Girolamini
⑫ Duomo

Further on Via dei Tribunali, Piazza dei Giro-lamini opens to your left. Here is the:

⑪ Chiesa and Quadreria dei Girolamini

These hold a treasure trove of artwork by great artists, including Luca Giordano, Pitro da Cortona, Francesco Solimena, Guido Reni, and the Cavalier d'Arpino.

Continue on Via dei Tribunali until you reach Via del Duomo. Make a left to the:

⑫ Duomo

Monumental in scope, this church actually houses two other churches, the paleochristian **Santa Restituta** and the 17th-century **Real Cappella del Tesoro di San Gennaro,** considered the most richly decorated chapel in Naples.

6 Shopping for Local Crafts

The best buys in Naples are Italian designer clothes and accessories, and antiques and crafts. Although you have to be careful—Naples is where fakes were invented, after all, back in the 17th or 18th century—you should be perfectly safe in the reputable shops that are listed here. **Chiaia** is where to go for the big names of **Italian fashion,** such as Valentino, Versace, Ferragamo, Prada, and local designer **Marinella** (Via Riviera di Chiaia 287; ✆ **081-7644214**), famous for classic and colorful ties. Nearby, you'll find some of the most reputable **antiques** dealers, such as **Regency House** (Via D. Morelli

The *Presepio*

Although the tradition of nativity scenes—called *presepio* in Italy—dates back to the 13th century, the art form really reached its peak in the 18th and 19th centuries when the aristocracy competed to acquire figurines for their mangers, modeled by the famous sculptors of the time. Nativity artists produced the terra-cotta parts (usually the head and limbs) that were then mounted on a mannequin of wire and *stoppa* (fiber), and richly dressed with precious silk clothes embroidered with gold. These figures represented popular characters and scenes, to the extent that they created somewhat faithful "pictures" of society at the time. These skilled artists-artisans were sculptors, goldsmiths, tailors, and scenographers, who created everything from the figures to the complicated settings—grottoes, buildings, rivers, and ponds—combining their crafts into the first examples of multimedia art.

The *presepio* tradition is still alive today, and Neapolitan mangers continue to go beyond typical nativity representations to depict current historical and political happenings. Among the figures you'll find on sale are such recognizable characters as Lady Diana, Mother Teresa of Calcutta, and even Versace. **Via San Gregorio Armeno** near the Duomo is where most of the historic workshops are located; the few artisans who have carried on their crafts from father to son have organized into a guild that protects their traditions. In the shops along this street, you'll find everything from characters to rocks, to grottoes, to miniature street lamps, and so on. At the back of the few authentic laboratories, you'll also find figurines carefully crafted in different sizes, from amazingly precise half-inch miniatures, to life-sized figures, to realistic sceneries. Unfortunately, this artistry doesn't come cheaply. Though a manger makes for a great souvenir, few customers can afford the real thing: A medium-sized hand-painted and -crafted terra-cotta shepherd can cost as much as 300€ ($375).

36; ⓒ **081-7643640**) and **Navarra** (Piazza dei Martiri; ⓒ **081-7643595**). Every third Saturday and Sunday of each month from 8am to 2pm (except in Aug), **Fiera Antiquaria,** or Antique Fair, ⓒ **081-621951**) is held in the Villa Comunale di Napoli on Viale Dohrn.

Opening hours for stores are generally Monday to Saturday from 10:30am to 1pm and from 4 to 7:30pm.

For more casual shopping and some specialty stores, try strolling popular **Via Toledo.** Here you will find the historical chocolate factory **Gay-Odin** (Via Toledo 214 and Via Toledo 427). You'll also find the elegant shops of the **Galleria Umberto I,** such as **Ascione 1855** (ⓒ **081-421111**) and its **cameo** workshop, where you can witness the delicate carving of agate and coral.

For crafts, the best place to shop is the *centro antico* ⟨⟨, where you'll find *presepio* workshops lining Via San Gregorio Armeno. The most reputable workshops are **Gambardella Pastori** (Via San Gregorio Armeno 40; ⓒ **081-5517107**) and **Giuseppe Ferrigno** (Via San Gregorio Armeno 8; ⓒ **081-5523148**).

The *centro antico* is also famous for its bookstores. Via San Biagio dei Librai, in particular, is lined with interesting shops. For antique prints and books, head to **Libreria Colonnese** (Via San Pietro a Majella 32; ✆ 081-459858).

7 Naples After Dark

A warm southern city, Naples is best experienced outdoors. Neapolitans know this, and they enjoy spending their evenings on the terraces of the city's many popular cafes. One of the best is **Gran Caffè Gambrinus** (Via Chiaia 1, in Piazza Trento e Trieste; ✆ 081-417582 or 081-414133). The oldest cafe in Naples, its original Liberty interior was decorated by Antonio Curri in the 1860s. Another very popular spot is **La Caffetteria** (Piazza dei Martiri 25; ✆ 081-7644243), frequented by the most elegant bourgeois of Naples who like to come here for evening aperitifs.

OPERA   **Teatro San Carlo** (Via San Carlo 98/f; ✆ 081-7972412 or 081-7972331; fax 081-400902; www.teatrosancarlo.it) is a world-class venue with a consistently high-level program. Performances take place Tuesday through Sunday, December through June. Tickets run between 45€ and 100€ ($56–$125); you'll get a 20% discount with an Artecard (p. 87).

Another great historic theater is **Teatro Mercadante** (Piazza Municipio 1; ✆ 081-5513396), which reopened recently with a prestigious program. Tickets are around 50€ ($63), depending on the performance; you'll get a 10% discount with an Artecard.

Another good venue for a musical evening is the **Centro di Musica Antica Pietà dei Turchini** (Via Santa Caterina da Siena 38; ✆ 081-402395; www.turchini.it). Ticket prices depend on the performance, with a 25% discount granted if you have an Artecard. The ticket prices at **Associazione Alessandro Scarlatti** (Piazza dei Martiri 58; ✆ 081-406011) also depend on the performance, with a 20% discount given to those with an Artecard (p. 87). For immersion in Neapolitan traditional music, try the **Trianon, Teatro della Canzone Napoletana** (Piazza Vincenzo Calenda 9; ✆ 081-2258285). Once again, ticket prices depend on the performance; you get a 10% discount with the Artecard.

BARS, DISCOS & CLUBS   Naples is a port, a cosmopolitan city, and a university town all in one, so its lively nighttime scene is not surprisingly eclectic and has something that will appeal to all tastes. Trendy bars and cafes stay open until the wee hours (at least until 2am) every day of the week, while clubs stay open even later—usually until 4 or 5am—but often only from Thursday to Saturday. While bars and cafes usually don't charge covers, club entrance costs around 14€ ($17).

The **roof bar** of the **Starhotel Terminus** (Piazza Garibaldi 91; ✆ 081-7793111) is a popular scene for Neapolitan socialites. Other good places to grab a drink range from quiet **Berevino** (Via Sebastiano 62; ✆ 081-290313), a popular *enoteca* (wine bar); to **Conoco Club** (Via Nilo 33; ✆ 081-5517784), a pub with a good beer selection and a relaxed atmosphere; to the sleek and exotic recently re-opened **Miami Bar Club** (Via Morghen 68C; ✆ 081-2298332).

For jazz, head to **Riot** (Via San Biagio 38; ✆ 081-5523231), which has a young ambience; for live Neapolitan bands, check out **Vibes Café** (Via San Giovanni Maggiore Pignatelli 10; ✆ 081-5513984), where you can dance inside or outside on the terrace in summer. Another good place for live music is **Il Re Nudo** (Via Manzoni 126; ✆ 081-7146272), where you can hear anything from jazz to South American groups.

An elegant nightclub worth checking out is **Chez Moi** (Via del Parco Margherita 13; © 081-407526) in the Riviera di Chiaia. Nearby **La Mela** (Via dei Mille; © 081-4010270) is not bad either; neither is **Tongue** (Via Manzoni 202; © 081-7690888) in Posillipo, a club with a good mix of gays and lesbians as well as a straight clientele.

For a more specifically gay spot, head for **Bar B** (Via Giovanni Manna, off Via Duomo; © 081-287681), a famous gay sauna—with Turkish and Finnish spas on three levels and with two bars and five dark rooms—that turns into a disco on Thursday and Saturday nights; music ranges from Latin to techno.

8 Vesuvius, an Easy Excursion from Naples

This dangerous volcano—it has demonstrated its destructive capacity more than once—is the sort of volcano that blows its top when erupting, Mount St. Helens style, instead of quietly oozing out lava, like the volcano on the Big Island of Hawaii. Dangerous as Vesuvius might be, though, people continue to live on its fertile slopes, as they have since antiquity (and since the last eruption in 1944). The most recent signs of activity were in 1999—some puffs of smoke, just to keep everybody on their toes.

Named Vesvinum or Vesuvinum after its vineyards, which were famous for their excellent wine even centuries ago, Vesuvius surprised everybody when it erupted in A.D. 79, since apparently nobody at that time knew it was an active volcano. Eruptions followed in 202, 472, 512, 1139, and 1306, but then a long period of quiet tricked everybody—until a 1631 eruption caused great destruction again. Other eruptions were in 1794 (nicely timed for Goethe's visit; a guide hauled him up through the poisonous smoke to look into the crater), 1871, 1906, and 1944.

GETTING THERE

You can get to Vesuvius by public transportation through **Circumvesuviana Railway** (© 800-053939; www.vesuviana.it), which leaves from Stazione Circumvesuviana (Corso Garibaldi, off Piazza Garibaldi; Metro: Garibaldi). A shuttle departs for the Mount Vesuvius park outside Ercolano Station, a 15-minute trip from Naples; the fare is 1.50€ ($1.90).

A good alternative is a guided tour from Naples (see earlier in this chapter), or a limousine service. Good choices are **ANA Limousine Service** (Piazza Garibaldi 73; ©/fax 081-282000) and **Italy Limousine** (© 081-8016184, 335-6732245, or 338-9681866; www.italylimousine.it). **Note:** All transportation gets you only as far as the park entrance at 1,017m (3,106 ft.) in altitude; you will have to climb an additional 264m (838 ft.) to reach the top at 1,281m (3,944 ft.) above sea level. Should you decide to descend into the crater with a guide, you'll have to arrange an additional hike.

WHAT TO SEE & DO

The only Continental volcano still active in Europe, Mount Vesuvius is enclosed within **Parco Nazionale del Vesuvio** (Mt. Vesuvius National Park). At 608m (1,994 ft.) is the **Observatory** (© 081-6108483; www.ov.ingv.it)—the oldest and one of the best volcano centers in the world. Established in 1841, it monitors Mount Vesuvius's activity and serves as a research center. You can visit its rich scientific library and its **Geological Museum** ⟨ (Via Osservatorio 14; © 081-6108483), which hold a vast collection of minerals and historical scientific instruments from the 18th century onwards.

Farther up at 1,017m (3,106 ft.) is the entrance to the park, with the **Centro Visite (Visitor Center;** C 081-7775720, 081-7391123, or 033-7942249), where you can sign up for a guided tour taking place daily from 10am to sunset. At the historical *osteria* you can have a bite to eat or a drink—including the famous local wine, Lacrima Christi, made from the vineyards on Mount Vesuvius. You can buy local products at a small shop. To reach the crater, you take the dirt trail that continues (over lava!) to the top. Descending into the **crater** ⍟, though, is possible only with a guide. You can arrange a trip at the visitor center or with the nonprofit organization **La Porta del Vesuvio** (C 081-274200; www.laportadelvesuvio.it; 9am–1:30pm). They organize a variety of tours of the volcano, from nature trails along the slopes, to scenic night tours (!) inside the crater.

Admission to the park is 4.50€ ($5.65); a guided tour to the crater costs 3€ ($3.75). The park is open daily from 9am until sunset; last admission is 1 hour before closing.

9 Pozzuoli ⍟⍟

18km (11 miles) W of Naples

Phlegrean Fields, the peninsula that surrounds the Gulf of Naples to the west, is a land of hills, craters, lagoons, and tarns. As a result, it boasts fantastic landscapes. Named the "burning fields" because of its active sulfur springs and boiling mud craters, the area was officially established as a national park in 1993. Because of its many warm and hot springs, its fertile soil, and good harbors on the coast, this was an important area during Greek and Roman times, as shown by the numerous ruins and remains that have been excavated in the area. The land's instability—eruptions as well as cyclical surging and subsiding of the land level—has created a varying coastline and caused the abandonment of inhabited areas, but it has also preserved entire ancient Roman neighborhoods. Highlights here are Pozzuoli, with its amphitheater and temples, Baia with its submerged Roman city, and Cuma with its Sybilla Cave.

Since Pozzuoli is just a few kilometers from Naples, you'd expect it to be downright suburban, but Pozzuoli is very much a town bustling with a life of its own—even though many of its residents commute to Naples for work every day. The town boasts sweeping views over the sea and the islands of Ischia and Procida on one side, and the island of Nisita (today linked to land) on the other. Rich in monuments from its antique past, Pozzuoli is also at the heart of the Phlegrean Fields, a beautiful national park replete with volcanic phenomena.

ESSENTIALS

GETTING THERE   Pozzuoli has become just another neighborhood of Naples and it is well connected by public transportation (see "Getting Around" at the beginning of this chapter). City bus no. 152, which starts in Piazza Garibaldi, near the Stazione Centrale, passes through the neighborhoods of Santa Lucia and Chiaia following the shoreline and ends its run in the center of Pozzuoli. It's slow, but very scenic. The Metro (line 2) is faster, and also ends in Pozzuoli.

Yet another possibility is the **Cumana Railroad** (C 800-001616); operating every 10 minutes between Piazza Montesanto in Chiaia and the Phlegrean Fields, from dawn till 9:20pm, it makes a stop in Pozzuoli.

Piazza della Repubblica in Pozzuoli is the departure point for the **ArcheoBus** (see box below), a dedicated bus for the various park sites, operating Friday to Sunday 9am to 7pm (ticket included in the Artecard). The ArcheoBus also stops by the Metro.

If you need a taxi, you'll find one in Piazza della Repubblica (© **081-5265800**).

WHAT TO SEE & DO

This lively small town was once the Greek colony of Dicearchia, founded in 530 B.C.; it then became the Roman Puteoli in 194 B.C., an important Roman harbor favored by the Roman emperors over Partenope (Naples), which had maintained closer allegiance to Greece. The town was destroyed by the barbarian Alaric in A.D. 410, but the acropolis, on a tufa stone promontory overlooking the sea, continued to be inhabited, and a new town slowly developed around it.

Rione Terra ☞   This is the original **Acropolis** and the oldest inhabited area of Pozzuoli. Located near the harbor, it has been progressively subsiding under the sea, so much so that it had to be abandoned in the 1970s. A large, ongoing excavation campaign begun in 1993 has uncovered a virtually untouched Roman town, sort of an underground Pompeii. The site is now open to the public. The tour, by advance reservation only, takes you along the streets of the town as it looked in 194 B.C. You'll proceed along the main *Decumano* (the central avenue running east-west) and some minor streets, where you'll discover shops, *osterie* (taverns), and a *pistrinum* (mill) along the way. Sculptures and other important objects from this site are on display in the Museo Archeologico dei Campi Felgrei in Baia. Since 2004, visitors have been allowed to tour the underground confines of the Palazzo Migliaresi. Seat of the town hall, it contains *ergastula* (slaves' cells), one of which still contains drawings by prisoners.

Largo Sedile di Porta, Pozzuoli. © **848-800288** or 063-9967050. www.pierreci.it. Admission 3€ ($3.75) plus .50€ (65¢) for reservation by phone, or 1.50€ ($1.90) online; children under 6 free. Cumulative ticket includes Museo Archeologico and Zona Archeologica in Baia; Anfiteatro Flavio and Serapeo in Pozzuoli; and Scavi di Cuma; plus Rione Terra; ticket valid 2 days 5.50€ ($6.90). Guided tours (45 min.) 3.50€ ($4.40). Sat–Sun 9am–7pm; ticket booth closes 30 min. before general closing.

Serapeo, aka Tempio di Serapide ☞   Named after the Egyptian god Serapis because of the statue found here during its excavation, this was not a temple at all but the town market, or *macellum* in Latin. The large porticoed structure, of which you can still see the perimeter—lined with ancient Roman shops and taverns—was built in the 1st century A.D. At its center are the remains of a temple, whose alabaster columns were used to decorate the Royal Palace in Caserta (see chapter 9). Interestingly, this ruin has been used to study the volcanic phenomenon called *bradisism* (alternated periods of subsiding and surging of the ground's level), which is typical of this area—you can still see little holes in the marble of the columns where they were submerged in water.

The ArcheoBus Flegreo

A great initiative, this bus was designed to serve the archaeological area and natural park of Phlegrean Fields. Operating between Piazza della Repubblica in Pozzuoli and the archaeological area of Cuma, it makes 16 stops along a loop convenient to all the points of interest of the park. Departures are every hour between 9am and 7pm from Pozzuoli, and the whole loop takes 90 minutes. The fare (8€/$10) is included in the Artecard (p. 87). At presstime the service was offered only Friday to Sunday, and it was not certain whether the schedule would remain the same throughout the year. Contact **SEPSA** (© **800-001616** toll-free within Italy; www.sepsa.it) for current information.

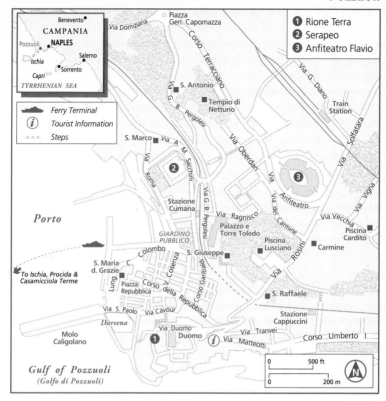

CAMPANIA
Benevento
Pozzuoli **NAPLES**
Ischia Salerno
Sorrento
Capri
TYRRHENIAN SEA

Ferry Terminal
(i) Tourist Information
Steps

❶ Rione Terra
❷ Serapeo
❸ Anfiteatro Flavio

Piazza Gen. Capomazza
Via Domiziana
Corso Terracciano
S. Antonio
Tempio di Nettuno
Via G. B. Pergolesi
S. Marco
Via A. M. Sacchini
Via Roma
❷
Via G. B. Pergolesi
Stazione Cumana
Via Ragnisco
Palazzo e Torre Toledo
Piscina Lusciano
Via del Carmine
Via Anfiteatro
❸
Via Oberdan
Via G. Diano
Train Station
Via Solfatara
Via Vecchia
Via Vigna
Piscina Cardito
Carmine
Via Rosini

Porto

GIARDINO PUBBLICO
Colombo
S. Maria d. Grazie
Lung.
Cosenza
S. Giuseppe
Piazza Repubblica
Corso della Repubblica
Corso Garibaldi
Via S. Paolo
Via Cavour
Darsena
Molo Caligolano
Via Duomo
Duomo
❶
(i) Via Matteotti
Via Tranvei
S. Raffaele
Stazione Cappuccini
Corso Umberto I

To Ischia, Procida & Casamicciola Terme

Gulf of Pozzuoli
(Golfo di Pozzuoli)

0 — 500 ft
0 — 200 m
N

Via Roma 10. ✆ 081-5266007. 4€ ($5); includes admission to Anfiteatro Flavio in Pozzuoli, Museo Archeologico and Zona Archeologica in Baia, and Scavi di Cuma. Daily 9am to 1 hr. before sunset; last entrance 1 hr. before closing time. Closed Jan 1, May 1, Dec 25.

Anfiteatro Flavio ⚑ Located in the upper part of town, where the roads to Cuma, Pozzuoli, and Naples met in Roman times, the Anfiteatro Flavio was the third largest amphitheater after the Colosseo and the amphitheater of Capua. Built by Vespasian, it is a grandiose sight, especially because of the perfect conservation of the walls and the vaulted ceilings under the arena. The theater, which could accommodate more than 20,000 spectators, is still used today for special musical events during the festival **Notti Flavie** (call ✆ **081-7611221** or 081-5261481 for the program).

Via Terracciano 75, Pozzuoli. ✆ **081-5266007.** Admission 4€ ($5); includes admission to Serapeo in Pozzuoli, Museo Archeologico and Zona Archeologica di Baia, and Scavi di Cuma. Daily 9am to 1 hr. before sunset; last entrance 1 hr. before closing time. Closed Jan 1, May 1, Dec 25.

Solfatara ⚑ Just outside Pozzuoli—but a 20-minute walk uphill—this large crater is the epicenter of the Phlegrean Fields' volcanic area. An important spa in the 19th century, today it attracts visitors who admire the impressive **volcanic phenomena:** bubbling hot mud, sulfurous hot water, and steam issuing from cracks in the soil. If you don't have time to visit all of Phlegrean Fields (see below), this is the one not-to-be-missed spot.

Via Solfatara 161, Pozzuoli. ℭ 081-5262341. www.solfatara.it. Admission 5.50€ ($6.90); 20% discount with Arte-card; children under 4 free. Daily 8:30am–7pm.

10 Baia & the National Park of Phlegrean Fields ⋆⋆

25km (15 miles) W of Naples

This gorgeous area mixes natural beauty and archaeological attractions with pictur-esque harbor towns. Resting on the coastal stretch that closes the Bay of Pozzuoli to the west, you'll find the picturesque fishing town of **Baia**—built over the Roman Baiae; the little town of **Bacoli**, over the ancient Roman town of Bauli; and, farther on, **Miseno** with its small harbor (once a crater), culminating with the promontory of **Capo Miseno.** Higher up inland is the ancient Greek colony of **Cuma** ⋆⋆, overlook-ing the sea on the two sides of the promontory, and interspersed with volcanic lakes.

GETTING THERE

If you are arriving in the area from Friday to Sunday, the easiest mode of transport is the **ArcheoBus** (p. 110), from Piazza della Repubblica in **Pozzuoli** (p. 109); this bus makes four stops in Baia and two in Bacoli and runs every hour from 9am to 7pm. (Tickets are included in the Artecard.)

During the rest of the week, we recommend using a taxi (same rates as in Naples; see "Getting Around" at the beginning of this chapter) to avoid cumbersome switches from the Metro to local buses. You'll find a taxi stand in Piazza della Repubblica in Poz-zuoli (ℭ 081-5265800), and another in Via Scarfoglio in Agnano (ℭ 081-5704162). Yet another is located at Piazzetta Centrale in Bacoli (ℭ 081-5235300). You can also take the Cumana train from Piazza Montesanto in Chiaia to the Lucrino stop, and there switch to the **SEPSA** (ℭ 800-001616 or 081-7354311; www.sepsa.it) coach line Lucrino-Torregaveta; get off at the Castello di Baia stop. Alternatively, SEPSA operates a coach from the Circumvesuviana Station on Corso Garibaldi in Naples; take the line called Monte di Procida/Torregaveta to the Castello di Baia stop.

THE NATIONAL PARK OF THE PHLEGREAN FIELDS ⋆⋆

This large volcanic area comprises several lakes, most with brackish waters, which also bear many remains from Roman and Greek times. The most famous is **Lake Averno,** near **Arco Felice**—an immense engineering feat realized under Emperor Domitian, when the mountain was cut and a viaduct was built for the passage of the Domitian Road. Both the arch and the Roman road below it are still visible.

Described by Virgil in the *Aeneid* as the entrance to the underworld, Lake Averno takes its name from the Greek phrase meaning "no birds," most likely because the area's volcanic vapors kept the animals at bay. The Romans decided to exploit the dan-gerous outpost for defense purposes: In 37 B.C., Marco Agrippa connected it to nearby Lucrino Lagoon and used it as a shipyard. Apparently, the Romans also used the area for play—on its eastern shore you'll find the remains of the great thermal baths known as **Tempio di Apollo.**

The largest of the volcanic lakes here is **Lake Fusaro** ⋆, farther south. Lake Fusaro was called *Acherusia Palus,* infernal swamp, by the ancients. In 1782, quite indifferent to the ancients' beliefs, Ferdinando IV Bourbon had the architect Carlo Vanvitelli (son of the famous Luigi) build a hunting and fishing lodge on a little island in the lake: **Casina Reale** ⋆. The elegant construction (today connected by a footbridge to the shore) boasts stunning views (Via Fusaro, Bacoli; ℭ 081-8687080; Sat–Sun 9am–1pm).

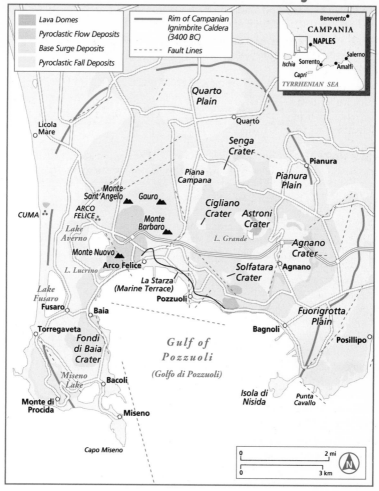

The following labels appear on the map:

Lava Domes
Pyroclastic Flow Deposits
Base Surge Deposits
Pyroclastic Fall Deposits

Rim of Campanian Ignimbrite Caldera (3400 BC)
Fault Lines

CAMPANIA
NAPLES
Benevento
Salerno
Ischia Sorrento Amalfi
Capri
TYRRHENIAN SEA

Quarto Plain
Licola Mare
Quarto
Senga Crater
Pianura
Piana Campana
Pianura Plain
Monte Sant'Angelo Gauro
Cigliano Crater
Astroni Crater
ARCO FELICE
CUMA
Monte Barbaro
L. Grande
Agnano Crater
Lake Averno
Monte Nuovo
Arco Felice
Solfatara Crater Agnano
L. Lucrino
La Starza (Marine Terrace)
Lake Fusaro
Pozzuoli
Fusaro
Baia
Fuorigrotta Plain
Torregaveta
Fondi di Baia Crater
Gulf of Pozzuoli
(Golfo di Pozzuoli)
Bagnoli
Posillipo
Miseno Lake
Bacoli
Monte di Procida
Miseno
Isola di Nisida
Punta Cavallo
Capo Miseno

0   2 mi
0   3 km
N

BAIA

Modern Baia is a lively fishing town built around a small harbor, where many of the ruins of Roman Baiae can still be seen. Indeed, the Roman town is in large part submerged under a few feet of water due to *bradisism,* a local geological phenomenon involving large patches of land that subside beneath the sea, only to resurface. The unsubmerged part here is rich enough to satisfy those who don't want to venture into the local waters.

Museo Archeologico dei Campi Flegrei ✮   This museum is housed in the scenic **Castello Aragonese,** built on a promontory over Baia in 1442 by Alfonso d'Aragona. Of the three sections of the museum, one holds artifacts from the excavations of **Baia** and **Miseno,** such as the **Sacello degli Augustali** and the famous **Complex of**

the **Ninfeo di Punta Epitaffio** (a ninfeo is a Roman kind of loggia or enclosed porch with columns) at the east end of Baia's bay. Another section displays a Roman collection of **plaster cast** fragments depicting the most celebrated Greek masterpieces. A third section on the upper floor holds the reconstruction of the **Ninfeo of the Emperor Claudius.**

The beautiful Castle Aragonese is worth seeing even if you are not interested in the museum's rich archaeological collections.

Via Castello 39, inside Castello Aragonese, Baia. ℭ 081-5233797 or 848-8002884. Admission 4€ ($5); includes admission to Anfiteatro Flavio and Serapeo in Pozzuoli, Zona Archeologica in Baia, and Scavi di Cuma. Tues–Sun 9am–8pm; ticket booth til 1 hr. before closing. Closed Jan 1, May 1, Dec 25.

Parco Archeologico Subacqueo di Baia ℛ   The elegant, ancient Roman summer resort of Baia, the Parco Archeologico has subsided several feet over the centuries and is now underwater. The submerged archeological area has been excavated and in places roped off and labeled for underwater visitors. Guided scuba tours are offered during summer and fall by the park; 35€ ($44) covers basic expenses including admission, insurance, boat, basic equipment, and use of the facilities onshore. The park can also be visited from above the water using the park's glass-bottomed boat for 35€ ($44); lunch is an additional 15€ ($19). Whichever way you choose to visit the site, exploring the ancient town's streets and the interiors of its beautiful villas should prove to be an eerie and magical experience.

Diving centers in the area are also authorized to guide scuba divers through the park; you can rent equipment as well from **Blue Point** (ℭ 081-8704444) and from **Cardone Sub** (ℭ 081-8706886). To rent a boat, contact **Associazione Barcaioli di Baia** (ℭ 081-8701222). If instead you'd like an organized boat excursion, try **Peppe Navigazione del Golfo** (ℭ 333-8877883) or the ferry company **Alilauro** (www. alilauro.it; ℭ 081-7611004 or 081-4972293). All the above companies are along the dock in the harbor.

Porticciolo di Baia. ℭ 081-5248169. www.baiasommersa.it. Admission 10€ ($13), plus 25€ ($31) for equipment, changing room, and boat; 20% discount on admission and 10% on scuba equipment rentals at the park with Arte-card. Mid-Mar to mid-Nov Tues–Sun 9:30am–1:30pm and 3:30–7:30pm.

Parco Archeologico Terme di Baia ℛℛ   The most celebrated of Roman baths, both for their therapeutic properties and their scenery, these were used by the VIPs of ancient Rome. Built by Emperor Ottaviano between 27 B.C. and A.D. 14, the baths took advantage of local, naturally occurring hot springs. Because the ground has subsided here, the original conditions no longer exist and there is little water left in the baths; still, incredible feats of **hydraulic engineering** remain for us to see. Connected to the Terme by a **footpath** is Parco Monumentale (see below); the short hike there is very pleasant but is best made downhill, starting from Parco Monumentale and proceeding down to the Terme.

Via Sella di Baia 22, Baia. ℭ 081-8687592. Admission 4€ ($5); includes admission to Anfiteatro Flavio and Serapeo in Pozzuoli, Museo Archeologico in Baia, and Scavi di Cuma. Tues–Sun 9am to 1 hr. before sunset; last entrance 1 hr. before closing time. Closed Jan 1, May 1, Dec 25.

Parco Monumentale ℛ   Excavations are ongoing in this large area covering 14 hectares (34 acres) of "historical landscape," where you can take a walk among the ruins of **imperial residences** and **elegant villas.** If you already have a ticket for the Parco Archeologico, you can descend the **footpath** ℛ connecting this park to the Parco Archeologico Terme di Baia (see above). The path starts from the **Esedra,** the

park's main square, and descends along the hill, providing beautiful views over the craters and the bay.

Via Bellavista, Baia. ⓒ 081-5233797. Free admission. Daily 9am to 1 hr. before sunset; last entrance 1 hr. before closing time. Closed Jan 1, May 1, Dec 25.

Scavi di Cuma ⓡⓡ   Founded in the 8th century B.C. as the first Greek colony in the western Mediterranean, the city of Cuma grew to be the coast's most important, eclipsing the nearby later Greek colony of Neapolis (today's Naples). It kept the Romans at bay for many years before being overtaken (see appendix A). Today, you can view the following remains of this great city: the **Acropolis,** part of the **fortified walls,** the **North Necropolis,** an **amphitheater** dating from the late 2nd century B.C. and the mysterious **Antro della Sibilla (Sybilla's Cave)** ⓡ. This huge tunnel, which was excavated through the mountain down toward the nearby lake, was probably built for defensive purposes. Some of the internal halls are decorated; these led to the legend that the Sybilla—the famous priestess of the god Apollo—received her postulants here, hence the tunnel's name. From the terrace outside the cave, a splendid **view** ⓡⓡ overlooks the harbor of Cuma. The Greek **Temple of Apollo** and **Temple of Giove** on the Acropolis—preserved only because they were transformed into churches in the Middle Ages—function as mirrors of the many cultures that came to this area after the Greeks, as they bear details from Sannites, Romans, and paleochristian users.

To get here when the **ArcheoBus** (p. 110) doesn't run, you can take a taxi from Pozzuoli, Bacoli, or Agnano (see "Getting There," earlier in this section). Public transportation is a bit more cumbersome; from the Fusaro stop on the Cumana Railroad, you'll have to switch to the **SEPSA** (ⓒ **800-001616** or 081-7354311; www.sepsa.it) coach line Miseno-Cuma and get down to the excavations.

Via Monte di Cuma 3, Pozzuoli. ⓒ 081-8543060. Admission 4€ ($5) includes admission to Anfiteatro Flavio and Serapeo in Pozzuoli, and Museo Archeologico and Zona Archeologica in Baia. Daily 9am to 1 hr. before sunset; last entrance 1 hr. before closing time. Closed Jan 1, May 1, and Dec 25.

TWO GOOD HOTELS IN THE AREA

Cala Moresca ⓡ   Picturesquely situated on Capo Miseno, this pleasant and welcoming hotel offers comfortable accommodations and lots of extras. Surrounded by a huge park, it has a rocky beach, a swimming pool, and outdoor activities such as tennis, squash, a playground, and a country trail. Guest rooms are large and bright; private balconies afford beautiful views.

Via Faro, 44 80070 Bacoli. ⓒ 081-5235595. Fax 081-5235557. www.calamoresca.it. 27 units. 135€ ($169); low season 115€ ($144). Rates include buffet breakfast. Children under 3 stay free in parent's room. AE, DC, MC, V. Free parking. Closed Dec 24–26. **Amenities:** Restaurant; bar; outdoor pool; outdoor tennis courts; basketball and squash courts; business center; room service; babysitting; laundry service. *In room:* A/C, TV, minibar, hair dryer, safe.

Santa Marta   This more moderately priced hotel offers excellent management, simple accommodations, and an ideal location near Arco Felice and the sea. The large and well-appointed units are pleasantly furnished with modern quality furniture, tiled floors, and good-sized bathrooms.

Via Licola Patria 28, 80072 Pozzuoli. ⓒ 081-8042404. Fax 081-8042406. www.santamartahotel.com. 35 units. 80€ ($100) double; 110€ ($138) triple; 130€ ($163) quad. Rates include buffet breakfast. Children under 3 stay free in parent's room. AE, DC, MC, V. Free parking. **Amenities:** Restaurant; bar; business center; babysitting; room service. *In room:* A/C, TV, minibar, hair dryer, safe.

WHERE TO DINE
Expensive
Misenetta ⭐ NEAPOLITAN   With upscale decor and food, and a lakeside location, this restaurant is perfect for a romantic dinner. The menu here is based on seafood, but you can get meat and vegetarian choices. Two standout dishes are *polpi in cassuola* (casserole of squid in a tomato-based sauce) and the more elaborate *ravioli di astice* (lobster ravioli). Superior desserts and a good wine list round out the meal.

Via Lungolago 2, Bacoli. ℂ 081-5234169. Reservations recommended on evenings and weekends. Secondi 18€–35€ ($23–$44). AE, DC, MC, V. Tues–Sun noon–3pm and 7–11pm.

Moderate
Garibaldi NEAPOLITAN   This seaside place makes for an excellent stop after a visit to the museum or the archaeological area of Baia. It takes advantage of its prime location by specializing in fish—simply prepared, but using fresh ingredients and traditional recipes. *Fusilli ai frutti di mare* (short pasta with seafood) is a perfect way to begin the meal, but you shouldn't miss out on the secondi: excellent *polpi in guazzetto* (squid in a tomato sauce), as well as some of the most flavorful grilled fish in the area.

Via Spiaggia 36, Bacoli. ℂ 081-52343. Reservations recommended on weekends. Secondi 8€–16€ ($10–$20). AE, DC, MC, V. Tues–Sun noon–3pm and 7–11pm.

Vecchio Ulivo ⭐ CAMPANIAN   This is a good choice if you want a romantic dinner without maxing out your credit card. The cuisine is traditional but prepared with a light hand and with delicious, fresh ingredients. The menu changes with market offerings, but you might find such hearty meals as *lasagne di pesce* (seafood lasagna) and *zuppa di pesce* (seafood stew).

Via Cupa della Fescina 35, Pozzuoli. ℂ 081-5241180. Reservations recommended. Secondi 11€–14€ ($14–$18). AE, DC, MC, V. Mon–Sat 7:30–11pm.

Inexpensive
Arturo al Fusaro ⭐ *(Finds)* NEAPOLITAN   This excellent restaurant offers traditional local cuisine in a pleasant decor, and at reasonable prices. The specialty is seafood, which is extremely fresh and served in a variety of ways, from appetizers, to pasta and rice dishes, to main courses. You might want to sample flawless *risotto ai frutti di mare* (seafood risotto); *vermicelli cozze e vongole* (thin spaghetti with mussels and clams); or one of the catches of the day prepared *all'acqua pazza* (in light herbed broth), grilled with herbs, or baked over a bed of potatoes.

Via Cuma 322, Bacoli. ℂ 081-8543130. Reservations recommended on weekends. Secondi 7€–12€ ($8.75–$15). AE, DC, MC, V. Daily noon–3pm and 7–10:30pm.

Cagi Da Ludovico *(Finds)* NEAPOLITAN   Keep this restaurant's address handy when you're in Pozzuoli and are looking for good food at moderate prices. Both seafood and meat, prepared traditionally, are the chef's forte here. *Spaghetti alle vongole* (spaghetti with clams) and *fettina alla pizzaiola* (beef in a tomato and oregano sauce) are particularly good.

Via Nicola Fasano 6, Pozzuoli. ℂ 081-5268255. Reservations recommended on weekends. Secondi 6€–12€ ($7.50–$15). AE, DC, MC, V. Tues–Sun noon–3pm and Tues–Sat 7:30–11pm.

Il Brontolone ⭐ *(Finds)* NEAPOLITAN   Offering traditional cuisine at moderate prices, Il Brontolone is one of the best restaurants in town. Not suprisingly, considering its location, the specialty is fish—but the menu includes many other choices.

Their *antipasti* buffet is famous for its variety and quality; you could make a meal just out of its dishes. We recommend sampling the entrees, too; there's everything from excellent *linguine all'astice* (linguine with lobster) to any number of wonderful fish dishes (baked with potatoes, grilled, or served *all'acqua pazza*).

Via Campana 121, Pozzuoli. Ⓒ 081-5266510. Reservations recommended on weekends. Secondi 6€–12€ ($7.50–$15). AE, DC, MC, V. Tues–Sun noon–3pm and 7–11pm.

Il Tucano PIZZA   It's a bit touristy, yes, but excellent pizza and traditional specialties make this restaurant worth a visit. The heir of the historical Trattoria Miramare, which existed in this same spot since 1929, Il Tucano serves up a large variety of pizzas—including the exceptional *quattro formaggi e gamberetti* (four cheeses and shrimp). The pizza here is served "by the foot"—you ask for a length, and they cut it and charge you accordingly. The owner has made a real effort to honor the old trattoria's menu of local specialties and to offer a wide selection of local wines.

Via Molo di Baia, Baia. Ⓒ 081-8545046. Reservations not necessary. Pizza 3€–8€ ($3.75–$10; charged by length). MC, V. Tues–Sun noon–midnight.

Taverna Alla Corte della Zia Pazza CAMPANIAN   Inspired by Italian cafes of the 19th century, Zia Pazza aims to create a relaxed atmosphere where diners can sample traditional, local dishes reinterpreted by the chef. The results are always good—sometimes excellent—as were the *risotto alla pescatora* (risotto with seafood) and *fusilli ai frutti di mare* (homemade pasta with seafood).

Pendio San Giuseppe 11, Pozzuoli. Ⓒ 081-3030202. www.allacortedellaziapazza.it. Reservations recommended on weekends. Secondi 6€–12€ ($7.50–$15). AE, DC, MC, V. Daily noon–3pm and 7–11pm.

5

Pompeii & Herculaneum: the Vesuvian Archaeological Area

Mount Vesuvius had been dormant for centuries when the great explosion of A.D. 79 occurred. At the time of the eruption, it seems that nobody knew it was a volcano, and its slopes—famous for the fertile soil and for the vineyards which produced an excellent wine—were heavily inhabited. Many towns and villages, as well as a number of estates, existed in the Vesuvian area, all of which were covered by lava or ashes. After the excavations of Pompeii, archaeologists kept at their work and have unveiled many other interesting sites. Although Pompeii is the most famous, it is hardly the only archaeological site worth a visit in the area. Herculaneum is less visited but more striking, because of how well the houses have withstood the ages. Also rarely visited by foreign tourists is the grandiose Roman

Villa of Oplontis, with its magnificent frescoes—it's a perfect stop if you don't have the taste or the time for a lengthier visit to Roman ruins.

Yet Roman ruins are not all this area has to offer. What attracted the ancient residents long ago remains: its thermal springs, the blue Mediterranean Sea, fertile land, and beautiful coastline. Though most foreign tourists limit their visit to Pompeii, if you take the time to look a bit deeper, you'll find that the Vesuvian area has much more to see—from the villas of Boscoreale and Boscotrecase to the thermal resort of Stabiae. All of the destinations we describe in this chapter make an easy day trip from Naples. You can also choose to stay in the Vesuvian area itself; the best options are Torre del Greco, Pompeii, and our favorite, Castellammare di Stabia.

1 Herculaneum ★★

9.5km (6 miles) SE of Naples

Herculaneum was covered by volcanic mud during the A.D. 79 Mount Vesuvius eruption, which quickly hardened to a semi-rock material. As a result, excavations have been much slower here than at Pompeii, and although the first Herculaneum discovery dates back to 1709, the uncovered area here is much smaller. Also, a large part of the ancient town lies under the modern one, which has slowed down the process further. The findings, though, are stunning, mainly because Herculaneum is thought to have been a glitzy seaside resort for wealthy Romans, and so boasts villas even more elaborate than those of Pompeii.

Although the first excavations started here in the 18th century—unfortunately damaging more often than benefiting the archaeology—research was often abandoned for long periods at a time due to the terrain's difficult access. As a result, little knowledge was gained about the town, and many doubts remain. It is believed that Herculaneum

The Vesuvian Area

was about a third of the size of Pompeii and was mostly a resort town, with little commercial and industrial activity. Researchers also believe that the town has existed since at least the 4th century B.C., and that there were about 5,000 inhabitants at the time of the disaster. Most of these inhabitants are assumed to have been wealthy; excavations have revealed a large number of elegant villas and apartment blocks for poor laborers, with a very small number of homes reserved for middle-class merchants and artisans.

ESSENTIALS

GETTING THERE   You can easily get to the archaeological area of Herculaneum by public transportation using the **Circumvesuviana** railway (© **800-053939** toll-free within Italy; www.vesuviana.it), which leaves from the Stazione Circumvesuviana (Corso Garibaldi, off Piazza Garibaldi; Metro: Garibaldi) to **Ercolano Scavi** (on either line, Sorrento or Poggiomarino) every half-hour; the 20-minute ride to Ercolano costs 1.70€ ($2.10). You can then get a shuttle bus outside the station to the archaeological site.

Driving is also possible, although we do not recommend it: Besides the terrible traffic, you'll encounter parking problems, and this is not quite a safe enough area to leave your car. If you insist, take the busy coastal road SS 18 out of Naples. Alternatively, take the autostrada A3 and exit at the sign for ERCOLANO-PORTICI.

Tips A Warning about Modern Ercolano

The modern town of Ercolano is relatively depressed and not exactly tourist-friendly. The only thing of interest besides the archaeological area is the show-room of a talented artist, a maker of **cameos** named **Biagio Piscopo** (Corso Resina 318; ℂ 081-7322736), conveniently located near the archaeological site. This laboratory has spilled over from the nearby town of Torre del Greco, where the art first developed and where you can buy some of the cameos that made the town famous. If you want to stay overnight, choose Torre del Greco (see below).

A good alternative to driving and public transportation is a guided tour from Naples (see chapter 4, p. 103).

EXPLORING THE ARCHAEOLOGICAL AREA ✸✸✸

Besides the **Artecard** (see box in chapter 4, p. 87), you can purchase a 3-day cumulative ticket including Herculaneum, Pompeii, Oplontis, Stabiae, and Boscoreale, for 18€ ($23).

Herculaneum Archeological Area   The first thing you'll notice about Herculaneum is its small size. This means it's easier to visit than Pompeii and, though it might first appear less impressive because of it small stature, the site's compact nature allows visitors to get a real feeling for the place. Throughout the site, you'll get the eerie feeling that the town was abandoned not long ago, instead of nearly 2,000 years ago. The volcanic mud that enveloped the site has also allowed for the unusual preservation of wood, from building structures to even room furnishings. As a result, you'll find incredibly rich examples of life during Roman times.

Herculaneum is in continuous evolution since the ongoing excavations continuously lead to new discoveries—such as a boat found near the water at Herculaneum in the 1990s, still filled with the corpses of victims caught in frantic postures, trying to get out to sea and safety. Recently, excavations have revealed part of an urban area that stretched from the water to the **Decumanus Maxim or Massimo** (the town's main street), but the rest of the town away from the water remains for the moment inaccessible under the buildings of modern Ercolano.

Some older sites have been recently reopened to the public, such as the **Villa dei Papiri** ✸✸. This grandiose villa—it stretched for over 250m (820 ft.) along the coast—was among the first discovered, back in 1750, and contained a rich cache of papyrus rolls and elegant sculptures, now in the Biblioteca Nazionale Vittorio Emanuele III and the Museo Archeologico Nazionale, both in Naples (see chapter 3). Opened to the public in 2004 after a lengthy restoration, the villa was built in A.D. 60, in a magnificent position on a cliff overlooking the sea, just outside Herculaneum to the west. You can visit the lower and upper floors—over 16 rooms are decorated with rich mosaic floors and frescoes—as well as the interior garden with pool and terrace. Access to the villa is separate from access to the Herculaneum excavations, and visits require an advance reservation (ℂ 081-7390963; www.arethusa.net). Admission is 2€ ($2.50).

Other highlights of a visit include the **Collegio degli Augustali (College of the Augustali),** with its marble floor and wall paintings, as well as the custodian's room—he was found inside the bed on view here. You should also tour the elegantly decorated

My, what an inefficient way to fish.

Ring toss, good. Horseshoes, bad.

Faster! Faster! Faster!

We take care of the fiddly bits, from providing over 43,000 customer reviews of hotels, to helping you find our best fares, to giving you 24/7 customer service. So you can focus on the only thing that matters. Goofing off.

travelocity®
You'll never roam alone.℠

©2005 Travelocity.com LP. All rights reserved. CST# 2056372-50.

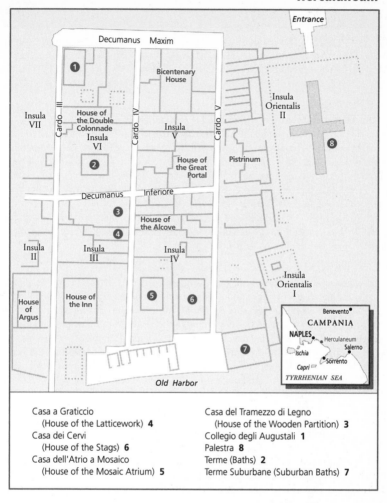

Casa a Graticcio
(House of the Latticework) **4**

Casa dei Cervi
(House of the Stags) **6**

Casa dell'Atrio a Mosaico
(House of the Mosaic Atrium) **5**

Casa del Tramezzo di Legno
(House of the Wooden Partition) **3**

Collegio degli Augustali **1**

Palestra **8**

Terme (Baths) **2**

Terme Suburbane (Suburban Baths) **7**

Thermal Baths and the **Casa del Tramezzo di Legno (House of the Wooden Partition)**, with its perfectly preserved facade. This state of preservation can be credited to the fact that most of the remains were solidly constructed villas used by the wealthy. The **Casa a Graticcio (House of the Latticework)** is particularly fascinating because it's one of the few well-preserved examples of poorer housing. Civic structures are not lacking, however, such as the **Palestra,** a monumental sports arena for competition and training. The **Casa del Mosaico (House of the Mosaic Atrium)** has an annexed shop, still showing the merchandise on the counter and cabinets with goods on the walls. Last, but hardly least, the **Casa dei Cervi (House of the Stags)** is the most elegant ruin in the excavated area, with terraces overlooking the sea and a high level of decoration.

Corso Resina, Ercolano. ⓒ **081-8575347**. www.pompeiisites.org. Guided tours reservations daily 10am–1:30pm 10€ ($13). Daily Nov–Mar 8:30am–5pm; Apr–Oct 8:30am–7:30pm. Last entrance 90 min. before closing.

2 Torre del Greco ★★

9.5km (6 miles) SE of Naples.

This modern seaside resort is a perfect base for an exploration of Herculaneum and the whole Vesuvian area. It has several hotels and restaurants based around the tourist flow, as well as a life of its own, focused around the traditional craft of cameo making.

ESSENTIALS

GETTING THERE AND AROUND You can easily get to Torre del Greco by public transportation using the **Circumvesuviana** railway (𝄐 **800-053939** toll-free within Italy; www.vesuviana.it), which leaves from the Stazione Circumvesuviana (Corso Garibaldi, off Piazza Garibaldi; Metro: Garibaldi) to Torre del Greco (on either line, Sorrento or Poggiomarino) every half-hour; the 25-minute ride costs 2€ ($2.50).

By car, take the very busy coastal road SS 18 out of Naples. Alternatively, take the autostrada A3 and exit at either TORRE DEL GRECO NORD or SUD.

Once in town, it's easiest to explore using a taxi. If you want to travel to other destinations, the Circumvesuviana railway (see above) links Torre del Greco with all the little towns around Mount Vesuvius.

EXPLORING TORRE DEL GRECO: CAMEO MAKING

Coral jewelry and cameos have a long history in Torre del Greco. The fishing of coral was a traditional activity since antiquity, when the art of the cameo was first invented. Lost during the Middle Ages, the craft boomed in the 19th century when local artisans found inspiration in the jewelry, found in the excavations of Pompeii and Herculaneum. In 1879 the Scuola di Incisione del Corallo (School of Coral Carving) opened. Today, it's called the **Istituto Statale per l'Arte del Corallo e l'Oreficeria**, and though the local coral beds are practically exhausted, the activity still flourishes, thanks to the use of corals and shells from the Pacific Ocean.

The **Istituto** has an annex at the **Museo del Corallo** ★★ (Piazza Palomba; 𝄐 **081-8811360**), where you can admire a largish collection stretching from the 18th century onward. Also in town is the private **Museo Liverino del Corallo e dei Cammei** ★★ (Via Montedoro 61; 𝄐 **081-8811225**)—it belongs to one of the historical cameo factories, which holds over 3,000 pieces from the 16th century onwards.

The number of cameo workshops in this area is quite large. Many of the most reputable congregate around Via Ettore de Nicola. At no. 1 is **Giovanni Apa** (𝄐 **081-8811155**), at no. 25 is **Antonino del Gatto** (𝄐 **081-8814191**), at no. 35 is **Baldo Liguoro** (𝄐 **081-8812600**), and at no. 38 is **Vincenzo Ricevuto** (𝄐 **081-8814976**). Other noteworthy workshops are **Fratelli De Simone** (Via Roma 4; 𝄐 **081-8829368**), **B. & E. Mazza** (Via Tironi 14; 𝄐 **081-8812665**), and **Giuseppe Pepere** (Via Friuli 11; 𝄐 **081-8834888**).

WHERE TO STAY

Hotel Holidays This family-run modern hotel caters mostly to Italian tourists and offers welcoming accommodations at a moderate price in a seaside location, only steps from the beach and a small distance from the area's major attractions. Guest rooms are spacious and nicely appointed, with tiled floors, comfortable furnishings, and modern bathrooms. Only the best rooms—with seaviews or private terraces—have air-conditioning and a minibar.

Via Litoranea 154, Santa Maria La Bruna, 80059 Torre del Greco. 𝄐 **081-8832170**. Fax 081-8836591. www.holidays hotel.it. 38 units. 75€–110€ ($94–$138) double. Rates include breakfast. Extra bed 25€ ($31). Specials available.

Children under 2 stay free in parent's room. AE, DC, MC, V. Free parking. **Amenities:** Restaurant; bar; concierge; business center; room service; babysitting; laundry service. *In room:* A/C, satellite TV, minibar.

Hotel Marad 🌴   Located in a quiet area and enjoying a great panoramic position, this is a relaxing place to take a break from the Roman ruins (be sure to take advantage of the pleasant garden and swimming pool). Guests have access to a spa and gym nearby. Rooms are quiet and well appointed, with quality furniture, tiled floors, and modern bathrooms.

Via San Sebastiano 24, 80059 Torre del Greco. ✆ 081-8492168. Fax 081-8828716. www.marad.it. 74 units. High season 140€ ($175) double; low season 120€ ($150) double. Rates include buffet breakfast. Specials available. Children under 3 stay free in parent's room. AE, DC, MC, V. Free parking. **Amenities:** 2 restaurants; bar; outdoor pool; spa; gym; concierge; business center; room service; babysitting; laundry service. *In room:* A/C, satellite TV w/pay TV, dataport; minibar.

Sakura 🌴 *Kids*   This hotel is more stylish than the Marad (see above), although both offer quality accommodations. The Sakura is surrounded by a large private park; public spaces are spacious and include outdoor activities, which children will like—there's even a *calcetto* field (calcetto is an Italian form of soccer, with five players on each side). The spacious guest rooms are individually decorated with classic and contemporary furniture; bathrooms are good-sized.

Via Ettore De Nicola 26, 80059 Torre del Greco. ✆ 081-8493144. www.hotelsakura.it. 80 units. 195€ ($244) double. Rates include buffet breakfast. Extra bed 45€ ($56). Specials available. Children under 6 stay free in parent's room. AE, DC, MC, V. Free parking. **Amenities:** Restaurant; bar; outdoor pool; outdoor tennis court; concierge; business center; room service; babysitting; same-day laundry service. *In room:* A/C, satellite TV, dataport, minibar, hair dryer, safe.

WHERE TO DINE

A major dining destination, Torre del Greco is popular with locals hailing from the whole region, who come here to sample the excellent local cuisine, famous for its fresh seafood dishes and D.O.C. wines. The whole Litoranea (seashore road) is lined with restaurants large and small, some more upscale and others simple shacks,; lots of others are hidden away on the inner streets. The town also has an array of excellent pizzerias—such as **Pizzeria la Bruna** (Via Nazionale 678; ✆ **081-8832431;** daily), which makes thoroughly good Neapolitan pizza and has a private garden.

Gaetano a Mare NEAPOLITAN/SEAFOOD   This is one of the town's best-established restaurants, favored by locals who love to come here on weekends for traditional cuisine and good wine (while the children play in the restaurant's playground). The menu is seasonal and based on the market, but you'll usually find an excellent *frittura* (medley of deep-fried seafood) and delicious *pasta alle cozze* (pasta with sauteed mussels). Catches of the day are prepared according to your choice, *all'acquapazza* (poached with an herb broth), or baked or grilled.

Via Litoranea 5, Torre del Greco. ✆ 081-8831558. Reservations recommended on weekends. Secondi 12€–22€ ($15–$28). No credit cards. Sat–Thurs noon–3pm and 7:30–11pm.

Chiarina A'Mmare 🌴 NEAPOLITAN/SEAFOOD   Another local favorite, this restaurant gets very crowded on weekends with locals craving seafood. The seasonal menu always includes traditional local favorites, of which we'd recommend *spaghetti zucchine e cozze* (spaghetti with mussels and zucchini), *frittelle di alghe* (seaweed fritters), *impepata di cozze* (mussels steamed with white pepper), and *pesce all'acquapazza* (fish cooked in a light tomato broth).

Via Calastro, Torre del Greco. ✆ 081-8812067. Reservations recommended on weekends. Secondi 12€–18€ ($15–$23). AE, DC, MC, V. Daily 12:30–3:30pm and 7:30–10:30pm.

Ristorante Pernice Salvatore *NEAPOLITAN/SEAFOOD* A bit more upscale than Gaetano a Mare or Chiarina A'Mmare, this restaurant offers both indoor and outdoor dining on its terrace. The menu is seasonal and depends on the day's market, but you'll usually find their delicious version of the *acqua pazza* (light herbed broth), and the *pesce al sale* (daily catch baked in a bed of salt; the salt bakes in all the natural flavors of the fish). Two of the most outstanding first courses are *risotto alla pescatora* (risotto with seafood), and *scialatielli ai frutti di mare* (fresh pasta with shellfish).

Via Ruggiero 45, Torre del Greco. ℂ **081-8832297.** Reservations recommended on weekends. Secondi 16€–28€ ($20–$35). AE, DC, MC, V. Daily noon–3pm and 7:30–11pm.

3 Oplontis *

20km (12 miles) SE of Naples.

Near the small harbor town of Torre Annunziata—famous for its flour mills and its pasta industry—the archaeological area of Oplontis covers a vast area where much remains to be excavated. Inhabited already in the 1st century B.C., Oplontis was an elegant residential resort where the very rich had their countryside villas; the name, indeed, might come from the Latin *opulentia* because of the luxury of the villas there. The remains here are spectacular and the size of the site is much more manageable than Pompeii or even Herculaneum.

ESSENTIALS

GETTING THERE You can easily get to Oplontis by public transportation using the **Circumvesuviana** railway (ℂ **800-053939** toll-free within Italy; www.vesuviana.it), which leaves from the Stazione Circumvesuviana in Naples (Corso Garibaldi, off Piazza Garibaldi; Metro: Garibaldi) bound for **Torre Annunziata-Oplonti Villa di Poppea** (on either line, Sorrento or Poggiomarino) every half-hour; the 30-minute ride costs 2€ ($2.50).

By car, take the autostrada A3 Napoli-Salerno and exit at TORRE ANNUNZIATA SUD. Then follow the signs for SCAVI DI OPLONTI.

EXPLORING SCAVI DI OPLONTI-VILLA DI POPPEA

This is the largest ancient Roman suburban villa ever discovered, declared a UNESCO World Heritage Site because of the unique quality of its frescoes. Scientifically excavated in the 1960s, only part of the site is visible to the public. The villa's entrance is at Via Sepolcri 12 (ℂ **081-8621755;** www.pompeiisites.org); admission is 5€ ($6.25) and includes same-day admission to Boscoreale and Stabiae. Besides the discount you can get with the **Artecard** (see box in chapter 3, p. ###), you can also purchase a 3-day cumulative ticket including Herculaneum, Pompeii, Oplontis, Stabiae, and Boscoreale, for 18€ ($23). The villa is open Sunday to Friday 8:30am to 5pm from November 1 to March 31 and from April 1 to October 31 from 8:30am to 7:30pm. Last admission is 90 minutes before closing time.

Impressions
Live in danger. Build your cities on the slopes of Vesuvius.
—Friedrich Nietzsche (1844–1900)

The great attraction of this archaeological site is the villa's decorations, left *in situ*—unlike Pompeii or Herculaneum where, except in the latest excavations, frescoes and mosaics have been removed to museums. It is possible, therefore, to have the unique experience of visiting a villa as it was at the time of the volcano's eruption (with a little support from your imagination). The frescoes and the stucco work here are also superb. Interestingly, the statuary—a very rich collection, second only to what was found in the Villa dei Papiri in Herculaneum—was found collected in a storeroom, and the villa appeared empty of the objects of daily life. Based on this, experts believe that at the moment of the eruption the villa was being restored—maybe as a consequence of the preceding earthquake of A.D. 62.

Oplontis was probably the property of the famous Poppea Sabina, the second wife of the Emperor Nero; an amphora bearing the name of her freedman and a vase bearing her mark were found on the villa's ground, thus giving evidence justifying the claim. The villa is enormous, with a large portico opening onto a garden with a huge pool surrounded by statues, and innumerable rooms, passages and cubicles, including a still-recognizable kitchen. Most of the interior was lavishly painted and many of the frescoes are still in very good repair, closely recalling the more well-known frescoes in the Villa dei Misteri of Pompei and in the Museo Archeologico Nazionale of Naples.

4 Pompeii ★★★

27km (17 miles) SE of Naples.

Pompeii is Italy's most famous archaeological site and with good reason: With an excavated area of 44 hectares (almost 109 acres), Pompeii is unique in the world. No other ancient town has been brought to light so completely. Discovered by chance during the excavations for a canal in the 16th century, the ruins of Pompeii were not recognized for what they were until larger explorations in the 18th century; scientific excavations started only at the end of the 19th century, but continued steadily until most of the ancient town was uncovered. Based on the recognition of the city walls—only partly excavated—Pompeii covered an area of 66 hectares (163 acres). Originally an Etruscan and then a Sannite town, it was colonized by the Romans in 80 B.C. At the time of the eruption, experts estimate the town could have held as many as 35,000 inhabitants.

GETTING THERE   You can easily get to Pompeii by public transportation using the Circumvesuviana railway (℗ **800-053939** toll-free within Italy; www.vesuviana.it), which leaves from the Stazione Circumvesuviana (Corso Garibaldi, off Piazza Garibaldi; Metro: Garibaldi) to Pompei Scavi on the Sorrento line every half-hour. *Note:* The Pompei stop on the Poggiomarino line is modern Pompei. The 45-minute ride to Pompei Scavi costs 2.20€ ($2.85); you can then easily walk to the archaeological site from the station.

By car, take the autostrada A3 and exit at POMPEI OVEST. Follow the signs for POMPEI CCAVI; the entrance to the site is only a short distance away.

GETTING AROUND   You can access the excavations from Porta Marina, on Via Villa dei Misteri, off the Circumvesuviana train station. Admission is 10€ ($13). Alternatively, and besides the **Artecard** (p. 87), you can purchase a 3-day cumulative ticket including Herculaneum, Pompeii, Oplontis, Stabiae, and Boscoreale, for 18€ ($23). The excavations are open November to March from 8:30am to 5 pm; and April to October from 8:30am to 7:30pm. Last entrance is 90 minutes before closing.

A Guided Tour with an Official Guide

Booking a tour through the **Ufficio Scavi** of Pompeii and Herculaneum is an excellent, even essential idea. You might spend a bit more, but you get to see much more as well: Official guides are allowed to show you restricted areas that cannot be accessed by regular visitors, and these include some of the best remains since these need extra protection. If you don't want to be left peeking through the gate of an ancient house, wondering what you are missing, book an official tour.

If you can't book in advance, don't panic (unless it is a busy weekend in high season). You can probably get a spot by signing up directly at the gate of either Pompeii or Herculaneum when you arrive.

The **Ufficio Scavi** (© 081-8575347; www.pompeiisites.org) offers thematic guided tours that are fascinating; they each focus on one aspect of the town's life, and some of them are seasonal—such as the **Vendemmia (Grape Harvest),** where you can visit the vineyards that produce an excellent red wine (the *Villa dei Misteri* label), using the techniques of 2,000 years ago. You can reserve these and other guided tours at © 081-8616405, or online at www.arethusa.net.

A note of caution: Given the extent of ground to cover, a visit here is quite demanding in time and energy. It's a good idea to bring a hat, sunscreen, water, and comfortable shoes; you don't want to have to leave because you're uncomfortable. We also recommend taking a guided tour. This will allow you to see more (since most of the houses are closed to the public, and official guides are allowed to show some of them). Because the site is so overwhelming, it is easy to miss some interesting attractions.

If you don't take a guided tour, at least buy the guidebook, complete with itineraries and photographs, for sale at the bookstore, located just after the ticket booth. They are available in various languages, including English.

THE EXCAVATIONS (SCAVI)

In Roman times, Pompeii was an important industrial and commercial town, with a complex layered society, which is reflected in the urban structures on view today. Besides elegant villas belonging to the richer citizens, there were blocks of more modest housing, as well as many shops, restaurants, hotels, and public buildings. The eruption covered Pompeii with volcanic ash and pumice stone, a much lighter material than in Herculaneum. As a result, the survivors of the disaster were able to retrieve some of their possessions, leaving less behind than in other locations. This also made it easier for the site to be excavated—and, unfortunately looted—in more recent centuries. You will recognize the different excavation styles: in the 19th and early 20th century, precious mosaics and frescoes were carefully detached and displayed in museums; the contemporary approach is to leave everything *in situ* to maximize visitors' experience of the place as it must have been.

Surrounded by walls, the city was much closer to the sea that it is now, since the water receded substantially since the days of the eruption. It had three centers: the **Forum;** the **Triangular Forum** with the **Theater District;** the **Amphitheatre,** and the **Palestra.** The rest of town was residential and commercial. Streets were lined with small shops, "bars," and *osterias* (taverns), and the walls were covered with red writing advertising the candidates to the local elections. You'll also see black charcoal graffiti,

Pompeii

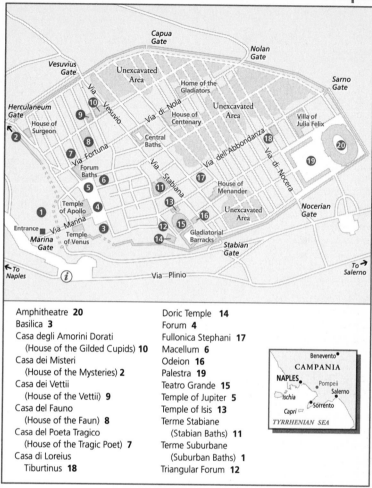

and painted signs for bars and shops. All these are still visible in the area of the so-called **Nuovi Scavi** (considered to be new excavations, although they started around 1911!) to the southeast of town.

The **Forum** is a large rectangular square covering over 17,400 sq. m. (58,000 sq. ft.) and surrounded by a portico on three sides. On the fourth is the **Temple of Jupiter,** from the 2nd century B.C., built over a high foundation. The Forum was decorated with bronze and marble statues of important citizens, but the niches stand empty because their objects were taken away shortly after the tragedy in A.D. 79. On the Forum opened the **Macellum,** the covered food market. At the opposite side, opening onto the street, was the **Basilica,** the largest building in town, which housed the meeting hall and tribunal.

The **Triangular Forum**—so called, as you would guess, because of its shape—is another large square which was surrounded by a portico. In the square are the ruins of the **Doric Temple** from the 6th century B.C. This was the heart of the **Theater District,** with the beautiful **Teatro Grande** ✺ from the 2nd century B.C. to the east, which could hold an audience of 5,000 for the most important theatrical representations. Farther on is the **Odeion,** or Small Theater, from the 1st century B.C., for music and mime shows, which could hold 1,000 spectators. Nearby is the **Temple of Isis** ✺, one of the best-conserved temples to this goddess to survive from antiquity. Also nearby are the **Terme Stabiane (Stabian Baths)** ✺, one of the town's three **public bath** establishments and among the finest conserved ancient baths in the world, with well-preserved decorations in mosaic, painting, and marble.

From the Forum, you can take **Via dell'Abbondanza,** the town's main commercial street, lined with shops of all kinds (the shops were under restoration at presstime but should be open again in 2007) and leading to the southeast of town—the most recently excavated area. One of the most curious shops is the **Fullonica Stephani ("Stephany's Dry-Cleaning");** the shop is on the ground floor and the owner's apartment on the second. Farther on is the **Casa di Loreius Tiburtinus,** with an elegant internal **loggia** ✺ bordering a long pool and decorated with small marble statues; at the end is the **Triclinium** with two beautiful **paintings** ✺✺. At the end of the road to the right is the **Palestra** for sports events, with a grandiose swimming pool and surrounded by plane trees (you can see the plaster casts of the stumps). Farther on is the **Amphitheatre,** the oldest Roman amphitheater in the world, built in B.C. 80, with seating for 1,000 people.

Among the other famous private houses here is the elegant **Casa dei Vettii (House of the Vettii),** with its magnificent paintings belonging to two rich merchants; they had just redecorated after the damages caused by the earthquake in A.D. 62. Besides several small paintings in a number of rooms in the house, you'll find the magnificent frescoed **Triclinium (Dining Room)** ✺✺, where you'll see figures and *amorini* (cupids) on Pompeiian red-and-black backgrounds. Behind it is the **Casa degli Amorini Dorati (House of the Gilded Cupids)** ✺—also beautifully decorated with frescoes and mosaics. It's famous for the walls in one of the bedrooms, made of disks of glass painted with cupids over gold leaf. Nearby is the **Casa del Fauno (House of the Faun),** the largest of private homes—it takes up an entire city block. This was an exquisite mansion, whose finest decorative pieces are now in the Museo Nazionale Archeologico in Naples. Also famous (though again, most of its paintings have been moved to Naples's museums), is the **Casa del Poeta Tragico (House of the Tragic Poet),** with the famous CAVE CANEM (BEWARE OF THE DOG) mosaic by the entrance, which has been copied many times.

From the Forum you can take the Via Consolare to the Via dei Sepolcri—a road lined with funerary monuments that leads outside the city walls towards the Porto Ercolano, Pompeii's harbor (about a ½-mile walk). There you'll find the **Casa dei Misteri (House of the Mysteries),** the most noteworthy suburban villa of Pompeii, famous both for its architecture—a dramatic terrace built over steeply sloping ground—and its paintings. Inside you'll find a largish room with a marble floor, and on its wall a large **painting** ✺✺ from the 1st century B.C., with several figures on a red background, which is thought to be related to the cult of Dionysus (Bacchus). Also outside the walls are the **Terme Suburbane (Suburban Baths)** ✺✺✺, opened to the public in 2002 after lengthy restorations. Contrary to the usual Roman custom, they are "mixed," for both men and women. The interior holds beautiful **frescoes** and **mosaic** decorations.

An interesting thing to do after visiting the archaeological area is to check out **Virtual Pompei,** a reconstruction of the ancient town and how it must have looked before the eruption. The showroom is at Via Plinio 105, in town (ⓒ/fax **081-8610500;** www.virtualpompei.it; 6€/$8; 10% discount with the Artecard; daily 11:30am–5pm).

WHERE TO STAY

Modern Pompei is famous for its **Santuario della Madonna del Rosario,** one of the major religious centers in Italy and a pilgrimage destination. It used to be that modern Pompeii was so run-down with cheap urban sprawl, slums, and the usual petty crime that comes with them that most visitors preferred to come for the day and stay elsewhere. The situation has notably improved, and there are now quite a few nice hotels—but you should still be very careful and avoid night strolls along deserted streets.

MODERATE

Hotel Bristol *(Kids)*   This modern hotel is not far from the centre and the Scavi, and it's quite close to the santuario. Family-run, it offers both courteous and personalized service. The ambience is relaxed and welcoming. Guest rooms are large and nicely appointed, with tiled floors and large modern tiled bathrooms. The large rooms are suitable for families.

Piazza Vittorio Veneto 1, 80045 Pompei. ⓒ **081-8503005.** Fax 081-8631625. www.hotelbristolpompei.com. 50 units. 90€ ($117) double; 110€ ($143) triple; 130€ ($169) quad. Rates include buffet breakfast. Children under 3 stay free in parent's room. AE, DC, MC, V. Free parking. **Amenities:** Restaurant; bar; concierge; business center; room service; babysitting. *In room:* A/C, TV, minibar, hair dryer, safe.

Hotel Forum *(Kids)*   If you want comfortable accommodations close to the Scavi, come to this family-run hotel. Some of the rooms open onto a garden, while others overlook the excavations—it makes for a pretty cool sight at night. Guest rooms are individually decorated, some with tiled floors, others with wooden floors; all have modern quality furnishings and good-sized bathrooms. The triples, quads, and quintuples are good choices for families.

Via Roma 99, 80045 Pompei. ⓒ **081-8501170.** Fax 081-8506132. www.hotelforum.it. 36 units. 90€ ($117) double; 110€ ($143) triple; 130€ ($169) quad; 150€ ($195) quint. Rates include buffet breakfast. Children under 3 stay free in parent's room. AE, DC, MC, V. Free parking. **Amenities:** Bar; lounge; concierge; free Internet point in lobby; babysitting. *In room:* A/C, satellite TV, minibar, hair dryer, safe.

Hotel Maiuri *   Although farther from the ruins and from the center of modern Pompeii than the other hotels we recommend, this is the best hotel in town, providing excellent and quiet accommodations at a moderate price. The hotel is modern, with completely soundproofed guest rooms opening onto the hotel's pleasant garden. A number of rooms are dedicated nonsmoking rooms. They even provide a bus shuttle to and from Naples's airport (for a fee).

Via Acquasalsa 20, 80045 Pompei. ⓒ **081-8562716.** Fax 081-8562716. www.maiuri.it. 30 units. 110€ ($143) double. Rates include buffet breakfast. Extra bed 30€ ($39). Children under 3 stay free in parent's room. AE, DC, MC, V. Free parking. **Amenities:** Restaurant; bar; concierge; business center; room service; babysitting; laundry service. *In room:* A/C, satellite TV, dataport, minibar, hair dryer, safe.

INEXPENSIVE

Motel Villa dei Misteri   This old-fashioned family-run hotel (the first Italian "motel" we've seen) has the advantage of being right at the excavations. Built in the

1930s, it has a certain charm. Some of the rooms are around the amphora-shaped pool, but most are in the main building. Rooms are spacious and well-appointed, with modern quality furnishings and tiled floors; some have private balconies.

Via Villa dei Misteri 11, 80045 Pompei. © 081-8613593. Fax 081-8622983. www.villadeimisteri.it. 40 units. 64€ ($83) double; 86 € ($112) triple. Children under 3 stay free in parent's room. DC, MC, V. Free parking. **Amenities:** Restaurant; lounge; outdoor pool. *In room:* A/C (9€/$12), TV/VCR/DVD, fax, dataport, minibar, hair dryer, safe.

WHERE TO DINE

Il Principe ⚔ NEAPOLITAN/ANCIENT ROMAN   In a dining room that attempts to recreate the luxury of Pompeii, this restaurant provides excellent food and a lively atmosphere. Right in the center of town, it also offers outdoor dining. The seasonal menu includes a large variety of dishes, and even some ancient Roman recipes, such as the *lagane al garum* (homemade egg-free pasta with an anchovy-paste sauce), which are actually pretty tasty. More modern choices include excellent *spaghetti alle vongole* (spaghetti with baby clams) and *fritto misto* (deep-fried calamari and shrimp).

Piazza Bartolo Longo. © 081-8505566. Reservations recommended. Secondi: 13€–18€ ($17–$23). AE, DC, MC, V. Tues–Sun 12:30–3pm and Tues–Sat 8–11pm.

Lucullus   Attempting to recreate the kind of atmosphere its namesake would have approved of—Lucullus was famous for his love of luxury—this restaurant is decorated with palm trees and copies of Roman statues. It's a good choice for its large buffet of *antipasti*, ranging from fish to vegetable dishes. The pasta is also good. The menu includes non-fish options, such as *fettuccine ai funghi* (homemade pasta with mushrooms) and grilled meat.

Via Plinio 129. © 081-8613055. Reservations recommended on weekends. Secondi 7€–15€ ($9–$20). AE, DC, MC, V. Wed–Mon noon–3pm and 7–11pm.

Ristorante President ⚔ NEAPOLITAN   This is a truly local favorite and one of the most upscale places to eat in the area, offering pleasant and cozy dining rooms and great service. The menu focuses on seafood, with appetizers like smoked swordfish or tuna and, for secondi, delicious pasta dishes such as the *paccheri allo scorfano, zucchine e vongole* (fresh homemade flat pasta with scorpion-fish, zucchini, and clams), and a variety of fish au gratin. The secondi come with a vegetable side dish—unusual, but most welcome. Desserts are excellent and strictly homemade.

Piazza Schettino 12. © 081-8507245. www.ristorantepresident.it. Reservations recommended on weekends. Secondi 12€–25€ ($16–$33). AE, DC, MC, V. Tues–Sun noon–3pm and Tues–Sat 7:30–11:30pm. Closed 2 weeks in Aug and 3 days for Christmas.

Zi Caterina ⚔ NEAPOLITAN   A cheaper choice than the places reviewed above, this restaurant is conveniently located between the Scavi and the center of town. It offers well-prepared, traditional food and good service, which appeals to locals. Try the vegetable appetizers, as well as the excellent *spaghetti alle vongole* (with clams).

Via Roma 20. © 081-8507447. Reservations recommended on weekends. Secondi 6€–15€ ($8–$20). AE, DC, MC, V. Daily noon–10:30pm.

5 Boscoreale ⚔

31km (19 miles) SE of Naples.

In ancient Roman times, this agricultural center on the slopes of Mount Vesuvius was populated with rural villas and farms, and was part of the northern suburbs of Pompeii. The situation hasn't changed much at all: it's still in an area of farms and vineyards (the adjacent Boscotrecase is famous for the production of *Lacrimae Cristi,* the amber-colored D.O.C. Vesuvian wine). To date, over 30 Roman villas have been found in Boscoreale—one with an incredible treasure hidden inside—but only one has been completely excavated.

ESSENTIALS

GETTING THERE   You can easily get here by public transportation using either the **Circumvesuviana** railway ((C) 800-053939 toll-free within Italy; www.vesuviana.it), which leaves from the Stazione Circumvesuviana (Corso Garibaldi, off Piazza Garibaldi; Metro: Garibaldi) to Boscoreale (on either line, Sorrento or Poggiomarino) every half-hour. The 25-minute ride costs 2.10€ ($2.50).

By car, take the autostrada A3 and exit at TORRE ANNUNZIATA; then follow the signs for COMUNI VESUVIANI and BOSCOREALE.

EXPLORING THE SCAVI DI BOSCOREALE & ANTIQUARIUM

Your first stop in town should probably be the **Antiquarium Nazionale Uomo e Ambiente nel Territorio Vesuviano** (Via Settetermini 15, Località Villaregina; (C) **081-5368796;** www.pompeiisites.org). This recently established museum (it opened in 1991) is divided into two sections. The first is dedicated to the daily life of a Roman farm and studies the techniques and objects related to agriculture and husbandry; the second focuses on archaeological findings from the area's villas and how they were structured differently from findings on the coast, which were solely dedicated to leisure. Admission to the whole complex is 5€ ($6.25) and includes same-day admission to Oplonti and Stabiae. Otherwise, besides the discount you can get with an **Artecard** (p. 87), you can also purchase a 3-day cumulative ticket including Herculaneum, Pompeii, Oplontis, Stabiae, and Boscoreale, for 18€ ($23). (The Scavi and the museum are open daily Nov 1–Mar 31, 8:30am–5pm; Apr 1–Oct 31 from 8:30am–7:30pm. Last admission is 90 min. before closing time. The museum is closed Jan 1, May 1, and Dec. 25.)

After visiting the Antiquarium Nazionale, proceed to **Villa Regina,** the only local Roman rural villa that's completely excavated. Located adjacent to the Antiquarium, this site was excavated in the late 1970s using only modern technology. Experts found a Roman rural villa, modest in size, with a residential space for the owner and an attached working farm producing wine and grains. The villa now appears complete with vineyards, as these have been replanted according to the paleo-botanical research performed during the excavation. Inside the buildings are the *torcularium* (the room for pressing grapes) and the cellar, which had a capacity of 10,000 liters (over 2,600 gallons).

Sweet Stop

If you have a sweet tooth like us, you'll love the local specialty, the *zandraglia.* Sold at pastry shops in the area, this traditional pastry is a sort of large sweet cookie shaped like a butterfly. It's also the main protagonist of the *Sagra della Zandraglia,* a fair dedicated to the pastry that's held on the second Sunday of July. For the best, head for the two Vaiano shops in town; one is near the excavations at Via Cirillo Emanuele 163 ((C) **081-5374372**); and the other is at Via Marra ((C) **081-8593732**).

Among the other partially excavated villas here, the most famous is the **Villa della Pisanella,** which was excavated in the 19th century. It, too, was dedicated to the production of wine, but most remarkably, a treasure trove of silver was also found here, including plates and other objects; these are now conserved in the Louvre museum in Paris. Another notable villa is the **Villa di Publius Fannius Synistor,** also excavated in the 19th century. It was decorated with beautiful frescoes, which were taken away and are now conserved—part in the archaeological museum of Naples, part in the Louvre in Paris, and part in the Metropolitan Museum of Art in New York.

6 Castellammare di Stabia ★★★

33km (20 miles) SE of Naples.

If you need some rest after sightseeing, then the small town of Castellammare di Stabia is the place for you. Opening like a fan onto the Bay of Naples, right before the beginning of the Sorrento peninsula, the town's beautiful location between beaches and hills has made it a popular resort since antiquity (when it was named Stabiae). Now, as then, the town attracts visitors to its natural springs—there are 28 of them, all told. Cicero used to spend his vacations here, as did many other prominent Romans, until the eruption of A.D. 79. The town was reborn after the disaster, although for a period its inhabitants had to take refuge in the mountains to escape from the incursions of Goths and Longobards. It has a long history of different rulers. In the 9th century, the citizens returned to build the castle, *Castrum a Mare,* which gave the name to the town. The Angevins later surrounded the town with walls, enlarged its harbor, and built the Royal Palace—immediately dubbed the *Casa Sana,* or "healthy house," for its renowned healing qualities. The Bourbons then created a shipyard that prospered, fueling the development of the town. Today, the shipyard remains one of the most important in Italy.

ESSENTIALS

GETTING THERE   You can easily get here by public transportation via either the regular railroad from Napoli Stazione Centrale, or by the Circumvesuviana rail (© **800-053939** toll-free within Italy; www.vesuviana.it), which leaves from Stazione Circumvesuviana (Corso Garibaldi, off Piazza Garibaldi; Metro: Garibaldi) to Castellammare (on the Sorrento line) every half-hour. The 35-minute ride costs 2.40€ ($3).

You can also take a **SITA** (© **081-5522176;** www.sita-on-line.it) bus from Naples or from the Capodichino Airport towards Sorrento; it stops in Castellammare di Stabia. By car, take the autostrada A3 and exit at CASTELLAMMARE DI STABIA; then follow the signs for CASTELLAMMARE DI STABIA: SS 145 leads directly into town.

GETTING AROUND   The best way to get around town is by taxi. As with every place in Italy, they don't cruise for customers but can be called at one of the two taxi stands in town: Piazza Matteotti (© **081-8706251**) and Piazza Unità d'Italia (© **081-8710577**).

VISITOR INFORMATION   The town tourist office (Piazza Matteotti 34; 80053 Castellammare di Stabia; © **081-8711334;** www.gotostabiae.it) holds information on both the cultural and leisurely aspects of Castellammare, including spas and the archaeological area.

Castellammare di Stabia

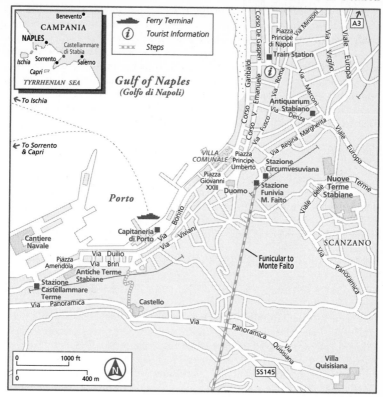

FAST FACTS

You'll find a **pharmacy** at Via Plinio il Vecchio 62 (℃ **081-8701077**). The **hospital** Ospedale San Leonardo is in Viale Europa (℃ **081-8729111** or 081-8715022). For an **ambulance,** dial ℃ **118.** You can call the **police** at ℃ **113** or at ℃ **112.** The post office is on Via Plinio il Vecchio 1 (℃ **081-3901511**) and is open Monday to Saturday 8am to 2pm. You'll find a Bank San Paolo in Corso Vittorio Emanuele 76 (℃ **081-8713501**).

EXPLORING THE ARCHAEOLOGICAL AREA

Excavations at Roman Stabiae started as early as the 18th century, and this is when a number of frescoes as well as sculptures and other precious objects were detached and taken away. "Archaeology," as it existed at that time, had different priorities; after the treasures were removed, the buildings were then usually covered again with dirt. Most of the findings from that time are now on display in the Archaeological Museum of Naples. The 1950s saw the start of the modern **excavations** (Scavi di Stabia, Via Passeggiata Archeologica; ℃ **081-8714541**), which brought to light part of the urban area and four villas, two of which have been excavated: **Villa Arianna** and **Villa San Marco.** These were richly decorated with frescoes, some of which are still *in situ,* while others have been removed to the **Antiquarium Stabiano** (Via Marco Mario 2,

© 081-8714541). *Note:* At presstime, the museum closed for restoration and no date was announced for its reopening. When it reopens, it should do so at a new location. Check with the local tourist office before your visit.

The so-called **Villa di Arianna** *✿* (Via Piana di Varano; *©* 081-274200; Tues–Sat 9am–2pm; Sun 9am–1pm) is a typical example of an ancient Roman patrician villa. Partly ransacked in the 18th century after it was discovered, it is located on the slope of the hill of Varano, just outside town to the northeast, and enjoys a panoramic position. To reach it, take Viale Europa and turn left onto the SS 366 towards Gragnano, and then immediately left again onto Via Piana di Varano.

The name of the villa (which has not been excavated in its entirety) comes from the most important of the paintings found inside, a beautiful **fresco** depicting the mythological Ariadne as she is discovered sleeping by Dyonisius. You can still admire the fresco in its original location in the summer *Triclinium* **(dining room)** together with another fresco depicting Ganimede taken by an eagle up to Jupiter. Another room had walls decorated with diagonal stripes of delicately **painted tiles**—many of which have been removed (some can be seen at the archaeological museum in Naples). Another interesting detail is the ramp leading to a tunnel that connects the villa with the bottom of the hill.

Farther along, on a lateral alley, is the entrance to the **Villa di San Marco** *✿* (Via Passeggiata Archeologica; Free admission; daily 9am to 1 hr. before sunset. Last admission is 1 hour before closing), another patrician villa whose name derives from the small 18th-century church nearby, now in ruins. One of the first ruins explored by the Bourbons in the 18th century, this villa was built in the 1st century B.C. as the residence of a rich family. Later enlarged in the 1st century A.D., it became quite extensive, with porticos, halls, private bathrooms (with the three key rooms of *calidarium, tepidarium* and *frigidarium*), all decorated with stucco, paintings and frescoes. This villa was in an excellent state of conservation until an earthquake in 1980. Despite the destructions caused by this earthquake, you can still visit many of the rooms and enjoy the views.

Within walking distance, you'll find the **Grotta di San Biagio** (St. Biagio's Grotto), a tufa stone quarry—used in Roman times for the construction of the villas in Stabiae—which was transformed into a paleochristian oratory in the 5th to 6th centuries A.D. The first bishops of Stabiae are buried here, making it one of the oldest Christian burial sites known to man. It is decorated with well-conserved frescoes and paintings that date from the 5th to 6th centuries and from the 9th to 10th centuries A.D., except for three frescoes by the entrance which are from the 14th century.

VISITING THE TOWN

Though modern in appearance, Castellammare has a number of worthy historical attractions, starting with its famous thermal establishments, such as **Antiche Terme Stabiane** (Piazza Amendola 18, off Via Brin.; Mon–Sat 7am–1pm), built in 1827 for King Ferdinando IV. Later enlarged—the original building was torn down and replaced with the current building in 1956—this establishment is down by the harbor and was constructed to use 17 natural sulfur springs with temperatures between 14°C and 17°C (57°F–67°F).

Newer thermal baths, called **Nuove Terme Stabiane** *✿✿* (Viale delle Terme 3; *©* 081-391311; www.termedistabia.com), opened in 1964 on the outskirts of town. You should head here if you want to enjoy just a single day at the spa. The waters in this state-of-the-art spa are recommended for digestive ailments and skin complaints, but beauty and relaxing treatments are available for everyone.

The most modern spa in the area was built near the **Villa Quisisana,** the monumental villa originally built by King Carlo II d'Angiò for his vacations ("qui si sana" means "here one heals"). Resting at an altitude of 173m (567 ft.) on the slopes of Monte Faito, the spa was restored in 1820 by Ferdinando I di Borbone and was only recently brought back to its original splendor for the new millennium.

As you cross the center of town, take note of the **Villa Comunale,** the public gardens opening onto the Gulf of Naples (off Piazza Giovanni XXIII, near the Stazione Circumvesuviana) with their gorgeous **Cassa Armonica** (bandstand)—a Liberty masterpiece created by Eugenio Cosenza in 1901.

Before you leave town, take some time to climb **Monte Faito** (1,100m/3,608 ft. high), for a great excursion and gorgeous views. Although you can drive, it is quite nice to take the **funivia (funicular)** starting from Piazza Stazione Circumvesuviana, in the center of town. It runs every half-hour. Round-trip fare costs 7€ ($8.75)

WHERE TO STAY
EXPENSIVE
Grand Hotel La Medusa 🏨🏨   This luxury hotel is our favorite in town. Housed in a 19th-century villa, it offers a romantic setting and professional service. Surrounded by a splendid park with a large oval fountain, it boasts plush public spaces and salons. Guest rooms are appointed with classic furnishings, fine linens and fabrics, beautiful tiled floors, and Oriental carpets, in keeping with the decidedly traditional yet elegant vibe.

Via Passeggiata Archeologica 5, 80053 Castellammare di Stabia. ℂ 081-8723383. Fax: 081-8717009. www.la medusahotel.com. 52 units. High season 190€–210€ ($238–$262) double; low season 150€–170€ ($188–$213) double. Rates include buffet breakfast. Extra bed 45€ ($56). Specials available. AE, DC, MC, V. Free parking. **Amenities:** Restaurant; bar; outdoor pool; outdoor tennis courts; concierge; business center; room service; babysitting; laundry service. *In room:* A/C, satellite TV, dataport; minibar, hair dryer, safe, radio.

MODERATE
Hotel dei Congressi 🏨 *Kids*   This is our second favorite hotel in town, offering elegance and a high level of service. Both its location—right across from the Terme di Stabia (see above)—and public spaces are splendid. Guest rooms are large and bright, with tasteful furnishings and ample bathrooms; some share superb panoramic views with the terraced swimming pool. The triple and quad rooms are a plus for those traveling as families.

Viale delle Puglie 75, 80053 Castellammare di Stabia. ℂ/ fax: **081-8722277.** www.hoteldeicongressi.it. 84 units. 100€ ($125) double; 120€ ($150) triple; 140€ ($175) quad; 150€ ($188) suite. Rates include buffet breakfast. Children under 3 stay free in parent's room. AE, DC, MC, V. Free parking. **Amenities:** Restaurant; bar; outdoor pool; concierge; business center; room service; babysitting; same-day laundry service. *In room:* A/C, satellite TV, minibar, hair dryer, safe.

Hotel Stabia 🏨   The Stabia is the best of Castellammare's historic hotels, serving guests since 1876. Housed in a neoclassical building, it offers professional service and fine accommodations. The historic feeling in the common spaces has been preserved, while the guest rooms have been done over with quality, modern furniture and tiled floors. All rooms come with private terraces and beautiful views.

Corso Vittorio Emanuele 101, 80053 Castellammare di Stabia. ℂ **081-8722577.** Fax: 081-8722105. www.hotel stabia.com. 97 units. 110€ ($138) double. Rates include buffet breakfast. AE, DC, MC, V. Free parking. **Amenities:** Restaurant; bar; piano bar; babysitting. *In room:* A/C, satellite TV, minibar, hair dryer, safe.

INEXPENSIVE

Hotel Villa Serena This small family-run hotel offers warm, personal service and good accommodations at moderate prices. Housed in a modern building, the hotel is spacious and painted in pastel colors, which is mirrored in the rest of the decor. It is surrounded by a garden and has a pleasant terrace under the trees. Guest rooms have new and entirely serviceable modern furnishings (think comfort, not style), tiled floors, and good-sized bathrooms.

Via Miscongiuri 1, 80053 Castellammare di Stabia. © 081-8710157. Fax: 081-8726561. www.hotelvillaserena.it. 60 units. 70€ ($88) double. Rates include breakfast. Extra bed 15€ ($19). Specials available. Children under 3 stay free in parents' room. AE, DC, MC, V. Free parking. **Amenities:** Restaurant; bar. *In room:* A/C, TV.

Hotel Montil *Finds* This small hotel overlooks the old fishing harbor and offers good accommodations right in the heart of town. Guest rooms are small but decorated with a personal touch (furnishings are not identical, so you won't feel like you're in a motel). Bathrooms are not large either, but the fixtures are modern and functional. The rates are an incredible steal given that you're down by the sea, and you benefit from a pretty view from your room.

Via Bonito 12, 80053 Castellammare di Stabia. © 081-8713538. Fax: 081-8711863. 30 units. 55€ ($69) double. Children under 2 stay free in parent's room. AE, DC, MC, V. Parking 12€ ($16). **Amenities:** Restaurant; concierge. *In room:* TV.

WHERE TO DINE

Giovanni di Pozzano *Finds* SORRENTINE/SEAFOOD Loved by locals, this traditional restaurant offers dining rooms and outdoor terraces enlivened by live music on weekend evenings. The menu changes with the seasons, but fresh homemade pasta and seafood are particularly well prepared year-round. We like the *cavatelli alle vongole* (a typical pasta, with clams), and the excellent *pezzogna al sale* (local fish baked in a salt crust).

Via Vecchia Pozzano 40. © 081-8026101. Reservations recommended on weekend evenings. Secondi 12€–18€ ($15–$23). AE, DC, MC, V. Wed–Mon noon–3pm and 7:30–11pm.

Tolino dal 1816 SORRENTINE/PIZZA This historic restaurant—as the name suggests, it's been around longer than a lot of countries—offers indoor and outdoor dining as well as a nice piano bar. The cuisine is traditional and focuses on seafood. You might try the delicious *linguine con zucchine* (linguine with zucchini) and the great *impepata di cozze* (steamed mussels with white pepper); they also make quality pizza.

Corso Vittorio Emanuele 13. © 081-8711607. Reservations recommended. Secondi 12€–21€ ($15–$26). AE, DC, MC, V. Wed–Mon 12:30–3:30pm and 8–11:30pm.

Osteria da Mena *Finds* This little trattoria offers well-prepared local specialties and a relaxed atmosphere. The homemade pasta is very good—when in luck, you'll find excellent *scialatielli ai frutti di mare* (with basil and shellfish), and the *frittura* (deep-fried medley of seafood) is crisp and juicy. You will also find meat on the seasonal menu, including excellent *pollo arrosto* (roasted chicken) or *arrosto di maiale* (pork roast).

Via Pietro Carrese 32. © 081-8713048. Reservations recommended. Secondi 11€–18€ ($14–$23). AE, DC, MC, V. Daily noon–3pm and 7:30–11pm.

6

The Land of Sirens:
Sorrento & its Peninsula

The beauty of Sorrento's coast is the sort that inspires myths, and indeed, this is where the Sirens are said to have waylaid travelers with their irresistible song in Homer's *The Odyssey*. Today, the pull of the sea and imposing rock-bound coast remain as strong as in Homer's day, attracting legions of visitors. Indeed, it is unlikely that you will feel alone here, especially if you come during the summer months. In spite of the crowds, this little town has its charms, with many lesser-known attractions and a peninsula that is among the most beautiful in the Mediterranean. A rocky point of land jutting into the sea and dominated by high mountains—the Monti Lattari—the peninsula of Sorrento has much more to offer than a seaside resort. You'll be able to hike rugged paths, discover towers and rural villages, explore ancient ruins, and sample a cuisine made with local cheeses and cured meats so good that they don't make it to the mainland.

The door to the Sorrento peninsula is Castellammare di Stabia. This is where you leave the highway if you are coming by car,

and it marks the beginning of this mountainous promontory projecting into the sea. About 20km (13 miles) long, the Castellammare di Stabia is a finger of land pointing to Capri—which is only 5km (3 miles) away at the closest point, at Punta Campanella. The peninsula also divides the Gulf of Naples from the Gulf of Salerno. Sorrento is the main town of the peninsula, located about midway to the tip on the northern shore, opening onto the Gulf of Naples. On the mountains above Sorrento and on the cliffs beyond are many villages connected by winding—and often bumpy—narrow local roads, which remain undiscovered precisely because of their inaccessibility. On the other side of the mountains is a very authentic and little-explored stretch of harsh and rocky coast; technically it's part of the famous Amalfi Coast, which is said to start at Positano, at the end of the Sorrento peninsula's southern shore. As happens so often in Italy, even in the midst of celebrated attractions and wall-to-wall tourists, you'll find yourself only a stone's throw from quieter byways and hidden pleasures.

1 Vico Equense ✦

Far less visited than its larger and more famous sister, Sorrento, Vico Equense is an elegant seaside resort. The town is built on a tufa stone platform overlooking the sea and is quite popular with Italian tourists, who seek it out especially in August. Foreign tourists are comparatively rare, which makes it a more special place to stay.

ESSENTIALS

GETTING THERE You can easily reach Vico Equense by public transportation via the **Circumvesuviana Railway** (Stazione Circumvesuviana on Corso Garibaldi in Naples, off Piazza Garibaldi; ✆ **800-053939;** www.vesuviana.it). The resort is about 40 minutes from Naples, and the ride costs about 3€ ($3.90).

You can also take a **SITA bus** (✆ **081-5522176;** www.sita-on-line.it); daily frequent service between Naples and Sorrento stops in Vico Equense. The ride takes about 45 minutes and costs 3.20€ ($4.15). From Naples's airport, Capodichino, you can take one of the seven daily shuttle runs made by **Curreri Viaggi** (✆ **081-8015420**) for 6€ ($7.80). The ride takes about 40 minutes.

If you are coming from Naples by car, take autostrada A3, at the sign for NAPOLI SALERNO, and exit at the sign for CASTELLAMMARE DI STABIA. If you are coming from north of Naples, do not take autostrada A30 for Salerno, which starts after Caserta on your way to Naples. Stay on the A1, until you see the signs for the A3; from the A3, follow the directions given above. From Castellammare, follow signs for VICO EQUENSE and SORRENTO to SS 145, the coastal road that will lead you to Vico Equense.

GETTING AROUND The best way to visit this small town is on foot—you can reach both the sea and the mountain trails by walking. If you want a taxi, call for one from Sant'Agnello or Sorrento (see below), or check the taxi stand on Piazza Umberto I.

VISITOR INFORMATION The **tourist office** is at Via San Ciro 16 (✆ **081-8015752;** fax 081-8799351; www.vicoturismo.it).

FAST FACTS You'll find a pharmacy on Via Roma 18 (✆ **081-8015525**). For first aid, the hospital, or an ambulance, dial ✆ **081-8729103.** You can call the **police** at ✆ **113** and the **fire department** at ✆ **115.** The post office is at Via San Ciro 57 (✆ **081-8016811**).

EXPLORING THE TOWN

Vico Equense is a very ancient town—excavations have found remains going back to the 6th century B.C., proving the existence of Oscan, Etruscan, and Greek occupants (evidenced by the **Necropolis** of Via Nicotera). Named *Aequa* during Roman times, the town survived the eruption of A.D. 79 and flourished until it was destroyed by the Goths in 553. It was then re-established by the Angevins in the 12th century with its new name; the town's center retains delightful medieval buildings from this era.

To enjoy Vico Equense, start by taking Via Filangeri off the main square, Piazza Umberto I, and turn right onto **Via Monsignor Natale,** the heart of the medieval town. Along this street, enter the splendid medieval courtyard at no. 3. Continuing on, you can enjoy the great view from **Largo dei Tigli,** and, retracing your steps to Vescovado, you can visit the **Chiesa dell'Annunziata** (Via Cattedrale; daily 8am–12:30pm and 3:30–7pm), a 14th-century church partially redone in the 17th century after the earthquake of 1688. In the upper part of town is a 13th-century castle, redone and enlarged in later centuries.

STAYING ACTIVE

As elsewhere on this peninsula, the best thing to do in Vico Equense is explore the sea and the mountains. Across from the Municipio in the center of town, you can take **Via Castello Marina,** the steep old footpath which, descending through olive groves, will lead you to Vico Marina, down on the seaside. There you will find small beaches

The Amalfi Coast & Sorrento Peninsula

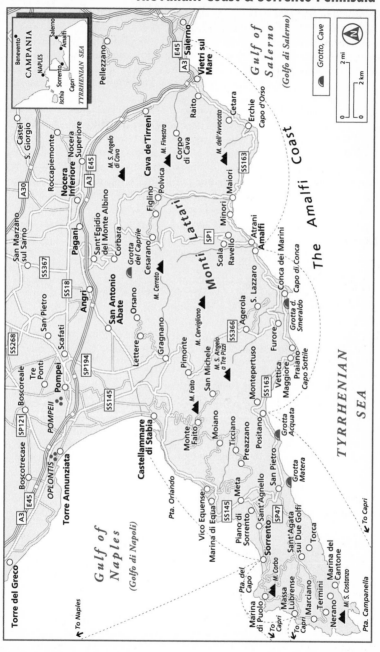

hidden inside picturesque coves. One of the nicest is **Marina di Equa,** west of a powerful defensive tower built in the 17th century.

Another great hike—but one that requires you to be moderately fit—is the series of old paths (which until the 19th century were the only communication links on this peninsula) leading to **Positano.** Although the area has been inhabited for thousands of years, the SS 163, the Amalfi Drive, dates only from 1840. Locals of previous centuries walked over mountain paths and used boats to work along the coast. Walking the succession of trails, you will need about 3½ hours to reach Positano. Follow the directions for Ticciano until you reach the **bridge over the Milo;** there, on your left, you'll find a dirt road to the pass of **Santa Maria al Castello** (altitude 685m/2,247 ft.). Just before the church, to your left, is the connection to **Sentiero degli Dei (Trail of Gods)** towards Nocelle (see later in this chapter). If you turn left at the dirt track just across from the church, you'll instead be led to the trail to Positano. When you reach a fork, the western branch climbs to Monte Comune (altitude 877m/2,877 ft.), with its sweeping views; the eastern branch is the descent to Positano. Along this descent are several uncertain passages around points of rock, so you'll want to contact the tourist office in town for a trail map.

If you're feeling less adventurous, you might instead visit one of the many *agriturismi* (farm houses) in the area. These are great places to have lunch and also to stay overnight; or you can drop by to experience the farm activities. This area is famous for its bee-keeping operations; one of the best places for a visit to the hives and a taste of the products is **Coop-Agrituristica La Ginestra** (Via Tessa 2, Santa Maria di Castello; ⓒ **081-8023211**).

WHERE TO STAY

In addition to the hotels below, consider the agriturismo **Coop-Agrituristica La Ginestra** mentioned above. They have a few nicely appointed rooms, and the food is delicious. The rates are 110€ ($125) for full board and 90€ ($112) with breakfast only.

Hotel Aequa *Finds*   Located in the heart of town by the medieval area, this hotel has been serving its guests since the 1940s and preserves the romantic atmosphere of the typical seaside abodes of this region. We love looking at the view of Mount Vesuvius from under the glorious wisteria on the terrace. Guest rooms are spacious and well appointed with hardwood floors and classic furnishings; bathrooms are modern and good-sized.

Via Filangeri 46, 80069 Vico Equense. ⓒ **081-8015331.** Fax 081-8015071. www.aequahotel.com. 70 units. 108€– 140€ ($140–$182). Rates include buffet breakfast. Children under 3 stay free in parent's room. AE, DC, MC, V. Parking: 10€ ($13). **Amenities:** Restaurant; bar; outdoor pool; solarium; room service; babysitting. *In room:* A/C, TV, minibar.

Mega Mare *Finds*   This panoramic hotel might not look like one of the most romantic abodes from the outside, but once you're inside you'll understand why we love it. It offers state-of-the-art service and a cliffside location overlooking the sea, all at a moderate price. The spacious guest rooms are quiet and full of light, and many of them afford the same wonderful views over the sea that you can enjoy from the hotel's public spaces.

Corso Caulino 73, 80069 Vico Equense. ⓒ **081-8028494.** Fax 081-8028777. www.hotelmegamare.com. 20 units. 135€ ($163) double. Low season 70€ ($88) double. Rates include buffet breakfast. Extra bed 35€ ($44). Children under 6 stay free in parent's room. AE, DC, MC, V. Free parking. **Amenities:** American bar; outdoor pool; room service; babysitting; laundry service. *In room:* A/C, TV, minibar, hair dryer.

Scrajo Terme ✿ This old-fashioned jewel is a short way out of town, off SS145, on a cliff overlooking the beach. Born as a thermal establishment back in the 19th century, it continues to offer a wide range of thermal therapies. The few guest rooms and public spaces overlook the shore in a cascade of terraces. Guest rooms are bright and well furnished and the hotel has a delightful ambiance.

Via Luigi Serio 10 (SS145), Località Scrajo, 80069 Vico Equense. © 081-8015731. Fax 081-8015734. www.scrajo terme.it. 7 units. 150€–220€ ($188–$275). Rates include buffet breakfast. Children under 3 stay free in parents' room. AE, DC, MC, V. Free parking. **Amenities:** Restaurant; bar; outdoor pool; full spa; room service; babysitting on request; laundry service. *In room:* A/C, TV, minibar, hair dryer, safe.

WHERE TO DINE

You can eat very well throughout Vico Equense, but in our opinion two places really make it special, though they are at opposite ends of the spectrum. For Italians, a journey with a good meal at its end is always worthwhile, and these are the kinds of places that cater to such taste.

The first restaurant is justly renowned **Ristorante Torre del Saracino** ✿✿ (Via Torretta 9; © **081-8028555;** secondi 15€–35€/$19–$44; Tues–Sun 12:30–3:30pm and Tues–Sat 7:30–11:30pm). Here the food is truly extraordinary. You can start with delectable *ravioli di pesce ripieni di verdure* (fish-and-vegetable ravioli)—one of the chef's specialties and a dish that made this restaurant famous. Continue with a masterful grilled fresh catch of the day, and finish with another specialty: *babà al rhum con crema pasticcera e fragoline di bosco.* This is an individual *babà* served with pastry cream and wild strawberries from the mountains nearby.

The town's other notable restaurant is **Da Gigino Pizza a Metro, L'Università della Pizza** ✿✿✿ (Via Nicotera 15; © **081-8798426** or 081-8798309; www.pizza metro.it; reservations not accepted; pizza 7€/$8.75 and up daily 12:30–3:30pm and 7pm–midnight), a sort of temple to pizza. Back in the 1950s, Gigino Dell'Amura invented a special pizza baked in a bread oven in a length so long that a visiting journalist suggested calling it *pizza a metro* (pizza by the foot). The special pizza—made with unique crispy dough and wonderful seasonings—quickly began to attract admirers, and today Dell'Amura's five sons maintain the tradition in a cavernous restaurant. Prepared in long strips, the pizza is sold literally by the foot (about 30cm, a very comfortable length), and the price depends on the topping. Not only do they serve the best Italian pizza in the world—really!—they offer delightful appetizers such as the local specialty, *frittelle di alghe* or seaweed fritters.

For a picnic and a taste of wonderful local specialties, head to **Da Gabriele** (Corso Umberto I 5), where you will find a great variety of local cheeses, including fresh mozzarella (which can be braided and studded with olives and prosciutto) and fresh cheese with rucola and red pepper.

2 Sorrento

39km (20 miles) SE of Naples.

Emperor Augustus and his successor, Tiberius, were two of Sorrento's early devotees. In later ages the town has been a preferred destination for artists and writers, as well as tourists. Although the presence of crowds may have dulled some of its magic, Sorrento still boasts charming, cobblestone streets in its historical center, colorful and fragrant flowers everywhere, a superb panorama from its *lungomare* (seafront), and lively nightlife.

ESSENTIALS

GETTING THERE   Sorrento is well connected through the **Circumvesuviana Railway** (Stazione Circumvesuviana on Corso Garibaldi in Naples, off Piazza Garibaldi; ℂ **800-053939;** www.vesuviana.it), which will take you all the way to Sorrento in about 50 minutes for about 3€ ($3.75).

Ferries are our favorite mode of transportation along this coast, and you can easily get to Sorrento by ferry and hydrofoil (only in the good season) with **Linee Marittime Partenopee** (ℂ **081-55513236**), **Navigazione Libera del Golfo** (ℂ **081-5527209**), and **Linee Lauro** (ℂ **081-5522838;** www.alilauro.it). All three make daily runs to and from Naples as well as to and from Ischia and Capri. The **Caremar** company (ℂ **081-5513882;** www.caremar.it) also has daily runs to Capri.

Ferries arrive and depart at the Marina Piccola in downtown Sorrento; from the harbor you can take one of the frequent yellow shuttle buses for the short climb to Piazza Tasso, Sorrento's main square.

SITA (ℂ **081-5522176;** www.sita-on-line.it) maintains regular bus service between Naples and Sorrento, as well as between Sorrento and Amalfi and Salerno. **Curreri Viaggi** (ℂ **081-8015420**) makes seven daily bus runs to Sorrento directly from Naples airport (Capodichino), with stops in Castellammare di Stabia, Vico Equense, Meta, Piano di Sorrento, and Sant'Agnello. The ride to Sorrento takes about 1 hour and costs 6€ ($7.50). *Note:* During the summer, traffic on the coastal road is absolutely abominable and can more than double the regular time.

Forget the car if you can—traffic is usually bad and, in summer, becomes downright horrible. If you must use a car, you can always rent one here (see "Getting Around" later on). To get here, take the exit marked CASTELLAMMARE DI STABIA off autostrada A3 NAPOLI SALERNO. Then follow signs for VICO EQUENSE, META DI SORRENTO, and SORRENTO. These will lead you to route SS 145, the Sorrento peninsula's coastal road. From Castellammare, the road proceeds to Meta di Sorrento, where it splits; one fork is the SS 163—the famed Amalfi Drive in the direction of Positano and Amalfi. Staying on SS 145 instead, you'll reach Sorrento; the road then loops up and across the mountains to reach SS 163 again on the other coast, close to Positano.

GETTING AROUND   The yellow shuttle buses (tickets 1€/$1.25 for 90 min. from tobacconists and newsstands) that connect the harbor with Piazza Tasso in the center of town and the Circumvesuviana Railroad station come in handy at times. Taxis are also useful, especially at night and for reaching some of the surrounding destinations; you'll have to call or go to one of the taxi stands in town, either at the harbor (ℂ **081-8783527**) or on Piazza Tasso (ℂ **081-8782204**).

If you choose to use Sorrento as your base for exploring the peninsula, a **car** will allow you a lot of freedom, but you don't necessarily have to drive it from Naples, because you can rent one here. If you feel up to it, you can use the most Italian means of transportation—the **scooter.** Because they are ideal for sneaking around cars lined up in summer traffic, scooters require drivers with quick reflexes and nerves of steel. We do not recommend one if you have never used a scooter before; if you have, it is a lot of fun and probably one of the best ways to get around this area. Try **Rent a Scooter** (ℂ **081-8771239**) or **Sorrento Rent a Car** (ℂ **081-8781386**), which rents both scooters and cars.

Another tantalizing possibility is to take a **limousine service.** Distances are short, so fares remain quite reasonable; most run about 35€ ($44) per hour for two people in a sedan (more for a minivan). A good company is **2golfi car service** (Via Deserto

30/e, 80064 Sant'Agata sui due Golfi; © **339-8307748** or 338-5628649; fax 081-5330882; www.duegolficarservice). You can also ask the concierge in your hotel—but make sure that the company he or she recommends uses new cars and minivans with air-conditioning (very important in summer), as well as trained, English-speaking drivers.

An even more romantic choice is to hire a **boat,** with or without a driver (a driver can double as a guide, which is an advantage), from one of the harbors to take you to secluded beaches or simply to the next village. **Nautica Sic Sic** (Marina Piccola; © **081-8072283** or 081-8785606; www.nauticasicsic.com; closed Nov–Apr) is a good place to rent boats; they go for 20€ ($25) and up, depending on the kind and size. The store also organizes cruises. Another good choice is **Tony's Beach** (Marina Grande; © **081-8785606**).

And surprising as it might seem, you can do a lot **on foot** in this area. The mountains are crisscrossed by a network of trails, most of which are well kept and well marked, with signs and arrows painted on rocks. Libraries and some newsstands in town carry the excellent *Carta dei Sentieri* published by CAI, the Club Alpino Italiano. It covers the **Monti Lattari, Penisola Sorrentina,** and **Costiera Amalfitana,** and costs 8€ ($9). Otherwise, contact the Massa Lubrense tourist office (see later in this chapter) for information on trails.

VISITOR INFORMATION The **AASCT tourist office** is at Via Luigi De Maio 35, off Piazza Tasso (© **081-8074033;** fax 081-8773397; www.sorrentotourism.com). It's open Monday to Saturday from 9am to 6pm; in July and August it's also open Sunday from 9am to 12:30pm. Besides a good city map, it carries copies of the excellent free magazine *Sorrentum.*

FAST FACTS You'll find a **pharmacy** on Corso Italia 131 (© **081-8781226**). The **hospital** is on Corso Italia 1 (© **081-5331111**). For an **ambulance,** dial © **118.** You can call the **police** at © **112, 113,** or **081-8075311;** and you can reach the **fire department** at © **115.** You will find several **ATMs** in town; one is at the **Deutsche Bank** (Piazza Angelina Lauro 22). The **post office** is at Corso Italia 210 (© **081-8781495**); it's open Monday to Friday from 8am to 6pm and Saturday from 8am to 12:30pm. For, a **taxi** call © **081-8782204** or 081-8783527; in Sant'Agnello call © **081-8781428.** For **Internet access,** go to **Sorrento info** (Via Tasso 19; © **081-8074000**).

EXPLORING THE TOWN

Sorrento has ancient Greek, Etruscan, and Oscan beginnings, and was colonized by the Romans in the 1st century B.C., when it became a valued resort for the affluent. But the town's history has been checkered, to say the least; this jewel by the sea has been fought over many times. After the fall of the empire it was taken by the Goths, and then reconquered by the Byzantines in A.D. 552. It remained part of the Byzantine Duchy of Naples until the 10th century. Having been conquered by the Prince of Salerno at the beginning of the 11th century, it succeeded in gaining its independence as a Duchy in 1067, and remained so until conquest by the Normans in 1133; it then passed into the hands of the Angevins. Saracen incursions and rivalry between the nearby towns of Vico Equense and Massa Lubrense made life difficult in Sorrento—and there was worse to come. The town was completely destroyed by Barbary pirates on the nights of June 12 and 13, 1558. Still, the town was immediately rebuilt, this time with numerous defensive towers along the surrounding coast and a new set of walls.

Some ruins of the medieval town remain, scattered around the center. Off the west side of **Piazza Tasso**—the heart of town—you can reach **Via Pietà,** where you can see Sorrento's oldest building. The facade of **Palazzo Veniero** (Via Pietà 14) still shows typical decorations (similar to wood marquetry) of the 13th century, while the ex-**Palazzo Correale** (Via Pietà 24) has its original 14th-century portal and two windows.

A few steps away, you might want to take a look at the beautiful 15th-century **Duomo,** the Cathedral of San Filippo and San Giacomo (Corso Italia 1; © **081-8782248;** daily 8am–noon and 4–8pm), with its striking Romanesque facade graced by a fresco over the portal, and flanked to its right by a short bell tower. The bell tower has five levels—three original and two added later—a majolica clock, and four antique columns at its base. Inside you can admire 14th- and 15th-century bas-reliefs and a wooden choir section decorated with marvelous intarsia.

A couple of blocks from Corso Italia is a newly established museum with a collection of 19th-century marquetry furniture, **Museo Bottega della Tarsia Lignea** ✻ (Via San Nicola 28; © **081-8771942** or 081-8782177; 8€/$9.20; Mon–Sat 10am–1pm; closed holidays). It is housed inside the beautifully frescoed 18th-century **Palazzo Pomaranci Santomasi,** in itself worth a visit.

On Piazzetta Padre Reginaldo Giuliani, off Via San Cesareo, is the elegant and very well-preserved 15th-century palazzo of **Sedile Dominova.** Off Via Luigi de Maio is Sorrento's second-most important church, **Basilica di Sant'Antonino** (Piazza Sant'-Antonino). Built in the 11th century over a preexisting oratory dedicated to Saint Anthony, it was later redone in the present baroque style, but the interior retains some 15th-century decorations.

Towards the sea, you will come upon a splendid 14th-century **cloister** ✻✻ hidden inside the 18th-century **San Francesco** church (Piazza Francesco Saverio Gargiulo; daily 8am–1pm and 2–7pm). Across from the church is the entrance to **Villa Comunale,** which has a panoramic terrace. From here, you can take the steep ramps descending to **Marina Piccola,** one of Sorrento's harbors, where you can enjoy the waterfront (there's no beach, however). The town's other harbor is **Marina Grande,** which is lined with restaurants and seaside establishments.

Off Piazza Tasso, **Via Correale** ✻ is one of the few streets that preserves the flavor of Sorrento's past. It leads to the **Museo Correale** (© **081-8781846;** www.museo correale.com; 8€/$9.20; Wed–Mon 9am–2pm), once the home of the brothers Alfredo and Pompeo Correale, counts of Terranova—an old aristocratic family of Sorrento—who donated their villa and private collections to the public. Stocked with its original furnishings, the museum offers magnificent views over the sea, but it has more to offer. The paintings and precious objects on display give an overview of decorative art from the 16th to the 19th centuries—from excellent Flemish paintings, to a collection of Italian and foreign porcelain from the reputedly best 17th- and 18th-century manufacturers. Continuing beyond the museum, you'll reach the attached little town of Sant'Agnello, with its gorgeous villas built in the past century or two, and many elegant hotels.

STAYING ACTIVE

Since it is a famous seaside resort, you would expect Sorrento to have beaches; well, think again. The shimmering sea here still fascinates in a way that rightly made this stretch of coast coveted for millennia. The coast's ruggedness, rocky and full of cliffs, is, of course, part of its charm—but the rocks make swimming difficult. For the best swimming in town, head to **Marina Grande** (there's not much of a beach, though).

Sorrento

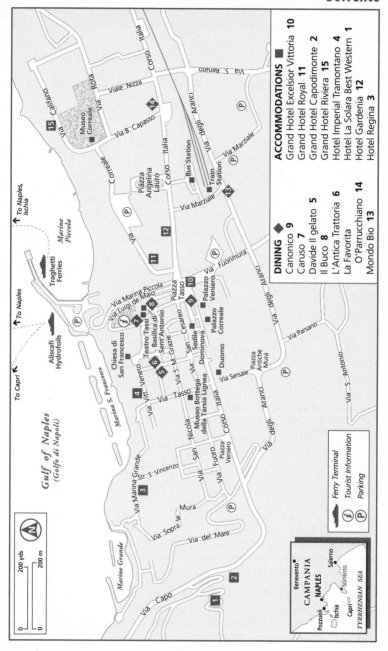

ACCOMMODATIONS ◼
Grand Hotel Excelsior Vittoria **10**
Grand Hotel Royal- **11**
Grand Hotel Capodimonte **2**
Grand Hotel Riviera **15**
Hotel Imperial Tramontano **4**
Hotel La Solara Best Western **1**
Hotel Gardenia **12**
Hotel Regina **3**

DINING ◆
Canonico **9**
Caruso **7**
Davide Il gelato **5**
Il Buco **8**
L'Antica Trattoria **6**
La Favorita
O'Parrucchiano **14**
Mondo Bio **13**

Ferry Terminal
ⓘ Tourist Information
Ⓟ Parking

Gulf of Naples
(Golfo di Napoli)

Marine Piccola

To Naples, Ischia
To Naples
To Capri

Traghetti Ferries
Aliscafi Hydrofoils

Marina S. Francesco
Marina Grande
Marine Grande

CAMPANIA
Benevento
NAPLES
Pozzuoli
Ischia
Capri
Sorrento
Salerno
TYRRHENIAN SEA

0 200 yds
0 200 m

Moments **Taking a Cooking Class**

If you like the local cuisine, you can sign up for a cooking class at the **Sorrento Cooking School** (Viale dei Pini 52; ⓒ **081-8783555;** www.sorrentocooking school.com). Classes last 3 hours and end with lunch or dinner, at which you eat what you prepared (or what the chef has, in the worst case), and drink local wine. Prices run about 120€ ($150) per class.

Most big hotels have private beaches—usually these resemble piers extending into the sea. For a real beach, go east to small **Marinella,** or farther east towards **Vico Equense** (see earlier in this chapter). Our favorite beach is the one at **Punta del Capo** ⓕ, west of town; above the beach are the ruins of the Roman **Villa of Pollio Felice,** and the so-called **Bagno della Regina Giovanna (Queen Giovanna's Bath)**—a small pool of water enclosed by rocks. This is a nice excursion to do on foot, from a trail starting at the Piazza of Capo di Sorrento, as well as by boat (see below).

Renting a boat here (see "Getting Around" earlier in this chapter) is recommended, because it will allow you to see the cliffs from the sea as well as the rocky coast's numerous ancient remains of elegant summer villas built by well-to-do Romans. Most often, only the grottoes and terraces that lined the descent to the sea from the villas above have survived over the centuries. The boat excursion to **Punta del Capo** (see above) is great; you reach the cove in about a half-hour. Another pleasant boat ride is the one to the **Grotta delle Sirene,** which lies eastward from Marina Piccola and past Sant'Agnello. We recommend renting a boat with a driver who can double as a guide and lead you to all the best spots.

Sorrento is also an excellent base for hiking excursions through the nearby mountains. One of the most beautiful of the area's hikes starts from Piazza Sant'Agnello in Sant'Agnello, from which you can take Via Bonaventura Gargiulo up to **Trasaella,** at an altitude of 196m (643 ft.), and then continue towards **Colli di Fontanelle** at an altitude of 343m (1,125 ft.). From the center of this village begins (across Via Belvedere) the trail to **Punta Sant'Elia** ⓕⓕⓕ, the point on the other side of the peninsula overlooking the Gulf of Salerno, just across from the little islands of LiGalli. (See "Getting Around," earlier in this chapter, for trail information.)

Hiring a guide will add to your experience; the best in the area is **Giovanni Visetti** (ⓒ **081-8089613;** www.giovis.com), an expert on this coast and its hinterlands, who organizes guided hikes of varying difficulty and cost.

WHERE TO STAY

This mecca of international tourism offers endless choices, both in Sorrento proper and in Sant'Agnello, to the east of town. Below are some of the very best.

EXPENSIVE

Albergo Cocumella This luxurious hotel is located in Sant'Agnello, within walking distance of Sorrento's center. It is housed inside a Jesuit monastery, which was turned into a hotel in 1822 and maintains its historical flavor. While here, you'll tread in the steps of such famous guests as Goethe and the Duke of Wellington, who enjoyed the magnificent park surrounding the hotel and the terrace overlooking the sea. Of course, rooms opening over the terrace are the most beautiful, but all rooms are furnished with the same 19th-century elegance and style, in keeping with the venerable atmosphere. If the weather's nice, this place offers barbecue lunches by the pool.

Via Cocumella 7, 80065 Sant'Agnello. ℂ 081-8782933. Fax 081-8783712. www.cocumella.com. 50 units. 312€–440€ ($388–$550) double; from 450€ ($563) suite. Rates include buffet breakfast. AE, DC, MC, V. Free parking. Closed Nov–Mar. **Amenities:** 2 restaurants; bar; outdoor pool; outdoor tennis court; health club; spa; concierge; room service; babysitting; laundry service. In room: A/C, satellite TV, minibar, hair dryer, safe.

Grand Hotel Excelsior Vittoria 🏵🏵🏵   This is the best hotel in Sorrento, and one of the best hotels in the world, housed in an impressive villa surrounded by a park right in the heart of town. Welcoming guests since 1834, this exclusive hotel has counted among its guests Lord Byron, Wagner, Oscar Wilde, and a long list of royalty. Still run by the same family (the Fiorentino) since its opening, it offers exquisite and individualized service. The elegant public spaces and terraces—still with the original 19th-century furnishings—are perfect places to enjoy a drink. The huge guest rooms are elegant abodes furnished with many antiques (and with all the modern comforts). From the hotel, private elevators take guests to the hotel's private beach-pier on Marina Piccola.

Piazza Tasso 34, 80067 Sorrento. ℂ **081-8071044.** Fax 081-8771206. www.exvitt.it. 105 units. 315€–380€ ($388–$475) double, from 525€ ($650) suite; low season 270€ ($338) double, from 370€ ($463) suite. Rates include buffet breakfast. Children under 3 stay free in parent's room. AE, DC, MC, V. Free parking. **Amenities:** 2 restaurants; bar; outdoor pool; private pier/beach; concierge; room service; babysitting; laundry service. In room: A/C, satellite TV, minibar, hair dryer, safe.

Grand Hotel Royal 🏵   This panoramic hotel offers a refined ambience and tasteful accommodations. One of the oldest hotels in Sorrento, it was completely renovated in 2003 and now offers modern rooms, a fabulous swimming pool, and relaxing public spaces, including a private beach. Guest rooms are large and bright, with classic furnishings, decorated tiled floors and bathrooms, and private terraces or balconies; most of the rooms have sea views.

Via Correale 42, 80067 Sorrento. ℂ **081-8073434.** Fax 081-8772905. www.manniellohotels.it. 100 units. 160€–300€ ($200–$375) double; from 375€ ($463) suite. Rates include buffet breakfast. Extra bed 40€ ($50). Specials available. Children under 3 stay free in parent's room. AE, DC, MC, V. Free parking. Closed Jan 7–Feb. **Amenities:** Restaurant; 3 bars; outdoor pool; concierge; business center; babysitting; room service; laundry service. In room: A/C, satellite TV, radio, minibar, hair dryer, safe.

MODERATE

Grand Hotel Capodimonte 🏵   If you like to swim, this is the place for you—the Grand Hotel is surrounded by a beautiful garden with a spectacular cascade of five large swimming pools. This family-run, modern hotel offers excellent amenities and beautiful views, together with friendly, personal service. The guest rooms are bright and furnished in a classic style, with pretty tiled floors and good-sized bathrooms; most of them have private balconies with views over the sea or the garden.

Via Capo 16, 80065 Sorrento. ℂ 081-8784555. Fax 081-8071193. www.manniellohotels.it. 90 units. 280€ ($350) double. Rates include buffet breakfast. Specials available. Children under 3 stay free in parent's room. AE, DC, MC, V. Free parking. **Amenities:** 2 restaurants; 2 bars; 5 outdoor pools; concierge; business center; room service; babysitting; laundry service. In room: A/C, satellite TV, radio, minibar, hair dryer, safe.

Grand Hotel Riviera   A modern hotel perched above the sea, this family-run operation offers beautiful accommodations and resort conveniences. Public spaces include a beautiful terrace, swimming pool, garden, and private beach accessible by a dedicated elevator. Guest rooms are spacious, with stylish furnishings upholstered in white or light pastels and a cool Mediterranean atmosphere. Their private terraces overlook either the sea or the private garden.

Via A. Califano 22, 80067 Sorrento. ☎ **081-8072011.** Fax 081-8772100. www.hotelriviera.com. 102 units. 208€–292€ ($250–$363) double. Children under 3 stay free in parent's room. AE, DC, MC, V. Free parking. Closed Nov–Mar. **Amenities:** Restaurant; American bar; outdoor pool; room service; babysitting; laundry service. *In room:* A/C, satellite TV, minibar, hair dryer, safe.

Hotel Imperial Tramontano   Another one of Sorrento's historic hotels, the Tramontano is housed in a former aristocratic palace that encloses two rooms of the house where the 16th-century Italian poet Torquato Tasso was born. Some of Sorrento's most famous visitors have stayed here, including Richard Wagner, Goethe, and Ibsen (who wrote the play *Ghosts* here). Surrounded by a beautiful garden, the hotel offers spacious guest rooms furnished with antiques. Guests have access through an elevator to the hotel's private beach.

Via Vittorio Veneto 1, 80067 Sorrento. ☎ **081-8782588.** Fax 081-8072344. www.tramontano.com. 116 units. 270€ double ($338); from 390€ ($488) suite. Rates include buffet breakfast. Specials are available. Children under 5 stay free in parent's room. AE, MC, V. Free parking. Closed Jan–Feb. **Amenities:** Restaurant; bar; outdoor pool; lounge; concierge; room service; babysitting; laundry service. *In room:* A/C, satellite TV, minibar, hair dryer.

Hotel La Solara Best Western ✹ *Kids*   Located in the upscale residential neighborhood of Sorrento, not far from the picturesque beach of Puolo, this modern hotel was taken over by Best Western in 2002. The chain has maintained the sunny, airy feeling in the guest rooms (decorated with tile-patterned floors and quality furnishings), while upgrading the common areas to a classier level with club chairs and ample room to enjoy a drink and the view. The spaciousness, as well as the amenities, are a plus if you are traveling with children (you'll spend a lot of time at the smaller, kidsize pool). Many of the rooms have sea views and private terraces.

Via Capo 118, 80067 Sorrento. ☎ **081-5338000.** Fax 081-8071501. www.lasolara.com. 40 units. 217€ ($263). Children under 3 stay free in parent's room. AE, DC, MC, V. Free parking. Closed Jan–Feb. **Amenities:** Restaurant; bar; lounge; Olympic-size outdoor pool; heated children's pool; concierge; room service; babysitting; laundry service. *In room:* A/C, satellite TV, dataport, radio, minibar, hair dryer.

INEXPENSIVE

Hotel Gardenia ✹ *Kids*   Guest rooms at this family-run, centrally located hotel are large and are simply but comfortably appointed with modern furniture and tiled floors; all rooms have private balconies. The hotel also has a state-of-the-art Olympic-size swimming pool and a fitness club. Families will love the pool and the possibility of triples and quads. Since the Gardenia is on the main street in town, it can get a bit noisy in summer—because of the tourists rather than cars: Corso Italia is closed to traffic from 7pm to 7am and again from 10am to 1pm.

Corso Italia 258, 80067 Sorrento. ☎ **081-8772365.** Fax 081-8074486. www.hotelgardenia.com. 30 units. 150€ ($188) double, 188€ ($225) triple, 225€ ($275) quad; low season 100€ ($125) double, 125€ ($150) triple, 150€ ($188) quad. Rates include buffet breakfast. Extra bed 25€ ($31). Specials available. Children under 3 stay free in parent's room. AE, DC, MC, V. Free parking. Closed Jan to mid-Feb. **Amenities:** Restaurant; bar; garden with piano bar in summer; outdoor pool; outdoor tennis court; concierge; babysitting; same-day laundry service. *In room:* A/C, satellite TV, minibar, hair dryer, safe.

Hotel Regina ✹   Just steps from the sea and Marina Grande, and a short walk from the center of town, this hotel offers simple and quiet accommodations at excellent prices. Guest rooms are functional, with good-sized bathrooms and balconies. About half of the rooms open onto the sea, and the rest have garden views. The hotel requires half-board, meaning that breakfast and dinner are included in your room rate.

Via Marina Grande 10, 80067 Sorrento. ⓒ **081-8782722.** Fax 081-8782721. 36 units. 95€–150€ ($119–$188) double. Rates include breakfast and dinner. Extra bed 25€ ($31). Specials available. Children under 6 stay free in parent's room. AE, DC, MC, V. Parking: 12€ ($15). Closed Nov 15–Jan 31. **Amenities:** Dining room; lounge; concierge; room service; babysitting; laundry service. *In room:* A/C, satellite TV, dataport, hair dryer, safe.

Johanna Park *(Finds)* This welcoming family-run hotel is built on the cliff on the west side of town and compensates for its relative distance from the town's center with large, well-lit guest rooms, each with a private terrace that allows for a fantastic views. The furnishings are pleasant and the new bathrooms are modern and good-sized (with both tub and shower). Though only a few years old, the hotel has been constructed to meet current standards. The furnishings—tiled floors; comfortable beds, desks, and chairs in dark woods—have an understated, tasteful feel. The common areas, too, choose tradition over glitz, in marble floors and potted palms.

Via Nastro Verde 25, 80067 Sorrento. ⓒ **081-8072472.** Fax 081-8073724. 30 units. 160€ ($200) double. Rates include buffet breakfast. Extra bed 25€ ($31). Specials available. Children under 6 stay free in parent's room. AE, DC, MC, V. Free parking. **Amenities:** Restaurant; bar; outdoor pool; concierge; room service; babysitting; laundry service. *In room:* A/C, satellite TV, minibar, hair dryer, safe.

Majestic Palace *✦* This elegant hotel enjoys a superior position overlooking the sea in nearby Sant'Agnello—you can easily walk to Sorrento from here along a scenic road in a half-hour or less. Surrounded by orange trees, it offers modern guest rooms, all with private balconies or terraces. Rooms are spacious and furnished with care: The tiled floors have woven rugs in the right places (by the bed), hardwood desks and furniture, and chandeliers. We especially like the hotel's common areas, which you'll actually want to use—a series of rooms separated by arched portals, with overstuffed chairs, antiques, statuary, paintings, and an old-world feel.

Via M. Crawford 40, 80065 Sant'Agnello. ⓒ **081-8072050.** Fax 081-8772506. www.majesticpalace.it. 96 units. 148€–188€ ($175–$225) double; 260€ ($325) suite. Rates include buffet breakfast. Specials are available. Children under 2 stay free in parent's room. AE, DC, MC, V. Free parking. Closed Jan 6–Mar 31 and mid-Nov to Dec 24. **Amenities:** 2 restaurants; 2 bars; outdoor pool; piano bar; concierge; business center; room service; laundry service. *In room:* A/C, TV, minibar, hair dryer, safe.

WHERE TO DINE

Sorrento's waterside and main streets are lined with restaurants big and small, traditional and modern, and the usually good food focuses on fresh fish and savory pastas. In addition to our suggestions below, remember that many of the hotels reviewed earlier also boast restaurants, often offering alfresco dining on terraces overlooking the sea—romantic settings for sunset dinners.

EXPENSIVE

L'Antica Trattoria *✦* CAMPANIAN This picturesque restaurant has served excellent food, mainly local specialties, for over 200 years. Their *antipasti* buffet is laden with a large array of seafood and vegetable dishes. Among the *primi,* let yourself be tempted by the house specialty: *spaghetti alla ferrolese* (spaghetti with a complicated seasoning of fish roe, shrimp, red cabbage, and cream). The lasagna and the seafood ravioli are also delicious. For a secondo, one of their specialties is fish cooked in a salt crust: It comes out savory and moist. When they offer *pezzogna,* do not miss the fish prepared in a spicy tomato and shellfish sauce.

Via Padre Reginaldo Giuliani 33. ⓒ **081-8071082.** Reservations recommended. Secondi 18€–35€ ($23–$44). AE, MC, V. Tues–Sun noon–3:30pm and 7–11:30pm; daily in summer. Closed Jan 10–Feb 10.

MODERATE

Caruso *✻* SORRENTINE   This elegant restaurant is dedicated to the famous Italian tenor who so loved Sorrento. The cuisine is among the best on this peninsula—where the competition is strong. The menu is seasonal, and you will find it difficult to get beyond the *primi:* delicious *ravioli all'aragosta* (lobster ravioli) or *ravioli con salsa di melanzane* (ravioli with an eggplant sauce), as well as *lasagne ai frutti di mare* (seafood lasagna) and tasty *riso con zucchine e gamberi* (rice with shrimp and zucchini). If you have room for a secondo, try the grilled fish. For dessert, *torta di arance e noci* (orange and walnut cake) is not to be missed if it's available.

Via Sant'Antonino 12. ✆ 081-8073156. www.ristorantemuseocaruso.com. Reservations recommended. Secondi 16€–32€ ($20–$40). AE, DC, MC, V. Daily noon–3:30pm and 7:30–11:30pm.

Il Buco *✻* CREATIVE SORRENTINE   Set by the ancient city gate, this new restaurant is housed in what was once a convent's wine cellar (with outdoor tables during summer). The restaurant's menu of fine, imaginative cuisine changes according to the daily market. Also offered are two tasting menus, one seafood-based and the other meat-based. Some of the pasta dishes have unusual, creative taste combinations, such as *fusilli alla zucca e gamberi* (homemade pasta with shrimp and pumpkin), or *ravioli di pesce ai peperoni* (seafood ravioli with sweet peppers). Don't forget to try the local wine—it's a standout.

Rampa Marina Piccola 5. ✆ 081-8782354. Reservations recommended. Prix-fixe menu: seafood 55€ ($69), meat 48€ ($60). Secondi 16€–22€ ($20–$28). AE, DC, MC, V. Daily noon–3:30pm and 7–11:30pm. Closed Jan.

INEXPENSIVE

Canonico *✻* *Value* SORRENTINE   This traditional restaurant right on Sorrento's main square is both handily located and a good value. Canonico offers professional service and well-prepared traditional cuisine. If you find it on the menu, try their beautifully made local specialty, *gnocchi alla sorrentina* (potato dumplings with fresh tomatoes and *mozzarella di bufala*). Another dish you aren't likely to see elsewhere is *paccheri di Gragnano* (local large pasta, a bit lasagna-like).

Piazza Tasso 5. ✆ 081-8783277. Reservations recommended on weekends. Secondi 8€–18€ ($9–$23). AE, DC, MC, V. Tues–Sun noon–3:30pm and 7–11:30pm.

La Favorita O'Parrucchiano SORRENTINE   Located right in the center of town, this venerable restaurant—in operation since 1868—boasts picturesque dining spaces,

---

A Gelato Break to Remember

The absolute best gelato parlor in the whole region—and maybe in the whole country—is **Davide Il gelato** *✻✻* (Via Padre R. Giuliani 39; ✆ 081-8072092), producing divine homemade gelato made with the typical fruits and specialties of this land. Among the 60 flavors (more or less, depending on the day), the most beloved are the sweet and deliciously creamy *noci di Sorrento* (Sorrento walnuts), the rich *cioccolato con canditi* (dark chocolate cream studded with candied oranges), the sinful *rhum babà* (rum-flavored cream with bits of soft cake), and the heavenly *delizia al limone* (a delectable lemon cream).

You'll definitely have to return, at least twice, or three, or four times, to taste them all.

---

including outdoor seating in a beautiful garden. They claim to have invented *cannelloni* (tubes of fresh pasta filled with meat and baked with tomato sauce and cheese). Whether that claim is true or not, the dish is just one of the excellent local specialties on hand. Try *ravioli alla Caprese* (ravioli filled with fresh cheese and seasoned with a sauce of fresh tomatoes and basil) or *frittura* (seafood medley, including calamari, shrimp, and small fish).

Corso Italia 71. (✆ **081-8781321**. Reservations recommended in the evening. Secondi 8.50€–14€ ($9–$18). MC, V. Nov 15–Mar 15 Thurs–Tues noon–3:30pm and 7–11:30pm; Mar 16–Nov 14 daily noon–3:30pm and 7–11:30pm.

Mondo Bio VEGETARIAN   If you are approaching a cholesterol overload or you like to eat vegetarian food, head for this tiny eatery, which doubles as a health food store. The food is strictly organic and the varying menu includes such typical fare as seitan and tofu, along with many other vegetable-based dishes (also vegan).

Via degli Aranci 146. (✆ **081-8075694**. Reservations not accepted. Secondi 5€–9€ ($6.25–$10). No credit cards. Mon–Sat 10am–3pm.

SHOPPING

Sorrento is famous for the bounty of its inland farms and groves: Lemons, walnuts, olive oil, and wine are staples. The local olive oil is special enough to have deserved a D.O.P. label: Penisola Sorrentina D.O.P.; it has an intense and fruity flavor with a sharp, almost peppery aftertaste. The wine has also earned a D.O.C. label, the Penisola Sorrentina, both red and white, called by some experts "the Beaujolais of Campania." And, of course, the cheese, a specialty of these mountains, is top-notch; nowhere more so than at **Apreda,** which has two locations: Via Tasso 6 (✆ **081-8782351**) and Via del Mare 20 (✆ **081-8074059**), where you can still get fresh ricotta made in traditional handmade baskets.

Until recent times, craft making was a popular art form here; sadly, though, it is slowly disappearing. Still, Sorrento has a strong tradition in lace and embroideries, and visitors can continue to buy lovely, intricate examples at **Luigia Gargiulo** (Corso Italia 48; ✆ **081-8781081**). Another of the town's traditional crafts is wood intarsia and marquetry furniture. **Gargiulo & Jannuzzi** (Piazza Tasso 1; ✆ **081-8781041**) has excelled in these crafts since the 19th century; today, you can visit the workshops to see demonstrations of this ancient technique following century-old patterns.

SORRENTO AFTER DARK

The narrow streets of Sorrento's *centro storico* come to life after dark, with cafes, restaurants, and lots of people enjoying the sweet nights. Locals as well as newcomers love sitting on the terrace of the **Fauno Bar** (Piazza Tasso; ✆ **081-8781135;** closed Nov) for an *aperitivo* (apertif).

Summer is when the music festival takes place in Sorrento, with concerts held throughout town. Venues include some of the best hotels (such as the **Albergo Cocumella**'s baroque chapel). The most famous and best performances are the classical music concerts held in the cloister of the **San Francesco church.** Ask at the tourist office for a schedule of events. Also, many restaurants and taverns in town offer live music together with dinner.

For more modern entertainment, head to Piazza Tasso and its two nightclubs: **Fauno Notte Club** (✆ **081-8781021;** www.faunonotte.it; cover 23€/$29); and **Matilda Club** (✆ **081-8773236;** cover 9€/$10). Both clubs have dancing—usually disco—but the first one has a more mature clientele and offers a colorful **Tarantella**

Show (traditional folk dance) between stretches of DJ music; shows are only held March through October (daily 9–11pm). Among the numerous pubs to choose from here, **Chaplin's Video Pub** (Corso Italia 18; ℭ **081-8072551**) and the **English Inn** (Corso Italia 55; ℭ **081-8074357**), located across from each other, both boast good beer selections and lively atmospheres—sometimes too lively on summer weekends. Farther along is the **Merry Monk** (Via Capo 6; ℭ **081-8772409**), another good pub with a good choice of beer.

If you like folk shows, **Teatro Tasso** (Piazza Sant'Antonino; ℭ **081-8075525**; www.teatrotasso.com; tickets 21€/$26 or depending on show) offers a revue of Neapolitan songs called *Sorrento Musical* Monday to Saturday at 9:30pm, but only from March to October. Another choice is **Circolo dei Forestierei** (Via Luigi de Maio 35; ℭ **081-8773012;** closed Nov–Feb), a live music bar with a beautiful terrace and shows every night.

One amusement that's very popular with Italians young and old alike is bowling. In Sorrento, you're guaranteed to find people practicing their strikes and spares at **Bowling** (Via Sant'Antonio; ℭ **081-8071348**).

3 Beyond Sorrento: Massa Lubrense & Punta Campanella

60km (38 miles) S of Naples.

Beyond Sorrento and Vico Equense, you'll find the most authentic part of this peninsula—with towns that manage to stay comparatively deserted even during the summer. Such a surprising feat has been accomplished via mundane means: terrible transportation. The train stops in Sorrento, and the main road (SS 145) bypasses Massa Lubrense completely, looping back towards the coast on the other side of the peninsula to join SS 163, the famous Amalfi Drive. The result is a little-visited, though ruggedly beautiful, corner that feels more remote than it is.

ESSENTIALS

GETTING THERE   All the small towns and villages described in this section can be easily reached from Sorrento, which is only a short **train** or **bus** ride from Naples. From Sorrento, the bus company **SITA** (ℭ **081-5522176;** www.sita-on-line.it) maintains regular service to Massa Lubrense and Sant'Agata sui due Golfi.

Alternatively, you can rent a car, take a taxi, or use a limousine service, such as **2golfi car service** (Via Deserto 30/e, 80064 Sant'Agata sui due Golfi; ℭ **339-8307748** or 338-5628649; fax 081-5330882; www.duegolficarservice).

If you are coming by **car** from Naples, take the exit marked CASTELLAMMARE DI STABIA on autostrada A3 NPOLI SALERNO, and follow signs for VICO EQUENSE and SORRENTO. These will lead you to SS 145, the Sorrento peninsula's coastal road. Take it all the way through Sorrento and stay on Via del Capo as it turns right. This is the narrow local road to Massa Lubrense, Nerano, and Sant'Agata sui Due Golfi.

GETTING AROUND   Renting a **car** is your most flexible option for the area, but a **scooter** is a fun option (as long as the weather's nice). **Taxis** and **limousine services** are other reasonably economical transport, since distances are rather short (see "Getting Around" in the Sorrento section of this chapter).

The best way to enjoy this ragged point of land, however, is by **boat.** You can rent a small launch from one of the many yards in the area, or have one of their captains take you where you want; or you can sign on for one of their organized excursions. In

Marina della Lobra, off Massa Lubrense, **Coop Marina della Lobra** (© 081-8089380; www.marinalobra.com) provides reliable boats. In Marina del Cantone, you can choose between **Cooperativa S. Antonio** (Via Cantone 47/C; © 081-8081638; www.cooperativasantonio.com) and its neighbor, **Nautica 'O Masticiello** (© 081-8081443, 081-8082006, or 339-3142791; www.masticiello.com).

If you are moderately fit, you should not miss the splendid **footpaths** crossing this area's hills and leading to breathtaking panoramic terraces and hidden coves down by the water. The whole area of Massa Lubrense includes 22 marked and maintained hiking paths with a total length of 110km (66 miles), lying within the projected national park of Punta Campanella. The Massa Lubrense visitor center (see below) can give you a free map of the foot and hiking paths.

VISITOR INFORMATION The main tourist office is the **visitor center of Massa Lubrense** (© 081-8089571; www.massalubrense.it). You can also get tourist information at the **Municipio (Town Hall) of Nerano** (© 081-8789083) and at **Sant'Agata dei due Golfi** (© 081-8789083).

FAST FACTS You'll find a **pharmacy** in Via Palma 16 (© 081-8789081). The **hospital** is in Sorrento (see earlier in this chapter). For an **ambulance,** dial © **118.** You can call the **police** at © **113** or 112, and you can reach the **fire department** at © **115.** The **post office** is on Viale Filangeri 40 (© 081-8789045).There is a **Deutsche Bank** on Viale Filangeri 26 (© 081-8089530).

EXPLORING MASSA LUBRENSE

In ancient times, Sorrento was one of Massa Lubrense's active rivals along this coast; today, the town's main opponent is modern transportation. Of course, the challenges involved in getting here have made it that much more attractive to a certain type of traveler. Massa Lubrense is quite popular with Italian tourists, who come here to enjoy its fantastic location over the cliffs (all with private vantage points) and its distance from the throngs of summer tourists.

Well established by the 10th century A.D., Massa Lubrense was destroyed by Carlo I d'Angiò, and rebuilt in the 14th century (higher up the hill for protection). Like the other towns along this coast, the town was later devastated by the Turks during the 16th century. Rebuilding began soon afterwards, including the construction of the 1512 ex-**Cattedrale Santa Maria delle Grazie** (Piazza Vescovado). This church was redone in the 18th century, retaining (in the transept and presbytery) nice examples of the original **majolica floor** ✿. From the terrace to the right of the church, you can enjoy a fantastic **view** ✿✿ over Capri.

From the Maria delle Grazie at the center of town, you can descend on foot to **Marina della Lobra,** a picturesque fishing village with a little harbor—and also one of the peninsula's rare stretches of sand. The sanctuary here—**Santa Maria della Lobra**—was built in the 16th century over a Roman temple, probably dedicated to Minerva. Inside you can see the original 17th-century wood-carved **ceiling** and the 18th-century **majolica floor.**

If you decide instead to continue towards **Annunziata** from the center of town, you will find yourself in the old Massa Lubrense. **Santissima Annunziata** is the original cathedral of Massa, which was destroyed in 1465 and redone in the 17th century. Nearby are the ruins of the castle—only one tower is standing—which was built in 1389. From the **Belvedere,** you can enjoy a **panorama** ✿✿✿ that encompasses the whole Gulf of Naples.

WHERE TO STAY

MODERATE

Hotel Bellavista Francischiello && This family-run hotel enjoys a wonderfully scenic position on the cliffs. Guest units are bright and comfortable, with tiled floors, spacious bathrooms, and private terraces (the sunset views, with Capri in the foreground, are amazing). Amenities include a swimming pool set on a garden terrace overlooking the sea, and a private beach. The attached restaurant, **Riccardo di Francischiello,** claims to be the heir of the historic **Antico Francischiello** next door (see "Where to Dine," later in this section); to settle the score you'll have to give each a fair trial.

Via Partenope 26, 80061 Massa Lubrense. ✆ **081-8789181.** Fax 081-8089341. www.francischiello.it. 28 units. 150€ ($188) double. Rates include buffet breakfast. Extra bed 30€ ($37). Children under 6 stay free in parent's room. AE, DC, MC, V. Free parking. **Amenities:** Restaurant; bar; outdoor pool; concierge; room service; babysitting; laundry service. *In room:* A/C, satellite TV, minibar, hair dryer, safe.

INEXPENSIVE

Ristorante Hotel La Primavera Another family-run hotel, this is a small and comfortable place, offering quiet accommodations and a relaxing atmosphere at moderate prices. The large guest rooms are pleasantly decorated and have good-sized bathrooms. Each unit has a private small terrace. The hotel's restaurant is quite good and offers local fare.

Via IV Novembre 3g, 80061 Massa Lubrense. ✆ **081-8789125.** Fax 081-8089556. www.laprimavera.biz. 20 units. 90€ ($112). Rates include buffet breakfast. Extra bed 25€ ($31).Children under 6 stay free in parent's room. AE, DC, MC, V. Free parking. Closed mid-Jan to mid-Feb. **Amenities:** Restaurant; bar; room service; babysitting; laundry service. *In room:* A/C, TV, hair dryer, safe.

WHERE TO DINE

For a snack or a more substantial meal, try the delicious local bread, which comes studded with your choice of salami, local walnuts, olives, or sweet peppers. Try **Antico Panificio Gargiulo** (Via Rivo a Casa 8) for a good sampling.

Antico Francischiello da Peppino && SORRENTINE This is one of the region's most famous restaurants, which has attracted customers all the way from Naples and beyond for decades. It has grown to a large size to accommodate its extensive clientele, but the atmosphere remains relaxed. We consider the fame justified: The food is really good and the service is professional. All the local specialties are prepared with practiced skill—the seafood tasting menu is a great choice, allowing you to try a large variety of dishes. You might find *cozze gratinate* (mussels au gratin), *gnocchetti verdi all'astice* (green potato dumplings with lobster), or *zuppa di pesce* (fish stew), all prepared with the freshest seafood. There is a rich buffet of *antipasti,* and the desserts are delicious. An *aperitivo* on the terrace here is an absolute must, especially at sunset.

Via Partenope 27, Massa Lubrense. ✆ **081-5339780.** www.francischiello.com. Reservations recommended on weekends. Secondi 12€–21€ ($15–$26). AE, MC, V. Thurs–Tues noon–3:30pm and 7–11:30pm; daily in summer.

Beitempi && SORRENTINE/CREATIVE This recently renovated restaurant serves simple but delicious local cuisine in pleasantly rustic small dining rooms (or on a terrace in clement weather). On the menu you might find such delicious specialties as the unusual *pasta e ceci coi gamberi* (thick soup of garbanzo beans, short pasta, and shrimp) or *fettuccine al peperoncino* (fresh homemade pasta with red pepper)—everything is simple, hearty, and satisfying. You can also take a break from seafood overload here: They prepare a great *misti di carne alla griglia,* a platter of several kinds of perfectly grilled meats. Homemade breads and desserts round out your meal—don't pass up the *delizia al limone* (small puff pastries filled with lemon-flavored cream), a traditional local dessert masterfully prepared here. You'll find several local wines among the fine selection.

Via Termine 3. Ⓒ 081-5330240. Reservations recommended on weekends. Secondi 8€–15€ ($9.20–$19). No credit cards. Thurs–Tues noon–3:30pm and 7–11:30pm; summer daily.

Il Grottino SORRENTINE   Under the shade of citrus plants and grapevines, this rustic trattoria serves local fare, nicely prepared. The menu is seasonal, but do be sure to try *pennette con le zucchine* (short penne pasta with zucchini) or *manicaretti ripieni di mozzarella e ricotta* (baked pasta filled with mozzarella and ricotta and served in a terra-cotta casserole). The winter menu includes platters of grilled meat, which you can enjoy in the small dining rooms containing fireplaces and arched ceilings. The local wine here is excellent.

Via Villaggio Caso 23. Ⓒ 081-8081012. Reservations recommended on weekends. Secondi 8€–16€ ($9.20–$20). No credit cards. Thurs–Tues noon–3:30pm and 7–11:30pm; daily in summer.

EXPLORING SANT'AGATA SUI DUE GOLFI 🌟🌟

Sant'Agata sui Due Golfi is located a short distance from the SS 145 and is the first village you'll encounter if you stay on the main road after Sorrento towards Positano. The crown of the area, so to speak, it is built on a mountain ridge. As the town's name suggests—*sui due Golfi* means "over the two Gulfs"—Sant'Agata has a commanding view over not one but two bays, Salerno and Naples. About 10km (6 miles) south of Sorrento, 14km (9 miles) west of Positano, and only 6km (4 miles) from the beach of Marina del Cantone, this pretty village makes a perfect base for exploring the surrounding area.

The village is focused around **Santa Maria delle Grazie,** a 17th-century church which contains a beautiful **altar** in colored marble and semi-precious stones.

From the center of town, you can take the road toward **Deserto** 🌟. Despite the name, it is a spectacular place with a long history of human habitation—it was a Carmelite hermitage, which then became a convent. At an altitude of 456m (1,496 ft.), it affords a famous **circular panorama** 🌟🌟🌟 over the Campanian coast, stretching all the way from Ischia to Punta Licosa, south of Paestum.

Alternatively, you can take the road to **Torca.** At 352m (1,155 ft.) above sea level, this is a nice village, only a few minutes away. From the village you can enjoy a beautiful view over LiGalli, Positano's small archipelago. You can also go on a great **hike** down to the so-called **Fiordo di Crapolla** and its beach. From the village of Torca, take Via Pedara, which will eventually turn into a dirt path. The trail descends a steep slope among olive groves and old farmhouses, and then among the rocks of a narrow crack in the cliff. As you descend on the western side of the cliff, you will see the ruins of the 12th-century abbey of San Pietro. Once at the bottom, you can access a small beach, where the ancient town of Capreolae (today Crappolla) was built. In fact, the ruins of a patrician Roman villa can still be seen here. The blue water beyond the cove is broken by many rocks—the very ones, it is said, where the Sirens wrecked the ships of innocent mariners. Figure on spending about 30 minutes for the descent.

WHERE TO STAY

Besides the hotels listed below, you can get one of the five suites at the elegant restaurant **Don Alfonso** or the delightful **Olimpia Relais** (see "Where to Dine" below).

Impressions

And lo! the Siren shores like mists arise.
Sunk were at once the winds; the air above,
And waves below, at once forgot to move;
Some demon calm'd the air and smooth'd the deep,
Hush'd the loud winds, and charm'd the waves to sleep.
Now every sail we furl, each oar we ply;
Lash'd by the stroke, the frothy waters fly. . .

—Homer, *The Odyssey*, book XII, lines 97–101,
translation Alexander Pope (1616)

Expensive

Hotel Iaccarino ＊＊＊   This elegant, quiet hotel offers classy accommodations among the filbert and chestnut trees around the town center. Built in 1890, the hotel was completely restructured in 1990. Kind service is one of the plusses you get in this family-run hotel, together with a quiet location and a swimming pool built on their scenic garden-terrace. Guest rooms are bright, with tiled floors and comfortable furnishings in a classic style. All rooms have private balconies opening over fantastic views.

Via Nastro Verde 4, 80064 Sant'Agata sui due Golfi. ⓒ 081-8780012. Fax 081-5330229. www.iaccarino.com. 90 units. 184€ ($225). Rates include buffet breakfast. Extra bed 35€ ($44). Children under 3 stay free in parent's room. AE, DC, MC, V. Free parking. Closed Oct–Apr. **Amenities:** Restaurant; bar; outdoor pool; concierge; room service; babysitting; laundry service. *In room:* A/C, satellite TV, minibar, hair dryer, safe.

Moderate

Grand Hotel Hermitage & Villa Romita ＊＊ *Kids*   Immersed in the green of its private park, this hotel offers excellent accommodations at moderate prices, both in the modern hotel and in the adjacent elegant country villa. The hotel's swimming pool is set in a panoramic garden-terrace and has a children's area with games. Guest rooms in both the hotel and the villa are comfortable, ample, and nicely furnished, and each comes with a private balcony. The hotel's restaurant offers excellent local cuisine.

Via Nastro Verde 9, 80064 Sant'Agata sui due Golfi. ⓒ 081-8780082 or 081-8782581 (winter). Fax 081-8780062. www.grandhotelhermitage.it. 76 units. 120€ ($150) double. Rates include breakfast. AE, V. Free parking. Closed Nov–Mar. **Amenities:** Restaurant; American bar; outdoor pool; concierge; room service; babysitting; laundry service. *In room:* A/C, satellite TV, minibar, hair dryer, safe.

Hotel delle Palme   Located right in the center of town, this pleasant hotel was created in the 1950s by adding onto a pre-existing 19th-century private villa (the hotel is still family-run). It is surrounded by a private park with a large swimming pool, and is decorated with period furniture and nice artwork. Guest units have modern furnishings and large bathrooms.

Corso Sant'Agata 36, 80064 Sant'Agata sui due Golfi. ⓒ 081-8780025. www.santagatasuiduegolf.it/dellepalme. 44 units. 95€–130€ ($119–$162) double. Rates include breakfast. AE. Free parking. **Amenities:** Restaurant; bar; large outdoor pool; concierge; room service; babysitting; laundry service. *In room:* A/C, satellite TV, minibar, hair dryer.

Inexpensive

Hotel Sant'Agata *Finds*   Close to the center of town and housed in a modern building, this hotel is a welcome addition to Sant'Agata. Guest rooms are spacious and pleasantly furnished, with tiled floors and modern bathrooms.

Via dei Campi 8/a, 80064 Sant'Agata sui due Golfi. ℭ 081-8080363. Fax 081-5330749. www.hotelsantagata.com. 28 units. 120€ ($150) double; ;lLow season 80€ ($100) double. Rates include breakfast. AE, MC, V. Free parking. **Amenities:** Dining room; bar; concierge; babysitting; laundry service. *In room:* A/C, satellite TV, minibar, hair dryer, safe.

WHERE TO DINE
Expensive
Don Alfonso 1890 ★★★ SORRENTINE/CREATIVE   Reputed to be the best restaurant in southern Italy, and a member of the Relais & Châteaux association, Don Alfonso does indeed offer superb everything: food, location, and service. The elegant dining rooms overlook the two imposing gulfs, and the ambience is welcoming and never stuffy. Lidia and Alfonso Iaccarino, in order to have a source of perfect ingredients, also started an organic farm—**Azienda Agricola Le Peracciole,** on Punta Campanella. All the food on the menu is prepared with produce and meats from this farm, while fish and cheese come from trustworthy local producers. They offer two prix-fixe menus, the *menu degustazione* (tasting menu) with a sample of their more creative dishes, and the *menu tradizione* (traditional menu) with their version of traditional Sorrentine classics. You can also choose from the extensive a la carte menu, which is seasonal. You might find *pesce spada ai ceci e al timo* (swordfish with thyme and chickpeas), *salame di cinghiale affumicato all'alloro* (smoked boar salami with bay leaves), or their simple roasted chicken (free-range, organically fed, and seasoned with fresh herbs—exquisite). Do ask to visit the century-old cellar, excavated in tufa stone, which spans three levels.

You can also sleep in the Locanda's few rooms, which they rent for 190€ ($238), including breakfast. At the shop on the premises you can buy olive oil, cured meats, limoncello, and other products from the farm, as well as a great variety of wines from the cellar. Note that cured meats are available only in winter and early spring.

Corso Sant'Agata 11. ℭ **081-8780026.** Reservations recommended. Secondi 22€–32€ ($28–$40). Prix-fixe *menu degustazione* 110€ ($138); *menu tradizione* 90€ ($112). AE, DC, MC, V. Tues–Sun 12:30–2:30pm and 8–10:30pm (Oct–May closed Tues). Closed mid-Jan through Feb.

Moderate
Villa Oasi of Olimpia Relais SORRENTINE   This is an excellent, moderately priced restaurant housed in a scenic villa, which also offers a few rooms. The cuisine is traditional but adds personal touches that attempt to rival Don Alfonso's (see above), in a much more down-to-earth, homey way. The seasonal menu is based on local produce and fish. You'll find excellent *pasta ai frutti di mare* (pasta with fresh shellfish) and such traditional dishes as *all'acquapazza* (catch of the day).

Via Deserto 26. ℭ **081-8080560.** www.oasiolimpiarelais.it. Reservations recommended. Secondi 12€–21€ ($15–$26). AE, DC, MC, V. Daily noon–3pm and 7:30–10:30pm.

SHOPPING
Excellent cheese abounds at any of the cheese makers in the area. You can get a taste of the local varieties of mozzarella—try the *treccia,* or the *scamorza,* or the delicious *triavulilli*—and the small *cacicavalli farciti* at **Caseificio Cordiale** (Via Campi 30; ℭ **081-8080888**); **Caseificio Savarese** (Via IV Novembre 19/a; ℭ **081-8789825**); and **Caseificio Valestra** (Via Bozzaotra 13, Località Monticchio; ℭ **081-8780119**).

At **Da Ferdinando** (Corso Sant'Agata 53; ℭ **081-8780196**), in addition to cheese, you can find a selection of the best typical farm products in the area, including olive oil, cured meats, dried fruits, and spirits.

EXPLORING NERANO & TERMINI

These small villages are the last stop on the peninsula, perched as they are on cliffs overlooking the gulfs. **Nerano** is a pleasant little village with an altitude of 166m (544 ft.). From the village you can easily descend—on foot or by car—a steep road to Nerano's "harbor," the fishing hamlet of **Marina del Cantone,** with its lovely beach. Opening onto the clear blue sea and dotted with small fishermen's houses, the beach is where locals keep their boats. Should you get tired of sunbathing and swimming here, you can try your hand at boating. Renting a boat (with or without driver) on this coast is a must: It allows you to discover small beaches, inlets, and hidden bays otherwise inaccessible from the high cliffs.

Termini is a delightful hamlet built on a natural terrace at 323m (1,059 ft.), overlooking Capri. The seashore here is a marine park, **Area Marina Protetta di Punta Campanella** (© 081-8089877; www.puntacampanella.org), extending all the way from Punta del Capo, near Sorrento, to Punta Germano, near Positano. From Termini, you can drive down the local road to **Punta Campanella,** the tip of the Sorrento peninsula with its famous lighthouse. The Greek and Roman **Temple of Minerva,** visible to all passing ships, used to rest near this lighthouse. Punta Campanella takes its name from the watchtower—built in 1335 and redone in 1566—and its bell, which warned of pirate incursions (*campanella* means small bell). Near the tower are the remains of a Roman villa. From a cliff to the east of the tower, you can look down into the wild, but protected, **Bay of Ieranto** 𝒜𝒜𝒜 (see below).

Punta Campanella *Finds* In addition to the drive to Punta Campanella described above, you can hike to this spot at the tip of the Sorrento peninsula. Although tourists flock to the seaside, few have enjoyed the experience of hiking this dramatic coast. From the village of Termini, take the sloping small street to the right of the central square. This road slowly descends to the hamlet of Cercito, and then continues down the **Vallone della Cala di Mitigliano.** This beautiful valley is filled with olive groves and typical vegetation (called *macchia mediterranea*) including scented *mirto,* a plant quite rare nowadays. The trail then crosses a plateau with large boulders and the ruins of **Torre di Namonte,** a medieval watchtower. Past the tower, the trail begins a steep descent towards the sea as the beautiful profile of Capri looms into view. You'll get clear views of Capri, with Monte Tiberio, Monte Solaro, and the Faraglioni, only 5km (3 miles) away. On the last part of the trail, you'll have a chance to walk the ancient Via Minerva, the original road that led to the Greek temple dedicated to Minerva once occupying this cape.

The olive groves in this area go back thousands of years, and were originally planted by the Greeks. They believed that olive oil was an invention of Minerva, the goddess of wisdom—we tend to agree with that—and brought gifts of olive oil to her temple. Nearby is the **Torre Minerva,** built in the 14th century to signal, with the sound of its *campanella* (bell), the arrival of the Saracen pirates. Today a modern lighthouse guards this dangerous cape and its waters, made treacherous by the many rocks in the Capri Narrows. The trail takes you from 300m (984 ft.) down to sea level; count on spending about 45 minutes for the descent and a bit more for the ascent. An even more picturesque—but longer, and more strenuous—alternative, is to take the trail that climbs from Termini to Mount San Costanzo, at 497m (1,630 ft.) above sea level; this then descends to Punta Campanella. Allow about 3 hours for this trail.

Bay of Ieranto 𝒜𝒜𝒜 You can reach the Bay of Ieranto from land over a trail that is quite steep at times and will take you a little over an hour, one-way. The best time to go is early afternoon. From Nerano, take the street at the right-hand side of the village, past the last houses. This street connects to a trail that climbs along the slopes of **Monte San Costanzo,** the westernmost peak of the **Monti Lattari.** The trail descends through typical vegetation, *macchia mediterranea,* and eventually descends the cliffs overlooking the sea, affording spectacular views. Once at the bottom, you'll find a beach and a cove of clear water where, in the afternoon, oblique sunlight creates the unique illusion that the water has disappeared and the boats are suspended in thin air.

An arrival here by boat is even more striking. If you're in the mood for a wonderful ride, rent a boat from Marina del Cantone and head—or have yourself driven to—the Bay of Ieranto. (Either of the boat companies we've listed earlier will work.) Count on about a half-day for the excursion. From the beach of Marina del Cantone, hug the coast heading southwest till you see the large Y-shaped promontory called *Sedia del Diavolo* ("Devil's Chair," a particularly appropriate name when you see it during a flaming sunset). As you pass the first arm of the Y with the medieval watchtower **Torre di Montalto,** you will discover a little bay, which is an introduction to the more spectacular bay that awaits you a little farther along. The splendid Ieranto—from the Greek *Hyeros Anthos,* meaning "Sacred Flower"—was declared a protected area in 1984 and, as a result, it remains a completely untouched haven. At the western end of the bay, you'll spot Punta Campanella, behind which are Costiera Sorrentina and the Gulf of Naples.

WHERE TO STAY

Taverna del Capitano *ℛℛ*   This small and comfortable hotel, right on the beach of Marina del Cantone, is a refuge of Mediterranean simplicity. Guest rooms are located above the restaurant, and all have terraces overlooking the sea. Both the restaurant and hotel are run by the Caputo family. You will want to stay here at least a week, just to soak in the clear sea and the warm sun—the hotel has a private beach. ***Note:*** Credit cards aren't accepted, so make sure you have cash.

Piazza delle Sirene 10, 80061 Massa Lubrense, Località Marina del Cantone. ℂ 081-8081028. Fax 081-8081892. www.tavernadelcapitano.it. 15 units. 130€ ($163). Rates include breakfast. Free parking on street. Closed Jan–Feb. **Amenities:** Restaurant; bar; babysitting. *In room:* A/C, TV.

WHERE TO DINE

Lo Scoglio *ℛ (Finds*   Opened in 1958 by the De Simone family, this restaurant is still run by Signora Antonietta with her children and nephews, all of whom will surely give you a warm welcome. Everything on the menu is made from local produce and other ingredients from family-run farms in the area. The simple *spaghetti con le zucchine* (spaghetti with zucchini) is excellent, as are *linguine di aragosta* (linguine with the local lobster) and, when available, tasty *zuppa di pesce* (soupy fish stew). All the fish here are not only caught by local fishermen but, whenever possible, kept alive in the restaurant's seawater fish tank. The desserts are homemade and rich without being heavy.

Piazze delle Sirene 15, Località Marina del Cantone. ℂ 081-8081026. Reservations recommended on weekends. Secondi 12€–28€ ($15–$35). AE, DC, MC, V. Daily noon–3pm and 7:30–10:30pm.

Quattro Passi SORRENTINE/CREATIVE   Come here when the weather's nice, and you can dine on a charming garden-terrace among lemon trees and bougainvillea. A somewhat formal atmosphere is matched by professional service and excellent food. The sophisticated appetizers might include *totano ripieno di provola con cozza gratinata e tortino di patate* (stuffed squid and mussels au gratin with potato torte). Among the primi are *pappardelle fave piselli e formaggio* (large fresh pasta with peas, fresh fava beans, and cheese shavings); and the secondi include intriguing choices like *rose di sogliola con capperi pomodorini e patate* (rosettes of sole with capers, cherry tomatoes, and potatoes). The bread is homemade and comes with flavored butter (citrus or herbs). For dessert try the local specialty, *delizie al limone* (puff pastry filled with lemon cream). Or try one of the more creative choices, such as the superb chocolate duo: chocolate torte with coffee ice-cream cake and orange sauce.

Via Vespucci 13, Marina del Cantone. ☎ 081-8081271. www.ristorantequattropassi.com. Reservations recommended on weekends. Secondi 21€–42€ ($26–$53). AE, MC, V. Thurs–Tues 12:30–3:30pm and Thurs–Mon 7:30–11pm; daily in summer. Closed Nov–Dec 25.

Taverna del Capitano ☆☆ This is our preferred restaurant on the peninsula, offering wonderful local homemade cuisine born from careful research and a great love for the produce of this land. The chef's free interpretation marries the tastes of the sea with those of the vegetable garden he personally supervises. There are three tasting menus at different prices and a menu a la carte, all seasonal; you might find *insalata di aragosta con verdure* (lobster and fresh vegetable salad), *zuppa di gamberi e cicorie selvatiche* (shrimp and dandelion soup), and *pesce alla salsa di agrumi* (fish in citrus sauce). Desserts, like everything else, are homemade. The wine list has a small but excellent selection of wines both regional and national.

Piazza delle Sirene 10. ☎ 081-8081028. Reservations recommended on weekends. Tasting menus 50€–80€ ($63–$100). Secondi 14€–28€ ($18–$35). AE, DC, MC, V. Wed–Sun 12:30–3:30pm and Tues–Sun 7:30–10:30pm; daily in summer. Closed 3 weeks in Jan.

The Amalfi Coast

Celebrated by tourists since the 19th century as one of the most beautiful stretches of coast in the world, the Costiera Amalfitana, or Amalfi Coast, was also well known during antiquity and the Middle Ages. Its unique views and plunging cliffs have inspired the works of many famous artists, from Giovanni Boccaccio to Richard Wagner. The small towns and hamlets along the Costiera have also been the preferred refuges of Henrik Ibsen, Pablo Picasso, Rudolf Nureyev and, more recently, Gore Vidal.

The Amalfi Coast is a magical landscape of cultivated cliffs hanging over a beautiful sea, interspersed with villages literally growing from the underlying rocks. Here and there, the mouth of a small river has created a natural harbor and a favorable nook for a larger town. Such is the case in Amalfi, the queen of the Costiera. The valley of its river allowed for the development of the paper mills that produced paper for much of Europe during the Middle Ages and well into the Renaissance, while its harbor became the shipyard that fueled Amalfi's political and commercial power.

Although they're the most famous towns here, Amalfi and Positano are not alone by the sea: They share the company of a number of smaller and lesser-known but delightful villages, such as Cetara, Minori, and Praiano. In between these towns and hamlets, small beaches are scattered at the bottoms of the cliffs— which make for beautiful, but sometimes forbidding, landscapes.

As you will rapidly discover, the landscape is almost vertical. The sea might be a thousand feet below you, but it is never far, even when you think you have gone well into the mountains. Ravello—the third most famous town of this coast—is the perfect example, but there are many other breathtaking views to be enjoyed from lesser-known settlements such as Tramonti and Agerola. For instance, the slopes of Monti Lattari will reward those daring enough to climb it with superb views and hidden hamlets.

In addition to swimming in the magical nearby sea, the best way to enjoy this region may be to hike one of its many mountain trails. The trails have been in use for thousands of years by local farmers and fishermen, and indeed, until very recently (the famed Amalfi Dr., Rte. SS 163, was built in 1840), they were the only way to travel from one hamlet to the next.

This area offers not only incomparable natural beauty, but a variety of historical and artistic monuments and an original architectural style, of which you'll see examples in both the larger towns and in smaller and less-frequented ones.

Be forewarned that a place famed for millennia can't be much of a secret anymore. The Amalfi Coast is one of the most visited seaside destinations in the world, and tends to get overcrowded during summer. Yet summer is when the Amalfi Coast is at its best, with innumerable art and cultural events. During this period, the sweet evening air is pervaded by the scent of citrus flowers—providing a perfect background for the area's numerous music festivals. In winter, everything is much quieter, as many places close down and the sea gets too cold to swim in. You may have the place all to yourself in these colder months, but you'll miss much of the spirit it shows when in full bloom.

1 Planning Your Trip to the Amalfi Coast

GETTING THERE When possible, we prefer to travel to this coast by ferry because we love approaching its destinations from the sea; indeed, you would sell yourself short if you didn't have a look at this stretch of coast from the water. **Alicost** (© 081-7611004 or 081-811986 in Naples; © 089-873301 or 089-871483 in Amalfi; and © **089-875032** or 089-811164 in Positano; www.lauroweb.com/alicost. htm or www.alilauro.it) maintains regular *aliscafo* (hydrofoil) and *motonave* (regular ferry) service from Naples, Sorrento, Salerno, and the islands of Capri and Ischia, to Positano, Amalfi, and Minori. Fares run between 1.50€ ($1.90) and 17€ ($21) depending on the distance and the boat. *Note:* You must make reservations at least 24 hours in advance. The **Metrò del Mare** (© **199-446644;** www.metrodelmare.com) operates between Naples and Salerno April through September, with stops in Amalfi and Positano. The ferry ride from **Molo Beverello** in Naples to Positano takes 75 minutes with the express line MM2, and about 2 hours with the local line MM3; count on 25 additional minutes to Amalfi on either ferry line. The special ticket **Terra&Mare** includes the ferry plus ground transportation for 45 minutes before and 45 minutes after the ferry link and costs 8.50€ ($11). **Cooperativa Sant'Andrea** (© **089-873190;** www.coopsantandrea.it) offers regular frequent service between Salerno, Vietri, Maiori, Minori, Cetara, Amalfi, Positano, and Sorrento, as well as special cruises and excursions, including to Capri; tickets are about 5€ to 9€ ($6.25–$11) depending on the distance.

SITA (© **081-5522176** in Naples and © 089-871016 in Amalfi; www.campania trasporti/sita or www.sita-on-line.it) maintains regular direct service from Naples, Sorrento, and Salerno to Amalfi and Positano; for most other villages and hamlets you need to switch in Amalfi (bus terminal on Piazza Flavio Gioia, © **089-871009**) to the local lines serving the area.

It may sound extravagant, but hiring a car with a chauffeur makes sense, especially if you plan to stay here only a day or two. This option is gaining popularity because its cost is relatively moderate and it has so many advantages. It removes the stress of driving and parking, it affords you complete comfort and your own pace, and your experienced local driver can double as a guide. You'll spend about 35€ ($44) per hour for two people in a sedan for a half-day trip; less for longer periods. We recommend **ANA Limousine Service** (Piazza Garibaldi 73, 80100 Napoli; ©/fax **081-282000**); **2golfi car service** (Via Deserto 30/e, 80064 Sant'Agata sui due Golfi; © **339-8307748** or 338-5628649; fax 081-5330882; www.duegolficarservice); and **Italy Limousine** (© **081-8016184,** 335-6732245, or 338-9681866; www.italylimousine.it). All of these use new cars with air-conditioning (very important in summer) and trained English-speaking drivers.

Myth or reality? Is the Amalfi Coast Drive as hair-raising as they say? Much depends on whom you ask. One of the world's most famous scenic drives, the whole stretch of road between Vietri sul Mare and Positano is only 36km (22 miles); and while the technical difficulty of the drive is moderate (easier than the road to Hana in Maui, let's say, but more difficult than the Pacific Coastal Highway), traffic and the

Neapolitan aggressive driving style can turn it into a headache for even the most experienced driver—and into a complete nightmare if you generally drive on spacious freeways in flat or gentle terrain. Alternative forms of transportation are well developed (see above), so you might do yourself a favor if you take advantage of one of those. On the other hand, if you want to explore this area in depth within a limited time period, having your own car with driver will provide you with more flexibility.

If you decide to drive, from the exit VIETRI SUL MARE on the *autostrada* A3 NAPOLI-SALERNO, follow the signs for VIETRI, MAIORI, AMALFI, and POSITANO; they will lead you to the famed SS 163, the coastal road which meanders all the way from Salerno to Positano and a bit beyond. Many of the villages and hamlets of the Amalfi Coast are right on SS 163—which is why the traffic is unbearable—and those that aren't on SS 163 are on well-indicated side roads off SS 163.

You can also reach SS 163 from Vico Equense and Sorrento heading east. You'll save about 20 minutes, but you'll be driving right at the edge of the cliff; for your peace of mind, choose the inner lane. In any case, you'll enjoy the best views only when you stop and park along this route. *Note:* Because of the solid traffic here in summer, local authorities enforce a system of "alternate plate number" permits, under which only cars with license plates ending in even numbers can circulate one day, and only those with uneven plate numbers on the other. Keep this in mind when making your plans.

GETTING ORIENTED   The Amalfi Coast opens onto the northern half of the Gulf of Salerno, and stretches from the town of Salerno westwards to Positano. Farther west, the Sorrento Peninsula begins, with Punta Campanella—the narrow point of land that divides the Gulf of Salerno from the Gulf of Naples (see chapter 6). There the SS 163 turns into SS 145, the coastal road of the Sorrento Coast, in the Bay of Naples. The other half of the Gulf of Salerno, from Salerno south, is the plain of Paestum, which we cover in chapter 9.

Starting from the Costiera's easternmost point, you will first find **Vietri sul Mare** and then **Cetara,** both mostly visited by local tourists. Proceeding west and passing Capo (Cape) d'Orso, you will enter the Bay of Amalfi. You'll then come, successively, to the villages of **Maiori, Minori, Atrani** and, finally, **Amalfi,** the queen of the Costiera. Between Maiori and Atrani are two local roads that proceed upward and inland following the beds of two streams: the road to **Tramonti** (turnoff in Maiori), and the one for **Scala** and **Ravello** (turnoff just after Minori).

The heart of the Amalfi Coast—and its busiest section—is its westernmost stretch between the Costiera's two most famous places, Amalfi and Positano. Past the cape that defines the Bay of Amalfi—Capo di Conca with **Conca dei Marini**—you will find another cape, Capo Sottile, with **Praiano** to the east and **Vettica Maggiore** to the west; this marks the entrance to the deep cove wherein lies **Positano.** At Conca dei Marini you will find the two turnoffs for the terribly steep but immensely rewarding mountain road for **Agerola** and **Furore** (one appears before you enter the village to the east, and the other turns up in Conca itself).

GETTING AROUND   **Ferries** are really convenient and a lot of locals use them instead of slogging along the local road, often completely clogged with traffic in summer. Vietri, Maiori, Minori, Cetara, Amalfi, and Positano are all connected by ferries (see above). Service is really frequent in the good season, when road traffic is at its worst, and with the hydrofoil, you can cut the travel time in half—views, though, tend to be less nice. To reach the other towns and hamlets not on the ferry routes, taking a **bus** (see above) is often the most convenient, and certainly the cheapest, way to get from one village to another. For example, the ride from Positano to Amalfi will take you about 20 minutes and cost you about 1.30€ ($1.65); the ride from Amalfi to Ravello takes only 12 minutes and costs 1.20€ ($1.50).

Other options are **taxi** (telephone numbers listed in "Fast Facts" for each destination) or **car service** (see above). Distances are short and therefore fares remain very reasonable. Make sure drivers use the meter or agree on a price before going. You can also hire a **boat,** with or without a driver, to take you to secluded beaches (or simply to the next town) from the harbors and marinas of Amalfi, Maiori, and Positano.

Renting a **car** is a possibility we don't recommend, especially in summer, but if you love to drive and hate the idea of getting stuck in traffic, you might like to try your hand at using an Italian **scooter** and play the locals' dangerous swerving game. You can rent both cars and scooters in Sorrento (see chapter 6); and scooters only in Positano at **Positano Rent a Scooter** (Viale Pasitea 99; © **089-8122077**). You'll spend about 40€ ($50) per day for a scooter at the height of summer.

As unlikely as it might seem, there is also much that you can do here **on foot** 🕸🕸. SS 163 has only been around since 1840; before then, trails and footpaths were the only ways to go (other than by sea). These paths are still used for bringing animals to pasture and are well kept and well marked. We suggest the best ones for each destination in the following sections, but if you are into serious **hiking,** you should contact the local tourist offices. You should also get the very good map published by the C.A.I. Club Alpino Italiano *Monti Lattari Penisola Sorrentina, Costiera Amalfitana: carta dei sentieri* sold for 8€ ($10) at the best newsstands and bookstores in Ravello, Amalfi, and Tramonti. You might also want to get in touch with **Comunità Montana Penisola Amalfitana** in Via Municipio, 84010 Tramonti (© **089-876354** or 089-876547), for info on guides and trails.

2 Vietri sul Mare & Cetara: Gates to the Costiera

Vietri is 5km (3 miles) west of Salerno and 20km (12 miles) east of Amalfi on SS 163. Cetera is 6km (3.7 miles) west of Vietri and 15km (9.3 miles) east of Amalfi on SS 163.

The Costiera begins just a few steps northwest of the pretty town of Salerno (see chapter 9), starting with the towns of **Vietri sul Mare** and **Cetara.** The easternmost section of the Amalfi Coast is less known and less crowded: Its two main centers are small working towns with well-established traditional craft industries. Vietri's main street, with its famous ceramic shops, gets a lot of tourist attention, but it usually makes for a hit-and-run shopping excursion, which leaves the area undisturbed. Vietri is indeed a great place for shopping, but it is also well worth a visit for its scenic seashore. Farther westwards, Cetara is a picturesque village with a still-active fishing tradition. It is a great place for a meal by the sea or for relaxing on the beach.

VIETRI SUL MARE

The gateway to the Amalfi Coast, Vietri is a pleasant little town by the sea, famous for its flourishing ceramic industry. Famous foreign artists, many of them German, worked in Vietri during the two World Wars, and their artwork brought this little town international fame. Today, its artistic ceramics are beloved by collectors from around the world. The town has more to offer than vases and plates, though; its key attractions are listed below.

The heart of town is Via Madonna degli Angeli, closed to car traffic and lined with ceramics shops. The first is the most famous—**Ceramiche Artistiche Solimene** 🕸

(Via Madonna degli Angeli 7; ℂ 089-212539 or 089-210048), one of Vietri's historical workshops. Besides visiting their showroom and buying ceramics, you can admire the building itself—a beautiful example of organic architecture from the 1930s by the Italian Paolo Soleri, who went on to work in the U.S. with Frank Lloyd Wright. Inside you can visit a rich collection of ceramics by various contemporary artists. You can see more ceramics—these from the 17th century—in the **San Giovanni Battista** church, where the outside cupola and the interior are decorated in painted majolica. The **panorama** ☜☞ from the square in front of the church is one of the prettiest of the coastal towns.

From Piazza Matteotti in the center of town, you can descend Via Costabile about a half-mile and arrive at the popular beach of **Marina di Vietri,** dominated by a watchtower which was transformed into a villa; if you cross its surrounding park you'll reach a small and more secluded beach. You can swim and sunbathe here at your leisure, although it tends to be crowded at the height of summer.

If you follow the road that heads out of town towards the southwest, after 2km (1 ¼ miles) you will get to **Raito** ☞, a picturesque little village of white-washed houses and gardens. Here is the **Museo della Ceramica** (Via Nuova Raito; ℂ **089-211835;** admission 2€/$2.50; Mon–Sat 9am–1pm; in summer also Thurs and Sat 5–7pm). Created in 1981, the ceramics museum is housed in the scenic Torretta Belvedere of historic **Villa Guariglia,** surrounded by a park. The museum's collection includes some masterworks and is organized into three sections: religious art; items of daily use; and the "German Period," with works created or inspired by the wave of foreign (mainly German) artists who came to work in Vietri between 1929 and 1947. Only 1km (½ mile) farther on is the little hamlet of **Albori** ☞, with its 16th-century church of **Santa Margherita ad Albori,** and prime sea views.

ESSENTIALS
VISITOR INFORMATION   The **Proloco tourist office** is inside the Municipal Building (Piazza Matteotti; ℂ **089-211285).**

WHERE TO STAY
Staying in the Vietri area is an excellent option if you want to visit the Costiera without paying through the nose for an ocean vista; this lesser-known resort is only steps away from the coast's famous and hip destinations, but it is relatively undiscovered (at least by most non-Italians).

Moderate
Hotel Raito ☞   Last renovated in 2004, this is the best hotel in this section of the Amalfi Coast. A modern luxury hotel, it enjoys a superior position high on the cliffs in the village of Raito, 3km (2 miles) south of Vietri. The spacious guest rooms are comfortable, with modern, stylish furnishings; most offer breathtaking views and balconies. All units have good-sized (and new) bathrooms. Guests can ride the free hotel shuttle bus down to its private beach. The hotel's **restaurant** is quite good and serves traditional local cuisine.

Via Nuova Raito 9, Frazione Raito, 84010 Vietri sul Mare. ℂ 089-210033. Fax 089-211434. 52 units. 250€ ($313) double. Rates include buffet breakfast. AE, DC, MC, V. Free parking. **Amenities:** Restaurant; bar; concierge; room service; babysitting; laundry service. *In room:* A/C, TV, minibar, hair dryer, safe.

Inexpensive
Hotel Bristol ⓕⁱⁿᵈˢ   This modern hotel is frequented mostly by Italians, and it enjoys a scenic position on cliffs overlooking the sea, yet near the center of town. A

2004 renovation ensures a uniform level of comfort; guest rooms are well appointed, with nice simple furnishings and modern bathrooms. All have sea views and some have private terraces with tables and chairs. Guests can use the hotel's private beach. The hotel's **restaurant,** offering traditional cuisine, is particularly good.

Via Cristoforo Colombo 2, 84019 Vietri sul Mare. ℂ **089-210800.** Fax 089-210216. www.hotelbristolvietri.com. 22 units. 95€ ($119) double; 105€ ($131) triple; 115€ ($144) quad. AE, DC, MC, V. Free parking. **Amenities:** Restaurant; bar; outdoor pool; concierge; room service; babysitting; laundry service. *In room:* A/C, satellite TV, minibar, hair dryer, safe.

Hotel La Lucertola *(Kids)*   This family-run hotel offers pleasant accommodations and cheerful service, just steps from the hotel's private beach. Moderate-sized guest rooms are simply furnished but decorated with care, and have tiled bathrooms. The hotel also offers a solarium and a children's playground with slides and swings, making this a good choice for families.

Via Cristoforo Colombo 29, Località Marina di Vietri, 84019 Vietri sul Mare. ℂ **089-210255.** Fax 089-210223. www.hotellalucertola.it. 32 units. 114€ ($143) double; low season 85€ ($106) double. Rates include buffet breakfast. Specials available. Children under 3 stay free in parent's room. AE, DC, MC, V. Free parking. **Amenities:** Restaurant; bar; business center; room service; babysitting; laundry service. *In room:* A/C, satellite TV, dataport, Wi-Fi.

Hotel Vietri   This small but comfortable hotel is located on the steep road that leads to the marina, and the shore is only a short walk away. Run by the D'Amico family, the hotel boasts guest rooms with tasteful furniture, tiled bathrooms, and sea views; some have poster beds and a private terrace.

Via Costabile 37, 84019 Vietri sul Mare. ℂ/fax **089-210400.** www.hotelvietri.com. 20 units. 105€ ($131) double; low season 95€ ($119) double. AE, V. Parking: 12€ ($15) in private garage. **Amenities:** Restaurant; bar; outdoor pool; Internet access in lobby; concierge; room service; babysitting; laundry service. *In room:* A/C, satellite TV, minibar, hair dryer, safe.

WHERE TO DINE

In addition to the restaurants reviewed below, you can have excellent meals at the restaurants of the hotels reviewed above..

Expensive

Sapore di Mare ♪ AMALFITAN/SEAFOOD   At this pleasant, upscale restaurant, you'll find imaginative variations on the seafood theme, made by using local ingredients. The menu is seasonal but you might find *fusilli ai gamberi e peperoni* (short pasta with shrimp and sweet peppers) or *pesce agli agrumi e mandorle* (fish baked with citrus and almonds). The menu always offers fresh seafood from the nearby sea, served grilled or baked.

Via G. Pellegrino 104. ℂ **089-210041.** Reservations recommended. Secondi 18€–22€ ($23–$28). AE, DC, MC, V. Fri–Wed 12:30–3pm; Mon–Wed and Fri–Sat 7:30–11pm; daily in summer. Closed Dec.

Moderate

La Locanda AMALFITAN   This old-fashioned restaurant combines good food with a cozy atmosphere. The seasonal menu includes a good selection of appetizers as well as wonderful pasta dishes. For a *secondo,* try the excellent *pesce al sale* (fish cooked in a salt crust). We also recommend the *frittura* (deep-fried medley of seafood).

Corso Umberto I 52. ℂ **089-761070.** Reservations recommended. Secondi 11€–18€ ($14–$23). AE, DC, MC, V. Tues–Sun 12:30–3pm and 7:30–11pm.

La Sosta ♪ AMALFITAN   Housed in a 19th-century relay station for carriage horses, this restaurant has charm to spare, as well as a traditional and well-prepared cuisine that's based on a seasonal menu. The offerings depend on the market, but you might find excellent *linguine con gli scampi* (linguine with prawns). The traditional desserts include a delicious *babà* (a rum-soaked cake filled with cream). The wine list is well rounded with both regional and national labels.

Via Costiera 6. © 089-211790. Reservations recommended on weekends. Secondi 12€–18€ ($15–$23). AE, MC, V. Thurs–Tues 12:30–3pm and 7:30–11pm. Closed Nov.

Taverna Paradiso *✸✸* AMALFITAN   If you are looking for a traditional trattoria with reasonable prices, this is the place for you. The Paradiso offers a warm atmosphere and traditional cuisine turned out by the Somma family. They excel at the homemade comfort food of this region. Start with *vermicelli avverniciati,* a sort of carbonara, and follow it with *salsicce e fagioli* (local sausages stewed with beans) or *costatelle di maiale con le pupacchielle all'agro* (pork ribs with a local vegetable). No matter what you choose to eat, wash down your meal with some of the menu's good local and regional wines.

Via Diego Taiani. © **089-212509.** Reservations recommended on weekends. Secondi 10€–18€ ($13–$23). AE, V. Tues–Sun 12:30–3pm and 7:30–11pm. Closed Aug 15.

Inexpensive
La Playa AMALFITAN   A good, inexpensive choice, this plain, modern restaurant offers simple local cuisine focusing on fish. We recommend the excellent homemade pasta, including tasty *scialatielli ai frutti di mare* (pasta with shellfish) as well as deliciously crisp *frittura* (deep-fried seafood) and the *grigliate* (grilled fish).

Via Costiera Amalfitana 24. © **089-761696.** Reservations recommended on weekends. Secondi 9€–15€ ($11–$19). AE, DC, MC, V. Wed–Mon 12:30–3pm and 7:30–11pm.

SHOPPING
Ceramics are very much a part of this little town's economy; if you are looking for a unique gift for yourself or for someone at home, chances are that you'll find it here. Enter Vietri's main street; the town will feel like an open-air showroom instead of a historic village or a laid-back resort. The display of color is incredible—the walls along the main streets are literally lined with beautiful tableware, ceramics of all kinds, and shelves burgeoning with variously shaped bowls and vases. After an initial pass-through, you should begin to see stylistic differences and be able to spot individual artists' showrooms–each characterized by a proprietary pattern and color palette. (We are very fond of the little goats that are the trademark of **D'Amore**—they have been imitated by many, so look for his signature on each piece.)

Recommended artists of long standing include **Ceramiche Artistiche Pinto** (Corso Umberto I 27; © **089-210271**); **Ceramiche Artistiche Solimene** (Via Madonna degli Angeli 7; © **089-212539**); and **Tortora & Giordano** (Via Travertino 17; © **089-211894**). Shops generally sell products from a variety of artists and most will ship your things home for you, but ask before buying.

VIETRI AFTER DARK
On most evenings during the summer season, **Villa Guariglia** (Via Nuova Raito; © **089-211835**) becomes the enchanting setting for classical music concerts; call the tourist information office for information on the program.

CETARA
Cetara has been an important fishing harbor since Roman times. Its name actually derives from the Latin *cetaria,* a tuna fishery, and the town is still the entire Costiera's

main fishing harbor. The town's *tonnare* (tuna-fishing facilities) are big complexes built mostly over the sea. Here, tuna are trapped in huge netting channels out at sea and brought to underwater cages. From there, the fish are pushed into a seawater pool, where they are killed and processed (this is definitely an industry, not a sport). Although canned tuna might not be high on your list of delicacies, you should taste the local tuna preserved in olive oil inside glass jars: The distinctive taste is so delicious you will find it hard to eat canned tuna again. This local industry is celebrated in July with the **Sagra del Tonno (Tuna Festival),** when preserved tuna and other local delicacies are sold in town; the festival also features music and other scheduled events. Contact the **Proloco tourist office** (Piazza San Francesco; ✆ **089-261474**) for more information.

The rest of the year, the key attraction in town is the **San Pietro** church, with its bright majolica cupola and 13th-century bell tower.

The best beach in the area is **Marina di Erchie.** It's located past the next village, only 2km (1.2 miles) west of Cetara. If you don't want to venture that far, there are small beaches by the harbor.

WHERE TO STAY

Hotel Cetus ✱ (Value (Kids)   This is a great hotel (although being the only one in the village gives it a decided advantage). Located in a spectacular panoramic location (hanging from a cliff) just out of town, the Cetus is your best choice if you decide to stay in this off-the-beaten-path village. For the Costiera, the price is a considerable value. Guest rooms are larger than average, comfortable, and bright, and have colorful tiled floors, bathrooms, and scenic views. The Cetus is particularly welcoming to children; it has its own sandy cove with umbrellas and chairs for its guests, along with a playground. Of the on-site restaurants—both upscale—Il Gabbiano offers excellent, traditional food (see below); and Falalella serves up gourmet international cuisine.

Corso Umberto I 1, 84010 Cetara. ✆/fax **089-261388.** 43 units. 260€ ($325) double; low season 130€ ($163) double. Rates include breakfast. Children under 3 stay free in parent's room. AE, MC, V. Free parking. **Amenities:** Restaurant; bar; concierge; room service; babysitting; laundry service; playground. *In room:* A/C, TV, minibar, hair dryer, safe.

WHERE TO DINE

Anchovies are the specialty here—be they roasted, grilled, deep-fried, or dressed with local herbs. In addition to fresh fish, you can buy locally prepared preserved anchovies and tuna at **Pescheria Battista Delfino** (Via Umberto I 78; ✆ **089-261069**) or at **Pescheria San Pietro** (Via Umberto I 72; ✆ **089-261147**).

Expensive

Il Gabbiano ✱ AMALFITAN   The breathtaking views from the panoramic dining room of this hotel restaurant are an important complement to any meal here. This is the perfect place to enjoy delicious fish while looking out to sea. The menu is small, but everything is freshly prepared according to market availability. They make a great *risotto alla pescatora* (seafood risotto) and tangy *fusilli al pesto con le vongole* (short pasta with pesto and clams). The wine list includes good local choices.

Corso Umberto I 1, SS 163. ✆ **089-261388.** Reservations recommended on weekends. Secondi 15€–32€ ($19–$40). AE, MC, V. Daily 12:30–3pm and 7:30–11pm. Closed Nov.

Moderate

Acquapazza ✱✱ AMALFITAN   This small and elegant restaurant is a good place to taste the local fish and experience high cuisine without spending a fortune. They prepare a wonderful array of *antipasti,* including *tortino di melanzane e alici* (fresh anchovy and eggplant torte), marinated tuna, and *carpaccio di pesce* (raw fish in a citrus sauce); and a number of tasty pasta dishes, such as *tubetti al ragù di pesce* (short pasta with a seafood and tomato sauce). For a secondo, you can pick your fish from the daily catch display, and have it prepared as you choose.

Corso Garibaldi 33. ✆ **089-261606.** Reservations recommended on weekends. Secondi 11€–15€ ($14–$19). MC, V. Tues–Sun 12:30–3pm and 7:30–11pm.

Inexpensive

San Pietro ✸✸ AMALFITAN   This down-to-earth trattoria has a small dining room and just a few tables under an arbor, where you can have a satisfying meal for very little money. The dishes of choice are grilled fish or *frittura* (deep-fried seafood), all extremely fresh and dependant on the offerings of the local market. They also prepare good pasta with sautéed shellfish.

Piazza San Francesco 2. ✆ **089-261091.** Reservations recommended. Secondi 8€–19€ ($10–$24). AE, MC, V. Wed–Mon noon–2:30pm and 7–10:30pm; daily in summer.

3 Mountains & Beaches: Maiori, Tramonti & Minori

Maiori is 15km (9 miles) west of Vietri and 6km (4 miles) east of Amalfi on SS 163. Tramonti is 11km (6½ miles) from Maiori. Minori is 18km (11 miles) west of Vietri sul Mare, and 3km (2 miles) east of Amalfi along SS 163.

Back when Amalfi was a powerful maritime republic, one of the few land accesses to its territory was the valley of the large stream, Reginna Maior, which comes into the sea at **Maiori** and lends its name to this village. This was an important little harbor in the Middle Ages and today is a pleasant village with both nice beaches and artistic attractions. Up the cliffs and well into the mountains are the ruins of the medieval castle of **Tramonti,** which has defended Amalfi from incursions over the ages. Tramonti should give you your first taste of the Costiera that exists closer to the sky—the Costiera that boasts truly unique views. At the mouth of a smaller stream—the Reginna Minor—lies **Minori,** a hamlet famous for its beaches. Ravello's notoriety often overshadows the other villages nearby, yet they are well worth your attention (it also secures comparative calm for them). Here you will find a few hidden art treasures, including an 11th-century monastery with beautiful frescoes.

MAIORI

Maiori opens onto one of the largest beaches of the whole Costiera—and, unfortunately, one of the most developed. Maiori, when it was an important town in medieval times, was surrounded by walls and defended by towers and castles, originally built in the 9th century. Today, only ruins remain of these walls and towers. The look of the village was also much changed by the flood of 1954, which destroyed the medieval heart of town. As in Amalfi and other towns along this coast, the Reginna Maior was covered over to gain building space, but the flood blew the lid off, causing the collapse of all the adjacent buildings. The town was rebuilt with a modern look. You can find more information on the town and its surroundings at the **AAST tourist office** (Corso Reginna Maior, 84010 Maiori; ✆ **089-877452;** www.aziendaturismo-maiori.it).

   Dominating the village from an impressive ramp of 108 steps is a memento of Maiori's glorious past, the **Collegiata di Santa Maria a Mare** (Corso Reginna Maior). Built in the 12th century, this church was redone in later times and is graced by a large majolica cupola. Inside is a precious collection of artwork from the 15th and 16th centuries. The richly carved, wooden ceiling in the main church and the crypt's majolica floor date from the same period. Adjacent to the church is the entrance to the museum, which protects more valuable objects of art from the church's past, dating from the 12th to the 18th centuries.

In the opposite direction of the church is the **beach,** which gets rather crowded in summer. From the beach, if you follow the cliff eastward, you will come to two grottoes. The first is frankly rather smelly, with its sulfur-magnesium mineral spring, but the other—**Grotta Pannone** ✻—is encrusted with stalactites and, particularly in the morning, takes on a color similar to the one of the famous Blue Grotto of Capri.

On your way to Maiori from Cetara, you'll pass **Capo d'Orso** ✻✻; the cape and the surrounding area—from Maiori to the west to the Torrente Bonea at the east—are protected natural areas. This is one of the most scenic stretches of the whole Amalfi Coast. Covering 1,235 acres, the protected area rests on a plateau with an average altitude of 70m (230 ft.) above sea level; the underlying limestone promontory has been eroded by the sea, and stones poke through the blanket of typical plants of the *macchia mediterranea,* creating a unique dolomitic landscape. A path leads to **Capo d'Orso Lighthouse** and its wonderful **panorama** ✻ (3.5km/2 miles east of the center of Maiori along the SS 163). Past the lighthouse and to the right is the fascinating **Abbazia di Santa Maria de Olearia** ✻ (Via Diego Tajani, Capo d'Orso; ✆ **089-877452;** daily 5–7:30 pm), locally known as the Catacombe di Badia. This incredible place was completely carved from the cliff's rocky face. Begun in the 10th century as a shrine dedicated to Santa Maria de Olearia, it was soon surrounded by a few cliff dwellings, which were then transformed into a monastery in the 11th century and frescoed. The main chapel has a vaulted ceiling and an apse, both decorated with 11th-century fresco work; underneath is the crypt, where the best-preserved frescoes depict the Virgin Mary and two saints.

WHERE TO STAY

Hotel San Francesco   In a quiet position a short distance from the sea, this hotel is surrounded by gardens and has a beautiful private beach. Housed in a modern building, the good-sized guest rooms are simply furnished in hardwood and wrought iron, with tiled floors and private balconies affording superior views (the balconies are covered, so you can use them at any time). Though the bathrooms aren't large, they do have quality, contemporary fixtures.

Via Santa Tecla 54, 84010 Maiori. ✆/fax **089-877070.** www.hotel-sanfrancesco.it. 44 units. 120€–140€ ($150–$175) double; low season 90€–110€ ($113–$138) double. Rates include buffet breakfast. Children under 3 stay free in parent's room. AE, DC, MC, V. Free parking. Closed mid-Oct to mid-Mar. Pets accepted. **Amenities:** Restaurant; bar; outdoor pool; room service; babysitting; laundry service. *In room:* A/C, satellite TV, minibar, hair dryer, safe.

Reginna Palace Hotel ✻   This elegant hotel sits right in the heart of Maiori, surrounded by a luxurious garden opening onto its private beach. The noteworthy swimming pool is filled with seawater. Guest rooms are spacious and furnished in contemporary style with fine fabrics and artistically tiled floors and bathrooms. A number of the rooms have views over the sea, and some have private balconies.

Via Cristoforo Colombo 1, 84010 Maiori. ✆/fax **089-877183.** Fax 089-851200. www.reginna.it. 67 units. 182€ ($228) double; low season 132€ ($165) double. Minimum 2 weeks' stay in Aug. Rates include buffet breakfast. Children under 3 stay free in parent's room. AE, DC, MC, V. Free parking. Closed Nov to mid-Mar. **Amenities:** Restaurant; bar; outdoor pool; room service; babysitting; laundry service. *In room:* A/C, radio, satellite TV, minibar, hair dryer.

WHERE TO DINE
Expensive
Faro di Capo d'Orso ☆☆ CREATIVE AMALFITAN   This is a special place, one where you'll want to come again and again, both for the haute cuisine and the magical atmosphere—the restaurant is set in an elegant glassed-in dining room with spectacular views over Capri and Ravello. The young chef, Rocco Iannone, loves the fruits of his region and takes the utmost care in combining them, with absolutely wonderful results. The menu changes with the seasons, the market, and his inspiration, with lots of raw or barely cooked fresh seafood. Among the innovative offerings you might find are *totanetti di paranza farciti di gamberetti bianchi* (local squid stuffed with white shrimp), or *linguine con ragù di calamaretti, pomodorini, prezzemolo e ricci di mare* (pasta with squid, cherry tomatoes, and sea urchins). The desserts are equally elaborate, and the wine list includes the very best from the local vineyards.

Via Diego Tajani 48. (℃ 089-877022. Reservations recommended. Secondi 18€–32€ ($23–$40). AE, DC, MC, V. Thurs–Mon 12:30–3pm and 7:30–11pm; in summer also open Wed. Closed 2 weeks in Jan.

Moderate
Mammato ⟨Value⟩ AMALFITAN   Located on the shorefront, this restaurant is popular with locals who come here to eat fish prepared according to the region's traditional recipes. This is a relaxed, local restaurant, decorated sparingly—in other words, it's a classic Italian place. Among the noteworthy classics of that cuisine are *scialatielli ai frutti di mare* (homemade pasta with basil and seafood), and *frittura* (deep-fried calamari and small fish).

Lungomare Amendola. (℃ 089-853683. Reservations recommended. Secondi 11€–18€ ($14–$23). AE, DC, MC, V. Wed–Mon 1–3:30pm and 8–11:30pm; daily in summer. Closed 2 weeks in Nov.

TRAMONTI
Up and inland from Maiori after about 11km (6½ miles) is the rural village of Tramonti. Its name comes from the Latin *intra montes* or "between the mountains," and so it is. The 13 historic *casali* (farms) that form the village are high above the sea, and each is graced by its own small church. The **Proloco tourist office** of Tramonti is inside the municipal building in **Polvica** (℃ **089-856820**). The highlight of an excursion to Tramonti is the **Valico di Chiunzi,** high in the mountains, at an altitude of 656m (2,152 ft.), with its spectacular **panorama** ☆☆☆ of the plain of Pompeii and Mount Vesuvius; picturesque ruins remain of its famous castle, now reduced to a single powerful tower.

One thing you must do here is sample the local wine—the *Tramonti,* one of the D.O.C. wines of the Amalfi Coast. Another local liquid specialty is *Concierto,* a very sweet liquor made with nine herbs and spices; it was first concocted in the 17th century in the **Convent Regio Conservatorio dei Santi Giuseppe e Teresa** (Località Pùcara; ℃ **339-1746893**), which you can still visit.

WHERE TO STAY
If you are looking for complete relaxation, the agriturismo **Azienda Agrituristica Le Chiancolelle** (Via Valico di Chiunzi, Località Campinola, 84010 Tramonti; ℃ **089-876339;** five units) offers a great alternative to regular hotels and restaurants. You'll get a deep immersion in nature while you are enticed by homemade and home-produced foods, including cured meats—from boar to pork—and good jams; much of their production is organic. Another great agriturismo nearby is **Azienda Agrituristica**

Mare e Monti (Via Trugnano 3, Località Campinola, 84010 Tramonti; ☏ **089-876665;** www.agriturismomaremonti.it; 2 units). There you will be pampered and plied with homemade delicacies ranging from jams made with the farm's organic fruits to sausages and cured meats made on the spot, all accompanied by the farm's own wine.

WHERE TO DINE

Da Nino ✦ AMALFITAN/PIZZA   Affectionately called "Ninuccio" (little Nino) by the locals, this trattoria offers a warm welcome and delicious specialties, made in large part with ingredients from the owners' farm. For an appetizer, taste the superb salamis and *sottoli* (vegetables preserved in olive oil) with homemade bread and local mozzarella. Follow this with a secondo of pasta or their whole-wheat pizza—the one with veggies *(con le verdure)* is particularly savory.

Via Pucara 39. ☏ **089-876184.** Reservations recommended on weekends. Secondi 8€–15€ ($10–$19). No credit cards. Wed–Mon noon–3pm and 7:30–10pm; daily in summer.

La Violetta *(Finds)* AMALFITAN   The views are gorgeous and the food is divine at this simple, honest restaurant. The hearty menu includes lots of salamis produced on the farm here, as well as homemade pasta and gnocchi. The *Risotto ai chiodini* (risotto with local wild mushrooms) bursts with flavor; and the grilled meats are superb. They also serve a good local red wine.

Via Valico di Chiunzi. ☏ **089-876384.** Reservations recommended on weekends. Secondi 12€–18€ ($15–$23). No credit cards. Tues–Sun 12:30–3pm and 7:30–11pm; daily in summer.

SHOPPING

This backcountry farming village has kept alive some traditional crafts that have since disappeared elsewhere. Here you will find **Amarante** (Via Corsano 15; ☏ **089-876715**), the showroom of a rare artist: a maker of chestnut-wood baskets. These solid baskets have traditionally been used for harvesting and carrying fresh lemons from the famed local orchards; the wood is steamed into shape and braided into baskets of any form and size. You can have one made to order.

Another of the area's traditional crafts is papermaking, an art that spread here from nearby Amalfi (see later in this chapter). **Antica Cartiera Amalfitana** (Via Nuova Chiunzi 14; ☏ **089-855432**), one of the original paper mills of Amalfi, still produces the delicate paper that made Amalfi famous, using traditional tools. You can buy quality filigree paper and visit the mill by appointment.

MINORI

Just west of Maiori—18km (11 miles) west of Vietri sul Mare, and only 3km (1¾ miles) east of Amalfi along SS 163—lies the village of Minori. Famous for its sandy beach, Minori is a picturesque little town nestled in a glorious setting of blue sea and citrus groves. Appreciated since antiquity, the village, with its small harbor inside a beautiful cove, was the arsenal of the Republic of Amalfi in the Middle Ages. Today, it comes alive in summer with vacationers enjoying its **beaches** and the **summer music festival;** for a schedule, contact the town's **tourist office** (Piazza Cantilena; ☏ **089-877087** or 089-877607; www.proloco.minori.sa.it).

The village is worth a visit at any time of year. Just a few steps from the little harbor you will find the **Cathedral,** the Basilica of Santa Trofimena. Built in the 11th century, it was completely redone in the 19th century; inside are some finely crafted

17th-century marble altars and the original crypt (restored in the 17th century) housing the remains of Saint Trofimena, Amalfi's protector saint. If you walk along the left side of the Basilica and turn right up a ramp of steps, you will reach the wonderful 12th-century **Campanile** 🐾🐾. The sole remnant of the church of Santa Annunziata, it still shows its original intarsia decorations.

Following the canalized stream—turning right from the beach through the narrow and winding local road—you will reach **Villa Romana, aka Villa Marittima** 🐾🐾 (Via Capo di Piazza 28; ℂ **089-852893;** Mon–Sat 9am to 1 hr. before sunset). One of the many Roman villas that existed in this area, Villa Romana dates from the 1st century A.D. and was discovered in 1932 but was not excavated until the 1950s. The villa was built on two floors around a vast courtyard, graced by a pool and surrounded by a portico. You can admire the hydraulic engineering that brought water to the pool, and the well-conserved rooms decorated with stucco work and remains of frescoes. One side of the portico opens onto the beautiful ninfeo, a hall richly decorated with frescoes and stucco work. Also architecturally interesting are the private thermal baths, which have been perfectly preserved. The staircase to the second floor is partially preserved, but you can climb its 29 steps to the **Antiquarium.** It contains a collection of artifacts and frescoes from this and nearby excavations.

WHERE TO STAY
Moderate
Hotel Caporal   This nice family-run hotel has relatively few units and offers simple and comfortable rooms with access to a private beach—just about everything you could ask for. If you plan to explore the area or spend time sunbathing, the Caporal is a good base (on-site amusements are few). Guest rooms are spacious, bright, and simple but well furnished. They have tiled floors and good-sized bathrooms; a number of them have balconies and overlook the ocean.

Via Nuova 20, 84010 Minori. ℂ **089-877408.** Fax 089-877166. 30 units. 130€ ($163) double. Rates include buffet breakfast. Children under 3 stay free in parent's room. AE, DC, MC, V. Free parking. **Amenities:** Restaurant; bar; room service. *In room:* A/C, satellite TV, minibar, hair dryer, safe.

Hotel Villa Romana 🐾🐾   Last restructured in 2000, this welcoming hotel is Minori's best and holds its own with anyplace on the Costiera. Its swimming pool, private beach, and terraces offer several ways to relax. Bright white walls, woodwork, and tile, as well as wrought iron and glass furniture, are used throughout to create a relaxed but tasteful atmosphere. The covered courtyard dining area is sunny, bright, and warm. The guest rooms are furnished in a similar manner, with some good quality copies of period pieces, but little in terms of wall art and knickknacks—in keeping with the hotel's almost "Mediterranean minimalist" feel.

Corso Vittorio Emanuele 90, 84010 Minori. ℂ **089-877237.** Fax 089-877302. www.hotelvillaromana.it. 50 units. 160€ ($200) double; low season 120€ ($150). Rates include buffet breakfast. Children under 3 stay free in parent's room. AE, DC, MC, V. Free parking. **Amenities:** Restaurant; American bar; outdoor pool; concierge; business center; room service; babysitting; same-day laundry service. *In room:* A/C, satellite TV, minibar, hair dryer, safe.

Inexpensive
Hotel Santa Lucia *Value*   Located only about 300 feet from the hotel's private beach, this small, family-run hotel offers pleasant accommodations and professional service. Guest rooms are simple, with tiled floors and modern bathrooms; most have private balconies. If the hotel doesn't have any vacancies, they will send you to their

annex—Pensione Isabella—right on the sea, with nice views but slightly more basic rooms. The combination of price and location near the sea here can't be beat.

Via Nazionale 44, 84010 Minori. ✆ 089-877142. Fax 089-853636. www.hotelsantalucia.it. 30 units. 95€ ($119) double; low season 75€ ($94). Rates include breakfast. Children under 3 stay free in parent's room. AE, DC, MC, V. Free parking. **Amenities:** Restaurant; bar; babysitting. *In room:* A/C, TV, minibar.

Settebello *Finds*   Located across from the archaeological area of Villa Romana, this little hotel is only a short walk from the beach. An unremarkable modern building from the outside, it has a pleasant interior showing a great deal of attention to taste and comfort. Decorated in white and blue, the common areas are quite spacious given the relatively small number of units. The hotel has large, simply furnished rooms with period reproductions, brightly tiled floors, and good-sized bathrooms with pedestal sinks and other touches that give it a traditional-but-not-old ambience. Many guest rooms have private balconies. Note that in August, you are obliged to take the "half-board" option, in which you are served breakfast and one of the two major meals in the hotel.

Via Nazionale, 39, 84010 Minori. ✆ 089-877494. Fax 089-877494. www.hotel7bello.it. 30 units. 80€ ($100) double; low season 60€ ($75) double. Rates include buffet breakfast. 116€/ $151 double with half-board (required in August). Children under 3 stay free in parent's room. AE, MC, V. Free parking. **Amenities:** Restaurant; bar; concierge; room service; babysitting; laundry service. *In room:* A/C (supplement), satellite TV, minibar (supplement), hair dryer, safe.

WHERE TO DINE
This area boasts several local specialties not to be missed. Try *sarchiapone,* a delicious dish of local squash filled with ground meat and ricotta and cooked in a tomato sauce. Another tasty invention is *'ndunderi*: gnocchi made of spelt flour and fresh cheese and served with a simple dressing of olive oil, cheese, and local fresh herbs (sometimes chopped walnuts).

Moderate
Capriccio AMALFITAN   This modern restaurant is run by the Russo family. Its friendly atmosphere is particularly enjoyable if you dine under the pleasant arbor (in good weather). The varied menu features a great selection of rich seafood *antipasti* and excellent pasta dishes, such as *gnocchetti piselli, funghi e frutti di mare* (potato dumplings with a shellfish, pea, and mushroom sauce), and *ravioli di pesce* (fish ravioli). The best *secondi* are *pesce al cartoccio* (market choice of fish cooked in a pouch with herbs), and *grigliate miste* (a medley of grilled seafood).

Via Capo di Piazza 6. ✆ 089-851279. Reservations recommended. Secondi 12€–25€ ($15–$31). AE, DC, MC, V. Wed–Mon 12:30–3pm and 7:30–11pm; daily in summer.

Il Giardiniello ⚜ AMALFITAN/PIZZA   Good food and a cozy atmosphere mark this restaurant, which is especially charming in the warm season, when you can dine in the lemon grove. The menu, not surprisingly, focuses on seafood—from a splendid *laganelle alla marinara* (fresh eggless pasta with squid, shrimp, arugula, and cherry tomatoes), a rich *riso al nero di seppia* (rice with squid ink), to satisfying *alici impanate con la provola* (fresh anchovies deep-fried with cheese). In the evening, they make pizza, and very good ones at that.

Corso Vittorio Emanuele 17. ✆ 089-877050. Reservations recommended. Secondi 11€–22€ ($14–$28). AE, DC, MC, V. Thurs–Tues 12:30–2:30pm and 7:30–10:30pm; daily in summer. Closed Jan.

Inexpensive
L'Arsenale ⚜⚜ AMALFITAN   Started in 1992 by the three brothers Proto, this small restaurant—it has a few tables under a portico outside—is a moderate, more-than-just-reliable choice on this coast. To the joy of many, the menu includes excellent

meat options besides the area's ever-present fish. A large variety of *antipasti* are comple-mented by tasty and often richly flavored homemade filled pasta, such as *tortelli con crostacei e porcini* (large ravioli with shellfish and porcini mushrooms), and *quadroni di carne con burro e salvia* (square meat ravioli seasoned with sage and butter). For a change of pace when it comes to the *secondi,* you might try the lamb or rabbit.

Via San Giovanni a Mare 20. © **089-851418.** Reservations recommended. Secondi 9€–15€ ($11–$19). AE, DC, MC, V. Fri–Wed 12:30–3pm and 7:30–11pm. Closed 3 weeks Jan–Feb.

La Botte *Finds* AMALFITAN/PIZZA   Located in a former church near the Villa Romana's archaeological area, the rustic decor of this popular restaurant offers a pic-turesque setting for a hearty meal. The menu includes an ample choice of pizza—36 kinds, in various sizes. The local cuisine has a creative twist; you will find not only the classic *scialatielli ai frutti di mare* (fresh homemade pasta with shellfish), but such ven-turesome choices as *ravioli con aragosta e crema d'asparagi* (lobster ravioli with cream of asparagus).

Via S. M. Vetrano 15. © **089-877893.** Reservations recommended on weekends. Secondi 11€–18€ ($14–$23). DC, MC, V. Tues–Sun 12:30–3pm and 7:30–11pm; daily in summer. Closed Feb.

Limoncello & other *Rosoli*

The typical liqueur of the region, *limoncello,* is the most famous of the sweet liqueurs made in the area from fruits and herbs—known as *rosoli.* The rarest are *Finocchietto,* made with wild fennel; *Lauro,* made with bay leaves; *Mirto,* made with myrtle; *Nocello,* made with walnuts; the rare *Nanassino,* made with prickly pears; and *Fragolino,* an extremely rare *rosolio* made with *frago-line di bosco,* the wild mini-strawberries from Monti Alburni.

Limoncello is probably the most versatile *rosolio.* You will find local ver-sions—and endless claims of paternity—from Vico Equense on the Sorrento Peninsula all the way to Vietri and beyond, to the islands of Ischia, Capri, and Procida. The liqueur's actual origin is probably the area of Maiori, Amalfi, and Vietri—although Sorrento has good foundations for its claim.

The fact remains that almost every family in Campania has its own recipe, passed on for centuries. The real version is made with Amalfi's special lemon—called *sfusato di Amalfi,* a particular lemon that has obtained the mark D.O.P. (the stamp of controlled origin for produce, similar to D.O.C. for wine). The Amalfi lemon is large, long, and light in color, with a sweet and very flavorful aroma and taste, almost no seeds, and a very thick skin.

Limoncello is sold in pretty, hard-to-resist bottles. If you plan to buy a few bottles as a gift, don't forget to give the recipient tips on how to use it. Always served very cold, the drink can be sipped as a digestive after a meal. It also makes an excellent lemon-flavored long drink—dilute with tonic water or seltzer. Some like it as a champagne cocktail (add a small quantity to a glass of champagne or prosecco). Another great variation is *granita*—dilute the *limoncello* with a light syrup made of sugar and water, and freeze the result, stirring occasionally.

SHOPPING

The area of Maiori is renowned for its *Sospiri,* aka *Zizz'e monache;* the first name translates as "sighs," and the second as "nuns' breasts." These are the sacred and profane names (but which is which?) for delicious, pale, dome-shaped small pastries filled with lemon cream. The best can be tasted at **Pasticceria De Riso** (see below), which makes the best sweets in the whole of Costiera.

Famous for its lemons, Minori is *the* place to buy authentic *limoncello.* **Limunciel** (Corso Vittorio Emanuele 9; ℂ 089-877393) was among the first to commercialize the local *rosolio;* at this shop you will also find rarer liqueurs such as *mandarino* (mandarin) and *fragoline di bosco* (wild strawberry), which they prepare in small batches according to their traditional recipe.

AFTER DARK

The **Summer Music Festival of Minori** (see earlier in this chapter) is a major attraction on the coast. The evening concerts—held in the open air, and made fragrant by the scent of lemon flowers—are particularly pleasant and well attended.

People also like to meet at the **Pasticceria De Riso** (Via Cantilena 20; ℂ 089-877396), to enjoy the best pastries of the whole Costiera, which excels particularly at lemon specialties. Another popular place on the seaside promenade is **Bar Umberto** (Via Roma 58; ℂ 089-877393), which makes a rich homemade ice cream.

4 Ravello ★★

6km (3.7 miles) NE of Amalfi, 29km (18 miles) W of Salerno, 66km (41 miles) SE of Naples.

High up in the mountains, Ravello is a terrace over the sea, overlooking the villages of Minori and Maiori. The focal point of the short stretch of coast between Maiori and Amalfi, it has been the refuge of VIPs since Positano lost some of its glamour to the tourist invasion that began in the 1980s. Although tourists invade Ravello, too, during the summer—Gore Vidal's decision to sell his villa here may have been the signal to the jet set that it is no longer cool—the lay of the land is such that the town remains an attractive retreat.

Ravello is connected to SS 163 by a sometimes dramatic mountain road that follows the valley of the stream Dragone, between Minori and Atrani. The town is largely pedestrian, with steep, narrow lanes and ramps of steps, and cars have to stop at the large public parking lot not far from the Duomo. Already celebrated by Boccaccio in his *Decameron* and by Turner in his paintings, Ravello is surrounded by luscious fields, vineyards, and citrus groves.

ESSENTIALS

VISITOR INFORMATION   The **AAST tourist office** (Via Roma 18, 84010 Ravello; ℂ 089-857096; www.ravellotime.it) is open October to April, Monday to Saturday from 9am to 6pm; May to September 9am to 8pm.

FAST FACTS   You'll find a **pharmacy** on Piazza Duomo (ℂ 089-857189). You can get **medical attention** at the Guardia Medica Castiglione di Ravello (ℂ 089-877208). For an **ambulance,** dial ℂ 118. Call the **police** at ℂ 113 or at ℂ 112. The **post office** is on Piazza Vescovado and is open Monday to Saturday 8am to 2pm. You'll find **Banca Monte Paschi di Siena** at Piazza Duomo 6 (ℂ 089-857120), and **Banca della Campania** at Via Roma 15 (ℂ 089-857872)—both with **ATMs.**

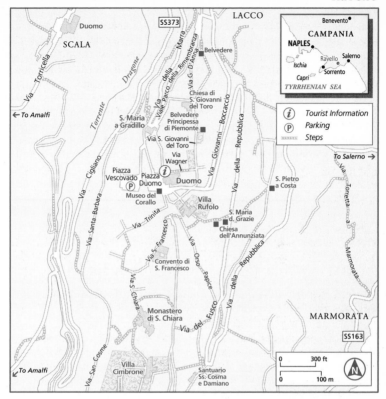

SPECIAL EVENTS The internationally famous **Festival di Ravello** (Via Roma 10, 84010 Ravello; ℂ **089-857096** or 199-109910 for reservations; fax 089-858422; www.ravellofestival.com) focuses on classical music, but it is also the occasion for other events, including jazz, dance, and visual arts. It is very popular (reserve well in advance) not only for the big names it attracts (among the participants in 2004 were Salvatore Accardo and the St. Petersburg Philarmonic), but for the magnificent settings. Performances are held at Piazza Duomo, Villa Rufolo, and Villa Cimbrone, among other venues. The festival is organized into several series, including the **Festival Musicale Wagneriano**—classical music concerts held in July in the garden of **Villa Rufolo** ✿—and the unique **Concerti dell'Aurora,** a group of concerts held at dawn (usually starting at 4am), to welcome the day in music. The festival runs July through September; prices depend on the event, and though some events have free admission, tickets for others can cost anywhere between 15€ and 130€ ($19–$163).

Music continues before and after the festival with concerts and events scheduled March through October. You can find information on these other events by contacting **Fondazione Ravello** (ℂ **089-858360;** info@fondazioneravello.it), or the **Ravello Concert Society** (ℂ **089-858149;** www.ravelloarts.org).

EXPLORING THE TOWN

According to local legend, Ravello was founded in the 5th to 6th centuries A.D. by Roman patricians fleeing barbarians who were ransacking Rome. The small town flourished in the Middle Ages, when it became part of the Republic of Amalfi. It was then the elected residence of some of the wealthiest merchant families of the republic, who created the numerous palaces that adorn this small town (many transformed into hotels today) and decorated the churches with works of high art. Often overlooked, the beautiful Romanesque church of **Santa Maria a Gradillo** 🏛🏛, dating from the 12th century, is the first architecturally noteworthy site you will see upon entering Ravello. Its intertwined arches, tall apses, and airy interior are all characteristic of the Arab-Sicilian style brought to town by the powerful merchant families who made their fortunes trading with Sicily, North Africa, Spain, and Asia. Until the earthquake of 1706 that destroyed it, the atrium in front of the church was used as the meeting hall for the nobles of Ravello.

The heart of town is **Piazza del Vescovado,** a terrace overlooking the valley of the Dragone, and the adjacent Piazza del Duomo. Taking Via Emanuele Filiberto, you will reach **Via San Giovanni del Toro** 🏛🏛, which has some of the most beautiful medieval palaces of Ravello, including the 11th-century **Casa Tolla,** today housing the **Municipio.** Crossing the **Belvedere Principessa di Piemonte,** you'll reach **Palazzo Sasso** (today Albergo Palumbo) and **Palazzo d'Afflitto** (now the Albergo Caruso Belvedere). You will arrive at **Piazza Fontana,** with its 13th-century **Convent of Sant'Augostino,** today transformed into the Hotel Parsifal.

Duomo 🏛🏛🏛   Dedicated to San Pantaleone, the patron saint of Ravello, this cathedral is a beautiful example of Romanesque architecture. Built between 1086 or 1087 by the Rufolo family, it was redone in the 12th century and then redecorated in the 18th century. The latest restorations have removed most of the baroque decorations that had affected (some might say afflicted) the interior. The beautiful facade, graced by three marble portals, is famous for the center arch's **bronze door** 🏛🏛, which was sculpted by Barisano da Trani in 1179 and cast in Constantinople. One of the nicest in Italy, it is decorated with 54 rectangular frames, each with different scenes of carved figures in relief. On the Duomo's right is the 13th-century **bell tower,** showing Arab and Byzantine influences. The Duomo's interior is divided into three naves, each with its own apse; in the central nave to the right is the beautiful **Ambone dell'Epistola** 🏛🏛🏛 from 1130, decorated with precious mosaics representing Jonah. Facing it to the left is the richly carved and decorated **Pergamo** 🏛🏛🏛 from 1272, a splendid work of art by Niccolò di Bartolomeo da Foggia. To the left of the main altar is the **Cappella di San Pantaleone,** built in 1643 for the relic of San Pantaleone. The saint was beheaded in Nicomedia on July 27, 305. On the anniversary of his death, his blood (contained in a vessel) miraculously liquefies. When the vessel is cracked, the second miracle occurs: No blood leaks from the cracked vessel. Beneath the church, the crypt houses a small museum where you can admire the elegant 13th-century **Bust of Sichelgaita della Marra** 🏛🏛, sculpted by Bartolomeo da Foggia, as well as several precious relic holders, including the **Bust of Santa Barbara** 🏛 in silver.

Piazza del Vescovado. 🕿 **089-858311** or 089-857122 for the museum. Duomo: free admission. Museum: 2€ ($2.50). Duomo daily winter 9am–1pm and 4:30–7pm; summer 8:30am–1pm and 3–8pm. Museum Mon–Sat 9:30am–1pm and 3–6:30pm. Bookshop and guided tours available.

Villa Rufolo 🏛🏛   In the center of town just to the right of the Duomo, this beautiful villa was built between 1270 and 1280 for the prominent Rufolo family, then passed on to the Gonfalone e Muscettola family in the 15th century. It was bought in 1851 by the Scotsman Francis Devile Reid, who partially restructured it and thereby affected its architectural harmony. A public building since 1975, the villa can be visited together with its beautiful **gardens** ℱ. The original architecture shows much Arab influence, especially in the detail of intertwined arches, which recurs in the **Entrance Hall** within the access tower and in the beautiful courtyard. The tower is also decorated with four statues representing symbols of charity and hospitality. The three-story main building is at the end of a tree-lined alley and opens over an **Inner Court,** a marvelous cloister with a double level of loggias over richly decorated and intertwined columns. The **Sala d'Aspetto (Receiving Hall), Salone (Main Hall),** and **Main Tower** also have interesting details. Across from the entrance is the famous **Terrace** ℱ, which was renamed Terrazza Wagner in memory of the German composer who wrote the Klingsor Garden scene in the second act of his *Parsifal* here because he was inspired by the terrace's view. Today, the view—which from 340m (1,115 ft.) above sea level is spectacular—is the setting for the *Concerti Wagneriani,* a summer festival of classical music.

Piazza Vescovado. ℂ **089-857657** or 089-857866. Admission 5€ ($6.25). Daily summer 9am–8pm; winter 9am–5pm.

Villa Cimbrone ℱ   Farther up from the center of town, this 14th- or 15th-century villa belonged to the noble family Acconciagioco, but was largely rebuilt in 1904 by its new owner, an eccentric English lord named William Beckett. The resulting mix of styles is somewhat disharmonious, but the villa and its gardens remain quite lovely. Inside you'll see two towers, the courtyard and, at the end of a delightful alley lined by statues, the famous **Belvedere Cimbrone** ℱℱℱ—famed for its awe-inspiring panorama. Between the sculptures which decorate the balustrade, you can look out at a view encompassing Atrani and the whole Gulf of Salerno down to the plain of Paestum and distant Punta Licosa. The villa accepts overnight guests in some of the rooms (see later in this chapter). *Note:* To visit, ring the bell at the entrance. Access to the path to the villa is only by foot and is rather steep.

Via Santa Chiara 26. ℂ **089-858072** or 089-857459. Admission 5€ ($6.25). Daily summer 9am–6pm; winter until sunset.

Museo del Corallo   Created in 1986, this small but extremely interesting museum has a wonderful collection of precious objects made of coral, including cameos, totaling over 600 pieces. Located on the premises of the workshop **Camo,** who specialize in this traditional art (see chapter 4 for more information), the collection stretches from ancient Roman pieces all the way to the 19th century. Particularly beautiful are the 16th-century **Crucifix** on a crystal cross and a **Madonna** from 1532. Be sure to note the 3rd-century-A.D. Roman amphora with a coral formation inside it, and a beautiful set of 14 cherub heads from the 18th to 19th centuries.

Piazza Duomo 9. ℂ **089-857461**. Free admission. Mon–Sat 9:30am–noon and 3–5:30pm.

Chiesa di San Giovanni del Toro ℱℱ   This 12th-century church, restored in 1715 after earthquake damage and again in the 1990s, is one of the most beautiful religious buildings in Ravello. The slender bell tower in Arab-Sicilian style rises beside a facade graced by a triple portal. A steep staircase descends on the right, allowing a view of the three high apses, each crowned by a dome and decorated with intertwined arcs. Inside, the church is divided into three naves by pointed arches supported by eight antique marble columns. The interior is decorated with 13th- and 14th-century frescoes, mosaics, majolica, stucco work, and bas-reliefs. Particularly beautiful is the 12th-century **pergamo** *✦* by Alfano da Termoli, as well as the 14th-century frescoes in the crypt's apse. The church is usually closed, but you can request a visit at Via San Giovanni del Toro 50.

Piazzetta San Giovanni del Toro 3. Donations encouraged. Visit by request (inquire at Via San Giovanni del Toro 50; daily 9:30am to 1 or 2pm and 3–5pm).

STAYING ACTIVE

Ravello lacks the beaches enjoyed by many of the other villages along this coast, but in compensation, it offers great opportunities for walks and serious hikes. The walks we suggest below are quite easy, allowing you to return by bus or taxi, but if you are more ambitious, you might undertake a complete loop of the two hikes below.

The **Monastero di San Nicola** makes for a pleasant and easy hike, since it only has a few small stretches of hillside but is very scenic. From the center of Ravello, take the road for Chiunzi for 1km (½ mile) towards the hamlet of Sambuco, 320m (1,050 ft.) above sea level (you can also get to this point by car). Descending from here a few steps to your right, you can reach the trail that climbs to the Monastery of San Nicola at an altitude of 486m (1,594 ft.). Plan on about 2 hours for the 9km (5.6-mile) hike. The monastery is currently under restoration, but you can still enjoy the great views. From the monastery, it is then possible to descend to Minori—or to Maiori if you prefer—in about a half-hour. Hiking the reverse route (starting from Minori or Maiori) is more demanding, but you can do it by taking the small road that connects Maiori with Minori and passes behind the Collegiata to reach the path that climbs gently towards the monastery. The trail becomes progressively steeper and more scenic until you reach the top. Figure on spending about 1 hour for the ascent from Maiori or Minori to the monastery.

Another scenic hike in the area is the one to Minori. From the center of Ravello, take another footpath—a charming mix of steps and hidden alleys—which descends all the way to Minori and the sea. Start from the alley to the left of Villa Rufolo, marked by a small fountain, at an altitude of 350m (1,148 ft.), and begin the descent. You will pass by the small 13th-century Annunziata church and by San Pietro church. You will then reach the hamlet of **Torello,** with its church of the Addolorata and graceful bell tower in Arab-Sicilian style. The picturesque walk will continue among olive trees all the way down to the sea and the village of **Minori.** The whole hike should take you only a half-hour; however, allow at least double that for the ascent.

WHERE TO STAY
VERY EXPENSIVE

Hotel Palumbo *✦*   This fascinating hotel occupies the 12th-century Palazzo Confalone. The key word here is refinement, with both guest rooms and public areas elegantly decorated and furnished with antiques. Guest rooms are not large, but many have private terraces with gorgeous views. The bathrooms tend to be lavish. The hotel grants access to a nearby swimming pool and to its private beach through shuttle service. Additional rooms have been created in the annex (a bit less luxurious), **The Palumbo Residence** (200€/$250 double; 430€/$538 half-board obligatory in high season).

Via San Giovanni del Toro 16, 84010 Ravello. ℂ 089-857244. Fax 089-858133. www.hotelpalumbo.it. 21 units. 660€ ($825) double, 870€ ($1,088) junior suite, 980€ ($1,225) suite; low season 380€ ($475) double, 460€ ($575) junior suite, 600€ ($750) suite. Rates include breakfast and dinner in high season and breakfast only in low season. Children under 3 stay free in parent's room. AE, DC, MC, V. Parking: 20€ ($25). **Amenities:** Restaurant; lounge; outdoor pool; concierge; room service; babysitting; laundry service. *In room:* A/C, TV, dataport, minibar, hair dryer, safe.

Palazzo Sasso ✮✮✮   This 11th-century palace was transformed into a hotel in 1880, and was the preferred retreat of the rich and famous until the 1960s. It then fell into ruin but was restored and reopened in 1997. Today, it has been transformed into an opulent hotel in a splendid location between plunging cliffs and steep mountainside. Guest rooms are luxuriously appointed with antiques. Some of them afford gorgeous views—the best are from room nos. 1, 201, 204, and 301, and suite 304. Some of the suites are as big as a good-size apartment, and even the lower-priced rooms are spacious (a few at the bottom of the scale have no view). Bathrooms are done up in marble, with large tubs and all the comforts you'd expect. The hotel, which offers a very high level of service, has a garden, a solarium, and an excellent restaurant.

Via San Giovanni del Toro 28, 84010 Ravello. ✆ 089-818181. Fax 089-858900. www.palazzosasso.com. 44 units. 296€–590€ ($370–$738) double; from 830€ ($1,038) suite. Rates include buffet breakfast. Children under 3 stay free in parent's room. AE, DC, MC, V. Free parking. Closed Nov to mid-Mar. **Amenities:** Restaurant; bar; 2 outdoor pools; concierge; room service; babysitting; laundry service; 1 room for those w/limited mobility. *In room:* A/C, TV, minibar, hair dryer, safe.

EXPENSIVE

Hotel Rufolo ✮   In the heart of Ravello, this family-run hotel overlooks the gardens of Villa Rufolo. Housed in a modern building, the interior, with white plaster and columns and arches everywhere, gives off a much older, traditional feeling. The hotel offers comfortable accommodations and friendly service. Guest rooms are different sizes, but all have reproduction and modern furnishings in a restrained decor. While all have varying views, the views from the common sun decks are always superb. The pool is tucked into an attractive garden.

Via San Francesco 1, 84010 Ravello. ✆ 089-857133. Fax 089-857935. www.hotelrufolo.it. 30 units. 240€–310€ ($300–$388) double; 400€–475€ ($500–$594) suite. Rates include buffet breakfast. Children under 3 stay free in parent's room. AE, DC, MC, V. Free parking. Closed Dec 22–28. **Amenities:** Restaurant; bar; outdoor pool; concierge; room service; babysitting; laundry service. *In room:* A/C, TV; dataport, minibar, hair dryer, iron.

Villa Cimbrone ✮✮   Could there be a better way to visit one of Ravello's main attractions (see earlier in this chapter) than to stay in it? This luxurious residence—today belonging to the Vuillemier family and once visited by the likes of Greta Garbo and Hillary Clinton—doubles as an exclusive hotel for those who don't mind the lack of access by car. (The hotel will send a porter to carry your luggage to the villa, but you'll have to do the 10-min. climb on foot.) The few guest rooms differ from each other, all affording great luxury and privacy, and are furnished with antiques. The less expensive rooms open onto the villa's park, while the others have private terraces overlooking the sea. The hotel's **restaurant** is open to the public and serves Amalfitan cuisine, with seafood its specialty.

Via Santa Chiara 26, 84010 Ravello. ✆ 089-857459. Fax 089-857777. www.villacimbrone.it. 19 units. 250€–450€ ($313–$563) double; 500€ ($625) junior suite; 650€ ($813) suite. Rates include breakfast. AE, DC, MC, V. Closed Dec–Mar. **Amenities:** Restaurant; bar; outdoor pool; concierge; same-day laundry service; room service. *In room:* A/C, TV/DVD, dataport, minibar, hair dryer, safe.

MODERATE

Hotel Giordano   This historic family-run hotel is set in a commanding location not far from Villa Rufolo. The entrance and lobby are sparely but handsomely decorated with fine antiques. The comfortable guest rooms are furnished with period or period-style pieces, with colorful tilework on the floors and in the bathrooms (the latter are up-to-date and functional, if a bit small). Public areas include a swimming pool and terraces, as well as some of the facilities of the nearby Villa Maria (see below).

Via San Francesco 1, 84010 Ravello. © 089-857170. Fax 089-857071. www.giordanohotel.it. 30 units. 170€–225€ ($213–$281) double, 280€ ($350) junior suite; low season 145€–200€ ($181–$250) double, 255€ ($319) junior suite. Rates include breakfast. Children under 3 stay free in parent's room. AE, DC, MC, V. Free parking in the hotel garage. Closed 4 weeks Feb–Mar. **Amenities:** Restaurant; bar; outdoor pool; concierge; babysitting; laundry service. *In room:* A/C, TV, minibar, hair dryer.

Villa Maria   This independent hotel is run by the same family that owns the Hotel Giordano (above). Housed in what was once a luxurious private villa, the site has a nice garden with views over the sea. The rooms, especially nice because of their brightness, are spacious and well-appointed, with a few antiques and otherwise quality hardwood furniture. The floors and bathrooms are colorfully tiled.

Via Santa Chiara 2, 84010 Ravello. © 089-857255. Fax 089-857071. www.villamaria.it. 30 units. 220€–280€ ($275–$350) double; low season 180€–240€ ($225–$300) double. Rates include breakfast. Children under 2 stay free in parent's room. AE, DC, MC, V. Free parking. **Amenities:** Restaurant; bar; outdoor pool; concierge; room service; babysitting; laundry service. *In room:* A/C, TV, minibar, hair dryer.

Hotel Marmorata *finds*   Housed inside an ancient paper mill perched on a cliff overlooking the sea, this charming hotel affords elegant accommodations (considering that it's owned by Best Western). The hotel is located right outside Ravello—you can walk up to town by way of the pedestrian Via Torretta a Marmorata. Guest rooms are comfortable and bright, all with sea views; the refined furnishings are in a nautical style, and the good-sized bathrooms are modern. Public spaces include a swimming pool and beautiful panoramic terraces, as well as access to the beach.

Via Bizantina, off SS 163, 84010 Ravello, Località Marmorata. © 089-877777. Fax 089-851189. www.marmorata.it. 20 units. 210€–260€ ($263–$325) double, 310€ ($388) junior suite; low season 120€–170€ ($150–$213) double, 220€ ($275) junior suite. Children under 3 stay free in parent's room. AE, DC, MC, V. Free parking. Closed mid-Nov to mid-Mar. **Amenities:** 2 restaurants; bar; outdoor pool; room service; babysitting; laundry service. *In room:* A/C, satellite TV, minibar, hair dryer, safe.

INEXPENSIVE

Hotel Bonadies *finds*   This historic hotel was opened in 1880 and is still run by descendants of the founder. Some of the antique furnishings in the rooms and common areas date from that time, while others are more modern. A renovation completed in 2000 brought the bathrooms and amenities up to date. Relatively small, the Bonadies is popular with Italians. The pool overlooks the hillsides plunging down to the sea; the beach can be accessed by the hotel's minivan shuttle. The hotel boasts a superior on-site restaurant.

Piazza Fontana 5, 84010 Ravello. © 089-857918. Fax 089-8571370. www.hotelbonadies.it. 36 units. 160€–220€ ($200–$275) double; low season 130€–190€ ($163–$238) double. Rates include breakfast. Children under 3 stay free in parent's room. AE, DC, MC, V. Free parking. **Amenities:** Restaurant; bar; outdoor pool; concierge; room service; babysitting; laundry service. *In room:* A/C, satellite TV, hair dryer.

Hotel Graal   Enjoying a scenic position, this small hotel offers great accommodations, moderately priced for such a fashionable part of town. The public areas are a bit faded, but guest rooms are bright and decorated in Mediterranean style with modern furnishings. They have good-sized bathrooms and balconies with sea views. The restaurant here is very good, with abundant shellfish choices (and a selection of meat dishes for those who've had their fill of seafood). Popular with locals who aren't staying at the hotel, the restaurant is open year-round.

Via della Repubblica 8, 84010 Ravello. ✆ 089-857222. Fax 089-857551. www.hotelgraal.it. 35 units. 123€–195€ ($154–$244) double; low season 98€–164€ ($123–$205) double. Rates include breakfast. Children under 3 stay free in parent's room. AE, DC, MC, V. Parking: 11€ ($14). Closed 4 weeks Feb–Mar. **Amenities:** Restaurant; bar; outdoor pool; babysitting. *In room:* A/C (11€/$14), TV.

WHERE TO DINE

In addition to our suggestions below, all the famous hotels in town (and some of the less famous) have good restaurants, usually offering romantic settings and ocean vistas, often at surprisingly moderate tabs. The **Villa Cimbrone**'s restaurant—just opened to the public—is particularly good.

MODERATE

Cumpà Cosimo 🄺🄸🄳🅂 AMALFITAN   Once a simple winery, this place has blossomed into a popular restaurant, favored by locals. Family-run since it opened in 1929—the second generation is still at the helm—it serves generous portions of homemade traditional dishes. The seasonal menu always includes mouthwatering pastas and particularly succulent secondi—you might find *zuppa di pesce* (fish stew) and a fine *fritto misto* (deep-fried medley of seafood), or roasted lamb with herbs. The staff is particularly accommodating to the needs of little ones, and allows half-portions.

Via Roma 44. ✆ **089-857156.** Reservations recommended. Secondi 11€–28€ ($14–$35). AE, DC, MC, V. Tues–Sun 12:30–3pm and 7:30–11pm; Apr–Oct daily.

Palazzo della Marra AMALFITAN CREATIVE   This much-admired restaurant offers hearty cuisine in the elegant setting of the 12th-century Palazzo della Marra. The menu varies depending on the local market and tends to offer traditional dishes with a twist. The focus is on meat; you might find *anatra affumicata con crema di finocchio* (smoked duck with fennel cream), or a juicy filet mignon. (The fresh pasta is excellent if you want something lighter.) Save room for dessert, especially if you can get the *tiramisu* made with pistachio cream.

Via della Marra 7. ✆ **089-858302.** Reservations recommended. Secondi 15€–27€ ($19–$34). AE, DC, MC, V. Wed–Mon 12:30–3pm and 7:30–11pm; Apr–Sept daily. Closed mid-Jan to mid-Feb.

INEXPENSIVE

Da Salvatore 🄺🄺 AMALFITAN   This simple restaurant offers local cuisine in a striking setting—the views are superb both from the dining room and the garden terrace, which is open for alfresco dining in warm weather. The style and atmosphere here are relaxed, with simple tables and chairs. You can choose fish or meat from among the traditional dishes, which include *gnoccoloni al pomodoro e basilico* (potato dumplings with fresh tomatoes and basil), grilled fish, and roasted veal. The restaurant has six guest rooms for rent.

Via Boccaccio 2. ✆ **089-857227.** Reservations recommended. Secondi 12€–18€ ($15–$23). AE, V. Tues–Sun 12:30–3pm and 7:30–11pm; Apr–Oct daily.

La Colonna AMALFITAN/PIZZA   This family-run restaurant is housed in a historic building from the 13th century, which was a *stabilimento vinicolo* (wine stable) of the Caruso wine-producing family. The homemade pasta is heartily recommended; special mention goes to the unique *spaghetti al limone* (lemon-flavored spaghetti), *lagane e totani* (fresh eggless pasta with sautéed squid), and *farfalle con vongole e rucola* (pasta with clams and arugula). The secondi include several fish delicacies probably unheard-of back home, such as *alici con fior di latte arrotolate e in foglie di limone* (fresh anchovies rolled in lemon leaves and filled with mozzarella). In the evening, excellent pizza is offered as well.

Via Roma 22. ℭ **089-857876**. Reservations recommended. Secondi 12€–18€ ($15–$23). AE, MC, V. Wed–Mon 12:30–3pm and 7:30–11pm; Apr–Oct daily.

RAVELLO AFTER DARK

Most locals spend their nights sipping an *aperitivo*—or nibbling on sweets—at one of the town's cafes. The activity can take on a theatrical air when the weather is nice and people-watching is at its prime. At the **Bar Calce** (Via Roma 2, next to the Duomo; ℭ **089-857152**), people gather for the excellent pastries and homemade ice cream. **Caffè Domingo** (Piazza Duomo; ℭ **089-857142**) has been run by the same family since 1929 and is famous for its *babà* (sponge cake) and *dolcezze al limone* (typical lemon pastries).

5 Off the Beaten Path: Atrani ⍟ & Scala

Atrani is 1km (½) mile east of Amalfi and 20km (12 miles) west of Vietri sul Mare. Scala is 6km (3½ miles) north of Amalfi.

Atrani is a small medieval town just east of Amalfi by the sea. Scala is a mountain town with defensive castles and an attached *borgo* (village). Though they are very different from each other, these two historic small towns both lie between Amalfi and Ravello, and they remain as unspoiled and picturesque as they were centuries ago.

ATRANI

This is the most picture-postcard-perfect village of the Costiera. It was built at the head of a narrow bay, where the Dragone—Ravello's stream—cuts deeply into the high cliffs, opening onto a small, protected beach. The town's little white houses seem to cling to the rocks; its medieval structure is perfectly preserved, with its narrow covered streets, ramps, and passageways crossing fragrant gardens. Atrani was the residence of choice for noble families of the Amalfi Republic. The heart of town is the picturesque **Piazza Umberto I** ⍟⍟, connected to the beach through a narrow lane. The 10th-century **San Salvatore de' Bireto** church, in Piazza Umberto I, was where Amalfi's doges were crowned and are still buried. (The doges were, as in Venice, elected political rulers.) The church was redone in the early 19th century, but much here is original, including the 12th-century carved portal and the 13th-century bell in its tower. Inside, the highlight is the splendid carved **transenna** ⍟⍟ decorated with two peacocks and dating from the 12th century. The original **bronze door** ⍟⍟ that closed the main portal, made in 1087 in Constantinople, was recently restored and is conserved inside the **Collegiata di Santa Maria,** a church that rises spectacularly to the east of town. The 13th-century building has been redone several times.

Atrani's fishing tradition is still quite active. The beach is the point of departure for the traditional *lampare,* fishing boats equipped with lights to attract fish at night. Unfortunately, the main road (SS 163) was built above the town—sometimes running over the roofs of the houses and cutting the town off from the sea with the pylons of the viaduct, which leaves only a few passages over which you can reach the beach. On the other hand, this inconvenience has contributed to protecting Atrani from development, making the town perhaps the most authentic one in the Costiera. The **beach** is small but charming and the waters are an exquisite blue. In addition to driving, you can take the **footpath** to Amalfi, a pleasurable and scenic 30- to 40-minute walk.

During the summer—mainly in July and August—the village is the site of a rich program of music and art; contact the **tourist office** at Atrani's Municipio (Via dei Dogi; ✆ **089-871185**) for a schedule of events.

WHERE TO STAY

Pensione Chez Checco *Value*　This small pensione-cum-restaurant was created in the 1960s and quickly became famous as the Costiera's first nightclub. Still family-run today, the nightclub has been transformed into a good restaurant, which works by reservation only. Above the restaurant are five simply furnished but cheerful rooms, where you'll be warmly welcomed by the friendly owners. The rooms are not large, and amenities are few. However, the modern furnishings are clean and comfortable, and the price is a bargain.

Via dei Dogi 9, 84010 Atrani. ✆ **089-872051.** 5 units. 60€ ($75) double. Rates include breakfast. No credit cards. Free parking. **Amenities:** Restaurant; bar. *In room:* TV.

WHERE TO DINE

In addition to the restaurants below, there's a good restaurant at **Chez Checco** (see above).

Moderate

'a Paranza 👁👁 AMALFITAN　This simple trattoria is popular for its seafood, and indeed, its menu is a triumph of seafood and traditional dishes. You can start with *frittelle di alghe* (seaweed fritters), follow that with *scialatielli alla paranza* (homemade pasta with small fish), and finish with *polipetti in cassuola* (squid stewed in a terra-cotta pot) or a crispy *grigliata* (grilled fish). The wine list is short but includes excellent local wines.

Via Traversa Dragone 1. ✆ **089-871840.** Reservations recommended. Secondi 12€–18€ ($15–$23). AE, DC, MC, V. Mid-Sept to May Wed–Mon 12:30–3pm and 7:30–10:30pm; daily in summer. Closed 2 weeks in Nov–Dec.

Inexpensive

Gennarino e' Zazza WINERY/PIZZA　This historic cellar-restaurant is always packed. They make an excellent pizza and, if you reserve 1 day ahead, they'll prepare a full meal with such traditional dishes as *baccalà* (stewed salted cod) or *trippa* (tripe). The place is so small that in summer they make pizza only to go.

Vicolo Carmine. ✆ **089-872255.** Reservations recommended. Pizza 5€–9€ ($6.25–$11). No credit cards. Mon–Thurs noon–3pm and Fri–Sat 7–11pm.

Le Arcate 👁👁 AMALFITAN/PIZZA　A popular address that is becoming an institution (the place has been in operation for over 30 years), this restaurant offers both indoor and outdoor dining. The menu is seasonal and focuses on local, simple dishes—homemade pasta with seafood, *panzerotti* (a sort of ravioli), *pesce all'acquapazza* (fish stewed in a light tomato broth), and *frittura* (deep-fried seafood). They also make tasty pizza.

Via G. Di Benedetto 4. ✆ **089-871367.** Reservations recommended. Secondi 8€–12€ ($10–$15). AE, DC, MC, V. Tues–Sun 12:30–3pm and 7:30–10:30pm; daily in summer.

SCALA

Only 6km (3½ miles) north of Amalfi, Scala is the oldest settlement in the area and was, together with Amalfi and Ravello, the heart of the Amalfi Maritime Republic.

Already established in Roman times, the town rises in a splendid position over the valley of the Dragone, opposite Ravello. A fortified town, its two castles—one guarding inland approaches, the other overlooking the sea—were connected by walls that enclosed the town completely. Some medieval palaces remain, such as **Palazzo d'Afflitto** with its beautiful **torrione (tower)**, where you can see an interesting bath in Arab-Sicilian style, covered by an elegant dome on arches similar to the one inside Palazzo Rufolo in Ravello. You can also visit **Casa Romano,** noted for its imposing entrance. While the first floor has been left as it was in medieval times, the second floor was completely redone and decorated with frescoes during the baroque period. The palace hosts several events, including the summer theater festival and a series of concerts. Contact the **Proloco tourist office** (Piazza Municipio; ✆ **089-858977** or 089-857325) for a schedule of events.

The 12th-century **Duomo** ✿ (Piazza Municipio 5; ✆ **089-857397;** daily 8am–1pm and 6–7pm), dedicated to San Lorenzo Martire, is an impressive church which was redone in 1615 and restored in 1980. A Romanesque portal and medieval sculptures decorate the façade; inside, the majolica floor is still in good condition. From the right nave, a staircase descends to the **crypt** ✿, which boasts a unique, surprisingly bright architecture. Some of the best art pieces are conserved here, including the 14th-century **funerary monument** ✿✿ for Marinella Rufolo, erected by her husband Antonio Coppola and uniquely decorated with colored enamel. Be sure to note the 13th-century **crucifix** over the main altar.

Around Scala you can also visit the several separate bourgs built on the surrounding hills. Each is a smaller replica of Scala's defensive structure—protected by two castles, one facing the sea and one guarding inland. All of these smaller bourgs can be reached by car of course, but also on foot, using the network of footpaths connecting them. These provide an excellent opportunity for short hikes. One of the easiest and most rewarding is the walk to the bourg of **Minuto,** only 1km (½ mile) south of Scala, where you'll find the **Chiesa della Santissima Annunziata** ✿✿, probably Scala's original cathedral. Built between the 11th and the 12th centuries, this church is one of the best examples of Romanesque architecture on the whole Amalfi Coast (and the view alone is worth a stop). The handsome covered portico was used in the Middle Ages as the town meeting place; the bell tower is remarkable for its rare octagonal housing. The three portals of the church's facade are decorated with Byzantine frescoes. Inside, the church is divided into three naves by antique columns. If you come here, be sure to visit the **crypt,** where you will find an important cycle of **12th-century frescoes** ✿✿, including a Christ Pantocraor that accurately represents Byzantine style. Note that the church is only opened for mass on Sunday (9:30–10:30am), but it can be visited upon request by asking at the parish house in Via Ficuciello.

STAYING ACTIVE

The mountainous area of Scala is unspoiled and authentic. The best (as well as the most exciting) way to visit it is on horseback. You can sign up for a pleasant **horse ride and guided excursion** in the countryside at local horse farms; the best are **Carmusina** (Via Casa Romana; ✆ **089-857904**), and **La Piccola California** (Via Sento; ✆ **089-858042**). If you prefer to walk, the best **hike** in the area is from **Campidoglio di Scala**—one of the bourgs connected to Scala, at an altitude of 470m (1,542 ft.). The first part is a ridge trail, extremely scenic and not very arduous. You can make the walk more challenging by descending all the way to Amalfi. Along the way you will find, on your left, the ruins of the 12th-century church of Sant'Eustachio. The trail continues through a natural rock formation in the form of an amphitheater, showing the ruins of ancient fortifications, called Castello. It finally reaches the waterfalls at the top of the Vallone delle Ferriere of Amalfi (see later in this chapter); here you are about halfway through the descent. If you wish, you can then walk down along the Vallone and reach Amalfi through the Valle dei Mulini. Figure on spending about 2 hours to get to the waterfall and an additional 2 hours to get to Amalfi.

WHERE TO STAY

Albergo La Margherita   Overlooking the valley of the Dragone, this hotel enjoys a delightful position, surrounded by greenery and quiet. Guest rooms are simply furnished, but all are comfortable and functional, with good-sized bathrooms. Guests can enjoy the large terraces and the pool, as well as the top-notch on-site restaurant (see below). The annex nearby—**Villa Giuseppina**—has added more rooms (same phone).

Via Torricella 31, 84010 Scala. ✆ **089-857106.** Fax 089-857219. www.lamargheritahotel.it. 30 units. 100€–120€ ($125–$150) double; low season 80€–100€ ($100–$125) double. Rates include breakfast. Children under 3 stay free in parent's room. No credit cards. Free parking. **Amenities:** Restaurant; bar; outdoor pool. *In room:* TV, minibar.

Hotel Zi 'Ntonio   Overlooking Ravello from the other side of the valley, this hotel offers comfortable accommodations with good views. A family-run establishment, the hotel basks in a quiet, warm atmosphere, surrounded by chestnut trees. Rooms come simply furnished but with modern bathrooms and amenities. The large terraces, garden, and pool are added attractions, and the restaurant is quite good (see below).

Via Torricella 39, 84010 Scala. ✆ **089-857118.** Fax 089-858128. www.zintonio.com. 22 units. 110€ ($138) double; low season 90€ ($113) double. Rates include breakfast. Children under 3 stay free in parent's room. No credit cards. Free parking. **Amenities:** Restaurant; bar; outdoor pool. *In room:* Hair dryer.

WHERE TO DINE

Da Lorenzo AMALFITAN/PIZZA   Overlooking the valley, Ravello, and the sea, this restaurant is in Santa Maria, one of the bourgs of Scala. The cuisine is simple and traditional, with homemade dishes focusing on fish in summer and meat in winter. The bread is made in a wood-burning oven that also turns out excellent pizza in the evening. Some of the best dishes here are *scialatielli ai frutti di mare* (fresh pasta with shellfish), *pappardelle con il coccio* (large pasta with a tasty local fish), *grigliata di gamberoni* (perfectly grilled large shrimp) in summer, and *scamorza alla brace* (grilled local cheese) and cured meats in winter.

Via Fra' G. Sasso, Frazione Santa Maria. ✆ **089-857921.** Reservations recommended. Secondi 10€–18€ ($13–$23). No credit cards. Thurs–Tues noon–2:30pm and 7:30–10:30pm; daily in summer.

La Margherita AMALFITAN   On the terrace and veranda of the hotel of the same name (see earlier), this restaurant offers great views over Ravello and a traditional cuisine to match. The seasonal menu always includes meat and fish. We recommend trying the homemade pastas, such as aromatic *fusilli con pomodoro a basilico* (short pasta with fresh basil and tomatoes) or *linguine con gli scampi* (linguine with prawns). Another specialty is *crespelle* (a sort of crepes with cheese and tomatoes). Also highly recommended are the eggplant Parmigiana and *peperoni ripieni* (stuffed peppers).

Via Torricella 31. ✆ **089-857106.** Reservations recommended. Secondi 11€–18€ ($14–$23). No credit cards. Wed–Mon 12:30–3pm and 7:30–10:30pm; daily in summer.

Zi 'Ntonio INLAND AMALFITAN   This excellent restaurant focuses on meat and vegetables, using ingredients from its own farm and serving local wine. You will find excellent *pasta e fagioli* (thick bean-and-pasta soup) and *carne alla brace* (beautifully grilled meat) in winter, or the special *rigatoni ortomare* (short pasta with fresh arugula and shellfish) in spring. Call in advance (it's worth it) to request the special *pollo all zi'Ntonio*, a chicken dish with herbs and wine. The *crespelle* (Italian crepes) are also very good.

Via Torricella 39. © **089-857118.** Reservations recommended. Secondi 11€–18€ ($14–$23). No credit cards. Daily 12:30–3pm and 7:30–10:30pm.

6 Amalfi ⋆⋆

34km (21 miles) W of Salerno, 61km (38 miles) SE of Naples.

The origins of Amalfi go back to ancient Roman times and even to the Byzantine Empire. Visitors often marvel that a town so small and picturesque was once a "maritime republic," but geography and the nature of those times help explain Amalfi's moment of global (or at least Western) prominence. The town declared its independence in A.D. 839, and its perfect strategic location—opening onto a natural harbor at the mouth of a valley rich in water, yet protected by the forbidding Monti Lattari from the incursions of both Turks and Normans—allowed Amalfi to develop into Italy's *first* maritime republic, before either Pisa or Venice. For 2 centuries, Amalfi was a maritime power to be reckoned with: Its navy kept the Turks at bay, and its maritime code–the Tabula Amalphitana—was recognized as law in the Mediterranean. The small republic was rich and cosmopolitan, and its coins were widely used across the Mediterranean, from the Greek empire to Africa to the Longobard territories. Amalfi also dominated the markets in spices, perfumes, silk, and valuable carpets.

Amalfi's toehold among the cliffs eventually became a liability, however; the limited size of its land area and comparable lack of military power obliged Amalfi to accept Norman rule in 1073. Pisa—which had developed into a powerful maritime republic itself in the meantime—then sacked Amalfi in 1135, and in 1143 a terrible seaquake destroyed large parts of the harbor, including the fortifications and the shipyards. The Amalfi of old was completely annihilated 5 years later, when the plague struck in 1348. Afterwards, Amalfi became a pretty fishing village, until it was rediscovered as a tourist destination by 19th-century travelers.

ESSENTIALS

VISITOR INFORMATION The **tourist office** is located inside Palazzo di Città (Corso delle Repubbliche Marinare 19, 84011 Amalfi; © **089-871107;** www.amalfi touristoffice.it). In winter, it is open Monday to Friday 8am to 1:30pm and Saturday 8am to noon; in summer it's open Monday to Friday 3 to 5pm.

FAST FACTS You'll find a **pharmacy** at Piazza dei Dogi (© **089-871063**). The **medical center** is at Via Casamare © **089-871449**); for an **ambulance,** dial © **118.** The **police** can be reached at © **113** or © **112.** The **post office** is at Via delle Repubbliche Marinare, next to the tourist office (© **089-872996**), and is open Monday to Saturday 8am to 2pm. Next door you will find a Deutsche Bank **ATM.**

SPECIAL EVENTS On the first Sunday of June, the **Historic Regatta of the Maritime Republics** is run, with turns being taken by each of the four historical towns—Genova, Pisa, Venice, and Amalfi. Amalfi's turn was in 2005, and will come again in 2009. Civic pride and thousand-year-old rivalries are at stake, and the boat races are run with pomp, athleticism, and great seriousness. The spectacular, colorful event is accompanied by parades and musical performances.

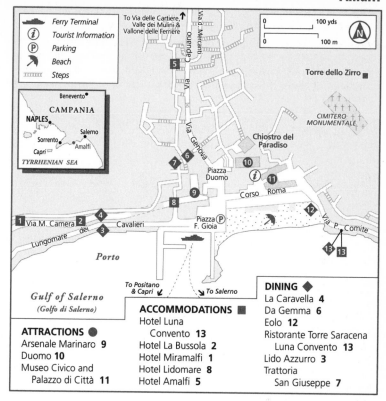

Map Legend

- Ferry Terminal
- ℹ️ Tourist Information
- Ⓟ Parking
- 🏖️ Beach
- Steps

0 — 100 yds
0 — 100 m

To Via delle Cartiere, Valle dei Mulini & Vallone delle Ferriere

Via dei Mercanti

Via Capuano

Via Genova

Torre dello Zirro

CIMITERO MONUMENTALE

Chiostro del Paradiso

Piazza Duomo

Corso Roma

Via P. Comite

Cavalieri

Piazza F. Gioia

Lungomare dei

Porto

CAMPANIA

Benevento

NAPLES

Sorrento

Capri

Amalfi

Salerno

TYRRHENIAN SEA

Gulf of Salerno
(Golfo di Salerno)

To Positano & Capri
To Salerno

ATTRACTIONS ●
Arsenale Marinaro 9
Duomo 10
Museo Civico and
  Palazzo di Città 11

ACCOMMODATIONS ■
Hotel Luna
  Convento 13
Hotel La Bussola 2
Hotel Miramalfi 1
Hotel Lidomare 8
Hotel Amalfi 5

DINING ◆
La Caravella 4
Da Gemma 6
Eolo 12
Ristorante Torre Saracena
  Luna Convento 13
Lido Azzurro 3
Trattoria
  San Giuseppe 7

EXPLORING THE TOWN

Full of mementos of its glorious past and decorated with gardens–olive trees, oranges, and lemons, the groves sloping all the way to the sea—Amalfi is a jewel of a small town. Its central square, **Piazza Flavio Gioia,** commemorates the inventor of the compass (or, at least, the man who perfected it for marine use), according to local legend. Indeed, Amalfi's mariners were the first in Europe to use the properties of magnetism for navigation, starting back in the 12th century; they provided material for the first nautical charts of the Middle Ages.

The medieval heart of Amalfi stretches from **Piazza Duomo** along **Via Genova** and **Via Capuano,** with typical covered porticos and narrow streets. To get its flavor, stroll under the Supportico Sant'Andrea Apostolo till you reach Largo Filippo Augustaricio. There, through a characteristic Arab-style trilobate arch, you can enter another covered passage, Campo de Cinnamellis—the seat, in medieval times, of Amalfi's spice market.

Be sure to visit the **Convento di San Francesco**—now Hotel Luna Convento (see later in this chapter). Its 16th-century watchtower over the cape to the east of town is an annex of the hotel. Here you can visit the well-conserved 13th-century cloister and the attached church.

Fun Fact **Amalfi by the Book**

Amalfi is best known to English readers from John Webster's masterpiece, **The Duchess of Malfi** (1623). This bloody tale of love, lust, and murder captures the scandalous side of Renaissance court life; what's more, it may actually be true. The original source is the **Novelle** of the Dominican priest Matteo Bandello (1485–1561), who served several courts and no doubt knew whereof he spoke.

Duomo 🏛🏛 This superb example of Arab-Norman architecture goes back to the 9th century, when the Republic of Amalfi was just gaining success. The majestic facade is decorated with a mosaic of gold leaf and majolica, with a magnificent 11th-century **bronze door** 🏛 made in Constantinople closing the main portal. The lovely Romanesque bell tower was finished in 1276. The Duomo was enlarged between the 16th and 18th centuries, when it was also given a baroque interior together with the majestic, imposing staircase leading to a beautiful atrium in black-and-white marble. It was renovated in 1891 and further restored in 1929, with respect for the 13th-century structures.

To the left of the Duomo is the breathtakingly beautiful cloister, the **Chiostro del Paradiso** 🏛🏛🏛, dating from 1266. The cloister, in Arab-Sicilian style, is decorated with interlaced arches over double columns, and was originally built as the cemetery for the city's religious and political elite. The site now holds a small museum with ancient Roman and medieval artifacts. Among the best pieces are the **Roman sarcophagus of Ottavio Rufo** 🏛, richly carved, and two other sarcophagi, also decorated with bas-reliefs. From the cloister you can gain access to the **Chiesa del Crocifisso,** the original cathedral of Amalfi dating from the 10th century, where other artworks are conserved. July through September, concerts are held in the cloister on Friday nights (see later in this chapter).

From the right nave of this church you can descend to the **Crypt,** the repository for the remains of the apostle St. Andrew, the protector saint of Amalfi. The crypt was built in the 13th century, when the remains of the saint were brought back from the 4th Crusade; it was redecorated in 1719. An interesting detail is that Andrew's face is missing— it was donated to the church of St. Andrew's in Patras, Greece. Over the main altar is the beautiful bronze **Statue of Sant'Andrea** by Michelangelo Naccherino.

Piazza del Duomo, 84011 Amalfi. ☎ 089-871059. Duomo: Free admission. Daily Nov–Feb 10am–1pm and 2:30–4:30pm; Mar and Oct 9:30am–5:15pm; Apr–June 9am–7pm; July–Sept 9am–9pm. Cloister: 3€ ($3.75). Daily June–Oct 9:30am–7pm; Nov–May 9:30am–5:15pm.

Museo Civico & Palazzo di Città The Palazzo di Città is Amalfi's Town Hall. On its southern wall hangs a famous **Pannello in ceramica** 🏛, a majolica panel relating key moments in Amalfi's history. Created in the 1970s by artist Diodoro Cossa, it is made of two series of large colored tiles, which you can read from left to right. It starts with the founding of Amalfi by a group of ancient Roman refugees and proceeds to the town's growth into an important commercial and political power in the Mediterranean, the building of the cloisters, and the arrival of the body of Saint Andrew. Then comes Amalfi's decline and its slow recovery—and along the way, the invention of the compass, and the production of paper. Inside the Town Hall, the **Museum** is interesting mostly for history buffs and concerns local events. It contains, however, at least one very important piece: the *Tabula Amalphitana,* the original Maritime Code written around the 11th century to regulate maritime traffic in the Mediterranean (this was enforced till at least the 16th century). The artifact was redeemed from Austria in 1929 and brought back to Amalfi. Also interesting are the original pastel drawings for the Duomo's mosaics by Domenico Morelli.

Piazza Municipio. ℂ 089-8736211. www.comune.amalfi.sa.it. Free admission. Mon–Fri 8am–1pm.

Arsenale Marinaro   Here at the Republic of Amalfi's shipyard, citizens built the vessels that maintained power over the Mediterranean back in the Middle Ages. Established in the 11th century, the shipyard was restored in the 13th century, and at its height, it could build galleys up to 40m (131 ft.) long, which were driven by both sails and oars. These were defined by their number of oars, which could number 108, 112,

Amalfi & the Industry of Papermaking

Amalfi is believed to be the first European location where paper as we know it today was made. The process was discovered by the Arabs and perfected in the Arab town of El-Marubig, where the original name *bambagina* referred to the special kind of paper that became known as *paper of Amalfi,* made from recycled cotton, linen, and hemp cloths. The process was then exported to Amalfi through the close commercial relationship the republic had with the Arab world. Considered less durable than parchment, paper was still forbidden in 1250 for public use, but the industry developed rapidly and Amalfi sold its paper far and wide throughout the Middle Ages and the Renaissance. Paper continued to be made by hand till the 18th century, when machines were finally introduced; at that time there were 16 paper mills in the area, 10 of which are still active today. The cloths (or rags) were reduced to a poultice in large vats and then strained in forms marked with the symbol of the paper mill. The paper was then pressed between layers of woolen felt to extract excess water, air dried, and finally "ironed." Even if it was considered inferior to parchment or vellum, this paper was of high quality: The oldest sheets still in existence date from the 13th and 14th centuries. The *bambagina* of Amalfi is still highly appreciated by many—for example, the Vatican uses Amalfi paper for its correspondence.

If you wish to visit one of the working mills, **Cartiera Amatruda** (Via Marino del Giudice; ℂ 089-871315) is still run by the original family, who welcomes visitors and will give you a tour of their facilities. **Antonio Cavaliere** (Via Fiume; ℂ 089-871954), one of the descendants of the ancient master papermakers, is another, smaller option. Antonio's specialty is paper with real dried flowers as filigree, ideal for very special letters.

Both shops produce paper of an almost forgotten quality, made completely by hand, which is sold to the most exclusive paper shops in Italy, Europe, and the U.S. The water for this craft still comes from the covered river that crosses town and was the key resource in the development of Amalfi's paper industry. Both workshops are open regular business hours.

or 120 for the largest ships. Only half of the building remains today—the other half, which reached into the sea, was destroyed by a series of great storms in the 14th century. However, you can still admire the building's beautiful architecture, such as its pointed arches and cross vaults resting over stone pillars. Between the Arsenale and the Porta della Marina you will find a tile panel depicting Amalfi's commercial empire in the Middle Ages; it was created by the artist Renato Rossi in the 1950s.

Via Matteo Camera, off Piazza Flavio Gioia. Free admission. Easter–Sept 9am–8pm.

Museo della Carta (Museum of Paper) This museum is the perfect place to learn more about the historical aspects of the local paper industry. Created inside one of the abandoned paper mills, it has a great collection of original tools and machines. It also maintains a library with over 3,000 texts on the origins of paper. If you are interested in the subject, you can visit two workshops in town (see "Amalfi & the Industry of Papermaking" box above).

Palazzo Pagliara Via delle Cartiere 23. (♪ 089-8304561. www.museodellacarta.it. Admission 3.40€ ($4.25). Tues–Sun 9am–1pm; daily in summer 10am–6pm.

STAYING ACTIVE

Amalfi used to have large **beaches,** but sea erosion and landslides have reduced the beach to two narrow strips on either side of the harbor. Most hotels on the waterfront have small private beaches carved out of the cliffs. You can also take the footpath to Atrani, an easy 15-minute stroll eastward, to the pretty beach there (see earlier in this chapter).

From the harbor at **Marina Grande** you can rent **boats**—with or without driver—to explore the nooks and crannies of this beautiful coast. Or you can sign up for an excursion. The most popular is the one to **Grotta dello Smeraldo** ☞☞ (see "Conca dei Marini," later in this chapter). **Cooperativa Sant'Andrea** (♪ 089-873190; www.coopsantandrea.it) offers a regular beach service to Duoglio and Santa Croce, only a few minutes away from Molo Pennello; boats leave every 30 minutes between 9am and 5 pm. They also have a regular service to Grotta dello Smeraldo leaving every hour between 9:30am and 3:30pm.

Amalfi is also a great starting point for a number of beautiful **hikes.** The most famous and popular is the pleasant and easy walk along **Valle dei Mulini (Valley of the Mills),** which is the valley of the Torrente Canneto, Amalfi's stream. Head up Via Genova from Piazza del Duomo and continue on as the street turns into a trail up the narrow valley of the river. The picturesque walk will lead you to the area known locally as the **Mulino Rovinato (Ruined Mill),** about 1 hour away. The area is so named because a great number of paper and flour mills used to reside in the valley. The flour mills were put out of business by the development of the pasta industry farther north in Torre del Greco, Torre Annunziata, and Gragnano, where the conditions were more favorable. In contrast, the paper mills continued to prosper until recently, and some are still active today.

The more demanding hike to the **Vallone delle Ferriere** ☞☞ was a favorite with 19th-century visitors doing the Grand Tour, who considered this valley one of the most beautiful areas in the whole of southern Italy. In fact, the valley has been declared a World Heritage Site by UNESCO, precisely because of its unique environment. The local limestone mountains were once at the bottom of the sea and have a dolomitic geology. The peculiarities of the area's geophysical configuration have made it into a sort of Mediterranean "lost valley," where plants and animals survive that have disappeared elsewhere on the European continent. Keep your eyes open for the special local fern *Woodwardia radicans,* a species alive since the quaternary or even the tertiary period, before glaciation. It shouldn't be too hard to spot: Its leaves grow up to 2m (8 ft.) in length. However, only a few plants remain. Other rare plants are *pinguicola hirtiflora,* a small carnivorous plant; and saffron, the most expensive spice in the world. Among the rare animals are several species of salamander, such as *salamandrina dagli occhiali* and *tritone italiano,* as well as a variety of birds. To reach the Vallone delle Ferriere, take the trail to the Valle dei Mulini (see above) and continue upwards as the rocky trail traverses through citrus groves and by picturesque waterfalls. The going is good but quite steep as you finally reach the ancient Ferriere (Iron Mills), with their imposing walls partly hidden by growth. Already extant in the Middle Ages, they were active until the 19th century. If you are in good shape, you can climb even further up to the waterfalls; the climb is short but steep. Allow 6 hours for the round-trip on the 12km (7.5-mile) trail.

A less demanding hike is the famous **Via degli Incanti (Trail of Charms),** which connects Amalfi to Positano. The trail is indeed bewitching, wending through the cultivated terraces and citrus groves of the Amalfi countryside. The hike is easy, with some moderately taxing passages, but due to its length—about 25km (15.5 miles)—most people choose to do only a section of it, or plan on doing the whole trip over several days. In either case, going from Amalfi to Positano is more demanding than going from Positano to Amalfi, so plan your hike accordingly. From Amalfi, follow the Via Maestra, the road that climbs through the outskirts of town; the trail is well marked.

WHERE TO STAY
VERY EXPENSIVE

Hotel Santa Caterina 😊😊   This is the most luxurious hotel in Amalfi, offering great, family-run service and a superb location hanging onto a cliff surrounded by terraces and gardens. The public spaces include a private beach (which you can reach by elevator or a winding garden path), a seawater swimming pool with a sun deck, a gym, a bar, an open-air restaurant serving very good food, luscious gardens, and citrus groves. Guest rooms are large and decorated in a refined manner, each with an antique piece among the furnishings, and luxurious bathrooms. Some of the suites are absolutely fantastic—Follia Amalfitana and Casa dell'Arancio, in particular. They are actually luxurious bungalows immersed in a citrus grove, with a private garden and a small pool.

Via Nazionale 9, 84011 Amalfi. © **089-871012.** Fax 089-871351. www.hotelsantacaterina.it. 70 units. 290€–360€ ($363–$450) double; from 580€ ($725) suite. Rates include buffet breakfast. AE, DC, MC, V. Parking: 15€ ($19). **Amenities:** 2 restaurants; bar; lounge; outdoor pool; health club; concierge; room service; babysitting; laundry service. *In room:* A/C, TV, dataport, minibar, hair dryer, iron, safe.

EXPENSIVE

Hotel Luna Convento 😊😊   Transformed into a hotel in 1822, the Hotel Luna Convento occupies Amalfi's watchtower dating from 1564, and the ancient Franciscan monastery founded by Saint Francis in 1222, complete with its beautiful original cloister and church. Just 273m (896 ft.) from the town's center, on the promontory protecting Amalfi's harbor, this family-run place counts Henrik Ibsen (who wrote *A Doll's House* here in 1879) among its famous guests. The space remains as artistically inspiring as ever: The hotel is surrounded by a garden, with sun terraces and a large seawater swimming pool carved out of the cliff. There is also a private, rather rocky beach and a highly praised gourmet restaurant where you have to make reservations long in advance. The watchtower houses a disco and piano bar, as well as another restaurant with fantastic views (see below). Guest rooms vary in size and decor, but all are bright and spacious, with sweeping vistas, commodious tiled bathrooms, and sometimes private terraces.

Via Pantaleone Comite 33, 84011 Amalfi. ⓒ **089-871002**. Fax 089-871333. www.lunahotel.it. 48 units. 240€ ($300) double; 540€ ($675) suite. Rates include buffet breakfast. Children under 3 stay free in parent's room. AE, DC, MC, V. Parking: 18€ ($23).. **Amenities:** 2 restaurants; American bar; outdoor pool; concierge; room service; babysitting; laundry service. *In room:* A/C, TV, minibar, hair dryer, safe.

MODERATE

Hotel La Bussola   It's not only monasteries and villas that have been converted to hotels—La Bussola is housed in the former Pastificio Bergamasco, a historic pasta-making factory. Located right on the seaside promenade, this hotel offers pleasant accommodations and kind, professional service. Guest rooms are bright and comfortable, with functional furnishings, colorful tiled floors, and modern bathrooms. The restaurant serves a variety of seafood and, of course, pasta.

Lungomare dei Cavalieri 16, 84011 Amalfi. ⓒ **089-871533**. Fax 089-871369. www.labussolahotel.it. 65 units. 124€–154€ ($155–$193) double; low season 94€–114€ ($118–$143) double. Rates include buffet breakfast. Children under 3 stay free in parent's room. AE, DC, MC, V. Free parking. **Amenities:** Restaurant; American bar. *In room:* A/C (10€/$13), TV.

Hotel Miramalfi *(Kids)*   Just outside the center of town to the west, this family-run hotel offers attractive rooms and a panoramic position. Perched on a rocky cliff on a point sticking out into the sea, the hotel has a view in every direction. It has its own private beach, as well as a pool at the foot of the cliff, which is accessible by elevator. It is therefore completely self-contained—kids can go back and forth to the beach, room, and pool without leaving the grounds. Guest rooms are modern in style with good-sized bathrooms; all have balconies and views overlooking the sea.

Via S. Quasimodo 3, 84011 Amalfi. ⓒ **089-871588**. Fax 089-871287. www.miramalfi.it. 49 units. 205€ ($256) double; 320€ ($400) suite. Rates include breakfast. Children under 3 stay free in parent's room. AE, DC, MC, V. Parking: 13€ ($16). Closed Nov–Dec 20. **Amenities:** Dining room; lounge; outdoor pool; concierge; room service; babysitting; laundry service. *In room:* A/C, satellite TV, dataport, minibar, hair dryer, safe.

INEXPENSIVE

Hotel Amalfi *(Finds)*   This quiet hotel with a nice citrus garden is hidden away in the medieval part of town, right by the Duomo. It offers comfortable accommodations at moderate prices and with friendly service. The simple guest rooms have modern furnishings chosen with care. Bathrooms, though small, are perfectly adequate.

Via dei Pastai 3, 84011 Amalfi. ⓒ **089-872440**. Fax 089-872250. www.hamalfi.it. 40 units. 120€–140€ ($150–$175) double; low season 80€–100€ ($100–$125) double. Rates include breakfast. Extra bed 25€ ($31). Children under 3 stay free in parent's room. AE, MC, V. Parking: 18€ ($23). **Amenities:** Restaurant; bar. *In room:* A/C (10€/$13), satellite TV, minibar, hair dryer, safe.

Hotel Lidomare *(Value)*   This is a great though small hotel offering friendly service and good accommodations for the money. Family-run, it is housed in a 13th-century building only steps from the beach. The spacious guest rooms have floors brightly patterned with tiles and are decorated with a mix of modern furniture and antiques. Bathrooms are on the small side but are perfectly kept. Some rooms have sea views and Jacuzzis.

Largo Duchi Piccolomini 9, 84011 Amalfi. ℂ **089-871332**. Fax 089-871394. www.lidomare.it. 15 units. 120€ ($150) double; low season 100€ ($125) double. Rates include breakfast. Children under 3 stay free in parent's room. AE, MC, V. Parking: 15€ ($19). **Amenities:** Lounge. *In room:* A/C, TV, minibar, hair dryer, safe.

WHERE TO DINE
VERY EXPENSIVE
La Caravella 🏵🏵🏵 AMALFITAN/CREATIVE   This is one of the best restaurants in the whole region. Chef Antonio Dipino has succeeded in marrying tradition with creativity, and so the dishes are sometimes elaborate, but simpler fare is also offered— and everything is made with fresh local ingredients. The seaweed fritters are an excellent appetizer, which you can follow with *tubetti di Gragnano al ragù di zuppa di pesce* (short pasta from Gragnano—bronze extruded—with a sauce of stewed seafood) and a superb *pezzogna* (local fish). For those who prefer meat or are tired of seafood, there are choices such as *ziti di Torre Annunziata ripieni di carne alla Genovese* (pasta tubes from Torre Annunziata—also bronze extruded—filled with meat, Genoese style). The desserts and the wine list are on par with the rest of the menu.

Via Matteo Camera 12. ℂ **089-871029**. Reservations required. Tasting menu 65€ ($81). Secondi 20€–30€ ($25–$38). AE, DC, MC, V. Wed–Mon noon–2pm and 7:30–10:30pm; daily in Aug. Closed mid-Nov to Dec 25.

MODERATE
Da Gemma *Kids* AMALFITAN   Serving customers for over a century, this venerable restaurant has racked up sheaves of reviews attesting to its quality. The atmosphere is upscale but relaxed enough to be kid-friendly. One of the most famous specialties is *paccheri con gamberetti* (homemade large pasta with shrimp). *Zuppa di pesce per due* (fish stew for two) is another winner. Don't forget to try the typical Amalfian side dish known as *ciambotta* (a mix of sautéed potatoes, peppers, and eggplant). For dessert try the simple homemade *crostata* (a thick crust topped with local citrus-fruit jam). Half-portions are available for children.

Via Frà Gerardo Sasso 9. ℂ **089-871345**. Reservations required. Secondi 15€–24€ ($19–$30). AE, DC, MC, V. Thurs–Tues 12:30–2:45pm and 7:45–10:30pm; daily in summer. Closed mid-Jan to mid-Feb.

Eolo 🏵 AMALFITAN   This is a classic-style restaurant of the no-nonsense kind Italians like—there are simple furnishings, but great attention is paid to the food and service. The seasonal menu focuses on seafood; you will find local traditional dishes such as *scialatielli ai frutti di mare* (homemade pasta with shellfish) and *frittura* (deep-fried medley of seafood).

Via Pantaleone Comite 3. ℂ **089-871241**. Reservations recommended. Secondi 15€–32€ ($19–$40). AE, DC, MC, V. Wed–Mon 12:30–3pm and 7:30–10:30pm. Closed 2 weeks in Jan–Feb.

Ristorante Torre Saracena Luna Convento 🏵🏵 AMALFITAN/ITALIAN   Great for an elegant dinner, the Torre Saracena, part of Hotel Luna Convento (see earlier in this chapter), is housed in a 16th-century watchtower and, not surprisingly, boasts superb views. The food is very good, too, with a varied seasonal menu which includes both local and common Italian dishes. From *fusilli ai frutti di mare* (short pasta with seafood), to pork chops, to grilled lamb on a bed of roasted and herbed potatoes, the menu ranges from seafood to meat—it's comprehensive, but uniformly good.

Via Pantaleone Comite 33. ℂ **089-871002**. Reservations required. Secondi 16€–25€ ($20–$31). AE, DC, MC, V. Daily 12:30–2pm and 7:30–9pm.

Christmas on the Amalfi Coast

Christmas *(Natale)* is always a special time in Italy, when lights and decorations create a suggestive atmosphere in even the smallest of hamlets. Natale on the Amalfi Coast is unique in its own way; the already picturesque villages and towns become truly magical with Christmas illumination, and you will find elaborate *presepi* (manger scenes, or creches) everywhere. However, the unique landscape of this coast plays a part even here; besides the more traditional location inside churches—such as the 10th-century church of **Santa Maria Maggiore,** whose very fine *presepi* dates from its redecoration in the 18th century (Largo S. Maria Maggiore, Amalfi)—*presepi* are placed in fountains and in grottos. Perhaps the most important of these is the one inside **Grotta dello Smeraldo** in Conca dei Marini (see "Conca dei Marini," later in this chapter), which becomes the point of arrival of a procession on December 24, and again on January 6 (Epiphany). Call the visitor center in Amalfi at ℭ **089-871107** for more information.

INEXPENSIVE

Lido Azzurro *(Kids* AMALFITAN   This simple restaurant enjoys a prime spot on the town's seaside promenade. The menu includes many kinds of pasta with seafood—*tubetti zucchine, vongole e cozze* (short pasta with clams, mussels and zucchini) is quite good. We recommend the day's fresh fish prepared either baked in a potato crust, or *all'acquapazza* (in a light tomato broth). A well-rounded children's menu makes this a good choice for families.

Lungomare dei Cavalieri. ℭ **089-871384.** Reservations recommended on weekends. Secondi 12€–18€ ($15–$23). AE, DC, MC, V. Tues–Sun 12:30–3pm and 7:30–10:30pm. Closed mid-Jan to mid-Mar.

Trattoria San Giuseppe *(Finds* AMALFITAN/PIZZA   Hidden away in the medieval part of town, this simple, down-to-earth place is a real local hangout. It's a great alternative to upscale dining, and the traditional food is of high quality. You can get a variety of pasta dishes as well as excellent pizza—probably the best in town.

Salita Ruggiero II 4. ℭ **089-872640.** Reservations recommended on weekends. Pizza 5€–10€ ($6.25–$13). Secondi 8€–12€ ($10–$15). No credit cards. Fri–Wed noon–2:30pm and 7:30–10:30pm.

AMALFI AFTER DARK

Summer is entertainment time in Amalfi, when musical events are held throughout town. Among the most striking are the piano and vocal concerts held in the **Chiostro del Paradiso** (Piazza del Duomo, off the Duomo's atrium) July through September on Friday evenings.

The town's other key entertainment is visiting one of its many pleasant cafes to sip an *aperitivo* or enjoy a *gelato*. On Piazza Duomo, try **Bar Francese** (Piazza Duomo 20; ℭ **089-871049**), with its elegant seating and excellent pastries. Overlooking the sea is **Gran Caffè di Amalfi** (Corso Repubbliche Marinare; ℭ **089-857874**), a standout for *apertivos*. For those with a sweet tooth, **Gelateria Porto Salvo** (Piazza Duomo 22; ℭ **089-871655;** closed Jan–Mar) is very popular—try the *mandorla candita* (candied almond) flavor. For other types of sweets, **Pasticceria Pansa** (Piazza Duomo 40; ℂ **089-871065;** closed Tues) has been creating delicious pastries since 1830.

If instead you'd like to explore the local wines, head to **Cantina San Nicola** (Salita Marino Sebaste 8; ℂ **089-8304559;** closed Sun) for its great atmosphere and wide selection of labels; they hold wine-tastings twice a week during the summer.

7 Between Amalfi & Positano: Conca dei Marini, Furore, Agerola & Praiano-Vettica Maggiore

Conca dei Marini is 5km (3 miles) W of Amalfi. Furore 10.6km (6½ miles) W of Amalfi. Agerola is 14.5km (9 miles) W of Amalfi. Vettica Maggiore is 6.5km (4 miles) E of Positano and 9km (5 miles) W of Amalfi.

The busiest stretch of the Costiera, the area between Amalfi and Positano, is studded with little towns both by the water and up the cliffs. These are often bypassed by tourists who make a beeline for more famous destinations—a boon for the traveler who chooses to tarry here. From the small seaside resort of Conca dei Marini, with its famous Emerald Grotto, you can take the road that winds up the cliff to Furore and continues to Agerola. Down by the sea are medieval Praiano and Vettica Maggiore, the two faces of the promontory a little distance west of Positano.

CONCA DEI MARINI

A delightful hamlet in a picturesque cove by the sea, Conca dei Marini is only a few miles west of Amalfi. Unbelievable as it might seem, this was once a powerful commercial center, whose ships crisscrossed the Mediterranean Sea. The quiet little town is famous today for its special *sfogliatella* (a pastry filled with cream and *amarene*— candied sour cherries in syrup— instead of the standard ricotta), which were invented in the 14th-century **Convento di Santa Rosa.** This delicious creation is celebrated with a special festival in August, **Sagra della Sfogliatella di Santa Rosa.** Summer is also the time for the **Summer Fest,** with a series of events including theater, ballet, and art shows. Contact the **Proloco tourist office** (ℂ **089-831301**) inside the Casa Comunale (town office) for a schedule of what's on.

The other famous attraction here is **Grotta dello Smeraldo** 𝒜𝒜 26km (4 miles) away on SS 163; admission is 5€ ($6.25), including the elevator down to sea level and the boat ride from the beach. The grotto is open daily, weather permitting, November to February from 9am to 4pm, and March to October from 9am to 7pm. This beautiful underwater grotto with karst formations of stalactites and stalagmites takes on a unique blue-green color in certain lights. Less famous than the Blue Grotto in Capri, the grotto is still impressive, measuring 30m (98 ft.) in length by 60m (197 ft.) wide, with a maximum depth of 24m (79 ft.). It was discovered in 1932 and is accessible only by boat or by swimming; inside, at a depth of 4m (13 ft.), you'll see the ceramic crèche that was submerged in the grotto in 1956. Admission includes the rowboat ride from the beach and the elevator from the SS 163, which runs high above the cliff. You can also take the hair-rising staircase, should you want more excitement. The grotto's entrance can be reached either by SITA bus (Positano-Amalfi line) or by launch service from Amalfi; launches operate between 9:30am and 4pm and cost 10€ ($13) round-trip.

WHERE TO STAY

Hotel Il Belvedere   This beautiful hotel is housed in a 19th-century villa built in a choice position on the cliffs, only minutes from the Emerald Grotto. The public spaces include a great seawater swimming pool overlooking the rocky private beach. The bright, large guest rooms are comfortably furnished with period furniture or reproductions, and have patterned tiled floors. Bathrooms are also nicely tiled, with modern fixtures. Each room has a small terrace (large enough for a table and chairs) with an ocean view.

Via Smeraldo, 84010 Conca dei Marini. © 089-831282. Fax 089-831439. www.belvederehotel.it. 40 units. 210€–230€ ($263–$288) double; low season 145€–170€ ($181–$213) double. Rates include buffet breakfast. Children under 2 stay free in parent's room. AE, DC, MC, V. Free parking. **Amenities:** Restaurant; bar; outdoor pool. In room: A/C, TV.

WHERE TO DINE

La Tonnarella ✶✶ AMALFITAN   This picturesque restaurant is best reached from the sea—call to be picked up by boat at the nearest harbor. It is also accessible from the road via a steep stairway descending from SS 163 to beach level. Of course, the menu's focus is fish, which is always extremely fresh and well prepared. You'll also find *risotto di mare* (with seafood and tomatoes), *pasta al forno* (lasagna), and *zuppa di pesce* (fish stew). Other strong suits are the *grigliate* (grilled seafood) and *fritto misto* (deep-fried medley of seafood).

Borgo Marinaro. © 089-831236. Reservations required. Secondi 11€–18€ ($14–$23). No credit cards. Daily 12:30–3pm and 7:30–11pm. Closed end of Sept to May.

FURORE

A village with a split personality, Furore is both a sparse hamlet high up on the cliffs and a scenic fishing hamlet down by the sea (its lower section occupies a lovely beach inside a deep fjord). Famous for its cliff vineyards, which produce an excellent D.O.C. wine, Furore is a very pleasant countryside area. The town is proud of its so-called open-air art gallery, with over 100 paintings and sculptures by artists from all over the world. Down by the sea is **Furore Marina,** a hamlet of a few fishermen's dwellings, called *monazzeri,* built on the little bit of beach at the bottom of the fjord. The famous fjord was cut into the high limestone cliff by the brook Schiato. It is so deep that when there's a storm, the sea rises with *furore* (rage—hence the name), flooding the *monazzeri.* Abandoned for a long time, these historic structures have been recently restored and transformed into showrooms and small jazz bars, and there is a quite active summer festival of art and music events. Call © 089-830525 for a show schedule, or the **Proloco tourist office** inside the Municipio (Via Mola, 84010 Furore; © 089-874100).

The small beach is very pleasant—especially in summer when one of the *monazzeri* houses a romantic small restaurant. The bottom of the fjord is accessible from the sea, passing under the arched viaduct of SS 163, and from the land by the steep stairway—200 steps—that starts from SS 163, just above the fjord. But perhaps the most romantic way to approach the bottom is via **Sentiero della Volpe Pescatrice (Fishing Fox Trail)** from Furore; the old trail was used by local peasant-fishermen to reach the *monazzeri.*

WHERE TO STAY & DINE

Albergo di Bacco ✶   Surrounded by vineyards, this hotel is set in a panoramic position, and offers comfortable accommodations and kind service. Founded in 1930, it is expertly run by the third generation of the family Ferraioli. Guest rooms are bright, and are simply but tastefully furnished. Each has a solarium and a small terrace. The hotel's restaurant is the wonderful **Antica Hostaria di Bacco** ✶✶ (© 089-874583), which offers a superb rendition of local traditional cuisine and very nice views. The homemade pasta is extraordinarily good; try *cavatelli ai capperi* (fresh pasta with a caper sauce) or *scialatielli ai frutti di mare* (a sort of tagliatelle, with shellfish). Other local specialties are *totani con patate* (stew of calamari with potatoes and cherry tomatoes), a dish typical of Furore; and, for dessert, *babà al Nanassino,* the classic Neapolitan sponge cake—but served here with a *rosolio* made with prickly pear, a well-kept family recipe. Of course, the wine to have here is the *Furore,* one of the Amalfi Coast's D.O.C. wines.

Via G.B. Lama 9, 84010 Furore. ✆ **089-830360.** Fax 089-830352. www.baccofurore.it. 18 units. 80€ ($100). Extra bed 20€ ($25). Children under 2 stay free in parent's room. AE, DC, MC, V. Free parking. Closed 1 week in Nov and Dec 24–25. **Amenities:** Restaurant; bar. *In room:* A/C, TV, minibar, hair dryer, safe.

La Volpe Pescatrice 🐟🐟 CREATIVE AMALFITAN   This gourmet restaurant offers refined cuisine and a beautiful setting within the luxury spa-hotel Furore Inn Resort. The dramatic sea view from its cliff location is pleasantly matched by the elegant interior and superb cuisine. The menu includes both surf and turf choices and varies daily, focusing on all the local foods and revised traditions. Of particular note are *spiedini di mazzancolle* (skewered grilled prawns), *coniglio alla cacciatora* (rabbit in a wine and tomato sauce), and the ever-present, sure-fire homemade pastas. The hotel —which doubles as a spa open to the public—is a whitewashed structure merging with the supporting cliff. The 22 panoramic guest rooms, all featuring tiled floors and modern furnishings, are offered at 404€ ($505) double and from 548€ ($685) suite. (Low-season prices are 220€/$275 double and from 300€/$375 suite.)

Via dell'Amore 1, Contrada Sant'Elia, 84010 Furore. ✆ **089-8304711.** Fax 089-8304777. Reservations recommended. Secondi 18€–29€ ($23–$36). AE, MC, V. Daily 12:30–3pm and 7:30–11pm. Closed 2 weeks Nov–Dec and 2 weeks Jan–Feb.

SHOPPING

If you would like to sample or take away some of the great local wine, **Cantine Gran Furor** (Via Lama 14; ✆ **089-874489**) is the place to go. The Cuomo family has taken care of their terraced vineyards for decades and has even been rewarded with D.O.C. certification.

AGEROLA

Farther up the cliff from Furore, the high plateau of Agerola is famous for its beauty and for its cattle and sheep, which produce the milk for which the Monti Lattari were named for (*latte* means milk). The region's best cheese comes from Agerola's farms— indeed, some of the best cheese in the country can be had here. A collection of farming hamlets, Agerola has its administrative center in **Pianillo,** where you'll also find the **Proloco tourist office** (Viale della Vittoria; ✆ **089-8791064**).

The most scenic of Agerola's bourgs is **San Lazzaro** where, past the church to the left, you will find the **Punta,** a natural terrace offering dramatic **views** 🐟🐟. Taking the road to the right of the church, you will find more awesome panoramas opening from the terrace by the ex-Castle Avitabile, and from the ruins of **Castel Lauritano** 🐟🐟🐟. The whole area offers unending **hiking** opportunities, including the demanding but extremely scenic 5-hour hike to the **Vallone delle Ferriere** waterfall, starting from San Lazzaro.

WHERE TO STAY

Albergo Ristorante Risorgimento   Last renovated in 2003, this welcoming hotel has been around since 1878. Your first clue that the owners are seriously interested in cuisine is the fact that the albergo side of the operation is smaller than the restaurant—there are 20 guest rooms, but the large restaurant-pizzeria seats 150. The restaurant serves a good pizza, as well as seafood, homemade pasta, and meat dishes such as rabbit and lamb. Guest rooms are comfortable and functional, with good-sized modern bathrooms. The simple rooms (moderate in size, but not small) have been tastefully decorated, with walls done in yellows and light ochres, color-coordinated furnishings, and wrought-iron beds.

Via Antonio Coppola 32, Località San Lazzaro, 84051 Agerola. ©/fax **081-8025072**. www.hotelrisorgimento.it. 20 units. 80€ ($100) double. Rates include breakfast. Children under 2 free in parent's room. AE, DC, MC, V. Free parking. **Amenities:** Restaurant; bar; tennis; laundry service. *In room:* TV.

WHERE TO DINE
La Taverna ✮ AGEROLA   This modern restaurant with a panoramic terrace offers excellent local cuisine, delicious in its simplicity. The *antipasti* can be a meal on their own, with a great choice of local cheeses, cured meats, and vegetable preparations. Of the homemade pastas, *pappardelle con funghi e tartufo* (large fresh pasta with mushrooms and truffles) and *spaghetti con i peperoni dolci* (spaghetti with sweet peppers) are truly special. For your secondo, do not miss the flavorful *grigliate* (artfully grilled local meats). All desserts are strictly homemade, too.

Via Radicosa 53, Località San Lazzaro. © **089-8025041**. Secondi 11€–18€ ($14–$23). No credit cards. Wed–Mon 12:30–3pm and 7:30–10pm. Closed Sept–Nov.

SHOPPING
Fresh cheese is a great food for a tasty snack or a picnic, and the inhabitants of these mountains are justly proud of theirs. To buy the famous *fiordilatte* of Agerola, as well as excellent *caciocavallo* and *scamorze,* head to one of the numerous cheese-making facilities. Among the best are **Caseificio Agerolina** (Via Tutti I Santi 6; © **089-8731022**); **Caseificio Belfiore** (Via Belvedere 35; © **089-8791338**); **Caseificio Fior di Agerola** (Via Galli 74; © **089-8791339**); and **La Montanina** (Via Carlo Poerio 30bis; © **089-8731022**).

PRAIANO-VETTICA MAGGIORE
A beautiful medieval village, **Praiano** sits 120m (394 ft.) above sea level on the slopes of Monte Sant'Angelo, only 6.5km (4 miles) east of Positano and 9km (5½ miles) west of Amalfi. To the west of Praiano, on the other side of Capo Sottile, is **Vettica Maggiore,** immersed in olive groves.

The preferred residences of the Amalfi doges—probably for the beautiful views it affords over Positano, Amalfi, and the Faraglioni of Capri—the two towns specialize in silk spinning and weaving, as well as coral fishing. Away from the tourist crowds, the towns are nestled harmoniously into their surroundings, with a graceful profusion of porticos and domes complementing the astounding natural beauty. You'll want to allot some time to walk through Praiano and Vettica Maggiore, admiring the architecture and the many medieval watchtowers. **San Gennaro** church, in Vettica Maggiore, is crowned by a beautiful oval dome tiled with colored majolica. Inside, the 18th-century majolica floor was rebuilt in 1966 according to the original design. The **view** from the church square is superb.

The beach of **Vettica Maggiore** is small but delightful, with wonderful clear waters. Nearby, via a somewhat tricky cliff trail, you can reach the secluded beach known as **Spiaggia della Gavitella;** it is a lot easier by boat—you can hire one in either town.

Also, just east of Praiano, a small road cut into the cliff leads down to the picturesque beach of **Marina di Praia** ★★.

Praiano's **tourist office** is at Via Capriglione (© **089-874557**), and Vettica Maggiore's is inside the Municipio (Via Nazionale; © **089-874456**).

WHERE TO STAY
Expensive
Grand Hotel Tritone   This elegant hotel offers gorgeous views and quiet accommodations. Completely surrounded by gardens and pines, it is built over a high cliff, with an elevator to the private beach below. On the grounds are a seawater pool and a picturesque chapel built inside a grotto. Guest rooms are well appointed and pleasantly furnished, many with sea views. Bathrooms are good-sized. The 12 suites are gorgeous, each with its own private terrace overlooking the water.

Via Nazionale, 840101 Praiano. © **089-874333.** Fax 089-813024. www.hoteltritone.com. 62 units. 270€–300€ ($338–$375) double; 380€ ($475) junior suite; 470€ ($588) suite. Rates include buffet breakfast. Children under 2 stay free in parent's room. AE, DC, MC, V. Free parking. **Amenities:** Restaurant; bar; outdoor pool. *In room:* A/C, satellite TV, minibar, hair dryer, safe.

Hotel Tramonto d'oro ★★   The name of this elegant hotel means "golden sunset," and indeed, you can enjoy wonderful sunsets over the sea from the guest room windows. On the hotel grounds, you'll find a large swimming pool and a gym; the beach is only a short distance away by the hotel's free shuttle. Guest rooms are spacious and filled with light, individually decorated in modern, contemporary styles with light woods and tiled floors.

Via G. Capriglione 119, 84010 Praiano. © **089-874955.** Fax 089-874670. www.tramontodoro.it. 20 units. 170€–250€ ($213–$313). Rates include buffet breakfast. Children under 4 stay free in parent's room. AE, DC, MC, V. Free parking. Closed Nov–Feb. **Amenities:** Restaurant; bar; outdoor pool; spa; health club; complimentary shuttle; babysitting. *In room:* A/C, TV/VCR/DVD, fax, dataport, minibar, hair dryer, safe.

Moderate
Hotel Onda Verde ★★   Perched on a cliff, this hotel hangs between sea and sky. It's actually made up of several separate villas, with differences in style but uniform amenities and service. Guest rooms are tasteful and well-appointed, with good-sized bathrooms; each unit has its own panoramic small terrace. The modern furniture has been keyed to the colors of the patterned tile floor and to the drapes and linens. The effect is restrained, comfortable, and easy on the eyes. Likewise, the hotel exudes a personal atmosphere and friendly service.

Via Terramare 3, 84010 Praiano. © **089-874143.** Fax 089-8131049. www.ondaverde.it. 20 units. 210€–240€ ($263–$300) double; low season 140€–210€ ($175–$263). Rates include buffet breakfast. Children under 3 stay free in parent's room. AE, DC, MC, V. Free parking. Closed Jan 7–Mar 20 and Nov 1–Dec 26. **Amenities:** Restaurant; bar. *In room:* A/C, satellite TV, minibar, hair dryer, safe.

Inexpensive
Hotel Il Pino   This family-run, modern hotel is only a few years old and offers very comfortable accommodations in a delightful location. Guest rooms are large, each with a private terrace with a water view. The beach is only a few minutes away by a pedestrian path. The hotel's restaurant on the terrace is very good; especially hard to pass up are *scialatelli ai frutti di mare* (fresh pasta with shellfish) and *grigliata di pesce* (grilled fish).

Via G. Capriglione 13, 84010 Praiano. © **089-874389.** www.hotelilpino.it. 16 units 124€ ($155) double; 150€ ($188) triple; 170€ ($213) quad. Rates include breakfast. Children under 2 stay free in parent's room. AE, DC, MC, V. Free parking. **Amenities:** Restaurant; bar. *In room:* A/C, TV, minibar.

Hotel Margherita ✦ *Finds*   This family-run hotel offers high-standard accommodations at moderate prices. The swimming pool and panoramic terraces are nice places to lounge, and the beach is only a few minutes away. Guest units are comfortable and well appointed, with tiled floors, modern furniture, and spacious bathrooms.

Via Umberto I 70, 84010 Praiano. © 089-874227. Fax 089-874628. www.hotelmargherita.info. 28 units. 100€ ($125) double; 140€ ($175) triple; 180€ ($225) suite. Rates include breakfast. Children under 3 stay free in parent's room. AE, DC, MC, V. Free parking. **Amenities:** Restaurant; bar; outdoor pool; health club; spa; room service; babysitting; laundry service. *In room:* A/C, TV/DVD, fax, dataport, minibar, hair dryer, safe.

Hotel Ristorante Alfonso a Mare ✦   This authentic little hotel is set among fishermen's houses just a few feet from the sea. The Fusco family will give you a warm welcome. The comfortable guest rooms are simply furnished in pleasant Mediterranean style, with beautiful majolica floors. The gardens are a wonderful place to relax—or to rest between your scuba lessons, which can be organized by the hotel (for a fee). They also have an annex on Via Umberto I, if you prefer to stay in town; guest rooms are similarly appointed but come a little cheaper. The hotel's restaurant is justifiably popular (see below).

Via Marina di Praia, 84010 Praiano. © 089-874091. Fax 089-874161. www.alfonsoamare.it. 16 units. 180€–210€ ($225–$263) double in Aug; 110€–140€ ($138–$175) double; low season 90€–110€ ($113–$138).. Aug rates include breakfast and dinner; other rates include breakfast only. Children under 2 stay free in parent's room. MC, V. Free parking. **Amenities:** Restaurant; bar; scuba lessons. *In room:* A/C, TV/VCR/DVD, fax, dataport, minibar, hair dryer, safe.

WHERE TO DINE
Expensive
Alfonso a Mare ✦✦ AMALFITAN   Locals love to come to this restaurant to gorge themselves on seafood prepared the traditional way while enjoying views of the nearby sea. Located within the hotel by the same name (see review above), it offers typical cuisine and a menu that varies with the market's offerings. You might find *canneroni ai totani* (pasta with squid) or *risotto alla pescatora* (seafood risotto). The *grigliate* (grilled seafood) is very tasty. The highly recommended house wine comes from the family vineyards.

Via Marina di Praia. © 089-874166. Reservations recommended on weekends. Secondi 18€–28€ ($23–$35). MC, V. Daily 12:30–3pm and 7:30–10pm.

Moderate
Da Gennarino a Mare ✦   Another of the area's traditional restaurants by the sea, this is located on the beautiful beach of Vettica Maggiore and is perfect for a meal after a swim. The menu changes daily, offering a small variety of simple down-home dishes based on seafood and fresh vegetables. You might be able to sample the *pezzogna*, a fish native to these waters, or *zuppa di pesce* (fish stew).

Spiaggia della Gavitella. © 089-874068. Reservations recommended on weekends. Secondi 11€–16€ ($14–$20). No credit cards. Daily 12:30–3pm and 7:30–11pm.

Ristorante Continental AMALFITAN/PIZZA   The terrace of this Bourbon villa is a perfect setting for a fine meal. The restaurant is run by the younger generation of the family that runs the hotel of the same name. They have chosen to stick to local cuisine, and they do it very well. *Penne con zucchine* (penne pasta with zucchini), *linguine ai frutti di mare* (linguine with shellfish), and *pesce con patate al forno* (fish baked with potatoes) are memorable classics. On Saturday nights, pizza from the wood-burning oven is served.

Via Roma 63. © 089-874084. Reservations recommended on weekends. Secondi 12€–18€ ($15–$23). No credit cards. Daily noon–2:30pm and 7:30–10:30pm. Closed mid-Nov to Mar.

Inexpensive

La Brace ✿✿ AMALFITAN   With a beautiful location, this is a cheap place to enjoy both good food and scenery. The menu has many simple home-cooked dishes, depending on the season, such as tasty *totani e patate* (squid and potatoes stew), and in winter *pappardelle al sugo di coniglio* (homemade pasta with rabbit ragout).

Via Capriglione 146, Vettica Maggiore. ℂ **089-874226.** Reservations recommended. Secondi 9€–14€ ($11–$18). AE, DC, MC, V. Oct–Mar Thurs–Tues 12:30–3pm and 7:30–11pm; daily in summer.

SHOPPING

Do you have a musician in the family? You might not have thought of purchasing a musical instrument while on your vacation, but once you've visited this artisan's workshop you might change your mind. At **Bottega Scala** (Via Roma 57; ℂ **089-874894**) the *liutaio* (stringed instruments maker) Pasquale Scala creates instruments using ancient techniques. Many of his clients are famous Italian musicians—one is Pino Daniele. He specializes in classic guitars and ancient instruments, from medieval to baroque.

PRAIANO-VETTICA MAGGIORE AFTER DARK

The popular nightclub **L'Africana** (ℂ **089-874042**) in Vettica Maggiore was a mythical hangout of the *Anni Ruggenti* (Roaring Years) of the sixties, when it was the destination of choice of VIPs and their trendy friends. Right by the sea, it is now experiencing a sort of second coming and is again a lively scene. Don't be surprised when at one point in the evening, you see a bunch of local fishermen pull their nets from the edges of the dance floor; they are off for the fresh catches for local restaurants. The club is open Friday and Saturday nights May and September, and daily June through August; it is closed October through April.

8 Positano ✶

17km (10 miles) W of Amalfi, 51km (101 miles) W of Salerno, 56km (35 miles) SE of Naples.

Hugging a semi-vertical rock formation, Positano is the quintessence of picturesque. Once one of the most exclusive retreats in Italy, the seaside has been thoroughly "discovered" but retains its elegance. Its unique mix of seascapes, colors, art, and cultural life has fascinated many famous artists, from Pablo Picasso and Paul Klee to Toscanini, Bernstein, and Steinbeck. Today, it is a preferred destination of tourists and fashionistas, coming to buy what has become known as "Positano Fashion" from the local designer showrooms and elegant boutiques.

ESSENTIALS

VISITOR INFORMATION   The **AAST tourist office** is at Via del Saracino 4, 84017 Positano (ℂ **089-875067;** www.aziendaturismopositano.it). It is open Monday to Saturday 8:30am to 2pm. It is also open 3:30 to 8pm between July and August.

FAST FACTS   You'll find a **pharmacy** on Viale Pasitea (ℂ **089-875863**). For an **ambulance,** dial ℂ **118.** You can call the **police** at ℂ **113** or at ℂ **112.** The **post office** is at the corner of Via G. Marconi (SS 163) and Viale Pasitea; it is open Monday to Saturday 8am to 2pm. You will find several banks with **ATMs,** including the Banco di Napoli on Piazza dei Mulini (ℂ **089-875797**).

SPECIAL EVENTS   **Summer Music** is an international chamber music festival that takes place from the end of August to the beginning of September every year.

The **Festival of the Assunta** is a lively event held August 14 and 15, when the violent attack of the Saracens and the Madonna's miraculous intervention are reenacted, accompanied by much noise and fanfare by Positanese of all ages. The histrionics include a fake fire and colorful historic costumes.

GETTING AROUND   Small orange buses make the loop of Viale Pasitea, Via Cristoforo Colombo, and Via G. Marconi (SS 163), stopping several times along the way. The buses run every half-hour, saving your tired knees from some of the town's endless steps. You can purchase the .80€ ($1) ticket on board.

A boat service links Marina Grande to Fornillo during the summer, with boats every half-hour.

EXPLORING THE TOWN

Luckily, crowds haven't affected Positano's unique location, and the town remains as picturesque as ever. Steep ramps of stairs replace streets. The typical pastel-colored houses—cubes with domed roofs and porticoes or loggias overlooking the sea—poke from the overflowing green of gardens and citrus groves. *Tip:* Wearing comfortable shoes without heels is a must here; otherwise, climbing the steep alleys and many steps will be an ordeal.

The heart of town is **Marina Grande,** the beach where fishermen used to haul up their boats. At its western end is the pier where ferries arrive and depart. From Marina Grande starts **Via Positanesi d'America** ☆☆—a cliffside pedestrian promenade, and the only flat street in Positano—which stretches along the shore past the cape of **Torre Trasita** to the smaller beach of **Fornillo.** Not far from Marina Grande is the **Collegiata di Santa Maria Assunta** ☆☆ (Piazza Flavio Gioia; © **089-875480;** daily 8am–noon and 4–7pm), founded in the 13th century and later decorated with a gorgeous majolica dome. Inside, you will find the famous *tavola* of the *Madonna Nera* (Black Madonna), an icon in 13th-century Byzantine style. The church is at the center of the **Festival of the Assunta** (see "Special Events," earlier in this section).

In our opinion, though, the best churches of Positano are the lesser-known ones. The small **Chiesa Nuova** (on Via Chiesa Nuova), restored in the 18th century, which has a striking colored **tile floor** ☆☆, one of the most beautiful in an area known for its colorful tile work. The **Chiesa di Santa Caterina** ☆☆ (Via Pasitea), built for the local Porcelli family, is another small architectural masterpiece in neo-Gothic style, with an elegant bell tower. Just west of Positano on SS 163 is the renowned **Belvedere dello Schiaccone** ☆☆☆, the best lookout on Amalfi Drive. At 200m (656 ft.) above sea level, it overlooks the archipelago of LiGalli and Capo Sottile over a palm and citrus grove, with the splendid Monte Sant'Angelo a Tre Pizzi in the background.

STAYING ACTIVE
SWIMMING & SUNBATHING

Positano is blessed with four delightful beaches besides the central **Spiaggia Grande** by the marina: **Fornillo** (linked by boat service from the Marina) to the west of town; and **La Porta, Ciumicello,** and **Arienzo** to the east. The sand is rather gray and pebbly, but the views are idyllic and the sea is clear and refreshing. You can rent a chair and umbrella at the reserved areas for about 15€ ($19) per day, or use the free but crowded public beach. Another beach, **Laurito,** is also a bit out of town, but you can easily reach it with the boat service offered by the restaurant Le Sirene (see "Where to Dine," later in this chapter).

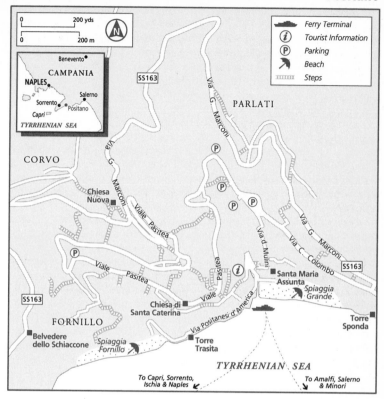

For a quieter swim, locals like to take a boat to the archipelago of **Li Galli (The Roosters).** You can rent a boat at Spiaggia Grande for between 8€ and 22€ ($10–$28) per hour, depending on kind of boat and length of rental. Privately owned, the four islands (Gallo Lungo, Castelluccio, Gallo dei Briganti, and La Rotonda) are where—according to Homer—the Sirens lived. Indeed, the other name of the archipelago is Sirenuse, from the Latin *Sirenusae,* meaning Sirens. According to legend, these beings attracted mariners with their magical singing and caused their ships to crash into the rocks. In Greek mythology, sirens were represented as birds with human faces and the bodies of fish (hence the name Li Galli, "The Roosters"). Once you skirt past the Sirens and arrive safely on Gallo Lungo, you'll spot a watchtower and the remains of a Roman villa; the archipelago is the site of the house where Rudolf Nureyev spent the last years of his life.

HIKING

Positano offers many hiking opportunities on the town's outskirts, in addition to the town's own steep streets. The most famous trail is **Sentiero degli Dei (Trail of the Gods)** ✹✹✹ linking Positano to Praiano. This is a trail of moderate difficulty, requiring some preparation, but it is—as its name suggests—a divine trail. Sections of it are a ridge trail, running high over the sea and affording magnificent views of the entire coast. Starting from Via Chiesa Nuova at the upper end of Positano, walk around to the right of the church and continue up the steps at the end of the lane. Cross the road and take the steps to the left; you'll see red and white markers. Allow yourself 5½ hours; you can then catch a bus back to Positano.

Another scenic trail is the climb to **Monte Tre Pizzi,** the highest of the Costiera at 1440m (4,723 ft.) in altitude. (If you are planning to reach the top, make sure you bring a warm windbreaker jacket and enough water.) Birdwatchers should love this trek, because you'll have many occasions to spot the raptors who nest in the area. The trail starts from the Guardia Forestale (Italian Rangers) station at an altitude of 700m (2,296 ft.). This magnificent trail wends among patches of pine trees and brooks. Eventually, you will reach the ancient village of **Santa Maria di Castello** with its spectacular natural terrace overlooking Positano (just up from the village). You can also reach Santa Maria di Castello by car, but you'll have to drive from Vico Equense, on the Sorrento side of the peninsula (see chapter 5). The top of the mountain is a bit farther up.

An easier hike is the ascent to **Nocelle** ☆☆, at an altitude of 443m (1,453 ft.). Here, in this little paradise where cars are not allowed, you can have an excellent lunch (or dinner) at **Ristorante Santa Croce** (make reservations in advance by calling ℂ **089-875319**). The trail starts at the end of Via Monsignor Clinque, in the upper part of town. Count on spending about 1 hour for the ascent; afterwards, you can return to Positano by bus. From Positano, you can also take **Via degli Incanti (Trail of Charms),** an easy trail that goes from Positano to Amalfi among terraces of citrus groves. The going is easy in this direction but more demanding from Amalfi. Be aware that the hike is about 25km (15.6 miles), so most people choose only a section. Alternatively, you can plan to do the whole trail at a leisurely pace, over several days.

WHERE TO STAY
VERY EXPENSIVE
Hotel Le Sirenuse ☆☆ This gorgeous 18th-century villa overlooking the bay is owned by the Marchesi Sersale family and was their residence until 1951. You may have seen the hotel featured in the film *Only You* with Marisa Tomei and Robert Downey, Jr.; if so, you'll get an idea of the hotel's romantic aura. Guest rooms are elegantly furnished, with antiques and period reproductions; many have gorgeous views, and all have private terraces and luxurious bathrooms. The hotel also has a swimming pool and a state-of-the-art health club-cum-spa. The buffet breakfast here is lavish. *Note:* Prices are significantly lower in the off season.

Via Cristoforo Colombo 30, 84017 Positano. ℂ 089-875066. Fax 089-811798. www.sirenuse.it. 63 units. 420€–780€ ($525–$975) double, from 1,000€ ($1,250) suite; low season 280€–400€ ($350–$500) double, from 550€ ($688) suite. Rates include buffet breakfast. Specials available. Children under 3 stay free in parent's room. AE, DC, MC, V. Parking: 20€ ($25). **Amenities:** Restaurant; 2 bars; lounge; outdoor pool; spa; health club; concierge; room service; babysitting; laundry service. *In room:* A/C, TV/DVD, dataport, minibar, hair dryer, safe.

Hotel San Pietro ☆☆☆ If you can afford it, this is *the* place to stay on the Amalfi Coast. One of the best hotels in the country (and in the world, in fact), it is a member of the Relais & Châteaux group but is still family-run. Affording luxurious accommodations and exceptionally professional service in a wonderful location just outside Positano, the hotel leaves nothing wanting. Elegant public areas have French windows opening onto the garden and the sea; spacious guest rooms are decorated with antiques, artistic tiled floors, and pink marble bathrooms. The private beach is accessible by elevator. The excellent restaurant offers fantastic views and a cozy terrace and garden (see later in this chapter).

Via Laurito 2, 84017 Positano. © 800-7352478 Relais & Châteaux toll-free in the U.S., or 089-875455. Fax 089-811449. www.ilsampietro.it. 60 units. 380€–510€ ($475–$638) double; 530€–990€ ($663–$1,238) suite. Rates include breakfast. AE, DC, MC, V. Free parking. Closed Nov–Mar. Amenities: Restaurant; bar; outdoor pool; outdoor tennis court; health club; spa; sauna; extensive water activities; concierge; room service; babysitting; laundry service. In room: A/C, TV, minibar, hair dryer, iron, safe.

EXPENSIVE

Buca di Bacco   Once a tavern—its nightclub was the meeting place for the local *dolce vita* back when Positano was an exclusive resort for VIPs—this spot has burgeoned into a popular restaurant-hotel over the years and looks posed for a new era of glory. Centrally positioned on the Marina Grande, the excellent hotel boasts beautiful rooms that are all large and well furnished. Most have balconies facing the sea, and six superior rooms have full seafront terraces. The less expensive guest rooms in the annexed buildings enjoy similar levels of comfort. The hotel's restaurant, **La Pergola,** is extremely popular, as is the less pricey snack bar.

Via Rampa Teglia 4, 84017 Positano. © 089-875699. Fax 089-875731. www.bucadibacco.it. 54 units. 175€–370€ ($219–$463) double; low season 144€–310€ ($180–$388) double. Rates include buffet breakfast. AE, DC, MC, V. Parking: 20€ ($25). Closed 2 weeks in low season. Amenities: Restaurant; bar; concierge; babysitting; laundry service. In room: A/C, TV, minibar, hair dryer, safe.

Covo dei Saraceni ❀   Situated directly over the sea, this hotel affords total relaxation in a natural environment. The core of the well-established hotel is a fisherman's house, which was enlarged in several stages and finally completely renovated. The result is the elegant hotel with an excellent location right on the marina, yet away from the hubbub. Guest rooms are large and comfortable, all with water views. The garden and seawater swimming pool here are also lovely. The very good restaurant on the premises may tempt you to sign up for full board.

Via Regina Giovanna 5, 84017 Positano. © 089-875400. Fax 089-875878. www.covodeisaraceni.it. 58 units. 284€ ($355) double, 376€–495€ ($470–$619) junior suite; low season 238€ ($298) double, 310€–429€ ($388–$536) junior suite. Rates include buffet breakfast. Children under 3 stay free in parent's room. AE, DC, MC, V. Parking: 18€ ($23). Closed Jan to mid-Mar. Amenities: Restaurant; 2 bars; outdoor pool; concierge; room service; babysitting; laundry service. In room: A/C, TV, minibar, hair dryer, safe.

Palazzo Murat   This 18th-century baroque palace near the marina is said to have been built for Gioacchino Murat, Napoleon's brother-in-law and later king of Naples. The five more expensive guest rooms in the historical part of the palace are decorated with antiques and original furnishings; the ones in the new wings are also very nicely appointed. All units have good-sized bathrooms, and most rooms have ocean views. The rich buffet breakfast is served in the delightful garden court when weather permits; in August and September this is the site of chamber music concerts.

Via dei Mulini 23, 84017 Positano. © 089-875177. Fax 089-811419. www.palazzomurat.it. 30 units. 230€–380€ ($288–$475) double. Rates include buffet breakfast. Children under 3 stay free in parent's room. AE, DC, MC, V. Parking: 20€ ($25) nearby. Closed Jan to week before Easter. Amenities: Restaurant; lounge; concierge; room service; babysitting; laundry service. In room: A/C, TV, minibar, hair dryer, iron, safe.

Villa Franca *(finds*   This delightful family-run hotel overlooking the sea is one of Positano's lesser-known, distinctive hotels. The common areas are decorated with reproduction artwork and fine tiles to evoke a neoclassical feeling. The motif continues in the elegant, comfortable guest rooms, all of which are decorated in Mediterranean style with bright artistic tiled floors and bathrooms; private balconies overlook the sea. The roof terrace has a 360-degree view over the town and a swimming pool with a solarium. An additional 10 rooms are in the less-inspired annex (the cheaper "standard" rooms are likely to be here; inquire when you book). The hotel's restaurant serves good food in a very romantic setting. Another nice feature is the free shuttle bus to the center of Positano.

Via Pasitea 318, 84017 Positano. ℂ **089-875655**. Fax 089-875735. www.villafrancahotel.it. 38 units. 190€–340€ ($238–$425) double. Rates include buffet breakfast. Children under 3 stay free in parent's room. AE, DC, MC, V. Parking: 18€ ($23). Closed Nov–Mar. **Amenities:** Restaurant; bar; lounge; outdoor pool; health club; spa; concierge; room service; babysitting; laundry service. *In room:* A/C, TV, minibar, hair dryer, iron, safe.

MODERATE

Albergo L'Ancora   Though not one of the most high-style choices in Positano, this moderately priced hotel offers good value. The large guest rooms have comfortable beds; some even have antiques. Some suites have private terraces with Jacuzzis. Staying here gives you free use of facilities at the Albergo's sister hotel, the seafront Covo dei Saraceni (which is considerably more expensive). The hotel's restaurant serves meals on the terrace.

Via Cristoforo Colombo 36, 84017 Positano. ℂ **089-875318**. Fax 089-811784. www.htlancora.it. 25 units. 180€–240€ ($225–$300) double; 270€–420€ ($338–$525) suite. Rates include buffet breakfast. Children under 3 stay free in parent's room. AE, DC, MC, V. Free parking. Closed Nov–Mar. **Amenities:** Dining room; lounge; outdoor pool; concierge; room service; babysitting; laundry service. *In room:* A/C (in most), TV, minibar, hair dryer, safe.

Casa Albertina ★★   This small, family-run hotel offers attentive service and great views. The famous Sicilian writer Luigi Pirandello had his usual abode in one of the beautiful guest rooms, and the rooms here do make you want to settle in. Each is individually decorated, with carefully chosen furniture and a simple, monochromatic theme; French doors open onto private balconies (with water views). When the weather's nice, breakfast is served on the terra-cotta tiled terrace. In the high season, rates include half-board (breakfast and dinner).

Via della Tavolozza 3, 84017 Positano. ℂ **089-875143**. Fax 089-811540. www.casalbertina.it. 20 units. Apr–Oct 230€–280€ ($288–$350) double with half-board (half-board required Apr–Oct). Nov–Mar 190€–230€ ($238–$288) double with breakfast. Rates include breakfast and half-board and lunch (or dinner)Children under 3 stay free in parent's room. AE, DC, MC, V. Parking: 22€ ($28) nearby. **Amenities:** Restaurant; bar; concierge; room service; babysitting; laundry service. *In room:* A/C, TV, dataport, minibar, hair dryer.

Hotel Marincanto   This hotel in an olive grove offers pleasant accommodations overlooking the sea. Panoramic terraces, a private beach, and open public spaces with white walls and handsome marblework create a perfect setting for relaxation. The large guest rooms are decorated in pastel colors, with wood, wicker, and glass furniture; bathrooms are tiled and have Jacuzzi tubs.

Via Cristoforo Colombo 36, 84017 Positano. ℂ **089-875130**. Fax 089-875595. www.marincanto.it. 25 units. 200€–230€ ($250–$288) double, 289€–336€ ($361–$420) junior suite; low season 165€–190€ ($206–$238) double, 245€–290€ ($306–$363) suite. Rates include buffet breakfast. AE, DC, MC, V. Parking: 21€ ($26). Closed Nov–Mar. **Amenities:** Restaurant; bar; outdoor pool; health club; spa; concierge; business center; room service; babysitting; same-day laundry service. *In room:* A/C, TV, minibar, hair dryer, safe.

Hotel Montemare ★   This family-run, tiny hotel is housed in what was once a private villa, and enjoys a panoramic position in the upper part of town. The beautiful arbor-shaded terrace, with views over Positano's beaches, is particularly delightful. Guest rooms are large and comfortable and come decorated with period furniture; all have good-sized modern bathrooms and small terraces overlooking the sea. The Cannavacciuolo family is supremely courteous and hospitable.

Via Pasitea 119 , 84017 Positano. © 089-875010. Fax 089-811251. 18 units. 155€–200€ ($194–$250) double; low season 130€–180€ ($163–$225) double. Rates include buffet breakfast. Children under 3 stay free in parent's room. AE, DC, MC, V. Parking: 18€ ($23). **Amenities:** Restaurant; bar. *In room:* A/C, TV, minibar, hair dryer, safe.

Hotel Savoia ★★   Nestled in the heart of Positano, this quiet, well-run hotel is just steps away from shops and the beach. Guest units are spacious, bright, and comfortably furnished (think good beds and roomy cabinets), with tiled floors and good-sized modern bathrooms. Some of the rooms have sea views, while others overlook the village. This place has been family run since 1936, and prides itself on courteous service.

Via Cristoforo Colombo 73, 84017 Positano. © 089-875003. Fax 089-811844. www.savoiapositano.it . 42 units. 130€–260€ ($163–$325) double; low season 100€–180€ ($125–$225) double. Rates include buffet breakfast. AE, DC, MC, V. Parking: 15€ ($19). Closed Dec–Feb. **Amenities:** Bar; concierge; babysitting; same-day laundry service. *In room:* A/C, satellite TV, minibar, hair dryer, safe.

INEXPENSIVE

California Residence   Run by the Cinque family, who are committed to making your stay comfortable, this is an especially good choice if you want to stay in Positano inexpensively. Housed in a historic building that was later restructured, the hotel offers a beautiful flowered terrace overlooking the seaside. Guest rooms are simply decorated, with tiled floors and pastel colors; the bathrooms are modern.

Via Cristoforo Colombo 141, 84017 Positano. © 089-875382. Fax 0812154. 10 units. 150€ ($190). Rates include buffet breakfast. AE, DC, MC, V. **Amenities:** Bar; babysitting; laundry service. *In room:* A/C, TV, minibar, hair dryer, safe.

Hotel Ristorante Le Sirene   Down on the beautiful small beach of Laurito, this restaurant-cum-hotel is open only in the summer. Run by the Migliaccio and Casola families, the hotel offers regular and frequent boat shuttle service to and from Positano's Spiaggia Grande, operating till midnight daily. Guest rooms are large and bright, with tiled floors; some come with sea views, while all have private large balconies. Guests have free access to the beach and to umbrellas and chairs; nonguests can access the beach for a fee. The restaurant, which is open to the public, serves traditional Italian cuisine on a romantic terrace overlooking the sea.

Via Spiaggia di Laurito 24, 84017 Positano. © 089-875490. Fax 089-875353. www.lesirenepositano.com. 8 units. 110€–120€ ($138–$150). Rates include breakfast. Extra bed 25€ ($31). Children under 3 stay free in parent's room. AE, V. Parking: 15€ ($19). Closed Oct–May. **Amenities:** Restaurant; bar; free shuttle to Positano. *In room:* Hair dryer.

Hotel Ristorante Pupetto   Right on the beach of Fornillo, only a short walk from Marina Grande along the seaside promenade, this family-run hotel was created in the 1950s above the popular restaurant of the same name (see below). Guest rooms are large, with simple furniture, whitewashed walls, and tiled floors, each with a private small terrace overlooking the sea. The hotel is accessible by elevator from the road above.

Via Fornillo 37, 84017 Positano. © 089-875087. Fax 089-811517. www.hotelpupetto.it. 30 units. 160€–200€ ($200–$250) double; low season 130€–160€ ($163–$200) double. Rates include buffet breakfast. AE, DC, MC, V. Parking: 13€ ($16). Closed mid-Nov to mid-Mar. **Amenities:** Restaurant; American bar; outdoor pool; health club; spa; concierge; business center; babysitting; room service; same-day laundry service. *In room:* A/C, TV, safe.

La Bougainville   This family-run hotel is quite small, having only 14 units, but it's a good choice if you don't mind sacrificing amenities for location—it sits in the heart of Positano only steps from the beach. Rates are very reasonable. Some of the guest rooms open onto flowery private terraces, where you can have breakfast in good weather; other rooms overlook the village. All are decorated with simple but quality modern furniture and pastel-colored tiled floors. Bathrooms are a good size.

Via Cristoforo Colombo 25, 84017 Positano. © **089-875047**. Fax 089-811150. www.bougainville.it. 14 units. 80€–95€ ($100–$119) double; low season 95€–130€ ($119–$163) double. AE, V. Closed Nov–mid-Mar. **Amenities:** Restaurant; bar; outdoor pool; health club; spa; concierge; business center; room service; babysitting; same-day laundry service. *In room:* A/C, TV, safe.

Rooms for Rent

Renting a room or a miniapartment with small cooking facilities might be a cheaper alternative when vacationing in Positano, especially for families. We recommend **Casa Maresca** (Via Lepanto 17; © **089-875679**); **Casa Soriano** (Via Pasitea; © **089-875494**); **La Fenice** (Località Chetrara, © **089-875513**); and **La Tavolozza** (Via Cristoforo Colombo; © **089-875040**).

WHERE TO DINE
Expensive

La Cambusa *AMALFITAN/FISH*   Baldo and Luigi created this restaurant in the 1960s vowing to serve traditionally prepared fish of the highest quality, and they have kept their promise. Only the freshest fish—brought in every morning by local fishermen—is prepared with techniques designed to bring out the natural flavors. Try *penne con gamberetti e rughetta* (penne pasta with shrimp and arugula); or our favorite, *spaghetti con le cozze di scoglio* (spaghetti with sautéed mussels and local cherry tomatoes). For the secondo, pick your fish from the display and have it prepared grilled or *all'acqua pazza* (with an herb broth).

Piazza Amerigo Vespucci 4. © **089-875432**. Reservations recommended. Secondi 12€–28€ ($15–$35). AE, DC, MC, V. Daily noon–3pm and 7:30–11pm.

Le Tre Sorelle AMALFITAN   Offering pleasant garden dining when the weather's nice, this restaurant serves up well-prepared, moderately priced food. The menu features homemade pasta, with *lasagne* (lasagna), *fusilli all cozze* (short pasta with mussels), and *ravioli* the high points; grilled fish and *polpi in cassuola* (octopus stewed in a terra-cotta dish) make fine *secondi*. Desserts are very good, too—sometimes you can get *ravioli al limone* (ravioli filled with a lemon-flavored ricotta-cheese mixture), a Positano specialty.

Via del Brigantino 23. © **089-875452**. Reservations recommended. Secondi 15€–28€ ($19–$35). AE, DC, MC, V. Wed–Mon 12:30–3pm and 7:30–11pm; daily Mar–Oct. Closed 2 weeks Nov–Dec.

Ristorante Il San Pietro *AMALFITAN/CREATIVE*   The restaurant of the famous San Pietro hotel, this place is positively bewitching and downright worthy of its acclaim. Exquisite cuisine combines with postcard-worthy views (indoors or in the garden and on the terrace), elegant Vietri dinnerware, and friendly professional service. The chef, Alois Vanlangenacker, uses local ingredients—mostly from the hotel's own farm—to create sophisticated concoctions but also deliciously simple dishes. From a perfect *risotto agli scampi e punte d'asparago* (risotto with prawns and asparagus tips), to *zuppa di borragine con fiori di zucchine alla ricotta* (borage soup with ricotta-filled zucchini flowers), to a unique *pollo ruspante in crosta di agrumi* (free-range chicken in a citrus crust), the menu features many pleasant surprises. Everything is homemade, including the pasta, the bread, and, of course, the desserts. The wine list is extensive and includes several wines by the glass.

Via Laurito 2, Positano. © **089-875455**. Reservations required. Secondi 25€–32€ ($31–$40). AE, DC, MC, V. Daily 12:30–3pm and 7:30–10:30pm. Closed Nov–Mar.

Moderate

Donna Rosa ⋆⋆ AMALFITAN   In the green outskirts of Positano, this is where locals come to eat homemade pasta and excellent seafood prepared by two sisters and served—in the good season—on a charming terrace overlooking the sea. The menu surprises you with excellent meats, such as *salsicce alla griglia* (grilled local sausages) and *agnello arrosto* (roasted lamb), in addition to a large variety of fish and shellfish—for instance, *scialatielli zucchine e vongole* (eggless pasta with clams and zucchini).

Via Montepertuso 97. ℂ 089-811806. Reservations recommended. Secondi 12€–21€ ($15–$26). AE, DC, MC, V. Wed–Mon 12:30–2:30pm and 7:30–10:30pm; June–July and Sept Wed–Sun 12:30–2:30pm; Jun–Sept daily 7:30–10:30pm. Closed 11 weeks Jan/Mar.

Da Adolfo ⋆ AMALFITAN/FISH   Don't even think of reaching this delightful beach restaurant from the road or you'll have to descend 450 rugged steps from the SS 163 above. Also running a beach operation with changing rooms, showers, and beach chair-and-umbrella rentals (6€/$7.50 for both per day), Adolfo offers a free shuttle service leaving Marina Grande every 30 minutes—you'll recognize the boat by the red fish on its side (daily 10am–1pm and 4–7pm; later on Sat nights in July and Aug). The restaurant has a great laid-back atmosphere, and the menu includes many simple local dishes. The varied antipasti include zesty vegetables and seafood—such as excellent *polpette di melanzane* (eggplant fritters), *spaghetti con le cozze* (spaghetti with sautéed mussels and tomatoes), and *grigliata di pesce* (medley of fresh grilled seafood).

Spiaggetta di Laurito. ℂ 089-875022. Reservations recommended. Secondi 12€–18€ ($15–$23). No credit cards. Daily noon–3pm; July–Aug also Sat 8pm–midnight. Closed Oct–May. Complimentary shuttle boat from Marina Grande.

Il Capitano   This is the restaurant of the Hotel Montemare (see above), where the Canavacciuolo family serves excellent typical dishes for guests and nonguests alike. The menu varies, but go for *spaghetti con alici, peperoncini verdi e pomodorini di Furore* (spaghetti with anchovies, green peppers, and the delicious cherry tomatoes from Furore) if it's available. From pasta to bread to breadsticks, their homemade goods are very tasty. They are justly proud of their wine cellar, which you can visit upon request.

Via Pasitea 119. ℂ 089-811351. Reservations recommended. Secondi 16€–31€ ($20–$39). AE, DC, MC, V. Dec 25 to mid-June Fri–Wed 12:30–3pm and 7:30–10pm; daily in summer. Closed Nov–Dec 25.

Pupetto AMALFITAN/FISH   This historic beach restaurant—it was here before the hotel bearing its name was built in the 1950s—offers dining under the shade of an arbor-terrace, right on the beach. The traditional menu offers lots of pasta with seafood, nicely grilled fish entrees, and a variety of *antipasti*. The bar terrace is perfect for a drink after a swim in the sea or in the hotel's pool.

Spiaggia di Fornillo. ℂ 089-875087. Reservations recommended. Secondi 12€–21€ ($15–$26). AE, DC, MC, V. Daily 12:30–3pm and 7:30–10pm.

Inexpensive

Da Vincenzo ⋆ AMALFITAN   In the small stone dining rooms of this family-run restaurant, you'll find great down-home local dishes. The menu changes regularly but you will always find *antipasti di mare* (a variety of tasty seafood appetizers) and scrumptious *panzerotti* (deep-fried square ravioli filled with ham and cheese). Other specialties are *panzerottini Margaret* (small square ricotta ravioli in a fresh basil and local cherry-tomato sauce), and *peperoni ripieni* (sweet peppers stuffed with olives, herbs, and cheese).

Viale Pasitea 172. ✆ **089-875128.** Reservations recommended. Secondi 8€–12€ ($10–$15). No credit cards. Daily 12:30–3pm and 7:30–10pm. Closed Nov–Feb.

Il Grottino Azzurro AMALFITAN/WINERY   Like Da Vincenzo above, this historic wine cellar has a simple menu of well-prepared traditional dishes, but the focus here is on meat, fresh homemade pasta, and wine. Locals come for *cannelloni* (delicious tubes of fresh pasta filled with meat and baked with cheese and tomato sauce), *parmigiana* (eggplant Parmesan), and succulent roasted chicken. Given the cellar location, you'll find a good number of local and regional vintages to quaff.

Via Guglielmo Marconi 158 (SS 163). ✆ **089-875466.** Reservations recommended. Secondi 8€–15€ ($10–$19). No credit cards. Thurs–Tues 12:30–3pm and 7:30–10pm; daily in summer.

Il Ritrovo *Finds* AMALFITAN   Here is a place where going off the beaten track to get to it bears dividends. Retreat to this pleasant restaurant high in the mountains if you want to escape heat and high prices. The menu is seasonal and focuses on meat and vegetables produced on the family farm. The medley of grilled meat is excellent, as is the free-range chicken baked with herbs. The restaurant has a cool arbor-covered terrace that makes it a perfect setting in the summer. *Note:* This restaurant is a bit farther out of town, but you can get here by taking the SITA to Montepertuso.

Piazza Cappella 77, Località Montepertuso. ✆ **089-811336** or 089-875453.   Reservations recommended. Secondi 8€–12€ ($10–$15). AE, DC, MC, V. Thurs–Tues 12:30–3pm and 7:30–10pm; daily in summer. Closed Jan.

La Chitarrina AMALFITAN/PIZZA   This simple, family-run trattoria a short distance from the town center offers great food. The menu varies with the market and includes both fish and local meat. Signora Giuseppina Marrone makes the bread and pasta in the open kitchen, while her children help with the service. Her specialties are *ravioli* and *gnocchi di patate* (potato dumplings), both delicious. In the evening they make a good pizza. Don't leave without trying the homemade desserts and the family's own *limoncello* or *mirto* (flavored with myrtle).

Piazza Cappella 75, Località Montepertuso. ✆ **089-811806.** Reservations not accepted. Secondi 8€–15€ ($10–$19). AE, DC, MC, V. Thurs–Tues noon–3pm and 7:30–10pm; daily in summer. Closed 2 weeks in Nov and Feb. Bus: SITA to Montepertuso.

SHOPPING 🎁🎁

All kinds of small shops and boutiques line the steep streets of Positano, many of them offering the colorful style that has become known as "Positano Fashion" around the world. The small tailoring boutiques of the 1960s, where you could have a dress or trousers made ready for fitting, have evolved into a widely appreciated, specialized craft. Local fashion designers have developed a unique style of colorful garments that are the embodiment of Positano's Mediterranean light and outlook. Wonderful summer clothes and beachwear—swimsuits are a specialty—await you in the elegant boutiques, as well as more dressy items. Most of the boutiques line Viale Pasitea. **Sartoria Maria Lampo** (Viale Pasitea 12; ✆ **089-875021**) is one of the remaining original 1960s boutiques, and is keeping to its reputation. Other favorites are **Pepito's** (Viale Pasitea 15; ✆ **089-875446**); **La Sirenetta** (Viale Pasitea, 29; and also Via del Saracino 35; ✆ **089-811490** or 089-875383); **Nadir** (Viale Pasitea 44; ✆ **089-875975**); **La Bottega di Brunella** (Viale Pasitea 76; ✆ **089-875228**); and **La Tartana** (Via della Tartana; ✆ **089-875645**).

Positano is also famous for its great handmade sandals. Some of the artisan shops will make them for you while you wait. Try **La Botteguccia** (Via Trara Genoino 13;

© **089-811824**); **Costanzo Avitabile** (Piazza Amerigo Vespucci 15; © **089-875366**); **Dattilo** (Via Rampa Teglia 19; © **089-811440**); or **Todisco** (Via del Saracino; © **089-875656**).

Among the town's many other boutiques, we really like the showroom-workshop of **Obrador** (Via Cristoforo Colombo 91; © **089-811049**), an Argentine artist who produces exquisite gold jewelry inspired by antiquity. He will work by commission only.

Positano also has a number of high-quality antiques shops, such as **Cose Antiche** (Via Cristoforo Colombo 21; © **089-811811**); **Le Myricae** (Via Cristoforo Colombo 27; © **089-875882**), with its splendid collection of Art Deco jewelry; **Objets Trouvés** (Viale Pasitea 230; © **089-811577**); and **Oggetti di Ieri** (Via Cristoforo Colombo 171).

POSITANO AFTER DARK

L'Incanto (Via Marina 4; © **089-811177**), by the sea at Spiaggia Grande, is perfect for a drink or a snack, and so is popular **Chez Black** (Via del Brigantino19; © **089-875036**) nearby. Not far away, **La Buca di Bacco** is a great place for a drink or a *granita*. All have good terraces for watching passers-by.

De Martino (Viale Pasitea 182; © **089-875082**) is a bar with live music on the terrace over the marina (they also make excellent coffee). The popular **Internazionale** (Via Marconi 306, by Chiesa Nuova; © **089-875434**) has a good wine selection and yummy pastries. If you have a sweet tooth, you will definitely like **La Zagara** (Via dei Mulini 8; © **089-875964**), where you can enjoy their excellent homemade ice cream and *granite* in various flavors—try the melon—in a marvelous garden of orange and lemon trees. Their famous pastry shop serves *torta positanese* (a local cake made with almonds), *delizie al limone* (lemon cream puffs), and *babarese,* a *babà* pastry filled with wild strawberries and whipped cream.

At the *enoteca* **I sapori di Positano** (Via dei Mulini 6; © **089-811116**), you can taste the best wines of the region, including the little-known local spumante, as well as a good selection of national wines. They produce small batches of quality *rosolio* (sweet liqueur) and excellent citrus marmalades. Another good wine bar is **Con Vinum** (Via Rampa Teglia 12; © **089-811461**), where a trendy local crowd comes to listen to live jazz on summer weekends and to sip at the good vintages.

If your thing is dancing, you should head for **Music on the Rocks** (Via Grotto dell'Incanto 51; © **089-875874;** www.musicontherocks.it), the two-level club owned by the same owners as Chez Black, with a disco and a quieter piano bar. The club is open Friday and Saturday nights in May and September, and daily June through August; it is closed October through April. Another choice is **L'Africana** in Vettica Maggiore (see earlier in this chapter).

8

The Jewels of the Gulf of Naples: the Islands of Capri, Ischia & Procida

Much of the splendor of Campania's coast is due to the islands that define the Gulf of Naples: Procida, Ischia, and Capri. Very different from each other, these three islands have enjoyed completely different fortunes as far as tourism is concerned. Capri, the most well known, has been a lively resort since antiquity, famous for the debauches of Tiberius. Ischia, also known to the ancient world, was noted for its spas, and has traditionally remained a place for relaxation. Procida was and still is a small fisherman's haunt, where locals continue to make their living from the sea and tourists are comparatively rare.

Ischia's sandy beaches, spas, and vineyards, as well as its bucolic atmosphere, appeal to the savviest of tourists. Noisy day-trippers tend to stay away; instead, they crowd Capri in the summertime (particularly its famous Blue Grotto), so much so that it is a real wonder that the lines to enter the famous attractions aren't any longer. Yet Capri, with its rough, strong landscape and dramatic vistas, remains a must-see even if you have to brave huge crowds.

So close to land that you can almost touch it, Procida is an easy, charming day trip from Naples. While Capri attracts the jet set and movie stars, Procida is a voyage to an earlier time.

Because of their proximity to the mainland, all of these islands are excellent destinations for a day trip. You can come early in the day, check in at one of the great park-spas with scenic outdoor facilities, and leave after a gourmet dinner. Of course, after darkness falls and the last ferryboat has gone, the islands become that much more romantic.

1 Ischia: Isola Verde & Island of Eternal Youth ★★★

42km (26 miles) NW of Naples and 20km (13 miles) W of Pozzuoli.

When the Greeks arrived on this coast more than 2,500 years ago, they first landed in Ischia. Only a few miles off the tip of Pozzuoli, Capo Miseno, Ischia was a perfect base from which the Greeks could reach the mainland. They quickly found what was to become their largest and most important city on this coast: Cuma, on the hill above the Phlegrean Fields and modern Pozzuoli (see chapter 4). Ischia knew little development during antiquity and the Middle Ages because of its very active volcano—788m-high (2,585-ft.) Monte Epomeo—which erupted for the last time in the 14th century. That is when the island's growing population led to the development of the spa industry with the opening of the first thermal establishment in Casamicciola Terme (see

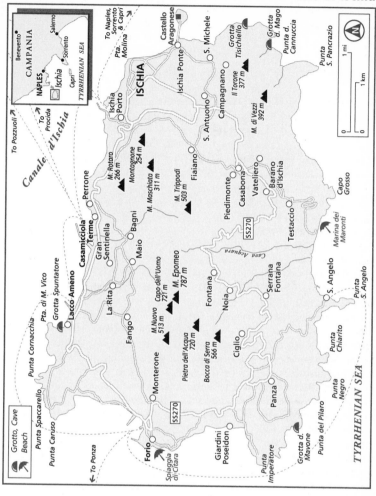

later) in 1604. The island itself, however, went relatively undiscovered by tourists until the 1950s, when well-to-do Italians came here in the hopes of finding an alternative to overcrowded Capri. Although Ischia is more popular now than it was then, the atmosphere is quieter than on Capri—partly because people who come here usually stay for several days and are looking for quiet, not celebrities.

Ischia is the largest of Campania's islands—its velvety slopes green with pine woods and vineyards—hence its nickname **Isola Verde (Emerald Isle).** Mount Epomeo—the volcano—has long been dormant, but the island shows significant volcanic activity with its many hot springs, mineral waters, and steam and hot mud holes. These are extensively used by the island's many spas; hence Ischia's other nickname, **Island of Eternal Youth.**

The island's shore alternates between rugged cliffs and beautiful beaches. You will appreciate the beaches all the more because they are a commodity almost completely lacking in the Sorrento peninsula, Capri, or the Amalfi Coast. Ischia's sandy beaches and spas are also perfect for day trips; a number of the island's modern facilities operate as day parks. If you are not into swimming or relaxation, you can visit the countryside, which is dotted with famous vineyards producing D.O.C. wines.

ESSENTIALS

GETTING THERE   Ferries and hydrofoils belonging to several different companies go back and forth between Ischia and the coast many times a day, especially in the summer. **Caremar** (② 081-5513882; www.caremar.it) runs ferries both from Pozzuoli (with a stop in Procida) and from Naples (Molo Beverello) and the company also runs hydrofoils from Mergellina. **Linee Lauro** (② 081-5522838) runs ferries from Molo Beverello in Naples, and its branch **Alilauro** (② 081-7611004; www.alilauro.it) runs hydrofoils from Mergellina. **SNAV** (② 081-4285555 or 081-4285111; www.snav.it) runs hydrofoils from Mergellina. The ride is about 40 minutes by hydrofoil for 11€ ($14) per person, while the ferry ride is about twice as long and costs roughly half as much, at 6€ ($7.50). If you want to bring your car, rates depend on the vehicle's size, but figure on spending about 35€ ($44).

In summer, you can also catch hydrofoils from Sorrento run by **Linee Marittime Partenopee** (② 081-55513236); **Navigazione Libera del Golfo** (② 081-5527209); and **Linee Lauro** (② 081-5522838; www.alilauro.it). Tickets cost 13€ ($16).

Most ferries land at Ischia Porto, but a few will make a stop in Casamicciola or in Forio.

GETTING ORIENTED   Ischia is a large island covering about 46 sq. km (18 sq. miles). The largest town is **Ischia,** on the eastern coast of the island, made up of two distinct neighborhoods, **Ischia Ponte** and **Ischia Porto.** This is where you are most likely to land. On the opposite coast is **Forío,** a lively resort with a wealth of bars and beaches. Between the two, on the north shore, you'll find **Lacco Ameno** and **Casamicciola Terme,** which basically make up one little town with many spas.

The southern half of the island, though it has fewer developed spas, has many beaches and natural mineral and hot springs. **Sant'Angelo** is the only village on the southern shore, while the main villages inland are **Serrara, Fontana,** and **Barrano d'Ischia.**

GETTING AROUND   Although larger than its surrounding islands, Ischia is not huge and can easily be toured using public transportation. SEPSA'S public **bus** system (② 081-991808 or 081-991828) works very well. One of its lines tours the island towards the right (*circolare destra* marked CD), and one circles towards the left (*circolare sinistra,* marked CS). Tickets are 1.20€ ($1.50) and are valid for 90 minutes; a daily pass costs 4€ ($5).

Motorettes—the local typical three-wheelers, which have replaced the once-common carriages—are another great way to get around, and operate as local **taxis** together with regular cabs. You can find taxi stands by the ferry terminals, or call them at ② 081-984998, 081-992550, or 081-993720.

If you would like to hire your own transportation, you can rent a scooter or a small car directly on the island from **Fratelli del Franco** (Via A. de Luca, Ischia Porto; ② 081-991334); they also rent bicycles.

VISITOR INFORMATION   The **AACST tourist office** of Ischia is at Via Sogliuzzo 72, 80077 Ischia (② 081-5074211; fax 081-5074230; www.infoischiaprocida. it). They also maintain an **information stand** on Corso Vittoria Colonna 116 in Ischia (② 081-5074231; www.ischiaonline.it; Mon–Sat 9am–noon and 2–5pm).

Either office should have a brochure, amusingly entitled *Lizard Trails,* which has descriptions and maps of the island's trails.

SPECIAL EVENTS   The **Festival of Sant'Anna** on July 26 is celebrated with evocative displays by the Aragonese Castle. The festival originated from the adoration of Saint Ann, the mother of Mary, who is believed to protect pregnant women. Originally, locals would sail to the small bay of Cartaromana with candles on their bows to honor the saint. Slowly, this tradition developed into the spectacular **Festa del Mare,** in which a procession of boats and floats crosses the water, and the castle and harbor are illuminated. If you are in the area around this time, be sure not to miss this memorable sight.

SPAS & THERMO-MINERAL TREATMENTS

With over 150 spas on the island, plus open-air facilities, including natural pools and steam holes, Ischia is a huge thermal resort. Experts have counted over 56 different mineral springs on the island, besides the numerous steam holes, hot mud, and sand. These natural resources are scattered across the islands' slopes and beaches, and are harnessed by the vast array of spa operators.

Most hotels have their own spas and will offer package stays including meals and basic spa services, such as the use of the thermo-mineral pools. However, a number of establishments specialize as spas and offer a greater variety of treatments, from medical uses addressing serious health concerns, to beauty care, and even to treatments for the mind's health with focus on stress relief. Some of these spas are beautiful enough that you should not miss them during your visit to Ischia; they are also worth a day trip. In the town of Ischia itself, the new **Ischia Thermal Center** ✹✹ (Via delle Terme 15, Ischia; ✆ **081-984376;** www.ischiathermalcenter.it) is a state-of-the-art establishment offering a wide range of medical and beauty treatments. Nearby, in **Casamicciola Terme,** you'll find four historical spas opening onto the village's famous **Piazza Bagni**—Terme Manzi, Belliazzi, Elisabetta, and Lucibello. Its neighbor is the new **Parco Termale Castiglione,** another thoroughly up-to-date facility which, according to the latest spa trend, offers thermo-mineral waters and mud treatments in a mix of indoor- and open-air facilities. It includes several pools at water temperatures ranging from 82°F to 104°F (28°C–40°C).

The historic **Terme della Regina Isabella** ✹✹ on Piazza Santa Restituta in **Lacco Ameno** (✆ **081-994322**) is the heart of this exclusive resort. They use two springs of radioactive waters, which—no matter what experts say—made us nervous; the radioactivity, of course, is low enough to be therapeutic and the settings are splendid. This is one of the most elegant spas on the island. In town you'll find several more trendy spas, such as **Parco Termale Negombo** (✆ **081-986152**) on the splendid little cove of **Baia di San Montano.**

In **Forio,** overlooking the splendid bay of Citara, is **Parco Termale Giardini Poseidon** ✹✹✹ (Via Giovanni Mazzella Citara, Forio d'Ischia; ✆ **081-907122** or 081-907420), an open-air facility with 22 pools (both relaxing and curative), a large private beach, and several restaurants. The spa's services are purported to offer psychosomatic relief; we highly recommend a soak in the pools whether you feel you need it or not.

Less well-known, the thermal facilities of **Serrara Fontana** ✹ include two very pleasant spas—**La Romantica** (Via Ruffano 11; ✆ **081-999059**); and **Terme San Michele** (✆ **081-999276**). Its **Parco Termale Giardini Aphrodite-Apollon** (✆ **081-999219**) is an indoor-outdoor facility with lovely grounds and pools.

EXPLORING ISCHIA PORTO & ISCHIA PONTE

One town with two faces, Ischia has a medieval and a modern harbor. The former—**Ischia Ponte** ✸✸—is the original settlement which began over and around the island promontory that guards the small natural harbor. The island-promontory has been fortified with a castle since as far back as the 5th century B.C.; the current one is the **Aragonese Castle** (Piazzale Aragonese, Ischia Ponte; ℂ **081-992834;** www.castellod ischia.it). This was connected to the main island by a bridge *(ponte)* when the Aragonese built the castle over the ruins of the previous fortifications. Among other interesting attractions, the castle houses the chilling **Museum of Torture Instruments and Weapons** (ℂ **081-984340;** 8€/$10; daily 9:30am–5pm; closed Nov–Feb). The last eruption on the island (in 1301) destroyed the village that stood nearby, between the castle and what is today's harbor, causing the population to resettle near the castle and around the bridge. This neighborhood is now the most picturesque and lively part of town.

The other half of town, **Ischia Porto** ✸, was founded after the Bourbons took over the island in the 18th century. The new kings fell in love with a villa-cum-spa built by a doctor, Francesco Buonocore, overlooking what was then a scenic lake, a little distance away from the village of Ischia. The Bourbons took over the villa, transforming it into a small palace—**Casina Reale Borbonica** ✸—which today houses the **Stabilimento Balneo–Termale Militare** (the military spa, not open to the public). They cut a channel into the sea to transform the lake (originally a volcano crater) into a large harbor. The modern harbor was inaugurated in 1854 and has been the island's major port ever since.

The two halves of town are connected by a promenade made up by Via Roma and Corso Vittoria Colonna—*il corso* in local parlance, stretching about 2km (1¼ miles). Along it you will find the 18th-century church **Santa Maria delle Grazie,** with its unusual tiled roof.

WHERE TO STAY
ISCHIA PONTE

Grand Hotel Punta Molino Terme ✸   Facing the Aragonese Castle and overlooking the bay of Punta Molino, this elegant, modern hotel offers great comfort, a high level of service, and beautiful views. On top of that, it has a full spa and a private beach (with chairs and umbrellas). The stylish public spaces mix modern furnishings with antiques. Guest rooms differ in shape; all are furnished with luxury fabrics and quality reproductions. Bathrooms have beautiful tiles, double sinks, commodious showers and bathtubs, and plenty of fluffy towels and bathrobes.

Lungomare Cristoforo Colombo 23, 80077 Ischia. ℂ 081-991544. Fax 081-991562. www.puntamolino.it. 90 units. 320€–430€ ($400–$538) double, 470€–570€ ($588–$713) suite; low season 250€–370€ ($313–$463) double, 410€–520€ ($513–$650) suite. Rates include buffet breakfast and dinner. Children under 2 stay free in parent's room. AE, DC, MC, V. Closed Nov–Apr 14. **Amenities:** Restaurant; lounge; 3 outdoor pools; health club; state-of-the-art spa; concierge; room service; babysitting; same-day laundry service. *In room:* A/C, TV, minibar, hair dryer, safe.

Hotel Terme Mare Blu ✸✸   Last renovated in 2004, this aristocratic residence facing the Aragonese Castle is not just beautifully situated, but beautifully decorated and run as well. The public spaces include delightful terraces overlooking the sea, and opportunities to swim (there are two pools and a private beach) and relax (at the spa, bar, restaurant, or lounge). The guest rooms are large and airy, with classic furnishings and brand-new fixtures giving you the best of both worlds.

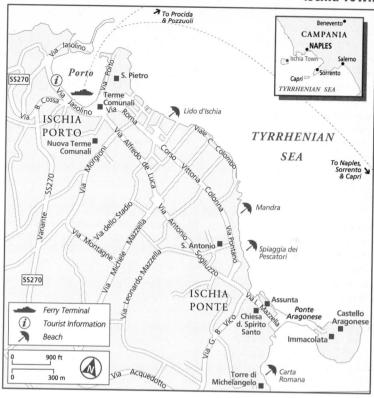

Via Pontano 36, 80070 Ischia. ℂ **081-982555.** Fax 081-982938. www.hotelmareblu.it. 40 units. 234€–306€ ($293–$383) double, 340€ ($425) suite; low season 136€–208€ ($170–$260) double, 242€ ($303) suite. Mid-Aug 7-day minimum stay and half-board. Rates include buffet breakfast. Children under 3 stay free in parent's room. AE, DC, MC, V. Closed mid-Oct to mid-Apr. **Amenities:** Restaurant; lounge; bar; 2 outdoor pools; private beach; health club; spa; concierge; room service; babysitting; laundry service. *In room:* A/C, satellite TV, minibar, hair dryer.

Miramare e Castello ⭐⭐ This is one of the best hotels in Ischia, offering elegance and refinement together with excellent service. Located at the entrance of the medieval *borgo* of Ischia Ponte, it has a full thermal spa with several pools and treatments. The bright, spacious guest rooms are tastefully furnished with tiled floors and color-coordinated bedspreads and furniture. Some have sea views—even from the bathroom—and a few have private terraces overlooking the sea and the hotel's private beach.

Via Pontano 5, 80070 Ischia. ℂ **081-991333.** Fax 081-984572. www.miramareecastello.it. 50 units. 270€–390€ ($338–$488) double, 490€ ($613) suite; low season 170€–290€ ($213–$363) double, 390€ ($488) suite. Mid-Aug 7-day minimum stay and half-board. Rates include buffet breakfast. Children under 5 stay free in parent's room. AE, DC, MC, V. Closed mid-Oct to mid-Apr. **Amenities:** Restaurant; bar; 3 outdoor pools; spa; concierge; room service; babysitting; laundry service. *In room:* A/C, TV, minibar, hair dryer, safe.

ISCHIA PORTO

Floridiana Terme *Finds* This is an exceptionally quiet hotel in the pedestrian area near the old harbor, housed in a gorgeous villa surrounded by greenery, and only a short walk from the sea. Guest rooms are bright and simply furnished but come equipped with all the comforts you'd expect from a quality hotel. Each room has a private terrace or balcony with a view.

Corso Vittoria Colonna 153, 80070 Ischia (NA). ℂ 081-991014. Fax 081-981014. www.hotelfloridianaischia.com. 64 units. 224€ ($280) double; low season 164€ ($205) double. Rates include buffet breakfast. Children under 2 stay free in parent's room. AE, DC, MC, V. Closed Nov–Mar. **Amenities:** Restaurant; bar; 2 outdoor pools; health club; spa; concierge; room service; babysitting; laundry service. In room: A/C, TV/VCR/DVD, fax, dataport, minibar, hair dryer, safe.

Grand Hotel Excelsior ℱ Formerly a private villa, this luxurious hotel enjoys a great panoramic view and offers top-notch service and amenities. Posh public spaces—from a panoramic pool, to a private beach, to a spa with beauty center—are complemented by beautiful guest rooms. The furnishings include wrought-iron bedsteads and designer tiled bathrooms; each room has a private patio-terrace. Note that the hotel only offers half-board, which means that breakfast and dinner are included in your room's rate.

Via E. Gianturco 19, 80077 Ischia. ℂ 081-991522. Fax 081-984100. www.excelsiorischia.it. 76 units. 300€–432€ ($375–$540) double, 470€–700€ ($588–$875) suite; low season 232€–364€ ($290–$455) double, 400€–580€ ($500–$725) suite. Rates include buffet breakfast and dinner. Children under 2 stay free in parent's room. AE, DC, MC, V. Closed mid-Oct to mid-Apr. **Amenities:** Restaurant; piano bar; 2 outdoor pools; minigolf course; health club; spa; concierge; room service; babysitting; laundry service. In room: A/C, satellite TV, minibar, hair dryer, safe.

Hotel La Marticana *Value* This small, family-run hotel is one of the few in town offering just accommodations instead of half-board. This will afford you more freedom but, on the other hand, less luxury. Guest rooms are not large but are comfortably furnished and open onto the pleasant garden. The friendly management will make you feel at home and give you pointers on enjoying the island.

Via Quercia 48, 80077 Ischia. ℂ 081-993230. Fax 081-3331787. www.lamarticana.it. 13 units. 130€ ($163) double; low season 68€ ($85) double. Children under 3 stay free in parent's room. AE, DC, MC, V. **Amenities:** Garden with barbecue; babysitting. In room: A/C (8€/$10 per day), TV, minibar, hair dryer; safe.

Jolly delle Terme This upscale but somewhat plain hotel (part of the Jolly chain) offers an excellent thermal establishment, several pools, access to a private beach, and a great garden, all at moderate prices. Guest rooms are spacious and furnished in classic style (with carpeting); bathrooms are good-sized.

Via A. De Luca 42, 80077 Ischia. ℂ 081-991744. Fax 081-993156. ischia@jollyhotels.it. 194 units. 259€–319€ ($324–$399) double, 329€–339€ ($411–$424) suite; low season 199€–259€ ($249–$324) double, 269€–279€ ($336–$349) suite. Rates include buffet breakfast. Children under 3 stay free in parent's room. AE, DC, MC, V. **Amenities:** 2 restaurants; piano bar; outdoor pools; health club; spa; concierge; business center; babysitting; laundry service. In room: A/C, satellite TV, pay TV, dataport, minibar, hair dryer, safe.

WHERE TO DINE

If an afternoon of hot mud treatments leaves you feeling you deserve a special dinner, you'll certainly be able to find one on this island. Ischia offers a lively dining scene, especially in the neighborhood of **Ischia Ponte** with its many restaurants and bars, and the exclusive **Via Porto**—called Rive Droite by the locals—lined with elegant nightclubs and restaurants.

ISCHIA PONTE

Alberto ℱ ISCHITANO This traditional restaurant is an excellent address for sampling the coast's seafood. The seasonal menu includes many regional specialties. Try, for instance, *polipo in cassuola* (squid cooked in a terra-cotta casserole), and superb *fusilli ai frutti di mare* (short pasta with shellfish). The traditional *antipasto* buffet will round out your meal with a bounteous selection of vegetable dishes.

Passeggiata Cristoforo Colombo. © **081-981259.** Reservations recommended. Secondi 12€–21€ ($15–$26). AE, DC, MC, V. Daily noon–3pm and 7–11pm.

ISCHIA PORTO

Damiano *✦* ISCHITANO At Damiano, the views and the food are equally tantalizing. The chef's specialties are seafood and fantastic homemade desserts, but the menu is varied enough that you can also find savory meat dishes, such as a tasty version of the local traditional *coniglio all'Ischitana* (rabbit in a spicy light tomato-and-herb sauce).

Via delle Vigne 30. © **081-983032.** Reservations recommended. Secondi 12€–22€ ($15–$28). DC, MC, V. Daily 8–11pm. Apr–June and Sept–Oct, also Sat–Sun 1–3pm. Closed Nov–Mar.

'O Purticciull' *Kids* ISCHITANO/PIZZA/SEAFOOD Opening right onto the harbor, this family-run restaurant—now in its the second generation—is proud to serve the freshest of seafood. An airy terrace and a cheery interior decorated in a light nautical theme provide two dining options. The food is the main attraction, of course; we recommend such dishes as *bucatini cozze e pecorino* (pasta with mussels and sheep's cheese), and their "Pizza D.O.C." (with buffalo mozzarella, local cherry tomatoes, olive oil, and basil). They welcome families, who should love the option of a two-sided dinner: elaborate seafood dishes for the parents and pizza for the kids.

Rive Droite, Ischia Porto. © **081-993222.** Reservations recommended. Secondi 6€–18€ ($7.50–$23). AE, DC, MC, V. Daily12:30–3pm and 7:30–11pm Apr–Oct; Wed–Mon 12:30–3pm and 7:30–11pm Nov–Dec. Closed Jan 7–Mar 20.

CASAMICCIOLA TERME

Located 6.5km (4 miles) northwest of Ischia Porto, this scenic village was founded in the 16th century to take advantage of the area's thermo-mineral springs. Its first spa opened its doors in 1604, but the village suffered a reversal of fortunes when it was destroyed by the earthquake of 1883. The village was immediately rebuilt closer to the shore, which had the happy effect of adding a beautiful beach to its other attractions. As a result of this history, the village now has two tiers: the **Marina** below by the sea; and **Majo,** the original settlement higher up the slope.

As you walk through the village, you'll come to **Piazza Bagni,** where some of the island's oldest spas are located; nearby are the **Parco Termale Castiglione** (see later in this chapter), and **Villa Ibsen,** where the famous Norwegian writer wrote *Peer Gynt.*

The D.O.C. Wines of Ischia

Ischia's vineyards produce wines that have been increasingly appreciated by connoisseurs; three even earned the D.O.C. label—a government recognition reserved only for those superior wines from specific areas that answer to severe requirements of consistently good quality and characteristics. The winning wines are the red Monte Epomeo, the Ischia (red and white), and the white Biancolella. Wine enthusiasts around the world have to thank the Greeks for this bounty, for it was they who recognized the local potential and planted the varieties of grape still used today to produce the area's wines.

LACCO AMENO ✪✪

Famous for its mushroom-shaped small island a few yards from the shore, Lacco Ameno is where the ancient Greeks established their first settlement on this coast, on the promontory of Monte Vico. The Greeks never developed this colony, daunted by the frequent—at that time—earthquakes and eruptions, and Lacco Ameno remained a little fishing harbor. In the 1950s, though, the famous Italian publisher Angelo Rizzoli decided to invest here in order to transform the place into an exclusive spa resort. His plan succeeded, and this former fisherman's *borgo* has become the most exclusive spa resort in Italy, offering numerous, and luxurious, hotel and villa options. Lacco is located 8km (5 miles) west of Ischia Porto.

On a more spiritual note, the town's **Sanctuary of Santa Restituta** (© 081-980706 or 081-980538) is an important Catholic pilgrimage site. Attached to the 19th-century sanctuary, the original church has undergone many face-lifts. Redone in the 14th century and redecorated in the 18th century, the church was built in the 11th century over a paleochristian basilica dating from the 4th or 5th century A.D.—which itself had been adapted from a Roman water cistern.

Nearby is **Lido di San Montano** ✪✪, the island's most picturesque cove, seat of some of the most exclusive spas in the area (see later in this chapter). Also nearby is **Villa Arbusto,** Angelo Rizzoli's own summer home and today the home of the **Museo Civico Archeologico di Pithecusae** ✪ (© **081-900356;** 3€/$3.75; Tues–Sun 9:30am–12:30pm and 3–6pm). The museum boasts important findings from the island's archaeological excavations and objects relating to the early Greek colonies from the 8th to the 5th centuries B.C., including the famous **Coppa di Nestore** from 725 B.C. with one of the oldest existing Greek inscriptions (appropriately, it celebrates the wine of Ischia!)

WHERE TO STAY

Albergo Villa Angelica *(Value)*   This small, family-run hotel is an excellent, moderately priced choice. Housed in a whitewashed Mediterranean building with arched doorways and passages, it has a welcoming atmosphere which extends from the public spaces to the guest rooms. These are quiet and cozy, with tiled floors and wrought-iron beds. Most have private terraces. The hotel offers a beautiful thermal swimming pool with a Jacuzzi in the garden.

Via IV Novembre 28, 80076 Lacco Ameno. © 081-994524. Fax 081-980184. www.villaangelica.it. 20 units. 130€ ($163) double; low season 100€ ($125) double. Minimum stay 3 days. Rates include buffet breakfast. Children under 2 stay free in parent's room. AE, DC, MC, V. Closed mid-Nov to mid-Mar. **Amenities:** Restaurant; bar; outdoor pool; spa; concierge; room service; babysitting; laundry service. *In room:* A/C, TV, minibar, hair dryer.

Hotel La Sirenella *(Finds)*   This family-run hotel right on the beach (La Sirenella's private property) offers bright guest rooms decorated in Mediterranean style at good rates. Public spaces include a pleasant lounge and a sunny terrace. Each guest room is large and bright with decorated tiled floors, and comes with a private terrace overlooking the sea. Note that from the last week in July to the last week in August, the hotel accepts only half-board.

Corso Angelo Rizzoli 41, 80076 Lacco Ameno d'Ischia. © 081-994743. Fax 081-994206. www.lasirenella.net. 20 units. 130€ ($163) double. Rates include buffet breakfast. Children under 3 stay free in parent's room. AE, DC, MC, V. Closed Nov–Mar. **Amenities:** Restaurant; piano bar; room service; babysitting; laundry service. *In room:* A/C, TV, minibar, hair dryer.

Hotel Regina Isabella ✪✪✪   Set in a beautiful location, this prestigious hotel offers fine accommodations, a state-of-the-art thermal establishment (see "Spa and

Thermo-Mineral Treatments" earlier in this chapter), and a private cove. The large guest rooms are decorated with a mix of contemporary and older furniture, and many have private balconies. Some of the floats in the hotel's private cove are equipped with chairs and umbrellas, suitable for lounging.

Piazza Santa Restituta 1, 80076 Lacco Ameno d'Ischia. ℂ 081-994322. Fax 081-990190. www.reginaisabella.it. 134 units. 228€–540€ ($285–$675) double; 990€ ($1,238) suite. Rates include buffet breakfast and dinner. 3-day minimum stay. Children under 3 stay free in parent's room. AE, DC, MC, V. Free parking. **Amenities:** 2 restaurants; 2 bars; 3 outdoor pools; full spa; concierge; room service; babysitting; laundry service. *In room:* A/C, satellite TV, dataport, minibar, hair dryer, safe.

Hotel Terme di Augusto *Value*   Located just a stone's throw away from the beach, this hotel is one of the best medium-range choices in town, with high levels of service and comfort. Guest rooms are good-sized, with tiled floors and modern bathrooms, and open onto the garden or the beach. The hotel's spa is small but offers a variety of treatments.

Viale Campo 128, 80076 Lacco Ameno d'Ischia. ℂ 081-994944. Fax 081-980244. www.termediaugusto.it. 118 units. 80€–110€ ($100–$138) double; 120€–170€ ($150–$213) suite. Rates include buffet breakfast and dinner. Children under 3 stay free in parent's room. AE, DC, MC, V. Free parking. Closed Dec 1–27. **Amenities:** 2 restaurants; 3 bars; outdoor pool; outdoor tennis courts; health club; spa; babysitting; concierge; limited room service; laundry service; rooms for those w/limited mobility. *In room:* A/C, TV, minibar, hair dryer, safe.

Hotel Terme San Montano *ℱ*   Surrounded by a lush garden and overlooking a private beach, this elegant hotel is a quiet retreat. The nautical-theme decor is repeated in the guest rooms, where headboards look like ship wheels, and portholes substitute for windows. Thankfully, the nautical vibe stops at the bathroom door; the bathrooms are good-sized and come with all the modern conveniences. All rooms are generous in size and the views are superb from those that overlook the sea.

Via Monte Vico, 80076 Lacco Ameno d'Ischia. ℂ 081-994033. Fax 081-980242. www.sanmontano.com. 77 units. 140€–250€ ($175–$313) double; 285€ ($356) suite. Rates include buffet breakfast and dinner. Children under 3 free in parent's room. AE, DC, MC, V. Free parking. Closed Nov–Easter. **Amenities:** Restaurant; 2 bars; lounge; 2 outdoor pools; outdoor tennis courts; squash courts; health club; spa; concierge; room service; babysitting. *In room:* A/C, satellite TV, minibar, hair dryer, safe.

FORIO *ℱℱ*

The least touristy of this area's large villages, Forio—13km (8 miles) west of Ischia Porto—has traditionally been known more for its wine and its medieval watchtowers than for its spas. A preferred retreat of writers and musicians for centuries, it is now appreciated by a large variety of artists—filmmaker Luchino Visconti, for example, had his villa here—as well as by tourists of all kinds.

The village's focal point is a masterful 15th-century watchtower, once the prison and today a museum (ℂ 081-3332934). The narrow streets are lined with little white houses hiding great little bars. Just outside the village to the north is the **Spiaggia di San Francesco,** named after a sanctuary (which can be visited). To the south is the most beautiful beach on the island, scenic **Spiaggia di Citara** *ℱℱ*, with thermo-mineral springs used by the great park-spa **Giardini di Poseidon** (p. 217).

WHERE TO STAY

Grande Albergo Mezzatorre *ℱℱ*   This is the best hotel in town, composed of modern buildings scattered in a 3-hectare (7-acre) wooded complex dominated by a 15th-century watchtower. The tower houses the lounge and the least expensive of the guest rooms. The other guest rooms—including the luxurious suites with private garden and Jacuzzi—are furnished in contemporary style, sleek yet warm and comfortable. The waterfront "infinity" pool (built so that the pool appears to stretch into the ocean beyond) offers beautiful views.

Via Mezzatorre, 80075 Forio d'Ischia. ℂ **081-986111.** Fax 081-986015. www.mezzatorre.it. 59 units. 290€–500€ ($363–$625) double; 610€–760€ ($763–$950) suite. Rates include buffet breakfast. Children under 4 stay free in parent's room. AE, DC, MC, V. Free parking. Closed Nov–Apr. **Amenities:** 2 restaurants; bar; outdoor pool; outdoor tennis courts, health club; spa; concierge; room service; babysitting; laundry service. *In room:* A/C, TV, minibar, hair dryer, safe.

Hotel Semiramis   Surrounded by greenery, this modern hotel is a good mid-range option. Guest rooms have colorful tiled floors in traditional patterns and good-quality furniture; some of the rooms have private balconies with ocean views. Potted palms dot the public spaces, creating a tropical atmosphere. There's a swimming pool; for those who prefer more bracing waters, the beach is only steps away.

Spiaggia di Citara, 80075 Forio d'Ischia. ℂ/fax **081-907511.** www.hotelsemiramisischia.com. 35 units. 114€–128€ ($143–$160) double; low season 90€–110€ ($113–$138) double. Rates include buffet breakfast. Extra bed 25€ ($31). Children under 2 stay free in parent's room. Specials available. AE, DC, MC, V. Free parking. Closed Nov–Mar. **Amenities:** Dining room; bar; outdoor pool; babysitting; laundry service. *In room:* TV, minibar, safe, ceiling fan.

Hotel Terme La Bagattella ⭐⭐ *Finds*   Housed in an elaborate villa with Moorish details and surrounded by a beautiful garden, this hotel has an excellent spa, offering both thermal and beauty treatments. Guest room decor is nautical in some and Moorish in others. The suites are particularly luxurious—with exposed beams on the white-washed ceilings, rich fabrics, and private terraces—but the regular rooms are very nice, too, either with private balconies, or direct garden access.

Via Tommaso Cigliano 8, 80075 Forio d'Ischia. ℂ **081-986072.** Fax 081-989637. www.labagattella.it. 40 units. 150€ ($188) double; low season 128€ ($160) double. Rates include buffet breakfast. Children under 2 stay free in parent's room. AE, DC, MC, V. Closed Nov–Mar. **Amenities:** Restaurant; bar; 2 outdoor pools; health club; spa; bike rentals; room service; babysitting; laundry service; bike rentals. *In room:* A/C, TV, minibar, hair dryer, safe.

WHERE TO DINE

La Romantica CAMPANIAN   Popular with tourists and locals, this venerable restaurant has welcomed VIPs as varied as singer Josephine Baker and heart surgeon Christian Barnard. The outdoor terrace, opening onto the old port, is delightful, but you can eat just as well inside. The menu focuses on fish, and you can depend on the *risotto alla pescatora* (seafood risotto), *pescespada al limone* (swordfish served with a lemon sauce), and other local favorites.

Via Marina 46. ℂ **081-997345.** Reservations recommended. Secondi 5€–12€ ($6.25–$15). AE, DC, MC, V. Daily noon–3pm and 7pm–midnight; closed Wed Nov–Mar.

Montecorvo ⭐ *Finds* CAMPANIAN   If you're in the mood for more than fish, this is the place for you. Popular with locals in the off season, it's also a good choice for traditional Ischitan food. The seafood is uniformly good, but you can also choose meat dishes, from a very good *coniglio all'Ischitana* (rabbit cooked with tomatoes and herbs in a terra-cotta casserole) to excellent roasted chicken with herbs.

Via Montecorvo 33. ℂ **081-998029.** Reservations required. Secondi 11€–20€ ($14–$25). AE, MC, V. Fri–Sun noon–3:30pm and 7pm–midnight.

Umberto a Mare ⭐⭐ CAMPANIAN/CREATIVE   This famous restaurant draws diners from as far away as Naples, who come for a weekend lunch or dinner (especially in fine weather, because of the romantic sunsets from the terrace overlooking the water). The choice of antipasti is large and always includes a variety of great vegetarian and seafood specialties, such as *insalata di mare* (seafood salad) and *melanzane a scapece* (eggplant in a vinegar sauce). However, don't stint on the pasta dishes like *pennette all'aragosta e agli asparagi* (short pasta with lobster and asparagus). Fish can be prepared imaginatively in dishes such as *tartare di palamita al profumo d'arancia* (tartare of local fish with citrus), or in the traditional way, grilled or *all'acqua pazza* (in a light herb broth).

Via Soccorso 2. (C) **081-997171.** www.umbertoamare.it. Reservations recommended. Prix-fixe menus 49€ ($61) and 59€ ($74),. Secondi 18€–32€ ($23–$40). AE, DC, MC, V. Tues–Sun noon–3:30pm and daily 7:30–11pm. Closed Jan 7–Mar and Nov–Christmas.

SANT'ANGELO ★★

This quiet fishing village on the southern shore, 11km (7 miles) south of Ischia Porto, is built around a diminutive harbor shaded by a tall promontory jutting from the sea and connected to the shore by a sandy isthmus (100m/300-ft. long). Closed to car circulation, it offers not only quiet, but a great beach and relaxed atmosphere. Far from the hype and the high-priced spa resorts, yet only minutes away from Ischia's most beautiful attractions and best outdoor park-spas, it makes an ideal base.

Inland of Sant'Angelo, you'll come to the two villages of **Serrara Fontana** ★★★ (9.5km/6 miles southwest of Ischia Porto), with its lesser-known but enjoyable spas; and **Barano d'Ischia** (4km/2½ miles south of Ischia Porto), with the most beautiful beach on the island, **Lido dei Maronti** ★★★, stretching for about 2km (1¼ miles).

WHERE TO STAY

Hotel Casa Celestino *(Value)*   This hotel is built vertically, hugging the cliff along the pedestrian promenade at the heart of the village. Guest rooms are large and bright, with spacious tiled bathrooms and private terraces (complete with table and chairs), as well as superb sea views. Reservations must be for a minimum of 7 nights, but you can try for last-minute availability.

Via Chiaia di Rosa, 80070 Sant'Angelo d'Ischia. (C) **081-999213.** Fax 081-999805. www.casacelestino.it. 20 units. 83€ ($104) double; 125€ ($156) suite. Rates include buffet breakfast. Extra bed 30€ ($38). Children under 5 stay free in parent's room. AE, DC, MC, V. Closed Nov–Dec. **Amenities:** Restaurant; bar; room service; babysitting; laundry service. *In room:* A/C, satellite TV, minibar, hair dryer, safe.

Hotel Loreley *(Finds)*   Housed in a modern whitewashed structure, this well-kept family-run hotel is set in a nicely landscaped garden, complete with a thermal water pool and harbor view. It combines quiet and beautiful views with a high level of service—all at moderate prices. Each bright, comfortably furnished guest room has its own balcony or terrace opening onto panoramic views over the sea.

Via Sant'Angelo 50a, 80070 Sant'Angelo d'Ischia. (C) **081-999313.** Fax 081-999065. www.hotelloreley.it. 30 units. 132€ ($165) double; low season 96€ ($120) double. Rates include buffet breakfast. Specials available. Children under 2 stay free in parent's room. AE, DC, MC, V. Closed mid-Oct to mid-Apr. **Amenities:** Restaurant; bar; outdoor pool; room service; babysitting; same-day laundry service. *In room:* A/C, satellite TV, hair dryer, safe.

Fun Fact Flower Power

Ischia's unusual volcanic characteristics have produced more than spa-perfect conditions. The fertile soil and unique subtropical climate have been so favorable to flowering plants and shrubs that you can find on the island 50% of the entire European patrimony of flower species, a number of them indigenous to Ischia.

Park Hotel Miramare ✦ Old-fashioned in style but not in spirit, this hotel has one of the only nudist-reserved areas on the island. It is also the most elegant hotel in Sant'Angelo. Opened in 1923 and run by the same family ever since, the hotel offers comfortable rooms furnished in a 1920s seaside style, with wicker and wrought-iron furniture as well as some antiques and quality reproductions. Guest room decor varies depending on the room's level and its location in the main building or in one of the two additions, Casa Apollo or Casa del Sole. All units are bright, with modern bathrooms and private balconies or terraces opening onto the sea. The hotel's spa includes 12 different pools, in case you're not feeling bold enough to venture to the nudist area.

Via Comandante Magdalena 29, 80070 Sant'Angelo d'Ischia. ℂ 081-999219. Fax 081-999325. www.hotelmiramare.it. 50 units. 156€–350€ ($195–$438) double; 560€ ($700) suite. Rates include buffet breakfast. Children under 3 stay free in parent's room. AE, DC, MC, V. Closed Nov 11–Apr 6. **Amenities:** 2 restaurants; bar; spa with pools; babysitting; laundry service. *In room:* A/C, TV, minibar, hair dryer, safe.

WHERE TO DINE
Trattoria il Focolare ✦ *Finds* CAMPANIAN This welcoming restaurant offers romantic dining and a more imaginative menu than those offered by most of the island's traditional restaurants. The offerings are seasonal but you can always find an excellent *frittura* (medley of deep-fried seafood) or *ravioli* with seafood. *Maiale arrosto* (pork roast) is usually available. The desserts are also good, including Neapolitan favorites such as *pastiera* (pie filled with ricotta and orange peels).

Via Cretajo al Crocefisso 3, Barano d'Ischia. ℂ 081-902944. Reservations recommended. Secondi 10€–18€ ($13–$23). AE, MC, V. Thurs–Tues 7:30–11:30pm; Sat and Sun also 12:30–3pm.

---

2 Romantic & Unspoiled Procida ✦✦

32km (20 miles) NW of Naples; 12km (8 miles) W of Pozzuoli; 7.8km (5 miles) W of Ischia.

Not well known among foreign tourists, Procida is an exclusive resort, popular with the rich and famous who have villas here, but also with local tourists, who often come just for the day or for dinner. We think both are excellent ideas.

Procida's landscape is dotted with pretty houses in tones of pink and yellow, contrasting with the green of citrus groves and gardens. Beyond the private residences, you'll find beaches and restaurants catering to various levels of taste and budget. And you won't find yourself competing with the kinds of crowds that can envelop Capri.

ESSENTIALS
GETTING THERE   Caremar (ℂ 081-5513882; www.caremar.it) runs a frequent ferry service from both Pozzuoli and Naples's Molo Beverello to Procida. The ride is about 15 minutes from Pozzuoli and 40 minutes from Naples and costs between 4.50€ ($5.65) and 8€ ($10). You can also catch a ferry to and from Ischia; the short ride is only 3€ ($3.75).

GETTING AROUND Given Procida's diminutive size (see below), the best way to see the island is definitely **on foot.** You can also take one of the four **public bus** lines run by **SEPSA** (ℂ 081-5429965). All of the buses start from Marina Grande; tickets are .80€ ($1) per ride. Or you can use an open **minitaxi**—you'll find stands at each of the three marinas and at the ferry terminal. Unfortunately, the island's short distances have not discouraged the use of cars by locals, so there are regular traffic jams, especially in the summer months.

VISITOR INFORMATION   The AAST maintains a small **tourist office** in Marina Grande near the ferry dock (© **081-8101968;** www.infoischiaprocida.it or www.procida.net), open May to September, Monday to Saturday from 9:30am to 1pm and 3:30 to 6pm; the rest of the year it's only open mornings. The nearby travel agency **Graziella** (Via Roma 117; © **081-8969191;** www.isoladiprocida.it) is another good resource for help with hotel reservations and boat rentals.

EXPLORING PROCIDA

The island is basically one whole village, interspersed with citrus groves and gardens and the occasional vineyard, developing northeast-southwest along one main street. The distance from Marina Grande—with the ferry terminal—on the northeastern tip of the island to Marina di Chiaiolella, all the way to the opposite end, is only about 3km (1¾ miles). Several side streets radiate from this main artery. Jutting from the southwestern tip, a bridge connects Procida to the little island of Vivara.

Marina Grande, or Marina di Sancio Cattolico, is the major harbor of the island, and the location of the ferry terminal. A few steps away, along the main street, **Via Principe Umberto,** is **Piazza dei Martiri,** the village's main square. From it you can climb to **Torre Murata,** the highest point of the island, fortified by 16th-century walls. This is where Procida's rulers had their residences, and where you can enjoy some of the most magnificent views of the island and its surroundings. As you climb, you will find a **belvedere** 🌣🌣 affording good views of the Marina di Corricella (see below); farther up beyond the Piazza d'Armi, you enter the **medieval citadel** of **Terra Casata** 🌣🌣🌣 and its belvedere with a magnificent view over the Gulf of Naples. On the square is the island's main church, **San Michele Arcangelo,** originally from the 11th century but redone in later times.

From Piazza dei Martiri, it is a short walk to **Marina della Corricella** 🌣🌣🌣, a picturesque and charming fishing harbor originally established in the 17th century. Its colorful houses and narrow streets surround the small port.

If you continue towards the southwestern tip of the island, you should not miss the detour to the left for **Punta Pizzaco** 🌣🌣🌣, from where you can enjoy one of the best views on the whole island.

Farther on, you'll finally reach **Marina di Chiaiolella** 🌣🌣 at the southwestern tip of the island. This crescent-shaped harbor was once the crater of a volcano and now is a pleasant marina, lined with little restaurants and bars. The harbor is dominated by the mountainous, tiny island of **Vivara,** attached to Procida by a bridge, and today a wildlife refuge run by the World Wildlife Federation. *Note:* The bridge has been under restoration since 1999 and still was at presstime, but in 2001 Vivara was connected to Procida by the world's longest Tibetan-style foot bridge, measuring 362m (1,188 ft.). Check with the tourist office when you arrive for guided tours.

One typical activity on Procida you should not miss is to an **excursion** 🌣🌣🌣 around the island. You can rent a boat, with or without driver, from any of the three harbors on the island: Marina Grande, Marina della Corricella, and Marina di Chiaiolella. You'll spend about 20€ ($25) for a 2-hour trip with a boat and driver.

WHERE TO STAY
PROCIDA, CHIAIOLELLA

Casa sul Mare *Finds*   Housed in a typical 18th-century building at the foot of Terra Murata (the historic *borgo* or village of Procida), this little-known, small hotel offers high-quality accommodations with beautiful views over the Marina di Corricella. The elegant guest rooms are furnished with taste, from beautiful tiled floors to wrought-iron bed frames. The view is really the focal point here, though—and each guest room enjoys one from a private terrace.

Salita Castello 13. *C*/fax **081-8968799**. www.lacasasulmare.it. 10 units. 160€ ($200) double; low season 90€ ($113) double. Rates include buffet breakfast. Children under 2 stay free in parent's room. AE, DC, MC, V. **Amenities:** Bar; babysitting; laundry service. *In room:* A/C, satellite TV, minibar, hair dryer, safe.

Hotel Celeste   This pleasant, family-run hotel near the Marina di Chiaiolella is a traditional structure where guest rooms open onto the outdoors. Some have private terraces, but others open onto the veranda, the inner courtyard, or the terrace/garden. All are simply furnished with tiled floors and small outdoor spaces with a table and chairs. The service is warm and welcoming; Signora Concetta and her family will give you individual attention. The view from the terraces and the solarium is nice.

Via Rivoli 6, 80079 Procida. *C* **081-8967488.** Fax 081-8967670. www.hotelceleste.it. 35 units. 154€ ($193) double. Rates include buffet breakfast. Children under 3 stay free in parent's room. AE, DC, MC, V. Closed Oct–Mar. **Amenities:** Restaurant; bar; room service; babysitting; laundry service. *In room:* A/C, TV, hair dryer.

Hotel Ristorante Crescenzo *Value*   Right on the marina, this small hotel attached to a popular restaurant of the same name (see below) has just a few rooms, allowing for special attention from the staff. Rooms are simply furnished with a somewhat nautical theme; bathrooms are plain but fully functional. Some of the rooms have balconies, while others have bay views.

Via Marina di Chiaiolella 33. *C* **081-8967255.** Fax 081-8101260. www.hotelcrescenzo.it. 10 units. 98€ ($123) double; 125€ ($156) triple; 158€ ($198) quad. Rates include breakfast. Children under 3 stay free in parent's room. AE, MC, V. **Amenities:** Restaurant; bar. *In room:* A/C, TV.

WHERE TO DINE

Caracalè *✿* ISCHITANO   This picturesque restaurant offers traditional cuisine and a lively atmosphere. The delicious food includes many local specialties, most focusing on seafood, but vegetarian and meat choices are also available. You will find a great *risotto ai frutti di mare* (seafood risotto) and, depending on the market, a variety of fish either grilled or served *all'acqua pazza*.

Via Marina Corricella 62. *C* **081-8969191.** Reservations necessary. Secondi 7€–12€ ($8.75–$15). AE, DC, MC, V. Daily noon–3pm and 7–11pm.

Conchiglia *✿* ISCHITANO   Somewhat more formal in atmosphere and elegant in decor than Caracalè, this is a good restaurant in the classic mold, serving dishes prepared according to tradition and seasonal seafood choices. You might find *linguine all'aragosta* (linguine with lobster) or *spiedini di mazzancolle* (prawn skewers), as well as grilled catches of the day.

Via Pizzaco, Discesa Graziella. *C* **081-8967602.** Reservations recommended. Secondi 12€–23€ ($15–$29). AE, DC, MC, V. Daily 12:30–3pm and 7:30–11pm. Closed Nov–Mar.

Crescenzo *✿✿* ISCHITANO   This popular restaurant, located in the hotel reviewed separately above, is one of the best on the island. Overlooking the romantic bay of Chiaiolella, it is moderate in price yet offers a well-rounded menu of traditional dishes, including both meat and seafood. The large array of *antipasti* includes such delicacies as *tortino di pesce spada* (swordfish cake) and *schiacciatine pesce spada e melanzane* (swordfish and eggplant fritters). You'll have a hard time choosing among the many pasta dishes, but we recommend *spaghetti cozze e broccoletti* (spaghetti with broccoli-rabe and mussels) and *spaghetti granchio e zucchine* (spaghetti with crab and zucchini).

Via Marina di Chiaiolella 33. ℂ **081-8967255**. Reservations required. Secondi 6€–15€ ($7.50–$19). AE, MC, V. Daily 12:30–2:30pm and 7:30–10:30pm.

3 Capri, the Faraglioni & the Blue Grotto ✶✶✶

33km (21 miles) SW of Naples.

Italy's most famous island, Capri (pronounced *cap*-ry, not ca-*pree*) is a dramatic rugged mountain soaring out of the sea at the tip of the Sorrento peninsula. A haunt for eccentric characters since antiquity (Roman Emperor Tiberius had his villa of pleasures, the Villa Jovis, here), Capri has been the preferred retreat of artists, movie stars, and other VIPs in modern times. Scottish writer Norman Douglas's novel *South Wind* (1917) is part homage to the island and part satire on its eclectic (and even mad) inhabitants. In recent years, though, all these personalities would have very little peace indeed, since the island is completely overrun with tourists May through October. Nights tend to be quieter, since many of the tourists come only for the day. You can come in the off season—Christmastime is popular with Italians—but you will find many businesses shuttered.

ESSENTIALS

GETTING THERE   Just as all roads lead to Rome, ferries leave for Capri from almost every harbor in Campania; you can get almost innumerable rides from Naples, as many companies make the trip either by regular ferry (a 90-min. trip), fast boat (about 50 min.), or hydrofoil (35 min.), with fares ranging from 6€ ($7.50) for the regular ferry *(traghetto)* to 12€ ($15) for hydrofoils. Ferries, fast boats, and some hydrofoils leave from Molo Beverello, where you will find **Caremar** (ℂ **081-5513882;** www.caremar.it); **SNAV** (ℂ **081-7612348**); and **NLG-Navigazione Libera del Golfo** (ℂ **081-5527209;** www.navlib.it), as well as the newly created **Metrò del Mare** (ℂ **199-446644;** www.metrodelmare.com).

The commuter fast-boat line MM4 makes one daily run to Capri at 4:25pm, with the return from Capri at 10:50am. The fare, a real bargain, is 4.50€ ($5.65), including ground transportation the 45 minutes before and 45 minutes after the ferry link. Most hydrofoils, on the other hand, leave from Mergellina's hydrofoil pier, where you will find SNAV (ℂ **081-4285555** or 081-4285111; www.snav.it) and NLG (ℂ **081-5527209;** www.navlib.it). *Note:* Hydrofoil service and the Metrò del Mare are suspended during winter because of bad weather. You can also easily reach Capri from **Castellammare di Stabia** with NLG (ℂ **081-5527209**) by fast ferry for 10€ ($13).

From **Sorrento,** you can take either a hydrofoil or ferry. At the Marina Piccola, off Piazza Tasso in downtown Sorrento, you will find **Linee Marittime Partenopee** (ℂ **081-55513236**), **Linee Lauro** (ℂ **081-5522838;** www.alilauro.it), **NLG** (ℂ **081-5527209;** www.navlib.it), and **Caremar** (ℂ **081-5513882;** www.caremar.it). You'll need to budget between 7€ ($8.75) for a ferry and 13€ ($16) for a hydrofoil. These companies also run to and from **Ischia** at the Marina Grande.

From the **Amalfi Coast,** you can catch ferries and hydrofoils from **Amalfi** (10€/$13 and 14€/$18), **Positano** (9€/$11 and 13€/$16), and **Salerno** (from Molo Manfredi; 11€/$14 and 15€/$19). You must make reservations in advance with your chosen company: **Alicost** (ℂ **081-7611004** or 081-811986; www.alilauro.it) or **NLG** (ℂ **081-5527209;** www.navlib.it).

GETTING ORIENTED   Mountainous Capri extends east-west with its major town, **Capri,** on the eastern half, and its second town—**Anacapri**—on the higher western half. They are separated by the highest peak on the island, **Monte Solaro,** which rises to an altitude of 589m (1,932 ft.). From the town of Capri you can descend to **Marina Grande** (the harbor with the ferry and hydrofoil docks) on the northern shore; and you can descend to the small harbor of **Marina Piccola** on the southern shore. You can also reach **Villa Jovis,** at the northeastern tip of the island, and the **Faraglioni** at its southeastern corner (see below). From Anacapri, you can take the funicular up **Monte Solaro** or travel to the northwestern corner of the island, where the famous **Blue Grotto** lies; you can also reach the southwestern tip of the island.

GETTING AROUND   Capri gets its name from the ancient Greek *kapriae,* meaning "island of the wild goats." Indeed, only goats can tread these steep slopes and cliffs with ease. There is also much that you can do here **on foot**—provided that you are moderately fit—by taking the old **footpaths** which were the only way to get around until very recently. They afford unique views and quiet—a rare commodity on Capri.

Ferries and hydrofoils arrive at Marina Grande, on the north shore. It is then quite a hike from there to the town of Capri, and you can take either the **funicolare (funicular)** or a **taxi.** *Note:* Because of the island's steepness, carry very little with you, or hire a porter. Wear comfortable shoes—stiletto heels are definitely not recommended. If you have mobility problems, count on using public modes of transportation to get around.

To fully enjoy all that the island has to offer, though, boats are the best form of transport. You can join an organized excursion or boat tour, or hire your own boat with or without mariner. The best place to find this kind of transportation is **Marina Grande;** there you'll find **Gruppo Motoscafisti** (www.motoscafisticapri.com) and **Laser Capri** (www.lasercaprisrl.com), offering **boat tours of the island** ✸✸✸ and excursions to the Faraglioni, the famous rock formations jutting from the sea. You'll spend about 19€ ($24) per person for a tour and 10€ ($13) for the Faraglioni excursion.

Regular **SIPPC buses** (© 081-9370420) offer service between Marina Grande, Capri, Marina Piccola, Anacapri, Faro (Lighthouse), and Grotta Azzurra. Tickets cost 1.30€ ($1.65) for either the bus or funicular. You can also get a 60-minute ticket for 2.10€ ($2.65) valid for one funicular run and unlimited bus runs during the time limit, or a day pass for 6.70€ ($8.40), valid for two funicular rides and unlimited bus service.

VISITOR INFORMATION   The **ACST** of Capri is at Piazzetta I Cerio 11 (© 081-8375308 or 081-8370424; fax 081-8370918; www.capritourism.com).

CAPRI TOWN ✸✸✸

This picturesque town is the heart of life on the island, with extensive shopping as well as numerous hotels—many of them among the coast's most glamorous—and a wide variety of restaurants and clubs. Social life radiates from the famous **Piazzetta** (Piazza Umberto I), a preferred spot for seeing and being seen. Off this diminutive square is the terrace of the **funicular** from **Marina Grande.** On the square is the 14th-century **Palazzo Cerio,** the most important example of medieval architecture remaining on the island. Inside, you can visit the **Museo Ignazio Cerio** (© 081-8376681), which has displays on the island's natural history.

From the square, you can take **Via Longano** to explore the old town. You can also take **Via Vittorio Emanuele III,** the town's main street. Past the famous **Quisisana hotel**—built in the 19th century as a sanatorium—and to the right on Via Ignazio Cerio, you can visit the **Certosa di San Giacomo** ✸ (© 081-8376218; free admission; Tues–Sun 9am–2pm), an important complex originally built in the 14th century and enlarged in the 16th and 17th centuries. It includes a church, a cloister, and a garden

Isle of Capri

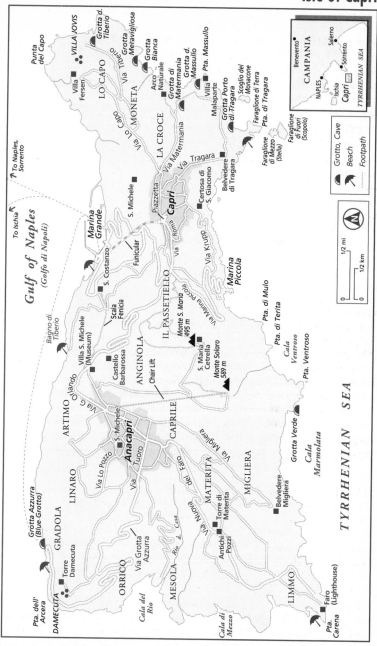

Punta del Capo

To Naples, Sorrento

To Ischia

Gulf of Naples
(Golfo di Napoli)

To Ischia

Bagno di Tiberio

Grotta Azzurra
(Blue Grotto)

Pta. dell' Arcera

DAMECUTA
Torre Damecuta

ORRICO

Cala del Rio

Cala di Mezzo

GRADOLA

LINARO

Via Lo Pozzo

MESOLA

Via Grotta Azzurra

Rio d. Cesa

Via Nuova del Faro

Via Grotta Azzurra

ARTIMO

Via G. Orlando

S. Michele
Anacapri

ANGINOLA

Castello Barbarossa

Villa S. Michele (Museum)

Scala Fenicia

S. Costanzo

Marina Grande

Funicular

S. Michele

Via Lo Capo

Via Matermania

LA CROCE

Piazzetta
Capri

Via Roma

Certosa di S. Giacomo

Via Tragara

Via Krupp

Marina Piccola

Via Mamma Piccola

IL PASSETIELLO

Monte S. Maria 495 m

S. Maria Cetrella

Monte Solaro 589 m

Chair lift

CAPRILE

Via Migliera

MATERITA

Torre di Materita

Antichi Pozzi

MIGLIERA

Belvedere Migliera

Grotta Verde

Cala Marmolata

LIMMO

Faro (Lighthouse)

Pta. Carena

TYRRHENIAN SEA

VILLA JOVIS

Grotta d. Tiberio

Grotta Meravigliosa

Grotta Bianca

Villa Fersen

LO CAPO

Via Tiberio

MONETA

Arco Naturale

Grotta di Matermania

Grotta d. Massullo

Pta. Massullo

Villa Malaparte

Scoglio del Monacone

Grotta Porto di Tragara

Faraglione di Terra

Pta. di Tragara

Faraglione di Mezzo (Stella)

Belvedere di Tragara

Faraglione di Fuori (Scopolo)

Pta. di Mulo

Pta. di Terita

Cala Ventroso

Pta. Ventroso

CAMPANIA

Benevento
Salerno
Sorrento
NAPLES
Ischia
Capri
TYRRHENIAN SEA

Grotto, Cave
Beach
Footpath

1/2 mi
1/2 km
0

Tragara

Impressions

. . . the creaking and puffing little boat, which had conveyed me only from Sorrento, drew closer beneath the prodigious island—beautiful, horrible and haunted—that does most, of all the happy elements and accidents, towards making the Bay of Naples, for the study of composition, a lesson in the grand style.

—Henry James, *Italian Hours,* 1909

with a belvedere affording great views. Continuing on Viale Matteotti, you'll reach the **Giardini di Augusto,** the public gardens with terraces from which you can enjoy some of the best **scenic vistas** 😊😊 in Capri.

From the town of Capri you can walk to the northeastern tip of the island—about 2.4km (1½ miles)—to **Villa Jovis** 😊😊, the best-preserved of the 12 villas built on the island by Roman emperors (Augustus, but especially the depraved Tiberius). Here and in his other abodes on the island—one for each of the most important gods of the Roman pantheon, Tiberius pursued illicit pleasures away from the prying eyes of the Roman Senate. The Villa Jovis—his main residence—covered over 5,853 sq. m (63,000 sq. ft.), including a glorious loggia, known as the **Loggia Imperiale,** a promenade on the edge of the cliff. The views from the villa are, to put it mildly, fit for an emperor of even the most jaded tastes (Viale Amedeo Maiuri; www.villajovis.it; 2€/$2.50; daily 9am–sunset; ticket booth closes 1 hr. early).

MARINA GRANDE

This, the largest harbor on the island, is where you'll land upon arriving in Capri. The village seems unspectacular and might even appear a bit drab, especially in comparison to the rest of the island. However, if you take the time to explore, you will find **San Costanzo** 😊, the oldest church on the island, dating back to the 5th century. Interestingly, when the church was enlarged in the 14th century, its orientation was turned 90 degrees so that the original apse can still be discerned in the right nave. A bit farther to the west are the ruins of the **Palazzo a Mare,** another of the Roman palaces on the island, followed by the **Bagni di Tiberio,** one of the island's best beaches (see later in this chapter).

MARINA PICCOLA 😊😊

This small harbor sits in a perfect position to overlook the famous **Faraglioni,** a collection of spiky, rocky structures that jut out of the sea a short distance from the coast (these grace most pictures of Capri). The structures are indeed very impressive; we like enjoying them from one of the beach clubs lining the bay on either side of the village of Marina Piccola. The stretch of beach to the east of the village is **Marina di Pennaulo** and the one to the west is **Marina di Mulo;** both were a favorite haunt for the jet-set in the 1950s and 1960s.

ANACAPRI 😊😊

Perched on the higher part of the island among hills and vineyards, Anacapri is just a hair-raising bus ride away. The trip along the cliff road is exhilarating in more ways than the treacherous driving, though. Off the main square of this pleasant village—**Piazza della Vittoria**—you can take **Via San Michele,** a picturesque street leading to **Villa San Michele** 😊 (© **081-8371401;** www.sanmichele.org; 5€/$6.25; Mar 9:30am–4:30pm,

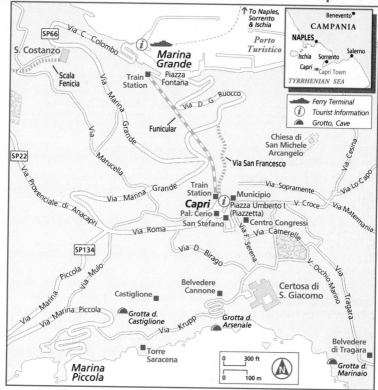

Apr 9:30am–5pm, May–Sept 9am–6pm, Oct 9:30am–5:30pm, Nov–Dec 10:30am–3:30pm), the home of the Swedish doctor and writer Axel Munthe, which was built in the 19th century and adapted from the ruins of a nearby villa. (The gardens are beautiful here, and the views from the terrace are superb.) Nearby is the **Church of San Michele,** with its beautiful **majolica floor** ✸.

If you long for still greater heights and thrills, from Piazza della Vittoria you can get a chairlift (Via Caposcuro 10; ✆ **081-8371428;** 4€/$5 one-way and 5.50€/$6.90 round-trip; Mar–Oct 9:30am–sunset; Nov–Feb 10:30am–3pm) to the top of **Monte Solaro** ✸✸, Capri's highest peak. The trip takes only 12 minutes, and the panorama from the top—particularly on a clear day—encompasses the whole stretch of coast and sea, including Mount Vesuvius and the two gulfs, Naples and Salerno.

Below Anacapri is the island's most famous attraction, the **Grotta Azzurra (Blue Grotto)** ✸✸. The magical colors of the water and walls of this huge grotto are indeed extraordinary, and writers have rhapsodized about it at length since its so-called "discovery" in the 19th century—discovery by foreign tourists, that is. In fact, the grotto was known since antiquity; on its southwestern corner, the Galleria dei Pilastri shows the remains of a small, ancient Roman dock. The Gallery is part of what appears to be a vast system of only partially explored caverns.

Unfortunately, this doesn't mean that you'll have a chance to explore on your own—especially if you come at the height of the season. During this period, motorboats line up outside the grotto, waiting for small rowboats—the only vessels allowed inside—to squeeze a few passengers at a time under the grotto's narrow opening (due to the sinking of the whole complex, the aperture now extends only about 1m/3 ft. above sea level). Because of the long lines, you'll be allowed inside the grotto only for a few minutes. Kids will love the adventure, conjuring up visions of secret pirate expeditions, but adults might find the experience wearisome, given the little time allotted for appreciating the grotto.

The grotto is open daily 9am to 1 hour before sunset; admission is 4€ ($5). The rowboats that take you inside—unless you want to swim in, which technically is allowed but not recommended—charge 4.50€ ($5.65). If you are taking a boat tour from Marina Grande instead, you'll pay about 17€ ($21) all-inclusive. Authorities have stepped in to prevent rip-offs but have forgotten to update prices with the cost of living, which has created some discontent among boat (especially rowboat) operators, who welcome tips.

STAYING ACTIVE
HIKING
From Capri's dramatic cliffs you can feast your eyes both on sea and land, with views stretching all the way over the Gulf of Naples and Mount Vesuvius, and along the Gulf of Salerno and the Amalfi Coast. Even if you are moderately fit, do not miss the opportunity to hike Capri's cliffs and soak in the beauty of its trails.

Before setting out, stop at the tourist office (see "Visitor Information" above), which can furnish you with a map of the paths.

One of the easiest paths is the short hike from **Capri to Marina Piccola;** from Via Roma in town, turn left onto Via Mulo. A series of steps and a dirt path will lead you down to the village through cultivated fields and gardens. A more demanding hike is the **Scala Fenicia (Fenician Staircase)** ⊛, which descends—or climbs, for the most intrepid—from **Anacapri to Capri.** Built by the Greeks in the 8th century B.C., it was the only access to the sea or to the village of Anacapri until 1877, when the current road was built. The steep path is basically a long staircase with 881 steps, along the slopes of the mountain, rewarding the daring with superb views. You can also climb **Mount Solaro** on a clearly marked dirt path (or descend it after taking the chairlift to the top).

SWIMMING
Capri's marvelous waters afford great swimming, which you can easily do from one of the paying beach clubs (*stabilimenti balneari*). The club will provide you with a changing cabin, towels, and a deck chair. One such place is **Bagni Nettuno** (Via Grotta Azzurra 46; © 081-8371362; 10€/$13; mid-Mar to mid-Nov, 9am–sunset) by the Blue Grotto. Technically, you could swim to the grotto from here, but it is not advisable to do so. If you must, go late in the day and during off season, when there's no boat traffic and the sea is calm (and, of course, go only if you are a strong swimmer). Another good paying club is **Bagni le Sirene** (© 081-8370221; same conditions) in Marina Piccola.

If you're looking for a public swimming spot, one of the better ones is **Bagni di Tiberio** ⊛, a nice, sandy beach accessible on the north side of the island, near the ruins of one of Emperor Tiberius's notorious villas. The beach is only about 1km (½ mile) from Marina Grande, but getting there involves a steep and rocky descent that can be arduous on the return leg. We recommend going by boat instead—you can get a passage there and back for 6€ ($7.50) from Marina Grande.

The best swimming in the area, though, is from a boat or at one of the rare but delightful small coves hidden among the cliffs and accessible only from the sea. From either of the two harbors (Marina Piccola or Marina Grande), you can hire a small boat to take you for a swim or to a secluded beach almost away from the tourist crowds; the fare is about 8€ ($10) per trip.

WHERE TO STAY

Capri offers a large number of accommodations in a wide range of styles and prices. As a rule of thumb, accommodations in Anacapri tend to be cheaper but also quieter than those in glitzier Capri town.

CAPRI
Very Expensive

Grand Hotel Quisisana ✦✦✦   This luxurious hotel offers positively mouthwatering accommodations and top-flight service. Built in the 19th century as a sanatorium (hence the name *qui si sana,* "here we heal"), it has become a favorite of all those who feel in need of pampering and can afford it. Guest rooms open onto wide arcades with superb views, and come in different decors ranging from modern to traditional, all with stylish details. The large bathrooms are done in marble or with designer tiles. Even if you don't stay here, come for an after-dinner drink at one of the elegant bars on the premises.

Via Camerelle 2, 80073 Capri. ✆ 081-8370788. Fax 081-8376080. www.quisi.com. 150 units. 250€–490€ ($313–$613) double; from 700€ ($875) suite. Rates include buffet breakfast. Specials available off season. Children under 3 stay free in parent's room. AE, DC, MC, V. Closed Nov to mid-Mar. **Amenities:** 2 restaurants; 3 bars; 2 outdoor pools; outdoor tennis courts; health club; spa; concierge; room service; babysitting; laundry service. *In room:* A/C, TV, dataport, minibar, hair dryer, safe.

Expensive

Hotel Punta Tragara ✦✦   Standing high on a cliff overlooking one of the best panoramas in Capri, this hotel is in a quiet location slightly away from the heart of things in Capri. Originally a luxurious private villa, it was designed by one of the greatest architects of the 20th century, Le Corbusier. Guest rooms have large windows and open onto private terraces or balconies. They feature modern furnishings, spacious bathrooms, and a restful ambience.

Via Tragara 57, 80073 Capri. ✆ 081-8370844. Fax 081-8377790. www.hoteltragara.com. 45 units. 300€–360€ ($375–$450) double; 400€–500€ ($500–$625) suite. Rates include buffet breakfast. Children under 3 stay free in parent's room. AE, DC, MC, V. Closed Nov–Easter. **Amenities:** 2 restaurants; lounge; nightclub; 2 outdoor pools; health club; concierge; salon; room service; babysitting; laundry service. *In room:* A/C, TV, minibar, hair dryer, iron, safe.

Luna Hotel ✦   This upscale and modern hotel enjoys a choice cliff-top location and offers luxurious accommodations and attentive service. Guest rooms are quiet and elegantly furnished with a mixture of pieces and styles. Bathrooms are spacious and tiled. Most rooms have private terraces overlooking the cliffs or the hotel's beautiful gardens.

Viale Matteotti 3, 80073 Capri. ✆ 081-8370433. Fax 081-8377459. www.lunahotel.com. 54 units. 170€–380€ ($213–$475) double; 440€ ($550) suite. Rates include breakfast. Children under 3 stay free in parent's room. AE, DC, MC, V. Closed mid-Oct to Easter. **Amenities:** Restaurant; lounge; outdoor pool; health club; spa; concierge; room service; babysitting; laundry service. *In room:* A/C, TV, minibar, hair dryer, safe.

Moderate

Hotel Certosella *(Finds*   This family-run small hotel is an excellent alternative to the island's more lavish resorts. The good-sized rooms are comfortable and furnished with care; most of them have sea views and private terraces. Bathrooms are not small, and a number of them even have Jacuzzis. The hotel is surrounded by a nicely kept garden with a pool.

Via Tragara 13, 80073 Capri (NA). ⓒ 081-8370713. Fax 081-8376113. www.certosella.com. 18 units. 170€–260€ ($213–$325) double. Rates include buffet breakfast. Children under 3 free in parent's room. AE, MC, V. **Amenities:** Restaurant; bar; outdoor pool; room service; babysitting; laundry service. *In room:* A/C, TV, minibar, hair dryer, safe.

Hotel Gatto Bianco *(Value)*

This is a good, family-run hotel, surrounded by greenery and moderate in price (for Capri). Guest rooms are large and well appointed, with pretty tiled floors and color-coordinated furnishings; they have either balconies or terraces. The relaxed vibe extends to the garden terrace, where breakfast is served when the weather's nice.

Via Vittorio Emanuele 32, 80073 Capri. ⓒ 081-8370203. Fax 081-8378060. www.gattobianco-capri.com. 20 units. 195€–220€ ($244–$275) double; 225€–325€ ($281–$406) suite. Rates include buffet breakfast. Specials available. Children under 3 stay free in parent's room. AE, DC, MC, V. Closed Nov–Mar. **Amenities:** Lounge; bar; beauty spa; babysitting; laundry service. *In room:* A/C, satellite TV, minibar, hair dryer, safe.

Hotel La Minerva

This cute family-run hotel with fewer than 20 units offers quiet accommodations and personal service just steps from the center of Capri. The bright, spacious guest rooms, pleasantly furnished in Mediterranean style, have beautiful hand-painted tiled floors, vaulted passages, and flowered terraces. Most rooms also have delightful views over the sea.

Via Occhio Marino 8, 80073 Capri. ⓒ 081-8377067. Fax 081-8375221. www.laminervacapri.com. 19 units. 150€–270€ ($188–$338) double; low season 110€–210€ ($138–$263) double. Rates include buffet breakfast. Children under 3 stay free in parent's room. AE, DC, MC, V. Closed Jan–Feb. **Amenities:** Bar; babysitting; laundry service. *In room:* A/C, TV, minibar, hair dryer, safe.

Villa Brunella *(Finds)*

Set in a panoramic position, this was a private villa until 1963, when it was transformed into its current incarnation as a pleasant family-run hotel. Guest rooms have a welcoming atmosphere and each double has its own flowered terrace or balcony with a sea view. Bathrooms are modest in size but come decorated with modern fixtures and designer tiles.

Via Tragara 24, 80073 Capri. ⓒ 081-8370122. Fax 081-8370430. www.villabrunella.it. 20 units. 240€–285€ ($300–$356) double; 320€–370€ ($400–$463) suite. Rates include buffet breakfast. Children under 3 stay free in parent's room. AE, DC, MC, V. Closed Nov–Apr. **Amenities:** Restaurant; bar; outdoor pool; room service; laundry service. *In room:* A/C, TV, dataport, minibar, hair dryer, safe.

Inexpensive

Villa Sarah

Located near Capri's orchards and vineyards, this family-run hotel is quiet, friendly, and affordable. Guest rooms vary in size and some are a bit small, but a number of them have private terraces. Only rooms on the upper floor have sea views, but the garden is so refreshing it doesn't really matter. Organic food is offered at breakfast. Book early, because the hotel is often full.

Via Tiberio 3/a, 80073 Capri. ⓒ 081-8377817. Fax 081-8377215. www.villasarah.it. 20 units. 165€–200€ ($206–$250) double. Rates include buffet breakfast. Children under 3 stay free in parent's room. AE, DC, MC, V. Closed Nov–Mar. **Amenities:** Bar; concierge; babysitting; laundry service. *In room:* A/C, TV, minibar, hair dryer, iron, safe.

ANACAPRI
Expensive
Capri Palace *(★★★)*

This is the best hotel in Capri, affording breathtaking views over the island and the gulfs, and absolutely perfect service. Richly decorated with artwork and antiques, it merges classical elegance with modern style, and is surrounded by a lovely landscaped garden. Guest rooms are furnished with taste; some of the comfortable beds come with canopies. The marble or designer tiled bathrooms come with quality linen. The four suites have a private garden with heated private pools. The on-site **Olivo** restaurant is excellent (see below).

Via Capodimonte 2b, 80071 Capri. ℂ **081-9780111.** Fax 081-8373191. www.capri-palace.com. 85 units. 265€–950€ ($331–$1,188) double; from 990€ ($1,238) suite. Rates include buffet breakfast. Specials available during off season. Children under 3 stay free in parent's room. AE, DC, MC, V. Closed Nov–Mar. **Amenities:** 2 restaurants; bar; lounge; outdoor pool; spa; concierge; room service; babysitting; laundry service. *In room:* A/C, TV, minibar, hair dryer, safe.

Moderate

Hotel San Michele ⋆   From its cliff-side location, this hotel affords beautiful views in its public spaces and in many of its guest rooms. Its panoramic garden is graced by the largest pool on Capri. The good-sized guest rooms are pleasantly furnished in a contemporary style and have modern bathrooms.

Via G. Orlandi 1, 80071 Capri. ℂ **081-8371427.** Fax 081-8371420. www.sanmichele-capri.com. 60 units. 150€–200€ ($188–$250) double; 360€ ($450) suite. Rates include breakfast. Children under 3 stay free in parent's room. AE, MC, V. Closed Nov–Mar. **Amenities:** Dining room; bar; large outdoor pool; concierge; room service; babysitting; laundry service. *In room:* A/C, TV, hair dryer, safe.

Inexpensive

Villa Carmencita *(Finds)*   This carefully kept, small modern hotel opens onto its private garden and is located in the modern part of Anacapri. It boasts comfortable and quiet accommodations at moderate rates. The spacious guest rooms are nicely—if simply—furnished, and come with tiled floors and private balconies. Ask about the interesting boating excursions organized by the hotel.

Viale T. De Tommaso 4, 80071 Capri. ℂ **081-8371360.** Fax 081-8373009. carmencita@capri.it. 20 units. 99€–147€ ($124–$184) double. Children under 3 stay free in parent's room. AE, DC, MC, V. Closed Nov–Mar. **Amenities:** Babysitting. *In room:* A/C, TV.

WHERE TO DINE

CAPRI

Expensive

La Cantinella ⋆ NEAPOLITAN   Near the Giardini di Augusto, this restaurant, housed in a beautiful 18th-century villa with scenic views, combines delectable cuisine with warm, professional service. Its menu changes daily but always includes seafood, meat, and vegetarian choices. You might find excellent *paccheri con frutti di mare e rucola* (fresh homemade largish pasta with shellfish and arugula) or superb *pezzogna al sale* (local fish baked in a salt crust). Desserts are always homemade and delicious.

Viale Matteotti 8, Capri. ℂ **081-8370616.** Reservations required for dinner. Secondi 21€–35€ ($26–$44). AE, DC, MC, V. Wed–Mon 12:30–3pm and 7:30pm–12:30am.

Moderate

Al Grottino ⋆ CAPRESE/NEAPOLITAN   Serving seafood and other Neapolitan specialties since 1937, this restaurant was a preferred hangout for VIPs in the 1950s. The food is still good, and you can choose from a variety of traditional Neapolitan comfort food, such as *frittura* (medley of deep-fried seafood) and *mozzarella in carrozza* (deep-fried mozzarella)—prepared in four different ways Excellent Caprese specialties are *zuppa di cozze* (a bean-and-mussel soup) and *ravioli alla caprese* (with fresh mozzarella and basil).

Via Longano 27, Capri. ℂ **081-8370584.** Reservations required for dinner. Secondi 12€–20€ ($15–$25). AE, MC, V. Daily noon–3pm and 7pm–midnight. Closed Nov–Mar.

Casanova ⭐ NEAPOLITAN/CAPRESE   Just a few steps from the *piazzetta,* this restaurant offers high-quality food at moderate prices. The setting is pleasant, with a more formal dining room and a tavern. You will find it hard not to fill yourself at the antipasti buffet, but save room for the fresh pasta (particularly the ravioli) and some special secondi, such as *totanetti affogati* (baby squid stewed in herbs and wine). The menu includes both meat and seafood. The excellent wine cellar holds a good selection of local wines.

Via Le Botteghe 46, just off Piazza Umberto, Capri. ⓒ 081-8377642. Reservations required for dinner. Secondi 11€–25€ ($14–$31). AE, DC, MC, V. Daily noon–3pm and 7–11pm. Closed Dec to mid-Mar.

La Colombaia del Grand Hotel Quisisana ⭐ CAPRESE   Even if hotel dining is not your thing, this romantic restaurant is worth trying. Housed in a gazebo in the Quisisana (p. 235) hotel's garden, it offers good, moderately priced food in a delightful setting. The service is what you'd expect from a luxury hotel (read: exceptional), and the simple menu includes local favorites such as *spaghetti ai frutti di mare* (with shellfish), *insalata caprese* (*mozzarella di bufala,* fresh tomatoes, and basil), and great desserts such as delicious *torta caprese* and *millefoglie* (cream napoleon).

Via Camerelle 2. ⓒ 081-8370788. Reservations recommended on weekend evenings. Secondi 15€–21€ ($19–$26). AE, DC, MC, V. Daily noon–3pm and 7–11pm.

Inexpensive

La Cisterna (Value) CAPRESE/PIZZA   This small, unpretentious restaurant serves well-prepared pizza and traditional dishes at very low prices. The menu varies but portions are always generous; you might find *lasagne verdi* (green lasagna), *zuppa di pesce* (seafood stew), *frittura* (deep-fried seafood), and the market choice of seafood served charbroiled or *all'acqua pazza* (poached in a light herb broth).

Via Madre Serafina 5. ⓒ 081-8375620. Reservations required. Pizza 4€–8€ ($5–$10). Secondi 7.50€–14€ ($9.40–$18). AE, DC, MC, V. Daily noon–3:30pm and 7pm–midnight; 11:30am–2pm and 6:30–11pm in winter.

La Pergola CAPRESE   Come here when the weather's nice—this pleasant and welcoming restaurant offers delightful alfresco dining in its private garden. The menu offers traditional local dishes like *spaghetti alle vongole* (with fresh clams), as well as local fish like *pezzogna all'acqua pazza* (a delicious fish in a light tomato sauce) and charbroiled swordfish.

Via Traversa Lo Palazzo 2. ⓒ 081-8377414. Reservations recommended. Secondi 11€–18€ ($14–$23). AE, DC, MC, V. Thurs–Tues 12:30–3pm and 7:30–11pm; daily in summer. Closed mid-Nov to Dec 25.

ANACAPRI
Expensive

Olivo of the Capri Palace ⭐⭐⭐ CAPRESE/CREATIVE   Housed in the most elegant hotel in Capri (see above), this is also the best restaurant on the island and in fact one of the best in the whole region. Chef Oliver Glowig keeps improving his already wonderful culinary feats with ever-changing seasonal menus. You will find both traditional dishes—such as an excellent version of *ravioli caprese* (mozzarella ravioli with tomatoes and basil)—and more creative ones, which are definitely the way to go for a special dinner. You can try these through a tasting menu *(menu degustazione)*—there's even a low-calorie one—or a la carte. Among the most tantalizing dishes are *gamberi rossi con asparagi e salsa alle mele verdi* (red king shrimp with asparagus and green apples), and *rombo in crosta di mandorle con purea di patate e porri in salsa all'Aglianico* (almond-crusted turbot with leek-and-potato puree and an Aglianico reduction sauce). A true delicacy is *penne con ragù di bufalo e cipolle rosse al pecorino di fossa* (short pasta with a sauce of buffalo, red onions, tomato sauce, and sharp sheep's cheese matured in a cave). Try one of the imaginative desserts for a grand finale—*zuppa di albicocche alle spezie con gelato alle mandorle* (spiced apricots with almond ice cream) is particularly good. The wine list, as you would expect at such a superior place, is extensive. The outdoor dining area is absolutely delightful.

Via Capodimonte 2b, Capri. ℂ 081-9780111. Reservations required. Secondi 25€–36€ ($31–$45). AE, DC, MC, V. Daily noon–3pm and 7–11pm. Closed Nov–Mar but open 10 days for New Year's.

Inexpensive

Rondinella ⭐ CAPRESE/PIZZA   This family-run restaurant is a good choice if you're after relaxation and quiet. They prepare many varieties of brick-oven pizza. Otherwise, the regular menu is traditional and you will find an excellent rendition of *ravioli alla caprese* (mozzarella, fresh tomatoes, and basil); *pezzogna all'acqua pazza* (local fish in a light tomato sauce); and *frittura* (deep-fried seafood medley), which they prepare particularly well. For dessert, local specialties such as *torta caprese* (almond cake) are excellent.

Via G. Orlandi 245, Anacapri. ℂ 081-8371223. Reservations required for dinner. Secondi 11€–16€ ($14–$20). AE, DC, MC, V. Daily noon–3pm and 7–11pm. Closed 2 weeks in Feb.

SHOPPING FOR LOCAL CRAFTS ⭐⭐

Dedicated shoppers will lose themselves in Capri's little shops. Many of the island's visitors return just to buy more of the locally made goods, especially the sandals and the jewelry.

One of the most famous shopping stops is **Carthusia**, a perfume maker that counts many stars among its customers. Its **laboratory** (Viale Parco Augusto; ℂ 081-8370368; daily 9:30am–6pm) has been concocting unique perfumes from local herbs and flowers since 1948. There are two outlets on the island, one in Capri (Via Camerelle 10; ℂ 081-8370368), and one in Anacapri (Via Capodimonte 26; ℂ 081-8373668). Both are closed from November to March.

Stylish sandals (handmade, of course) can be found at **Canfora** (Via Camerelle 3; ℂ 081-8370487) in Capri, and at **L'Arte del Sandalo Caprese** (Via Orlando 75; ℂ 081-8373583) in Anacapri.

Finally, the island has an old jewelry-making tradition. You can admire—and purchase—fine examples at **La Perla Gioielli** (Piazza Umberto I 21; ℂ 081-8370641).

9

Salerno, Paestum & the Cilento

Salerno is the last (or the first, depending on your approach) stop on the Amalfi Coast, and the largest town of southern Campania. The refuge of artists for centuries past, it's still very much a hideaway today. Though it remains mostly undiscovered, it has an abundance of artistic, historic, and cultural offerings for those who do make the trip.

Salerno also stands at the door of the Cilento, one of Italy's best-guarded secrets. Covering most of the southern part of Campania, this region offers breathtakingly beautiful hills and valleys, and a splendid coast where cliffs and promontories protect wonderful beaches

overlooking crystal-clear waters. The best part of the Cilento has been made into a protected national park, the second-largest national park in Italy. Cilento was also the area where the ancient Greeks built some of their most important colonies, whose grandeur is still visible in the unique ruins of Paestum.

This region is popular with Italians during the summer, but you'll encounter mostly locals here the rest of the year. Foreign tourists usually see the temples of Paestum and move on, completely missing out on the Cilento's wild interior, scenic shores, and wonderful cuisine.

1 Salerno

55km (34 miles) SE of Naples.

The most important harbor of Campania after Naples, Salerno used to be the region's capital. It is often overlooked by those in haste to run off to Amalfi, Positano, or Paestum. But to overlook this area would be a mistake. This laid-back—and even a bit provincial—town is rich in history, culture, and beauty. Surrounded by scenic mountains and opening onto the bay, some say (and we agree) that its *lungomare* (seafront) is the most beautiful on this coast; the lack of crowds makes it all that much more enjoyable than Sorrento's more famous coast. Of course, there are trade-offs. Salerno is far larger than any town on the Amalfi Coast (though far smaller than Naples), a bustling modern Italian city of 150,000 people. Virtually every square inch of tiny Amalfi is picturesque, which can't be said of Salerno's 60 sq. km (23 sq. miles). On the other hand, Salerno has many beauties, and for the most part you won't be sharing them with foreign tourists but with Italians.

The medieval heart of Salerno is very picturesque. An Etruscan and Campanian town founded around the 6th century B.C., Salerno was absorbed into Magna Gracca, the Greek colonial possessions in southern Italy and Sicily. It became a Roman colony in 194 B.C. Over time, it acquired greater importance as Paestum (located farther south) declined in prestige, and it eventually became an independent principality under the Longobards in the 9th century A.D. It emerged as an important cultural center in

Salerno

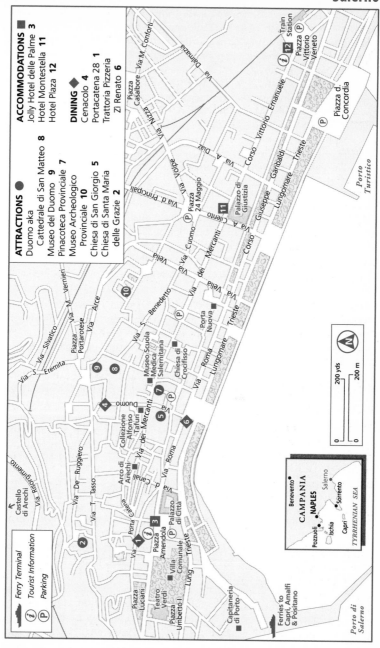

ATTRACTIONS ●
Duomo aka
  Cattedrale di San Matteo **8**
Museo del Duomo **9**
Pinacoteca Provinciale **7**
Museo Archeologico
  Provinciale **10**
Chiesa di San Giorgio **5**
Chiesa di Santa Maria
  delle Grazie **2**

ACCOMMODATIONS ■
Jolly Hotel delle Palme **3**
Hotel Montestella **11**
Hotel Plaza **12**

DINING ◆
Cenacolo **4**
Portacatena 28 **1**
Trattoria Pizzeria
  Zi Renato **6**

Ferry Terminal
i Tourist Information
Ⓟ Parking

0   200 yds
0   200 m

241

medieval and Renaissance times, and its renowned medical school (Scuola Medica Salernitana) paved the way in the establishment of modern medicine.

The principality passed successively to Normans, Swabians, Angevins, and then Bourbons, but in the meantime its political and cultural importance declined in proportion as Naples's power increased. Salerno sank back into the quiet life of a smallish provincial town until World War II, when it became the capital of Allied-controlled Italy. Unfortunately, the severe bombing in the months during military operations caused enormous destruction. The reconstruction and expansion that followed gave the town its modern look, especially to the southeast and northeast of the seafront. Luckily, much of the medieval part of town and the 19th-century waterfront were preserved. Since the 1990s, these areas have been the focus of a successful restoration and valorization campaign, which has brought the old sections of Salerno back to their original splendor.

ESSENTIALS

GETTING THERE   By Train   You can easily reach Salerno by train from anywhere in Italy and abroad, since it is a major stop on the Reggio Calabria line from Rome. Service from Naples is very frequent; trains leave every 10 to 30 minutes. It's cheap as well: the 35-minute ride to Salerno costs only 5.40€ ($6.75). Don't expect a view of the Amalfi Coast on the way down, however. Because of the steepness of the coast, the train line passes well inland.

By Bus   SITA (© **089-226604** or 089-405145) maintains regular bus service between Salerno and Naples; buses leave about every half-hour. You can purchase tickets from the **Bar Cioffi** (Corso Garibaldi 134) in front of the bus stop. Frequent service is also available for the Amalfi Coast and the Sorrento peninsula, with buses leaving from Piazza Vittorio Veneto every hour.

Bus lines operated by the town transportation authority **CSTP** (© **800-016659;** toll-free within Italy, or 089-487001; www.cstp.it) connect Salerno with Paestum and the National Park of the Cilento (line no. 34 from Piazza della Concordia). For Pompeii, use line nos. 4 and 50 from Salerno's Piazza Vittorio Veneto. It takes an hour to get from Salerno to Pompeii, and just slightly more than that to get from Salerno to Paestum. Getting to the Cilento can take up to 4 hours, depending on where you are going. For example, Agropoli, at the near end of the Cilento, is only 1 hour and 20 minutes from Salerno.

By Ferry   Travel by ferry is our favorite means of transportation, especially in the summer, when roads tend to be crowded. Salerno is a major harbor and you will find that ferries travel not only to the major destinations in Campania—Naples, Ischia, Capri, Amalfi, Positano, and Sorrento—but also to other ports in the Mediterranean. **Alicost** (© **089-234892** or 089-227979) runs both ferry and hydrofoil service from **Molo Manfredi** in downtown Salerno to and from Amalfi, Capri, and Ischia, with stops in Positano, Minori, and Sorrento. Fares run between 1.50€ ($1.90) and 14€ ($18) depending on the distance, and you must make reservations at least 24 hours in advance. **Metrò del Mare** (© **199-446644;** www.metrodelmare.com) operates two lines—the express line MM2 and the local line MM3 between **Molo Beverello** in Naples and Molo Manfredi in Salerno, with stops in Amalfi and Positano. The service runs April through September. The express line MM2 takes about 2 hours. A special ticket called **Terra&Mare** costs 8.50€ ($11). The ride includes the ferry plus ground transportation for the 45 minutes before and 45 minutes after the ferry link.

In addition, **Caronte & Tourist** (© 800-627414; toll-free within Italy or 089-2582528; www.carontetourist.it) travels from Salerno to Catania and Messina, while **Grimaldi Ferries** (© 081-496444; www.grimaldi-ferries.com) travels from Salerno to Malta (La Valletta), Tunis, Valencia in Spain, and Palermo in Sicily. Call or check the websites for price and schedule information.

Travelmar (© 089-2227979) offers regular service to the Amalfi Coast (six daily runs to Amalfi and Positano, with two stopping also in Minori) from Piazza della Concordia. For Capri, there are two daily runs from the Molo Manfredi in the commercial harbor. **Alicost** (© 089-873301) offers regular hydrofoil service from Molo Manfredi: two daily runs to Capri, three to Amalfi and Positano, and one to Ischia.

By Car Salerno is an easy drive from most destinations in Campania. From Naples, take the A3 autostrada marked NAPOLI-SALERNO. This highway ends at Salerno, so there is no difficulty knowing where to exit. Follow signs for the city center.

GETTING AROUND Although large compared to the compact towns of the Amalfi Coast, Salerno is actually a moderately sized town stretching along its waterfront. The town has a good **public bus** stystem run by **CSTP** (© 800-016659 toll-free within Italy, or 089-487111; www.cstp.it); most bus lines start or pass by Piazza Vittorio and the train station. Of course, **taxis** are another excellent resource (see "Fast Facts" below). However, distances are not long. You can easily see the town **on foot.** From the train station on **Piazza Vittorio Veneto,** the pedestrian street and major shopping strip begins: **Corso Vittorio Emanuele.** At its end, it leads into **Via dei Mercanti,** at the heart of Salerno's medieval center (see later in this chapter). Parallel to it towards the sea are **Corso Garibaldi/Via Roma** and the famous seafront promenade, **Lungomare Trieste.**

VISITOR INFORMATION The **AACST tourist office** for Salerno is at Via Roma 258 (© 089-224744). The tourist office for the whole province, including the Cilento, is the **EPT** of Salerno (Via Velia 15, 84100 Salerno; © 089-230411; www.crmpa.it/ept). They also maintain an office in Piazza Vittorio Veneto, at the train station (© 089-614259), which is open Monday to Saturday from 9am to 2pm and 3 to 8pm (until 7pm in winter). In advance of your visit, you can check out what's going on in Salerno at www.salernocity.com.

FAST FACTS You'll find the pharmacy **Farmacia del Leone** (© 089-231439) at Corso Vittorio Emanuele 223. The **hospital Ruggiero d'Aragona** is on Via San Leonardo (© 089-67111). For an **ambulance**, dial © 118. Dial © 113 for the police or an ambulance, © 115 for the fire department, and © 116 for ACI road assistance. You will find several banks and **ATMs** in Salerno along Corso Vittorio Emanuele; a convenient one is the branch (with ATM) of the **Banca Nazionale del Lavoro** in the train station. The main **post office**—housed in a majestic building—is at Corso Garibaldi 203 and is open Monday to Saturday from 8am to 2pm. There are taxi stands in front of the railway station (© 089-229947); Piazza Amendola (© 089-229963);a and Piazza XXIV Maggio (© 089-229171); or you can call **Radiotaxi** Salerno at © 089-757575.

SPECIAL EVENTS The **Salerno Film Festival Linea d'ombra (Salerno Film Festival of the Shadow Line)** ✦ is a major international event, dedicated to new talents in Europe and focusing on the theme of the passage from adolescence to adulthood—the "shadow line" of maturation, a term coined by Joseph Conrad and taken as the fesitval's motto. The festival (Piazza Sant'Agostino 13, 84121 Salerno; © 089-2753673;

fax 089-2571125; www.shadowline.it) is now an annual weeklong event that takes place in April; it celebrated its 10th year in April 2005. Besides films, it includes a number of interesting musical events.

Another important festival is **Salerno Etnica (Ethnic Salerno),** a music festival focusing on music as an expression of culture and tradition. It is held in September during the celebration for Salerno's patron saint, San Matteo (in Piazza Alfano I, in front of the cathedral; and in Piazza Amendola); admission is free. Contact the tourist office for a schedule of events.

During the Ravello Music Festival (see chapter 7), concerts are also held in the monastery of Santa Maria della Mercede in Salerno; contact the Festival office for a schedule of events.

EXPLORING SALERNO

Prepare yourself for a surprise once you get to the **Lungomare** ✹✹✹, one of Campania's best-kept secrets. Lined with palm trees and opening onto the seascape of the Costiera Amalfitana and Cilentina, this is the most beautiful seafront promenade in the whole region—and one of the best in Italy. Also, thanks to a large restoration project, the waterfront was completely pedestrianized in 1990.

At the Lungomare's western end is the **Villa Comunale** (Piazza Amendola, between Lungomare Trieste and Via Roma), a pleasant and orderly public garden dominated in the background by the **Castello di Arechi.** This castle (Via Benedetto Croce; ✆ **089-233900;** www.castellodiarechi.it; free admission; daily 7am–noon and 4–7:30pm) was originally built by the Byzantines, probably over older fortifications, and took on its current aspect in the 16th century, under Spanish rule. Now housing special events, it's worth a visit for its panorama. It can be reached by car or taxi, or on foot—a steep 40-minute climb along a pedestrian ramp.

Opening onto the western side of the Villa Comunale is the **Teatro Verdi** ✹ (Piazza Luciani; ✆ **089-662141;** daily 8am–2pm and 4–8pm), the historic theater inaugurated on April 15, 1872, with *Rigoletto* by Giuseppe Verdi. A recent restoration has brought the beautiful baroque and neoclassical decorations back to life, including the magnificent hall with its frescoed ceiling by Domenico Morelli, and the bronze of musician Pergolesi from a plaster sculpture by Giovan Battista Amendola. The theater hosts many important concerts and performances (see later in this chapter).

The medieval heart of town begins across from Teatro Verdi; it's the second main reason to visit Salerno after the Lungomare. The exclusive shopping street **Via di Porta Catena** leads into charming **Piazza Sedile del Campo,** the medieval market square, graced by the beautiful **Fontana dei Delfini (Fountain of the Dolfins)** ✹ and the **Palazzo dei Genovesi** (at no. 3)—today a school—with its grand **portal** ✹. Off the square in Via Roteprandi you'll find the **Sant'Andrea de Lama** church—one of the oldest medieval buildings in Salerno—with its pretty 12th-century bell tower and, a few steps farther, the even older **Sant'Alfonso** church (10th c.), with recently restored Longobard frescoes inside.

Also off the square, **Via dei Mercanti** ✹ begins. Today, as in medieval times, it is the town's major shopping street. This is where you'll find some of the best boutiques and most elegant stores in town. Off to the left is the **Vicolo dei Sartori** with the **Palazzo Fruscione** ✹, notable for its medieval decorations, including a pretty loggia and intertwined arches. Not far off, on Vicolo Adalberga, is the ancient **Palatine San Pietro a Corte** church ✹. Its 11th-century frescoes have survived, and excavations have revealed successive strata from the modern period to the Roman baths below.

Farther along Via dei Mercanti is the 10th-century **Chiesa del Crocifisso** ⚜⚜ (Piazza Matteotti 1; ℂ **089-233716**; daily 9am–noon and 4–7pm), famous for its beautiful 13th-century **frescoes** in the main and right apses of the crypt. One depicts the Crucifixion and the other three saints; this fresco is reproduced in mosaics over the main altar of the church above.

Duomo/Cattedrale di San Matteo ⚜⚜⚜ One of Italy's most important medieval churches, the Duomo was built in 1076 and consecrated in 1085, after the rediscovery of the relics of Saint Matthew the Evangelist. Restructured several times, its interior is filled with mosaics, paintings, and other important art pieces. What you see from the square is the Facciata dell'Atrio (Facade of the Atrium) with, to its right, the **Sala San Lazzaro** divided into two naves. They are believed to have been the Main Hall of the **Scuola Medica Salernitana** (**Salerno Medical School**). A 17th-century staircase leads to the 11th-century Romanesque portal known as **Porta dei Leoni,** with its finely carved architrave. Beyond is the elegant **Atrium** ⚜, surrounded by a portico decorated with stone and tufa intarsia and dominated by the Romanesque **bell tower** ⚜⚜. The tower dates from the first half of the 12th century and is 56m (184 ft.) high. (You can get a better view of the bell tower from Via Roberto il Giscardo, to the right of the Duomo.) Under the portico is a rich collection of Roman sarcophagi and a number of medieval tombs; to the right of the Duomo's facade, a door leads to the adjacent street and the **Museo del Duomo** (see below). The **central portal** of the Duomo's actual facade is beautifully carved, and is closed by two **bronze doors** ⚜⚜ cast in 1099 in Constantinople.

The interior—a Latin cross with three naves—was gravely damaged in the earthquake of 1688, and more of the original decoration was lost during 18th-century restoration. An amazing quantity of impressive artwork still exists, however. In the central nave are two magnificent **ambones** ⚜⚜⚜; the smaller is from the 12th century and the larger, with the monumental **candle holder** ⚜ in front, is from the 13th century. The 13th-century ambone has 12 red and gray granite columns blossoming with birds, figures, and vegetation. On the ambone's facade, note the remarkable mosaic showing a sinner with a snake biting him in the breast, and an eagle digging his talons into the unfortunate sinner's head. Both ambones are attached to the choir, which is also extremely ornate: the sides glow with mosaics from 1175, as does the floor, whose mosaics date from 1181.

The right apse is the **Cappella delle Crociate (Chapel of the Crusades)** ⚜⚜, where the Crusaders had their weapons blessed before leaving for the Holy Land. Fine 13th-century mosaics and later frescoes cover the walls and ceiling. Conserved under the altar are the remains of the famous Pope Gregorio VII, who died in exile in Salerno in 1085.

The rest of the church holds other important art and Roman, medieval, and Renaissance funerary monuments. In the left nave, you can view the grandiose **Monument of the Queen Margherita Durazzo** ⚜⚜ by Antonio Baboccio da Piperno and Alessio di Vico of 1435. Below the cathedral is the baroque crypt, holding relics of saints. Piazza Alfano I. ℂ **089-231387**. Daily 10am–6pm. Free admission.

Museo del Duomo ⚜⚜ This museum holds an important collection of local art, starting from the Roman period and extending to the 18th century. One of the most impressive rooms is the one holding the ivory collection. It has a number of beautiful carvings, but the greatest of all is the 12th-century *paliotto* (altar front) ⚜⚜⚜, with

54 carved scenes by different artists—of the four missing frames, one is in the Louvre in Paris, one in Berlin, one in Budapest, and the last in the Met in New York. In the other rooms are several other important pieces, including paintings and bas-reliefs from the 16th century, and paintings by such artists as Andrea Vaccaro, Luca Giordano, Jusepe de Ribera, and Francesco Solimena. The museum also has a collection of illuminated manuscripts from the 13th and 14th centuries.

Via Monsignor Monterisi. ℰ 089-239126. Free admission. Daily 9am–6pm.

Pinacoteca Provinciale Housed in the 17th-century Palazzo Pinto, this picture gallery holds, in addition to the palace's original collection, the most important paintings found in Salerno's abandoned or ruined churches and buildings—works of art dating from the 15th to the 18th centuries—and a number of later paintings. The best pieces are the 15th-century triptych of the *Madonna in Trono tra i Santi Francesco, Bernardino, Antonio e Ludovico;* and the 16th-century polyptych by Andrea Sabatini da Salerno of *Madonna delle Grazie e i Santi Antonio, Agostino e Michele Arcangelo.* The gallery holds paintings by Giovanni Battista Caracciolo and Francesco Solimena as well.

Via Mercanti 62. ℰ 089-2583073. www.pinacoteca.provinciasalerno.org. Admission 3€ ($3.75). Tues–Sat 9am–1pm and 4–7pm; Sun 9am–1pm.

Museo Archeologico Provinciale Tucked away in the beautiful complex of the 11th-century Convent of San Benedetto and the Castelnuovo (a royal palace), and slated to be expanded to the nearby Norman Royal Palace in future years, this museum holds a rich collection stretching from remote archaeological periods—the 11th century B.C.—to Roman times. The objects on display come from excavations in the area of Salerno and its province, down to Palinuro. Special permanent exhibits include Roman Salerno—focusing on the Roman colony; Fratte di Salerno, the pre-Roman town; and pre-Roman ambers, with amber jewels and other objects from the town's early history. If you are interested in archaeology, you'll love the feature that allows you to visit the labs where recent finds are restored and where you can watch the experts at work.

Via S. Benedetto 28. ℰ 089-231135. www.comune.salerno.it. Free admission. Mon–Sat 9am–8pm.

Chiesa di San Giorgio ℱ Built in 1647 over an 8th-century church, this is the most beautiful baroque church in Salerno. An atrium with a carved portal stands in front of the imposing facade, and the interior is typically baroque, with ornate gilded stucco and numerous frescoes and paintings. The fresco cycle depicting the *Passion of Christ* in the cantoria, as well as the *Crucifixion* and *San Benedetto* in the transept, are all by Angelo Solimena. *San Michele* (over the 4th altar to the right) and the frescoes of the large chapel are by Franceso Solimena, and other paintings are by Andrea da Salerno. A beautiful carved wooden pulpit is supported by four lions.

Via Duomo 19. ℰ 089-228918. Daily 9:30am–12:30pm.

Chiesa di Santa Maria delle Grazie This 15th-century church was part of the convent of the Girolamini and, from its terrace outside, you can enjoy a scenic **view** over the town and the bay. Inside, over the main altar, is a beautiful painting by Cristoforo Scacco of 1493 depicting *Madonna delle Grazie.* More paintings and other precious objects are conserved in the tiny museum and picture gallery in the sacristy, highlights of which are *Madonna col Bambino* and *San Francesco* by Andrea Vaccaro.

Largo Luciani 1, off Via De Ruggiero. Daily 9am–noon and 4–7pm. Free admission.

WHERE TO STAY

MODERATE

Jolly Hotel delle Palme ✿✿   Location on the beautiful seaside promenade, within walking distance of both the medieval center and the harbor, makes this the best hotel in town. It's also a very comfortable hotel, with a chain's uniformly polite service and consistent styling. Guest room decor is sober and functional; bathrooms are good-sized and modern. The hotel's restaurant is not bad—the food is good enough, but the atmosphere and ambience are rather bland.

Lungomare Trieste 1, 84121 Salerno. ℂ **089-225222**. Fax 089-237571. www.jollyhotels.it. 104 units. 163€ ($204) double; 230€ ($288) junior suite; low season 124€ ($155) double; 210€ ($263) junior suite. Rates include buffet breakfast. Specials available. Children under 6 stay free in parent's room. AE, DC, MC, V. Free parking. **Amenities:** Restaurant; bar; concierge; business center; room service; babysitting; laundry service. In room: A/C, satellite TV, minibar, hair dryer, safe.

INEXPENSIVE

Hotel K ✿   South of the center of town, in the modern part of Salerno, this recently renovated (in 2004) and welcoming hotel has been proudly run by the Bartoli family since 1964. Housed in a modern building, it overlooks the sea and offers nicely appointed accommodations and good service. The spacious units have contemporary modern furniture and good-sized, tiled bathrooms. Each room has a private balcony overlooking the sea or the hotel's garden-courtyard; some have Jacuzzis and safes. Guests have free access to the hotel's Internet point in the lobby.

Via D. Somma 47, 84129 Salerno. ℂ **089-752720**. Fax 089-725515. www.hotelk.it. 53 units. 95€ ($119) double; 110€ ($138) triple; 113€ ($141) quad. Rates include breakfast. Children under 3 stay free in parent's room. AE, DC, MC, V. Free parking. **Amenities:** Snack bar; bar; concierge; business center; room service; babysitting; laundry service. In room: A/C, TV, minibar.

Hotel Montestella ✿   This family-run hotel, last renovated in 2000, has a very central location in the pedestrian area between the train station and the medieval center. The good-sized guest rooms come with comfortable, modern furnishings. The bathrooms are medium-sized, with new fixtures.

Corso Vittorio Emanuele 156, 84122 Salerno. ℂ **089-225122**. Fax 089-229167. www.hotelmontestella.it. 40 units. 90€ ($113) double. Rates include breakfast. Extra bed 25€ ($31). Specials available. Children under 3 stay free in parent's room. AE, DC, MC, V. Parking: 10€ ($13). **Amenities:** Bar; concierge; room service; babysitting; laundry service. In room: A/C, TV, minibar, safe.

Hotel Plaza   This hotel is housed in a large neoclassical building across from the railway station. Inside, it has been completely modernized, and the decor is modern throughout. The guest rooms are not large; but they are certainly adequate, with simple furnishings, carpeting, and either tubs or showers in the bathrooms.

Piazza Vittorio Veneto 42, 84123 Salerno. ℂ **089-224477**. Fax 089-237311. www.plazasalerno.it. 42 units. 100€ ($125) double. Rates include buffet breakfast. Extra bed 30€ ($38). Children under 3 stay free in parent's room. AE, DC, MC, V. Parking: 12€ ($15). **Amenities:** Bar; concierge; room service; babysitting; laundry service. In room: A/C, satellite TV, minibar, hair dryer, safe.

La Vecchia Quercia   A few miles outside Salerno, on the hills surrounding the town, this *agriturismo* offers an idyllic rural retreat on a farm with a long family history. The few guest rooms and suites are nicely furnished in, of course, country style. The excellent food—served in the elegant dining room of the 18th-century main building—is based completely on local produce and specialties.

Via Montevetrano 4, 84099 San Cipriano Picentino, Località Cantina. ℂ **089-882528**. Fax 089-882010. www.lavecchia quercia.it. 8 units. 100€ ($125) double; from 110€ ($138) suite. Rates include buffet breakfast. Extra bed 25€ ($31).

Children under 3 stay free in parent's room. AE, DC, MC, V. Free parking. Closed mid-Jan to Feb. **Amenities:** Restaurant; bar; babysitting; laundry service. *In room:* A/C, tea kettle, minibar.

WHERE TO DINE

Since it's a lively university town, it's not surprising that Salerno's streets are lined with *pizzerie* and *trattorie,* especially in the medieval center. This can, however, make it difficult to find upscale or formal dining. We've selected the best options below.

MODERATE

Cenacolo ☮☮ SALERNITAN CREATIVE   Located across from the Duomo, this is the best restaurant in Salerno—which might not seem a great achievement in a town that favors cheap eateries, but the food is indeed very good. Owner and chef Pietro Rispoli brings together the best flavors of the region—fresh herbs and vegetables, seafood, local meats, and cheeses—sometimes in new combinations. The menu varies regularly, but you might find *mousse di tonno con composta di pomodori* (tuna mousse with tomato jam), *cavatelli con salsa di zucchine* (a delicious creation of homemade pasta with a sauce of zucchini, lemon peel, anchovies, and local provolone cheese), or *mazzancolle con verdurine grigliate e capperi fritti* (local prawns with grilled garden vegetables and fried capers). The breads and the pastas are exclusively homemade; the wines and cheeses are superb.

Piazza Alfano I 4. ✆ 089-238818. Reservations recommended. Secondi 15€–21€ ($19–$26). AE, DC, MC, V. Tues–Sun 12:30–3pm; Tues–Sat 7:30–11pm. Closed 3 weeks in Aug.

Portacatena 28 *Finds* SALERNITAN CREATIVE   This tiny restaurant in the medieval center of Salerno was recently opened with the ambition of bringing creative

---

Salerno after Dark

If you limit your time in Salerno to the day and only view the lungomare, the principal sights, and all the people rushing to and from work before you head away from town, you'd miss out. As a university town, Salerno could hardly exist without nightlife and places to hang out. The **Bogart Cafe** (Via Rafastia 9; ✆ 089-252288) is a disco on weekends, and at other times it's a place to have a drink or a snack. **Fabula** (Via Porto 1, ✆ 340-1403144) is another popular club which also has live music. Die-hard club aficionados have even been known to drive to **Ciclope,** all the way down at the foot of the Cilento in **Marina di Camerota** (see later in this chapter).

Then, of course, there are Salerno's contributions to the Italian craze for pubs. **Galleon** (Via Roma 254-56; ✆ 089-250938) is a cozy place whose walls are decorated with nautical art and curios. For upscale nightlife, heading the top of the list is the above-mentioned **Teatro Verdi** (Piazza Luciani; ✆ 089-662141; daily 8am–2pm and 4–8pm) which, true to its namesake, is sometimes the venue for Italian opera. It also presents classic or contemporary plays, which won't be interesting if you don't understand Italian. However, musical and dance performances are offered as well. To find out the schedule for the period of your visit, you can check with the **tourist office** or visit **www. salernocity.it.**

cuisine to Salerno's depressed—according to gourmets—culinary scene, and as such it succeeds very well. The seasonal menu focuses on meat—an unusual and welcome choice; if it's offered, try the complex and subtle *risotto con porcini, quaglia e tartufo nero* (risotto with porcini mushrooms, quail, and truffle). They also offer a first-rate tasting menu. The wine list focuses on local varieties unlikely to be found elsewhere.

Via Portacatena 28. ⓒ 089-235659. Reservations recommended. Prix-fixe tasting menu 40€ ($50). Secondi 14€–18€ ($18–$23). AE, DC, MC, V. Daily 12:30–3pm and 7:30–10pm.

INEXPENSIVE

Trattoria Pizzeria Zì Renato ⭐ SALERNITAN/PIZZA   This is the quintessence of the Italian trattoria, with a welcoming owner-patron, red-and-white-checked table-cloths, and a romantic yet casual mood set by candles. The pizza is very good and the menu includes well-prepared local dishes, such as *scialatielli ai frutti di mare* (fresh pasta with shellfish) and grilled seafood, as well as a variety of hearty, stick-to-your-ribs meat dishes.

Via Roma 170. ⓒ **089-228018**. Reservations recommended for dinner. Pizza 5€–9€ ($6.25–$11). Secondi 6€–12€ ($7.50–$15). AE, DC, MC, V. Daily 12:30–3pm and 7:30–10pm.

SHOPPING

Shopping is not Salerno's forte. As far as clothing is concerned, the town isn't big enough to have its own boutique scene and designers, and so it relies on national chains or local clothiers who stock fairly conservative and utilitarian clothing for the workplace (you are also in the south now, where customs, manners, and dress are more traditional). You'll also find the pottery of nearby **Vietri** (see chapter 7), but we recommend you go to the source. There is one great exception to Salerno's relatively unexceptional shopping: **Salerno Trading Art Project** (Via Tasso 3; ⓒ **089/2580761**), a showroom for jewelers, ceramic artists, glassmakers, and other artisans, located in the old center of the town.

2 The Magical Ruins of Paestum ⭐⭐

35km (22 miles) S of Salerno, 100km (62 miles) SE of Naples.

The fabled ruins of Paestum are everything they are reported to be: Enormously evocative, the three Greek temples (in an excellent state of conservation) occupy a grassy plain that really gives off the sense of a vanished, ancient city. The town walls are intact as well. The temples are a unique sight, especially at sunset, and in spring and fall when Paestum's roses—praised since antiquity—are in bloom. The archaeological area can be reached as a day trip from anywhere in Campania; plan on spending a couple of hours exploring the temples and an hour for the museum, but count on a whole day to fully take advantage of all of the attractions here.

Situated in an area inhabited since the paleolithic period, Poseidonia—the Greek name for Paestum—was established as a Greek colony in the 7th century B.C., around the same time that the nearby temple of Hera Argiva (see later in this chapter) was built. The town flourished for a couple of centuries but, in the 4th century B.C., it was overtaken by a local mountain people—the Lucanians. The decline was reversed when, in 273 B.C., the Romans established the colony of Paestum, which quickly grew wealthy from its agriculture and commerce. Paestum was progressively abandoned at the beginning of the Middle Ages and the inhabitants moved farther up the hills—a common pattern at the time, when Saracen attacks put every town on this coast in danger. In addition, the slow sinking of the ground transformed the plain of Paestum into marshes, which resulted in the spread of malaria.

Normans eventually gained a foothold here and, in the 11th century, removed much of the statuary from the abandoned buildings of the Greek city. After that, the ruins remained undisturbed—although their existence was known—until the nearby roads were developed centuries later. That's when the monuments were first studied and given their current designations.

ESSENTIALS

GETTING THERE   You can get to Paestum by public transportation, either by train or bus, but you have to switch in Salerno. **Trains** depart Salerno for **Paestum** and **Capaccio-Roccadaspide,** also called Capaccio Scalo (Capaccio's train station), every 2 hours (call © 892021 toll-free in Italy for schedules). The first station is about a half-mile from the archaeological area, and the second is about 3.2km (2 miles) away. Several **bus** lines connect Salerno with Paestum; buses leave from Piazza della Concordia, near the train station. **SCAT** (© 0974 838415) offers five daily runs from Salerno and Agropoli.

By car, you can take autostrada A3, marked SALERNO-REGGIO CALABRIA, and then take the exit marked BATTIPAGLIA. You can also take the local **Strada Litoranea** (Shore Rd.) from Salerno, following signs for PAESTUM.

GETTING AROUND   If you decide to explore the Cilento from Paestum, you can rent a car from **Travelcar** on Via Magna Grecia (© 0828-811034; www.travelcar.it), or from one of the other companies in town, which also offer car service with a driver—the best way to enjoy a tour of the area, especially if you have limited time. Here are some of the best operators in town: **Leonardo D'Onofrio** (Via Cesare Pavese 27, Paestum; © 0828-721107 or 339-3201101); **Autonoleggi Meridionali Di Filippo** (Via Fratelli Arenella 3, Capaccio; © 082-8821045 or 082-8821452); and **Fratelli Di Filippo** (Capaccio Scalo; © 082-8724707).

VISITOR INFORMATION   AACST is at Via Magna Grecia 151, not far from one of the temple entrances and from the Archaeological Museum's entrance (© 082-8811016; www.infopaestum.it; Mon–Sat 9am–3pm, Sun 9am–1pm; in July and Aug, Mon–Sat 9am–7pm, Sun 9am–1pm). You will also find a **Pro Loco tourist office** in the Town Hall (Via V. Emanuele; © 082-8812111; fax 082-8812239).

EXPLORING THE ARCHAEOLOGICAL AREA

Paestum's temples are ranked among the best-preserved Greek temples in the world, second only to the Theseion in Athens. When they were first excavated in the 17th century, they were thought to be a basilica and two temples, one to Neptune and one to Ceres. Later excavations and studies showed that the first two buildings were actually part of one unique sanctuary complex dedicated to Hera, while the third one was a temple dedicated to Athena. The names, however, stuck.

Admission to the temple area is 4€ ($5); the museum's admission fee is also 4€ ($5); the cumulative ticket for both is 6.50€ ($8.15). The temples are open daily 9am to sunset; the museum is open daily 9am to 7pm and closed the first and third Monday of each month; both are closed January 1, May 1, and December 25. You can access the temples from three entrances: One on Via Magna Grecia across and up from the Archaeological Museum and tourist information office; one on Via Magna Grecia by the Temple of Neptune; and the third through the ancient southern gate in the town walls, **Porta della Giustizia (Justice Gate).**

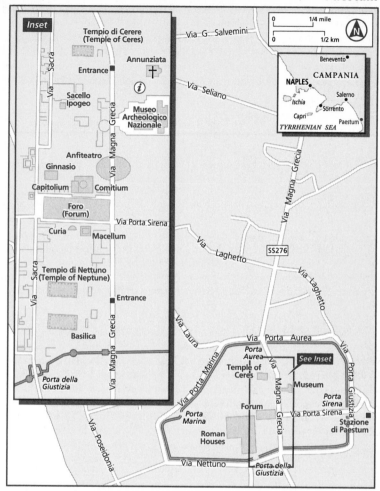

The **Basilica** ✹✹✹ is the oldest of the three temples, built in 550 B.C. in Doric Archaic style. The 50 columns of its monumental portico still stand, showing the pot-bellied profile typical of archaic temples; the roof and the pediment have long ago fallen down. In front is a partially ruined sacrificial altar and, on its side, the square *bothros*—the sacrificial well where the remains were thrown.

To the right of the Basilica is the grandiose **Temple of Neptune** ✹✹✹, whose restoration was just finished in 2004. Built around 450 B.C., it is covered in local travertine marble, which glows a magical gold color when hit by the sun's rays. Its perfect proportions and a number of architectural tricks—the columns at the corners have an elliptical section instead of round, and the horizontal lines are slightly convex instead of perfectly straight—give it slender elegance and power at the same time; it is considered the best example of a Doric temple in the world. It is also one of the best preserved temples around—its roof and pediments are mostly intact. At the temple's front are two sacrificial altars; the smaller was built by the Romans in the 3rd century B.C. to replace the oldest and largest. Based on the rich trove of findings in and around the temple, most experts believe that it was dedicated to Hera Argiva, the goddess of fertility and maternity—the same goddess honored in the sanctuary near the mouth of the Sele River (see later in this chapter). Others, though, think it might have been dedicated to Apollo, and still others think that it was an Olympeion, a temple dedicated to Zeus. Several other smaller religious buildings, all dedicated to Hera, have been discovered near the temple, in the area that stretches towards the Forum.

The third temple is on the opposite side of the town, across the **Forum**—one of the oldest rectangular Roman forums in existence, lined by Doric porticos. In the past, the Forum was surrounded by a number of ceremonial and public buildings, including what must have been the town's *capitolium,* the temple dedicated to Jupiter, Juno, and Minerva, built in the 3rd century B.C. To the west of the Forum runs **Via Sacra (Sacred St. or Sacred Way);** it still has its Roman pavement but was originally laid out by the Greeks to connect the various temples and ceremonial centers of Paestum. About 12km (7½ miles) long, it originally connected the Greek town of Poseidonia to the ancient temple of Hera and, in Roman times, led to the Roman amphitheater and the Forum. The Via Sacra climbs the plateau of the so-called **Temple of Ceres** ⚜⚜, which was actually dedicated to the goddess Athena. Built at the end of the 6th century B.C., it was transformed into a church in medieval times; that is why, inside its portico, you will see three Christian tombs.

A short distance from the Temple of Athena, off the Via Magna Grecia—the old state road that cut through the middle of the archaeological area of Paestum, plowing right through the Roman amphitheater—you will find the Paestum's **Museo Archeologico Nazionale (National Archaeological Museum)** ⚜⚜ (Via Magna Grecia 917; © **0828 811023;** www.infopaestum.it). Inside are all the finds from the excavations of Paestum itself—including a 6th-century-B.C. **Statue of Zeus** ⚜⚜ from the Forum, and a beautiful collection of 6th-century-B.C. **vases** with red or black figures. You'll also see objects from the nearby necropolis, including the famous **Diver's Tomb** ⚜ from the 5th century B.C., decorated with beautiful frescoes; and the superb paintings and objects from the **Lucanian Tombs** dating from the 6th to the 3rd centuries B.C. One whole area of the museum is dedicated to the architectural remains from the **Sanctuary of Hera Argiva** (see later in this chapter), including the complete **frieze** ⚜ of metopes and triglyphs; a number of the metopes are unfinished, which helps shed light on the carving techniques.

Impressions

And I myself, were I not even now
Furling my sails, and, nigh the journey's end,
Eager to turn my vessel's prow to shore,
Perchance would sing what careful husbandry
Makes the trim garden smile; of Paestum too,
Whose roses bloom and fade and bloom again.

—Virgil, *Georgics*

The lesser-known attraction of Paestum is the impressive set of **walls** ⍟, which completely surrounded the town, one of the few complete sets of walls left from antiquity. Originally built by the Greeks, the walls were restored by the Lucanians and then the Romans. Measuring 5m (18 ft.) thick on average, with several square and round towers, they mark a pentagonal perimeter of 4,750m (15,580 ft.), with four main gates at the four cardinal directions. You can make a complete tour here; if time is short, you might focus on the western side, which is the best preserved. It includes the **Porta Marina;** there you can climb the walls and walk on the patrol paths, enjoying the great views over coast and ruins.

EXPLORING THE SANCTUARY OF HERA ARGIVA

In the late 1930s, two young archaeologists succeeded where others had failed over the previous 200 years: They discovered the ruins of the famous sanctuary to Hera Argiva. This large complex, existing since the 7th century B.C. and said to have been founded by the mythical Jason—the one of the golden fleece—flourished during antiquity in spite of a few mishaps, such as being damaged by the eruption of Mount Vesuvius in A.D. 79, when ejecta rained down and pulverized a portico's roof. Unfortunately, in the Middle Ages people used temple limestone to make lime, and all traces of the complex were afterwards lost.

Eleven kilometers (6¾ miles) north of Paestum, this was one of the most famous temples of Magna Grecia (the Greek cities outside Greece), located near the only easy landing place on this stretch of coast, on the left bank of the Sele River and little more than a mile from its mouth. The sinking of the ground and the growth of marshes completely obliterated all traces of the sanctuary, which was actively searched for from the 18th century on. Finally, Paola Zancani Montuoro and Umberto Zanotti Bianco almost single-handedly located and excavated the site, bringing to light the few ruins that we can see today—little more than the foundations of the main temple, some remains of the smaller and older temple called the *thesaurus,* and a portico with attached buildings. All the decorations—metopes and votive statuettes—are conserved in the National Archaeological Museum of Paestum (see above). Near the archaeological area, in a restored farm 9km (5 ½ miles) from Paestum, you will find the newly created **Museo Narrante del Santuari di Hera Argiva** (Masseria Procuriali; ℭ **0828-811016;** www.infopaestum.it; Tues–Sat 9am–4pm). Termed a "narrating museum," this permanent exhibit is a wonderful multimedia installation with panels, sound effects, images, and videos about the discovery and significance of the sanctuary.

The cult of Hera—Minerva in Latin—was powerful in antiquity and remained so in later times, as shown by the sanctuary of the **Madonna del Granato** where the Madonna holds a pomegranate, the characteristic symbol for Hera and Minerva. This interesting example of syncretism shows the continuation of the cult of Hera Argiva into Christian times, and disproves the notion that, after the rise of Christianity, paganism disappeared. The sanctuary of the Madonna del Granato was built in the 11th to 12th centuries on the road to Capaccio Vecchia, and is still an important pilgrimage destination—nowadays it is open only on August 15. It also offers a unique panorama over the valley of Paestum and the Gulf of Salerno.

MARINA DI PAESTUM (PAESTUM'S BEACH) ⍟

Though it's famous for its archaeological area, Paestum is also a great seaside destination. If lying on the beach is your thing, this is the place to do it; the sea is warm and great for swimming, too. Paestum's shore extends for miles; many of the hotels we recommend are actually on the beach. Located relatively far from large towns, these beaches are popular with local vacationers, who use them mainly in August; otherwise they are less crowded than more famous parts of the Italian coast.

WHERE TO STAY

EXPENSIVE

Savoy Beach Hotel ♨ *Kids*   This luxurious hotel sits right by the archaeological area and not far from the beach. The extensive public spaces—including a garden with outdoor swimming pool and waterside romantic dining—are the perfect places to relax after a day spent visiting the temples. The large guest rooms, furnished with care, include wooden floors, classic furniture, occasional antiques, Oriental carpets, and marble bathrooms; the suites are particularly elegant. The best thing of all for families, though—and a rare occurrence in Italy—is that this hotel offers a kindergarten for young children and on-site babysitting.

Via Poseidonia 41, 84063 Paestum. ℂ 082-8720100. Fax: 082-8720807. www.worldhotels.com. 42 units. 200€ ($250) double, 320€ ($400) suite; low season 138€ ($173) double, from 220€ ($275) suite. Rates include buffet breakfast. Specials available. Children under 3 stay free in parent's room. AE, DC, MC, V. Free parking. **Amenities:** Restaurant; bar; indoor and outdoor pool; health club; spa; children's center; concierge; business center; room service; babysitting; same-day laundry service. *In room:* A/C, satellite TV, dataport, minibar, hair dryer, safe.

MODERATE

Mec Paestum ♨♨   This family-run luxury hotel, just steps from the beach and within walking distance of the archaeological area, is our preferred hotel in the area. Housed in a modern building, guest rooms are comfortable, large, and furnished with good taste, in a modern style. The new, spacious bathrooms all come with Jacuzzi tubs. Each room has a private small terrace with a view—often over the hotel's own private beach.

Via Tiziano 23, Località Sterpinia, 84063 Capaccio. ℂ 082-8722444. Fax 082-8722305. www.mechotel.com. 52 units. 170€ ($213) double, from 250€ ($313) suite; low season 90€ ($113) double, from 200€ ($250) suite. Rates include buffet breakfast. Extra bed 30€ ($38). Children under 2 stay free in parent's room. AE, DC, MC, V. Free parking. **Amenities:** Restaurant; bar; outdoor pool; concierge; business center; room service; babysitting; laundry service. *In room:* A/C, satellite TV, dataport, minibar, hair dryer.

Strand Hotel Schuhmann ♨   This pleasant hotel offers beachside accommodations not far from the archaeological area. Guest rooms are quiet and well appointed, each with a balcony or a small private terrace with a view. Bathrooms are good-sized. Guests have access to the private beach and use of beach equipment (chairs, umbrellas, and showers). The hotel building's terrace offers wonderful views over the Gulf of Salerno and Capri.

Via Marittina, Località Laura, 84063 Capaccio. ℂ 082-8851151. Fax 082-8851183. www.hotelschuhmann.com. 53 units. 190€ ($238) double; low season 120€ ($150) double. Rates include half-board. Children under 3 stay free in parent's room. AE, DC, MC, V. Free parking. **Amenities:** Restaurant; lounge; concierge; room service; babysitting; laundry service. *In room:* A/C, TV, dataport, minibar, hair dryer.

INEXPENSIVE

Hotel Ariston ♨   This luxury hotel is located a couple of miles from the archaeological area, in the little town of Laura. Surrounded by a garden complete with sports equipment and swimming pool, the hotel is not far from its private beach—10 minutes away on foot—but the hotel offers complimentary shuttle service and a beach bar. Guest rooms are quite spacious and come furnished with good-quality modern furniture; bathrooms are substantial and new.

Via Lauran 13, Località Laura, 84040 Capaccio. © **082-8851333**. Fax 082-8851596. www.hotelariston.com. 110 units. 130€ ($163) double; low season 100€ ($125) double. Extra bed 20€ ($25). AE, DC, MC, V. Free parking. **Amenities:** Restaurant; bar; outdoor pool; outdoor tennis court; health club; state-of-the-art spa; concierge; business center; room service; babysitting; same-day laundry service; soccer fields; basketball field; billiards room. *In room:* A/C, satellite TV, dataport, minibar, hair dryer, radio.

Hotel Esplanade   Acquired in 2004 by Best Western, this hotel remains one of the better ones in Paestum, retaining some unique touches and public spaces, including a pleasant garden, swimming pool, and private beach. It offers comfortable guest rooms with modern furniture, new bathrooms, and private balconies.

Via Poseidonia, Località Laura, 84063 Capaccio. © **082-8851043**. Fax 082-8851600. www.hotelesplanade.com. 28 units. 138€ ($173) double; low season 64€ ($80) double. Rates include breakfast. Specials available. Children under 2 stay free in parent's room. AE, DC, MC, V. Free parking. **Amenities:** Restaurant; bar; outdoor pool; concierge; room service; babysitting. *In room:* A/C, satellite TV, minibar.

Tenuta Seliano 🏞🏞   If you like being pampered in a countryside surrounding, this pleasant *agriturismo* will be perfect for you. Set in a 19th-century hamlet, the picturesque buildings have been turned into lodgings with large, comfortable guest rooms and a decor with country-style elegance and good taste. A well-groomed garden with swimming pool and some 91 hectares (200 acres) of land complete the property. The excellent cuisine prepared by Mrs. Bellelli—who also offers classes—completes the service. You can choose to have all your meals at the farm, or only breakfast.

Via Seliano, in Borgo Antico (Capaccio Scalo), 84063 Paestum. © **082-8723634**. Fax 082-8724544. www.agriturismo seliano.it. 14 units. 115€ ($144) double; low season 70€ ($88) double. Rates include full breakfast. Children under 2 stay free in parent's room. AE, DC, MC, V. Free parking. Closed Nov–Dec 27 and Jan 7–Feb 28. **Amenities:** Dining room; lounge; outdoor pool; babysitting; laundry service. *In room:* A/C, TV.

WHERE TO DINE
EXPENSIVE
Ristorante Nettuno 🏞 SALERNITAN   This picturesque restaurant is literally right beside the ruins of Paestum, housed in a 2nd-century-B.C. tower opening onto a charming garden. Appropriate for the surroundings, the cuisine is traditional, and the menu includes both meat and fish choices. You'll find *crespoline* (savory crepe stuffed with mozzarella and ham), and excellent pasta dishes, as well as a variety of secondi.

Via Nettuno, Paestum. © **082-8811028**. Reservations recommended. Secondi 15€–23€ ($19–$29). AE, DC, MC, V. July–Aug daily noon–3:30pm and 8–11:30pm; Sept–June Tues–Sun noon–3:30pm.

MODERATE
Il Granaio dei Casabella 🏞🏞 SALERNITAN CREATIVE   Not far from the walls of ancient Paestum, this countryside *residenza* offers refined dining and a delightful veranda overlooking an internal garden. You may be surprised by the delicious *granatine di lardo ai frutti di mare* (little rolls of lard filled with shellfish); *gnocchi con zucca e gamberi in zimino* (potato dumplings with shrimp, pumpkin, and a spinach-and-herb sauce), or *risotto carciofi e aragosta* (rice with lobster and artichokes). For something simpler, try the grilled fish. If after dinner you would like to spend the night, the hotel has a few rooms to let.

Villa Casabella, Via Porta Marina, 84063 Paestum. © **082-8721014**. Fax 082-8721977. Reservations recommended. Secondi 12€–18€ ($15–$23). AE, DC, MC, V. Daily 12:30–3pm and 7:30–10pm.

Le Trabe 🏞🏞 SALERNITAN CREATIVE   This is a beautiful restaurant, located in a lovely setting of gardens and streams inside a romantic old mill. The menu is seasonal and changes often, with such preparations as *taccozzette gamberi e porcini mantecati al* *provolone* (homemade pasta with shrimp and porcini mushrooms baked with provolone cheese) or *filetto di cernia all'uva* (grouper filet with grapes).

Via Capo di Fiume, Capaccio Scalo. ⓒ 082-8724165. Reservations recommended. Secondi 12€–18€ ($15–$23). AE, DC, MC, V. Daily 12:30–3pm and 7:30–10pm.

INEXPENSIVE

Nonna Sceppa ⌖ SALERNITAN CREATIVE   This large, classic restaurant offers well-prepared, traditional food with a twist. The specialty is homemade pasta. The seasonal menu merges tradition and creativity. You might find imaginative *fagottini di gamberi e zucchine gratinati* (small zucchini rolls filled with shrimp and baked with cheese), a classic and masterfully prepared *rombo al forno con patate* (turbot baked over a bed of potatoes), or a traditional *tiano di carne* (ragout of sausages, pork ribs, and pork rind).

Via Laura 53, Capaccio Scalo. ⓒ 082-8851064. Reservations recommended. Secondi 9€–14€ ($11–$18). AE, DC, MC, V. Daily 12:30–3pm and 7:30–10pm.

3 The National Park of the Cilento ⍟⍟⍟

110km (68 miles) S of Naples.

Established as a National Park in 1991, this is the second-largest national park in Italy, offering a variety of landscapes, from the mountains of the Alburni with their beautiful grottoes, to the massif of Mount Cervati, the highest in Campania, to the splendid promontory of Cape Palinuro—so justly praised by Virgil.

Inhabited since prehistoric times, the Cilento is rich in archaeological and architectural mementoes of the various civilizations that inhabited the area, from the Villanovians of prehistoric sites such as Sala Consilina, to the Lucanians, Greeks, Romans, Byzantine, Longobards, and Normans. Most of the medieval castles, churches, monasteries, convents, and palaces are in the interior part of the Cilento region—including the splendid Certosa di San Lorenzo—both the interior and the coast hold surprises of immense natural beauty.

In 1997, the park was declared part of the Biosphere Preservation program of UNESCO for its unique natural environment, rich in rare plant species, such as the primula of Palinuro—the flower that is the symbol of the park—and the wild orchid of San Giovanni a Piro. Natural attractions include rugged mountains such as Monte Cervati (1,898m/6,225 ft.) and Monte Alburno (1,742m/5,714 ft.). Here you'll find some of the most interesting caves in the world, such as the extensive grottoes of Castelcivita (over 4km/2½ miles); natural sinkholes, where rivers temporarily disappear underground (the most famous being the Bussento River, which remains underground for about 6km (3¾ miles); and the gorgeous rocky coast, with some of the clearest waters in the Mediterranean.

ESSENTIALS

GETTING THERE   The best way to explore the park is by private car, with or without a driver. You can easily get either one from the several agencies in Paestum (p. 250). If you are taking a car service with a driver, you can get a pretty good overview of the area in a day, but of course, if you are not pressed for time, you can easily find enough to do for several days.

If you wish to use public transportation, Salerno's transportation authority **CSTP** (Piazza Matteo Luciani 33, Salerno; ⓒ **800-016659** toll-free within Italy, or 089-487001; www.cstp.it) runs several lines from Napoli, Pompeii, and Salerno to Paestum,

Vallo della Lucania, Agropoli, Santa Maria di Castellabate, Acciaroli, and Pollica, connecting the coast with the interior of the Cilento. Other companies offering coach service to various towns and villages inside the park are **Curcio Viaggi** (© 089-254080; www.curcioviaggi.it), with lines from Rome and Salerno to Sicignano degli Alburni, Padula, Scario, and Polla; **Autolinee SLA** (© 097-321016; www.slasrl.it), also serving Padula and the Vallo di Diano; **SCAT** (© 097-4838415) serving Salerno, Agropoli, Paestum, Santa Maria di Castellabate, and other little towns along the coast; **La Manna** (© 097-5520426), offering runs from Salerno to Padula and Polla; and **Giuliano** (© 097-4836185), offering service between Naples and Salerno to Capaccio Scalo, Paestum, Roccadaspide, Agropoli, Vallo della Lucania, and Pioppi. **SITA** (© 089-226604) has lines from Salerno to Capaccio Scalo, Pertosa, and Polla.

GETTING ORIENTED   The park covers an area of almost 182,000 hectares (450,000 acres) extending from the autostrada A3 area marked SALERNO-REGGIO CALABRIA to the east, to the Tyrrhenian sea to the west. The northernmost part is occupied by the mountains of the Alburni, divided from the massif of the Cilento to the south by Route SS 166, which goes from Paestum to Atena Lucana, passing by Roccadaspide. From Paestum, two roads run southeast: One that follows the line of the coast—Route SS 267, right by the water, and the larger SS 18 that runs more inland. On the eastern side of the park is the Vallo di Diano, a fertile plateau crossed by the

Tanagro River, and once a lake in prehistoric times; the autostrada A3, as well as the local road SS 19, run alongside it.

EXPLORING THE CARTHUSIAN MONASTERY OF SAN LORENZO 🏛🏛🏛

Located about 98km (59 miles) southeast of Salerno on the slopes of the hill under the little town of Padula, this is one of the largest monasteries in the world and among the most interesting in Europe for its architectural beauty and rich collection of artistic treasures.

You can easily reach the monastery by public transportation; there are five train connections a day from Salerno (to Battipaglia, where you switch to a bus shuttle), as well as direct coach service from Piazza della Concordia in Salerno with **Curcio Viaggi** (© 089-254080; www.curcioviaggi.it). The company offers coach service from Firenze and Siena as well. **Autolinee SLA** (© 0973 21016; www.slasrl.it) also has service from Naples. An option is to hire a car service from Salerno or from Paestum (see earlier in this chapter).

By car, take the autostrada A3 marked NAPOLI-SALERNO-REGGIO CALABRIA. From the exit, PADULA-BUONABITACOLO, continue onto SS 19, following the signs for PADULA.

An extremely rich monastery during its existence, the **Certosa di San Lorenzo** (© 097-577484 or 097-577745; Sun and holidays 8am–sunset, on other days, call before your visit because the schedule often changes) occupies an area of 51,500 sq. m (554,341 sq. ft.) in a complex of buildings and courtyards. If you're impressed by numbers, then you'll like this: The Certosa has 320 halls, 52 staircases, 100 fireplaces, 13 courtyards, and 41 fountains. Suppressed as a monastery in 1866, it has recently been reopened to the public after extensive restorations, including repair of some of the damage due to the earthquake of 1980. It is now the setting for important cultural events and international exhibits, not the least of which is the Ravello Music Festival (see chapter 7), which schedules a number of concerts on the grounds every year.

Established in 1306, the monastery was built over a long period of time and was terminated only during the first years of the 19th century. As a result, the original medieval structures have been redecorated in baroque style, including the facade and most of the interior, turning it into one of the most important baroque works of art in the whole country. Among the most striking attractions is the first **cloister** 🏛🏛, near the entrance to the monastery, dating from 1561 and graced by an elegant portico and fountain. Inside the church, teeming with baroque decoration, you can see two impressive **choirs** 🏛🏛🏛 inlaid with intarsia artwork in wood; one dates from 1503 and was for the monks, while the other, designed by Giovanni del Gallo in 1507, was meant for the lay brothers. Near the church is the original cemetery from 1552, now a **cloister.** The later, larger cemetery is in a separate part of the splendid 17th-century **main cloister** 🏛🏛🏛. The huge space is focused upon a central fountain and surrounded by two levels of porticos decorated with beautiful carvings along the perimeter. Along the portico you can see the monks' cells—not "monastic" at all, these were mini-apartments of three to four rooms with private porticos and small gardens, and even a workshop/studio above for some. Less enviable, perhaps, are other aspects: notice the small opening through which food was received, and the aperture through which monks were given a light at night, both by the entrance door to the cell. (The monks rarely came out of these chambers because they had sworn a vow of seclusion.)

Through a beautiful **staircase** housed inside an octagonal tower, you can climb to the upper floor, where you'll see the **Monk's Promenade** *R* around the cloister and the **Apartments of the Prior** *RR*.

The monastery also houses the **Museo Archeologico della Lucania Occidentale** (© **800-219661** toll free within Italy, or **097-577745;** 3€/$3.75; Tues–Sat 8am–1:15pm and 2–3pm; Sun 9am–1pm) in what were the original library and reception halls. The collection ranges from the 9th century B.C. to the Roman age, displaying artifacts and findings from the necropolis of the Vallo di Diano nearby.

The monastery lies by the ancient little town of Padula, a Lucanian and then a Roman town. Though the town is rich in history, one of the more interesting historical notes is that this was the original hometown of the legendary New York policeman Joe Petrosino, one of the first to fight the Sicilian Mafia until he was killed on the job in 1909. You can stay in town at the atmospheric hotel **Villa Cosilinum** (Corso Garibaldi, Località Sant'Eligio, 84034 Padula; © **097-5778615;** fax 0975 778800; www.villacosilinum.it; 140€/$175 double including buffet breakfast), which offers elegant accommodations and an excellent restaurant. An option is the **Grand Hotel Certosa** (Viale Certosa 41; 84034 Padula; © **097-577126;** fax 097-577046; www.certosa.it; 90€/$113 double including breakfast), which has warm hospitality, a swimming pool, and a good restaurant-pizzeria. You can also eat well at the **Taverna Il Lupo** (Via Municipio; © **097-5778376**) and at **do' Giulino** (Viale Certosa; © **097-577335**).

EXPLORING THE MOUNTAINS
VALLO DELLA LUCANIA

For a leisurely visit of Cilento's massif, the best plan is to drive along the scenic road (SS 18) that crosses through the park from the town of **Vallo della Lucania**—the official seat of the park (Palazzo Mainenti, Via F. Palombo; © **097-4719911;** www.pncvd.it). Proceed all the way down to the pretty seaside village of **Scario.** Make sure that you stay on the local road, because for the first half of the way, a newer—and much less scenic—section of SS 18 was built west of the old one. The whole itinerary is about 62km (38 miles) long on a good but quite winding road.

You can eat and stay over at the **Hotel Mimì** *R* (Via Ottavio De Marsilio 1; 84078 Vallo della Lucania; © **097-44302;** fax 0974 4214; 70€/$88 double and 110€/$138 suite); a good alternative is **La Chioccia d'Oro** *R* (Via Biblio di Novi Velia, Vallo della Lucania; © **097-470004;** closed Sept 1–10), which specializes in homemade pasta.

SINKHOLES

The limestone composition of this area's mountains has caused rivers to carve beautiful narrow valleys into the green slopes of the Cilento. Occasionally, rivers sink underground for several miles before reemerging. The most spectacular of such **sinkholes** is the enormous one of the Bussento River, which disappears near the little town of **Caselle in Pittari**, only to reappear in **Morigerati** *RR*, several miles to the south. Morigerati is a very pretty medieval town well worth a visit in itself. If you choose to do so, you should stay and eat at the **Hotel Cavaliere** (Via Rione Nuovo 12, 84030 Caselle in Pittari; © **097-4986804**). You can get a good meal, light or elaborate, at the restaurant and pizzeria **Zi' Filomena** (Via Roma, Caselle in Pittari; © **097-4988024**). To delve more deeply into the regional cuisine, try the excellent *agriturismo* **Al Castello** *R* (Piazzetta XI Novembre 3, Morigerati; © **097-4982085**) in the ancient *borgo* of Morigerati, which serves organic food from their own farm.

EXPLORING THE GROTTOES OF CASTELCIVITA ★★★

A number of splendid grottoes are in this area, of which about 400 have been explored to date. The most famous (and justly so) are the **Grotte di Castelcivita** (© 082-8975524; www.grottedicastelcivita.it), which happily are also the most accessible. The entrance is near the small agricultural town of Controne. To get there from the autostrada A3 marked NAPOLI-SALERNO-REGGIO CALABRIA, take the exit marked SERRE, onto SS19 towards Serre; turn right on SS 488 following directions for ROCCA D'ASPIDE. The grottoes are a few miles down a road that branches to the left after Controne and just before the bridge over the Calore River; the whole stretch is very scenic, running along the slopes of the Alburni and overlooking the river valley(from Paestum, take SS 166 and turn left on SS 488 at Rocca d'Aspide). Inhabited since paleolithic times up until the Bronze Age, the grottoes are composed of a central section of galleries and halls, which have been fully studied and are electrically illuminated. Lateral chambers that depart from the main core have been only partially explored. Part of an astounding succession of large galleries and natural halls extending for 4.8km (almost 3 miles), each of the spaces is very different; some have beautiful stalactite and stalagmite formations, others have multicolored concretions, such as the so-called *Tempio*. But the most spectacular are the grottoes in the farthest section of the itinerary, which are striking both for the beauty of their crystals and the variety of colors. Remember to bring a jacket to keep you warm, even in summer—temperatures stay pretty cool year–round way down here.

You'll find a snack bar by the entrance of the grotto, or you can eat a more substantial meal at the nearby **Taverna Degli Antichi Sapori** ★ (Via Nazionale 27, Controne; © 082-8772500; Wed–Mon noon–3pm and 8–11pm), where you can taste the local food staple, the famous beans of Controne, prepared in several traditional ways—with porcini mushrooms, with homemade pasta, stewed, and so on.

GROTTOES OF PERTOSA, AKA OF THE ANGEL ★★

Another of Cilento's famous caves is the **Grotta dell'Angelo** (© 097-5397037; www.grottadell'angelo.sa.it; Tues–Sun 9am–5:30pm), also called Grotta di Pertosa for the name of the nearby small town. Created by a subterranean river, they are perhaps even more magnificent than those of Castelcivita above, but a bit less accessible. You can reach them from the part of autostrada A3 signed NAPOLI-SALERNO-REGGIO CALABRIA: take the exit POLLA onto SS 19 and follow the signs for PERTOSA; you will find the parking area a short distance off the road to the left. Also inhabited in prehistoric times (pile-dwellings during the Neolithic period, when the water level was higher; and more regular dwellings during the Bronze and early Iron Ages), the caves were also used during Lucanian and Roman times and, from the 11th century on, by Christians, when they were consecrated to Saint Michael.

A visit here is an adventure. After crossing the first cave on a raft guided by a metal wire—it is submerged by water—you will be welcomed by a picturesque waterfall. Here you disembark and continue on foot, through the main branch of the grotto (two others open on your right, one completely occupied by the water of the subterranean stream, and the central one rather plain). Hall after hall contains marvelous formations of stalactites and stalagmites intertwined and in different shapes; others are covered with pure crystal accretions.

You can stay and eat at **Ristorante Hotel Motel Forum** (Strada Statale 19, 84035 Polla; © 097-5391323; fax 097-5391133; www.motelforum.it; 50€/$63 double), conveniently located nearby the highway exit; it calls itself a motel, but it has the feeling of a countryside hotel, with spacious, cozy rooms and a good restaurant, popular with locals. They serve a selection of traditional dishes as well as flavorful pizza. You can also stay at **Hotel Grotte Cafaro** ๑ (Via Muraglione 33, 84030 Pertosa; ✆ **097-5397045;** fax 097-5397043; www.hotelgrotte.it), a quiet, smaller hotel surrounded by greenery. Their restaurant is excellent—you can even take classes on homemade pastas, for which they have much expertise. The welcoming **Ristorante Villa delle Rose** (Contrada Arnaci 1, Pertosa; ✆ **097-5397262;** Wed–Mon) has a children's playground and garden.

HIKING & MOUNTAINS
If you would rather stay well aboveground and you are into serious hiking, the area's best climb is **Monte Alburno** (1,742m/5,714 ft.) ๑๑๑, also called Monte Panorama because, true to its name, it offers sweeping views over the whole region. Two trails start from **Sicignano degli Alburni,** off SS 19 not far from Serre, one climbing directly to the western peak and another branching out at 1,400m (4,600 ft.) for the eastern peak on one side and the western one to the other; allow at least 4 hours for either climb.

If you plan to hike, your best bet for accommodations is to stay at one of the several excellent *agriturismo* in the area; at **Agriturismo Zito–Acqua della Battaglia** (Contrada Acqua della Battaglia, 84029 Sicignano degli Alburni; ✆ **082-8973790;** agriturismozito@tiscalinet.it), you can take riding lessons and tours. At the **Azienda Agrituristica Sicinius** (Contrada Piedi la Serra 22, Frazione Scorzo, 84029 Sicignano degli Alburni; ✆/fax **082-8973763;** www.sicinius.com; 52€/$65 double), you can take hiking tours and taste their organic products. You can also eat at **La Taverna do' Scuorzo** (Via Nazionale 139, 84029 Sicignano degli Alburni; ✆ **082-8978050**); or at **Trattoria Tre Braci** (Via Nazionale 19, 84029 Sicignano degli Alburni; ✆ **082-8978007**).

Separated from the Alburni by a few lower hills, the massif of the Cilento is Campania's loneliest wilderness, well off the beaten track and one of the least inhabited areas in Italy. The population is concentrated on the dramatically beautiful coast, while the inland area is comparatively abandoned despite its few roads. The region's highest mountain is **Monte Cervati** ๑๑๑; at 1,898m (6,225 ft.), it is a dramatic sight, especially in the summer, when it turns blue from its extensive lavender fields. You can climb to the top from the little town of **Sanza** on SS 517, where two different trails begin; allow about 6 hours for the ascent on either one.

In the area, you'll find a few *agriturismo,* such as **La Bussentina** (Contrada Agno, 84030 Sanza; ✆ **097-5322527;** fax 097-5322250), located in a panoramic locations. Two other agriturismo are **La Sontina** (Contrada Verlingieri, 84030 Sanza; ✆ **09-75322346**); and **Il Giardino dei Ciliegi** (Località Vesolo Contrada Matina, 84030 Sanza; ✆ **097-5322344**). You can also eat well and stay at the small hotel in town, **Il Gabbiano** (Via Fontana Vecchia 26, 84030 Sanza; ✆ **097-5322370**). Another good restaurant is **4 G** (Via Val d'Agri 6, 84030 Sanza; ✆ **097-5322058**), with such down-home favorites as homemade pasta and charbroiled lamb and kid.

THE COSTIERA CILENTANA
The National Park extends all the way to the shore, where the mountains drop into the sea—creating a dramatic coastline of high cliffs and small coves interspersed by lovely beaches. From the flat plain of the Sele and Paestum rivers, the cliffs rise in a series of promontories; small green valleys from Agropoli descend for a stretch of 100km (62

miles) of coast. This coast has become popular with Italians in the summer, who come to enjoy the usual seaside activities, as well as the area's pristine beauty..

The best way to explore this area is by car, but if you have the time, each of the little towns along the coast is well-served by frequent bus service from Salerno, as well as from other towns in the region (see earlier in this chapter). The road south along the coast begins as Route 267, and then changes to the 447, but it's really the same winding highway following the edge of the sea, so you are unlikely to get lost.

AGROPOLI ✵✵✵

The first town you encounter coming from Paestum is **Agropoli,** lying 49km (30 miles) southeast of Salerno. To discover this picturesque fishing town, you have to first cross through the modern districts that surround it and take the ramp that climbs the promontory to the **medieval *borgo*** ✵✵. Beyond the original **gate** you'll enter a delightful little town dominated by a powerful castle to the east and opening onto a beautiful bay. Below are the small **harbor** ✵✵ and a **seafront promenade** ✵✵.

Probably founded by the Byzantines in the 5th century A.D., Agropoli was taken over by the Saracens in 882, who used it as their base until 1028, when they were chased out by the allied forces of Salerno and Capua. You can visit the partially ruined castle originally built by the Byzantines, and walk along the walls that enclose the three towers; from there you can enjoy a fantastic **view** ✵✵✵ over the coast, stretching all the way to Punta Campanella and Capri.

Agropoli is a good place to find a number of nice hotels and restaurants. You can have a meal or stay overnight at **Il Ceppo** ✵ (Via Madonna del Carmine 31, 84043 Agropoli; ✆ **097-4843044;** fax 097-4843234; www.hotelristoranteilceppo.com; 80€/$100 double including breakfast). This pleasant, family-run hotel is small, with a pretty garden and well-furnished, comfortable rooms. The good restaurant is favored by many locals. A shuttle can take you to the beach. **La Colombaia** ✵✵ (Via Piano delle Pere, 84043 Agropoli; ✆ **097-4821800;** fax 097-4823478; www.lacolombaiahotel.it; 100€/$125 double including breakfast) is also family-run but a bit more elegant. The charming villa, surrounded by olive groves, has a swimming pool. The tastefully furnished rooms have sea views. **Hotel Ristorante Carola** (Via Carlo Pisacane 1, 84043 Agropoli; ✆ **097-4826422;** fax 097-4826425) and **Hotel Ristorante Il Gambero** (Via San Marco 234, 84043 Agropoli; ✆/fax **097-4822894;** www.gambero.it; restaurant closed Tues) are other good options. If you just want to eat, the best restaurant in town is **Il Ceppo,** with our second choice Il Gambero (see above).

CASTELLABATE & SANTA MARIA DI CASTELLABATE ✵✵

The next town farther south along the coast, about 19km (12 miles) from Paestum, is **Santa Maria di Castellabate.** The coast road has to take a jog inland just south of Agropoli because of impassable Monte Tresino, which goes right down to the sea. Therefore, be sure to follow signs for Santa Maria di Castellabate and the SS 262 as you leave Agropoli (avoiding the small road that branches off to the right and is marked as going to Monte Tresino, where it dead-ends). There are two beautiful beaches in Santa Maria di Castellabate: The larger one to the north has very fine sand, and the smaller one nearby to the south boasts a pine grove. The stretch of sea before Santa Maria is a **Biological Protected Area and Marine Park.** It affords some interesting snorkeling and scuba diving; for guides and equipment, head for the **Centro Subaqueo** (Via Marina Castellabate; ✆ **097-4961060**), the best operator on the whole coast. Inland but nearby is the hill town of **Castellabate,** built around its 12th-century castle. This delightful medieval bourg offers a great cultural-historical break from the natural attractions. Its history goes back to Roman times and, like the rest of Campania, has been held by and wrested from many hands and cultures.

If you decide to stay overnight, you can do so at **La Mola** ⚲ (Via A. Cilento 2, 84048 Castellabate; ② **097-4967053;** fax 097-4967714; www.lamola-it.com; 114€/ $143 double; 124€/$155 suite including breakfast). This elegant B&B is housed in a villa enjoying a commanding position overlooking the sea; guest rooms are comfortable, and each has a private balcony with a view. The small **Hotel Villa Sirio** (Via Lungomare De Simone 15, 84072 Santa Maria di Castellabate; ② **097-4961099;** fax 097-4960507; www.villasirio.it; 200€/$250 double including breakfast; 290€/$363 half-board obligatory in July and Aug) is pricier but lovely, with punctilious service. It is housed in a historic palace right on the sea, and offers guest rooms with private balconies—most with sea views.

Also on the shore, you can have a great meal at **Da Carmine** ⚲ (Via Ogliastro Marina, 84060 Castellabate; ② **097-4963023;** fax 097-4963900; www.albergodacarmine.it), an enthusiastic supporter of the Mediterranean diet, which is suspiciously similar to the typical cuisine of the Cilento: Dishes are prepared with unsaturated fats (olive oil), fish, and fresh seasonal vegetables. The establishment also has a few guest rooms, most of them with sea views. Another good place to eat is **La Taverna del Pescatore** (Via Lamia, 84062 Castellabate; ② **097-4968293;** Tues–Sun noon–3pm and 7–11pm; closed Nov–Mar), where you can have a splendid *zuppa di pesce* (fish stew) with local fresh seafood.

If a seaside vacation is what you are after, **Club Hotel Residence L'Approdo** (② **390-974966001;** fax 390-974966500; www.lapprodo.it; 122€–152€/$153–$190 double including breakfast; 208€–258€/$260–$323 double with half-board in July and Aug) is a modern resort-style hotel. It offers suites and mini-apartments, a restaurant with an outdoor terrace, a private cove, two beautiful swimming pools (one for children with a slide), a children's playground, and a variety of healthy and athletic pastimes (sea kayaking, archery, aerobic classes). Moreover, there are even special programs for children aged 3 and older, run by specialized instructors, as well as organized excursions. During July and August the hotel accepts only Saturday-through-Saturday weeklong reservations, but you can check for last-minute availability.

ACCIAROLI ⚲⚲

South of Castellabate, the local coastal road (here SS 267) becomes even more scenic and stays so all the way down to the end of the park. The little towns along the coast are charming, particularly **Acciaroli** and the attached medieval **Pioppi.** At 80km (50 miles) southeast of Salerno, Acciaroli is a tourist and fishing harbor and was the preferred hideaway of Ernest Hemingway, who stayed here several times. The little town is built on a promontory dominated by a Saracen square defense tower overlooking the harbor, and is noted for its small 12th-century Annunziata church down by the sea.

Hotel Ristorante La Vela (Via Caracciolo 96, 84060 Pioppi; ② **097-4905025** or 097-4905172 in winter; fax 0974-905140; www.lavelapioppi.com; 162€/$203 double with half-board; low season 110€/$138 double with half-board) offers nicely appointed rooms and a private beach. **La Playa** ⚲ (Via Nicotera 135, 84041 Acciaroli; ② **097-4904002;** fax 0974-904225; www.hotellaplaya.it; 90€/$113 double including breakfast; in Aug, reservations made for Sat through Sat only), has bright rooms (with private terraces), a private beach with umbrellas and chairs, an organic foods restaurant, and a free shuttle to the hotel's saltwater farm and nature preserve, Tenuta degli Eremi. There you can hike or take a donkey excursion to the national preserve. Another pleasant hotel in the area is **Il Faro,** which has a large beach (Via Nicotera 151, 84041 Acciaroli; ©/fax **097-4904389;** www.hotelilfaro.it; 144€/$180 double; low season 65€/$81 double; Aug one week–Sat through Sat stay.) The hotel might have last-minute availability.

THE ARCHAEOLOGICAL AREA OF VELIA 🌸🌸

Lesser known and farther south than Paestum, the archaeological area of **Velia** and its acropolis are important stops if you are interested in antiquity. Originally called Yele, then changed to Elea, this town was first an Italic settlement, and was taken over by Greek colonists around 540 B.C. Elea, like other settlements in southern Italy, saw an influx of Greeks fleeing from the Persian wars in the 6th century B.C. One of them is said to have been the Ionic poet and philosopher Xenophanes, traditionally held to be the founder of the important **Eleatic School** of philosophy that flourished here. The most important of the Eleatics was **Zeno of Elea,** who died around 430 B.C. He is most famous for his paradoxes, the best-known of which is his proof that motion is impossible. A controversial figure for centuries, Bertrand Russell said that in the modern period Zeno's rediscovered ideas inspired "a mathematical renaissance." Not only an intellectual center but also a rich commercial and fishing harbor, Elea was allowed to maintain its Greek language even after it fell under the rule of the Roman empire.

Archaeological excavation started here in the 1920s, and the archaeological area (SS 447 at its intersection with SS 267, Marina di Ascea; © **097-4971409**) includes both the **lower town,** with portions of the walls from the 4th and 5th centuries B.C., and houses originally from the same period but modified in Roman times around the south gate. Also of note are the Roman thermal baths, with beautiful mosaics in the **Frigidarium** and the **Acropolis.** (You can climb to the famous **Porta Rosa** 🌸🌸 here, on a stretch of the original Greek pavement.) The Acropolis holds the ruins of a theater and of an Ionic temple (partially covered by the Norman castle built over it); to the east are the ruins of a sanctuary to Poseidon. From there you can walk along the walls—a well-preserved section lies to the north.

Access is from Marina di Ascea, near the Angevin Tower; the excavations are open daily from 9am to sunset; admission is 2€ ($2.50).

PALINURO 🌸🌸🌸

Still farther south (41km/25 miles from Acciaroli), you'll find the highlight of this shore, **Palinuro** and its famous cape. The town is a fishing and resort harbor set among olive groves in a picturesque bay protected by the promontory of Cape Palinuro. You can walk to the lighthouse, from where you can enjoy a sweeping panorama.

The Cyclops

You may think that here in this paradise of hiking, spelunking, and swimming, you are far from the nightlife of the city. In fact, the legendary **Ciclope** (SS 562, Località Mingardo, Marina di Camerota; © **0974-930318;** www.ilciclope.com) is a club like no other. It occupies four limestone caves of the kind that are found throughout the Cilento. Open only during the summer months, Ciclope features live music on some nights and a DJ on others. "Atmospheric" doesn't begin to cover this weird mixture of the natural and the hip. It's also not the easiest place to find, so take a cab from Marina di Camerota (see below), or download directions from the club's website in advance.

But the real must-do activity here is a **boat tour** ⚜ of the promontory, on which several grottoes open. The most beautiful is the **Grotta Azzurra** ⚜⚜—yet another blue grotto, but less mobbed than the more famous one on Capri—which takes on a wonderful blue coloration especially around noon and sunset. In the harbor you'll easily find boats for rent with or without crew; contact the **Cooperativa dei Pescatori** in the harbor (℃ **097-4931233**). Another marvelous boat excursion is to the little fishing and resort harbor of **Marina di Camerota** (see later in this section), which you can reach in 1½ hours and enjoy gorgeous views over the rocky coast.

A pleasant family-run hotel is **America** ⚜⚜ (Via Bolivar, 848–4059 Marina di Camerota; ℃ **097-4932131;** fax 097-4932177; www.americahotel.it; 185€/$231 double including breakfast; low season 70€/$88 double), located in a nice spot surrounded by olive trees, and offering well-appointed guest rooms, a playground for children, and a swimming pool. Another good hotel is **Hotel La Conchiglia** ⚜⚜ (Via Indipendenza 52; ℃ **097-4931018;** fax 097-4931030; www.hotellaconchiglia.it; 116€/$145 double including buffet breakfast; in Aug 190€/$238 double with halfboard). It has a number of rooms overlooking the sea (these also happen to be more attractively decorated). **Hotel Lido Ficocella** (Via Ficocella 56, 84064 Palinuro; ℃ **097-4931051;** fax 097-4931052; www.lidoficocella.com; 150€/$188 double with half-board; low season 82€/$103 double with half-board; closed Nov–Mar) offers bright and welcoming rooms on a dramatic cliff above the ocean. For more elegant accommodations and a beautiful swimming pool (also with a sea view), try the **Grand Hotel San Pietro** ⚜⚜ (Corso Carlo Pisacane; 84064 Palinuro; ℃ **097-4931466;** fax 097-4931919; www.grandhotelsanpietro.com; 250€/$313 double, 300€/$375 junior suite; low season 112€/$140 double, 124€/$155 junior suite; closed Nov–Mar).

As far as eating goes, **La Taverna del Porto** (Via Porto 48, Palinuro; ℃ **097-4931278**) is a good restaurant-cum-pizzeria right by the water. **Da Carmelo** ⚜ (SS 562, Località Isca, 84064 Palinuro; ℃ **097-4931138;** fax 097-4930705; www.dacarmelo.it; 120€/$150 double with breakfast; low season 60€/$75 double with breakfast) is also good, and has recently added a hotel and residence (miniapartment).

MARINA DI CAMEROTA ⚜⚜

Only about 10km (6 miles) south of Palinuro along the scenic coastal road (which at this point is named SS 562—watch that you don't turn off onto the SS 562d, which branches off and heads inland a few kilometers south of Palinuro), this wonderful seaside resort is famous with locals for its pristine coastline and variety of beaches—sandy or rocky—as well as its coves, grottoes, towers, and great scuba-diving opportunities. A good hotel and restaurant in the area is **Albergo Delfino** (Via Bolivar 45, 84059 Marina di Camerota; ℃ **097-4932239;** fax 097-4932979; www.albergodelfino.com; 85€/$106 double; low season 40€/$50 double), which offers pleasant accommodations overlooking the sea, good service, and an array of excursions and activities, including scuba diving, trekking, and horseback riding. Other good establishments to keep in mind are: scenic **Baia delle Sirene** (Via Sereni 29, 84059 Camerota; ℃ **097-4932236;** fax 097-4932122; www.baiadellesirene.it; 200€/$250 double with half-board; low season 66€/$83 double; closed mid-Oct to Mar) overlooking the beach of the **Baia della Calanca** ⚜, a little distance from the town; and **Hotel La Scogliera** (Via Lungomare Trieste, 84059 Marina di Camerota; ℃ **097-4932019;** fax 097-4932391; www.albergolascogliera.it; 160€/$200 double; low season 108€/$135 double; closed Nov–Mar).

10

Campania's Well-Kept Secrets: Caserta, Benevento & Avellino

Somewhat mysteriously, many of Campania's best spots remain unknown to most foreign tourists and even to many Italian ones; the tranquil, yet lively, towns of Caserta, Benevento, and Avellino are at the top of that undiscovered list. These towns probably owe their quiet and semi-forgotten states to their location—all three lie away from the main train line that goes from Rome to Naples and Reggio Calabria, but they are close enough to Naples and the Amalfi Coast that they're easily overshadowed, in spite of their first-rate attractions. Most people probably think (as we did on our first visits) that they will come back to see these three towns *after* seeing Naples, but no one never does: The Costiera awaits, and then Paestum, Capri, Sorrento. . . .

As a result, Caserta remains a quiet little town a bit north of Naples, though it is the perfect beginning for a trip through Campania, an ideal place for easing into this different culture without being overwhelmed by the hectic pace of Naples. The spirit here is akin to the Neapolitan one, but in a much more subdued way. The same can be said of Avellino, where you can feel the Campanian spirit very clearly. Benevento, on the other hand, has historically been under the influence of Rome, rather than Naples, and so it has a unique local culture. Like Caserta, both Avellino and Benevento make excellent departure points for the rest of Campania. Yet the attractions—the unique Reg-

gia in Caserta, the ancient Roman ruins of Santa Maria Capua Vetere and Benevento, the little towns of Sant'Agata dei Goti and Sant'Angelo dei Lombardi, and the Sanctuary of Montevergine near Avellino—are worth a trip all by themselves.

Caserta is just a few miles to the north of Naples. From a small medieval town, it gained international status when the Bourbon kings in the 18th century chose it as the site of their palace. Though geographically close, the two Capuas—Santa Maria Capua Vetere and Capua proper—are very different. Capua was such an important city in Roman times that it was considered *the* major city of the Roman Empire after Rome. The names are a bit confusing: the city that was called Capua by the Romans is today called Santa Maria Capua Vetere (St. Mary Old Capua), whereas today's Capua was *Casilinium* in ancient Roman times, and was Roman Capua's harbor on the Volturno River. Both small towns lie a few minutes away to the west of Caserta.

Farther inland, and to the northeast of Naples, lies Benevento, with its mysterious heritage of witchcraft and Roman art. It holds many surprises, from a round church to a collection of Egyptian art (the result of a local cult of Isis that lasted into late Roman times). Surrounding the town is a beautiful area still little urbanized and rich in natural beauty.

Also to the east and inland of Naples lies mountainous Irpinia—the land of another original Italic people, the Irpini. This is a place of green hills and mountains, topped by medieval towns and castles. Avellino is the capital of this region, renowned for the quality of its food.

Here, you'll be able to do the kind of tour Italians love to do, stopping at each little hill town for a quick visit to the local monuments and a lengthier assessment of the local cuisine and wine.

1 Caserta

17km (11 miles) NW of Naples.

Of uncertain origin—some say that Caserta was founded by the Sannites or the Romans, and others by the Longobards, who would have moved here from Capua in the 13th century—this town developed modestly in medieval times. However, after a sleepy period of several centuries, everything changed when the Bourbons made Caserta the site of a palace explicitly meant to rival Versailles. The new town down on the plain developed around the Royal Palace to serve the needs of the court, while the old town up in the mountains (Caserta Vecchia) was nearly abandoned. Caserta then flourished in the 19th century as a business center for small industry for the whole area. The newer part is not enormously interesting, but the Old Town is a delightful medieval hill town, beautifully situated and mostly preserved.

ESSENTIALS

GETTING THERE   Caserta is easily reached by train from Naples. Trains leave Napoli Stazione Centrale every 10 to 20 minutes for the 30-minute trip to Caserta. Caserta's **railway station** is in Piazza Giuseppe Garibaldi 1 (© 0823-325479), only a few steps from the Reggia, on the other side of Piazza Carlo III.

Caserta is also easily reached by car, from either Rome or Naples, on autostrada A1 by following the sign for ROMA-NAPOLI, taking the exit marked CASERTA NORD, and following the signs for CASERTA CENTRO. Coming into town, you will see signs for SAN LEUCIO, CASERTA VECCHIA, and the REGGIA.

VISITOR INFORMATION   The **EPT information office** is on Piazza Dante at the corner with Via Douhet (© 0823-321137; www.casertaturismo.it). It is open Monday to Saturday from 9am to 7pm.

FAST FACTS   You'll find a **pharmacy** on the Corso Trieste not far from the entrance to the Reggia (Farmacia D'Errico, Corso Trieste 47; © 0823-326147). The **hospital** *(ospedale civilie)* is nearby, at Via Tescione Gennaro 1 (© 0823-304964). For an **ambulance,** dial © 0823-321000. You can call the **police** at © 112 and the **fire department** at © 115. The **post office** is on Viale Ellittico, off Viale Douhet, and is open Monday to Saturday from 8am to 2pm. For a **taxi,** call © 082-3322400 or © 082-3326919.

GETTING AROUND   The great attractions of Caserta are not concentrated in one area, but everything can be easily reached with a short car or taxi ride. While the Reggia is in the center of the new town, near the train station, the medieval town is about 10km (6 miles) up the hill that overlooks the new town to the east, and is easily reached by a road that starts off Via Medaglie d'Oro: Follow the signs reading CASERTAVECCHIA. San Leucio is on top of a smaller hill at the northern outskirts of town, off the Via Provinciale (from Piazza Vanvitelli, proceed north following the signs for San Leucio). If you don't have a car, you can go to one of the **two taxi stations** in town, on Piazza Garibaldi across from the train station (© 082-3322400); and on Via Ferrara (© 082-3326919).

EXPLORING THE TOWN

While the one reason to visit Caserta is the splendid artistic monument of the Royal Palace, do not miss out on the other attractions, which are well worth a visit.

Reggia di Caserta 🏵🏵🏵   Like a visit to Versailles outside of Paris, a visit to the Reggia is bound to stir up feelings of amazement at how such a place could be built. Simply put, this is one of the most beautiful royal palaces in the world, and the architectural undertaking can't help but seem immense. Even more than Versailles, the Reggia is a masterpiece of harmonious architecture and decorative arts. (If it seems otherworldly, it may be because the Reggia was used as a location for *Star Wars: Episode I—The Phantom Menace*).

Bourbon King Carlo III built the Reggia after deciding to move the kingdom's capital away from Naples, which he considered too open to attacks from the sea; he also wanted a palace of his own to rival the courts of Paris, London, and Madrid. Designed by the famous architect Luigi Vanvitelli in 1751, the Reggia was built using only the best materials and workmanship from all over Italy. The first stone was laid in 1752, but the Reggia took so long to build that it was finished 1 year after the architect's death in 1774, and its interior was fully completed only in 1847. Measuring over 45,000 sq. m (484,376 sq. ft.), it is divided into four wings, each surrounding a courtyard. From the main gallery—very scenic, with a view all the way to the large waterfall at the end of the park (see below)—a glorious **staircase** 🏵 brings you to the magnificent **octagonal vestibule,** decorated with precious marble in various colors. (People with limited mobility can gain access by a special elevator; ask at the ticket booth.) The scale is almost stupefying. There are 116 stairs, flanked by niches containing sculptures that allude to the grandeur of the kingdom. The two sculpted lions by Pietro Solari and Paolo Persico are among the most familiar symbols of the Reggia.

At the top of the stairs, you reach the door to the **Cappella Palatina (Palatine Chapel)** 🏵, which is graced by a gallery with 13 columns—some of which still show the damage from the 1943 bombings. The chapel was partly inspired by the one at Versailles and, like everything else at the Reggia, has imposing dimensions (37m/120 ft. long). Once inside, you will see the royal box from which the king and queen observed services over the entrance. On the main altar is the model in wood of the ciborium that should have been realized in precious stones but never was. (*Note:* the chapel was closed for restoration at presstime.)

To the left of the stairs are the **Appartamenti Storici (Royal Apartments)** 🏵🏵. The "new" apartment *(appartamento nuovo)* had a public function; these rooms were decorated between 1806 and 1815 with stuccoes, bas-reliefs, and more frescoes. The **Sala di Marte** 🏵 celebrates military virtues, with nine beautiful bas-reliefs by Valerio Villareale and a large ceiling fresco by Antonio Galliano depicting mythological scenes from Virgil's *Iliad.* The **Sala del Trono (Throne Room),** inaugurated in 1845, is dazzling, encrusted with gild stucco and 46 medallions depicting all the kings of Naples, from the Norman Roger I to Ferdinand II.

The so-called "old" apartment *(appartamento vecchio)* was the first to be inhabited: This section of the palace was used by Ferdinando IV and his wife Maria Carolina of Austria from 1780 on. Beautifully furnished and decorated with frescoes, these were the private rooms of the queen and king. First come the "conversation rooms," decorated according to seasonal themes by Antonio Dominici (*Primavera* and *Autunno,* or spring and fall) and Fedele Fischetti (*Estate* and *Inverno*—summer and winter). Spring and summer make up the receiving room and sitting room, respectively, while fall is

Caserta

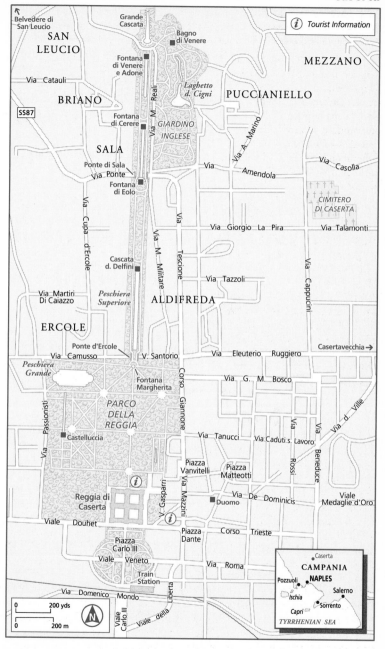

Belvedere di San Leucio

SAN LEUCIO

Grande Cascata

Bagno di Venere

MEZZANO

Fontana di Venere e Adone

Via Catauli

BRIANO

Laghetto d. Cigni

PUCCIANIELLO

SS87

Fontana di Cerere

GIARDINO INGLESE

SALA

Via M. Reali

Via A. Marino

Via Casolla

Ponte di Sala

Via Ponte

Via Amendola

Via Cupa d'Ercole

Fontana di Eolo

CIMITERO DI CASERTA

Via Giorgio La Pira

Via Talamonti

Via Tazzoli

Via Cappucini

Cascata d. Delfini

Via M. Militare

Via M. Tescione

Via Martiri Di Caiazzo

Peschiera Superiore

ALDIFREDA

ERCOLE

Ponte d'Ercole

Via Camusso

V. Santorio

Via Eleuterio Ruggiero

Casertavecchia →

Peschiera Grande

Fontana Margherita

Corso Giannone

Via G. M. Bosco

PARCO DELLA REGGIA

Via Passionisti

Via Tanucci

Via Caduti s. Lavoro

Via d. Ville

Castelluccia

Piazza Vanvitelli

Piazza Matteotti

Via Rossi

Via Beneduce

Reggia di Caserta

V. Gasparri

Via Mazzini

Via De Dominicis

Viale Medaglie d'Oro

Duomo

Viale Douhet

Piazza Dante

Corso Trieste

Piazza Carlo III

Viale Veneto

Via Roma

Caserta

CAMPANIA

Via Domenico Mondo

Train Station

Viale Carlo III

Viale della Libertà

NAPLES

Pozzuoli

Ischia

Salerno

Sorrento

Capri

TYRRHENIAN SEA

0   200 yds
0   200 m

(i) Tourist Information

(i)

(i)

the dining room, and winter is the smoking room. After these come the bedroom, the king's study, and the queen's parlor. Notice the magnificent **Murano glass chandeliers** ✴, the **carved chairs and sofas** ✴ by Nicola and Pietro Di Fiore—masterpieces of neoclassical Italian furniture—and the **paintings by Jacob Philipp Hackert** ✴, a court painter who was kept very busy by the Bourbons. Goethe called him an "inveterate hard worker," who not only painted prolifically but gave drawing lessons to the royal children and delivered lectures (note his scenes of the kingdom's harbors in the receiving room and the scenes of royal sites in the king's study). Finally, you'll come to the three rooms of the library—notice the frescoes in the third room by Friederich Heinrich Függer, said to contain hidden Masonic meanings, a subject which deeply interested the queen—and to an oval hall which contains the magnificent *presepe reale* **(royal manger scene)** ✴✴. This is a manger scene of gigantic proportions with dozens of figures in the typical Neapolitan tradition, carved by the leading wood sculptors of the time.

Also off the octagonal vestibule is the permanent exhibit **Terrae Motus,** composed of over 70 artworks by Italian and foreign contemporary artists—such as Andy Warhol and Keith Haring—in reaction to the terrible earthquake of 1980 that shook Campania.

Parco della Reggia (Reggia Gardens) ✴✴ is magnificent and correspondingly enormous (it covers about 120 hectares/296 acres); it is the most celebrated of Italian gardens in the world, graced by a number of fountains and pools. The park stretches from the palace to the nearby hills along a central path 3.2km (2 miles) long, offering a unique view of the large waterfall that feeds the fountains of the park. The waterfall—and the Caroline Aqueduct that carries the water to it from Monte Taburno 40km (25 miles) away—is artificial and was designed and built by Luigi Vanvitelli. (Today, the water is recirculated thanks to pumps, and the aqueduct instead feeds the town's supply.) Among the fountains depicting mythical events, the most spectacular is the **Fontana di Eolo (Fountain of Eolus)** ✴✴, a large construction of grottoes and figures representing the palace of the wind god. Above it and up the hill is a system of **three fountains** ✴, Fontana di Cerere (Fountain of Ceres), Fontana di Venere e Adone (Fountain of Venus and Adonis), and Fontana di Diana e Atteone (Fountain of Diana and Atteonis)—the highest—from which you can enjoy a superb **view** ✴. To the right of this last fountain is the entrance to the **Giardino Inglese (English Garden)** created for Queen Maria Carolina di Borbone by Carlo Vanvitelli (the son of Luigi), who designed the architectural part; and by the English botanist and landscaping artist Andrea Graefer, who created the rest. Covering over 30 hectares (74 acres), it is a perfect romantic realization, with a lake, a spring, and a small temple, all decorated with ancient Roman statues from Pompeii. The queen also indulged her infatuation with the Masons here, and the garden is full of hidden symbols and esoteric references. It is accessible only by guided tour.

Given the size of the park, it is a good idea to make use of the bus that goes from the park's entrance to the Fontana di Diana; you can also take the bus one-way and return on foot. We recommend a horse-carriage tour, which is very romantic and in tune with the spirit of the place. However, the carriages go only as far as the Fontana di Eolo (the rest of the way is too steep).

On weekend nights June through October, you might be able to book a special tour. **Percorsi di Luce nella Reggia (Paths of Light in the Reggia)** ✴ is a unique festival that uses music and visual and performing arts to help you discover the Reggia, the famous gardens, and the kings that inhabited it. The tours are narrated by art historians and accompanied by light effects, 18th-century music, short performances, and multimedia presentations. Started in 2003, the festival is not well established; at presstime, there was a threat of cancellation due to lack of funds. Call ahead at ⓒ **0823-4480840** or 0823-462078 to find out, or check online at www.percorsidiluce.it. (Reservations are required admission is 18€/$23; children under 6 free.)

You can always book a guided tour during regular opening hours with professional art historians by contacting **Arethusa** (ⓒ **0823 448084;** www.arethusa.net), the society that manages some aspects of Italian national artistic sites. They charge 3.60€ ($4.50) for a 1½-hour visit.

A cafeteria inside the Reggia, just before the entrance to the gardens, is open nonstop during visiting hours. In summer, you'll find a snack bar at the entrance to the English Gardens.

Viale Douhet. ⓒ **0823-277430** or 0823-277111. www.reggiadicaserta.org. Admission to apts 4.50€ ($5.65); gardens 2.50€ ($3.15); both 6€ ($7.50). Audioguides 3.50€ ($4.40). Guided tours through Arethusa 3.60€ ($4.50). Bus shuttle to Diana Fountain 1€ ($1.25) round-trip. Horse carriage to Eolus's Fountain 10€ ($13) per person round-trip. Royal Apartments: Wed–Mon 8:30am–7:30pm; last admission 30 min. prior to closing. Park: Wed–Mon 8:30am–sunset; last admission 2 hr. prior to sunset. English Gardens: guided tours every hour 9:30am to 3 hr. before sunset.

Casertavecchia ✸✸ This is considered one of the better-preserved medieval *borgos* in of all Italy, built around the wonderfully unique 12th-century cathedral, and just up the hill from the castle (today in ruins). The town was partially abandoned in the 18th century, when the king built his palace in the valley below—and required part of the population to move there as well. This helped preserve the old town above, which has survived practically intact.

Dedicated to St. Michael, the **Cathedral** ✸✸ was built by the Normans using elements of the pre-existing paleochristian church and of a nearby temple to Jupiter; it is a great example of the Norman-Arab style. The church is built of tufa stone—like the rest of the town—with delicate highlights in white marble: the three portals, the window frames, the decorative columns, and a number of zoomorphic sculptures. The dome is covered by a beautiful *tiburio*—a sort of roofed tower—where the Arab influence is readily visible. The octagonal structure has geometric designs in alternate yellow and gray tufa stone, with an ornate intertwining of arches supported by little white columns. Inside you can admire the mosaic altar baptismal font from the 4th century. Besides the beautiful facade is the 13th-century bell tower, under which passes the main street of the town; it is topped by an octagonal roof and decorated in similar fashion to the cathedral.

Behind the Duomo, on the main street, is the **Chiesetta dell'Annunziata,** a Gothic church built at the end of the 13th century; the portico was added in the 18th century, but behind it you can admire the original facade with the beautiful marble portal. Farther on is the 11th-century **Norman Castle;** most of its original structure—a central core with six towers—is in ruins, but the powerful main tower remains.

The rest of the *borgo* is a pleasant place to stroll. The narrow medieval streets retain their original paving, and all along it you notice stone archways and preserved medieval details. Not surprisingly, the town is a preferred dinner destination for locals, who come to enjoy the food, the view, and the atmosphere, especially in the warm season and on weekends. In September, Casertavecchia hosts a well-established music and art festival, Settembre al Borgo. Between the last Monday of August and September 15, the *borgo* comes alive with concerts, theater, and dance (call Caserta's tourist office for the program at ⓒ **082-3321137**).

The Radical Philosophy of Gaetano Filangeri

Little known to most, the important Neapolitan jurist and philosopher Gaetano Filangeri was in frequent correspondence with Benjamin Franklin during the years of the American Revolution and the elaboration of the American Constitution. Franklin obtained several copies of Filangeri's main work, the six-volume *The Science of Legislation*, and tried to include some of the principles in the U.S. Constitution.

Filangeri's work was cut short by his early death in 1788, and the sixth volume is only an outline, However, the other volumes had begun to appear in 1780 and met with great success, and have been translated into English, French, German, and Spanish.

Born near Naples in 1752 as Prince of Arianello, Filangeri was an encyclopedist and a reformer; his work was central to the birth of a liberal movement in Southern Italy, and some of his ideas continue to be rediscovered to our own day. He was particularly strong on public education, which he believed to be the foundation of everything, leading to happy, healthy, satisfied citizens. Hence he considered that public education was also the foundation of public tranquillity. Among his other ideas, he believed that honesty was the primary social virtue, and that merit should be the only distinction among individuals . . . ideas as much in need today as in his own time.

Strada Provinciale per Casertavecchia. Duomo: Piazza Vescovado. ✆ 082-3371318. Duomo and Chiesetta: Free admission. Daily 9am–1pm and 3:30–6pm; till 7:30pm in summer.

San Leucio ⃰ In 1789, Ferdinando IV established a colony on this hill, only a couple of miles from the Reggia, around a small church of probable Longobard origin. To make the colony economically independent, the king promoted the production and manufacture of silk, establishing a silkworm farm and a weaving factory. He also endowed the colony—with the help of his liberal minister Bernardo Tanucci—with completely innovative laws and organization—based on the political philosophy of Gaetano Filangeri, which were quite radical even by today's standards (above). Education was obligatory and free from the age of 6 up, and only those skilled in their job were allowed to marry and have children. There was no distinction between sexes, and every manufacturer had to contribute a portion of their gains to the common fund for those who became invalids from poor health or old age. The factory became famous for its precious fabrics. Though today the farm has disappeared, the weaving factory is still operating (privately, under the Stabilimento Serico De Negri) and the craft is still alive, with expert artisans weaving damasks, brocades, and other fabrics of international reputation.

Opening onto Piazza della Seta, the original colony is very scenic, with ordered rows of houses offering beautiful views over the Reggia and the surroundings. Following a small road to the right past the building that housed the silk factory, you will find the **Casino Reale di Belvedere,** a small (compared to the Reggia) palace in the delightful green surroundings of a park; this was the king's hunting preserve and a smaller part of the Palazzo Reggia's park. The **Royal Apartments** ⃰⃰ are richly frescoed with **allegoric**

scenes on the ceilings painted by Fedele Fischetti; those in the queen's bathroom are by Philipp Hackert. The view from the **Belvedere** ✦✦ is superb. In the casino, an exhibit of original weaving machinery is still in working order—you can ask to see one functioning. The **Museo della Seta (Silk Museum)** contains a display of a large number of the wonderful original fabrics produced in this unique environment.

If you choose to climb the road that leads towards the left (below the steps of the original silk factory on Piazza della Seta), you will find the **Casino di Caccia (Hunting Lodge)** of the Aquaviva princes—the original owners of the estate—and the **Vaccheria,** the stables where Ferdinand established the colony's first weaving activity before he built the village.

Piazza della Seta, off Strada Statale SS87. ✆ **800-411515** or 082-3301817. 5€ ($6.25). Mon–Sat 9:30am–5:30pm. Closed Jan 1, Easter, August 15, and Dec 24–25.

WHERE TO STAY
NEAR THE REGGIA

Hotel Europa   This is considered (together with the Jolly below) the best hotel in town, with large, comfortable rooms—only a few steps from the Reggia and the railway station. Although it has all the comforts—including a fitness room and a billiard room, comfortable mattresses in the guest rooms, and modern bathrooms—it is far from plush: The furnishings are functional and the decoration is minimal. There are also mini-apartments (suites with small utility kitchens that sleep four). The restaurant near the hotel—Via Roma—is very good (see "Where to Dine," below).

Via Roma 19, 81100 Caserta. ✆ **082-3325400.** Fax 082-3325400. www.hoteleuropacaserta.it. 62 units. 120€ ($150) double; 150€ ($195) suites. Rates include buffet breakfast. Extra bed 30€ ($38). Specials available. Children under 3 stay free in parent's room. AE, DC, MC, V. Parking: 15 € ($19). Closed Dec 31–Jan 1. **Amenities:** Bar; health club; concierge; business center; room service; babysitting; laundry service. In room: A/C, TV, minibar, hair dryer.

Hotel Jolly Caserta   Housed in a large pink building of modern style, the Jolly has over a hundred rooms and gives you the standards and uniformity you expect from a chain hotel (it may not be charming and quirky, but it is clean and comfortable). The medium-sized rooms have large beds; decor and furnishings are modern.

Viale Vittorio Veneto 13, 81100 Caserta. ✆ **082-3325222.** Fax 082-3354522. www.jollyhotels.it. 107 units. 138€ ($173) double. Rates include buffet breakfast. Extra bed 30€ ($38). Specials available. Children under 16 stay free in parent's room. AE, DC, MC, V. Free parking. **Amenities:** Restaurant; bar; concierge; conference room. In room: A/C, satellite TV, minibar, hair dryer, safe.

IN SAN LEUCIO

Hotel Belvedere   Located in San Leucio, this hotel offers good value in terms of amenities and prices. The spacious modern rooms have wood floors and functional furniture, including comfortable beds. Some have balconies or small terraces, and all have good-sized bathrooms. Note that the "health club" is more outdoor recreation area than indoor fitness center.

Via Nazionale Sannitica 87, Località Vaccheria, 81100 Caserta. ✆ **082-3304925.** Fax 082-3485914. www.hotel belvederesanleucio.it. 35 units. 80€ ($100). Rates include buffet breakfast. Extra bed 20€ ($25). Children under 6 stay free in parent's room. AE, DC, MC, V. Free parking. Small pets allowed. **Amenities:** Restaurant; bar; disco; health club; concierge; business center; room service; laundry service. In room: A/C, TV, hair dryer, safe.

IN CASERTAVECCHIA

Hotel Caserta Antica   Located near the old *borgo,* this hotel has accessibility and comfort to spare—an on-site restaurant, the bar, a terrace, meeting rooms and, best of all, a 14m×8m (45 ft.×26 ft.) swimming pool. The rooms are simply—sometimes spartanly—decorated, but are cozy enough. There are doubles, triples, and quads; that most units have balconies is a plus.

Via Tiglio 41, Localitá Casertavecchia, 81100 Caserta. ℂ 082-3371158. Fax 082-3371158. www.hotelcaserta-antica.it. 25 units. 75€ ($98) double; 88€ ($114) triple; 110€ ($140) quad. Rates include breakfast. Extra bed 20€ ($25). Children under 6 stay free in parent's room. AE, DC, MC, V. Free parking. **Amenities:** Restaurant; bar; outdoor pool; concierge. *In room:* A/C, TV, safe.

WHERE TO DINE
NEAR THE REGGIA
Ciacco ℛ CAMPANIAN/CASERTAN   This simple restaurant, favored by locals, especially for the midday meal, prepares and serves good food in a pleasant atmosphere. They always have a variety of fish dishes—*pasta alle cozze e vongole* (pasta with mussels and clams) is excellent—and a number of meat choices, including very tasty local sausages.

Via Maielli 39. ℂ 0823-216491. Reservations recommended for dinner. Secondi 7€–12€ ($8.75–$15). AE, DC, MC, V. Daily 12:30–3pm and 7–10:30pm.

Mastrangelo CAMPANIAN/CASERTAN   Similar in clientele to Ciacco above, this is also a good local restaurant, with an ample choice of dishes. The menu varies, but it always includes both surf and turf options, true to the Casertan tradition. The homemade *cannelloni di pesce* (homemade tubes of pasta filled with seafood) are very good, as is the daily catch *all'acqua pazza* (cooked in a light tomato-and-herb broth).

Piazza Duomo 5. ℂ 0823-371377. Reservations recommended for dinnder. Secondi 8€–12€ ($10–$15). AE, DC, MC, V. Daily 12:30–3pm and 7–10:30pm.

Via Roma ℛ CAMPANIAN/CASERTAN   This is the best restaurant in town, but don't be put off by the formal atmosphere and the elegant decor: The service is very welcoming and accommodating, and the food's excellent. You'll find a seasonal menu offering traditional specialties as well as more sophisticated innovations based on local ingredients, such as *pappardelle con mazzancolle e porcini* (homemade pasta with local shrimp and porcini mushrooms), and roasted pork. *Note:* Although it's next door to Hotel Europa, this is a stand-alone restaurant.

Via Roma 21. ℂ 0823-443629. Reservations recommended for dinner. Secondi 9€–14€ ($11–$18). AE, DC, MC, V. Daily 12:30–3pm and 7–10:30pm.

IN SAN LEUCIO
Antica Locanda CAMPANIAN/CASERTAN   This atmospheric restaurant right in the picturesque piazza in the heart of San Leucio offers well-prepared, traditional, and local dishes as well as a number of regional favorites. The menu changes often, but you should always find the excellent *scialatielli ai frutti di mare* (homemade eggless pasta with seafood) and grilled baby pig.

Piazza della Seta 8. ℂ 0823-305444. Reservations recommended on weekends. Secondi 8€–12€ ($10–$15). AE, DC, MC, V. Daily 12:30–3pm and 7–10:30pm.

IN CASERTAVECCHIA
Da Teresa ℛ CASERTAN/PIZZA   This restaurant enjoys the best location in Casertavecchia, with a beautiful terrace and a garden offering great views over Caserta and—on good days—all the way to the sea beyond. The restaurant is large and includes a regular dining room and a picturesque inner courtyard with seating. In addition to good-quality pizza, they have an extensive menu of local specialties. They also offer four excellent prix-fixe menus (including a primo, a secondo, a side dish,

and a dessert). The dishes vary daily, but the always-available *menu del Ghiottone* (gourmet menu) offers such choices as *cinghiale alla brace* (charbroiled wild boar). The *menu tipico* offers local dishes such as *misto alla brace* (charbroiled mixed platter with local vegetables, meats, and sausages).

Via Torre 6, Casertavecchia 81020. ℰ **082-3371270.** www.dateresa.com. Reservations recommended for dinner. Secondi 7€–13€ ($8.75–$16); also choice of 4 prix-fixe menus 13€–20€ ($16–$25). AE, DC, MC, V. Thurs–Tues 11:30–3pm and 7–midnight.

CASERTAVECCHIA AFTER DARK

Caserta has a lively—albeit small—cultural scene, consisting mostly of concerts of classic, pop, and jazz music; theater (in Italian, of course); and special folkloric events based on Caserta's major historical attractions: the Reggia, the Belevedere, and Casertavecchia. The best source of information is the online magazine (in Italian only) *CasertaMusica.com*. The tourist office (see earlier in this chapter) can also help.

2 Ancient Rome's Second Rome: Santa Maria Capua Vetere ✦

6.5km (4 miles) W of Caserta and 24km (15 miles) NW of Naples.

The history of Capua is a bit like that of the mythical phoenix: cyclically achieving greatness and splendor, only to be destroyed down to the ground. Starting as a small Oscan (one of the local Italic populations) village that was transformed by the Etruscans into a town in 589 B.C., Capua was taken over by the Sannites (the Italic population of the Benevento region) in 438 B.C. The town, located in a fertile area, grew rapidly to become—according to the Roman historian Livy—the richest and largest town in Italy outside of Rome. Allied with the Romans, it committed the mistake of trying to go its own way and was punished with complete political annihilation in 211 B.C. In 89 B.C., the Romans decided to rebuild a colony there, and the town rapidly grew again to become one of the major cities of the Roman Empire. The Via Appia, *regina viarum* (queen of all roads) of the ancient Romans, was created to unite Rome and Capua; it was the first large road the Romans built (the 1st "consular" road, as they are still locally called) and was later extended all the way to Brindisi, the harbor on the eastern Apulian coast. This was the highway for all the precious goods from Asia, and Roman Capua (today called Santa Maria Capua Vetere) was a major stop.

Capua prospered even through the barbarian invasions after the end of the empire, but in A.D. 840 it was completely destroyed by the Saracens. The fleeing population decided to rebuild Capua on the ruins of the nearby Casilinum, the small harbor on the Volturno River. At the location of old Capua, only a church remained standing (today, it is the Duomo). A new village developed from the ruins around the church, and once again it prospered, slowly growing into the lively and flourishing modern town of Santa Maria Capua Vetere. With a modern-day population double that of nearby Capua, the Capuans are definitely a resilient people!

ESSENTIALS

GETTING THERE   You can get to Santa Maria Capua Vetere by train from Rome. First, take the train to Caserta, then switch to a local train for the short ride to Santa Maria Capua Vetere. Alternatively, you can get a train from Naples at the Stazione Centrale, which takes about a half-hour.

Arriving by car is simple: From either Rome or Naples on autostrada A1, take the exit marked CASERTA NORD. Follow the signs for SANTA MARIA CAPUA VETERE; you will find yourself on a local road that actually retraces the original route of the Roman Appian Way. You can also take this road directly from Caserta, continuing west on Viale Douhet past the Reggia and out of town. Arriving from Caserta and the highway, you will find two parking lots off the main road to your left, one behind Piazza San Pietro, and another off Via F. Pezzella, which you can take from Corso Garibaldi.

VISITOR INFORMATION   You can find information at the **Pro Loco office** in the Municipio (Via Albana, Inst. Lucarelli; ✆ **0823-700589;** Mon–Fri 9am–1pm). Otherwise, you can get information online through the Caserta **EPT** (www.caserta turismo.it).

FAST FACTS   You'll find a **pharmacy** in Piazza San Francesco, not far from the amphitheater (Farmacia Salsano, Piazza S. Francesco 6; ✆ **0823-798583**). The hospital is **Casa di Cura Santa Maria della Salute** (Via Avezzana 6; ✆ **0823-812522**). For an **ambulance,** dial ✆ **118.** You can call the **police** at ✆ **113** or at ✆ **112.** The **post office** at Piazza Resistenza 1 (✆ **0823-818411**) is open Monday to Saturday from 8am to 2pm.

EXPLORING THE TOWN

Santa Maria Capua Vetere is a small town that can be easily visited on foot. During your strolls, keep an eye out for archaeological remains, which are everywhere: pieces of column, sculpted busts of gods and goddesses, and capitals, all incorporated into more modern buildings over the centuries. The most important ancient Roman attractions are off the ancient Appian Way—the central stretch of it is called Corso Aldo Moro—that runs east-west from Piazza San Pietro to **Arco di Adriano (Hadrian's Arch).** Located at Capua's western entrance on the ancient Via Appia, this was a majestic triumphal monument composed of three arches. Today the marble finish has disappeared and only one arch remains—the southern one—though you can see the three brick pillars that supported the central arch.

At no. 210 of the Corso, you'll see the remains of a Roman house, **Casa di Confuleio Sabbio** (discovered by chance during excavations on a building site in 1955), which dates from the 1st century B.C. It was the home of a freedman, a merchant specializing in the production of *sagum:* the heavy woolen cape worn by soldiers and—in a less refined version—by slaves and paupers. At the corner of the Corso and Via Galatina is the large building that housed the prisons until only a few decades ago; under it are the remains of a **Criptoportico,** an ancient Roman covered promenade that is believed to have been part of the *Capitolium,* the town's major temple in Roman times. It received light from 80 windows and was decorated outside by 30 statues inside niches. Until the 17th century, this was a favorite local promenade; however, in the 18th century, after a temporary transformation into a Franciscan convent, it was used as stables by the Bourbons and, in the 19th century, as a prison.

Anfiteatro Campano ✺✺   Second in size only to the Colosseum in Rome, this Roman amphitheater was probably built around A.D. 3, enlarged in 119 by the Emperor Hadrian, and further embellished by Emperor Antoninus Pius. It remains majestic in spite of having been used—like so many Roman buildings in Italy—as a mine for quality marble and construction materials over the centuries. It was also picked apart in the 9th century onwards during searches for bronze and lead (the building's large stone components were broken apart to get at the heavy metal clamps that held them together). Some of its columns and stones were even used to rebuild the town and the Duomo (see below). This practice—common throughout the

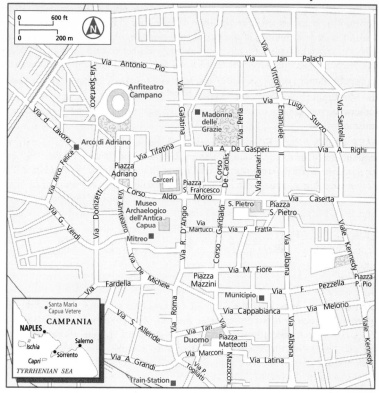

Roman world in the centuries after the fall of the empire—could be called an early version of recycling.

Judging from what remains, though, the amphitheater must have been quite a sight back in those days. Four stories tall, it was completely covered in travertine stone, with each marble bust of a god serving as the keystone for each of the 240 arches (80 for each of the three lower floors), and full-length statues under the arches of the second and third floors. You can still see the carved keystones over the main entrance (busts of Ceres and Juno). The giant arena has a maximum length of about 170m (557 ft.) and can seat over 60,000 people. The corridors below the arena are relatively well conserved and still show traces of stuccoes and frescoes; this is where the gladiators waited between combats (if they had survived, of course). It is also where all the scene props were kept and where the bestiary—home of the fighting animals—was located. One of the small rooms here was transformed into a Christian oratory in the 9th century, and you can see the remains of the paleochristian altar and paintings that rested here. The garden in front of the amphitheater has been turned into an open-air museum, where you can admire many of the fragments of the original decorations of the amphitheater as well as other buildings in town. Among the objects on display is the beautiful 2nd-century **mosaic** ✦ depicting Nereides and Tritons.

Also in the garden is the building housing the **Museo dei Gladiatori (Gladiators' Museum)** ✛, a permanent exhibit dedicated to gladiatorial fights. On display are four suits of gladiator armor as well as a model reconstruction of the amphitheater, and an animation of a gladiator fight. Spartacus, the slave made famous by the 1960 Stanley Kubrick film, was a graduate of the gladiator school located near this amphitheater.

Piazza Ottobre, off Piazza Adriano. ✆ 0823-798864. Admission 2.50€ ($3.15); includes Museo dei Gladiatori, Museo Archeologico dell'Antica Capua, and Mitreo. Tues–Sun 9am–5:30pm.

Duomo ✛✛   Dedicated to Santa Maria Maggiore, this church was originally built in A.D. 432 by Saint Simmaco—Capua's bishop—over the Grotto of Saint Prisco and the catacombs. In A.D. 787, Arechi II added the two external naves. The church was restored nearly a thousand years later in the baroque period, when in 1666 the apse was completely rebuilt; it was further redecorated in the 18th and 19th centuries. The interior is quite suggestive, with five naves supported by columns borrowed from the nearby amphitheater and Roman temples, topped with Corinthian capitals. Among the artworks not to miss are the carved Renaissance **cyborium** ✛ in the chapel at the end of the right-hand nave; the **wooden choir** ✛ in the apse; the **organ;** and the chapels opening off the left-hand nave—gated **Cappella del Conforto** ✛✛, with a beautiful altar in colored marble inlay, and **Cappella della Morte** ✛, featuring more notable inlay work at the end of the nave.

Via Sirtori 3, off Piazza Matteotti. ✆ 0823-846640. Free admission. Daily 9am–12:30pm and 4:30–6pm.

Mitreo ✛   Built between the 2nd and 3rd centuries A.D., this is one of the few remaining ancient temples dedicated to the god Mithras (a cult of Persian origin, which became diffused in Rome during the 1st century A.D.). Discovered by chance in 1922, the temple site is very well conserved. Its vaulted ceiling is decorated with green and red six-pointed stars and a large fresco of Mithras sacrificing a white bull. On the lateral walls above the stalls, you'll see remains of fresco decorations depicting the seven stages of initiation into the cult of Mithras. Ask at the ticket booth of the Anfiteatro Campano if you want to arrange a visit.

Vicolo Mitreo, behind the Museo Archeologico dell'Antica Capua. ✆ 0823-844206. Included in Anfiteatro Campano admission (see above). Tues–Sun 9am–6pm.

Museo Archeologico dell'Antica Capua ✛   If you have the time, this museum is an important stop, since it displays a large collection of work ranging from the beginning of Capua in the 10th century B.C. to its flourishing as a Roman town in the 1st century A.D. Housed in the Torre di Sant'Erasmo—a suggestive tower originating before the Longobards—the museum was inaugurated in 1995, consolidating findings from the area's various archaeological excavations. The museum is chronologically arranged, showing jewels, weapons, pottery, and artwork consistent with each period; most come from funerary collections.

Via Roberto D'Angiò 48, off Corso Aldo Moro. ✆ 0823-844206. Included in Anfiteatro Campano admission (see above). Tues–Sun 9am–6pm.

3 Capua & its Churches ✛

11km (6½ miles) W of Caserta and 28km (17 miles) NW of Naples.

In Roman times, this lively little town at a bend in the Volturno River was the fluvial harbor Casilinum, serving the nearby town of Capua (today's Santa Maria Capua Vetere; see above), and guarding an important bridge of the Appian Way. Towards the end

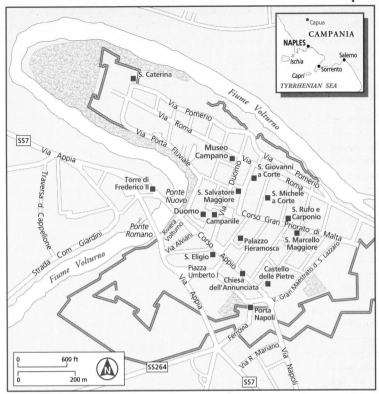

of the Roman Empire, Casilinum was progressively abandoned as the needs for the bridge's defense disappeared. It was brought back to life when Capua's inhabitants took refuge here after their town was destroyed by the Saracens in A.D. 840. They came with all they could save from their old town, even the town's name, so that Casilinum was renamed Capua. Its strategic position made it into an independent principality, though it was repeatedly besieged by various powers until the unification of Italy in 1860. As the seat of a bishopric, it played an important religious role throughout the centuries, which is still visible in its many churches.

ESSENTIALS

GETTING THERE   By train, you can reach Capua from Rome by changing at Caserta. From Naples, trains leave directly for Capua from all stations; the trip takes less than an hour. If you're traveling by car from either Rome or Naples, take the exit marked CAPUA of autostrada A1 (ROMA-NAPOLI). Take Via Appia, following the signs for CAPUA; the town is to your left after you cross the bridge over the Volturno River.

From Caserta, take Viale Douhet past the Reggia and follow it westward out of town; it will become Via Appia and pass through Santa Maria Capua Vetere. You will find a parking lot off Via Appia at Piazza Umberto I, near the center of town.

VISITOR INFORMATION   The **tourist office** of the Pro Loco is in the Municipio, located at Piazza dei Giudici 6 (© **0823 962729**). Hours are Monday to Friday from 9am to 1 pm. Otherwise, you can get information online through the Caserta **EPT** (www.casertaturismo.it).

FAST FACTS   You'll find a **pharmacy** at Via Duomo 32 (© **0823-961224**). The **hospital** (*ospedale civile* in nearby Caserta) can be reached at © **0823-627397.** For **first aid,** dial © **18.** You can call the **police** at © **112.** The **post office** (© **0823-620511**), at Via Pier Delle Vigne 3, is open Monday to Saturday from 8am to 2pm. For a **taxi,** call © **0823-963142** or 0823-963521.

EXPLORING THE TOWN

Small in scope, Capua maintains the feeling of an ancient town—it helps, too, that its fortifications are intact, as well as many of its churches and two of its castles. The old Appian Way crossed the center of town (today named Corso Appio), coming off the old Roman bridge to the west—it remained perfectly functional until 1943, when it was destroyed by bombing during World War II. It has since been rebuilt. The Appian Way exits the city at the 15th-century gate, **Porta Napoli,** to the east. Just before the gate along Via Andreozzi is the **Castello delle Pietre,** the 11th-century Norman castle; you can admire its remaining powerful crenellated tower—there were four originally. Off the Corso Appio is **Piazza dei Giudici,** the central square of Capua, where Via Duomo begins. It is graced by the 13th-century church and Arch of Saint Eligio and the 16th-century **Palazzo del Municipio (Municipal Building).** On its facade, you can see several marble details taken from the Anfiteatro Campano of Santa Maria Capua Vetere, including six arch **keystones** with relief **busts** ✿ of divinities (Jupiter, Neptune, Mercury, Juno, Ceres, and Mars), which were originally keystones of the arches in the Anfiteatro Campano of Santa Maria Capua Vetere (see earlier in this chapter). Other Roman remains have been incorporated into buildings around town, such as the bas-relief of **Via Pier delle Vigne** (also off Corso Appio) at no. 26; on that same street, at no. 34, you will find a picturesque Renaissance house with an arched courtyard designed by Guido da Maiano, as well as a couple of interesting churches.

If you visit during Carnival, do not miss the grand parade and the many shows organized for the occasion (contact the **EPT** in Caserta © **0823-321137** for a schedule of events). Capuans claim the paternity of **Pulcinella** (p. 296), and the holiday is celebrated with great pride by the local population. The whole town participates in the festivities, which include theater and cabaret shows with famous professionals. The performances are often farcical, and sometimes reflect on recent political events.

Duomo, aka Cattedrale di Santo Stefano e Sant'Agata ✿✿   Originally founded in 856 and redone in 1120, this Duomo was almost completely rebuilt in 1724 and redecorated in 1850. Then, after the much-altered structure was severely damaged by bombing in 1943, it was rebuilt according to its original plan, using many of the original materials. The columns of the beautiful atrium, built in the 11th century, are topped by Corinthian capitals of the 3rd century. The Duomo's 9th-century bell tower still stands, supported at its base by four ancient Corinthian columns. Among the medieval sculptures decorating the bell tower, you can admire three Roman bas-reliefs from the amphitheater in Santa Maria Capua Vetere (see earlier in this chapter).

Inside the church, a range of artwork dates from the 12th century to the present. (Note the splendid, lavishly decorated 13th-century **ceremonial candle holder.**) In the **Cappella del Sacramento** at the end of the right-hand-side nave is a beautiful **altar** made of marble and precious stones. The *Assunta* in the presbytery behind the altar is by Francesco Solimena. The two green columns supported by carved lions on the modern pulpit's sides were part of the original 13th-century **ambo.** Under the presbytery is the **crypt** with a small chapel decorated on the outside with mosaic and other pieces from the ancient ambo. The **Cappella del Corpo di Cristo,** adjacent to the cathedral, houses the **Museo Diocesano** (© **0823-961081;** admission 3€/$3.75; open daily 9:30am–1pm and 3:30–7pm), where you will find the church's **treasure,** including a collection of Islamic carved crystal dating from the 11th and 12th centuries, as well as fragments of the cathedral's original majolica floors, and a number of 15th- and 16th-century paintings.

Piazza Landolfo, off Via Duomo. © **0823-961081.** Free admission. Daily 8–11am and 5:30–7:30pm.

Museo Campano &&   Housed in the Palazzo Antignano, and graced by a bizarre 15th-century **portal** & in Catalán-Moorish style (at no. 76 of Via Roma), the museum was established in 1874. It is dedicated to the art, religion, and history of Campania. The museum's holdings are extremely rich, and are divided into two sections: Archaeological finds are on the first floor, and medieval displays are on the second.

The archaeology section includes collections of Oscan (the Osci were the local Italic population), Etruscan, and Roman art from a number of sites in the area. Among the Etruscan-Oscan pottery are beautiful black plates with fish decorations (from the 4th century B.C.). The star of the show, however, is the unique collection of **Le Madri (The Mothers)** &&, in room nos. V through IX. This is a whole group of statues and architectural structures with Oscan inscriptions, which were found in a field near Santa Maria Capua Vetere. They pertain to an Oscan sanctuary that was active between the 6th and 1st centuries B.C. and was dedicated to the Italic goddess of fertility and maternity, Matuta. Several of these figures, carved in tufa stone, show mothers offering their children to view and (probably) thanking the goddess for the gift of maternity.

Among the other high points of the museum is a **Roman mosaic** found in the temple of Diana Tifatina near Sant'Angelo in Formis, on the second floor in room no. X. In the medieval section, you'll see a large display of stone carvings, mainly from the 10th to the 13th centuries; in room no. XXVI, you'll find the internationally famous collection of **Sculture Federiciane (Federician Sculptures)** &, a group of marble sculptures from the castle built by Federico II in 1239 in Capua. Among the works on display here are portraits of Federico himself. One of the greatest of medieval rulers, he was crowned king of Sicily at the age of 4 and became Holy Roman Emperor in 1220, participated in the Sixth Crusade, and crowned himself king of Jerusalem in 1229. He was called **Stupor Mundi,** or "wonder of the world," but he was excommunicated twice by distrustful popes.

Also on the second floor is the picture gallery, displaying paintings from the 15th to the 18th centuries, as well as earlier artwork such as a 12th-century fresco saved from a local church. All of this does not exhaust the museum's holdings; there is also a library of 40,000 volumes and 1,000 parchment manuscripts, some of the most striking of which are on display.

Via Roma 68, off Via Duomo. © **0823-961402.** www.museocampano.it. Free admission. Tues–Sat 9am–1:30pm and Sun 9am–1pm.

Sant'Angelo in Formis 🎭🎭🎭 This is one of the most fascinating medieval churches in Italy, graced with magnificent original frescoes and enjoying an ideal position on the slopes of Mount Tifata, the mountain overlooking Capua.

Sant'Angelo can be easily reached from Capua by the bus line for Sant'Angelo in Formis. You can also get there by car; from Capua's town center, take Via Roma and continue out of town following the signs for S. ANGELO IN FORMIS. You'll come first to the village and then, higher up along the road, to a church standing alone in the square. On clear days, the view from the square stretches all the way out to Ischia.

The basilica was built over the ruins of the **Tempio di Diana Tifatina**—the most important pre-Christian sanctuary in this region. The construction date of the original church is unknown, but it's believed to have existed in the 10th century. In 1073, after the church was bequeathed to the famous monastery of Montecassino, it was completely rebuilt to its current form by the abbot Desiderio of Montecassino, who also established the sanctuary as an important religious site. The church is famous both for its architecture and for its frescoes, which display unique characteristics of the Romanesque-Campanian style. The portico in front of the church has one round central arch, while the lateral ones are pointed arches typical of Islamic architecture. Under the portico you will see the first series of frescoes, with a wonderful **Saint Michael** 🎭🎭 from the 11th century, and others from the 12th and 13th centuries.

Inside, the basilica is divided into three naves by 14 columns topped with beautiful antique Corinthian capitals. Little remains of the 11th-century mosaic floor—you'll see some at the end of the right nave—and parts of the marble floor are original to the temple of Diana (dated by an inscription from 74 B.C.). The greatest attraction is really the **frescoes** 🎭🎭🎭 that decorate the whole interior. They were painted by the local school, which followed Byzantine models and iconography. Along the sides of the central nave is the cycle depicting scenes from the Old and New Testaments; on the inner facade is the Giudizio Universale (the Last Judgment).

Piazza della Basilica di Sant'Angelo in Formis. ✆ 0823-960492. Free admission. Sun and holidays 10am–4pm year-round; summer Mon–Sat 9:30am–noon and 3–7pm; winter Mon–Sat 9:30am–12:30pm and 3–6pm.

WHERE TO STAY

Hotel Capys 🎭 This modern, family-run hotel offers the best lodgings in Capua. Located in the town's new part, out of Porta Napoli, off the Via Appia in the direction of Castel Volturno (you'll need to use a cab or your own transportation), the hotel provides excellent service. The exterior's modern look does not prepare you for the pleasant, carefully furnished guest rooms. Some rooms open onto the very pretty interior garden, and others have small terraces; bathrooms are good-sized and modern.

Via Santa Maria la Fossa 24 (off SS Appia), 81043 Capua (CE). ✆ 0823-961299. Fax 0823-961299. www.hotel capys.it. 45 units. 95€ ($119) double; low season 75€ ($94) double. Rates include breakfast. Extra bed 20€ ($25). Specials available. Children under 6 stay free in parent's room. AE, DC, MC, V. Free parking. **Amenities:** Restaurant; bar; concierge; room service; babysitting; laundry service. *In room:* A/C, TV, minibar, hair dryer, safe.

Masseria Giòsole *(Finds)* If you want a taste of the countryside and don't mind staying outside town, this picturesque farm will be perfect for you. It offers very comfortable and well-appointed rooms, done up in a tasteful country style, with idyllic views over green fields and shady trees. The wonderful meals served here are created with the farm's own produce. If you have a car, this makes an optimal base for a visit to Capua, Santa Maria Capua Vetere, or Caserta. Indeed, the farm is only a short distance from Capua, on the western bank of the Volturno River, though you might find it difficult to tear yourself away for your explorations.

Via Giardini 31 (off Via Appia, west of the Volturno River bridge), 81100 Capua (CE). © **0823-961108.** Fax 0823-968169. 13 units. 120€ ($150) double. Rates include half-board. Extra bed 30€ ($38). Specials available. Children under 6 stay free in parent's room. AE, DC, MC, V. Free parking. Closed Dec 31–Jan 1. **Amenities:** Restaurant; babysitting. *In room:* A/C, TV, hair dryer.

WHERE TO DINE

You'll find a number of good restaurants outside the center of Capua, along Via Fuori Porta Roma, the urban part of Via Appia on the western bank of the Volturno in the modern part of town. Choices are more limited in the heart of town.

Ristorante Eredi Romano CAPUAN   Very central, this restaurant is a bit more formal than the Oasi (below) and is favored by locals, especially for midday meals. The menu varies but always includes a variety of very well-prepared primi—the *rigatoni cacio e pepe* (short pasta with cheese and black pepper) was very good, as was the *panzotti* (a sort of ravioli) served with local *mozzarella di bufala* and fresh tomatoes. Afterwards, you can enjoy classic secondi, often seafood offerings that change daily according to the market.

Piazza Duomo 6. © **0823-622755.** Reservations recommended in the evening. Secondi 9€–16€ ($11–$20). AE, DC, MC, V. Daily 12:30–3pm and 7:30–11pm.

Ristorante Pizzeria L'Oasi PIZZA   You can't beat this simple restaurant for convenience—it's right on Piazza Duomo. The food is good and the "no-frills" atmosphere youthful. Pizza, the house specialty, is available with a variety of toppings. The regular restaurant menu offers a good choice of dishes; while the pasta is good, expect it to be simple, not gourmet.

Piazza Duomo 6. © **0823-622755.** Reservations recommended in the evening. Secondi 6€–14€ ($7.50–$18). AE, DC, MC, V. Daily noon–3pm and 7–11pm.

4 Bewitching Benevento ⊛

51km (31 miles) E of Caserta and 86km (53 miles) NE of Naples.

Known as the Salem of Italy for its infamous but curious reputation for witchcraft, Benevento is also renowned for its art and culture. Still, suffering and strife have been the lot of this ancient town, inhabited since around the 7th century B.C. Originally called Malies, or Maloenton, it was an important Sannite town, which opposed the Romans (bad move) and was soundly defeated in 275 B.C. As a sign of goodwill after winning the city, the Romans changed its name to *Beneventum,* but that didn't really help: The city continued to be much fought over through the ages. In turn, it was taken over by the Goths, the Byzantines, and then the Longobards—who established it as a principality. It was then attacked by the Popes, who kept their hold over the city in spite of the sack by Federico II. Benevento finally knew some quiet in the 16th century and was relatively peaceful under the Roman church state rule, but it was almost completely destroyed by the earthquake of 1688. The city's archbishop—who, in later years, was to become Pope Benedetto XIII—rebuilt the city and supported its cultural and spiritual development. The reborn Benevento enjoyed a new period of prosperity until World War II, when the town was heavily bombarded in 1943—65% of it, including important monuments, was destroyed, and 2,000 people died. The town has recovered since and has become a lively and pleasant provincial town with a very marked character—the influence of Rome really differentiates it from the rest of Campania.

ESSENTIALS

GETTING THERE Benevento is easily reached by train from Naples in about 1 hour and 15 minutes; service is relatively frequent, with 12 daily runs from Monday to Saturday (fewer on Sun). From Rome, the trip takes about 2 hours and 20 minutes, and there are eight daily runs (fewer on Sun). The **railway station** (© 0824-50159) is in Piazza Colonna 2, to the north of town.

If you are driving, from Caserta take autostrada A30 in the direction marked by the sign SALERNO; after a few kilometers you'll see signs for the A16 in the direction of AVELLINO and BARI. Take the exit signed BENEVENTO and continue on the short stretch of highway to the town. From Naples, take autostrada A3 in the direction marked AVELLINO and the A16; take the exit signed ENEVENTO.

VISITOR INFORMATION The local **tourist office EPT** is excellent (Via Nicola Sala 31; © 0824-319911 or 0824-319931; www.eptbenevento.it) and maintains an **information office** in Piazza Roma 11 (© 0824-319938).

FAST FACTS You'll find a **pharmacy** in Piazza Orsini 13 (© 0824-21590). The hospital is **Ospedale Fatebenefratelli** at Viale Principe di Napoli 14–16 (© 0824-50374). For an **ambulance,** dial © 118 or the **Croce Rossa Italiana** (© 0824-315000). You can call the **police** at © 112. There is a **post office** (© 0824-24074) in Piazza Colonna Vittoria, where the railway station is located. It's open Monday to Saturday from 8am to 2pm. For a **taxi,** dial © 0824-50341.

GETTING AROUND The center of Benevento is small but extends uphill, so you might want to use public transportation instead of walking the whole way. Several city buses go from the train station to the historic center; the best are nos. 1 and 7, both going by Trajan's Arch and up to the Rocca dei Priori (see below). Before boarding, you will have to buy bus tickets at a tobacconist's or a newsstand; tickets cost .65€ (80¢) and are valid for 90 minutes.

You can also take a **taxi;** the stand (© 0824-50341) is by the railway station in Piazza Colonna.

EXPLORING THE TOWN

Benevento is one of the nicest towns in Campania, high on a hill at the heart of a hilly green valley. It has some wonderful monuments, most of them along the historic town's main street, **Corso Garibaldi;** this stretches from Piazza IV Novembre, at the top of the hill, to Piazza Cardinal Pacca, farther down to the west. Only part of the ancient wall that surrounded the town is still visible, but at the top of the hill you can see the castle: **Rocca dei Rettori,** on Piazza IV Novembre. In accordance with a practice typical in Italy, the fortress—built by the Pope in 1321—was constructed over a Longobard castle, which itself had been built over a Roman fortress that protected the Appian Way and the road to Avellino. The Rocca was recently restored and houses Benevento Provincial Government as well as the historical section of the Museo del Sannio (see below). Also off the square is the delightful **Villa Comunale** ⊛, the public gardens designed in the late 19th century by Alfredo Denhart. They were recently restored at great expense (about 7 million dollars), including the beautiful Liberty-style fixtures (such as the lamps and the benches, which are original). The charming bandstand is a new copy of period design. The park here has a wonderful view over the surrounding valley.

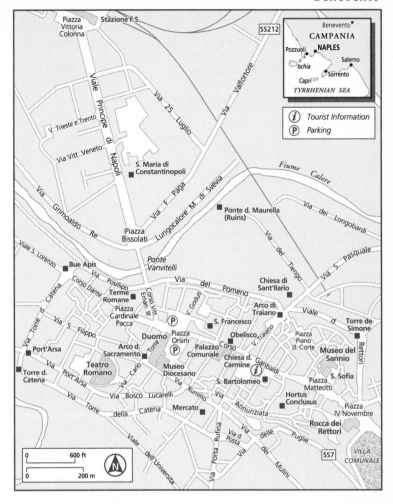

Arco di Traiano (Trajan's Arch) ✰✰✰ This is quite simply the best conserved—it's practically pristine considering its 2,000 years of age—ancient Roman triumphal arch in the world. The lengthy restoration—mainly a careful cleaning that took 14 years—was completed recently (2001) and the arch is again visible in all its glory. Built between A.D. 114 and 117 by Rome to honor the Emperor Trajan, it was located at the beginning of the Via Traiana, what was then a new—and shorter—route that led from Benevento to Brindisi, the harbor that was Rome's gateway to the eastern Mediterranean. The arch's reliefs celebrate the deeds of this illuminated leader, who enlarged and strengthened the Empire while implementing a generous social policy and numerous public works. During the Middle Ages, this superb work of art was enclosed in the city walls and used as the main gate into town (hence the local name for the arch: Port'Aurea), which contributed to its conservation. The nearby church,

Sant'Ilario a Port'Aurea ⚜ (Via San Pasquale, off the Arco di Traiano; ✆ **0824-21818**), a Longobard church from the 10th century, houses a permanent exhibit on the arch and on life in Rome under the Emperor Trajan.

Via Traiano, off Corso Garibaldi.

Duomo ⚜ The first version of this church goes back to the 7th century A.D., when it had only a central nave. After consecration in A.D. 780, during Longobard domination, two naves were added in the 9th century and two others in the 12th century. The structure was then restored and redecorated in the 18th century, at which point it became known as one of the most beautiful Romanesque churches in Italy. However, the bombing of 1943 destroyed almost the entire ancient church, sparing the facade and the bell tower (one of many sad examples in Italy of artworks that survived a dozen centuries of strife, only to be wrecked by modern madness). The elegant Romanesque facade, done in the Pisan style of striped marble, is from the 13th century; it is decorated with arches, animal statues, and a loggia topped by carved capitals alive with figures. The beautiful rose window in the center of the loggia was decorated with a mosaic, which was lost during the bombing. The richly carved jambs of the central portal date from the 12th century; they once bracketed 13th-century sculpted bronze doors which were considered rivals of the famous ones of Florence's baptistery; unfortunately, the door was blown to pieces by the bombing. What was saved has been restored, and you can now see the 72 frames that composed the doors displayed inside the church. The top 43 are decorated with scenes from the life of

The Witches of Benevento

Legend has it that Benevento is a land of witches, and has been for thousands of years. The origins of the legend lie with the Egyptian cult of Isis—goddess of magic and mystery among other things—which found fertile ground in Benevento during the Roman era. The cult remained an important force here even after the cult was replaced by Christianity in other parts of Italy. When the Longobards from Central Europe took the town in A.D. 571, they imported their own religion, a nature cult based on the adoration of the god Wothan and his sacred walnut tree. They elected an old walnut near the **Ponte Leproso** as the town's sacred tree. (The Ponte Leproso was a bridge built by the Romans over the Sabato River at the Via Appia's entrance to Benevento. The bridge is still in use today; you can see it by taking a short walk west of the Teatro Romano). Around this walnut tree the Longobards held their nocturnal open-air rituals which, combined with knowledge of the cult of Isis and the vivid imagination of the locals, gave rise to the witchcraft legend. At the same time, the *Noce di Benevento*—the walnut tree of sorcerers and witches—became famous.

The Longobards were converted to the Catholic religion by Saint Barbato, the town's bishop, in the 7th century A.D. Revelry around the walnut tree ended (partly because the bishop was skeptical enough to cut down the sacred tree). Nevertheless, the witches remained, some say, and can still be seen dancing by the site on certain nights. . . .

Christ, from the Annunciation to the Ascension. In the bottom 29, local religious personalities—including the archbishop and 24 bishops—are well represented and named. The bell tower, to the left of the facade, was built in the 13th century and is decorated with marble carvings of Roman origin.

On the left side of the Duomo is the Piazza Orsini with the recently restored 18th-century *Fontana delle Catene,* a monumental fountain dedicated to Benevento's Archbishop Orsini, who became Pope Benedetto XIII. The **Museo Diocesano**—housed partly in the crypt and partly in the Palazzo Arcivescovile (Piazza Orsini 27; ℭ **0824-54717**)—holds remains from the destroyed Duomo, including the little that was left of the extremely rich treasure after the bombing.

Piazza Duomo. ℭ 082-447591. Free admission. Daily 9am–12:30pm and 5–7pm.

Museo del Sannio ✦

Originating in the 19th century, this art museum has been enlarged and completely reorganized over the years. It was moved to its present location at the beginning of the 20th century. The archaeological and medieval sections, including the picture gallery, are located in the monastery of Santa Sofia, whereas the historical section is in the Rocca dei Rettori on Piazza IV Novembre. Among the most interesting items on display is the collection of Egyptian art coming from the local temple of Isis (built by the notoriously cruel Emperor Domitian in A.D. 88). It was decorated both with statues imported from Egypt and others produced locally in the Egyptian style—including a portrait of Domitian in Egyptian attire. In addition, you'll be hard pressed to find a better reminder of the cosmopolitanism of the Roman Empire than the authentic Egyptian temple here, complete with statues of Anubis and Thoth, buried in the middle of Campania.

Among the other archaeological remains in the museum are some beautiful sculptures, mostly Roman copies from original Greek art. The medieval section includes great sculptural examples, and the picture gallery holds a collection stretching from the 15th to the 20th century, including major names such as Francesco Solimena *(Madonna col Bambino e i Santi)* and Carlo Maratta *(Sacra Famiglia).*

The historical section of the museum (inside the Rocca dei Rettori) displays important documents and signatures of famous historical figures who played important roles in the town's history. The view from the castle is great.

Piazza Matteotti. ℭ 0824-21818 or 0824-28831. Admission 3€ ($1.65). Tues–Sun 9am–1pm.

Santa Sofia ✦

This medieval church's unique design singles it out as an architectural marvel; it shows the merging of pagan and Christian cultures. Begun in 762 by the Longobard Arechi II when he became Duke of Benevento, the church's star-shaped structure is composed of a central hexagon, covered by a dome, and supported by six powerful columns; around this are eight square pillars and two columns topped by Corinthian capitals. The pillars are aligned with the surrounding walls, which are part circle and part star, creating a strange perspective. In the apse you will see fragments of a great cycle of frescoes from the 8th century, representing, among other things, scenes of the life of Saint Zaccaria; the surrounding walls, however, are decorated with representations of nature derived from pagan symbols.

Outside the church and isolated from it is the bell tower, which was redone in 1703. Attached to the church is the convent of the order of Benedictine nuns founded at the same time as the church. It became one of the most powerful monasteries in Italy during the 12th century, famous for its type of writing, which became known as *"scriptorium Beneventanum."* The monastery houses the **Museo del Sannio** (see earlier in this section), from which it is possible to access the elegant **cloister** ✴. This is another structure of interwoven cultural heritages, with elegant Moorish arches and Romanesque columns, each of them decorated with strange, fantastic, or everyday scenes, from boar hunts to pilgrimages. *Note:* The church was under restoration at presstime and no date was announced for the reopening. The cloister, however, can still be visited.

Piazza Matteotti. (C) 0824-21206. Free admission. Daily 10am–noon and 4:30–7pm.

Teatro Romano ✴ The few spectacular remains of Roman amphitheaters—the arenas for circus performances such as the Coliseum in Rome and the Anfiteatro Campano in Santa Maria Capua Vetere—sometimes make us forget how important real theater, such as drama, comedy, and poetry as well as music, were to Roman culture. Theaters for these events (the classic hemicycle) were ubiquitous, to the extent that even little towns had one or more in their possession. Few of them remain, though, which makes this ruin all the more special. Built in the 2nd century A.D. and restored under the ruler Caracalla, its first level, and a portion of the second, still stands with parts of the halls. The seating area is also well preserved; only the third floor was lost. The path that leads from the ticket booth to the theater takes you past all sorts of sculptures, capitals, and massive hunks of marble that once graced the structure. With a diameter of 90m (295 ft.), the theater could contain up to 20,000 spectators. During summer, the theater is still used for opera performances and classical dramas (contact the tourist office for a schedule of events).

Via Port'Arsa. (C) 0824-29970. Admission 2€ ($2.50). Wed–Mon 10am–5pm.

WHERE TO STAY

Grand Hotel Italiano ✴ This hotel is family-run (since 1920) and is also the best in town, offering excellent service and very well-thought-out accommodations. It is conveniently located not far from the train station, in a pleasant, residential part of town with lots of shops; the center of town is a 15-minute walk or a short bus ride away. The large guest rooms have very comfortable beds, and the bathrooms are modern. All are done up in a modern and functional style, but are pleasing to the eye (not spartan, and not Ikea-ridden, either). The parking area in the rear courtyard is locked behind a gate (if you get there early and there is space). The restaurant on the premises is very good (see below).

Viale Principe di Napoli 137, 82100 Benevento. (C) 0824-24111. Fax: 0824-21758. www.hotel-italiano.it. 71 units. 62€–103€ ($78–$129). Rates include buffet breakfast. Children under 3 stay free in parent's room. AE, DC, MC, V. Limited free parking inside. **Amenities:** Restaurant; bar; concierge; business center; room service; babysitting; laundry service. *In room:* A/C, TV, dataport, minibar, hair dryer.

Hotel Villa Traiano ✴ Benevento's most elegant hotel is housed in a neoclassical villa in the heart of town, only a few steps from Trajan's Arch. Completely restored, it offers elegant and pleasant accommodations, with antique and reproduction furniture, good-sized guest rooms, and fairly spacious marble bathrooms. The roof garden and the veranda are great places to relax, and boast views of the famous arch.

Viale dei Rettori 9, 82100 Benevento. (C) 0824-326241. Fax 0824-326196. www.hotelvillatraiano.it. 19 units. 100€–120€ ($125–$150). Rates include buffet breakfast. AE, DC, MC, V. Free street parking. **Amenities:** Restaurant; bar; concierge; business center; room service; laundry service. *In room:* A/C, TV, dataport, minibar, hair dryer.

President Hotel In the center of town, this modern hotel caters to a business clientele and tourists alike. The rooms are airy and open, with hardwood floors and furniture.

Decor is simple, functional, and tasteful, the beds large and comfortable. The hotel's public areas are also roomy, with plenty of space to relax.

Via Perasso 1, 82100 Benevento. © 0824-316716. Fax 0824-316764. www.hotelpresidentbenevento.it. 69 units. 90€–120€ ($113–$150) double. Rates include buffet breakfast. Children under 5 stay free in parent's room. AE, DC, MC, V. Free parking. **Amenities:** Restaurant; bar; concierge; business center; room service; laundry service. *In room:* A/C, TV, dataport, minibar, hair dryer.

WHERE TO DINE

Antica Trattoria Pascalucci 🥢🥢 *Finds* FISH/SANNITE   Located on the Appia Way between Benevento and San Giorgio del Sannio, this restaurant is famous for its attentive service and large menu of tasty local peasant cuisine—this is the kind of place where Italians like to go on a family outing on weekends or for a special dinner with friends. Erminia De Cicco is faithful to the Sannite tradition and prepares top-notch fish dishes and grilled meats. Start with the *antipasti* for a taste of local cured meats and *sottoli* (delicious vegetables prepared and kept in olive oil).Continue with *tubetti alle cozze* (short pasta with mussels) or *fusilli ai funghi porcini* (fresh pasta with porcini mushrooms). You can then attack the secondo, choosing between perfectly grilled meats or *pesce al forno in umido* (fish baked with tomatoes)—the type of fish depends on the market. Simply wonderful.

Via Lanassi 2, Località Piano di Cappelle. © 0824-778400. Reservations recommended. Secondi 9€–22€ ($11–$28). AE, DC, MC, V. Daily noon–3pm and 7:30–11:30pm.

Nunzia 🥢 BENEVENTAN   This is a welcoming, family-run restaurant where you'll enjoy the local cuisine and feel as if you were invited into the home of a Beneventan host. You'll also spend very little, so it's not surprising that this place is very popular with locals. Be sure to come early, or make a reservation. The highlights are the *primi* and the soups, which might include tasty *spaghetti e piselli* (pasta with peas) and delicious *pasta e ceci*. If they have it, do not miss their specialty, *baccalá con capperi e olive* (salt cod in an olive-and-capers sauce).

Via Annunziata 152. © 0824-29431. Reservations recommended for dinner. Secondi 6€–12€ ($7.50–$15). MC, V. Mon–Sat noon–3pm and 7–11pm.

Pizzeria Baffo D'oro 🥢 PIZZA   This excellent pizzeria is located in a residential area not far from the train station. The menu includes classics like *pizza margherita* as well as specialties such as a pizza covered with local sausages. The ample choice of appetizers includes very good *bruschetta* (rustic bread toasted and seasoned with olive oil and fresh tomatoes).

Via Diacono, off Via Principe di Napoli. © 0824-443372. Reservations recommended on weekends. Pizza 5€–10€ ($6.25–$13). MC, V. Daily 7–11pm.

Restaurant of the Grand Hotel Italiano BENEVENTAN   The Grand Hotel Italiano is where locals come for a well-prepared meal in an elegant, formal setting; the excellent service is a pleasant plus. The menu is small but changes daily and always includes a few dishes inspired by local culinary traditions. You might find excellent *gnocchi ai porcini e allo speck* (potato dumplings with a heart of cheese and porcini mushrooms, served with a creamy sauce with smoked ham); or a stew of tender bits of pork with a sauce of pickled peppers.

Viale Principe di Napoli 137. © 0824-24111. Reservations recommended. Secondi 6€–11€ ($7.50–$14). AE, DC, MC, V. Daily noon–2:30pm and 7:30–11pm.

Ristorante Pizzeria Traiano ✯ BENEVENTAN/PIZZA　Excellent local cuisine and great pizza (available only in evening) make this a popular place—more so than say, Pizzeria Baffo D'oro, reviewed above. Open the almost unnoticeable entrance door and you'll find yourself in a crammed little restaurant with two small dining rooms, usually filled with people happily downing large dishes of food. This place is particularly famous for its variety of *antipasti* that come either as appetizers or as side dishes—try *involtini di melanzane* (eggplant rolls) if they have them. The restaurant is also famous for its homemade desserts. Both antipasti and desserts are on display near the entrance. Pasta dishes—such as *spaghetti alle cozze e vongole* (with mussels and clams)—are also excellent.

Via Manciotti 48. ℭ **0824-25013.** Reservations recommended for dinner. Secondi 6€–11€ ($7.50–$14). MC, V. Wed–Mon noon–2:30pm and 7:30–11pm.

Taverna Paradiso, aka Di Orazio *Finds*　Hidden away in one of the narrow streets right in the heart of town, this reliable restaurant serves traditional fare that's popular with locals. The atmosphere is livelier than at the Grand Hotel above and more down-to-earth. On the seasonal menu you might find great *tagliatelle ai carciofi* (fresh home-made pasta with sautéed fresh artichokes), or a mean pork stew with vegetables.

Via Mario La Vipera 33, off Viale dei Rettori. ℭ **0824-42914.** Reservations recommended. Secondi 8€–14€ ($10–$18). AE, DC, MC, V. Wed–Mon 1–3pm and 7–11pm.

SHOPPING FOR LOCAL PRODUCTS

Benevento is famous for its *torrone* (Italian nougat) and the liqueur known as *Strega* (the name means—what else—"witch"), a secret mixture of 17 herbs and spices that's great poured over fruit salads and ice cream (it's a little too syrupy to drink straight).

While Strega is not for everyone, torrone is a wonderful delicacy made of egg whites, honey, hazelnuts, and almonds, and sometimes enriched with chocolate and citrus essences. Already known in Roman times—historian Tito Livio mentions it in his writings—torrone attained European fame in the 17th century, when the Beneventan candy makers created what are today's traditional varieties: crumbly torrone covered with dark chocolate or with lemon, orange, or coffee icing. Among the best makers in town are **Alberico Ambrosino** (Corso Garibaldi 111; ℭ **0824-28546**); **Umberto Russo** (Via Gaetano Rumno 17; ℭ **0824-24472**); and **Fabbriche Riunite Torrone di Benevento** (Viale Principe di Napoli 113; ℭ **0824-21624**), a consortium of local torrone producers. You will also find a torrone Strega, which is excellent, and some delicious *caramelle* (small hard candies with a soft center) filled with "cream of Strega" (the Strega version of Bailey's) liqueur.

This region is also well known for its wines, as it counts an uncommonly high number of D.O.C. vintages. Standouts include Aglianico del Taburno, Solopaca, Guardiolo, Sannio, Sant'Agata dei Goti, and Taburno. Another famous wine from this area is the refreshing Falanghina, a white wine with an aromatic bouquet and a dry flavor.

5 Around Benevento: the Land of the Sannites ✯

Valle Caudina (Montesarchio) 18km (11 miles) SW of Benevento; Valle Telesina (Telese Terme) 17km (10½ miles) NW of Benevento ; Val Fortore (Pietrelcina) 12km (7½ miles) NE of Benevento

As you leave Caserta on your way to Benevento, you'll enter the land of the Sannites, one of the original Italic people who occupied this part of Italy before the coming of the Greeks. This is a region rich in history and natural beauty, where great artistic treasures lie amidst green hills and valleys. One of the greatest draws here, though, is that few people are clued in enough to visit (it's not uncommon to be the only foreign tourist in a hotel), allowing the area to maintain its authenticity. Local culture in this region is very much alive, with each town claiming to be different not only from the rest of Italy, but from other towns a few miles away. If you have a car and the where-withal, we suggest that you make a trip here as soon as possible to soak up the unique atmosphere while you still can.

VALLE CAUDINA 🕰🕰

This beautiful valley, dominated by the Monte Taburno, is where the Appian Way passes between Capua and Benevento. From Benevento, take the SS7 (the Appian Way) and follow the sign MONTESARCHIO. The old town of **Montesarchio,** 18km (11 miles) southwest of Benevento, is picturesque, but it has been surrounded by modern devel-opment (aka sprawl). The 15th-century **Castle** is an imposing fortress which was used as a political prison until the 19th century. Outside of town, you can make a pleasant **excursion** to the national park of **Monte Taburno** (www.parcotaburno.it). From the 1,394m-high (4,572-ft.) mountain, you can enjoy a splendid **panorama** 🕰🕰; this, by the way, is the mountain and the starting point of the aqueduct that Vanvitelli built to bring water to the Reggia in Caserta. To reach the trail, take the scenic local road marked VITULANO at the eastern edge of town; it passes under the Castle of Montesar-chio and climbs the mountain. After 14km (8½ miles) you will reach Piano Caudio where, at a fork in the road, you need to bear left towards the **Rifugio-Albergo Taburno,** a bar/restaurant, at an altitude of 1,050m (3,444 ft.). This is where the trail to the summit starts; it's a fairly easy climb that will take about an hour.

For a good meal, head to **Ristorante 'O Pignatiello** 🕰 (Via Vecchia Annunziata 2; © 0824-847470); alternatively, you can find good pizza at **Pizzeria Tangredi** 🕰 (Via Vitulanese 108; © 0824-831446). You can also eat very well and, of course, stay overnight at the **Cristina Park Hotel** 🕰🕰 (Via Benevento 102, 82016 Montesarchio; © 0824-835888; www.cristinaparkhotel.it; 105€/$131 double) or at **Hotel La Siesta** (Via Vitulanese 123, 82016 Montesarchio; © 0824-834675; 55€/$69 double).

Continuing on SS7 out of Montesarchio and then turning onto the local road, you'll reach the pretty mountain town of **Airola,** 26km (16 miles) southwest of Ben-evento. The town is dominated by its scenic castle and by a beautiful 16th-century **Chiesa dell'Annunciata.** This church's attractive facade is by Luigi Vanvitelli; its inte-rior holds equally interesting artwork.

Eventually, you'll get to medieval **Sant'Agata dei Goti,** 36km (23 miles) from Ben-evento. This ancient little town of Sannite origin takes its name from a colony of Goths who were allowed to establish themselves here after their defeat in the battle of Mount Vesuvius in A.D. 553. Located in the Valle Caudina, it enjoys a scenic position high on a cliff of tufa stone. Although Sant'Agata dei Goti was among the towns in the area most damaged by the earthquake of 1980, and the local economy was deeply depressed, the town still boasts a number of attractions. Famous for its beautiful churches and medieval atmosphere, it also has a decidedly urban structure, which was built accord-ing to a unique semicircular plan. The 10th-century **Duomo,** redone in the 12th cen-tury, contains fragments of the beautiful mosaic floor and, in the crypt, the original frescoes from the 10th century. The 13th-century **Chiesa dell'Annunziata** is graced by a richly decorated 16th-century portal, the inside of which holds a beautiful painting of the *Annunciazione* by a 15th-century Catalán master. The 11th-century **Chiesa di**

San Menna is also well worth a visit, with its simple interior still embellished by large fragments of the original mosaic floor.

While in town, stop for a gelato at the local **Bar Gelateria Normanno** (Via Roma 65; © 0823-953042), which makes its own delicious ice cream in many unusual flavors (try the delicious *bacio Normanno*), and a proprietary *spumone all'Annurca* (a sort of sherbet-shake made with the renowned local apple). For a real meal, head to **Ristorante L'Antro di Alarico** (Piazza Duomo; © 0823-717454) or to **Ristorante La Taverna dei Goti** (Piazza Castello, inside the Castello Ducale, across from the church of San Menna; © 0823-953494). For a really special treat, make a reservation at **Agriturismo Mustilli** (Vico dei Fiori 20, 82019 Sant'Agata dei Goti; © 0823-717433; www.mustilli.com; 75€/$94 double), which serves superb meals prepared with its farm's produce: homemade pasta *(ravioloni, cavatelli, pacche)* with seasonal sauces, such as wild mushroom in the fall and wild asparagus in the spring; *agnello* (lamb); *arista di maiale* (pork roast); *brasato* (beef in wine and vegetable sauce); and desserts made with the tasty local apples *(annurche di Sant'Agata)*. You can stay overnight in one of their six rooms inside the 18th-century Palazzo Rainone in the historic center of Sant'Agata.

VALLE TELESINA

Following the ancient road that leads to Telese from Benevento, you'll discover villages and small towns full of history and character. From Benevento, take SS 372 in the westerly direction indicated by signs for TELESE TERME. Just a few miles after Benevento, you can take a detour for **Torrecuso** , a beautiful medieval *borgo* with a scenic castle, high on a cliff that affords a superb panorama. Continuing on SS 362, you'll enter the area of **Solopaca,** from the name of the village that dominates the vineyard area; it produces one of the best D.O.C. wines of the Sannio. You can have a good meal in town, accompanied by excellent local wine, at **Ristorante La Torretta** (Via Bebbiana 21, Solopaca; © 0824-977310).

Continuing on SS 362 for 17km (11 miles), you'll get to **Telese Terme,** a green and pleasant little town, famous for its spa. The town's sulfur thermal springs, beneficial to skin and ear ailments as well as respiratory illnesses, suddenly appeared after the earthquake of 1349—one of the rare cases of a natural disaster's silver lining. The spa—called **Terme di Telese** (© 0824-976888; www.termeditelese.it)—is in a beautiful park where pavilions and pools have been built over the natural springs. They offer a wide range of services, ranging from baths to mud applications to more complicated therapies. From the Terme's park, you can set out on an easy walk (only 1km/½ miles southeast) to the pretty **lake of Telese** , a perfect spot for a picnic.

In lieu of a picnic, head to **Locanda della Pacchiana** (Viale Minieri 32; © 0824-976093) for a typical Sannite meal and good local wine; or go a bit farther on to **Ristorante La Pergola** (Viale Minieri 252; © 0824-975528), which also serves local Sannite cuisine and a choice of seafood in a slightly more formal atmosphere. Or you can opt for a meal at the best hotel in town, **Grand Hotel Telese** (Via Cerreto 1, 82037 Telese; © 0824-940500; fax 0824-940504; www.grandhoteltelese.it; 140€/$175 double, 200€/$250 suite), which offers elegant accommodations as well as spa treatments. At the other end of the spectrum, in the countryside, you can stay overnight at **Hotel del Lago** (Via Panoramica del Lago 1; Telese Terme; © 0824-976221; www.hoteldellago.3000.it; 52€/$65 double).

Thermal springs in the area were already famous in antiquity, as shown by the ruins of **Telesia** ⌖, only a couple of miles out of town to the west. This was a Sannite and then Roman town; you can still see the whole set of walls and, inside, remains of pavement, a theater, and three thermal baths. Just outside the walls is an amphitheater.

Leaving Telese Terme, you can continue towards **Guardia Sanframondi,** a picturesque medieval town dominating the surrounding valley, only 9km (5½ miles) away. Built around the **medieval castle**—from where you can enjoy a fantastic view ☞—the *borgo* has important churches rich in art, such as the **Chiesa dell'Annunziata** and **San Sebastiano.** You can stay—or just have an excellent meal with a view—at **Hotel Ristorante Il Cervillo** ☞ (Strada Provinciale Guardia-Cerroto, Località Cervillo; ☏ **0824-861047;** www.ilcervillo.it; 52€/$65 double); the restaurant is closed on Wednesday.

Farther up the mountains, in another 5.5km (3 miles) you'll reach **Cerreto Sannita** ☞☞. Completely rebuilt after the earthquake of 1688, the town is a harmonious ensemble in late baroque style, with many interesting churches—the **Cattedrale,** and the churches of **San Martino** and of **San Gennaro** are the most noteworthy—and *palazzi.* The town is famous for its ceramics, an art imported to the area after the earthquake when artists from the king's manufactures of Capodimonte moved here. Today, local artists in Cerreto and in the nearby village of **San Lorenzello** continue the tradition of crafting 18th-century Capodimonte porcelains. You can see a complete historic display at the **Mostra Permanente della Ceramica Antica e Moderna** (Piazza L. Sodo, off Corso Umberto I; ☏ **0824-861337** or 0824-861700). There's another at the **Museo Civico e della Ceramica** (Corso Umberto I, inside the church of San Gennaro and the Convent of Sant'Antonio; ☏ **0824-815211**). If you're more interested in buying wares, try the showroom **Keramos** (Via Nicotera 84; ☏ **0824-861463**).

In Cerreto, you can stay and eat at the hotel restaurant **A' Capuana** ☞ (Via Lupariello 6, 82032 Cerreto Sannita; ☏ **0824-861002;** www.acapuana.it; 65€/$81 double) or at the restaurant hotel **La Vecchia Quercia** (Via Cerquelle 25, 82032 Cerreto Sannita; ☏ **0824-861263;** www.vecchiaquercia.com; 70€/$88 double). In San Lorenzello you can eat at **Archimagicus** (Via Monterbano; ☏ **0824-860098**) or at the **Pizzeria Velardi** (Via Telese 66; ☏ **0824-861627**).

Continuing farther north into the mountains for 11km (6½ miles), you'll reach the picturesque medieval town of **Cusano Mutri** ☞☞, with its stone houses, the churches of Santi Pietro e Paolo and San Giovanni, and its Norman castle. The road then proceeds to **Pietraroja,** a little mountain town famous for the **Parco Geopalentologico di Pietraroja** ☞ (☏ **0824-868000;** www.geologi.it/pietraroja), a geo-paleontological site rich in fossils. A famous fossil of a baby dinosaur, Scipionyx Samniticus, was found here.

VAL FORTORE ☞

This area is the home of the famous Padre Pio (Father Pius), who died in 1968 and was canonized by Pope John Paul II in 2002. He was born in **Pietrelcina** and became an important figure for his work with kids and teenagers; his town has now become a pilgrimage site. Even if you are not particularly religious, the excursion is well worth it, if only for the ride alone—the meandering road takes you through scenic green mountains that afford great views. From Benevento take SS 212; Pietrelcina is only about 12km (7½ miles) away.

Once in Pietrelcina, you can eat a very good meal as well as lodge at **Lombardi Park Hotel** (Via Nazionale, SS 212, 82020 Pietrelcina; ☏ **0824-991144;** www.lombardiparkhotel.it; 100€/$125 double); the restaurant (☏ **0824-991206**) is closed on Tuesday. You can also eat well at **Trattoria Il Foro dei Principi** (Via S. Paolo; © **0824-991634;** closed Tues) and at **Trattoria Bacchus** (Via dell'Orto 8; © **0824-991366;** closed Mon).

Continuing on scenic road SS 212 for 6km (3¾ miles) after the town of Pietrelcina, you'll reach the pretty hill town of **Pesco Sannita.** If you are a *torrone* lover, you can proceed a bit farther (15km/9 miles) to **San Marco dei Cavoti** ⊛. While the road here is much less scenic, the town really does make the best *torrone* (Italian nougat) in the world, so you'll be rewarded for the trek. In the medieval *borgo,* they hold the delicious **Festa del Torrone (Torrone Festival)** in December. The specialty here is bite-sized *torroncini* covered with dark chocolate. Among the best are the *baci* from **Premiata Fabbrica Cavalier Innocenzo Borrillo** (Via Roma 66; © **0824-984060**); and the torroncini produced by other descendants of this same illustrious clan of sweet-makers, such as **Anna Maria Borrillo** (Via Martiri di Bologna 18; © **0824-984939**) and **Dolciaria Borrillo** (Contrada Catapano 22; © **0824-995099**). Even farther away in the mountains is the picturesque village of **Montefalcone di Val Fortore,** with its ruined castle—it was destroyed in 1809 because it became a refuge for bandits—affording sweeping views over the whole valley. Here you will find another famous torrone artisan: **Antonina Petrillo** (Vico San Vincenzo 2; © **0824-969266**).

You can eat in town at two very good restaurants: **Ristorante Il Leone d'Oro** (Via Papa Giovanni XXIII; © **0824-984782**) and **Ristorante La Pergola** (Via Beviera 48; © **0824-984080**).

6 Avellino ⊛⊛ & the Hill Towns of Irpinia ⊛⊛

35km (22 miles) S of Benevento and 54km (34 miles) E of Naples.

To the east of Naples lies the green province of Irpinia, inhabited since prehistoric times by the Irpinians, another original Italic people. Though defeated by the Romans in 290 B.C., the Irpinians were not subdued for another 200 years. That was in 80 B.C., with the foundation of the Roman colony named *Abellinatium* (later changed to *Abellinum*). After being conquered by the Longobards and then the Normans, this area finally knew a period of political quiet under Bourbon rule. The dangerous political situation pushed the local populations to build away from the pretty valleys, high on the hills and mountains, in search of positions easier to defend. This has structured the province as we see it today, with green valleys spreading beneath little mountain towns and villages.

The pretty scenery here is really a bonus, however: The real reason to visit is the food—considered the best in Campania and among the best in Italy.

AVELLINO

The capital of Irpinia, Avellino is not to be confused with the prosperous Roman town of *Abellinum*—which became today's Atripalda. Avellino grew out of what was originally a fortified village built by the Longobards near the site of Roman Abellinum (3km/2 miles to the west); the older city was abandoned because it was too difficult to defend. The population moved up to the new Avellino, which became an important town because of its strategic position dominating the road between Benevento and Salerno. Unfortunately, little remains of the ancient town because of the numerous earthquakes that have hit the area—last and not least the one of 1980, whose terrible economic repercussions are still felt here. However, the little that is left from antiquity is worth seeing and certainly justifies a visit.

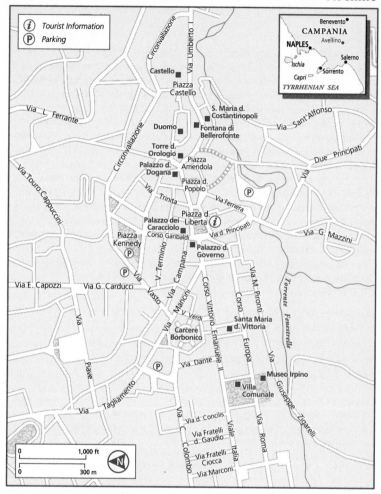

GETTING THERE   Avellino is easily reached by train from Benevento and Salerno in about 40 minutes and 30 minutes, respectively, by direct train. From Naples you need to change in Salerno, but the trip still takes only about 1½ hours. Avellino's train station is in Via Francesco Tedesco (© **892021**).

If you are driving (which we highly recommend for this area), take the autostrada A30 towards the sign for SALERNO from Caserta; after a few kilometers you'll see signs for the A16 in the direction of AVELLINO. From Naples, take autostrada A3 and follow the sign for AVELLINO. Once there, you'll want to leave your car in a parking lot. If you have luggage in your car, you'll want a garage. The covered garage in Via Terminio 20 (© **0825-23574**) is an excellent one, charging only 2€ ($2.50) per hour for a basic car.

TOURIST INFO   The local tourist office is at Piazza della Libertà 50 (© **0825-74732**) and is open Monday through Friday 8am to 2pm and 2:30 to 4:40pm;

Pulcinella

Pulcinella, the famous white-dressed, black-masked, pizza- and spaghetti-eating character, is the Campanian counterpart to the Venetian masks of the *Commedia dell'Arte*. His familiar figure has become a sort of local hero, and plays an important role in celebrations, especially during **Carnival**. Many towns in Campania have claims for the paternity of this character—Capua for one—but the truth is more complicated. In Acerra (a little town just north of Naples), a tailor named Andrea Calcese "Ciuccio" is supposed to have invented Pulcinella sometime before his death around 1656 (you can still see his house in town at Via Suessola 6). Ciuccio did not actually invent Pulcinella; he popularized him after a farmer from Giffoni created him.

According to historians, though, the Pulcinella character already existed in the *Atellane* (traditional theatrical farces with typical characters, similar to the *Commedia dell'Arte,* which were common in Campania during the late Roman Empire), and that his name was derived from *pullicenus,* late Latin for "chick."

Whatever its origins, you will probably encounter Pulcinella at various turns if you travel through this region.

Saturday 9am to 1pm. The **EPT** office for the province is at Via Due Principati 5 (© **0825-74731** or 0825-74695; fax 0825-74757; www.eptavellino.it).

FAST FACTS You'll find a **pharmacy** in Corso Vittorio Emanuele 11 (© **0825-35097**). You will find a number of banks and **ATMs** along Corso Vittorio Emanuele II, such as the **Banca di Roma** (Corso Vittorio Emanuele II 35; © **0825-24737**). The **hospital San Giuseppe Moscati** is at Via Cristoforo Colombo 20 (© **0825-23343** or 0825-36891). For an **ambulance,** dial © **118.** You can call the **police** at © **113** or at © **112.** The **post office** is at Via Francesco De Sanctis 3, off Corso Europa (© **0825-781209**).

SPECIAL EVENTS The town is famous for **Carnevale Irpino,** the festival organized for the celebration of Carnival. Included are traditional performances, the most famous of which is **Zeza.** Taking its name from the wife of the famous character Pulcinella, this musical farce narrates the adventures of the Zeza family when their daughter Porzia decides to get married to Don Zenobio. Parades are an important part of the festival; one of the best is **Concorso della Zeza,** a large mummer competition. Contact the **EPT** (Piazza Libertá 50; © **0825-74732,** 0825-74731, or 0825-74695) for a schedule of events.

EXPLORING THE TOWN

The heart of town is the beautiful **Piazza della Libertà,** graced by a central garden with three fountains and a view of the mountain of Montevergine, looming above. To the north of the square is the 18th-century **Palazzo Caracciolo,** built by the princes of Avellino and today the seat of the provincial government; to the west is **Palazzo del Governo**—a Dominican convent until 1807. To the square's west runs **Corso Vittorio Emanuele,** the elegant shopping strip mall where locals love to come for their evening promenade. If instead you take **Via Giuseppe Nappi** to the east, you come to the medieval heart of town, which stretches between the cathedral and the ruins of the castle, and still shows the typical street structure. **Piazza Amendola,** the small, triangular square at the end of Via Giuseppe Nappi, has to its left the medieval **Palazzo della Dogana,** redone in the 17th century and decorated with ancient Roman busts (of the charming emperors Caligula, Nero, and Commodus) and a statue of Prince Marino Caracciolo. The building was eventually turned into a movie theater, though restoration is pending since a fire partially destroyed it. From this square—where you can see the baroque **Torre dell'Orologio (Clock Tower)**—you can take **Corso Umberto I,** one of the original streets crossing the medieval town towards the ruins of the **Castello.** Built in medieval times, it was ruined during the Spanish wars at the beginning of the 18th century.

Duomo, aka Cattedrale dell'Assunta 𝒜 This 12th-century church was redone and added to in following centuries. The elegant facade is neoclassical, as are the decorations inside. The cathedral holds many masterpieces, including a beautiful tabernacle by Giovanni da Nola that you can admire in the chapel to the right of the main one. Also take note of the 16th-century carved choir at the back of the church, in the apse. Under the Duomo, you'll find the Cripta dell'Addolorata, or Church of Santa Maria dei Sette Dolori. It was created in the 17th century by adding a nave to the original Romanesque crypt and is decorated with frescoes and with Roman and medieval capitals. From the presbytery you can access the courtyard, where you can see remains of the original Longobard church and the partially restored Romanesque bell tower, decorated with Roman marble inscriptions from Abellinum.

Piazza Duomo. Free admission. Daily 9–11am and 5–7pm.

Museo Irpino 𝒜𝒜 Across from the pleasant Villa Comunale, the public park between Corso Vittorio Emanuele and Corso Europa, this museum is housed in a modern building. It focuses on the artistic and cultural developments of the region, from its prehistory onwards, and is divided into three sections. The extensive archaeological collection displays findings from the surrounding archaeological areas, starting with remains dating back to 4000 B.C. and extending all the way to the 6th century A.D., the end of the Roman era. Among the most interesting findings are those—in room nos. II and III—from the aeneolithic necropolis of Madonna delle Grazie (near Mirabella Eclano), including the reconstruction of the tomb of a tribal chief, buried with his dog. (By the way, "aeneolithic" means the transitional period between the neolithic and the Bronze Age; we looked it up.) A rich collection of statues, carvings, and coins comes from the archaeological area of Aeclanum, also near Mirabella Eclano. A number of findings document life in the old Abellinum, including a great **mosaic** 𝒜 from the 1st century (in the entrance hall), ceramics, fragments of frescoes, and the funerary collection from the 2nd-century **tomb of a young woman** 𝒜, all in room nos. VIII and IX. A new hall displays the recent findings from the Sanctuary of the Goddess Mefite, a cult going back to the 6th century B.C. that persisted through the Roman era. These were found in a site near the Passo di Mirabella.

The modern section of the museum includes a **picture gallery** with a collection of 17th- and 18th-century Neapolitan masters, as well as a grandiose 18th-century artistic *presepio* and a rich collection of **porcelain** from the late 18th century to the early 19th century. The 19th-century picture collection has been moved to the Carcere Borbonico (see below). The museum also holds a section dedicated to the **Risorgimento;** on display are documents and other materials showing the role of Irpinia in the Italian struggle for unification.

Corso Europa. ℭ 0825-38582. Free admission. Sun–Fri 8:30am–2pm.

Carcere Borbonico This interesting hexagonal building once housed the prisons of the Bourbon kings and has recently been converted into a cultural space and exhibition gallery. It now houses part of the modern section of the Museo Irpino, the Pinacoteca. *Note:* Building restoration and the installation of the picture gallery in this new location were ongoing at presstime. Only the paintings relating to the 19th century had been moved, and access was limited. Check with the local tourist office for the state of completion and opening hours.

Piazza d'Armi, off Via Mancini. ℭ 0825-38582. Free admission to Pinacoteca. Pinacoteca: Mon–Fri 8:30am–2pm. Carcere: Hours depend on events and exhibits.

WHERE TO STAY

Hotel De La Ville 🎯 With its central location, luxury service, and elegant, romantic vibe, this place wins the prize for best hotel in town. Guest rooms are large and well appointed with all the comforts, and the nice bathrooms are good-sized. Public spaces are spacious and furnished with elegance—down to a garden complete with swimming pool (heart-shaped, no less). You certainly won't starve, either: Of the hotel's four quality restaurants, our favorites are **Il Cavallino,** which serves traditional and historical Neapolitan and Irpinian dishes, and **La Terrazza,** which offers romantic outdoor dining.

Via Palatucci no. 20, 83100 Avellino. ℭ 0825-780911. Fax 0825-780921. www.hoteldelaville.it. 69 units. 210€ ($263) double; from 360€ ($450) suite. Rates include buffet breakfast. Children under 6 stay free in parent's room. AE, DC, MC, V. Parking: 10€ ($13). **Amenities:** 4 restaurants; bar; disco; outdoor pool; concierge; business center; room service; babysitting; laundry service; billiard room. *In room:* A/C, satellite TV w/pay movies, dataport, minibar, hair dryer, safe.

Viva Hotel *Value* Right in the heart of town, not far from the medieval center, this hotel used to belong to the Italian Jolly chain and was completely refurbished in 2004. Guest rooms are what you'd expect from a chain, with classic and functional furnishings, but all are spacious and have new bathrooms. The hotel's restaurant is top-notch and the hotel has an Internet point free for its guests.

Via Tuoro Cappuccini 97, 83100 Avellino. ℭ 0825-25922. Fax: 0825-780029. www.vivahotel.it. 72 units. 180€ ($225) double; low season 110€ ($138) double. Rates include buffet breakfast. Children under 6 stay free in parent's room. AE, DC, MC, V. Free parking. **Amenities:** Restaurant; bar; concierge; business center; room service; babysitting; laundry service. *In room:* A/C, satellite TV, minibar, hair dryer, safe.

WHERE TO DINE

Antica Trattoria Martella AVELLINESE This is the best restaurant in Avellino, serving difficult-to-find specialties in an elegant yet down-to-earth style. The vaulted ceilings, the wooden chairs with straw seats, the white tablecloths, and the attentive service re-create an old-fashioned atmosphere, which is perfect for sampling the varied seasonal menu. If they have it, try the unusual *fusilli affumicati* (a homemade pasta lightly smoked) and, of course, do not miss *tagliatelle al tartufo nero,* seasoned with the famous local black truffles.

Via Chiesa Conservatorio 10. ℭ 0825-31117. www.ristorantemartella.it. Reservations recommended. Secondi 9€–14€ ($11–$18). AE, DC, MC, V. Daily 1–3pm and 8–11pm.

Da Giorgio AVELLINESE/NEAPOLITAN This is a superior restaurant with no frills: The cuisine is local at its best, offering a variety of homemade pastas with seasonal sauces, as well as a great variety of seafood. The *fusilli ai frutti di mare* (homemade pasta with seafood) is particularly delicious. If you are tired of fish, treat yourself to *coniglio alla cacciatora* (rabbit in an olive-and-caper sauce).

Via De Renzi 18. ℂ 0825-34947. Reservations recommended for dinner. Secondi 7€–14€ ($8.75–$18). AE, DC, MC, V. Tues–Sun noon–3pm and 7–11pm. Closed July.

Da Mario AVELLINESE In this down-to-earth trattoria, you'll find all the local dishes prepared in a hearty, home-cooking style, from *cavatelli* (a kind of shortish pasta) and *ravioli*, to *brasato* (beef in wine sauce), *agnello* (lamb), and *coniglio arrosto* (rabbit). Do not expect elegance—this is not a fancy, trendy place, but a traditional local restaurant where you will get good food and service. The local wine is excellent.

Via Laura Beatrice Oliva Mancini 15. ℂ 0825-26499. Reservations recommended for dinner. Secondi 6€–12€ ($7.50–$15). AE, DC, MC, V. Mon–Sat noon–3pm and 7:30–11pm.

I Moti Carbonari PIZZA For a younger atmosphere and some of the best pizza around, head to this popular restaurant. They prepare pizza according to the best Neapolitan tradition but add imagination to the toppings. They'll accommodate most of your wishes, within reason.

Via De Concilis 20. ℂ 0825-782534. Reservations recommended on weekends. Secondi 5€–9€ ($6.25–$11). AE, DC, MC, V. Daily 7–11pm.

Ristorante La Fontana AVELLINESE/NEAPOLITAN Located in the medieval part of town, this place has a well-rounded menu with both meat and seafood specialties. Their homemade pasta is tasty, and they make a mean *pappardelle ai funghi porcini* (homemade large tagliatelle with porcini mushrooms). They excel at fish, though; you'll be happy with *cavatelli cozze e vongole* (homemade pasta with mussels and clams) and *polipi in guazzetto* (squid in a tomato sauce) when they are on the menu.

Corso Umberto I 32. ℂ 0825-756209. Reservations recommended. Secondi 8€–16€ ($10–$20). AE, DC, MC, V. Daily noon–4pm and 5:30pm–3am.

SANTUARIO DI MONTEVERGINE ✿✿✿

Very close to Avellino, this sanctuary with an annexed monastery (ℂ 0825-72924; www.santuariodimontevergine.it) is famous for its art and for the **splendid view** ✿, encompassing the whole valley down to Mount Vesuvius and the Gulf of Naples. The panorama is beautiful enough—some say—to justify your whole trip to Campania: Do not come only for the view, however, unless you are sure of a sunny day! The mountain can be quite dour in overcast conditions; in really bad weather, we wouldn't even attempt the drive up (you might find the road closed anyhow).

Teatro Gesualdo

The main theatrical venue in Avellino is Teatro Gesualdo (Piazza Castello; ℂ 0825-756403). As in other provincial cities, the theater must be all things to all people, hosting dramatic productions (in Italian, naturally), as well as music, comedy, and whatever else comes to town. If the music is orchestral, of course, you won't have any trouble understanding it.

Located almost at the top of Mount Montevergine, at an altitude of 1,270m (4,166 ft.)—the summit rises 1,493m (4,897 ft.)—the sanctuary is a popular pilgrimage destination which attracts over a million people every year, especially between May and September. You can reach it easily from Avellino by taking SS 7bis and then by switching to SS 374 in the direction of Mercogliano; follow the signs there for MONTEVERGINE up the winding mountain road. The whole trip from Avellino is 21km (13 miles) long.

Founded by Guglielmo da Vercelli in 1119 for his order of the Verginiani—San Guglielmo Day is June 25, an occasion for important celebrations—the sanctuary is composed of a hostel, the monastery, a museum and gallery, and **two churches.** The smaller, original church was probably consecrated in 1124; the huge new basilica, finished in 1961, is nestled into the older one at a right angle, over the original church's left nave.

In the presbytery of the **New Church,** rich in marble decorations, you can admire the so-called *Throne of the Madonna,* the great 13th-century painting of the **Madonna di Montevergine** *&*. On each side of the new presbytery, small doors lead to the **Old Church.** Built in the 12th century, the Old Church was completely redecorated in the 17th century but still shows its Gothic structure. In the presbytery, you will see the splendid 17th-century **main altar** *&*, a masterpiece of intarsia in marble and precious stones. In the apse is a beautiful carved choir from the 16th century. At the end of the right nave is the Gothic **Cappella del Sacramento,** holding a magnificent 13th-century **baldaquin** *&* in mosaic, and the ornate 15th-century marble **cyborium** *&*. The church is rich in funerary monuments with amazing stone inlay work, such as the grandiose **Monument to Caterina Filangeri** from the 15th century, located at the end of the right nave to the left, before the Cappella del Sacramento. The Gothic portal of the original church is also very beautiful, and warmer than the rather austere modern style of the new construction.

The **Abbey Museum** contains a range of artistic and archaeological items. The star of the collection is the 13th-century **Sedia Abbaziale (Abbey's Throne).** The monastery itself can be visited only by men. Interesting elements show the 17th-century structure. From the monastery, you can take the car up the road for 1.5km (1 mile) to the trail head to the mountaintop. The short walk takes only about 15 minutes, and from the summit you can enjoy an even better panorama than from the sanctuary.

If all this visiting made you a bit hungry, you'll find several restaurants in Mercogliano, such as **Hotel Ristorante Caterina** (Viale S. Modestino 40, 83013 Mercogliano, AV), where you can also stay overnight; up at the sanctuary, you can have a meal at **Hotel Ristorante Romito Santuario** (Piazza Montevergine 7, 83013 Mercogliano, AV), which also accepts guests.

EN ROUTE TO MIRABELLA ECLANO

Leaving Avellino in an easterly direction, you will come to a fork in the road. Bear left, and follow the signs for PRATA DI PRINCIPATO ULTRA. This village is only about 11km (6½ miles) north of Avellino and is famous for its **Basilica dell'Annunziata** *&&&*, located 1.3km (¾ miles) north of the village. The church (✆ **0825-961019**), which was recently restored, is considered one of Irpinia's most important monuments. Built by the Longobards, it still shows remains of a paleochristian catacomb and a 6th-century basilica. From the modern little church you will access an elliptical **apse,** carved in the tufa stone. This is believed to be from the 7th century and at its end has a fresco of *Madonna and Saints* dating to the 8th century. At the end of a courtyard to the left of the church is the entrance to the grotto, a Christian catacomb going back to the 3rd and 4th centuries and decorated with frescoes, altars, and sarcophagi.

Retracing your steps to the main road, you can take the scenic local route pointed to by the signs PRATO LA SERRA and SERRA. Continue in the direction of the sign for PIETRA DE FUSI, passing over the highway, and switch to the SS 90 at the sign for PASSO DI MIRABELLA. This will eventually take you to **Mirabella Eclano,** at 47km (29 miles) northeast of Avellino. This lively little town is located in the heart of one of the country's most important archaeological areas. Mirabella grew over the ruins of Acquaputida, the town founded in the 11th century after Aeclanum (see below) was abandoned due to Saracen attacks. Acquaputida, though, didn't have a long life: It was partially destroyed by natural catastrophes and civil wars in the 14th century. If you take a stroll in the streets, you will see many marble carvings and inscriptions from Roman and medieval times built into the walls of the houses, like mementoes or fossils of the town's turbulent past. In the main square of the upper part of town you can visit **Santa Maria Maggiore** church, with its beautifully carved and painted *Crocefisso* 🎨 from the 12th century, a Romanesque masterpiece by a Campanian artist.

Only 3.5km (2 miles) to the southwest (follow the signs for TAURASI) is the important **Eneolithical Necropolis of Madonna delle Grazie** 🎨. Dating back to 2000 B.C., these tombs were excavated in the tufa stone and have given up a rich collection of artifacts; most are on display in the Museo Irpino of Avellino (see earlier in this chapter). What's really awe-inspiring here is the feeling that comes from standing on a site where a culture thrived 1,200 years before the founding of Rome.

Back on SS 90, just before you reach **Passo di Mirabella,** are the ruins of **Aeclanum** (📞 **0825-449175**). One of the most important Sannite centers, the Aeclanum was taken by the Romans in 89 B.C. and became an important stop on the Via Appia. Aeclanum was destroyed in A.D. 662 during the wars against the Longobards, and the town of Quintodecimo was built on its ruins—which survived until the 11th century when it, too, was destroyed in the wars between Byzantines and Saracens. In the archaeological area you can see many remains of the Roman town, including segments of the walls, the theater, and the market square, as well as portions of houses and shops. The most important findings are conserved in Avellino's Museo Irpino (see earlier in this chapter).

If you choose to linger in the area, we recommend staying and dining at comfy **Hotel Mirabella** (Via Bosco, 83036 Mirabella Eclano; 📞 **0825-449724;** fax 0825-449728; 62€/$78 double); or at **Hotel Ristorante Aeclanum** (Via Nazionale, 83030 Passo di Mirabella; 📞/fax **0825-449065;** 38€/$48 double), which has the bonus of a swimming pool.

ON THE WAY TO SANT'ANGELO DEI LOMBARDI

Going east out of Avellino, bear right at the fork in the road with the sign for ATRIPALDA. Only 3.5km (2¼ miles) east of Avellino, **Atripalda** is a smallish agricultural town founded in the 11th century by the Longobards near the ruins of Roman **Abellinum** 🎨🎨. Although the large archaeological area has been used as a marble and construction-material "quarry" for centuries, you can see the ancient walls with semicircular towers and, inside the walls, the ruins of a large Roman house. In the center of Atripalda you can visit the **Collegiata di Sant'Ippolisto** 🎨 and its **crypt,** which was part of the **Specus Martyrum,** the subterranean structure where Saint Ippolisto and the other martyrs of Abellinum, killed by the notoriously cruel Emperor Domitian, are buried. The crypt is decorated with a beautiful fresco of a Christ Pantocrator from the 14th century. If you want to stop for the night, **Hotel Malaga** (Via Appia 95, Atripalda; ℂ **0825-611501;** fax 0825-623323; www.hotelmalaga.it; 80€/$100 double; 120€/$150 suite) offers very nice accommodations at moderate prices.

Continuing east, you will come to **Montemarano** ⚜ 19km (12 miles) east of Atripalda. Built on the top of a hill, it has a well-preserved **castle.** Another interesting attraction is the **Chiesa dell'Assunta,** where you can admire the nicely carved 16th-century portal and, inside, a unique 15th-century **folding chair,** decorated with delicate carvings and a *Sacra Famiglia* by Andrea Vaccaro; the seat was used by the bishop until recent times. This ancient little town is also famous for its **Carnival** celebrations. Festivities start on January 17—the feast of Sant'Antonio Abate—and continue until Mardi Gras (Fat Tuesday). During the first weeks of Mardi Gras, groups of dancers and musicians, guided by a Pulcinella, tour the little town asking for offerings, but as Carnival ripens, the events multiply, including the now rare ritual of the *Tarantella,* the famous frenzied dance that has become a subject of study for ethnographers. Among the lighter events are farcical performances and the traditional Parade of the Pulcinella, in which the entire town's Pulcinella characters participate. Contact the **UNPLI Provinciale** (Via Derna 7; ℂ **082-524013**) for a schedule of events.

A few miles east of Montemarano, you can follow the signs for MONTELLA and then for PIANO DI VERTEGLIA, which will take you on a scenic road (SS 574) along the slopes of **Mount Terminio** ⚜⚜. This is an area of great natural beauty and is considered part of the Regional Park of the Monti Picentini. The little town of **Montella** is famous for its chestnuts, which are not only flavorful but are very easy to separate from the skin. For a taste of the local cuisine, try **Ristorante La Bussola** ⚜ (Piano di Verteglia; ℂ **0827-609020;** Tues–Sun noon–3pm and 7–10:30pm; no credit cards). You can also make a reservation at the Agriturismo Pericle (see below).

If you decide to stay overnight, the best choice is the **Agriturismo Pericle** ⚜ (Via Sottomonticchio; ℂ **0827-69239** or 329-6175778; www.agriturismopericle.it), a wonderful organic farm offering elegant country-style accommodations, and scrumptious meals prepared with their products. The menu is, not surprisingly, seasonal but very varied: They raise organic pork (think sausages, salami, and wonderful roasts), rabbits, guinea hens, ducks, and geese, along with a bounty of wild mushrooms, truffles, and chestnuts (for wonderful desserts). They also produce their own wine, an excellent Aglianico. Besides eating, you can go horseback and bicycle riding. Moreover, if you like the cooking, the chef, Mamma Rina, gives cooking classes!

If you're set on a regular hotel, we recommend **Conca d'Oro** (Via M. Cianciulli 25; ℂ **0827-61244;** 72€/$90 double) in town; or **La Faia** ⚜ (Via Altopiano Verteglia; ℂ **0827-61247;** 35€/$44 double), which is a bit out of town but pleasantly situated.

For hikers, several trails lead to the summit of the surrounding mountains, including the highest of them, the Terminio, at an altitude of 1,806m (5,924 ft.). Most trails start at the **Rifugio Principe di Piemonte,** housed in the old church of Verteglia (when it is open you can get some refreshments). Contact the **Comunità Montana Terminio Cervialto** (Via Don Minzoni 2, 83048 Montella [AV]; ℂ **0827-609411;** www.cmterminiocervialto.it) for more information on the trails. For a guided excursion, contact **Ekoclub Montella** (ℂ **0827-61534** or 0347-8605435; ekoclubmontella. freeweb.org).

SANT'ANGELO DEI LOMBARDI ✿✿✿

From the top of its hill, this ancient little town overlooks the beautiful surrounding valley. Founded by the Longobards, it was famous for its many monuments; unfortunately, the town was severely damaged by the earthquake of 1980, which completely destroyed a number of important buildings. However, restorations have been underway ever since, and although some are not completed, the town's artistic riches are quite enjoyable. The **Norman Castle** is among the monuments under restoration that can be visited; the Normans probably chose this site for strategic reasons, but you can enjoy the beautiful view over the valley of the Ofanto River. The 11th-century **Cathedral** has been restored and is now completely accessible. Redone in the 16th century, it has a late-Renaissance portal. Inside are several funerary monuments, including the 17th-century **Sepolcro Cecere,** at the beginning of the right nave.

About 1km (½ mile) out of town to the northwest is the **Convento di San Marco** ✿✿, once a powerful monastery, holding a collection of many works of art, including paintings and monumental tombs; as of presstime, however, it is being restored from damage caused by the 1980 earthquake.

At 6.5 km (4 miles) to the southwest is the famous **Abbazia Di San Guglielmo al Goleto** ✿✿✿ (✆ 0827-24432; www.goleto.it), one of the most scenic attractions of southern Italy. Founded by San Gulgielmo da Vercelli around 1133, this is the abbey where the saint died in 1142. Originally a double monastery, it was very influential until the end of the 14th century. The women's section was suppressed in 1505, while the other half was annexed to the Abbey of Montevergine near Avellino. It was finally closed in 1807 and the body of Saint Guglielmo was moved to Montevergine. The monastery has been saved from ruin by restoration, and since 1989, it has again been the seat of a religious community. The huge monastery is surrounded by powerful walls visible at a distance over the mountain, and is organized around two cloisters. In the left cloister you can admire the facades of the two churches which were built one over the other, the top one Gothic (from the 13th century), and the bottom one Romanesque (from the 12th century). Also in this cloister are the ruins of the 18th-century church. Stone steps lead to the top church, a wonderful artistic masterpiece with harmonious proportions and elegant decoration. Around the second cloister is the abbey itself, with the massive defense tower built in the 12th century using blocks from a Roman mausoleum. The abbey is open daily from 8am to 1pm and 6 to 8pm.

We suggest you dine nearby in the memorable **Ristorante Il Porcellino** ✿✿ (Via Campoluongo; ✆ 0827-23694), only a couple of minutes away. Here you can delight in local cuisine. The menu is based on homemade pastas and a variety of grilled meats. In winter they make wonderful soups.

For a restaurant in town, try **Trattoria Di Nicola Carmela** (Via Giostra 28; ✆ 0827-24648; daily noon–3pm and 7–11pm). You can also go to **O' Matetore** (Via San Pietro; ✆ 0827-23829; Sat–Thurs 8am–midnight); it offers a menu of typical dishes. Alternatively, try **Pizzeria Di Petito** ✿ (Piazza Francesco De Sanctis; ✆ 0827-23416; Mon–Sat noon–3pm and 7–11pm; no credit cards) for excellent pizza.

If you want to spend the night, you can do so at **Bed & Breakfast Casa Alberico** (Via San Marco; 83054 Sant'Angelo dei Lombardi; ✆ 0827-23642; casa.alberico@ virgilio.it).

Appendix A: Campania & the Amalfi Coast in Depth

A land of ancient civilizations, Campania has been inhabited since at least 4000 B.C., as shown by the many excavated necropolises here. A wonderful and fertile land, it attracted many people, who frequently fought for possession of it over the past 3,000 years. Its three main sections each had slightly different historical fates: the plains in the region's northern part and the hinterland of Naples—the *Campania Felix* of the Romans; the mountainous Sannio dominated by Benevento; and, to the south, the Amalfi Coast and the Cilento.

This appendix covers the basic makeup of this region, with essays on history, culture, art, food, and wine.

1 A Look at the Past

This brief survey of Campania's long and complex history is oriented toward the Amalfi Coast, but the rest of Campania is covered as well. Once we hit the Renaissance, the focus shifts primarily to Naples and its surroundings, which became the center of power in the region.

THE GREEKS

After a short stop on the island of Ischia, Calcidians founded the city of Cuma in 750 B.C., the first Greek city of Magna Grecia—the Greek cities outside the mainland. Cuma became a beacon of Greek civilization in Italy. Their expansion into the region, though, was contested by the Etruscans (see below). In spite of this, they established other important colonies in the current area of Naples: first Partenope around 680 B.C., then Dicearchia (Pozzuoli) in 531 B.C., and then Neapolis in 470 B.C. In the meantime, Greeks from Sibari founded Posidonia (Paestum) in 600 B.C. and Elea (Velia) in 540 B.C.

Greeks won two major battles in Cuma against the Etruscans, one in 524 B.C. and

the final in 474 B.C. Nevertheless, weakened by their fights with the Etruscans, they could not resist the Sannite invasion in the 5th century B.C.

THE ETRUSCANS

While the Greeks colonized Campania's coast, the Etruscans colonized the inner plains, the rich agricultural areas around Capua, which they founded in the 9th century B.C., and south all the way down to the hinterland of Paestum. They, too, were weakened by their fights for supremacy in the region against the Greeks (see above), so that when the Sannites began their expansion, Etruscan power in the area came to an end.

THE SANNITES

This mountain people, originally from nearby Abbruzzo, had been expanding south in the Appennines, with an economy based on sheep husbandry. Also a warrior culture, they established a flourishing civilization in Benevento and then moved towards the coast in the 5th century B.C., causing conflict with both Greeks and Etruscans.

Sannite attacks were successful; they took over Capua in 424 B.C. and then took Cuma 3 years later in 421 B.C. Their influence quickly expanded to other cities such as Neapolis, Pompeii, and Herculaneum and gave birth to a new civilization, the Oscans (see below).

The inland Sannites of Beneventum, in the meantime, came into opposition with the Romans who, by the 4th century B.C., had started their expansion southward. This led to the three famous Sannite wars. It took Rome from 343 B.C. to 290 B.C. to overcome the Sannites. The strongly independent Sannites, however, kept creating problems for the Romans. Finally, Beneventum was destroyed and later rebuilt as a Roman colony.

THE LUCANIANS

Another Italic mountain population, the Lucanians came from the nearby region of Basilicata. Slightly less belligerent than their Sannite cousins, they also started a migration towards the coast. They took over Posidonia (Paestum) in 400 B.C., but failed to overcome Elea (Velia). Like the Sannites farther north, they merged with the existing Greek population into the cultural melting pot that became the Oscans (see below).

THE OSCANS

After their victories over the Greeks and Etruscans, the Sannites in the plains merged culturally with Etruscans and Greeks, giving birth to the Oscan civilization. This original population had strong Sannite roots, blending important cultural elements of the other two civilizations in a way that created a unique individual character with its own language. They made their capital in Capua.

Over time, the Oscans became so distinct from the original Sannites, however, that they actually shifted their support to Rome during its conquest of Campania.

THE ROMANS

The Romans took advantage of the opposition between the Oscans and the Sannites to extend their influence in the region. In exchange for allegiance to the Republic, Rome bestowed Roman citizenship, with the right to vote and decide on public affairs (but with the obligation of military service). Citizen colonies were set up as settlements of Roman farmers after the original people had given allegiance (voluntarily, or by sheer force). This worked better with the Oscans than with the Sannites, who continued to oppose Rome even after they lost the war (see above). The Romans founded Paestum in 273 B.C., Beneventum in 268 B.C., then Salernum and Puteoli (modern Pozzuoli) in 194 B.C. These cities were fortified and linked to Rome by the famous Roman roads, such as the Appian

---

Dateline

- **4000 B.C.** Local people are already organized in villages and active in commercial exchange with other Mediterranean groups.
- **800 B.C.** The first Greek settlements appear along the southern coast. Cuma and Ischia are founded.
- **600 B.C.** Parthenope is founded over Monte Echia (behind Piazza del Plebiscito

in modern Naples) by Greek colonists. In the meantime, the Etruscans have been establishing colonies in the interior of Campania, as far down as the Sele River, inland of Paestum.

- **524 B.C.** The first battle of Cuma between Etruscans and Greeks is won by the Greeks.
- **474 B.C.** The second battle of Cuma occurs, when allied Cumans and Syracusans defeat the Etruscans.

- **400 B.C.** The Sannites descend from their inland towns on the hills towards the plains and the sea. They occupy Capua in 424 B.C. and Cuma in 421 B.C.
- **343–290 B.C.** The three Sannite wars between Romans and Sannite end with a Roman victory, but the Sannites continue to rebel.

continued

Way, which led to Capua, then Beneventum, and then all the way to Brindisi, on the Ionian Sea on Italy's eastern coast.

In this way, a stern Roman culture was added to the pre-existing local mixture. The social war from 91 B.C. to 88 B.C.—and, even more so, the civil war instigated by the dictator Sulla from 82 B.C to 81 B.C.—caused great destruction in Campania, especially to the rebellious Sannio region, which was almost completely wiped out. Peace came again with the advent of Rome's first emperor, Gaius Octavius Augustus.

Under the Empire, Campania was completely Romanized, but its agricultural strength was slowly supplanted by the production of Africa and Spain, leading to a strong local recession.

When the Empire ended in A.D. 395, the richest plains of Capua and Paestum had been abandoned and were in the throes of a malaria epidemic; the population was forced to found new villages up in the mountains, a situation that would not improve dramatically until the 20th century.

THE BYZANTINE & THE LONGOBARDS

With the end of the Roman Empire, barbarian invasions began. The Goths from the north invaded the region in 410, while the Vandals from Africa sacked and destroyed Capua in 456; the Byzantines counterattacked against the Goths and finally drove them out in 555; but (only a few years later, in 570), the Longobards arrived from the Appennines and took over the interior. The Byzantines struggled to maintain power but eventually lost, keeping only the harbors of Naples, Sorrento, and Amalfi; even Salerno was occupied by the Longobards in 630.

The Longobards' aristocracy oppressed Latin populations, but the yoke was lifted a bit when the Longobards converted to Catholicism thanks to the bishop of Benevento, Barbato; the conversion allowed the monasteries to begin operating again, and their role in preserving classical culture was immense. Later, (in the 13th century) the Abbey of Monte Cassino, in northern Campania, would be, for a time, the home of the greatest philosopher-theologian in Europe, St. Thomas Aquinas.

In the second half of the 8th century, the Longobard prince Arechi II moved his court from Benevento to Salerno, causing an increasing tension between the two towns, which resulted in civil war and the splitting of the Longobard realm into two independent principalities in 849. This marked the beginning of the end for the Longobards; in the 10th century, Capua also became an independent principality, after having been destroyed

- **275 B.C.** Rome defeats the rebellious Sannites of Maluentum and changes the name of the town into Beneventum, turning it into a Roman colony in 268 B.C.
- **273 B.C.** Rome establishes a colony in Paestum.
- **211 B.C.** Rome completely defeats the Sannites of Capua and turns that town into a Roman colony as well.
- **194 B.C.** The Romans refound Pozzuoli with the

name of *Puteoli*, as well as Salerno.
- **A.D. 79** On August 24, Mount Vesuvius erupts, burying the prosperous towns of Pompeii, Herculaneum, and Stabiae.
- **476** Romolo Augustolo, the last Roman emperor, dies inside the *castrum lucullanum*—today's Castel dell'Ovo,

- **5th century** Campania is divided between Goths, Longobards, and Byzantines.
- **553** The Byzantines chase the Goths from Naples and establish a duchy.
- **570** The Longobards descend from the Appennines and eventually take Benevento.
- **839** Amalfi chases out the Longobards who had occupied the city 3 years before.
- **9th century** Naples and Amalfi, allied with Gaeta,

by the Saracens in 841 and refounded on more secure grounds.

In the meantime, Amalfi became independent from the Byzantine Duchy of Naples and started gaining strength and power as a maritime commercial republic, maintaining strong contact with both the Byzantine and the Muslims in the East.

THE SARACENS

The Arab period in Sicily began in 827. Taking advantage of the Longobards' civil war, the Saracens—Arabs who had started out in the region as mercenaries—took over a few small harbor towns (particularly Agropoli in 882), and started attacking and sacking the other towns along the coast.

Under these repeated assaults, the once-prosperous coastal towns of Campania became deserted, as the people sought refuge in the hills and the countryside. Some of the towns were then reborn, often in more defensive locations and surrounded by heavy fortifications.

THE NORMANS, SWABIANS & ANGEVINS

Things changed with the arrival of the Normans, who reintroduced the concept of central government and unity in southern Italy. Their first base was Aversa, near Naples, established in 1029, and from there they rapidly expanded their conquest to Capua in 1062, Amalfi in 1073, and Salerno in 1076, where they established their capital until Naples was also annexed to the kingdom in 1139. The Normans then proceeded south and won over Sicily, displacing the Arabs who had ruled the island for 2 centuries.

Salerno became a splendid town and a beacon of culture and learning, thanks to the development of its medical school, the first and most important medical center of the whole Western world. Benevento, on the other hand, had passed appraisal by the power of the Popes in 1051 and stayed so until the unification of Italy in 1860.

The Normans introduced feudalism, a repressive social system that discouraged individual economic initiative, and which undermined the very base of the kingdom. When the dynasty became weaker, it passed to the Swebians and then to the Angevins. The feudal chiefs in Sicily revolted and attacked the central monarchy in the famous "Sicilian Vespers" of 1282. Led by Aragonese elements, the Angevins resisted and succeeded in retaining their power in Campania, but the Cilento—right at the border of the reduced kingdom, and the coastal towns suffered immense casualties and depopulation.

In the mid-13th century, the Angevins had established the capital in Naples, which flourished, but the kingdom's interior was

---

defeat the Saracens and the Muslim Turks (who had established themselves in Licosa in 845), in Agropoli in 882, and at the mouth of the Garigliano River in 883.

- **915** The Arab colony at the mouth of the Garigliano River is defeated and the Arabs are forced out.
- **10th & 11th centuries** Amalfi's Maritime Republic reaches its apogee.

- **1030** The Norman Rainolfo Drengot obtains the county of Aversa, opening the way to the establishment of Norman rule in Campania.
- **1139** Naples surrenders to Ruggero II, and becomes part of the Norman kingdom of Sicily.
- **1194** The Swabian dynasty replaces the Norman one in the southern Kingdom.
- **1225** Birth of St. Thomas Aquinas at Rocca Secca.

- **1266** The Angevins defeat the Swabians in the battle of Benevento, taking over the kingdom. Carlo I transfers the capital from Palermo to Naples.
- **1442** The kingdom passes to the Aragonese dynasty. It changes hands several times during the rest of the century.
- **1503** The French are finally driven from Naples, and the

continued

abandoned to heavy feudal rule, which smothered commerce and economic activity and led to extreme poverty, which in turn fostered the growth of groups of bandits in the hills who made all road communication unsafe. The legacy of these centuries of stagnation and misrule persists to this day. The situation worsened still when the rule of the kingdom shifted to Spain.

SPANISH RULE

Spanish rule was seemingly so backward that even many histories of Naples contain a large blank spot for this 2-century-long period. The main events of Spanish rule were revolts against it—in 1547, 1599, 1647, and 1674, to name the major ones. The former kingdom of Naples was ruled by a Spanish viceroy, and the resulting extraction of taxes and the imposition of authoritarian rule were onerous. Philip IV called Naples "a gold mine which furnished armies for our wars and treasure for their protection." The Spanish did build some great palaces and churches, though it is perhaps symbolic that Naples's Palazzo Reale was built for King Philip III, who never lived here. The great plague also occurred during this period, and wiped out half the population.

THE BOURBONS

During the tangled period of the War of Spanish succession in the early 18th century, Naples was ruled by Austrians for 27 years. Naples regained its independence in 1734, with Carlo di Borbone. The independence of the kingdom of Naples was at last recognized by Spain and the Papacy. Carlo revitalized the kingdom, improving the roads, draining the marshes in the area of Caserta, and creating new industries—such as the silk manufacturers in San Leucio, the ceramic artistry in Capodimonte, and the cameo and coral industries in Torre del Greco. The improvements continued during the 10 years of Napoleonic power, when the feudal system was completely dismantled and land was redistributed, creating new administrative and judicial structures. This gave new life to the provinces but, once the Bourbons returned, they were unable to strike a balance with the developing bourgeoisie. The region was thus poised for rebellion when Garibaldi arrived and brought about the unification of Italy in 1861.

A UNITED ITALY

Thanks to the brilliant efforts of Camillo Cavour (1810–61) and Giuseppe Garibaldi (1807–82), the Kingdom of Italy was proclaimed in 1861. Victor Emmanuel (Vittorio Emanuele) II of the House of Savoy, king of Sardinia, became the head of the new monarchy.

Unfortunately, if the new kingdom was politically good for Campania, it was

---

kingdom falls under Spanish rule.
- **1509** Naples refuses the establishment of the Inquisition. The attempt to establish the "Santo Oficio" fails again in 1547: Naples will be the only town in the Catholic world to successfully stave it off.
- **1528** Naples almost falls to the French, but Admiral Andrea Doria sides with the

Spaniards and secures a victory.
- **1558** The Saracens—in this case, the Barbary pirates— sack Sorrento.
- **1631** On December 16, Mount Vesuvius erupts again, killing over 3,000.
- **1647** Masaniello's Rebellion, a revolt against Spanish taxes and oppression, is led by a fish peddler in Naples.
- **1656** The plague seizes Naples for 6 months. Half of

Spaniards and secures a victory.
- **1558** The Saracens—in this case, the Barbary pirates— sack Sorrento.
- **1631** On December 16, Mount Vesuvius erupts again, killing over 3,000.
- **1647** Masaniello's Rebellion, a revolt against Spanish taxes and oppression, is led by a fish peddler in Naples.
- **1656** The plague seizes Naples for 6 months. Half of

disastrous for Campania's economy: The northern government imposed heavy taxes, and the centralized administration paid little attention to local differences and needs. This killed the burgeoning industry that had been developing thanks to the Bourbons' paternalism and protection. Despite these setbacks, though, towards the end of the 19th century the coastal area started to develop the agricultural specialties that still exist today.

FASCISM & WORLD WAR II

Fascism achieved little success outside the urban area of Naples and was mostly embraced by prefects and notables in the rest of Campania. The region paid a heavy toll during World War II, when it was heavily bombarded in preparation for the Allied landing on September 8, 1943, when 55,000 Allied troops stormed ashore. Known as the "Salerno Invasion," it actually involved landings in a long arc from Sorrento and Amalfi to as far south as the area of Paestum. The Nazis occupied the region and set up a desperate resistance, retreating slowly for long months just north of Caserta along the Garigliano River. This involved one of the war's most notorious battles, the several-months siege of Monte Cassino, which left the ancient monastery a heap of rubble. The Nazis destroyed as much as they could during their retreat, sacking and vandalizing everything—even the most important section of the Naples State Archives was burned.

In September 1943, Naples revolted and managed to chase out the occupiers, only days before the Allied forces arrived in the city. Other towns' insurrections resulted in horrible massacres; men and women organized guerrilla groups against the Nazis, hiding out in the mountains and hills and striking mostly at night, while the Allies bombarded their towns and cities. After many hard months of fighting, Campania was finally freed in June 1944.

THE POSTWAR YEARS

In 1946, Campania became part of the newly established Italian Republic— although Naples had given its preference to the monarchy in the referendum—and reconstruction began. Even though the war had left Italy ravaged, the country succeeded in rebuilding its economy. By the 1960s, as a member of the European Community (founded in Rome in 1957), Italy had become one of the world's leading industrialized nations, prominent in the manufacture of automobiles and office equipment. Campania was slow to recover; the terrible destruction that it suffered, the plague of corruption, plus the rising development of the Camorra, Campania's Mafia-like organization, hindered the region's development more than others.

---

the population—over 200,000 people—is killed.

- **1707** The Austrian Habsburgs obtain Naples as a result of the Spanish succession wars.

- **1734** The kingdom of Naples recovers its independence with the Bourbon dynasty.

- **1799** In Naples, insurrection leads to the establishment of the short-lived Parthenopean Republic.

- **1806** After several battles, the kingdom of Naples is taken over by the French.

- **1816** The Bourbons take back the kingdom.

- **1840** The road SS 163—the famous Amalfi Drive—is opened to traffic.

- **1860** On September 7, Garibaldi enters Naples; Campania becomes part of the new Kingdom of Italy.

- **1940** On September 9, "Operation Avalanche," the

Allied landings around Salerno, begins. On November 1, Allied planes bomb Naples. It is the first of 105 attacks that will cause over 22,000 deaths.

- **1943** On October 1, Allied troops are welcomed into a Nazi-free Naples.

- **1946** The Italian Republic is officially established in Naples, although the city had

continued

The great earthquake (10 on the MCS scale) that hit the region on November 23 gave it another push back, causing great destruction and economic hardship—over 3,000 people died, especially in the provinces of Avellino and Salerno, at the heart of the quake.

In the 1990s, a new Naples mayor and new regional government began investing more time and money in the restoration of Campania's artistic treasures, the reorganization of old museums, and the creation of new museums throughout the region. Just as important, the new government declared war on corruption and criminality. The millennium celebrations and the Papal Jubilee of 2000 brought about further renovations. Results have been spectacular; the center of Naples has been transformed from a depressed state into a sort of open-air museum with tons of artistic and historical attractions.

At the same time, the escalating war against the Camorra in Naples has attracted much press attention over the past year or so, casting doubt on the city's safety. In our opinion, however, the accounts are sensationalized. Life in the historical part of the city has remained virtually untouched by Camorra violence, and improvements continue to be made, to the extent that Naples's artistic treasures, as well as the attractions of the whole Campania region, become more and more accessible to visitors every day.

2 Art & Architecture in Campania

ITALIAN ARCHITECTURE AT A GLANCE

While each architectural era has its own distinctive features, there are some elements, general floor plans, and terms common to many. Also, some features might appear near the end of one era and continue through several later ones.

From the Romanesque period on, most churches consist either of a single wide **aisle** or a wide central **nave,** flanked by two narrow aisles. The aisles are separated from the nave by a row of **columns** or by square stacks of masonry called **piers,** usually connected by **arches.**

This main nave/aisle assemblage is usually crossed by a perpendicular corridor called a **transept** near the far east end of the church so that the floor plan looks like a **Latin Cross** (shaped like a crucifix). The shorter, east arm of the nave is the holiest area, called the **chancel;** it often houses the stalls of the **choir** and the **altar.** If the far end of the chancel is rounded off, it's called an **apse.** An **ambulatory** is a curving corridor outside the

given its preference to the Monarchy in the referendum.

- **1950s** Naples grows explosively, with 80,000 dwellings built within a decade.
- **1980** On November 23, a violent earthquake (10 on the MCS scale) produces great destruction, especially in the provinces of Avellino and Salerno, causing over 3,000 deaths.

- **1993** Antonio Bassolino is elected mayor of Naples. A major cleanup, restoration, and anti-crime campaign begins.
- **1994** The G7 meeting is held in Naples, attended by the heads of state of the seven leading industrialized countries.
- **1995** The historic center of Naples is included in the UNESCO list of World Heritage. The archaeological

areas of Pompeii, Herculaneum, and Torre Annunziata, as well as the Reggia of Caserta and the Amalfi Coast, are added in 1997.
- **2005** In the early part of the year, a crime war between rival Camorra factions gets international press, but historic Naples is unaffected.

altar and choir area, separating it from the ring of smaller chapels radiating off the chancel and the apse.

Some churches, especially after the Renaissance when mathematical proportion became important, were built on a **Greek Cross plan,** with each axis the same length, like a giant "+" (plus sign). By the baroque period, funky shapes became popular, with churches built in the round or as ellipses.

It's worth pointing out that very few buildings (especially churches) were built in only one particular style. Massive, expensive structures often took centuries to complete, during which time tastes changed and plans were altered.

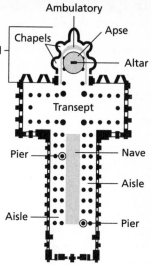

Church Floor Plan

CLASSICAL: GREEKS & ROMANS (6TH CENTURY B.C. TO A.D. 4TH CENTURY)

The **Greeks** settled Sicily and southern Italy, and left behind some of the best-preserved ancient temples in the world.

The **Romans** made use of certain Greek innovations, particularly architectural ideas. The first to be adopted was post-and-lintel construction (essentially, a weight-bearing frame, like a door). The Romans then added the load-bearing arch. Roman builders were inventive engineers, developing hoisting mechanisms and a specially trained workforce.

Identifiable Classical architectural features include these:

- **Classical orders.** These were usually simplified into types of column capitals, with the least ornate used on a building's ground level and the most ornate used on the top: Doric (a plain capital), Ionic (a capital with a scroll), and Corinthian (a capital with flowering acanthus leaves).

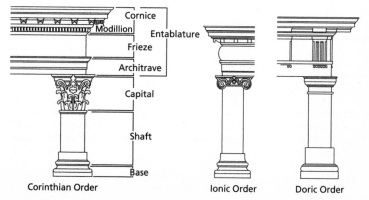

Classical Orders

- **Brick and concrete.** Although marble is traditionally associated with Roman architecture, Roman engineers could also do wonders with bricks or even prosaic concrete—concrete seating made possible such enormous theaters as Rome's 2.4-hectare (6-acre), 45,000-seat Colosseum.

Most **Greek Temples** in the *Magna Graecia* of southern Italy were built in the 5th century b.c., Doric style, including those at **Paestum** south of Naples, and in Sicily at **Segesta** and **Agrigento,** including the remarkably preserved Temple of Concord. **Greek theaters** survive in Sicily at Taormina, Segesta, and Syracuse (which was the largest in the ancient world).

One of the best places to see **Roman** architecture, of course, is Rome itself, where examples of most major public buildings still exist. These include the sports stadium of the **Colosseum** (A.D. 1st c.), which perfectly displays the use of the Classical orders; Hadrian's marvel of engineering, the **Pantheon** (A.D. 1st c.); the brick public **Baths of Caracalla** (A.D. 3rd c.); and the **Basilica of Constantine and Maxentius** in the Roman Forum (A.D. 4th c.). By the way, Roman basilicas, which served as law courts, took the form of rectangles supported by arches atop columns along both sides of the interior, with an apse at one or both ends; the form was later adopted by early Christians for their first grand churches.

Three **Roman cities** have been preserved, with their street plans and, in some cases, even buildings remaining intact. These are famous, doomed **Pompeii** and its neighbor **Herculaneum** (both buried by Vesuvius's A.D. 79 eruption), as well as Rome's ancient seaport **Ostia Antica.**

ROMANESQUE (A.D. 800 TO 1300)

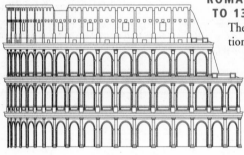
Colosseum, Rome

The Romanesque took its inspiration and rounded arches from ancient Rome (hence the name). Romanesque architects concentrated on building large churches with wide aisles to accommodate the masses, who came to hear the priests say Mass but mainly to worship at the altars of various saints. To support the weight of all that masonry, walls had to be thick and solid (meaning they could be pierced only by few and rather small windows), resting on huge piers, giving churches a dark, somber, mysterious, and often oppressive feeling.

Identifiable Romanesque features include:

- **Rounded arches.** These load-bearing architectural devices allowed architects to open up wide naves and spaces, channeling all the weight of the stone walls and ceiling across the curve of the arch and down into the ground via the columns or pilasters.
- **Thick walls.**
- **Infrequent and small windows.**
- **Huge piers.**

- **Blind arcades.** A range of arches was carried on piers or columns and attached to a wall. Set into each arch's curve was often a lozenge, a diamond-shaped decoration, sometimes inlaid with colored marbles.

- **Stripes.** Created by alternating layers of white and light-gray stones, this banding was typical of the Pisan-Romanesque style prominent in Pisa and Lucca. The gray got darker as time went on; by the late Romanesque/ early Gothic period, the pattern often became a zebra of black and white stripes.

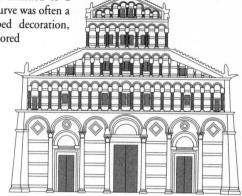

Cathedral, Pisa

- **Stacked facade arcades.** Another typical Pisan-Romanesque feature was a tall facade created by stacking small, open-air loggias with columns of different styles on top of one another to a height of three to five levels.

Modena's Duomo (12th c.) marks one of the earliest appearances of rounded arches, and its facade is covered with great Romanesque reliefs. **Abbazia di Sant'Antimo** (1118), outside **Montalcino,** is a beautiful example of French Romanesque style. **Milan's Basilica di San Ambrogio** (11th–12th c.) is festooned with the tiered loggias and arcades that became hallmarks of the Lombard Romanesque.

Pisa's Cathedral group (1153–1360s) is typical of the Pisan-Romanesque style, with stacked arcades of mismatched columns in the cathedral's facade (and wrapping around the famous Leaning Tower of Pisa) and blind arcading set with lozenges. **Lucca's Cattedrale di San Martino and San Michele in Foro** (11th–14th c.) are two more prime examples of the style.

GOTHIC (LATE 12TH TO EARLY 15TH CENTURIES)

By the late 12th century, engineering developments freed architecture from the heavy, thick walls of the Romanesque and allowed ceilings to soar, walls to thin, and windows to proliferate.

In place of the dark, somber, relatively unadorned Romanesque interiors that forced the eyes of the faithful toward the altar, where the priest stood droning on in unintelligible Latin, the Gothic interior enticed the churchgoers' gaze upward to high ceilings filled with light. The priests still conducted Mass in Latin, but now peasants could "read" the Gothic comic books of stained-glass windows.

The style began in France and was popular in Italy only in the northern region. From Florence south, most Gothic churches were built by the preaching orders of friars (Franciscans and Dominicans) as cavernous, barnlike structures.

Identifiable features of the French Gothic include:

- **Pointed arches.** The most significant development of the Gothic era was the discovery that pointed arches could carry far more weight than rounded ones.
- **Cross vaults.** Instead of being flat, the square patch of ceiling between four columns arches up to a point in the center, creating four sail shapes, sort of like the underside of a pyramid. The "X" separating these four sails is often reinforced with ridges called ribbing. As the Gothic progressed, four-sided cross vaults became six-sided, eight-sided, or multisided as architects played with the angles.

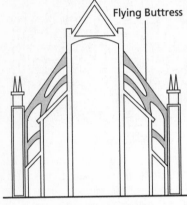

Cross Section of Gothic Church

- **Tracery.** These lacy spider webs of carved stone grace the pointy ends of windows and sometimes the spans of ceiling vaults.
- **Flying buttresses.** These free-standing exterior pillars connected by graceful, thin arms of stone help channel the weight of the building and its roof out and down into the ground. To help counter the cross forces involved in this engineering sleight of hand, the piers of buttresses were often topped by heavy pinnacles, which took the form of minispires or statues.
- **Stained glass.** Because pointy arches can carry more weight than rounded ones, windows could be larger and more numerous. They were often filled with Bible stories and symbolism written in the colorful patterns of stained glass.

The only truly French-style Gothic church in Italy is **Milan's massive Duomo & Baptistry** (begun ca. 1386), a lacy festival of pinnacles, buttresses, and pointy arches. **Siena's Duomo** (1136–1382), though started in the late Romanesque, has enough Giovanni Pisano sculptures and pointy arches to be considered Gothic. **Florence** has two of those barnlike Gothic churches: **Basilica di Santa Maria Novella** (1279–1357) and **Basilica di Santa Croce** (1294). The decorations inside **Santa Maria Sopra Minerva** (1280–1370), **Rome**'s only Gothic church, are all of a later date, but the architecture itself is all pointy arches and soaring ceilings (though, hemmed in by other buildings, its interior is much darker than most Gothic places).

RENAISSANCE (15TH TO 17TH CENTURIES)

As in painting, Renaissance architectural rules stressed proportion, order, classical inspiration, and mathematical precision to create unified, balanced structures. It was probably an architect, **Filippo Brunelleschi,** in the early 1400s, who first truly grasped the concept of "perspective" and provided artists with ground rules for creating the illusion of three dimensions on a flat surface.

Some identifiable Renaissance features include:

- A sense of proportion
- A reliance on symmetry
- The use of classical orders

One of the first great Renaissance architects was Florence's Filippo Brunelleschi (1377–1476). He often worked in the simple scheme of soft white plaster walls with architectural details and lines in pale gray *pietra serena* stone. Among his masterpieces in **Florence** are the Basilica di Santa Croce's **Pazzi Chapel** (1442–46), decorated with Donatello roundels; the interior of the **Basilica di San Lorenzo** (1425–46); and, most famous, the ingenious **dome** capping **Il Duomo** (1420–46). This last truly exemplifies the Renaissance's debt to the ancients. Brunelleschi traveled to Rome and studied the Pantheon up close to unlock the engineering secrets of its vast dome to build his own.

Il Duomo, Milan

Urbino architect **Bramante** (1444–1514) was perhaps the most mathematical and classically precise of the early High Renaissance architects, evident in his (much-altered) plans for **Rome's St. Peter's Basilica** (his spiral staircase in the Vatican Museums has survived untouched). Also see his jewel of perfect Renaissance architecture, the textbook **Tempietto** (1502) at San Pietro in Montorio on the slopes of Rome's Gianicolo Hill, where church officials once thought that St. Peter had been crucified (as a plus, the little crypt inside is a riotous rococo grotto).

Renaissance man **Michelangelo** (1475–1564) took up architecture late in life, designing **Florence's Medici Laurentian Library** (1524) and **New Sacristy** (1524–34), which houses the Medici Tombs at Basilica di San Lorenzo. In **Rome,** you can see his facade of the **Palazzo Farnese** (1566) and one of his crowning glories, the soaring **dome of St. Peter's Basilica,** among other structures.

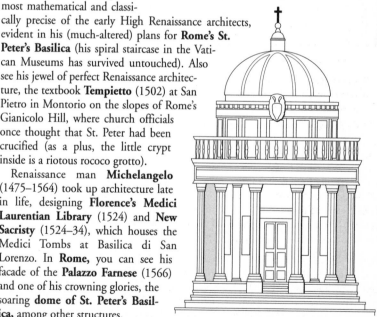

Tempietto, Rome

The fourth great High Renaissance architect was **Andrea Palladio** (1508–80), who worked in a much more strictly classical mode of columns, porticoes, pediments, and other ancient temple–inspired features. His masterpieces include **Villa Foscari** and the great **Villa Rotonda,** both in the **Veneto** countryside around Vicenza. His final work is **Vicenza's Olympic Theater** (1580), an attempt to reconstruct a Roman theater stage as described in ancient writings. Other designs include the Venetian church **San Giorgio Maggiore** (1565–1610). He had great influence on architecture abroad as well; his "Palladian" style informed everything from British architecture to Thomas Jefferson's Monticello.

BAROQUE & ROCOCO (17TH TO 18TH CENTURIES)

More than any other movement, the **baroque** aimed toward a seamless meshing of architecture and art. The stuccoes, sculptures, and paintings were all carefully designed to complement each other—and the space itself—to create a unified whole. This whole was both aesthetic and narrative, with the various art forms all working together to tell a single biblical story (or often to subtly relate the deeds of the commissioning patron to great historic or biblical events). Excessively complex and dripping with decorative tidbits, **rococo** is kind of a twisted version of the baroque.

Some identifiable baroque features include:

- **Classical architecture rewritten with curves.** The baroque is similar to Renaissance, but many of the right angles and ruler-straight lines are exchanged for curves of complex geometry and an interplay of concave and convex surfaces. The overall effect is to lighten the appearance of structures and add movement of line and vibrancy to the static look of the classical Renaissance.
- **Complex decoration.** Unlike the sometimes severe and austere designs of the Renaissance, the baroque was playful. Architects festooned exteriors and encrusted interiors with an excess of decorations intended to liven things up—lots of ornate stucco work, pouty cherubs, airy frescoes, heavy gilding, twisting columns, multicolored marbles, and general frippery.
- **Multiplying forms.** Why use one column when you can stack a half-dozen partial columns on top of each other, slightly offset, until the effect is like looking at a single column though a fractured kaleidoscope? The baroque loved to pile up its forms and elements to create a rich, busy effect, breaking a pediment curve into segments so that each would protrude farther out than the last, or building up an architectural feature by stacking short sections of concave walls, each one curving to a different arc.

Trevi Fountain, Rome

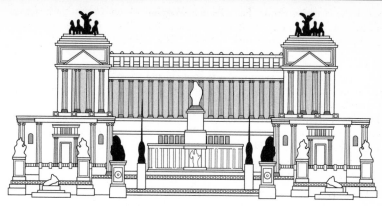

Vittorio Emanuele Monument, Rome

The baroque flourished across Italy. Though relatively sedate, Carlo Maderno's facade and Bernini's sweeping elliptical colonnade for **Rome's St. Peter's Square** make one of Italy's most famous baroque assemblages. One of the quirkiest and most felicitous baroque styles flourished in the churches of the Apulian city **Lecce.** When an earthquake decimated the Sicilian town of **Noto** near Syracuse, it was rebuilt from scratch on a complete baroque city plan; the streets and squares made viewing platforms for the theatrical backdrops of its churches and palaces.

For the rococo—more a decorative than architectural movement—look no further than **Rome's Spanish Steps** (1726), by architect de Sanctis, or the **Trevi Fountain** (1762), by Salvi.

NEOCLASSICAL TO MODERN (18TH TO 21ST CENTURIES)

As a backlash against the excesses of the baroque and rococo, architects began turning to the austere simplicity and grandeur of the classical age and inaugurated the **neoclassical** style by the middle of the 18th century. Their work was inspired by the rediscovery of Pompeii and other ancient sites.

In the late 19th and 20th centuries, Italy's architectural styles went in several directions. The **Industrial Age** of the 19th century brought with it the first genteel shopping malls of glass and steel. The country's take on the early-20th-century Art Nouveau movement was called **Liberty Style.** Mussolini made a spirited attempt to bring back ancient Rome in what can only be called **Fascist architecture.** Since then, Italy has built mostly concrete and glass **skyscrapers,** like the rest of the world, although a few architects in the medium have stood out.

Some identifiable features of each of these movements include:

• **Neoclassical.** The classical ideals of mathematical proportion and symmetry, first rediscovered during the Renaissance, are the hallmark of every classically styled era. Neoclassicists reinterpreted ancient temples as buildings and as decorative, massive colonnaded porticos.

• **Liberty Style.** Like Art Nouveau practitioners in other countries, Italian decorators rebelled against the era of mass production by stressing the uniqueness of craft. They created asymmetrical, curvaceous designs based on organic inspiration (plants and flowers), and they used such materials as wrought iron, stained glass, tile, and hand-painted wallpaper.

- **Fascist.** Deco meets Caesar. This period produced monumentally imposing and chillingly stark, white marble structures surrounded by statuary in the classical style.

Of the **neoclassical, Caserta's Royal Palace** (1752–74), outside Naples, was a conscious attempt to create a Versailles for the Bourbon monarchs, while the unbelievably huge (and almost universally derided) **Vittorio Emanuele Monument** (1884–1927) in Rome, which has been compared to a wedding cake or a Victorian typewriter, was Italy's main monument to reaching its *Risorgimento* goal of a unified Italy.

The **Industrial Age** created glass-domed shopping arcades in giant "X" shapes in both **Milan** and **Naples. Liberty** style never produced any surpassingly important buildings, although you can glimpse it occasionally in period storefronts.

Fascist architecture still infests corners of Italy (although most of the right-wing reliefs and the repeated engravings of DVCE—Mussolini's nickname for himself—have long since been chipped out). You can see it at its best in Rome's planned satellite community called **EUR,** which includes a multistory "square Colosseum" so funky that it has been featured in many a film and music video, and in **Rome's Stadio Olimpico** complex.

The **mid–20th century** was dominated by **Pier Luigi Nervi** (1891–1979) and his reinforced concrete buildings, **Florence's Giovanni Berta Stadium** (1932), **Rome's Palazzeto dello Sport stadium** (1960), and **Turin's Exposition Hall** (1949).

CAMPANIA ART & ARCHITECTURE IN DEPTH

Campania's fertile and rich lands have attracted various peoples since prehistoric times, so it's not surprising that the territory bears the marks of the many civilizations. Campania boasts Italy's richest trove of monuments from antiquity, with superb Greek ruins and unique Roman remains. You'll also find medieval castles and towns, Longobard, Norman, and Norman-Sicilian (or Arabo-Norman) architecture, and some of the richest collections of Renaissance and baroque monuments in Italy. However, art here didn't die with modern times—Naples continues to be a lively center of artistic life, especially in music and the figurative arts.

PREHISTORY

The islands and mountains of Campania are home to a huge trove of prehistoric art, from the grottoes of Palinuro and Marina di Camerota, to the necropolis of Mirabella Eclano, to the beautiful painted terra cottas of the Grotta delle Felci in Capri, to the rich Grotta di Pertosa near Salerno. Prehistoric Italy is probably the least appreciated aspect of Italian history, but it's fascinating.

THE LEGACY OF THE ETRUSCANS & THE GREEKS ON LOCAL ITALIC ART

The Greeks and the Etruscans started to introduce their artistic styles to Campania in the 9th century B.C. From the ruins of **Cuma**—the first Greek colony in Italy—to the wonderful temples of **Paestum,** to the acropolis of **Velia,** Campania is rich with examples of Greek architecture, and the region's jewelry and metal work bear the mark of Etruscan influence. Etruscan and Greek style were deeply embedded in the art of the local Italic populations when the Sannites took over the region in the 5th century B.C. The best examples of Italic art are the marvelous statues from the Sanctuary of the

Goddess Matuta in **Santa Maria Capua Vetere;** and in particular the superb wall paintings from the tombs of **Cuma, Capua,** and **Paestum** in, the archeological museums of Naples, Capua, and Paestum.

THE ROMANS

With its harbors, fertile plains, and thermal waters, Campania was a key region for the Romans when it came to local artistic development. To the great private homes built along the coasts and on the islands—especially in **Herculaneum, Pompeii, Oplontis,** and **Boscoreale**—Rome added many grand public buildings, such as the amphitheater in **Capua Vetere;** the triumphal arch in **Benevento;** the villas of **Minori, Pozzuoli, Baia;** and the rich collections now in the museums of Naples, Capua, and Salerno.

THE BYZANTINES, THE NORMANS & THE LONGOBARDS

Most of the early examples of art and architecture of the Middle Ages suffered from extensive damage, particularly by the Longobards. Only with the citizens' conversion to Catholicism and then with the arrival of the Normans did Byzantine art have a rebirth. The cathedrals of **Capua, Salerno,** and **Amalfi** are the richest examples of medieval art in the area, together with the **Basilica of Sant'Angelo in Formis,** the cathedral of **Sant'Agata dei Goti,** and the cathedral of **Casertavecchia,** as well as the Sanctuary of **Montevergine** and the cloister of Sant'Antonio in **Ravello.**

Campania also boasts several examples of magnificent medieval bronze doors, such as the ones in the cathedrals of Amalfi, Atrani, and Salerno. Classic Romanesque and Arab and Sicilian architecture intersect in these cathedrals. So do many of Campania's local cloisters, such as Amalfi's cathedral and the ex-convent of the Capuchins, Ravello's Palazzo Rufolo, and Sorrento's cloister of Saint Francis.

RENAISSANCE & BAROQUE

When the Angevins moved the capital of their kingdom to Naples, the enormous artistic development that was the Renaissance exploded in Campania. Famous artists came here from Tuscany—Lello da Orvieto, Giotto, Tino da Camaino, and Donatello—while local artists emerged on the scene: Roberto d'Oderisio, Niccolò di Bartolomeo da Foggia, and Colantonio, the teacher of Antonello da Messina. The results are visible in the many churches of Naples and in the Castel Nuovo.

In Salerno, the local painter Antonio Sabatini da Salerno gained renown in the early 16th century. Some of the most powerful examples of Campanian High Renaissance style are in Naples, where many Italian artists were active, including Rossellino, Benedetto and Giuliano da Maiano, fra' Giocondo, and Giovanni da Verona; Pietro Bernini, Giorgio Vasari, Polidoro da Caravaggio, and Antonio Solaro. The chapels of Monteoliveto and the Duomo in Naples are some of the best from this period.

In the 17th century, Caravaggio visited Naples and gave birth to the "Neapolitan School" of painting, which flourished in the 17th and 18th centuries under such names as Battistello Caracciolo, Andrea Vaccaro, Francesco Guarini, and Luca Giordano. Other Italian artists active in Naples during that period were Artemisia Gentileschi and Domenichino.

As with the rest of Italy, baroque art eventually gained dominance in Naples. The painter Francesco Solimena, together with the sculptors Domenico Antonio Vaccaro (son of Lorenzo), and Giuseppe Sanmartino, were among its most famous practitioners. Among the many area architects, Luigi Vanvitelli, with his work on the Reggia di Caserta, emerged as the preeminent figure. Music by such important artists as G. B. Pergolesi and Domenico Cimarosa was also produced during this period.

CONTEMPORARY ART

The 19th and 20th centuries saw the continuation of Campania's artistic potential, with the School of Posillipo (Anton Pitloo, Salvatore Fergola) and later the Scuola di Resina in the 19th century, the Gruppo Sud, and the Gruppo 1858 in the 20th century. Modern painters such as Domenico Morelli and Francesco Paolo Michetti, along with sculptors such as Francesco Jerace, gained fame in the early 20th century, while one of the more contemporary artists to emerge is the painter Gianni Pisani. While the most famous composers of Italian opera generally hailed from other cities, the region did produce probably the most famous operatic performer of all time: Enrico Caruso, who was born in Naples in 1873.

3 Gastronomia Campania & its Wines (A Taste of Campania)

Food has always been one of life's great pleasures for the Italians. This has been true even from the earliest days: To judge from the lifelike banquet scenes found in Etruscan tombs, the Etruscans loved food and took delight in enjoying it. The Romans became famous for their never-ending banquets and for their love of exotic and even decadent treats, such as flamingo tongues.

Much of the Naples's cookery of **Naples** (spaghetti with clam sauce, or with ragù [meat sauce], meatballs, pizzas, fried calamari, and so forth) is already familiar to North Americans because so many Neapolitans moved to the New World and opened restaurants. However, Campanian cuisine has an enormous list of specialties that are much lesser known, especially those from the region's other provinces. **Avellino,** for example, shares many specialties with Naples, but also has a number of unique typical dishes which come from the mountain tradition, such as dishes flavored with **truffles,** and the delicious cakes made with **chestnuts,** both typical local products. **Benevento,** instead, has a completely different cuisine, reflecting its distinct history—it was part of the church's kingdom from the Renaissance onwards—and because of its strong Sannite heritage. Beneventan cuisine favors meat over fish and includes a large number of specialties made with pork and wild boar.

PASTA, MOZZARELLA & PIZZA

The stars of Campanian cuisine are so well known, they have become epicurean symbols of the nation: Italian cuisine as a whole is associated with pasta, pizza, and mozzarella. Yet these three creations were a direct consequence of the fertility and characteristics of Campania, defined by the Romans as *"Campania Felix,"* or the happiest and most perfect of countrysides. To this day, Campania is considered one of the most important and even ideal agricultural provinces around.

Famous for the quality of their **pasta** since the 16th century, the many mills of the Monti Lattari, at the beginning of the Sorrento peninsula, are counted among the best producers of pasta in the world (the ones in Gragnano are particularly renowned). The pasta here is still *trafilata a bronzo* (extruded through bronze forms), a procedure that leaves the pasta slightly porous, allowing for a better penetration of the sauce for tastier results (as opposed to steel forms, which makes the pasta perfectly smooth).

This region created the kinds of pasta that we eat today—*penne, fusilli, rigatoni,* and so on, each type strictly defined: *spaghetti* is thicker than *vermicelli,* and both are thicker than *capellini.*

The warm plains of Campania are also home to the rare native buffalo, which is still raised in the provinces of Caserta and Salerno. Campanians have made **mozzarella** with delicious buffalo milk for centuries and look with disdain on what we all know as mozzarella—the similar cheese made with cow's milk—to which they refer a different name, *fiordilatte* (literally, "flower of milk"). Indeed, once you've tasted the real **mozzarella di bufala,** with its unique delicate flavor and lighter texture, you'll surely be converted too, and will look down on regular mozzarella as an inferior kind of cheese. It's delicious as is, or try it in the *caprese,* a simple salad of sliced mozzarella, fresh tomatoes, and basil seasoned with extra-virgin olive oil.

Putting together the wheat, the mozzarella, and the third famous produce of this region, the tomato, Neapolitans one day invented **pizza.** The unique local tomatoes—especially those produced on the slopes of Mount Vesuvius—have basically no seeds: Imagine a tomato with no central cavity (no spongy, white stuff, either), but filled just with fruit meat, both flavorful and juicy. These are the *pomodoretti,* or small tomatoes of Mount Vesuvius. Obviously the result couldn't be anything but a bestseller, and pizza quickly spread from Naples throughout the world.

Be forewarned that many tourists, however, are disappointed by Neapolitan pizza. Here the dough and the tomatoes are the key ingredients—together with the olive oil, of course—and cheese is an option. The traditional "Neapolitan pizza" is actually called "marinara," with a thick crust that is crunchy on the outside and covered with fresh tomatoes, olive oil, and oregano. Funny enough, what Romans and the rest of Italy call Neapolitan pizza (pizza Napoletana, with tomatoes, cheese, and anchovies) is referred to here in Naples as "Roman pizza" (alla Romana). Therefore, cheese lovers beware! If you ask for a Neapolitan pizza in Naples, you'll be offered a marinara, with no cheese at all.

The second traditional pizza in Naples is the *margherita.* Named after Margherita di Savoia, queen of Italy, who asked to taste pizza during her residence in the Royal Palace of Naples before the capital was moved to Rome, the pizza bears the colors of the Italian flag: basil for the green, mozzarella for the white, and red for the tomatoes. The new pizza met with immediate favor, eventually surpassing the popularity of its older counterpart. Pizza evolved with the addition of a large variety of other toppings, but purist pizzerias in Naples (such as Da Michele in Naples— see chapter 3) that serve only these two types. In Naples, you can also taste another wonderful type of pizza: ***pizza fritta.*** This wonderful creation is served only in truly old-fashioned places where a double round of pizza dough is filled with ricotta, mozzarella, and ham, and deep-fried in a copper cauldron of scalding olive oil. It arrives as puffy as a ball, but as you poke into it, the pizza flattens out, allowing you to delve into the delicious (though not exactly cholesterol-free) dish.

ANTIPASTI E CONTORNI

Italian delight in food has remained strong in Campania throughout the centuries, seemingly in spite of the region's poverty. In fact, the region's poverty prompted the development of an important local characteristic when it comes to food: expediency. Ease and quickness, and making something out of almost nothing, were the driving forces behind Campanians coming up with some of the most delicious, yet simplest, concoctions in the history of cuisine. Check out the *antipasti* buffet of any good restaurant, and you'll be certain to find variety, from scrumptious vegetable dishes to seafood preparations like *sauté of shellfish,* delicious mussels and clams sautéed in a pan with garlic and olive oil. Alternatively, go for *polipetti in cassuola* or *affogati* (squid cooked with a savory tomato-and-olive sauce inside a terra-cotta small casserole). Among the vegetables, do not miss the typical *zucchine a scapece,* a round of zucchini fried in olive oil and seasoned with tangy vinegar and fresh mint dressing (the same preparation is sometimes used for eggplant); or *involtini di melanzane* (a roll of deep-fried eggplant slices, filled with pine nuts and raisins, and warmed up in a tomato sauce) and, when in season, the *friarelli,* a local vegetable that is a cousin to broccoli but much thinner; it's often sautéed with garlic and red pepper, and is at its best paired with local sausages.

SOUPS & PRIMI

One of the most surprising and delicious associations you'll come across here is the delicious *zuppa di fagioli e cozze* (beans and mussels soup), which is common south of Naples and on Capri; another good and unique soup is the *minestra maritata,* a thick concoction of pork meat and a variety of fresh vegetables. The simple comfort food *pasta e patate* (pasta and potatoes smothered with cheese) will surprise you by how tasty it is. At the other end of the spectrum, the elaborated *sartù* (a typical Neapolitan baked dish made with seasoned rice filled with baby meatballs, sausages, chicken liver, mozzarella, and mushrooms) matches the difficulty of its preparation with the satisfaction of eating it.

Our preferred dish is the local pasta, including *scialatielli* (a fresh, homemade, eggless kind of noodles), served with sautéed seafood *(ai frutti di mare).* Another delicious, but more difficult-to-find pasta, is homemade *fusilli;* they can be served with all the traditional sauces: *con le vongole* (with clams), *zucchine e gamberi* (shrimp and zucchini), or *al ragù* (a meat sauce, where many kinds of meat can be cooked with tomatoes, including *braciole,* a meat *involtino* with pine nuts and raisins).

SECONDI

The cuisine of Naples—shared by most of Campania's coast—focuses on seafood, and some of the best main courses are made with fish. The *frittura* (*fritto misto* elsewhere in Italy) of shrimp and calamari is always a great pleasure, and here you will also find other kinds, such as the *fragaglie* (very small fish). The local version of *zuppa di pesce* is not often offered, but it is a delicious fish stew. Much more common and equally delicious are the *polpi affogati* or *in cassuola,* squid or octopus slowly stewed with tomatoes and parsley. Large fish is served grilled, with a tasty dressing of herbs and olive oil; *all'acqua pazza,* poached in a light broth made of a few tomatoes and herbs; or *alle patate* (baked over a bed of thinly sliced potatoes, and absolutely delicious). You might also find it *al sale* (cooked inside a crust of salt) to keep retain its moisture and flavors. Finally, if you have a taste for lobster, you should not miss out on the rare and expensive local clawless variety—*astice.*

For the turf, you might try *coniglio alla cacciatora* (rabbit with wine and black olives), a very tasty creation typical of Ischia; *brasato,* beef slowly stewed with wine and vegetables; *braciola di maiale*— a pork cutlet rolled and filled with prosciutto, pine nuts, and raisins cooked in a tomato sauce; or the simpler meat *alla pizzaiola,* a beef cutlet sautéed in olive oil and cooked with fresh tomatoes and oregano.

SWEETS

If Sicilians are famous for having a sweet tooth, Neapolitans come in a close second, with many delicious specialties on offer. Naples is famous for its *pastiera,* a cake traditionally prepared for Easter but so good that it is now offered year-round in most restaurants. Whole-grain wheat is soaked, boiled, and then used to prepare a delicious creamy filling with ricotta and orange peel in a thick pastry shell.

Another famous dessert is *babà;* a soft, puffy cake soaked in sweet syrup with rum and served with pastry cream. The famous *sfogliatelle* (flaky pastry pockets filled with a sweet ricotta cream), are so good with typical Neapolitan coffee that you shouldn't leave without tasting them; a special kind from Conca dei Marini on the Amalfi Coast is the *sfogliatella Santa Rosa,* filled with pastry cream and *amarene* (candied sour cherries in syrup) instead of ricotta, which was invented in the 14th-century Convento di Santa Rosa.

Each town in Campania, including the smaller villages, has some kind of sweet specialty, such as the *biscotti di Castellammare,* shaped like thick fingers several flavors, and the several lemon-based pastries from the Sorrento and Amalfi regions: *ravioli al limone* (filled with a lemon-flavored ricotta mixture) from Positano; the *Sospiri* ("Sighs")—also called *Zizz'e Nonache* ("Nuns' Breasts") depending on which aspect you focus; the taste or the look. (The dome-shaped small, pale pastries filled with lemon cream) come from Maiori and Minori; and *dolcezze al limone,* the typical lemon pastries of Sorrento (small puff pastries filled with lemon-flavored cream).

AND SOME VINO TO WASH IT ALL DOWN

Italy is the largest wine-producing country in the world (more than 1.6 million hectares/4 million acres of soil are cultivated as vineyards). Grapes were cultivated as far back as 800 B.C., probably introduced by the Greeks, and wine has been produced ever since. However, it wasn't until 1965 that laws were enacted to guarantee consistency in winemaking and to defend specific labels. Winemakers have to apply to have the right to add "D.O.C." *(Denominazione di Origine Controllata)* on their label, and only consistently good wines from specific areas receive this right. The "D.O.C.G." on a label (the "G" means *garantita*) applies to even better wines from even more strictly defined producing areas. Vintners who are presently limited to marketing their products as unpretentious table wines—*vino da tavola*—often expend great efforts lobbying for an elevated status as a D.O.C.

Of Campania's five provinces, Benevento is the one with the largest number of D.O.C. wines, including the **Aglianico del Taburno, Solopaca, Guardiolo, Sannio, Sant'Agata dei Goti,** and **Taburno,** but Avellino is the only one with three D.O.C.G. wines: the wonderful **Taurasi,** considered to be one of the best Italian red wines, up there with Brunello and Barolo; the **Greco di Tufo,** straw-yellow and dry, with a delicate peach-almond flavor; and the **Fiano di Avellino,** a dry and refreshing white wine which received its D.O.C.G. label only in 1993.

From the volcanic soil of Vesuvius comes the amber-colored **Lacrima Christi** ("Tears of Christ"), and from the area of Pozzuoli, the D.O.C. **Campi Flegrei.** With meat dishes, try the dark mulberry-colored **Gragnano,** in the Sorrento peninsula, which has a faint bouquet of faded violets; and **Penisola Sorrentina.** From the islands come the **Ischia** red and white, and the **Capri.**

The Amalfi Coast also has its share of D.O.C. wines. the **Costa d'Amalfi** includes the **Furore**—white, red, and dry rosé—the red **Tramonti,** and the **Ravello**—white and dry with an idea of gentian, the rosé dry with a delicate violet and raspberry bouquet and with a slightly fuller body, and a red with the most body.

Produced in the Salerno area, the **Castel San Lorenzo** red and rosé are D.O.C., but there is also a *barbera* (fizzy red), a white, and a *moscato* (sweet). Farther south is the **Cilento,** another excellent D.O.C.

From Caserta come the *Falerno,* the D.O.C. *Galluccio,* and the D.O.C. *Asprino d'Aversa,* which is light and slightly fizzy.

Campania also excels at the preparation of *Rosolio,* sweet liquor usually herb- or fruit flavored, prepared according to recipes passed down by families for generations. The most famous is *limoncello,* a bright yellow drink made by infusing pure alcohol with the famous lemons from the Amalfi Coast, but others deserve similar fame, like the rare *nanassino,* made with prickly pears; and the *finocchietto,* made with wild fennel.

Appendix B:
Molto Italiano

1 Basic Vocabulary

English	Italian	Pronunciation
Thank you	**Grazie**	*graht*-tzee-yey
You're welcome	**Prego**	*prey*-go
Please	**Per favore**	*pehr* fah-*vohr*-eh
Yes	**Sì**	see
No	**No**	noh
Good morning or Good day	**Buongiorno**	bwohn-*djor*-noh
Good evening	**Buona sera**	*bwohn*-ah *say*-rah
Good night	**Buona notte**	*bwohn*-ah *noht*-tay
How are you?	**Come sta?**	*koh*-may *stah*
Very well	**Molto bene**	*mohl*-toh *behn*-ney
Goodbye	**Arrivederci**	ahr-ree-vah-*dehr*-chee
Excuse me (to get attention)	**Scusi**	*skoo*-zee
Excuse me (to get past someone)	ermesso	pehr-*mehs*-soh
Where is . . . ?	**Dovè . . . ?**	doh-*vey*
the station	**la stazione**	lah stat-tzee-*oh*-neh
a hotel	**un albergo**	oon ahl-*behr*-goh
a restaurant	**un ristorante**	oon reest-ohr-*ahnt*-eh
the bathroom	**il bagno**	eel *bahn*-nyoh
To the right	**A destra**	ah *dehy*-stra
To the left	**A sinistra**	ah see-*nees*-tra
Straight ahead	**Avanti**	ahv-*vahn*-tee
	(*or* **sempre dritto**)	(*sehm*-pray *dreet*-toh)
How much is it?	**Quanto costa?**	*kwan*-toh *coh*-sta
The check, please.	**Il conto, per favore**	eel kon-toh *pehr* fah-*vohr*-eh
When?	**Quando?**	*kwan*-doh
Yesterday	**Ieri**	ee-*yehr*-ree
Today	**Oggi**	*oh*-jee
Tomorrow	**Domani**	doh-*mah*-nee

English	Italian	Pronunciation
Breakfast	**Prima colazione**	*pree*-mah coh-laht-tzee-*ohn*-ay
Lunch	**Pranzo**	*prahn*-zoh
Dinner	**Cena**	*chay*-nah
What time is it?	**Che ore sono?**	kay *or*-ay *soh*-noh
Monday	**Lunedì**	loo-nay-*dee*
Tuesday	**Martedì**	mart-ay-*dee*
Wednesday	**Mercoledì**	mehr-cohl-ay-*dee*
Thursday	**Giovedì**	joh-vay-*dee*
Friday	**Venerdì**	ven-nehr-*dee*
Saturday	**Sabato**	*sah*-bah-toh
Sunday	**Domenica**	doh-*mehn*-nee-kah

NUMBERS

1	**uno** (*oo*-noh)	30	**trenta** (*trayn*-tah)
2	**due** (*doo*-ay)	40	**quaranta** (kwah-*rahn*-tah)
3	**tre** (tray)	50	**cinquanta** (cheen-*kwan*-tah)
4	**quattro** (*kwah*-troh)	60	**sessanta** (sehs-*sahn*-tah)
5	**cinque** (*cheen*-kway)	70	**settanta** (seht-*tahn*-tah)
6	**sei** (say)	80	**ottanta** (oht-*tahn*-tah)
7	**sette** (*set*-tay)	90	**novanta** (noh-*vahnt*-tah)
8	**otto** (*oh*-toh)	100	**cento** (*chen*-toh)
9	**nove** (*noh*-vay)	1,000	**mille** (*mee*-lay)
10	**dieci** (dee-*ay*-chee)	5,000	**cinque milla** (*cheen*-kway *mee*-lah)
11	**undici** (*oon*-dee-chee)	10,000	**dieci milla** (dee-ay-chee *mee*-lah)
20	**venti** (*vehn*-tee)		
21	**ventuno** (vehn-*toon*-oh)		
22	**venti due** (*vehn*-tee *doo*-ay)		

2 A Glossary of Italian Architectural Terms

Abside (Apse)   Half-rounded extension behind the main altar of a church. Christian tradition dictates that it be placed at the eastern end of an Italian church, the side closest to Jerusalem.

Ambo or **Ambones**   Pulpit, either serpentine or simple in form, erected in an Italian church.

Atrio (Atrium)   Courtyard, open to the sky, in an ancient Roman house; the term also applies to the courtyard nearest the entrance of an early Christian church.

Baldacchino or **Ciborio (Baldachin, Baldaquin,** or **Ciborium)**   Columned stone canopy, usually placed above the altar of a church; spelled in English.

Basilica   Any rectangular public building, usually divided into three aisles by rows of columns. In ancient Rome, this architectural form was frequently used for places of public assembly and law courts; later, Roman Christians adapted the form for many of their early churches.

Battistero (Baptistery)   Separate building or a church area where the rite of baptism is held.

Calidarium   Steam room of a Roman bath.

Campanile   Church's bell tower, often detached.

Capitello (Capital)   Four-sided stone at the top of a column, often decoratively carved. The Greek classic architectural styles included three orders: Doric, Ionic, and Corinthian.

Cariatide (Caryatid)   Column carved into a standing female figure.

Cattedrale (Cathedral)   The church where a bishop has his chair.

Cavea   The curved row of seats in a classical theater; the most prevalent shape was that of a semicircle.

Cella   The sanctuary, or most sacred interior section, of a Roman pagan temple.

Chiostro (Cloister)   Courtyard ringed with a gallery of arches or lintels set atop columns.

Chiesa   Church

Cornice   The horizontal flange defining the uppermost part of a building, especially in classical or neoclassical facades.

Cortile   Courtyard or backyard.

Cripta (Crypt)   Church's underground chapel, mostly used as a burial place, usually below the choir.

Cupola   Dome.

Duomo   A town's most important church, usually also a Cathedral.

Foro (Forum)   The main square and principal gathering-place of any Roman town, usually adorned with the city's most important temples and civic buildings.

Ipogeo (Hypogeum & Hypogee)   Adjective describing any subterranean structure, a temple, a chamber, or a chapel. Often used as a tomb.

Loggia   Roofed balcony or gallery.

Navata (Nave)   Each of the longitudinal sections of a church or basilica, divided by walls, pillars, or columns.

Palazzo   Palace or other large building, usually of majestic architecture.

Pergamo   Pulpit.

Piano Nobile   The floor of a palazzo reserved for the owner's use (usually the second floor), as opposed to the floors used by the house staff and for other services.

Pietra Dura   Semiprecious stone, such as amethyst and lapis lazuli.

Portico   A porch with columns on at least one side, usually for decorative purposes.

Presbiterio   Area around the main altar of a church, elevated and separated by columns or, in the oldest churches, by a screen (transenna), which was traditionally reserved for the bishop and the officiating clergy.

Pulvino (Pulvin)   A typical structure of Byzantine architecture consisting of a four-sided stone, often in the shape of a truncated pyramid and often decorated with carvings of plants and animals, which connected the capital to the above structure.

Putto   Artistic representation of a naked small child, especially common in the Renaissance.

Stucco   A building compound composed of sand, powdered marble, lime, and water. Stucco is applied to a surface to make it smooth, or used to create decorative reliefs.

Telamone or Atlante   Statue of a male figure used as structural support.

Terme   Thermal baths or spa, such as the ancient Roman ones.

Timpano (Tympanum)   The triangular wall—sometimes decorated with reliefs— between the cornice and the roof.

Transenna   Screen (usually in carved marble) separating the presbytery from the rest of an early Christian church.

Travertino (Travertine)   Type of porous limestone—white, pale yellow, or pale reddish in color—commonly found in Central Italy.

3 Campanian Menu Terms

Acqua pazza   Light herbed broth used to poach fish.

Agnello   Lamb, usually grilled or baked.

Antipasti   Succulent tidbits served at the beginning of a meal (before the pasta). The choices might be sliced cured meats, seafood (especially shellfish), and cooked and seasoned vegetables.

Aragosta   Lobster.

Babà   Puffy soft cake soaked in rum and served with pastry cream.

Baccalà   Dried and salted codfish usually prepared as a stew.

Braciola   In the rest of Italy this means chop, usually lamb or pork; here it refers to an *involtino* filled with raisins and pine nuts and cooked in *ragù* sauce, a meat-based tomato sauce.

Brasato   Beef braised in white wine with vegetables.

Bruschetta   Toasted peasant-style bread, heavily slathered with olive oil and garlic and often topped with tomatoes.

Bucatini   Thick hollow spaghetti.

Calzone   Filled pocket of pizza dough, usually stuffed with ham and cheese, and sometimes other ingredients. It can be baked or fried.

Cannelloni   Tubes of fresh pasta dough stuffed with meat, fish, or vegetables and then baked with cheese, tomato sauce, and sometimes béchamel (creamy white sauce).

Caprese   Salad of fresh tomatoes and fresh mozzarella, seasoned with fresh basil and olive oil.

Carciofi   Artichokes.

Carpaccio   Thin slices of raw beef, seasoned with olive oil, lemon, pepper, and slivers of Parmesan. Sometimes raw fish is served in the same style but without the cheese.

Cassuola   Small terra-cotta casserole; also the process of cooking something in terra cotta—usually squid or octopus.

Coniglio alla Cacciatora   Rabbit cooked in wine with olives and herbs.

Cozze   Mussels.

Fagioli   Beans.

Fiordilatte   Type of *mozzarella* made with cow's milk.

Fragaglie   Very small fish, usually served deep-fried.

Fresella   Whole-wheat rustic bread served as a salad with fresh tomatoes, fresh basil, salt, and olive oil. The special bread is sold in the shape of flat rounds.

Friarelli   Local type of thin broccoli sautéed with olive oil, garlic, and red pepper and often served with sausages.

Frittata   Italian omelet.

Frittura   Deep-fried medley of seafood, usually calamari and shrimp.

Frutti di Mare   Translated "fruits of the sea," it refers to all shellfish.

Fusilli   Spiral-shaped pasta; the traditional one is fresh and home-made.

Gelato (Produzione Propria)   Ice cream (homemade).

Gnocchi   Dumplings usually made from potatoes (*gnocchi alla patate)* or from semolina (*gnocchi alla romana)* and often served with a tomato sauce.

Granita   Flavored ice, usually with lemon or coffee.

Insalata di Mare   Seafood salad (usually including octopus or squid) seasoned with olive oil, lemon, sometimes vinegar, and whatever the chef fancies—usually parsley and other herbs and spices.

Involtini   Thinly sliced beef, veal, pork, eggplant, or zucchini rolled, stuffed, and sautéed, often served in a tomato sauce.

Melanzane   Eggplant.

Minestra Maritata   Thick soup of pork meat and vegetables.

Minestrone   Rich and savory vegetable soup usually sprinkled with grated *parmigiano*.

Mozzarella di Bufala   Typical Campania cheese, this is an unfermented cheese, made exclusively from fresh buffalo milk, boiled, and then kneaded into a rounded ball, and served fresh. What is called *mozzarella* in the rest of Italy and abroad is mere *fiordilatte*, a similar kind of cheese made with cow's milk.

Panna   Heavy cream.

Panzerotti   Reminiscent of ravioli, panzerotti is half-round in shape and deep fried. They can be savory—filled with ricotta, ham, and mozzarella—or sweet, in which case they are filled with jam.

Parmigiano   Parmesan is a hard and salty yellow cheese usually grated over pastas and soups but also eaten by itself; the best is *parmigiano-reggiano*. A pale imitation is *grana padano*.

Pastiera   Sort of a thick pie filled with a creamy mixture of wheat grains, ricotta, and candied orange peels. Traditionally prepared for Easter but sold all the time now.

Peperoni   Green, yellow, or red sweet peppers (not to be confused with pepperoni, which doesn't exist in Italy).

Pesce al Cartoccio   Fish baked in a parchment envelope and seasoned with whatever the chef fancies.

Pesce Spada   Swordfish.

Pesto   Fresh basil, garlic, and olive oil, finely chopped into a paste.

Pizza   Among the varieties is *margherita* (with tomato sauce, cheese, fresh basil, and memories of the first queen of Italy, Marguerite di Savoia, in whose honor it was first made by a Neapolitan chef); *marinara* (w/tomatoes and oregano); and *romana* (tomatoes, cheese, and anchovies). Quite hilariously, these are the same toppings that in Rome make the pizza *napoletana*.

Pizzaiola   Process in which something (usually a slice of beef or a filet of fish) is cooked in a tomato-garlic-oregano sauce.

Polipetti   Squid.

Polpo or **Polipo**   Octopus.

Ragù   Meat-based tomato sauce, where the chef's imagination rules.

Ricotta   Soft, bland cheese served very fresh and made from sheep's milk or, in lesser-quality versions, from cow's milk.

Risotto   Italian rice, cooked with wine and other ingredients to a creamy consistency.

Risotto alla Pescatora   Rice cooked with wine, a little tomato, and lots of fresh seafood.

Sartù   Delicious baked rice dish in which a crown of rice is filled with baby meatballs, mozzarella, sausages, and other ingredients.

Scapece   For this special preparation for zucchini and eggplants, the vegetables are fried, then seasoned with vinegar and fresh mint.

Semifreddo   Frozen dessert; usually ice cream with sponge cake.

Seppia   Cuttlefish (a kind of squid); its black ink is used for flavoring certain sauces for pasta and risotto dishes.

Sfogliatella   Flaky pastry filled with a sweet ricotta mixture.

Sogliola   Sole.

Soffritto   Typical Neapolitan sauce made with pork tidbits cooked at length in a tomato sauce with olive oil and red pepper.

Spaghetti   Long, round, thin pasta, served different ways: *al ragù* (meat sauce), *al soffritto* (see above), *al pomodoro* (with fresh tomatoes), *ai frutti di mare* (with a medley of sautéed seafood), and *alle vongole* (with clam sauce) are some of the most common.

Spiedini   Pieces of meat grilled on a skewer over an open flame.

Tagliatelle   Flat egg noodles.

Tonno   Tuna.

Torta Caprese   Rich cake made with chocolate and almonds.

Tortelli   Pasta dumplings stuffed with ricotta and greens.

Vermicelli   Very thin spaghetti.

Zabaglione or **Zabaione**   Egg yolks whipped into the consistency of a custard, flavored with Marsala, and served warm as a dessert.

Zuccotto   Liqueur-soaked sponge cake, molded into a dome and layered with chocolate, nuts, and whipped cream.

Zuppa Inglese   Sponge cake soaked in custard.

Index

FROMMER'S® COMPLETE TRAVEL GUIDES

Alaska
Amalfi Coast
American Southwest
Amsterdam
Argentina & Chile
Arizona
Atlanta
Australia
Austria
Bahamas
Barcelona
Beijing
Belgium, Holland & Luxembourg
Belize
Bermuda
Boston
Brazil
British Columbia & the Canadian
  Rockies
Brussels & Bruges
Budapest & the Best of Hungary
Buenos Aires
Calgary
California
Canada
Cancún, Cozumel & the Yucatán
Cape Cod, Nantucket & Martha's
  Vineyard
Caribbean
Caribbean Ports of Call
Carolinas & Georgia
Chicago
China
Colorado
Costa Rica
Croatia
Cuba
Denmark
Denver, Boulder & Colorado Springs
Edinburgh & Glasgow
England
Europe
Europe by Rail

Florence, Tuscany & Umbria
Florida
France
Germany
Greece
Greek Islands
Hawaii
Hong Kong
Honolulu, Waikiki & Oahu
India
Ireland
Italy
Jamaica
Japan
Kauai
Las Vegas
London
Los Angeles
Los Cabos & Baja
Madrid
Maine Coast
Maryland & Delaware
Maui
Mexico
Montana & Wyoming
Montréal & Québec City
Moscow & St. Petersburg
Munich & the Bavarian Alps
Nashville & Memphis
New England
Newfoundland & Labrador
New Mexico
New Orleans
New York City
New York State
New Zealand
Northern Italy
Norway
Nova Scotia, New Brunswick &
  Prince Edward Island
Oregon
Paris
Peru

Philadelphia & the Amish Country
Portugal
Prague & the Best of the Czech
  Republic
Provence & the Riviera
Puerto Rico
Rome
San Antonio & Austin
San Diego
San Francisco
Santa Fe, Taos & Albuquerque
Scandinavia
Scotland
Seattle
Seville, Granada & the Best of
  Andalusia
Shanghai
Sicily
Singapore & Malaysia
South Africa
South America
South Florida
South Pacific
Southeast Asia
Spain
Sweden
Switzerland
Texas
Thailand
Tokyo
Toronto
Turkey
USA
Utah
Vancouver & Victoria
Vermont, New Hampshire & Maine
Vienna & the Danube Valley
Vietnam
Virgin Islands
Virginia
Walt Disney World® & Orlando
Washington, D.C.
Washington State

FROMMER'S® DOLLAR-A-DAY GUIDES

Australia from $60 a Day
California from $70 a Day
England from $75 a Day
Europe from $85 a Day
Florida from $70 a Day

Hawaii from $80 a Day
Ireland from $90 a Day
Italy from $90 a Day
London from $95 a Day

New York City from $90 a Day
Paris from $95 a Day
San Francisco from $70 a Day
Washington, D.C. from $80 a Day

FROMMER'S® PORTABLE GUIDES

Acapulco, Ixtapa & Zihuatanejo
Amsterdam
Aruba
Australia's Great Barrier Reef
Bahamas
Berlin
Big Island of Hawaii
Boston
California Wine Country
Cancún
Cayman Islands
Charleston
Chicago

Disneyland®
Dominican Republic
Dublin
Florence
Las Vegas
Las Vegas for Non-Gamblers
London
Los Angeles
Maui
Nantucket & Martha's Vineyard
New Orleans
New York City
Paris

Portland
Puerto Rico
Puerto Vallarta, Manzanillo &
  Guadalajara
Rio de Janeiro
San Diego
San Francisco
Savannah
Vancouver
Venice
Virgin Islands
Washington, D.C.
Whistler

FROMMER'S® CRUISE GUIDES

Alaska Cruises & Ports of Call

Cruises & Ports of Call

European Cruises & Ports of Call

FROMMER'S® DAY BY DAY GUIDES

Amsterdam	London	Rome
Chicago	New York City	San Francisco
Florence & Tuscany	Paris	Venice

FROMMER'S® NATIONAL PARK GUIDES

Algonquin Provincial Park	National Parks of the American West	Yosemite and Sequoia & Kings
Banff & Jasper	Rocky Mountain	Canyon
Grand Canyon	Yellowstone & Grand Teton	Zion & Bryce Canyon

FROMMER'S® MEMORABLE WALKS

Chicago	New York	Rome
London	Paris	San Francisco

FROMMER'S® WITH KIDS GUIDES

Chicago	National Parks	Toronto
Hawaii	New York City	Walt Disney World® & Orlando
Las Vegas	San Francisco	Washington, D.C.
London		

SUZY GERSHMAN'S BORN TO SHOP GUIDES

Born to Shop: France	Born to Shop: Italy	Born to Shop: New York
Born to Shop: Hong Kong, Shanghai	Born to Shop: London	Born to Shop: Paris
& Beijing		

FROMMER'S® IRREVERENT GUIDES

Amsterdam	Los Angeles	Rome
Boston	Manhattan	San Francisco
Chicago	New Orleans	Walt Disney World®
Las Vegas	Paris	Washington, D.C.
London		

FROMMER'S® BEST-LOVED DRIVING TOURS

Austria	Germany	Northern Italy
Britain	Ireland	Scotland
California	Italy	Spain
France	New England	Tuscany & Umbria

THE UNOFFICIAL GUIDES®

Adventure Travel in Alaska	Hawaii	Paris
Beyond Disney	Ireland	San Francisco
California with Kids	Las Vegas	South Florida including Miami &
Central Italy	London	the Keys
Chicago	Maui	Walt Disney World®
Cruises	Mexico's Best Beach Resorts	Walt Disney World® for
Disneyland®	Mini Las Vegas	Grown-ups
England	Mini Mickey	Walt Disney World® with Kids
Florida	New Orleans	Washington, D.C.
Florida with Kids	New York City	

SPECIAL-INTEREST TITLES

Athens Past & Present	Frommer's Exploring America by RV
Cities Ranked & Rated	Frommer's NYC Free & Dirt Cheap
Frommer's Best Day Trips from London	Frommer's Road Atlas Europe
Frommer's Best RV & Tent Campgrounds	Frommer's Road Atlas Ireland
in the U.S.A.	Retirement Places Rated

FROMMER'S® PHRASEFINDER DICTIONARY GUIDES

French	Italian	Spanish

THE NEW TRAVELOCITY GUARANTEE

EVERYTHING YOU BOOK WILL BE RIGHT, OR WE'LL WORK WITH OUR TRAVEL PARTNERS TO MAKE IT RIGHT, RIGHT AWAY.

*To drive home the point,
we're going to use the word "right" in every single sentence.*

Let's get right to it. Right to the meat! Only Travelocity guarantees everything about your booking will be right, or we'll work with our travel partners to make it right, right away. Right on!

Here's a picture taken smack dab right in the middle of Antigua, where the guarantee also covers you.

The guarantee covers all but one of the items pictured to the right.

For example, what if the ocean view you booked actually looks out at a downright ugly parking lot? You'd be right to call – we're there for you. And no one in their right mind would be pleased to learn the rental car place has closed and left them stranded. Call Travelocity and we'll help get you back on the right track.

Now, you may be thinking, "Yeah, right, I'm so sure." That's OK; you have the right to remain skeptical. That is until we mention help is always right around the corner. Call us right off the bat, knowing that our customer service reps are there for you 24/7. Righting wrongs. Left and right.

Now if you're guessing there are some things we can't control, like the weather, well you're right. But we can help you with most things – to get all the details in righting,* visit **travelocity.com/guarantee**.

*Sorry, spelling things right is one of the few things not covered under the guarantee.

I'd give my right arm for a guarantee like this, although I'm glad I don't have to.

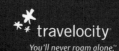

travelocity
You'll never roam alone.

IF YOU BOOK IT, IT SHOULD BE THERE.

Only Travelocity guarantees it will be, or we'll work with our travel partners to make it right, right away. So if you're missing a balcony or anything else you booked, just call us 24/7. 1-888-TRAVELOCITY.

travelocity
You'll never roam alone